Was 70 CE a Watershed in Jewish History?

On Jews and Judaism before and after the Destruction of the Second Temple

Edited by

Daniel R. Schwartz and Zeev Weiss
in collaboration with Ruth A. Clements

BRILL

LEIDEN • BOSTON
2012

This book is printed on acid-free paper.

Library of Congress Cataloging-in-Publication Data

Was 70 CE a watershed in Jewish history? : on Jews and Judaism before and after the destruction of the Second Temple / edited by Daniel R. Schwartz and Zeev Weiss in collaboration with Ruth A. Clements.
    p. cm. — (Ancient Judaism and early Christianity, ISSN 1871-6636 ; v. 78)
Includes index.
    "This volume presents revised versions of lectures given in January 2009 at a Jerusalem symposium sponsored by Hebrew University's Scholion Center for Interdisciplinary Research in Jewish Studies"—Preface.
    ISBN 978-90-04-21534-4 (hardback : alk. paper)
    1. Temple of Jerusalem (Jerusalem)—Congresses. 2. Judaism—History—To 70 A.D.—Congresses. 3. Jews—History—To 70 A.D.—Congresses. I. Schwartz, Daniel R. II. Weiss, Zeev, 1959–.

BM655.W37 2012
296.09'014—dc23

BM
655
.W37
2012

2011038377

In Cooperation with Scholion Library
The Mandel Institute of Jewish Studies
The Hebrew University of Jerusalem

ISSN 1871-6636
ISBN 978 90 04 21534 4

MIX
Paper from
responsible sources
FSC® C008919

PRINTED BY AD DRUK BV - ZEIST, THE NETHERLANDS

Was 70 CE a Watershed in Jewish History?

Ancient Judaism and Early Christianity

Arbeiten zur Geschichte des antiken Judentums und des Urchristentums

VOLUME 78

The titles published in this series are listed at brill.nl/ajec

CONTENTS

PART IV

SACRED TEXTS: EXEGESIS AND LITURGY

PART V

COMMUNAL DEFINITION—POMPEY, JESUS, OR TITUS: WHO MADE A DIFFERENCE?

PREFACE

This volume presents revised versions of lectures given in January 2009 at a Jerusalem symposium sponsored by Hebrew University's Scholion Center for Interdisciplinary Research in Jewish Studies. The symposium was organized by the 2006–9 Scholion research group on "Religions of Place and Religions of Community" (*Dat HaMaqom veDat haQahal*). During the three years of its tenure at Scholion, the eight members of that group—Gideon Aran, Esther Chazon, Ori Schwarz, Nadav Sharon, Michael Tuval, Naama Vilozny, and the two undersigned—devoted weekly seminars to various aspects of the transformation of Judaism in antiquity from a religion with a central Temple to one without; this symposium was an opportunity for us to share our views with colleagues from Israel and a small number of scholars we were able to invite from abroad. The introductory essay to this volume, which schematically surveys the history of scholarship of the basic issue addressed by our group, and by this symposium, explains the approach we adopted in planning the conference and, consequently, this volume.

On behalf of the members of our research group, we would like to thank all of the participants in the symposium, who devoted much time and effort both to the symposium itself and to the preparation of their papers for publication. Along with them, we would also thank most sincerely the wonderful staff of Scholion, beginning with its academic head, Prof. Israel Jacob Yuval, and its quondam administrative director, Ms. Zohar Marcovich, for their unfailing support and counsel. They made this symposium—as indeed all three years of our tenure in Scholion—an exceptionally positive and fruitful experience and, we hope, a fitting confirmation of the vision of the Mandel Foundation, which so generously funds Scholion. The other members of the Scholion team likewise contributed to the success of our project, each in his or her particular domain, and we thank them all as well, as also Dr. Ruth Clements, who saw to the final preparation of the manuscript for publication, and also consented to enrich this volume with a contribution of her own. We are likewise grateful to the editorial staff at Brill Academic Publishers, in particular Ms. Mattie Kuiper and Dr. Tessel Jonquière, for their pleasant and efficient assistance in seeing this book through the publishing process in a timely fashion. We owe, finally, a special debt to Ms. Maya Sherman, who is now the administrative director of Scholion but was then our group's "assistant"— a title which is an egregious understatement. The truth is that "whatever they did, actually she did it" (Gen 39:22), in planning and executing the conference, and we are very grateful to her for all her help.

Daniel R. Schwartz   Zeev Weiss
Jerusalem, May 2011

ABBREVIATIONS

ABD	*Anchor Bible Dictionary*
AJA	*American Journal of Archaeology*
AJSReview	*Association for Jewish Studies Review*
ANF	*Ante-Nicene Fathers.* Edited by Alexander Roberts and James Donaldson, with A. Cleveland Coxe. 1885–1896. 10 vols. Repr. Grand Rapids, 1969–1973
ANRW	*Aufstieg und Niedergang der römischen Welt: Geschichte und Kultur Roms im Spiegel der neueren Forschung.* Part 2, *Principat.* Edited by Hildegard Temporini and Wolfgang Haase. Berlin and New York, 1974–
BA	*Biblical Archaeologist*
BAI	*Bulletin of the Asia Institute*
BASOR	*Bulletin of the American Schools of Oriental Research*
Bib	*Biblica*
BibInt	*Biblical Interpretation*
BN	*Biblische Notizen*
BSOAS	*Bulletin of the School of Oriental and African Studies*
ByzF	*Byzantinische Forschungen*
BZ	*Biblische Zeitschrift*
CBQ	*Catholic Biblical Quarterly*
CIJ	*Corpus inscriptionum judaicarum*
CP	*Classical Philology*
CPJ	*Corpus papyrorum judaicorum.* Ed. V.A. Tcherikover, A. Fuks and M. Stern. 3 vols. Cambridge, Mass., 1957–1964
DJD	Discoveries in the Judaean Desert. Oxford, 1955–2010
DOP	*Dumbarton Oaks Papers*
DSD	*Dead Sea Discoveries*
ErIsr	*Eretz-Israel*
ETL	*Ephemerides theologicae lovanienses*
FJB	*Frankfurter Judaistische Beiträge*
GLA	*Greek and Latin Authors on Jews and Judaism.* Edited by M. Stern. 3 vols. Jerusalem, 1974–1984
HAR	*Hebrew Annual Review*
HR	*History of Religions*

HTR	*Harvard Theological Review*
HUCA	*Hebrew Union College Annual*
IEJ	*Israel Exploration Journal*
JAAR	*Journal of the American Academy of Religion*
JAOS	*Journal of the American Oriental Society*
JBL	*Journal of Biblical Literature*
JEA	*Journal of Egyptian Archaeology*
JJS	*Journal of Jewish Studies*
JNES	*Journal of Near Eastern Studies*
JQR	*Jewish Quarterly Review*
JR	*Journal of Religion*
JRS	*Journal of Roman Studies*
JSJ	*Journal for the Study of Judaism in the Persian, Hellenistic and Roman Periods*
JSNT	*Journal for the Study of the New Testament*
JSP	*Journal for the Study of the Pseudepigrapha*
JSQ	*Jewish Studies Quarterly*
JTS	*Journal of Theological Studies*
LCL	Loeb Classical Library
LSJ	Liddell, H.G., R. Scott, H.S. Jones, *A Greek-English Lexicon.* 9th ed. with revised supplement. Oxford, 1996
LTP	*Laval théologique et philosophique*
MGWJ	*Monatsschrift für Geschichte und Wissenschaft des Judentums*
NEAEHL	*The New Encyclopedia of Archaeological Excavations in the Holy Land.* Edited by E. Stern. 4 vols. Jerusalem, 1993
NETS	*A New English Translation of the Septuagint.* Edited by Pietersma and B.G. Wright; Oxford, 2007
NovT	*Novum Testamentum*
NTS	*New Testament Studies*
OTP	*The Old Testament Pseudepigrapha.* 2 vols. Edited by J.H. Charlesworth; New York, 1983–1985
PAAJR	*Proceedings of the American Academy of Jewish Research*
PEQ	*Palestine Exploration Quarterly*
QDAP	*Quarterly of the Department of Antiquities in Palestine*
RA	*Revue d'assyriologie et d'archéologie orientale*
RB	*Revue biblique*
RevQ	*Revue de Qumrân*
RivB	*Rivista biblica italiana*
SCI	*Scripta classica Israelica*

SPhA   *Studia Philonica Annual*
ST   *Studia theologica*
USQR   *Union Seminary Quarterly Review*
TDNT   *Theological Dictionary of the New Testament.* Edited by
          G. Kittel and G. Friedrich. Translated by G.W. Bromiley.
          10 vols. Grand Rapids, 1964–1976
TRE   *Theologische Realenzyklopädie.* Edited by G. Krause and
          G. Müller. Berlin, 1977–
TLZ   *Theologische Literaturzeitung*
TZ   *Theologische Zeitschrift*
ZAW   *Zeitschrift für die alttestamentliche Wissenschaft*
ZDPV   *Zeitschrift des Deutschen Palästina-Vereins*
ZPE   *Zeitschrift für Papyrologie und Epigraphik*

LIST OF CONTRIBUTORS

Dr. Gideon Aran, The Hebrew University of Jerusalem

Dr. Hanan Birenboim, The Hebrew University of Jerusalem, and Jacob Herzog College, Gush-Etzion

Prof. Gideon Bohak, Tel-Aviv University

Dr. Esther G. Chazon, The Hebrew University of Jerusalem

Dr. Ruth A. Clements, The Hebrew University of Jerusalem

Prof. Jörg Frey, University of Zurich

Prof. Martin Goodman, University of Oxford

Dr. Noah Hacham, The Hebrew University of Jerusalem

Prof. Martha Himmelfarb, Princeton University

Dr. Jutta Leonhardt-Balzer, University of Aberdeen, Scotland

Prof. (emer.) Lee I. Levine, The Hebrew University of Jerusalem

Prof. Jodi Magness, University of North Carolina at Chapel Hill

Dr. Paul Mandel, Schechter Institute of Jewish Studies, Jerusalem

Prof. Daniel R. Schwartz, The Hebrew University of Jerusalem

Dr. Ori Schwarz, The Hebrew University of Jerusalem

Nadav Sharon, The Hebrew University of Jerusalem

Prof. Michael D. Swartz, Ohio State University

Michael Tuval, The Hebrew University of Jerusalem

Dr. Naama Vilozny, The Hebrew University of Jerusalem

Prof. Zeev Weiss, The Hebrew University of Jerusalem

INTRODUCTION: WAS 70 CE A WATERSHED IN JEWISH HISTORY? THREE STAGES OF MODERN SCHOLARSHIP, AND A RENEWED EFFORT

Daniel R. Schwartz

The overarching issue addressed by the papers in this volume, whether 70 CE should be considered a watershed in Jewish history, has been the object of discussion for more than a century and a half, but the results are still far from unambiguous. In undertaking a project like this it might be well to recall at the outset, as an inspiration but also as a warning, the experience of one of the founding fathers of our profession, Heinrich Graetz.[1] First, inspiration: In 1846, before he began publishing his *Geschichte der Juden*, which eventually filled eleven volumes, Graetz published an ambitious programmatic essay on the structure of Jewish history, in which he took the schematic position that all of Jewish history, from the earliest times reflected in the Bible until his own day, divides into three major eras.[2] Of these, the first, which ended with the destruction of the First Temple, was that of a people in its land; the second, which ended with the destruction of the Second Temple, was that of a religious community in its land; and the third, which continued from 70 CE until Graetz's own times, was that of a religious community in exile.

I believe, on the one hand, that especially in our age of specialization we should be inspired by such a daringly broad and elegant view, and challenged by it to try our hands, too, at making sense of the big picture, at trying to find a meaningful forest that unites all of our trees. On the other hand, however, Graetz's example should also serve as a warning, for it turned out that his grand project fell on its face insofar as our period is concerned. True, things started

---

[1] For the coming discussion of Graetz, see the details in D.R. Schwartz, "Jews, Judaeans and the Epoch that Disappeared: H. Graetz's Changing View of the Second Temple Period," *Zion* 70 (2004/5): 293–309 (in Hebrew).

[2] For an easily accessible reprint of this 1846 essay, see H. Graetz, *Die Konstruktion der jüdischen Geschichte* (Berlin, 1936). For an English version, see: H. Graetz, *The Structure of Jewish History, and Other Essays* (trans. and ed. I. Schorsch; New York, 1975).

out according to plan: When in 1853 Graetz began his grand project with the publication of his first volume, vol. IV, on the post-70 period, he designated it prominently, in accordance with his programmatic scheme, as the first volume of those on the *Dritter Zeitraum der jüdischen Geschichte: Vom Untergange des jüdischen Staates bis auf die neueste Zeit, von 70 bis 1850 nach der üblichen Zeitrechnung.*[3] However, when the hapless but honest Graetz then sat down to write up vol. III, on the Second Temple period, which was supposed to be the second era, he concluded that it was not an era at all. Rather, Graetz concluded that the first four hundred years after the destruction of the First Temple were best handled as a continuation of the first era, and that—more importantly for the present context—he could not really point to what changed in 70.[4] The result was that the second volume he published (vol. III, 1856) was dedicated to the 230 years from the death of Judah Maccabee until 70 CE but not assigned to any era at all, and so things were to remain in all editions of his eleven-volume *Geschichte*: Vols. I–II are labeled prominently as devoted to the first era, down to the Hasmonean revolt, and vols. IV–XI are just as prominently labeled as devoted to the last era(s),[5] but vol. III is not said to deal with any era at all. The second era simply disappeared from the scheme.[6] Graetz's grand project thus testifies not only to the perils of committing oneself to an a priori conception, and to Graetz's honesty in abandoning it, but also, and most importantly for us here, it warns us of the difficulty of pinning down the significance of the destruction of the Second Temple.

---

[3] H. Graetz, *Geschichte der Juden* (Leipzig, 1853), 4:1 (the title of the volume's introduction); see also p. 7, where, correspondingly, he offers an introduction to this particular volume under the rubric: *Erste Periode des dritten Zeitraums: Die talmudische Zeit.* This volume, the fourth of this *Geschichte*, was the first published.

[4] Graetz's difficulty with this period is easily seen by comparison of the introductions of the volume in each of its first three editions: his continual rewriting and waffling tell the story well, and also explain why in the end he gave up and published the fourth edition (1888) without an introduction. See my "Jews, Judaeans," 305–6.

[5] In fact, Graetz eventually decided to end the third era with his vol. X, in the mid-eighteenth century, so as to allow his final volume, optimistically, to open a fourth era—a point that need not detain us here.

[6] The only remnant of it seems to be in the concluding sentence of vol. III (p. 457 in the 1856 ed.), where Graetz comments on the comparison of end of the first *Zeitraum*, in the days of Jeremiah, to the end of the second *Zeitraum*, in the days of Josephus. This corresponds to the vision of his 1846 *Konstruktion*, not to the *Geschichte* itself, where Jeremiah comes four hundred years before the end of the first *Zeitraum*.

What engendered Graetz's difficulties was his original a priori fram-ing of Jewish history as a neat triad that characterized the Second Temple period as the era of *a religious community in its land*. In fact, in preparing vol. III he realized that the Jewish world of the Second Temple period was chock full both of Jews abroad, such as those of Alexandria, and also of politically-oriented Jews, such as those who established the Hasmonean state and those who later attempted to restore a Jewish state by rebelling against Rome. Moreover, neither of these types was exceptional or marginal, and Graetz in fact found them quite interesting.[7] These discoveries, however, scuttled his origi-nal scheme.

But if one of the two roots of Graetz's original error was to under-estimate the significance of politics for Jews in our period, other defenders of the assumption that 70 was a watershed have erred by overstating that same element. I refer to those many who write as if 70 meant the demise of a Jewish state—which is simply not true. The end of the Jewish state had come already in 63 BCE, when Pompey conquered Hasmonean Judea; or at least in 6 CE, when Rome put an end to even the Herodian vassal state and incorporated Judea directly into the empire. Although to get around that problem some scholars have used the more nebulous term *Staatswesen* rather than *Staat*, just as Zeitlin would later begin with "State" but conclude with "Com-monwealth," to the same end,[8] such recourse to evasive terminology merely underlines the fact that already many decades before 70 there had been no Jewish state. In this light, we can understand why the central modern account of Jewish history of our period that is written from a political point of view in fact defines the period without any particular regard for 70.[9]

But if the criterion historians normally use for defining periods—who is ruling the people or country in question?—does not point to 70 as a watershed, what, if anything, does? It is not easy to say. Culture,

---

[7] Note that Graetz's vol. III is the only one that went through four editions in his own lifetime, and that it grew spectacularly—from 572 pages in the first edition to 858 in the fourth. No other volume grew anywhere near as much.

[8] See, for example, A. Bertholet, *Das Ende des jüdischen Staatswesens* (Tübingen, 1910); S. Zeitlin, *The Rise and Fall of the Judaean State: A Political, Social and Religious History of the Second Commonwealth* (3 vols.; Philadelphia, 1962–1978). For other similar material, see N. Sharon's paper, below, pp. 417–18.

[9] E.M. Smallwood, *The Jews Under Roman Rule, From Pompey to Diocletian: A Study in Political Relations* (Leiden 1976, 1981²).

for a prime alternative candidate, will not do. Note, for example, that although Menahem Stern opened his long survey of "The Period of the Second Temple"[10] with the arrival of Alexander the Great, thereby bespeaking the view—not at all surprising for the compiler of *Greek and Latin Authors on Jews and Judaism*—that it is the encounter with Greek culture (nearly two hundred years after the construction of the Second Temple!) that was most epoch-making,[11] he nevertheless ended his survey with 70 CE, although no one would suggest that the Jewish-Greek encounter ended then. That encounter continued quite intensely for another several hundred years, until the rise of Islam in the seventh century;[12] indeed, more recently David Biale's *Cultures of the Jews* (2002), although divided like Graetz's original scheme into three parts, brought the first era down to the seventh century.

Nor, it seems, do religious criteria dictate a break at 70. For Emil Schürer, for example, it was clear that the period of Jewish history relevant for those interested in understanding the birth of Christianity ("aus dem Schoose des Judenthums in der Fülle der Zeiten") continued down until 135 CE.[13] Similarly, for Judaism, such a standard survey as Judah Goldin's is entitled "The Period of the Talmud (135 BCE–1035 CE)"—that is, it begins two centuries before 70 (with John Hyrcanus—the rabbis' "John the High Priest") and ends almost a millennium later, when the more or less concomitant death of Hai Gaon

---

[10] In H.H. Ben-Sasson, ed., *A History of the Jewish People* (Cambridge, Mass., 1976), 183–303.

[11] For the same orientation, see esp. his "Judaism and Hellenism in Palestine in the Third and Second Centuries B.C.E.," in *Acculturation and Assimilation: Continuity and Change in the Cultures of Israel and the Nations* (ed. Y. Kaplan and M. Stern; Jerusalem, 1989), 41–60 (reprinted in his *Studies in Jewish History: The Second Temple Period* [ed. M. Amit, I.M. Gafni, and M.D. Herr; Jerusalem, 1991], 3–21 [both in Hebrew]); and two Hebrew volumes he edited (and contributed to substantially): *The Diaspora in the Hellenistic-Roman World* (Jerusalem, 1982/83); *The Hellenistic Period and the Hasmonean State (332–37 BCE)* (Jerusalem, 1981).

[12] As was emphasized especially by M.D. Herr, "Hellenism and the Jews in Eretz Israel," *Eshkolot* n.s. 2–3 (1976/77–1977/78): 20–27 (in Hebrew). See also L.I. Levine, *Judaism and Hellenism in Antiquity: Conflict or Confluence?* (Seattle, 1998).

[13] E. Schürer, *The History of the Jewish People in the Age of Jesus Christ (175 BCE–135 CE)* (ed. G. Vermes et al.; 3 vols.; rev. English ed.; Edinburgh, 1973–1986). The German words cited in parentheses are from the first line of the German version (*Geschichte des jüdischen Volkes im Zeitalter Jesu Christi* [Leipzig, 1901³⁻⁴], 1:1); it is remarkable how sensitivities about gender-charged language and Christian supersessionism suppressed both images in the new, sanitized, version: "Since it was from Judaism that Christianity emerged in the first century A.D." (*History*, 1:1).

and birth of Rashi pointed to a shift from East to West.[14] In a very basic way, however, we might add that Goldin's view corresponds to that of the ancient rabbis themselves, who—despite the fact that for halakhic purposes they sometimes distinguish between "the days of the Temple" and "the present era"[15]—in their most central historical document (the first two chapters of the Mishnaic tractate *Abot*) detail the sequence of generations that transmitted the Torah from Sinai via the second century BCE to the second century CE but nowhere mention the destruction of the Temple, or of Jerusalem. Indeed, they do not hint at any historical event at all. The history which interested the editor of those chapters was "in the world but not of the world," as one of his contemporaries, working in another context but with a similar attitude toward this world, would put it (*Epistle of Diognetus*, ch. 6). If the Romans destroyed the Temple, that was sad, but the rabbis' world could still "stand" without it, on the universally accessible pillars of justice, truth, and peace (*m. Abot* 1:18).[16]

But if neither politics, culture, nor religion justify the view of 70 as a watershed in Jewish history, it would seem that the notion, however intuitive it would seem, should have to go. In fact, however, the hypothesis that it was nevertheless a watershed derives from doubts about the view just now exemplified by Goldin and *Abot* 1–2. To understand this, we should review, however briefly and schematically, three phases in modern scholarship concerning the nature of Judaism in antiquity. More particularly, I would address three stages in the modern understanding of the relationship between priestly Judaism and rabbinic Judaism in antiquity—for my point of departure is Abraham Geiger's discovery, and popularization in his *Urschrift* (1857), of

---

[14] Goldin's survey appeared in L. Finkelstein, ed., *The Jews: Their History, Culture, and Religion* (2 vols.; Philadelphia, 1949), 1:115–215. Correspondingly, the next chapter in that compendium (1:216–49), by C. Roth, is entitled "The European Age in Jewish History."

[15] See, for example, *m. Ma'aser Sheni* 2:5; *m. Bikkurim* 2:3. Note, however, that—as I.M. Gafni has emphasized—even "this era" does not always mean "post-Destruction;" see Gafni's "Concepts of Periodization and Causality in Talmudic Literature," *Jewish History* 10/1 (Spring 1996): 33.

[16] For the argument that, in general, until the third century, the rabbis paid the destruction of the Temple little attention, see G. Stemberger, "Reaktionen auf die Tempelzerstörung in der rabbinischen Literatur," in *Zerstörungen des Jerusalemer Tempels* (ed. J. Hahn; Tübingen, 2002), 207–15. He suggests that this might have arisen out of a desire to dampen apocalyptic hopes and rebelliousness, but other explanations are possible.

the fundamental distinction in ancient Judaism between priestly Judaism and Pharisaic/rabbinic Judaism, a distinction which has proven itself to be quite basic and meaningful, a fruitful key to the understanding of much of what we can see in the Jewish world of the Second Temple period.[17] The stages of scholarship I will set out developed within the parameters of that basic division, which has maintained itself, *mutatis mutandis*, until today. Where they differ is with regard to which of those two types of Judaism was more popular and widely accepted before and after 70.

THE FIRST STAGE

In the first stage, until the middle of the twentieth century, it was generally held, on the basis of such texts as the Mishnah and Josephus' statements about Pharisaic hegemony, which dovetail well with New Testament statements about the Pharisees' enjoying authority and "sitting on the seat of Moses" (Matt 23:2), that the Pharisees, who were identified with the scribes and also with the rabbis, enjoyed nigh universal authority among the Jews of the Second Temple period. Although everyone knew that there were other sects, as Josephus and other evidence indicates, these were assumed to be marginal. Thus for example, in 1864, just a few years after the appearance of Geiger's *Urschrift*, we find a prominent Protestant scholar, Adolf Hausrath, pronouncing with regard to the pre-70 world of Judea in which Josephus grew up, that:

> This people was in the hands of its scribes.[18] The rabbis ruled the market and the home, the Temple and the school; they were the people's

---

[17] A. Geiger, *Urschrift und Übersetzungen der Bibel in ihrer Abhängigkeit von der innern Entwicklung des Judentums* (Breslau, 1857). See also his "Sadducäer und Pharisär," *Jüdische Zeitschrift für Wissenschaft und Leben* 2 (1863): 11–54. A few years after Geiger's work put the theme on the map, J. Wellhausen popularized it in his *Die Pharisäer und die Sadducäer: Eine Untersuchung zur inneren jüdischen Geschichte* (Greifswald, 1874). For surveys of scholarship in this field, see J. Le Moyne, *Les Sadducéens* (Paris, 1972), 11–26 ("Panorama de la recherche depuis Abraham Geiger," whose work "ouvre la période moderne des investigations" in this field [p. 11]); and R. Deines, *Die Pharisäer: Ihr Verständnis im Spiegel der christlichen und jüdischen Forschung seit Wellhausen und Graetz* (Tübingen, 1997).

[18] The term *Schriftgelehrten*, which is so popular in German scholarship concerning our period but bespeaks the assumption—contradicted by P. Mandel in this volume—that Pharisaic sages (like good Protestant preachers) taught primarily on the basis of Scripture, is something of a hybrid of the Greek *grammateus* and the Hebrew *hakham*

teachers, priests, physicians, judges, and statesmen. Without them no marriage was contracted, no child circumcised, no contract formulated, no judgment given, no matter of state performed. They sat on the seat of Moses and what they said was an oracle for the people...[19]

But even if some would back away from such sweeping generalizations, these seemed to be what the literary evidence offered, if taken at face value, as there was then no particular reason not to. Accordingly, one can piece together a more or less univocal chorus of scholarship in the next generations, featuring—to choose representative voices from different sectors—such central works as Schürer's handbook, which ruled the field in the decades around the turn of the twentieth century, and which claimed that the Pharisees enjoyed hegemony in the Jewish world beginning in the early first century BCE and "für alle Folgezeit"; George Foot Moore's volumes in the late 1920s on normative Judaism; and Gedalia Alon's work in the decade thereafter, predicated on the premise that "it is a known fact that from the days of the Hasmoneans and onwards the Pharisees constituted the vast majority of the nation, and hence, generally speaking, we have to regard the history of Jewry in our period, in all spheres, as also reflecting the history of the Pharisees."[20] Apart from various details, the only major issue was whether one wanted to defend the type of Judaism represented by those ancient Pharisees, who administered "life under the Law,"[21] or, rather, condemn it and use it to explain why, in the fullness of time, a new type was required.[22] One way or the other, all agreed that the

---

and has no apt English equivalent. Note, in any case, that the next sentence equates them with the rabbis.

[19] A. Hausrath, "Über den jüdischen Geschichtschreiber und Staatsmann Flavius Josephus," *Historische Zeitschrift* 12 (1864): 288 (my translation).

[20] E. Schürer, *Geschichte des jüdischen Volkes im Zeitalter Jesu Christi* (3 vols.; Leipzig, 1901²⁻³), 2:336 ("die ganze Leitung der inneren Angelegeneiten lag in ihren Händen [...] unter allem Wechsel der Regierungen, unter Römern und Herodianern, behaupteten die Pharisäer ihre geistige Hegemonie"); G.F. Moore, *Judaism in the First Centuries of the Christian Era* (3 vols.; Cambridge, Mass., 1927–1930); G. Alon, *Jews, Judaism and the Classical World* (Jerusalem, 1977), 22 (translated from a Hebrew article that appeared originally in 1934/35). Note that the passage in Schürer survived largely intact in the new English edition; although a footnote is added, referring to Morton Smith's argument (see below, n. 24) that Josephus' emphasis on the Pharisees' supremacy reflects post-70 developments, no attempt is made to grapple with the implications of that argument. See Schürer, *History*, 2:402 and n. 74.

[21] See, for example, I. Abrahams, "Professor Schürer on Life under the Jewish Law," *JQR* o.s. 11 (1898/99): 626–42.

[22] For surveys of this literature, see Deines, *Die Pharisäer*, and K. Hoheisel, *Das antike Judentum in christlicher Sicht: Ein Beitrag zur neueren Forschungsgeschichte* (Wiesbaden, 1978).

Pharisees were the most popular and most authoritative type of Judaism during the Second Temple period, all agreed that the rabbis were their heirs, and, therefore, all agreed that the destruction of the Second Temple didn't change much, apart from eliminating whatever power base their competitors had had.

THE SECOND STAGE

Within two decades of the appearance of Moore's *Judaism* and Alon's pronouncement about what we all know about the Pharisees' hegemony, the Qumran finds began to turn everything upside down. By their very existence, they showed there were quite a lot of interesting things in the world of ancient Judaism about which the rabbis gave us no inkling—and, as especially a seminal article by Morton Smith pointed out,[23] this put a question mark alongside the rabbis' claims that they enjoyed hegemony, suggesting that these claims should be taken as seriously as any political party's claim that "the people supports us." It didn't take long for arguments to be found to undercut Josephus' statements about Pharisaic hegemony as well.[24]

The importance of this for our issue is in the priestly nature of the sectarian scrolls from Qumran and so, apparently, of the community that produced them.[25] Since putting priestly Judaism on the map in a very serious and intensive way[26] bolstered, perforce, in numerous ways

---

[23] M. Smith, "Palestinian Judaism in the First Century," in *Israel: Its Role in Civilization* (ed. M. Davis; New York, 1956), 67–81 (reprinted in his *Studies in the Cult of Yahweh* [ed. S.J.D. Cohen; 2 vols.; Leiden, 1996], 1:104–15).

[24] See already Smith, "Palestinian Judaism," 74–78 (in his *Studies*, 109–13). For the continuation of this branch of research, see below, n. 36.

[25] That "priestly" is an appropriate adjective for the Qumran community is indicated by its frequency in scholarly literature, whether in relation to the topics the Scrolls address, the diction and metaphors they use, or the identity of the leadership they mandate (e.g., "only the sons of Aaron shall rule concerning law and property and according to them shall all decisions be made concerning all matters of the people of the community"—*Manual of Discipline* 9:7). The priestly nature of the Qumran community has lately been emphasized, quite rightly, by R. Elior, in her *Memory and Oblivion: The Mystery of the Dead Sea Scrolls* (Jerusalem, 2009 [in Hebrew]). It is unfortunate that another aspect of her volume (her emphasis on the unreliability of first-century accounts of the Essenes that do not point up their priestly orientation, which has mistakenly been taken to imply that the Essenes did not exist) has received disproportionate attention.

[26] For one of the early expressions of this in the wake of the Qumran discoveries, see E. Stauffer, "Probleme der Priestertradition," *TLZ* 81 (1956): 135–50.

both general and specific, the importance of the Temple of Jerusalem and its priesthood, the upshot for our issue was a new assessment of 70: In the light of Qumran, the events of 70, which destroyed the Temple and thereby deprived the priesthood of its power base, will indeed have been quite a watershed. Correspondingly, the new rabbinic center at Yavneh, and the success that it quickly attained, will have been a *novum* in comparison with the priestly Judaism that was regnant in the pre-70 period.

That is where scholarship had moved by the 1970s. The decade started off with a boom with the three volumes of Jacob Neusner's *The Rabbinic Traditions about the Pharisees before 70* (1971), a massive work that concluded with a long and critical review of all preceding scholarship that had assumed the hegemony of the Pharisees and their continuity with the later rabbis, dwelling upon the errors and uncritical assumptions of that construct.[27] As the 1970s moved on, additional analyses carried forward this critique. Thus, for some prominent examples:

- other studies by Neusner argued and also popularized the irrelevance and lack of reliability of the post-70 evidence of Josephus, the New Testament, and the rabbis, concerning the nature of Judaism and the popularity of rabbinic Judaism in the pre-70 period;[28]
- Joseph Blenkinsopp emphasized, in 1974, Josephus' *priestly* orientation;[29]
- In an extended *JSJ* debate about "Orthodoxy" in the first century, Lester L. Grabbe's contribution, which opened by highlighting the importance of Smith's earlier article, tended to emphasize the centrality of the Temple and the sacrificial cult;[30]

---

[27] *Rabbinic Traditions*, 3:320–68.

[28] For his most popular statement of this, see J. Neusner, *From Politics to Piety: The Emergence of Pharisaic Judaism* (Englewood Cliffs, N.J., 1973).

[29] J. Blenkinsopp, "Prophecy and Priesthood in Josephus," *JJS* 25 (1974): 239–62.

[30] N.J. McEleney, "Orthodoxy in Judaism of the First Christian Century," *JSJ* 4 (1973): 19–42; D.E. Aune, "Orthodoxy in First Century Judaism? A Response to N.J. McEleney," *JSJ* 7 (1976): 1–10; L.L. Grabbe, "Orthodoxy in Judaism of the First Century: What are the Issues?" *JSJ* 8 (1977): 149–53; and N.J. McEleney, "Orthodoxy in Judaism of the First Christian Century: A Response to David E. Aune and Lester L. Grabbe," *JSJ* 9 (1978): 83–88.

- E.P. Sanders, in his 1977 study of the Jewish background of Paul, developed the notion that we should think of a "common Judaism" rather than Pharisaic or rabbinic Judaism;[31]
- and a new contribution by Smith, in 1978, argued that the references to "Pharisees" in the Synoptic Gospels were late and reflected not what things were like in Jesus' day, but rather the post-70 ascent of the rabbis.[32]

Similarly, the 1980s saw scholarship assimilate the new halakhic material from Qumran (especially the *Temple Scroll*, which had been published in the late 1970s, and *Miqṣat Maʿase ha-Torah*, which was circulating one way or another in the 1980s long before it was published "officially" in 1994). From a 1980 article by Joseph Baumgarten to a longer end-of-the-decade piece by Yaakov Sussmann,[33] these materials were shown to indicate both the vitality and validity of the Geigerian distinction between priestly and rabbinic Judaism and, concerning the period of the Temple, that even in this most rabbinic of fields, halakhah, the Pharisees and their laws were not alone. It is accordingly not at all surprising that, writing around the same time as Sussmann, David Goodblatt, in his "The Place of the Pharisees in First Century Judaism: The State of the Debate,"[34] surveyed the field and concluded that Smith was right that the Pharisees' "place" was more or less on the margins.[35] Similarly, around that very same time Steve Mason tidied up the evidence supplied by Josephus: if it had always

---

[31] *Paul and Palestinian Judaism* (London, 1977). To appreciate the significance of this book in our present context, it is enough to note the contrast between its title and that of its main predecessor, which appeared when the Qumran scrolls had yet to make their impact: W.D. Davies, *Paul and Rabbinic Judaism* (London, 1948). For a review of the debate about "common Judaism," see G. Stemberger, "Was There a 'Mainstream Judaism' in the Late Second Temple Period?" *Review of Rabbinic Judaism* 4 (2001): 189–208; and *Common Judaism: Explorations in Second-Temple Judaism* (ed. W.O. McCready and A. Reinhartz; Minneapolis: Fortress, 2008).

[32] M. Smith, *Jesus the Magician* (San Francisco, 1978), 153–57.

[33] J.M. Baumgarten, "The Pharisaic-Sadducean Controversies about Purity and the Qumran Texts," *JJS* 31 (1980): 157–70; Y. Sussmann, "The History of the Halakha and the Dead Sea Scrolls: Preliminary Observations on *Miqṣat Maʿase ha-Torah* (4QMMT)," *Tarbiz* 59 (1989/90): 11–76 (in Hebrew). For a shorter English version of the latter, see idem, "The History of Halakha and the Dead Sea Scrolls," in *Qumran Cave 4.V: Miqṣat Maʿase ha-Torah* (ed. E. Qimron and J. Strugnell; Oxford, 1994), 170–200.

[34] *JSJ* 20 (1989): 12–30.

[35] "The evidence in hand, especially that composed by the end of the first century: Josephus and the New Testament, does not support the view that Pharisaic Judaism comprised 'orthodoxy' in the first century. Nor does it support the claim that the

been bothersome for the priest vs. Pharisee model that a Jerusalemite priest like Josephus should have been a Pharisee, as he reports (*Life* 12), and should have said such nice things about them, Mason argued that a proper understanding of Josephus will show that in fact he did not claim to be a Pharisee and that in fact, in general he was hostile towards them.[36] Mason's argument bolsters the fundamental dichotomy between priests and Pharisees/rabbis and also strengthens the basic notion that priests were in charge as long as the Temple stood—a point Mason underlined elsewhere as well in those years.[37] These studies reinforce the basic assumption that something very significant must have changed when the carpet was pulled out from under the priesthood with the destruction of the Temple in 70.

That was the second stage of our topic, which granted hegemony to the priesthood in the Second Temple period and thereby (whether or not that was the focus) emphasized the significance of the destruction of the Temple. We may round out this stage of research with reference to Ezra Fleischer's 1989/90 study, claiming that the liturgy of communal Jewish prayer was a total innovation of the post-70 period,[38] and—a few years later—with Francis Schmidt's fascinating *La pensée du Temple* (1994),[39] which attempted to draw second-story conclusions from the new appreciation of the vitality and importance of Temple-centered priestly Judaism in the late Second Temple period. Indeed, on the other side of the ocean, Shaye J.D. Cohen's textbook on the period was still defending, in 1987, the concomitant notion that 70 should be seen as defining a new period, "the rabbinic period"[40]—although his discussion of periodization is not without qualifications that already anticipate the next chapter of our story.

Pharisees dominated Jewish society in *provincia Iudaea*" (Goodblatt, "Place of the Pharisees," 28–29).

[36] S. Mason, "Was Josephus a Pharisee? A Re-Examination of *Life* 10–12," *JJS* 40 (1989): 31–45; and idem, *Flavius Josephus on the Pharisees: A Composition-Critical Study* (Leiden, 1991).

[37] Mason, "Priesthood in Josephus and the 'Pharisaic Revolution,'" *JBL* 107 (1988): 657–61.

[38] E. Fleischer, "On the Beginnings of Obligatory Jewish Prayer," *Tarbiz* 59 (1989/90): 397–441 (in Hebrew). This study, which appeared in the same volume as Sussmann's ("History of the Halakha"), is one of the main points of reference for E.G. Chazon's study in the present collection.

[39] Paris, 1994. English translation: *How the Temple Thinks: Identity and Social Cohesion in Ancient Judaism* (trans. J.E. Crowley; Sheffield, 2001).

[40] S.J.D. Cohen, *From the Maccabees to the Mishnah* (Philadelphia, 1987), 18–19 (= 6–7 in 2d ed., 2006).

The Third Stage

Namely, even when positing the continued use of "the rabbinic period" for the post-70 era, Cohen was justifying this usage primarily on the basis of the change in the language and nature of the sources most useful for students of the history of Jews and Judaism: with the end of Josephus' account, at 70, those who would study the history of the Jews become dependent upon the rabbinic corpus. Cohen notes, however, that that fact about sources does not entail the claim that the rabbis enjoyed great popularity and/or authority after 70. On the contrary, Cohen emphasized that although the rabbis would eventually be "the 'winners' of ancient Jewish history," nevertheless,

> in the second to sixth centuries the rabbis were not nearly as dominant as they would become later, and the concept "the rabbinic period" slights the rabbis' opponents (the losers) and falsely implies that after 70 CE all Jews accepted the rabbis as their leaders and followed the way of rabbinic Judaism.[41]

Indeed, others too were already at work during the heyday of the second stage in preparing a third stage of scholarship, undermining the traditional notion of the rabbis' post-70 domination of Judaism even as they were undermining the other pillar of both previous stages: the assumption that the priests dropped out of competition after 70.[42]

Thus, first of all, the notion of rabbinic popularity and authority even after 70 was coming under fire, with one work after another arguing that here too, claims for rabbinic hegemony had been greatly overstated. We can draw a straight line from Goodblatt's *Rabbinic Instruction in Sassanian Babylonia* (1975), which argued that the great Babylonian yeshivot of the talmudic period were not so great nor so much yeshivot as mere study circles, to Cohen's 1981/82 survey of epigraphic evidence from all around the Jewish world, a survey that yielded no support for the notion that rabbis enjoyed any special role in synagogues in Palestine or the Diaspora or that their presence in the Diaspora was anything more than "meager."[43] Such adumbrations

---

[41] Ibid., 18 (6 in 2d ed.).

[42] For a review of this aspect of third-stage scholarship on "The Extent of the Rabbinic 'Movement' and Its Relationship to Other Jews," see S.S. Miller, *Sages and Commoners in Late Antique 'Erez Israel* (Tübingen, 2006), 7–17.

[43] S.J.D. Cohen, "Epigraphical Rabbis," *JQR* 72 (1981/82): 1–17; see his conclusions on pp. 16–17.

came to fruition in the 1990s with the publication of Cohen's work on the role of the rabbis in ancient Jewish society, which concluded that this role was quite minimal until the third century;[44] Catherine Hezser's work on the rabbinic movement in Roman Palestine, which argued that the movement as such was small and scattered;[45] and Hannah Cotton's work that emphasized how little rabbis and rabbinic law are reflected in Judean papyri of the second century CE.[46] On the basis of all of this and more, which pushed the rise of rabbinic authority down to the third century,[47] the road was not very long to Seth Schwartz's *Imperialism and Jewish Society* (2001), which argued that Judaism basically disappeared between the second and fourth centuries; any rabbis who maintained allegiance to it must have been few and far between.[48]

This development was reinforced, moreover, by growing doubts about the second axiom shared by both previous stages of scholarship: that the priesthood dropped out of the competition after 70. Such doubts allowed the priests to step into the vacuum being created by the minimizing of the rabbis' role. The theory that the priests, *qua* priests, maintained (or rehabilitated) themselves and their prestige after 70 therefore garnered considerable support; although that began only slowly, in the mid-eighties, lately it has flourished.[49] Especially the

---

[44] See idem, "The Place of the Rabbi in Jewish Society of the Second Century," in *The Galilee in Late Antiquity* (ed. L.I. Levine; New York, 1992), 157–73, where the final conclusions include: "They had little inclination and availed themselves of few opportunities to propagate their way of life among the masses. Their judicial authority extended to a few circumscribed topics only. The rabbis were but a small part of Jewish society, an insular group which produced an insular literature. They were not synagogue leaders…" A fuller version of this essay appeared, with the same conclusions, as "The Rabbi in Second-Century Jewish Society," in *The Cambridge History of Judaism, Vol. 3: The Early Roman Period* (ed. W. Horbury, W.D. Davies, and J. Sturdy; Cambridge, 1999), 922–90.

[45] *The Social Structure of the Rabbinic Movement in Roman Palestine* (Tübingen, 1997). For a good measure of the shift from the second stage to the third, see the review of this volume, in *JQR* 90 (1999/2000): 483–88, by L.I. Levine, author of *The Rabbinic Class of Roman Palestine in Late Antiquity* (Jerusalem and New York, 1989).

[46] See esp. H.M. Cotton, "The Rabbis and the Documents," in *Jews in a Graeco-Roman World* (ed. M. Goodman; Oxford, 1998), 167–79.

[47] For this see also Levine's assessments—below, at n. 58.

[48] A relevant passage from his volume is quoted below, at n. 57. For the scholarly roots of Schwartz's approach, see esp. M. Satlow's review in *JQR* 95 (2005/6): 155–56.

[49] See, for example, R. Kimelman, "The Conflict between the Priestly Oligarchy and the Sages in the Talmudic Period (on Explication of PT *Shabbat* 12:3, 13C = *Horayot* 3:4, 48C)," *Zion* 48 (1982/83): 135–48 (in Hebrew); D. Trifon, "The Jewish Priests from the Destruction of the Second Temple to the Rise of Christianity"

synagogue, that quintessential institution of the Jewish community, has been claimed as a space more for the priests than for the rabbis,[50] who are now often thought of as more at home in their ivory tower, the *bet midrash*.[51]

Put quite simply, if schematically and paradoxically, scholarship today is thus, for many serious practitioners, in both total agreement and total disagreement with scholars of Hausrath's day a century and a half ago, and even those of Moore's and Alon's day seventy or eighty

---

(Ph.D. diss., University of Tel-Aviv, 1985 [in Hebrew]); D.M. Goodblatt, "The Title 'Nasi' and the Ideological Background of the Second Revolt," in *The Bar-Kokhba Revolt: A New Approach* (ed. A. Oppenheimer and U. Rappaport; Jerusalem, 1984), 113–32 (in Hebrew; see also idem, "The Priestly Component in Ancient Jewish Nationalism," in idem, *Elements of Ancient Jewish Nationalism* [New York, 2006], 71–107); M. Goodman, "Sadducees and Essenes after 70 CE," in *Crossing the Boundaries: Essays in Biblical Interpretation in Honour of Michael D. Goulder* (ed. S.E. Porter et al.; Leiden, 1994), 347–56; P.S. Alexander, "What Happened to the Jewish Priesthood after 70?" in *A Wandering Galilean: Essays in Honour of Seán Freyne* (ed. Z. Rodgers et al.; Leiden, 2009), 5–33.

[50] That this is quite a recent development, totally part of the third stage of scholarship in this field, is shown strikingly by the fact that as late as 1992, when Levine asked who ran the ancient synagogue if the rabbis did not he offered three candidates (local community; wealthy urban aristocrats; patriarchs) but did not even mention the priests; by 2000, however, he had a whole chapter on the priests in the synagogue, positing "a far more prominent role for priests in the synagogue setting than has been heretofore assumed." Compare L.I. Levine, "The Sages and the Synagogue in Late Antiquity," in *The Galilee in Late Antiquity* (ed. L.I. Levine; New York, 1992), 219, to idem, *The Ancient Synagogue: The First Thousand Years* (New Haven, 2000), 500; cf. below, n. 53. See, inter alia, M.D. Swartz, "Sage, Priest, and Poet: Typologies of Leadership in the Ancient Synagogue," in *Jews, Christians, and Polytheists in the Ancient Synagogue* (ed. S. Fine; London, 1999), 101–17; O. Irshai, "The Role of the Priesthood in the Jewish Community in Late Antiquity: A Christian Model?" in *Jüdische Gemeinden und ihr christlicher Kontext in kulturräumlich vergleichender Betrachtung (5.–18. Jahrhundert)* (ed. C. Cluse, A. Havercamp, and I.J. Yuval; Hannover, 2003), 75–85 (for a more detailed Hebrew version, see idem, "The Priesthood in Jewish Society of Late Antiquity," in *Continuity and Renewal: Jews and Judaism in Byzantine-Christian Palestine* [ed. L.I. Levine; Jerusalem, 2004], 67–106).

[51] That distinction between *bet midrash* and *bet knesset* is another innovation of recent decades. In the wake of a fortuitous epigraphic discovery (an inscription published early in the 1970s; see D. Urman, "Public Structures and Jewish Communities in the Golan Heights," in *Ancient Synagogues: Historical Analysis and Archaeological Data* [ed. D. Urman and P.V.M. Flesher; 2 vols.; Leiden, 1995], 2:432–33) that directed scholarly attention to the issue, additional positive and negative evidence for the distinction was found (see already Urman's "The House of Assembly and the House of Study: Are they One and the Same?" in Urman and Flescher, *Ancient Synagogues*, 1:232–55); given the way the thesis fits right into the trend we are discussing, towards limiting the rabbis' role, it has flourished. See, for example, Levine, "Sages and the Synagogue," 203–5 (emphasizing the distinction between *bet midrash* and synagogue and that rabbis were at home in the former; see also L.I. Levine, *The Ancient Synagogue*, 449–51); Irshai, "Priesthood in Jewish Society," 82–99. In the present volume, see esp. Z. Weiss's and M.D. Swartz's essays.

years ago. They agree that not much changed before and after 70. But, while the earlier scholars held that the Pharisees/rabbis ruled before and after, today "the more or less scholarly consensus of minimizing rabbinic authority"[52] minimizes rabbinic authority both before and after 70 and tends to leave the priests regnant before 70—and, the way things are going, may soon enthrone them after 70, too.[53]

TOWARD A FOURTH STAGE?

It can be fascinating, and quite instructive, to look back at the way an issue has been addressed over a century and a half; to contemplate the interplay of data, discoveries, methodologies, and predispositions; and to observe the way new hypotheses turn up when the requisite antecedents had prepared the way.[54] Truth be told, however, there is at times something somewhat frustrating about these discussions. As

---

[52] As Satlow puts it ("Review," 153). On this consensus, see now H.I. Newman, "The Normativity of Rabbinic Judaism: Obstacles on the Path to a New Consensus," in *Jewish Identities in Antiquity: Studies in Memory of Menahem Stern* (ed. L.I. Levine and D.R. Schwartz; Tübingen, 2009), 165–71.

[53] For the sake of completeness, however, note that some of those who emphasize the importance of the priests in Byzantine Palestine view this status as a *novum*, not as a matter of continuity. Note in this connection that the 2005 second edition of Levine's *The Ancient Synagogue* adds the limitation "of Late Antiquity" after the word "setting" in the passage quoted above in n. 50, along with a new footnote (n. 57) citing scholars who hold that the priests' ascent to prominence was new (pp. 528–29). So too ibid., 476 n. 43. See also D. Stökl Ben Ezra, "Templisierung: Die Rückkehr des Tempels in die jüdische und christliche Liturgie der Spatantike," in *Rites et croyances dans les religions du monde romain* (ed. J. Scheid; Vandœvres, Genève, 2007), 231–287.

[54] As a case in point, note how, given the centrality of the Yavneh story in the traditional history of the self-institutionalization of rabbinic Judaism after the destruction of the Temple, Cohen's 1984 study fit right into what the second stage of scholarship required while Boyarin's work in the past decade fits right into the third. Cohen explained the Yavnean accomplishment ("building a grand coalition" that tolerated difference) as an innovation of the first-century rabbis that allowed them to become powerful, while Boyarin explained the Yavneh stories as the editorial creation of a much later period. See S.J.D. Cohen, "The Significance of Yavneh: Pharisees, Rabbis, and the End of Jewish Sectarianism," *HUCA* 55 (1984): 27–53, and, inter alia, D. Boyarin, "The Yavneh-Cycle of the Stammaim and the Invention of the Rabbis," in *Creation and Composition: The Contribution of the Bavli Redactors (Stammaim) to the Aggada* (ed. J.L. Rubenstein; Tübingen, 2005), 237–89. Or, for another example, note that the same decade that saw the rise of the conception of the continued (or renewed) influence of priests *qua* priests in Palestinian Judaism despite 70 was also witness to the phrasing of the issue as programmatic vis à vis Qumran: F. García Martínez, "Priestly Functions in a Community without Temple," in *Gemeinde ohne Tempel/Community without Temple* (ed. B. Ego et al.; Tübingen, 1999), 303–19.

long as the issue is phrased so broadly as, "Were the rabbis popular
and authoritative in the X century?" while the evidence supplied by
our sources (especially the rabbinic sources) is almost always scattered
and anecdotal, and while we certainly have no access to anything comparable to modern statistics or public opinion polls, there will always
be some evidence for one side of the question and some for the other.
Too often the debate, no matter how penetrating, turns out to be about
how much collateral significance one wants to ascribe this or that bit
of evidence which, taken by itself, both sides are willing to accept; too
often do our debates recall arguments as to whether a cup is half full
or half empty.

If, for example, Philo reports in passing about something that once
happened when he made a pilgrimage to Jerusalem (*De providentia*
2.107), does that indicate that he, or Hellenistic Jews in general, regularly made such pilgrimages? And further, does this bespeak a significant devotion to priestly Judaism? Or should we rather limit ourselves
to concluding that even regarding Philo, all we know is that he once
went on a pilgrimage—and perhaps even ratchet up the significance
of that by underscoring that Philo was rich and religiously committed
and well-documented, so his silence about other visits makes broader
conclusions all the more difficult? Should we, indeed, underline—with
Folker Siegert[55]—the fact that when Philo says that he made the pilgrimage "in order to pray and to sacrifice," he gives precedence to
prayer, for which he had no particular need to go to Jerusalem? Who
can say?[56] Or, for another example, if the Mishnah reports an incident in which both "the sages" and "the priests" dealt with the same
calendrical issue (*m. Rosh HaShanah* 1:7), shall we assume that such
competition and attendant confusion concerning such a basic element
in the fabric of social life as the calendar was the rule or the exception?
Who knows for sure?

Thus, for example, when Seth Schwartz first writes in his chapter
on "Rabbis and Patriarchs on the Margins," with regard to the second–fourth centuries, that "some Jews, probably a very small number (among them were the rabbis) still insisted on the importance
of the Torah, of Judaism, in their symbolic world, and these Jews,

---

[55] So, most recently, F. Siegert ("Philo and the New Testament," in *The Cambridge
Companion to Philo* [ed. A. Kamesar; Cambridge, 2009], 194), in the context of drawing lines from Philo to prophetic and New Testament criticism of the Temple cult.
[56] See J. Leonhardt-Balzer's contribution to this volume.

convinced of their elitist status, tried to insinuate their way into general Palestinian society," but then emphasizes that their real role was only "peripheral and weak" and so "we need...to keep the rabbis to one side if we wish to understand the character of Jewish society between 70 and 640—a fortiori between 70–350,"[57] one wonders whether the evidence, which admittedly points in two directions, can indeed be resolved very clearly in favor of one. But one might also wonder, when reading Lee I. Levine's 1992 report of a consensus that "the rabbis were not the universally recognized authorities of the period, but neither were they without influence,"[58] or Stuart S. Miller's 2006 assessment that "the rabbinic movement was neither as ubiquitous as was once thought, nor as diminutive as some have recently maintained,"[59] whether—however well-founded such assessments may be—the time has not come for another phrasing of the issue.

In planning our conference, accordingly, we decided to prescind from the basic question, "Who, if anyone, and—accordingly—what type of Judaism, if any, was regnant among the Jews before and after 70?" and to cast our net more broadly, to take in a fuller array of elements in the lives of Jews of the period. We asked experts in numerous fields, including some areas that might be assumed a priori to have been affected by the Destruction and others apparently isolated from that event, to go over their materials and, each in his or her own field, compare what they found from before 70 to what they found from the period after 70. Furthermore, we asked them, if they did find changes, to consider what might have caused them.

The answers we got were something of a mixed bag. This is not surprising. If the present survey of the ups and downs of a century

---

[57] Schwartz, *Imperialism and Jewish Society*, 103–4.

[58] Levine, "Sages and the Synagogue," 202. So, too, ibid. 207–8: after emphasizing how little evidence there is for rabbinic involvement in synagogues in the second century, he continues: "In contrast, from the mid-third through the fourth centuries the number of sources attesting to rabbinic involvement in synagogue affairs increases dramatically, undoubtedly reflecting a more significant presence"; but a few paragraphs later he concludes that "despite this increase in source material, rabbinic involvement in synagogue activities nevertheless appears sporadic and limited in scope."

[59] *Sages and Commoners*, 446 (in the last chapter of a detailed study that is basically a response to Hezser and S. Schwartz). See, similarly, the debates in the section entitled, "In the Wake of the Destruction: Was Rabbinic Judaism Normative?" in *Jewish Identities in Antiquity: Studies in Memory of Menahem Stern* (ed. L.I. Levine and D.R. Schwartz; Tübingen, 2009).

and a half has shown that learned and reasonable people espoused views very different from one another, and even diametrically opposed to one another, and if we began by recalling that when the dean of Jewish historians thought about the big picture he was sure 70 was a watershed but when he turned to the details he just couldn't pin it down, we must realize that this is a topic that is not susceptible to easy generalizations. There are tensions in the evidence, and, accordingly, the papers in this volume present:

- disagreements concerning the assessment of basically the same dossier as to *how attached Diaspora Jews were to the Temple cult* (Leonhardt-Balzer, Hacham, and Tuval) and some suggestive comparative evidence that the faithful, if they are so disposed, are quite capable of maintaining meaningful religious contact with a place with which they have no real contact (Schwarz);
- different subdossiers pulling different ways, such as those concerning *art* (if Vilozny underlines the rise of figural art in exorcism following the Destruction and suggests that this bespeaks a need for something to replace the Temple cult, Levine argues that it was the local context of Jewish communities, rather than anything relating to the Temple or its destruction, that determined the type of art they would employ) and *synagogue life* (Swartz finds something of a virtual continuation of sacrifice, while Weiss finds no support for the thesis that priests had a special role in the synagogue);
- fields such as *liturgy*, in which, as Chazon shows, there is both change and continuity despite the expectation that this field, at least, would be directly and intensively affected by the Destruction;
- fields in which things definitely changed between the first and second century but where it is not clear that the change was actually due to the Destruction—so Mandel on *biblical interpretation as a basis for law* and Frey on *Johannine Christianity*;
- an area such as *exorcism formulae* (Bohak), which apparently reflects a world of its own that could maintain itself more or less unchanged despite the events in our world;
- reasons to think that the *polarity between priests and nonpriests* was less than clear-cut, either because the priests themselves insisted on binding themselves to the Torah (Himmelfarb); or because there is reason to associate priesthood with zealotry and not merely with Aaronic descent (Aran); or because there is reason to doubt the assumption that rabbinic preoccupation with purity indicates competition with priests (Birenboim);

- evidence that might indicate continued *sectarianism* long after 70, which would suggest that the Destruction did not change much with regard to this well-known aspect of pre-70 Judaism (Magness);
- reasons to think that Judeans had gotten used to the loss of state-hood long before 70 (Sharon), but could not accept, without two more wars, the loss of the Temple (Goodman)—a conclusion that corresponds with the argument that it was only after 135 that Christian observers began to consider the events of 70 as final and epoch-making (Clements).

It is in the nature of things that collective volumes do not put forward unified theses. What unites our volume is, rather, the common phrasing of the question, the common quest. Our volume reflects the views of individual scholars, presented in this manner to our colleagues and other interested readers after having had the benefit of the comments and criticism of the small number of scholars we were able to bring together for the conference. We are confident that making these papers available to the scholarly community at large will allow them to make significant contributions to the discussion both of the specific issues that they address and of the larger issues of the structuring of Jewish history, with which this quest began. Who knows, perhaps scholars looking back at this issue in a few generations will discern here, and in similar works by other scholars, the beginning of a fourth stage, building on the insights of the preceding three along with whatever the future will bring.

PART I

SONS OF AARON AND DISCIPLES OF AARON:
PRIESTS AND RABBIS BEFORE AND AFTER 70

"FOUND WRITTEN IN THE BOOK OF MOSES": PRIESTS IN THE ERA OF TORAH

Martha Himmelfarb

Sometime in the middle of the fifth century BCE, the Persian governor of Yehud intervened in the affairs of the Jerusalem Temple (Neh 13:4–9). While the governor was away in Persia, the high priest Eliashib had designated a room in the Temple for the use of Tobiah the Ammonite. Tobiah was a long-standing enemy of the governor (Neh 2:10, and *passim*), and the governor must have understood Eliashib's friendship with Tobiah as a sign of hostility. Thus on his return to Jerusalem the governor ejected Tobiah and had the room purified and returned to its former use. Eliashib may have been the high priest, but the governor had the power of the state behind him.

The governor in question was, of course, Nehemiah, hero of the biblical book bearing his name, a pious Jew, or at least so the book of Nehemiah presents him, as well as a Persian civil servant. Eliashib's response to Nehemiah's interference is not preserved for us. He would probably have insisted that he knew more about how the Temple should operate than a mere layman like Nehemiah and that Nehemiah could hardly be more concerned about maintaining its purity than he. He might also have claimed that the rules he had learned at his father's knee made it perfectly acceptable to give space in the Temple to a pious Gentile such as Tobiah, who after all bore a Yahwist name. Yet no matter what Eliashib said, Nehemiah was the governor, and he won the argument because he had the power to enforce his views.

But the editors of the book of Nehemiah were not content with Nehemiah's victory.[1] They also wanted to show readers that his behavior was not arbitrary. Thus they placed the account of the confrontation

---

[1] There is no consensus about the process of composition of the books of Ezra and Nehemiah. For a recent discussion with extensive references, see J.L. Wright, *Rebuilding Identity: The Nehemiah Memoir and Its Earliest Readers* (Berlin, 2004). I am not persuaded, however, by Wright's account of the passages under discussion here (189–204, 315–17).

over Tobiah immediately after a report on the reading of "the Book of
Moses" on the day of the dedication of the wall around Jerusalem:

> ...It was found written in it that no Ammonite or Moabite should enter
> the congregation of God forever because they did not greet the children
> of Israel with bread and water and they hired Balaam to curse them,
> but our God turned the curse into a blessing. And it happened, when
> they heard the Torah, that they separated all foreigners from Israel. (Neh
> 13:1–3)[2]

The chronological relationship between the dedication of the wall and
Nehemiah's confrontation with Eliashib is not entirely clear since
the narrative implies that the dedication of the wall took place in the
thirty-second year of Artaxerxes (Neh 5:14, 6:15), the year in which
Nehemiah was away. But whatever the historical reality, if any, the
placement of the reading of the Book of Moses has the advantage
of implicitly justifying the expulsion of Tobiah from the Temple by
appeal to the Book's prohibition of Ammonites in the congregation of
God. Thus the book of Nehemiah represents Nehemiah's interference
in the Temple not as the work of an angry governor threatened by a
high-ranking official's alliance with his enemy, but as the act of a pious
Jew concerned for the sanctity of the Temple and the requirements of
the Book of Moses.

By the "Book of Moses," the editors surely meant the same work
that Ezra read to the assembled Judeans as the "Book of the Torah
of Moses" (Neh 8:1), though the specific rules and practices that the
books of Ezra and Nehemiah attribute to works bearing a variety of
similar names make it difficult to identify these books with the Torah
as we know it today.[3] Clearly, however, the Book of Moses included
material we find in Deuteronomy: the law excluding Ammonites and
Moabites from the congregation of the Lord in Deut 23:4–7 offers the
same explanation for their exclusion as the passage from Nehemiah,
in almost identical language.

---

[2] All translations of the Bible and other ancient texts are mine unless otherwise
indicated.

[3] C. Houtman, "Ezra and the Law: Observations on the Supposed Relation between
Ezra and the Pentateuch," in *Remembering All the Way: A Collection of Old Testament
Studies Published on the Occasion of the Fortieth Anniversary of the Oudtestametische
Werkgezelschap in Nederland* (Leiden, 1981), 103–15. For names of the book in Ezra
and Nehemiah, see ibid., 104 n. 67. For the collection of material attributed to the
book, see 104–6. I am not convinced by Houtman's conclusions, however.

But whatever the contents of the work, the editors' strategy for justifying the expulsion of Tobiah from the Temple demonstrates the potentially revolutionary implications of the existence of an authoritative text. Deuteronomy was published in 622 BCE, decades before the destruction of the First Temple, when a king still sat on the throne in Jerusalem; indeed its publication was part of the program of reform undertaken under the patronage of King Josiah. Yet Deuteronomy placed all Israel, including the king and his priests, under its authority.[4] Similarly, in the incident just discussed, Nehemiah, a layman with no claim to priestly authority, was able to appeal to the text to justify what in an earlier day would have been understood by one and all as a usurpation of the high priest's prerogative.

Now I would like to turn to a passage from the Mishnah that describes another instance of lay interference in the domain of the priesthood on the basis of an authoritative text. On the eve of the Day of Atonement, according to the passage, the elders of the court make the high priest take an oath: "Sir high priest, we are the representatives of the court, and you are our representative and the representative of the court. We adjure you by Him who makes His name dwell in this house that you change not a word of all that we have said to you" (*m. Yoma* 1:5). By the end of the Second Temple era, the period to which the Mishnah refers, there can be no doubt of the existence of the Torah as we have it. The Mishnah itself does not explain why the oath is necessary, but according to other rabbinic sources the Pharisees and Sadducees differed in their interpretation of the instructions of Leviticus 16 and thus on the proper procedure for the high priest's incense offering.[5]

More than the ritual of any other day of the year the ritual of the Day of Atonement depends on the high priest. Yet the passage from the Mishnah claims that the high priest had to swear to follow the instructions of representatives of the court, experts who need not have been priests of any kind, much less connected to a high priestly family. The assumption of the court's ability to make the high priest do its bidding may well be rabbinic fantasy, of a piece with the claim in the next mishnah (1:6) that only if the high priest was himself a sage

---

[4] Reform and regulation of the cult and thus of its priests is one of the central concerns of Deuteronomy. For the king, see esp. the "Law of the King," Deut 17:14–20.

[5] *T. Yoma* 1:8; *y. Yoma* 1:7; *b. Yoma* 19b, 53a; *Sipra Aḥarei Mot* 3.11.

was he permitted to expound Scripture on the evening of the Day of
Atonement; otherwise disciples of the sages were to expound before
him. But even if it is fantasy, the Mishnah points clearly to the tension
between the Torah and traditional priestly authority. Only because the
laws of the Temple ritual of the Day of Atonement are contained in
the Torah is it possible to imagine the court contesting the way the
high priest chose to perform the ritual.

The Torah's impact on the power and autonomy of the priesthood
is also evident in a variety of texts from the period between Nehemiah
and the Mishnah. One striking example is 4QMMT, which offers an
extended critique of the way priests perform their rituals, leading the
people astray through their errors. The critique derives its power from
its repeated references, implicit and explicit, to passages in the Torah.[6]
The priests attacked by 4QMMT would presumably have defended
their practices, and their defense would surely have involved contesting 4QMMT's interpretation of particular passages. This sort of dispute is possible only because both parties acknowledge the authority
of the text.

The appeal to the Torah in other works critical of priests in the
Second Temple period is often implicit. Thus the Book of the Watchers and *Aramaic Levi* criticize, without ever citing the Torah, the same
priestly marriage practice that 4QMMT objects to.[7] For these writings
to have cited the Torah would have been anachronistic for their fic-
tive settings in the pre-Sinaitic period; nonetheless, their authors must
have assumed that readers could be counted on to make the connection to the Torah's laws. True, priests could certainly ignore the criticism of these works, whose authors, unlike Nehemiah, had no means
to impose their positions. Nevertheless, the idea that priestly practice
was open to discussion on the basis of the contents of the Torah could
not fail to weaken the traditional authority of the priesthood.

---

[6] On the use of Scripture in 4QMMT, see M.J. Bernstein, "The Employment
and Interpretation of Scripture in 4QMMT: Preliminary Observations," in *Reading
4QMMT: New Perspectives on Qumran Law and History* (ed. J. Kampen and M.J.
Bernstein; Atlanta, 1996), 29–51.

[7] M. Himmelfarb, "Levi, Phinehas, and the Problem of Intermarriage at the Time
of the Maccabean Revolt," *JSQ* 6 (1999): 1–23; eadem, *A Kingdom of Priests: Ancestry
and Merit in Ancient Judaism* (Philadelphia, 2006), 25–28. To the references there, add
Bernstein, "Employment," 46, in tentative support of reading the passage in 4QMMT
as insisting on priestly endogamy.

The texts just discussed leave no doubt of the public character of the Torah during the Second Temple period, in the sense that a learned elite had access to copies that it studied carefully. The ideal of universal access to the authoritative text is expressed in Deuteronomy, which decrees public reading every seven years in Jerusalem during the festival of Sukkot (Deut 31:10–11), but the evidence for nonelite access is much more limited. Public reading every seven years would hardly guarantee lay familiarity with the text, and in fact there is little evidence to confirm that such reading was practiced during the Second Temple period. Indeed, evidence for any kind of public reading is quite limited, and it exists primarily for the Diaspora. Nor is there much evidence before the first century CE for the institution in which ordinary people would be most likely to acquire their knowledge of the Torah—the synagogue.[8]

Despite the paucity of evidence, D.M. Goodblatt has recently argued for knowledge of the Torah as one of the central components of Jewish national identity in the Second Temple period. After surveying the limited evidence, he points to another kind of evidence that, in his view, strongly suggests a practice of public reading of the Torah in Judea from the third century BCE on: the significant number of manuscripts of books of the Torah that survive among the Dead Sea Scrolls, at Masada, and at sites in the Judean desert associated with the Bar Kokhba revolt, which must represent only a very small fraction of what once existed. Goodblatt argues that the only way to understand the numbers in light of the likely size of the population of Judea and its low level of literacy is to see the scrolls of the Torah as "performance texts," intended for public reading.[9] If Goodblatt is correct, then even

---

[8] D.M. Goodblatt, *Elements of Jewish Nationalism* (Cambridge, 2006), 28–43.

[9] Goodblatt, *Elements*, 43–48. He cites Keith Hopkins's comment that even for ancient Egypt, with its favorable climatic conditions, "the survival ratio [for texts] could be lower than 1:10,000" ("Conquest by Book," in *Literacy in the Roman World* [ed. M.K. Beard et al.; Ann Arbor, 1991], 133 n. 2). Goodblatt suggests that in Judea one might expect an even lower survival ratio because the climate is not as favorable: it is no accident that the manuscript finds come from the Judean desert. My papyrologist colleague AnneMarie Luijendijk expresses (in private correspondence) some skepticism about Hopkins's ratio, and I might add that Hopkins himself is more cautious than the quotation above might suggest: he goes on to say that the three surviving copies of the *Oracle of the Potter* reflect the existence of anywhere from three to more than 35,000 copies. Nonetheless, whatever the appropriate ratio, it is hard not to be impressed by the number of scrolls of books of the Torah found at a small number of sites in the Judean desert.

illiterate people were in a position to form opinions about whether priestly practice conformed to the dictates of the Torah. Even if he is not, there can be no doubt that the existence of a written document enabled at least a small group of learned experts to compare reality to what the Torah prescribed.

Many scholars have assumed that the authors of texts such as 4QMMT, the Book of the Watchers, and *Aramaic Levi* were priests, on the assumption that only priests would be sufficiently interested in the details of priestly practice to criticize the mistaken behavior of other priests. I reject this assumption: if the fate of the people of Israel depended on what priests did in the Temple, surely even nonpriests would have wanted to see it done right. Still, it is quite likely that the authors of at least some of these texts were of priestly ancestry, for priests appear to have made up a significant portion of the learned class of Judean society in the Second Temple period. Ezra, "a scribe expert in the Torah of Moses" (Ezra 7:6), to whom the books of Ezra and Nehemiah attribute the establishment of the Torah as the constitution of the Jewish people, was a priest by ancestry. Joshua ben Sira at the beginning of the second century BCE is often thought to have been a priest; he was undoubtedly a scribe by profession. But even if the authors of 4QMMT, the Book of the Watchers, and *Aramaic Levi* were priests, they offered their criticism of priestly practice not on the basis of access to priestly tradition but on the basis of the text of the Torah.

Yet if the Torah made their life difficult, priests had only themselves to blame for it.[10] Nehemiah cites a passage from Deuteronomy as the justification for overruling Eliashib, but the oath that elders of the court make the high priest swear is necessary because of a dispute about a ritual described in P, the priestly source of the Torah. In most ancient Near Eastern societies, knowledge of how the cult and other rituals were to be performed was restricted to priests, and the written instructions were kept secret.[11] But the priests of ancient Israel—or at least those of them who stood behind P—chose to make public the central aspects of their task in documents that became part of the Torah. We

---

[10] So, too, J.W. Watts, *Ritual and Rhetoric in Leviticus* (Cambridge, 2007), 60–61.

[11] J. Milgrom, *Leviticus 1–16* (New York, 1991), 143–44; A.L. Oppenheim, completed by E. Reiner, *Ancient Mesopotamia: Portrait of a Dead Civilization* (rev. ed.; Chicago, 1977), 181, 186–87, 192–93; S. Sauneron, *The Priests of Ancient Egypt* (trans. D. Lorton; new ed.; Ithaca, N.Y., 2000), 35–36, 81, 91.

have already seen the consequences of the publication of P: criticism from lay people, who were now in a position to form an opinion about how well priests were doing their job, and from unhappy priests, who now had objective criteria to point to.

The Torah contains a second body of priestly material in addition to P, the Holiness source known as H—a somewhat later work that concerns itself not only with cultic and ritual matters but also with the ethical behavior required for Israel to be a holy people.[12] H understands the entire land to be holy and thus, like the sanctuary according to P, subject to defilement. As a result, lay people become more important to maintaining sacred space in a state of purity. Thus, H's efforts to enlarge the definition of holiness also involve a certain shift of power away from the priesthood.[13] My discussion here, however, focuses on the laws of P, which are concerned exclusively with the cult and ritual practices and are thus in some sense the most essentially priestly.

There is no consensus about the date of P, or even whether it is preexilic or postexilic,[14] but for our purposes this does not really matter. For if P preceded Deuteronomy, it seems reasonable to conclude that priestly willingness to publish a presentation of the central priestly activities grew out of the same appreciation of the power of the written text reflected in Deuteronomy. If, however, its publication followed Deuteronomy, it was presumably in imitation of Deuteronomy, with the intention of confirming the status of the cult in the era of the Torah of Moses.

Although much of P consists of narrative, it is the laws of the first part of the book of Leviticus (chs. 1–16) and a significant portion of the book of Numbers that are of interest here. Many of these laws are instructions for the sacrificial cult or other rituals performed by priests. Yet the rhetoric of these laws formulated by priests and requiring priestly participation is inclusive. Again and again God tells Moses to report his words to the children of Israel;[15] only rarely is Moses told

---

[12] My understanding of H and its relationship to P is most indebted to I. Knohl, *The Sanctuary of Silence: The Priestly Torah and the Holiness School* (Minneapolis, 1995).

[13] Himmelfarb, *Kingdom of Priests*, 62–63.

[14] For a recent discussion of the state of the question, with extensive bibliography, which favors a postexilic date, see J. Blenkinsopp, "An Assessment of the Alleged Pre-Exilic Date of the Priestly Material in the Pentateuch," *ZAW* 108 (1996): 495–518.

[15] E.g., Lev 1:2; 4:1; 5:20; 7:22; 12:1.

to report them specifically to Aaron and his sons.[16] Sometimes God addresses priestly laws to both Moses and Aaron,[17] but he speaks to Aaron alone only rarely and in extraordinary circumstances.[18] Thus the priestly authors emphasize that the laws are directed to all Israel even when they can be fulfilled only with the assistance of priests. It is also noteworthy that P requires lay participation in the process of sacrifice.[19] This practice stands in contrast to that of other ancient cults in which priests performed rituals out of view of the laity.[20] In other words, the decision to make public the rules of the cult can be seen as part of a larger priestly world view that is quite distinctive in the ancient Near East.

One other aspect of the public character of P should be noted. For all that many modern readers find the priestly laws excessively detailed, there is a great deal they do not tell us about how rituals were to be performed. Presumably this missing information was part of the living tradition of priestly practice that young priests learned as they came of age to serve. It is noteworthy that Isaac's instructions to Levi in *Aramaic Levi*, a work composed in pre-Hasmonean times, cover just the sort of subjects one would expect such oral tradition to include, such as directions for additional ablutions beyond those decreed by the Torah, an exhortation to avoid getting blood on priestly garments, and a list of types of wood suitable for use on the altar. Although there are some points concerning which the instructions in *Aramaic Levi* appear to stand in tension with the rules of the Torah, such as the order in which the various parts of the sacrificial ritual are to be performed, there is nothing to suggest that they reflect sectarian objections to the laws of the Torah, and they may well reflect actual Temple practice.[21] The descriptions of the working of the Temple in the *Letter*

---

[16] E.g., Lev 6:1, 18.

[17] E.g., Lev 11:1; 13:1; 14:33; 15:1.

[18] Lev 10:8.

[19] E.g., Lev 1:4–5; 3:2, 8.

[20] Milgrom, *Leviticus 1–16*, 143–44.

[21] See M. Himmelfarb, "Earthly Sacrifice and Heavenly Incense: The Law of the Priesthood in *Aramaic Levi* and *Jubilees*," in *Heavenly Realms and Earthly Realities in Late Antique Religions* (ed. R. Boustan and A.Y. Reed; Cambridge, 2004), 106–16; and L.H. Schiffman, "Sacrificial Halakhah in the Fragments of the *Aramaic Levi Document* from Qumran, the Cairo Genizah, and Mt. Athos Monastery," in *Reworking the Bible: Apocryphal and Related Texts at Qumran. Proceedings of a Joint Symposium by the Orion Center for the Study of the Dead Sea Scrolls and Associated Literature and the Hebrew University Institute for Advanced Studies Research Group on Qumran,*

of Aristeas, perhaps from the second century BCE, and in the mishnaic tractate *Tamid*, from the beginning of the third century CE, even if they are entirely the product of their authors' imaginations, offer a good indication of another kind of material missing in the priestly material of the Torah: principles for integrating the rather individualistic picture of sacrifice in the Torah into the institutional framework of the Temple. Both rhetoric and content, then, make it clear that P is not a handbook written for priests that was later published in the Torah. Rather, it was written to represent the central aspects of priestly responsibilities not only to priests but to the entire people of Israel.[22]

Nehemiah's confrontation with Eliashib and the elders' admonishment of the high priest on the eve of the Day of Atonement demonstrate the potential for tension between priests and expert interpreters of the Torah. Yet the composition of P shows us that the priestly authors of P operated like scribes. The presentation and arrangement of P's laws reflect a tradition of scribal practice parallel to other biblical and ancient Near Eastern scribal traditions.[23] The colophon, "This is the torah of…," which serves to organize a significant portion of the material of Leviticus and Numbers (Lev 6:2, 7, 18; 7:1, 11, 37; 11:46; 12:7; 13:59; 14:2, 32, 54, 57; 15:32; Num 5:29; 6:13; 19:14), is the priestly counterpart to the characteristic colophons of prophetic and wisdom literature.[24] The scribal activity of the transmitters of the priestly corpus can also be detected in specifications, clarifications, and exegetical resolution of tensions or contradictions within the corpus.[25] In the Second Temple period, as already noted, the combination of priestly ancestry and scribal profession in a single individual was by no means unusual. Indeed, the combination comes to represent an

---

15–17 January, 2002 (ed. E.G. Chazon, D. Dimant, and R.A. Clements; Leiden, 2005), 177–202.

[22] Watts, *Ritual*, offers a full-scale rhetorical analysis of Leviticus 1–16 (though without much attention to chaps. 12–15), which he sees as priestly propaganda for the Aaronides' monopoly on sacrifices, though he is more respectful of priests and their motives than this summary might suggest.

[23] Thus M. Fishbane, *Biblical Interpretation in Ancient Israel* (Oxford, 1985), 26–32.

[24] Fishbane, *Biblical Interpretation*, 78–79; idem, "Biblical Colophons, Textual Criticism and Legal Analogies," *CBQ* 42 (1980): 438–49, esp. 439–43; idem, "Accusations of Adultery: A Study of Law and Scribal Practice in Numbers 5:11–31," *HUCA* 45 (1974): 25–45, esp. 32–35.

[25] Fishbane, *Biblical Interpretation*, 166–70, 189–94, 197–99, 209–10, 216–17, 220–28.

ideal. Thus Enoch in the Book of the Watchers is explicitly a "scribe of righteousness" and implicitly a priest, while the high priest Simon the Righteous is represented as the twin of Wisdom herself in the Wisdom of Ben Sira. Teaching also figures as a priestly duty in H (Lev 10:11),[26] and frequently in Deuteronomy and in a variety of exilic and postexilic works.[27] True, it does not figure as a priestly duty in P, but the very existence of P suggests the importance of priests who were also scribes for the very formation of the Torah.

In several influential articles over the past two decades D.R. Schwartz has argued that the fundamental difference between the priestly law of the Second Temple period (that is, the law of the Sadducees and Qumran sectarians) and Pharisaic-rabbinic law is that priestly law is realist while Pharisaic-rabbinic law is nominalist.[28] By this Schwartz means that the priestly system understands the laws of the Torah as reflecting and revealing the way the world really is (acts are prohibited by the Torah because they are bad) while the Pharisaic-rabbinic system understands the laws to create that reality (acts are bad because they are prohibited by the Torah).[29] In Schwartz's view it stands to reason that priests, who owe their status to the natural fact of descent, would view the world in realist terms, while Pharisees and rabbis, who derive their authority not from nature but from expertise in the law

---

[26] Knohl, *Sanctuary of Silence*, 68–69; Milgrom claims that vv. 10–11 of Lev 10 "comprise a late interpolation" (*Leviticus 1–16*, 617).

[27] Milgrom notes 2 Kgs 17:27; Ezek 22:26; 44:23; Hag 2:11; Mal 2:7 (*Leviticus 1–16*, 52).

[28] See esp. "Law and Truth: On Qumran-Sadducean and Rabbinic Views of the Law," in *The Dead Sea Scrolls: Forty Years of Research* (ed. D. Dimant and U. Rappaport; Leiden and Jerusalem, 1992), 229–40; "Between Sages and Priests in the Time of the Second Temple," in his *Studies in the Period of the Second Temple* (Jerusalem, 1996), 403–19 (in Hebrew); "From Priests on Their Right to Christians on Their Left? Toward the Interpretation and Development of a Mishnaic Story (*m. Rosh HaShanah*)," *Tarbiz* 74 (2004–2005): 21–41 (in Hebrew); "Arguments a minore ad majus (*qal vahomer*)—Sadducean Realism," *Massekhet* 5 (2006): 145–56 (in Hebrew). Those who have embraced Schwartz's analysis include C. Werman and A. Shemesh (see the references in Schwartz, "Arguments," 146 n. 3); D. Rothstein ("Sexual Union and Sexual Offences in *Jubilees*," *JSJ* 35 [2004]: 363–84, esp. 371); and E. Regev ("On Blood, Impurity, and Body Perception in the Halakhic Schools in the Second Temple and Talmudic Period," *AJS Review* 27 [2003]: 1–22, esp. 16–17 [186–87], 22 [181] [in Hebrew]).

[29] "Arguments," 145–46; see also the discussion of specific examples in "Law and Truth," 231–35. Schwartz cites Y. Silman, "Halakhic Determinations of a Nominalist and Realistic Nature: Legal and Philosophical Considerations," *Dine Israel* 12 (1984–1985): 249–66 (in Hebrew), as the source for his use of the categories ("Law and Truth," 230 n. 8; "Arguments," 145 n. 2).

itself, would embrace nominalism. In response to critics, Schwartz has revised his argument to take account of a significant amount of realism in Pharisaic-rabbinic law.[30] He now suggests that the best evidence for the underlying characteristics of each system is to be found in polemical contexts and that the disputes between the two schools of law demonstrate that the Pharisaic-rabbinic system is fundamentally nominalist.[31]

Though I find Schwartz's argument provocative and stimulating, I am skeptical about the claim that the fundamental difference between priestly and Pharisaic-rabbinic law is the difference between realism and nominalism. In fact, I must admit that I am not persuaded that such a fundamental difference exists, nor am I convinced that there was a unified corpus of priestly law that stood in contrast to protorabbinic law in the late Second Temple period, as the scholarly consensus holds.[32] The point I would like to make here, however, is independent of the perhaps eccentric views to which I have just confessed. The point is this: there are significant nominalist elements in the foundational text of priestly law, the P document itself. Though Schwartz's argument concerns later interpretations of biblical law rather than biblical law itself,[33] I believe that an analysis of P is nonetheless relevant to it. For if my understanding of P is correct, it calls into question Schwartz's claim that the hereditary character of priestly authority predisposes priests to legal realism.

The topics from P that I would like to consider, very briefly, are skin afflictions in human beings and plague in houses, both termed *tsara'at* in the text of Leviticus. Schwartz comments on these laws in his first article on the realism/nominalism divide, suggesting that they provide evidence for priestly realism before the Second Temple

---

[30] Schwartz, "Arguments," 147–48. Schwartz also notes an instance of nominalism in priestly law (148, esp. n. 10), but he clearly perceives rabbinic realism as the problem for his argument, presumably because there are more examples of rabbinic realism than of priestly nominalism. This imbalance fits the argument of J.L. Rubenstein, "Nominalism and Realism in Qumranic and Rabbinic Law: A Reassessment," *DSD* 6 (1999): 180–83, that realism is the default mode for legal systems; see below. Rubenstein ("Nominalism," 157–83) offers the most extended critique of Schwartz of which I am aware; for other criticism and responses to Schwartz's argument, see Schwartz, "Arguments," 146 nn. 4, 6.

[31] "Arguments," 147–48.

[32] Himmelfarb, *Kingdom of Priests*, 112–14; A.I. Baumgarten, *The Flourishing of Jewish Sects in the Maccabean Era* (Leiden, 1997), 56, 75–80.

[33] As Schwartz notes ("Law and Truth," 236).

period, but also noting "some nominalist element" in the particular law for plague in houses that I discuss below.[34] My goal is not to call into question Schwartz's claim of realist elements in P but rather to insist on the presence of significant nominalist elements as well. And though I focus here on one category of P's purity laws, I am confident that a careful examination of the entirety of P's laws would yield other examples of nominalism.

P's purity laws constitute a system in the sense that the rules for one type of impurity allow us to deduce rules for others. Thus, for example, although Lev 15:19–24 does not mention bathing as part of the process of purification from menstrual impurity, it is clear from elsewhere in the Bible (2 Sam 11:14) that bathing was required, as the rules for purification from other types of genital discharge imply.[35] The organic character of the system fits a realist understanding of purity and impurity; a nominalist approach would presumably understand each type of impurity, defined by its own laws, as distinct from the others and without any bearing on them. P's understanding of the way in which impurity is transmitted also reflects a realist conception.[36]

Yet P's laws for plague in houses include a remarkable instance of legal nominalism:

> When you enter the land of Canaan that I give you as a possession, and I inflict an eruptive plague upon a house in the land you possess, the owner of the house shall come and tell the priest, saying, "Something like a plague has appeared upon my house." The priest shall order the house cleared before the priest enters to examine the plague, so that nothing in the house may become unclean; after that the priest shall enter to examine the house. (Lev 14:34–36, NJPS)

A realist view of impurity would surely presume the contents removed from the house to be impure on the basis of their exposure to plague before it was diagnosed.

---

[34] The passage in which Schwartz discerns realism concerns the person who has already been declared pure by the priest after having been quarantined for the required two periods of seven days with ambiguous symptoms (Lev 13:31–37). The immediate designation of the afflicted person as impure is realist in Schwartz's view: the priest obviously got the facts wrong the first time and corrects his mistake. A nominalist approach would require starting the whole process over ("Law and Truth," 236). The discussion of nominalism in the law for plague in houses appears in a footnote ("Law and Truth," 236–37 n. 22).

[35] Himmelfarb, *Kingdom of Priests*, 89–90.

[36] See Rubenstein, "Nominalism," 170–71, who argues that rabbinic laws about transmission of impurity also reflect a realist view.

Another indication of the presence of nominalist elements in P emerges from comparison to ancient Mesopotamian rituals for treating fungus in houses. These rituals understand the fungus as an omen of disaster and require its removal in an effort to avert the disaster.[37] But while the green or red eruptions of plague in houses (Lev 14:37) sound quite unpleasant, P does not see them as an omen, nor does it suggest that they reflect any wrongdoing on the part of the owner of the house. In light of the realist attitude toward fungus indicated by the Mesopotamian rituals, the absence of a connection in P between plague in houses and immorality or an external evil can be seen as reflecting a nominalist approach to impurity: the house is impure because the rules say so.

Nor is P's nominalist understanding of the impurity of tsara'at limited to plague in houses. Elsewhere in the Bible, skin afflictions are quite explicitly described as punishment for sin. Thus, in a story in the book of Numbers, Miriam is visited with skin afflictions for speaking ill of Moses (Num 12:10), while in the book of Chronicles, King Uzziah is struck with scale disease in response to his arrogant attempt to offer incense in the Temple (2 Chr 26:16–19). P, in contrast, never mentions sin in its laws of skin afflictions.[38]

True, there is a certain tension between P's understanding of impurity and portions of the rituals P decrees for purification, such as the release of a bird as part of the process of purification from skin afflictions (Lev 14:4–7). This ritual is an adaptation of Mesopotamian and Hittite rituals in which birds are released to carry away illness, headache, or sin.[39] But P never claims that skin afflictions are the result of sin, so there is no sin to remove.[40] And while P appears to understand skin afflictions as disease, since it speaks of the sufferer being healed

---

[37] Milgrom *Leviticus 1–16*, 865; see also S. Meier, "House Fungus: Mesopotamia and Israel (Lev 14:33–53)," *RB* 96 (1989): 184–92.

[38] The same is true of P's view of menstrual impurity (Himmelfarb, *Kingdom of Priests*, 89).

[39] Milgrom, *Leviticus 1–16*, 834–35. Milgrom notes that the scapegoat ritual of the Day of Atonement, which has a similar function, has been transformed to make it more suitable to P's worldview.

[40] Note, however, that Milgrom finds evidence that P shared the popular view of the relationship of skin afflictions to sin in the four different sacrifices P requires as part of the process of purification from scale disease (Lev 14:10–20); Milgrom sees these as an effort to expiate all possible types of wrongdoing that might have led to the affliction (*Leviticus 1–16*, 858). Even if P's rituals take account of the popular understanding, however, this does not mean that P shares this view.

(Lev 14:3), the impurity and the disease are not coextensive. Someone whose entire body is covered with the afflictions, though surely ill, is pure (Lev 13:13), and the ritual of purification does not take place until after the disease is gone (Lev 14:3). Thus it is neither sin nor disease but only impurity that the bird carries away. Once again P's attitude toward impurity should be characterized as nominalist: skin afflictions cause impurity not because they are a sign of immorality or disease, but because the rules say so.

In his critique of Schwartz, J.L. Rubenstein argues that *living* legal systems are always realist because laws change when a society's understanding of reality changes. Rubinstein thus takes it as obvious that biblical law is realist. What nominalism there is in rabbinic law reflects the distance of the rabbis from the society in which the biblical law they interpreted took shape; if the Dead Sea texts display even less nominalism, it is a result of their greater proximity, both chronological and ideological, to the society of the First Temple period.[41] Rubenstein's general formulation about living legal systems may be correct, but, as we have just seen, the worldview reflected in P's purity laws stands at some distance not only from that of other ancient Near Eastern societies but from that of its own society as well. Despite the fact that their claim to authority rested in their priestly ancestry, then, the authors of P not infrequently took the nominalist approach Schwartz identifies with the rabbis.

I would like to conclude my discussion of P with Milgrom's suggestive reading of the negotiations between Aaron and Moses after the death of Aaron's sons (Leviticus 10) as P's consideration of the relationship between priestly and nonpriestly authority.[42] In the passage Moses rebukes Aaron's surviving sons, Eleazar and Ithamar, for failing to eat the goat of the purification offering brought on behalf of the people before the deaths of Nadab and Abihu (Lev 9:15) as prescribed (Lev 6:19). In response to Moses' criticism, Aaron points to the disaster that has just befallen his family as justification for their behavior, and Moses accepts Aaron's answer (Lev 10:19–20). The story thus

---

[41] "Nominalism," 180–83.
[42] Milgrom, *Leviticus 1–16*, 57, 626–27; for a discussion of why P thought Aaron's sons shouldn't eat of the purification offering and the meaning of Aaron's justification for his sons' behavior, see ibid., 635–40.

represents Aaron as a greater expert in ritual matters than Moses,[43] but, more striking in a work composed by priests, it nonetheless makes Moses the authority to whom Aaron must answer. In accordance with his view that P dates to the period of the First Temple, Milgrom understands the story as acknowledgment of priestly subservience to prophetic authority.[44]

Whatever the intention of the authors of the passage, the passage as it stands clearly subordinates Aaron to Moses despite giving Aaron the last word. And the attitude of this story toward Moses does not stand alone in the priestly corpus. As already noted, P repeatedly depicts priestly rules as communicated to Aaron and his sons through Moses, a picture that makes Moses the ultimate authority even as it diminishes tension between priestly authority and the authority of Moses. Finally, it is worth remembering that even if the authors of the story understood Moses as a prophet, by the middle of the Second Temple period Moses would have been understood also as the archetype of the scribes, the expert interpreters of the Torah of Moses.

But despite the similarities between priests on the one hand and scribes or rabbis on the other, there is no denying a crucial difference: as Schwartz insists, priests are born, scribes and rabbis are made. Priesthood in ancient Israel was in a sense a profession, and young priests must have undergone some kind of training before undertaking the responsibilities of priesthood. But even if skill or aptitude made one priest a better priest than another, no amount of skill or aptitude could make anyone a priest if he could not claim to be a descendant of Aaron.

In a way the hereditary character of ancient Israel's priesthood is surprising. The constellation of ideals and attitudes just discussed would be better served by a priesthood constituted more along the

---

[43] For P, despite his role in Aaron's ordination, Moses is not a priest (Milgrom, ibid., 57: Moses does not get the right thigh, and the theophany occurs only after Moses has completed his task and when Aaron and his sons are officiating).

[44] Watts, *Ritual*, offers a somewhat similar reading but emphasizes that the passage is attempting to restore to priests some of the authority they have lost to the Torah (114–17). In contrast, Fishbane, *Biblical Interpretation*, 226–28, understands the passage as an exegetical effort to resolve the tension between the account in Leviticus 9 and the laws of Lev 6:9–11. Furthermore, Fishbane believes that what Moses hears and accepts in Lev 10:20 is not Aaron's words, but an oracle of the Lord. Knohl, *Sanctuary*, takes Lev 10:6–11 as H's work, connected to H's laws for mourning by the high priest (Lev 21:10–12) (68–69).

lines of a civil service, so that becoming a priest would be more like
becoming a scribe. In fact, other ancient Near Eastern priesthoods
were not hereditary, although certain prestigious priestly offices might
tend to run in families.[45] And the stakes were higher for Jews, who
had only a single national priesthood on which to rely, than for other
peoples of the ancient Near East, who had a variety of priesthoods to
serve the cults of multiple gods.

There is, to be sure, a certain paradox in the existence of a national
priesthood in ancient Israel. If, as the Torah demanded, all Israel was
to be a "kingdom of priests and a holy nation" (Exod 19:6), what need
was there for a special class of priests? This problem certainly occurred
to the writers of the Torah, who put a similar question into the mouths
of the wilderness rebels: "All the assembly is holy, every one of them,
and the Lord is in their midst. Why then do you exalt yourselves over
the congregation of the Lord?" (Num 16:3).[46] Yet for the most part
ancient Jews lived with the tension between the holiness of all Israel
and the existence of a special class of priests without too much difficulty. They seem to have come to the conclusion that, in the words of
4QMMT, while all Israel was holy, the priests were holy of holies.[47]

The tension between ancestry and merit, on the other hand, did
cause some ancient Jews considerable anxiety. The concern is clear
as far back as the epic strand of the Torah, which suggests that the
descendants of Levi earned the priesthood by putting their ancestor's
violent tendencies to pious use in the service of Moses and the Lord
after the incident of the Golden Calf (Exod 32:26–29). Above I noted
that Enoch in the Book of the Watchers and Simon the Righteous in
the Wisdom of Ben Sira reflect an ideal that combines priestly and
scribal elements. But the combination can also be seen as an effort to
alleviate anxiety about the hereditary right to priestly office by supple-
menting it with a claim based on wisdom and piety.[48]

Most priests, however, probably lost little sleep over the problems
inherent in their hereditary right to their office and felt no need to

---

[45] Milgrom, *Leviticus 1–16*, 52–53 and references there.

[46] The account of the rebellion appears to consist of three strands: the rebellions of
Korah and the Levites, of the "leaders of the assembly" (Num 16:2), and of Dathan and
Abiram. The passage quoted above belongs to the strand associated with the leaders of
the assembly. For a recent discussion, see Knohl, *Sanctuary*, 73–85. Knohl identifies
the question as coming from the H source, which makes it all the more interesting.

[47] 4QMMT B 75–82; see Himmelfarb, *Kingdom of Priests*, 27–28.

[48] Ibid., esp. 51–52.

reimagine the Jewish priesthood as a meritocracy. Thus, though P offers an account of how Phinehas earned the high priesthood for himself and his descendants, it does not present the priestly status of Aaron and his descendants as something they somehow earned but, rather, as God's choice, in contrast to the epic strand's account of the ordination of the Levites. A similar attitude is reflected in *Aramaic Levi* and the writings of Josephus. *Aramaic Levi* praises wisdom and has Levi encourage his sons to acquire it (*ALD* 82–105), but the wisdom in question is practical and secular, Joseph's sphere rather than Levi's; for the task of the priest, proper ancestry—a subject about which *Aramaic Levi* feels strongly (*ALD* 17–18)—is enough.[49] Similarly, after the destruction of the Second Temple Josephus brags of both his priestly ancestry and his learning, but he seems to see them as two separate claims to prestige and does not draw a connection between them.[50] I think it is safe to assume that most priests and most Jews as well shared the confidence of *Aramaic Levi* and Josephus that descent from Aaron was enough for priests, as, after all, the Torah itself decreed.

Furthermore, the problematic fact of being defined by genealogy was not unique to the priesthood. It was shared by the entire people of Israel. Just as the odds of individual priests fulfilling their mandate for holiness were not very high, so too the odds of the people of Israel achieving holiness were low, for the very same reason. Thus, sectarians intent on actualizing holiness moved away from a genealogical definition of Israel. The *Damascus Document* claims that the true Israel was constituted by members of the sect alone. The Qumran *yaḥad* went even further. The *Rule of the Community* has little to say about Israel. Rather, the members of the *yaḥad* are Children of Light, set apart from the creation of the world from the Children of Darkness, that is, the Gentiles and all Jews who were not members of the sect. Like the sectarians of the Scrolls, early Christians rejected genealogy in favor of holiness, though more consistently than the sectarians of the Scrolls they understood the true Israel to include believers of both Jewish and Gentile ancestry.[51]

---

[49] Ibid., 25–28, 47–50.

[50] Ibid., 50–51; see references to Josephus there.

[51] Himmelfarb, *Kingdom of Priests*, 115–42. On early Christian self-understanding as an *ethnos*, see D.K. Buell, *Why This New Race: Ethnic Reasoning in Early Christianity* (New York, 2005). See also P. Townsend, "Another Race? Ethnicity, Universalism, and the Emergence of Christianity" (Ph.D. diss., Princeton University, 2009), which includes a critical assessment of Buell.

In contrast to the Jewish priesthood, the rabbis constituted a profession or class in which membership was determined at least in theory by aptitude, skill, and piety. In reality, family and social status played a very significant role;[52] but even if the story of the poor shepherd who became Rabbi Akiva is fiction, it is a fiction that reveals something about rabbinic self-understanding. One great advantage of the way in which the rabbinic class was formed is that it made rabbis somewhat more likely than priests to live up to the standards they set for themselves. Yet despite the way they constituted their own class, the rabbis nonetheless embraced a genealogical definition of the people of Israel. I have argued elsewhere that their insistence that descent from Abraham in itself was enough for membership in the holy people and that all Israel had a portion in the world to come was in considerable part a response to Christian efforts to deny the title Israel to descendants of Abraham according to the flesh even as they claimed it for descendants of Abraham according to the promise.[53]

What difference, then, did 70 make? My argument has been that despite the inherent tension between the authority of priests and the authority of the Torah, the ancient Israelite priesthood as represented in the P document was in many ways surprisingly close in its ethos or at least its ideals to the scribes of the Second Temple period and even to the rabbis of the period after the Destruction. The authors of the priestly corpus of the Torah would perhaps have been offended that Nehemiah and the elders of the court scolded high priests as Nehemiah's memoir reports and the Mishnah instructs. But the priestly authors would have embraced the idea that the behavior of the high priest and all other priests should conform to the mandates of the authoritative text. Perhaps they would have differed with the rabbis of the Mishnah over the procedure for the high priest's incense offering. But the difference would have been over the meaning of Leviticus 16, not over the authority of the passage.

But with the permanent loss of the Temple, any tension between the Temple and the Torah was resolved once and for all in favor of the Torah. Priests retained a certain prestige on the basis of their ancestry,

---

[52] S.J.D. Cohen, "The Rabbi in Second-Century Jewish Society," in *The Cambridge History of Judaism vol. 3: The Early Roman Period* (ed. W. Horbury, W.D. Davies, and J. Sturdy; Cambridge, 1999), esp. 941–43, 948–56, 974–77.

[53] Himmelfarb, *Kingdom of Priests*, 160–85.

but in the absence of the Temple they had no claim to power. Yet the triumph of the Torah was incomplete, for without a Temple or political sovereignty many of its dictates could no longer be carried out. Some scholars have argued that the rabbis had little use for priests and Temple and did their best to minimize their importance.[54] My own view is that the rabbis were somewhat less unenthusiastic about the Temple and hostile to priests than these scholars claim.[55] But either way, despite the priests' loss of their traditional tasks, the rabbis could not fail to acknowledge their significance and to anticipate the restoration of those tasks at the eschaton—because the Torah demanded it. Thus, even as the authors of the P document opened their descendants to the scrutiny of Torah experts and thus diminished priestly authority, they succeeded in securing for the priesthood a permanent place in the imagination of the heirs of those experts.

---

[54] See, e.g., P. Schäfer, "Rabbis and Priests, or: How to Do Away with the Glorious Past of the Sons of Aaron," in *Antiquity in Antiquity* (ed. G. Gardner and K. Osterloh; Tübingen, 2008), 155–72.
[55] Himmelfarb, *Kingdom of Priests*, 165–70.

THE OTHER SIDE OF ISRAELITE PRIESTHOOD: A SOCIOLOGICAL-ANTHROPOLOGICAL PERSPECTIVE

Gideon Aran

INTRODUCTION

My paper treats a less-discussed aspect of the ancient Israelite priesthood: the fact that the sons of Aaron, or rather, the biblical grandsons of Aaron and their offspring, in both the literal and figurative sense, were both officiants in the sacrificial cult and zealots for God. Thus we may speak of two Aaronic genealogies and, in parallel, of two Aaronic legacies—the priestly and the zealous. Furthermore, I will contend that these two legacies are fundamentally linked and partially overlapping. Indeed, in a way we may speak in terms of one genealogy, or, one legacy, which is priestly/zealous—a combined social-cultural motif that is not without its inner tensions.

The question at the root of the present volume—was 70 CE really a watershed?—is indirectly answered by the very method of my study, which goes back to the legendary Israelite crossing of the Jordan at the time of the symbolically charged passage from the desert to the land of Canaan (Numbers 25). From this primeval beginning my study extends to the survey of other paradigmatic scenes in ancient, medieval, and modern times; it concludes with some observations on relevant typical offshoots in our own generation. Nevertheless, it is clear that my study is a-historical. First, its center of gravity is present-day phenomena. Second, it is essentially analytic and conceptual, or rather theoretical. Third, many of the data processed in this study comprise a mixture of collective memory and sacred materials wherein there is no earlier or later but, rather, an absolute presentness, which is acutely sensed, and wherein there is much that is not scientifically proven, but nevertheless, persuasive and genuine from the point of view of the ardent believers—mythological truth or canonical fact.

I am a sociologist-anthropologist who studies high-energy true believers,[1] charismatic strong religion,[2] Jewish and other super-

---

[1] E. Hoffer, *The True Believer* (New York, 1951).
[2] S. Appleby, G. Almond, and E. Sivan, *Strong Religion* (Chicago, 2003).

religiosity,[3] and political religion (rather than religious politics).[4] My academic interest centers on the points where religion or religiosity meets social movements, cultism, direct action, extremism, and violence. This phenomenon of religious radicalism, particularly when it resorts to coercive or subversive aggression, has been manifested in variegated ways in the past and is still quite conspicuous and effective today. Its dramatic actualization in the last four decades has been labeled "fundamentalism," both in public discourse and academic discussion.[5]

"Fundamentalism"—basically the ultra-politicization of a holy scripture—has replaced several other terms, the most popular of which was "fanaticism." However, while "fanaticism" is no longer in vogue, it is of some heuristic value. True, use of the term is often criticized because it bears a negative connotation. However, although the word has become derogatory it is nonetheless worthwhile to subject it at least to a cursory examination, especially from an etymological point of view. In its Latin origin "fanaticism" is related to *fanum*, "a place solemnly consecrated to a god—a temple (with land around it)." The reference is to the deity spirit that typically filled classical shrines and inspired the local priestly cadres to behave enthusiastically, that is, to fulfill their sacred duties in a zealous manner. Apparently, then, the association of priesthood with a zealous type of worship is not uniquely Jewish.

However, rather than both "fundamentalism" and "fanaticism," I prefer the term "zealotry" for describing and analyzing the phenomenon of violent religiosity, particularly Jewish religious violence. For one thing, zealotry is both *etic* and *emic*: that is, the term is used by observers—academic and laymen—and at the same time by the "natives" and "practitioners" themselves.[6] It is universal and local as well, and it can be used by outsiders in a derogatory sense but also by insiders, voluntarily and proudly, as a self-designation. Since "zealotry"

---

    [3] G. Aran, "Religiosity and Super-Religiosity: Rethinking Jewish Ultra-Orthodoxy," *Numen* (2012): forthcoming.

    [4] G. Aran, "Jewish-Zionist Fundamentalism," in *Fundamentalisms Observed* (ed. M. Marty and S. Appleby; Chicago, 1991).

    [5] The most scholarly ambitious and influential example is the Fundamentalism Project of the American Academy of Arts and Sciences, which culminated in five volumes published by the University of Chicago, from *Fundamentalisms Observed* (1991) to *Fundamentalisms Comprehended* (1996).

    [6] J. Cresswell, *Qualitative Enquiry and Research Design* (London, 1998).

can be charged with both negative and positive valuation, we may treat it neutrally.

Another reason for preferring the term zealotry is its mythico-historical depth. Zealotry is a key concept in a long and ample tradition still alive, an integral and intriguing component of a great religious and national culture. A major thrust of my work has been the attempt to unearth the deep strata of the concept of zealotry by rereading various Jewish sacred texts (the Bible and its traditional interpreters, *Aggadah* and *Midrash*, etc.) from the point of view of the social sciences. This paper is part of an undertaking to deconstruct the religious and social-political complex of which zealotry is a core element.

In my extensive field research I have discovered that present-day zealots relate themselves to past zealots, or rather to priests *cum* zealots. The latter serve as source of legitimization and guidance for the former. The priest-zealots of old have heirs today who look up at them as objects of identification and models for emulation. Thus, for example, I am acquainted with a certain group of radical North American Protestants involved in anti-black and anti-Jewish aggression. The name it uses is: "The Order of the Phineas Priesthood."[7] I am also acquainted with an order-like group of Israeli settlers in the Occupied Territories[8] involved in anti-Palestinian and anti-leftist aggression; it has adopted the pseudo-patronymic "Son of Phineas."[9] Conventionally, such borrowing or adoption of the names of great historical or mythological figures expresses not only sympathy and solidarity with them but also a presumption to have a sanction to act "in their name," in accordance with the way they are thought to have behaved, and to monopolize the spirit that motivated them.[10]

In my comparative social study of religious violence, I thus found that present-day zealots relate themselves to a very old and ramified legacy featuring ancient legendary zealots, especially the great biblical father of all zealots—Phineas. The latter has been the source of inspiration or, rather, of obligation, and the role model for Jewish zealots—and to a lesser degree for Christian zealots—from earliest times. In

---

[7] R.K. Hoskins, *Vigilantes of Christendom: The History of the Phineas Priesthood* (Lynchburg, Va., 1997).

[8] Particularly in Hebron.

[9] That is, an adherent named "Jack Roth" would call himself "Jack, son of Phineas, Roth."

[10] Cf. I.J. Yuval, "*Moses redivivus*—Maimonides as a 'Helper to the King' Messiah," *Zion* 72 (2006/7): 161–88 (in Hebrew).

order to better understand the zealots of our epoch and place I have reexamined the biblical subculture (counterculture?), at the epicenter of which the idea of zealotry is located.

First, I compiled a list of the prominent archetypical mythico-historical zealots. The list holds no surprise—it is indeed a classical roster of figures regarded by both adherents and students of Judaism as zealots par excellence. At the head of the list is, of course, Phineas, followed by Elijah[11] and a few other biblical figures: Levy son of Jacob, the Levites, maybe Ezra as well.[12] Then come Mattathias and the Hasmoneans, the Sons of Zadok from Qumran, the Zealots of the First Revolt against the Romans, and the Bar Kokhba rebels. All the above and some others as well are closely linked to one another. They are "family relatives" in several ways.[13]

The enumerated cases, conceived of as paradigmatic, are the basis of my attempt to construct an "ideal type" of zealotry. An ideal type—or pure type—is a (hypothetical) analytical model which is similar to known and typical empirical cases though not necessarily fully identical with any of them. The Weberian concept of *Idealtyp* is not meant to refer to moral ideals, perfect things, or a statistical average, but to an amalgamation of particular characteristics common to most (classical) cases of a given phenomenon. To quote Weber, it is formed by a one-sided accentuation of one or more points of view and by the synthesis of a great many diffuse and discrete concrete individual phenomena that are usually present although occasionally absent. The ideal type is an effective tool in comparative social study. Each empirical case may be analyzed in light of the ideal, that is, in terms of the characteristics of the model that it possesses and that it lacks.[14]

My study of Jewish zealotry, using ideal-type methodology, has produced some interesting findings which I have discussed elsewhere.[15] In the present forum I would like to raise just one issue concerning zealotry: its intriguing association with priesthood. My main argument

---

[11] According to a well known Jewish tradition Phineas and Elijah were one and the same person; see L. Ginzberg, *The Legends of the Jews* (Philadelphia, 1968), 6:316–17 n. 3.

[12] One may add the first prophet, Moses, as well.

[13] Cf. the Wittgensteinian idea of family resemblance: L. Wittgenstein, *Philosophical Investigations* (2d ed.; Oxford, 1963), 32 (§67).

[14] M. Weber, *The Methodology of the Social Sciences* (trans. and ed. E. Shils and H.A. Finch; New York, 1997); S.J. Hekman, *Weber, the Ideal Type, and Contemporary Social Theory* (Notre Dame, Ind., 1983).

[15] G. Aran, *Jewish Zealotry: Past and Present* (forthcoming).

here concerns a certain homology and close affinity between zealots and priests, particularly high priests—a point which may be suggestive when, in the context of this conference, we consider what disappeared with the destruction of the Second Temple and the consequent apparent cessation of the central, Temple-oriented, function of the priesthood.

At first glance, zealotry and Jewish priesthood appear opposite, representing, for example, the excessively discussed dissonance of charisma vs. routine, or of deviance vs. conformity. Nevertheless, despite the obvious contrast and tension between zealotry and priesthood there is an especially telling resemblance and kinship between these two types of religious virtuosity. In fact, the above association is so powerful that one may justifiably speak in terms of the "zealot-priest complex."

In my several years of research devoted to religious extremism, I have tried to further the understanding of zealotry by examining its linkage to priesthood. Here, however, I would focus on the parallel and opposite enterprise, namely, on enriching our understanding of priesthood by examining its linkage to zealotry. For the particular purpose of this volume I tentatively shift my concern, accordingly, from zealots to priests, or rather from the priestly dimension of zealots to the zealous dimension of priests.

Before elaborating on the relationship between zealots and priests, however, I must briefly present one hypothesis to be substantiated by later argumentation. The Pentateuch says: "And he (Phineas) and his progeny after him shall have it, the covenant of everlasting priesthood, because he was zealous for his God."[16] Therefore it is commonly held that an act of zealotry is the basis for the claim to monopoly on the priestly privileges. The zealous act, we may add, is also—although perhaps not unavoidable—the ultimate culmination and consummation of the priestly career and mission. In other words, perfect manifestation of priesthood in its pure and consistent form betrays the fundamentals of zealotry.

---

[16] Num 25:13. Various observers contend that the Phineas episode was inserted into the sacred narrative by the Aaronites in order to solidify their claim to the hereditary high priesthood. Similarly, there is speculation concerning the Hasmoneans' manipulation of the priority of Jehoiarib in the list of the priestly families; see R.R. Hutton, "Jehoiarib," in *The Anchor Bible Dictionary* (ed. D.N. Freedman; New York, 1992), 3:666.

Zealot and Priest: Affinities

In the following I shall briefly survey some aspects of the affinity
between the two phenomena, or two models, embodied in the paradigmatic figures of the zealot and the priest:

a) *The genealogical dimension and the professional-class dimension*
According to the sacred texts, all ancient mythico-historical zealots
who serve as paradigms for present-day zealots were—with no exceptions—priests (or Levites), as well.[17] They were priests both by heredity
and by career, that is, they were born priests and they worked in the
priesthood—and it was the priesthood that engendered their lifestyle,
socioeconomic status, political interest, etc. Elitism is just one deriva-
tive of these characteristics.

b) *The legendary and functional dimension*
The unique initiative that made these figures worthy of praise and
heavenly rewards, namely, the bold deed for which they were granted
eternal priesthood, in short, their very act of zealotry, could be seen
as sacrificial, thus as typically priestly. This act is an actual killing,
subject to many detailed restrictions which amount to cultic rules. It
is symbolic bloodshed for the purpose of purification and expiation,
a dramatic murder aiming to mediate between the community and
the divine, an assassination with theurgic effect conducted on stage
in front of the public.[18] But the above characteristics also define the
act of *qorban*, sacrifice—which is the privileged specialization of the
priesthood.

   Turning now from the priestly nature of zealotry to the zealous
nature of priesthood, let us note the obvious: The essence of Jewish
priesthood is the Temple cult and the epitome of that is the sacrificial
act—which is certainly an act of (religious) violence.

c) *The ideological dimension: The zealot-priest ethic*
Both zealots and priests are patriots. In modern terminology, their
fundamental "political" orientation is nationalistic and hawkish. Note

---

[17] See the lists at nn. 11–12 of the prominent archetypical Israelite cases of zealotry.
[18] R. Girard, *Violence and the Sacred* (Baltimore, 1989); M. Bourdillon and
M. Fortes, eds., *Sacrifice* (London, 1980).

not only the freedom-fighter-priest-cum-zealot Hasmoneans, but also the priestly core of the anti-Roman rebels,[19] and—moving back to biblical models—the chauvinist enterprise of Phineas (vs. the Moabites—Numbers 25) and Levi (vs. the Shechemites—Genesis 34).

d) *The physical and personality dimension: The zealot-priest* habitus
It is reasonable to assume that both zealots and priests have tough stomachs and hard heads. From various aggadic sources there emerge the contours of the mentality and the body of the priests—and they remind us of those that characterize zealots. Both are activists and practical; hot-blooded and aggressive; crude; moralist; strict; exacting; masculine; daredevil. Correspondingly, both are physically strong and quick; manually skillful; alert and incisive; sensual. Note the mention of the priests running up the ramp to the altar (*t. Kippurim* 1:12) and the portrait of them, in the *Letter of Aristeas* (§§92–93), as competitive athletes.[20] The description of the priestly routine in the Temple as "synaesthetic," utilizing all the senses (seeing, hearing, touching, and smelling), applies to the zealot, too.[21]

e) *Worldview: The zealot-priest conception of reality*
More specifically, I refer here to the priestly and zealous perspective on the sacred. Schwartz defines the priests' legal interpretation of the sacred as naturalist or realist (as opposed to the rabbinic nominalist interpretation).[22] I would rather characterize their attitude as essentialist and immanentist.[23] Thus it is also categorical, static, and

---

[19] D.M. Goodblatt, "Suicide in the Sanctuary: Traditions on Priestly Martyrdom," *JJS* 46 (1995): 10–29; idem, "Priestly Ideologies of the Judean Resistance," *JSQ* 3 (1996): 225–49.

[20] "The service of the priest is in every respect unsurpassed in the physical strength (required of them).... With both hands they take up the legs of the calf, each of which for the most part are more than two talents' weight, and in a wonderful manner throw them with each hand to the correct height (for the altar) and do not miss in their aim" (C.T.R. Hayward, *The Jewish Temple: A Non-Biblical Sourcebook* [London, 1996], 28–29). For an intriguing analysis of this portrait of the priesthood, see A. Glucklich, *The Road to Qumran* (Tel-Aviv, 2006), 57–58 (in Hebrew).

[21] See Glucklich, *The Road to Qumran*.

[22] D.R. Schwartz, "Law and Truth: On Qumran-Sadducean and Rabbinic Views of Law," in *The Dead Sea Scrolls: Forty Years of Research* (ed. D. Dimant and U. Rappaport; Leiden and Jerusalem, 1992), 229–40.

[23] Ascribing ultimate reality to the essence that inheres in a thing; regarding it as having innate existence or universal validity rather than as being socially or intellectually constructed; assuming that the really real nature of things is contained within

dichotomous. Such orientation applies to zealots, too. Both zealot and priest resemble the Authoritarian Personality, (often associated with a closed mind, rigidity, obsessiveness, and to a certain degree also fascist inclinations).[24]

The last three common characteristics (c, d, e) can be subsumed, if anachronistically and generally, under the description of both priests and zealots as proto-Zionists of sorts.[25]

f) *The symbolic dimension: The thematic of the zealous and priestly imagination*
Zealots and priests stand in the center of a triangle, the three corners of which are: Blood—Purity (and Danger)—Passion (libido). This motif will be developed later.

ZEALOT AND PRIEST: APPARENT DISCREPANCIES

Notwithstanding my emphasis here on the affinity of zealotry and Jewish priesthood, the fundamental distinctions, if not contradictions, between them, should not be ignored. It is, however, precisely the oppositions between the two that make their similarities revealing.

Conventionally, zealots and priests are seen as different and contrary in at least three senses:

First, Israelite priesthood is founded on the hereditary principle.[26] In sociological terms it is based on ascription whereas zealotry depends on achievement.[27] Unlike priesthood, zealotry is not automatic and guaranteed in advance. While priesthood is particularistic, zealotry is universalistic. In principle, zealotry is potentially open to anybody; it is democratic, so to speak. Priesthood, in contrast, is aristocratic by definition.

Second, the priest is obsessed with procedures. The priestly act is patterned according to ample and detailed prescriptions. Any devia-

---

their innermost rather than beyond them; denying reality that transcends the empirically perceived.

[24] T. Adorno et al., *The Authoritarian Personality* (New York, 1950).
[25] Cf. D.R. Schwartz, "Does Religious Zionism Tend to Sadduceeism?" *Eretz Acheret* 24 (November, 2005): 72–76 (in Hebrew).
[26] M. Himmelfarb, *Kingdom of Priests: Ancestry and Merit in Ancient Judaism* (Philadelphia, 2006).
[27] T. Parsons, *Societies* (New York, 1961).

tion from the minute priestly norm borders on sin and might prove harmful. Zealotry, in contrast, is spontaneous and even creative in a way. The zealous act bypasses prevalent binding procedures, thus challenging their hegemony.

Third, priesthood is highly conformist and fully institutionalized; actually it comprises the establishment. In contrast, zealotry betrays primeval surge. It is completely uninstitutionalized and antiestablishment by implication, a type of anarchism.

The above three points partially overlap. Their commonality boils down to the classic opposition between tradition, routine and authority on the hand, and charisma on the other. Yet, does priesthood have no charismatic qualities? And is there no zealot tradition and zealot authority? I would like to add a few comments on zealots and priests that somewhat mitigate the opposition between the two types, qualify the differences between them, and refine our understanding of each of them.

We can come at the hereditary versus merit or excellence issue from both sides. On the one hand, despite its hereditary privileges, priesthood, too, is conditioned by and related to the need to meet high moral and cultic standards. As mentioned earlier, the priestly position was awarded to virtuous brave individuals who excelled in religiosity, such as Phineas and Mattathias. Similarly, it is known that even well-established priests who violate the rules of the game risk their status. If they are economically or politically corrupt, or ritually defiled, they might be ousted.[28]

On the other hand (and perhaps more controversially), there inheres a quasi-hereditary core in zealotry that makes it resemble priesthood. To begin with, zealotry is not just an individual quality but also a collective one. Actually, in some cases it is a family or tribal trait. Note the Levites, whose murderous inclination comes by birth and kinship affiliation.[29] True, zealotry appears to be an impulsive reaction. However, impulses are contingent on chromosomal heritage.

It is true that the substance of the zealot's act is but of a moment—sudden, sharp and brief. Zealotry is not normal, neither a gradual or continuous state nor a predictable development or outcome of

---

[28] See, for example, the biblical case of the high priest Abiathar (1 Kgs 2:26–27; see also *b. Yoma* 73b), and later stories about the priests Menashe (Josephus, *Ant.* 11.302–312) and Alcimus (2 Macc 14:3).

[29] See the massacre in the aftermath of the sin of the golden calf, Exodus 32.

conscious intention and systematic effort. In fact, any premeditation, training or preparation for the zealot's act may invalidate and preempt it in advance.[30] Nevertheless, it must be underlined that the zealot's passionate surge is not capricious, accidental, or random. It is a behavioral corollary of an innermost unique quality. It is the acting-out of some unknown inherent nature. Fundamentally zealotry is a potentiality. One identifies a zealot only in retrospect. Even the zealot himself is not aware of his true value until the critical moment. Zealotry is an innate and predestined attribute. It is, in other words, like a genetic flaw that is effective and discovered only in maturity.

Another issue concerns the zealot's act as a rite. While zealotry seems to be primordial and rowdy, it is in fact subject to harsh discipline that defines and conditions it. For example: Phineas' zealous act, viewed as the act of an ideal type, would have been invalidated had it not been committed in the "real time" of the sexual act (not even a single second after the act),[31] or, if not carried out in public, that is, in the presence of at least ten persons.[32] Practically zealotry is strait-jacketed—so much so that it becomes hardly possible. Indeed, it is reasonable to assume that traditional Judaism made zealotry such a demanding and complicated cultic operation in order to minimize, or rather to nullify, the probability of it actually happening. According to that tradition, the zealot's act, very much like the sacrificial priestly act, cannot be committed under just any conditions. Its specific time and place are essential requisites for this rite, just as for any other sacrament. The hallowed celebration of the zealous act must be performed in a very particular way—and if not committed accordingly, it is judged as a severely punishable act of murder pure and simple.

Now we turn to the institutional status of zealotry. First, while the zealot appears to undermine traditional law, in his own understanding and that of his many admirers he actually conforms to the true spirit of the law, right in tune with the original intention of the divine lawgiver. Some believe that if his act is indeed truly a zealous one, it is synchronized with the heavenly rhythm. A present-day zealot I know,

---

[30] B. Sanh. 82a ("If someone comes to consult [about doing an act of zealotry] he is not to be instructed [to do it]").

[31] Ibid. ("Had Zimri separated himself [from the Midianite woman] before Phineas killed him, he would have been executed for killing him").

[32] See, for example, the commentary of R. Obadiah Bertinoro (15th/16th century) to m. Sanh. 9:6, printed in standard editions of the Mishnah.

who is also a Bible scholar, claims that the essence of Phineas-like zealotry is timing. The zealot's test is to act exactly when God wills it; not
a second before or after. Furthermore, while the zealot undoubtedly
challenges the religious and political authorities, and therefore might
be thought to be antithetical to the authoritative priesthood, it must
be recognized that, at the same time, he actually volunteers to serve
those authorities by performing an indispensable and costly task they
cannot (afford to) carry out by themselves. Zealotry is an urgent high-
risk mission that absolves impotent authorities (Moses and the Elders
in the Moabite Desert, for instance) from fulfilling their responsibility.
The zealot's act implies subversion. The authorities, however, neutral-
ize the subversive danger by coopting zealotry.

HYBRIDITY

Despite the linkage and resemblance between zealot and priest, their
association is problematic. Conceiving the two as one entity—zealot-
priest, or, priest-zealot—is suggestive, however. Once we speak of one
entity, the contradiction between the two types is transformed into an
inner contradiction within a so-called social "hybrid."[33] The tension
contained within the priest-zealot figure makes this figure a culturally
potent and fascinating one. The zealot-priest is at one and the same
time a legalist and traditionalist, yet a charismatic one.[34] He is stringent but impulsive, and so forth.

At this point I would like to suggest a somewhat daring hypothesis,
possibly a heuristic metaphor. Let us envision *priesthood as zealotry
in a golden cage*. By this I mean to suggest that we consider Israelite
priesthood, centered on the sacrificial rite, to be an ingenious way of
pre-empting the likely damages of zealotry while channeling its violent
energies toward controllable and desirable ends. Zealotry is adapted,
contained and tamed by introducing it into the Temple, the heart of
the establishment, and thus becoming the axis of the Jerusalemite cult.

---

[33] This concept is mainly used with regard to identity hybrids, such as transgen-
der and transnational. See, for example, *Hybrid Identities: Theoretical and Empirical
Examinations* (ed. K.E.I. Smith and P. Leavy; Leiden, 2008).
[34] Cf. the Weberian typology of the three variants of authority: traditional, legal,
and charismatic; H.H. Gerth, and C. Wright Mills eds., *From Max Weber: Essays in
Sociology* (London, 1948).

As mentioned earlier, the world common to both zealots and priests is marked by the trinity of blood, libido, and purity. First, the two religious virtuosi—zealot and priest—are what the Bible would call "people of blood" (2 Sam 16:7–8; Ps 26:9; 55:23; 59:2; 139:19; Prov 29:10); both can be lethal. Two comments are in order here. 1) The violent act of both priest and zealot is termed slaughter (*shehitah*).[35] Their blood-spilling activity conforms to a complex system of ritual norms. 2) Both roles allow for forms of killing exempt from criminal jurisdiction, and, more generally, not subject to legalities.[36]

As for libido: In the case of the paradigmatic zealous act, sexuality is quite self-evident. Witness the way Phineas reacts to harlotry: striking at a copulating couple; aiming at their genitals; simulating a sexual act. Similarly, the Shechem story (Genesis 34), which ends with Levi perpetrating a massacre, opens with an intercourse (rape?) and continues on to a story of mass circumcision (castration?).

In the case of priests, sexuality is more subtle. At times, however, it is quite blatant, as in the biblical treatment of the *sotah* (Numbers 5)—the woman suspected of adultery.[37] Here, the priest conducts a sexual ritual par excellence.[38] In addition, priests regulate the community's and their own sexuality. They also supervise the ritual cleansing of menstrual and other impurities that affect sexual organs and activity (Leviticus 15), and apply special marital restrictions to their own class (Leviticus 21). As we have learned from Freud, Foucault, and others, such aggressive puritanism is another form of coping with sexuality.

The third issue to consider is purity. While purity is the priest's middle name, it preoccupies the zealot as well. Analytically we should distinguish between ritual (bodily and sexual) purity and racial (ethnic-national) purity. Phineas, like Levy and Mattathias, fought the type of

---

[35] Thus, for example, the Greek verb used in 1 Macc 2:24 to describe the assassination of the man upon the altar by Mattathias—who is said to have been zealous, and compared in v. 26 to Phineas—is the same as that used for the ritual act of slaughter. See N. Martola, *Capture and Liberation: A Study in the Composition of the First Book of Maccabees* (Åbo, 1984), 218.

[36] Note that the talmudic discussion of the case of a priest who serves while impure rules that he should not be tried in court by his fellow priests. Rather, "the young priests crush his skull with an axe" (*m. Sanh.* 9:6).

[37] On this biblical law and its development in the Mishnah (*Sotah*) and other rabbinic literature, see L. Grushcow, *Writing the Wayward Wife: Rabbinic Interpretations of Sotah* (Leiden, 2006).

[38] The priest tears the woman's clothes as low as her bosom, unties the tresses of her hair, fastens her torn clothes with a girdle below her breasts, etc.

assimilation created by bodily-sexual impurity that engenders tribal impurity. Their zealous acts are acts of national purification, aimed at dissociating the Israelites from the fornicating Moabite women, the lustful Shechemite men eager to join the club, and the Hellenized Jews who do not circumcise their sons.

Concluding Remarks: Policing Borders

Blood, passion and purity bring us to the issue of boundaries—the boundaries of the individual body on the one hand, and those of the collectivity, on the other. The relationship between the two types of boundaries is now a matter of common knowledge in the social sciences owing to the work of Mary Douglas.[39] One of her more striking anthropological insights refers to a situation in which the collectivity's boundaries are violated and consequently the group's identity is threatened. In such a situation there emerges a special sensitivity in the group ethos regarding keeping body boundaries intact and under control.[40] This thesis is helpful in explaining why the biblical narrative in Numbers 25 (the Phineas story), set in the plains of Moab before the people cross the Jordan on the way into the Land, focuses so much attention on the regulation of physical contact between Israelites and Gentiles. The same holds for the situation during the Return to Zion in the days of Ezra (see esp. Ezra 9–10!) and during the early Hasmonean period (see esp. 1 Macc 1:11–15).

A salient expression of the priestly preoccupation with body boundaries is the relatively large space devoted by the Torah to the subject of bodily flow (ziva—gonorrhea, as well as menstrual blood, semen, and the like; Leviticus 15). Concerning zealotry, we have repeatedly mentioned its focus on instances of the transgression of the boundaries between the Israelite and the Other. The zealot's initiative aims at securing the tribal boundaries so as to avoid assimilation.

The zealot and the priest—two variations upon religious virtuosity—may thus be seen as being in charge of the protection of Israel's borders. Metaphorically speaking, they serve in the "sacred" Border

---

[39] M. Douglas, *Purity and Danger: An Analysis of Concepts of Pollution and Taboo* (London, 1988).

[40] See, for example, J. Okely, *The Traveller-Gypsies* (Cambridge, 1983).

Police of mythico-historical Israel. In this context, it is relevant to
note another lesson that classical anthropology teaches us, namely,
that those responsible for guaranteeing the integrity of collective identity are themselves often especially sensitive to the question of borders. This sensitivity derives from their own marginal social position,
between and betwixt, neither here nor there.[41] In other words, those
entrusted with the holy task of guarding the group's frontiers occupy
a problematic social status. Located in the proximity of the border
they are liminal and hybrid. Naturally enough, their own identity is
confused and full of tension.[42]

It is not coincidental, for example, that the contemporary Border
Police of the State of Israel—charged with the task of keeping Jews and
Palestinians apart—includes a large representation of Druze, Ethiopians and "Russians" (immigrants from the former Soviet Union)—three
elements whose Israeliness is somehow questionable and incomplete.
Excelling in policing the borders facilitates their integration in the center of society. All of the above, I would suggest, is true with regard
to the priests and zealots who policed the borders of ancient Israel.
Zealots, first of all, are liminal and hybrid: praised and canonized but
kept at arm's length; heroes but deviants; enjoying high rewards but
risking a fatal penalty; a priori suspect and circumscribed, yet idolized
in retrospect. A zealot is an acrobat walking a tight rope.

And priests? They are organically linked to the people of Israel but
at the same time a distinct caste relegated to its own elevated enclave.
Even marital ties between them and the rest of the people are not
a trivial matter (see Lev 21:7; Ezek 44:22; Josephus, *Ant.* 3.276–277).
Moreover, priests are positioned in the middle, neither in heaven nor
on earth, representing the divine vis à vis the community and the community vis à vis the divine. Indeed, priests (and Levites), being liminal,
are the only ones who do not own land (Deut 18:1–2). Another aspect
of the priests' hybrid nature: They shed blood but are the champions
of seeking peace.[43]

---

[41] V. Turner, *The Ritual Process: Structure and Anti-Structure* (New York, 1991).
[42] Cf. Y. Bilu, *Without Bounds* (Jerusalem, 1993 [in Hebrew]).
[43] Cf. *m. Avot* 1:12: "Be of the disciples of Aaron—a lover of peace and seeker of
peace."

Thus, the two types of Israelite boundary specialists are subject to limitations and obligations. Nevertheless they are privileged. They are exempt from certain normative demands enforced upon other Jews, including norms regarded as elementary and natural—specifically, norms that concern murder.

The privileges of priesthood are well known. The priests enjoy offerings and emoluments that provide them with a comfortable living. Another basic social norm is qualified when applied to priests: in particular instances they are licensed to kill a person outside of court's jurisdiction.[44] But that, of course, reminds us of zealots.

The other side of legitimizing some strictly defined and rare forms of murder is the perilous venture the boundary guardians take upon themselves. Boundary policing is in any event risky—and, indeed, zealots and priests also undertake "professional risks"—the hazard of those living on the brink, who experience liminality and challenge the limits.

The two virtuosi embark upon a journey loaded with action. In the zealot's act there inheres an element of provocation, a certain life-or-death gamble. Zealots who are intent on killing (slaughter) know well enough that they too might be killed if they fail to conform to the detailed specifications of their mission. So, too, however, there were severe professional risks that threatened the mission of the priest, especially the high priest. The source of danger is the unmediated proximity of the sacred. This is another species of liminality which is known to be lethal. Note especially, in this regard, the dangerous situation of the high priest on the Day of Atonement.[45] We know the intricate preparations and security measures taken prior to his deep bold intrusion into the realm of liminality—the Holy of Holies. There was no certainty of his surviving it. Thus, both the zealous and the priestly acts harbor a murderous potentiality and also a suicidal potentiality. Both contain not only aggression but at the same time also victimhood. Both priest and zealot initiate violence and may be its victims as well.

---

[44] See above, n. 36.

[45] Cf. *m. Yoma* 5:2. "The entrance of the High Priest into the Holy of Holies on the Day of Atonement was not only a great privilege, offering the rare opportunity of catching a glimpse of the Deity, but was also fraught with great danger (of immediate death, etc.)" (J.Z. Lauterbach, *Rabbinic Essays* [New York, 1973], 72–75).

In conclusion one may speculate that both priests and zealots seek—even if only subconsciously—to die for God. In a sense, the priest-zealot is a (potential) martyr, reminding us, inter alia, of the juxtaposition of martyrdom and rebellion in the Jewish resistance to Rome in the days of Bar Kokhba.[46]

---

[46] Compare also the willingness to die for God celebrated in 4 Maccabees and in the stories of the Ten Martyrs (G. Reeg, ed., *Die Geschichte von den zehn Märtyren* [Tübingen, 1985]). Although the latter were composed later than the Second Rebellion, the fact that they became linked to that rebellion is not accidental.

"A KINGDOM OF PRIESTS":
DID THE PHARISEES TRY TO LIVE LIKE PRIESTS?

Hanan Birenboim

Part of the usual construction of the "watershed" issue is the assumption that there was competition between Pharisaic/rabbinic Judaism and Sadducean/priestly Judaism. One formulation of that competition assumes that adherents of the former aspired to appropriate priestly status. True, there is no doubt that several streams in Second Temple Judaism reflect a desire to appropriate the status of priests for non-priests.[1] But did the Pharisees attempt to create a "kingdom of priests" in the sense of a community in which all would be considered priests or priestly? Many scholars answer this question in the affirmative and claim that the Pharisees attempted to allow all Israel (or, at least, all members of their group) to share in holiness, that is, to share as much as possible in the privileges and obligations of the priests.[2] In the following, I will consider this question and attempt to cast light on one of the most important characteristics of the conflict between the Pharisees and the Sadducees/priests.[3]

The view that the Pharisees tried to live like priests has been put most coherently and influentially by Jacob Neusner. He first studied rabbinic passages which include either the name of someone known to have been a Pharisee or the schools of Hillel and Shammai. Then he proceeded to an analysis of the mishnaic laws, in order to stratify the material chronologically. At the conclusion of his study he defined

---

[1] See M. Himmelfarb, "'A Kingdom of Priests': The Democratization of the Priesthood in the Literature of Second Temple Judaism," *Journal of Jewish Thought and Philosophy* 6 (1997): 89–104. But see also D.R. Schwartz, "'Kingdom of Priests'—A Pharisaic Slogan?" in idem, *Studies in the Jewish Background of Christianity* (Tübingen, 1992), 57–80, pp. 59–61.

[2] For a survey of the research on this question, see Schwartz, ibid., 67–70.

[3] A. Geiger was among the first to link the Sadducees with the priests. See Schwartz, ibid., 67. But when I speak of Sadducees/priests, I mean to include the Dead Sea Scrolls community, since they too shared a priestly view. On this see D.R. Schwartz, "Law and Truth: On Qumran-Sadducean and Rabbinic Views of Law," in *The Dead Sea Scrolls: Forty Years of Research* (ed. D. Dimant and U. Rappaport; Leiden, 1992), 229–40.

the Pharisees as being essentially a pure-food club, concerned above all with table fellowship and eating ordinary food in a state of purity. He attributed to the earliest layer of the Mishnah the same concern that he had previously attributed to the Pharisees, and proposed that Hillel, at the beginning of Herod's reign, had converted the group from a political party into a table fellowship sect:[4] "Eating one's secular...unconsecrated food in a state of ritual purity as if one were a Temple priest in the cult was one of the two significations of party membership."[5]

This conclusion conforms very well to the critical reading of Josephus' description of the Pharisees proposed by Morton Smith.[6] Smith noted that the portrait of the Pharisees is different in each of Josephus' major works, and argued that the *Jewish War* presents the more historically accurate portrait, reflecting the fact that the Pharisees "had no real hold either on the government or on the masses of the people."[7] Following Smith, Neusner argued that Josephus' work contains no description of Pharisaic political activity under Herod; on this basis he developed the hypothesis that the Pharisees, after being politically active in Hasmonean times, retreated from politics during the reign of Herod. The hostility between the king and the Pharisees forced the latter to withdraw from the political scene and concentrate instead on the construction of a spiritual world based on the punctilious observance of all the commandments of the Torah. The Pharisees' dominant ideal was the stringent observance of purity laws, in particular with regard to the eating of nonsacred food in a state of ritual purity.[8] That the

---

[4] J. Neusner, *The Rabbinic Traditions about the Pharisees before 70* (3 vols.; Leiden, 1971), 3:305.

[5] Ibid., 3:288.

[6] See M. Smith, "Palestinian Judaism in the First Century," in *Israel: Its Role in Civilization* (ed. M. Davis; New York, 1956), 67–81, pp. 74–78.

[7] Ibid., 81.

[8] "The Pharisees determined to concentrate on what they believed was really important in politics...to achieve elevation of the life of all of the people, at home and in the streets, to what the Torah had commanded: *You shall be a kingdom of priests and a holy people.* Such a community would live as if it were always in the Temple sanctuary of Jerusalem. Therefore the complicated and inconvenient purity laws were extended to the life of every Jew in his own home. The Temple altar in Jerusalem would be replicated at the tables of all Israel" (J. Neusner, *From Politics to Piety: The Emergence of Pharisaic Judaism* [Englewood Cliffs, N.J., 1973], 146). See also L.I. Levine, "On the Political Involvement of the Pharisees under Herod and the Procurators," *Cathedra* 8 (1978): 23–27 (in Hebrew). It should be noted that according to Neusner, the biblical perception is that the purity laws are limited to the Temple precincts alone (*Judaism: The Evidence of the Mishnah* [Chicago, 1981], 211).

Pharisees were a table fellowship sect can also be learned, according to Neusner, from the Gospels' picture of them.[9]

But Neusner's arguments are untenable. First and foremost, E.P. Sanders has already shown that Neusner's characterizations of the Pharisees as they appear in rabbinic literature are based on false assumptions.[10] Moreover, Daniel Schwartz has argued very convincingly that several of Josephus' accounts of the Pharisees derive from Nicolaus of Damascus; he has underlined the hostile tone of those passages,[11] thus rebutting Smith's argument that the assertions of Pharisaic influence in *Antiquities* were pro-Pharisaic propaganda. Furthermore, Schwartz has noted that Nicolaus clearly attests to Pharisaic political activity under Herod; and he has also pointed, *pace* Neusner, to indications that such activity continued during the first century CE.[12]

Neusner's thesis, however, has been accepted by many scholars. Thus, for example, Roland Deines has expanded it and offered new evidence in its favor. Surprisingly, however, Deines' case is based upon the opposite assumption: namely, that the Pharisees' political power was at its zenith during the reign of Herod. The new ruler had distanced himself from the Sadducean aristocracy and promoted the emergence of a new social elite; this elite included recent arrivals from the Diaspora such as Hillel the Babylonian, who became the Pharisees' leader.[13] Deines states that, beginning in the middle of the first century BCE, the Pharisees were responsible for a religious revolution that mainly stressed the religious experience of the individual[14] and was characterized by an attempt to adhere to a "priestly" way of life outside the Temple precincts.[15] According to Deines, one expression of this tendency was the fact that, although the origin of the synagogue in the

---

[9] Neusner, *From Politics to Piety*, 67–80.

[10] E.P. Sanders, *Jewish Law from Jesus to the Mishnah* (Philadelphia, 1990), 166–84.

[11] D.R. Schwartz, "Josephus and Nicolaus on the Pharisees," *JSJ* 14 (1983): 158–62. The negative tone of several of these passages is also basic for the thesis of S. Mason, *Flavius Josephus on the Pharisees* (Leiden, 1991)—although his conclusions are composition-critical rather than source-critical.

[12] "Josephus and Nicolaus," 166 n. 27.

[13] See R. Deines, *Jüdische Steingefässe und Pharisäische Frömmigkeit: Ein Archäologisch-Historischer Beitrag zum Verständnis von Joh 2, 6 und der jüdischen Reinheitshalacha zur Zeit Jesu* (Tübingen, 1993), 16.

[14] Ibid., 3–7.

[15] Ibid., 11–15. He asserts (173), contrary to Neusner (*Judaism: The Evidence of the Mishnah*, 211), that the observance of ritual purity outside the bounds of the Temple has its roots in the Bible, and so is not a Pharisaic innovation.

Land of Israel was in the Hasmonean period, in the days of Herod it turned into a place in which the Torah was learned and interpreted—a development that both bespoke the Pharisaic view that emphasized the individual's religious experience and also served to popularize that view among the people.[16] Another expression of the same tendency was the use of stone vessels, which were first manufactured in the Land of Israel in the second half of the first century BCE. The sudden emergence of this industry in Galilee and in Judea, particularly in Jerusalem and its environs, along with its absence from many other regions, both in the Land of Israel and elsewhere, indicate that this was an exclusive Jewish industry.[17] Judging from the wide distribution and large quantities of stone vessels, they were by no means a luxury item. Deines suggests that the need to observe the purity laws outside the Temple, following the Pharisaic religious revolution, provided the impetus for the enormous surge in the production, marketing, and use of stone vessels, since according to rabbinic halakhah they are not susceptible to ritual impurity.[18] Their wide distribution points to the considerable influence of the Pharisees, as well as to the adoption of the Pharisaic ideal by many sectors of Jewish society. This can also explain the use of ritual baths, which likewise became widely distributed in this period.[19] The increased Pharisaic influence is also implied by the widespread use of ossuaries as receptacles for the bones of the deceased at this time, an innovation that Deines[20] associates with the spread of the Pharisaic doctrine of resurrection of the dead and immortality of the soul.[21]

Although Deines thus assembles diverse archaeological finds and seems to succeed in giving them a coherent explanation, his thesis should be rejected for several reasons. First, concerning synagogues: As Levine has noted, there is no evidence that points to a connection between the Pharisees and the early synagogue. Nothing in the early

---

[16] Ibid., 6–8.

[17] See Y. Magen, *The Stone Vessel Industry in the Second Temple Period: Excavations at Hizma and the Jerusalem Temple Mount* (Jerusalem, 2002), 162.

[18] Deines, *Steingefässe*, 18–19. See also Magen, *Stone Vessel Industry*, 146–47.

[19] See R. Reich, "*Miqva'ot* (Jewish Ritual Immersion Baths) in Eretz-Israel in the Second Temple and the Mishnah and Talmud Periods" (Ph.D. diss., The Hebrew University of Jerusalem, 1990), 109, 126, 140–41, 148, 150, 152 (in Hebrew).

[20] Following L.Y. Rahmani, "A Jewish Tomb on Shahin Hill, Jerusalem," *IEJ* 8 (1958): 105.

[21] Deines, *Steingefässe*, 4–10. Regarding Pharisaic influence and power, see also M. Hengel and R. Deines, "E. P. Sanders' 'Common Judaism', Jesus, and the Pharisees," *JTS* 46 (1995): 29–35.

synagogue liturgy is particularly Pharisaic.[22] Thus, Pharisaic involvement in the development of the synagogue cannot be proved. Regarding ritual baths, it should be noted that these were already in use at the end of the second century BCE or the beginning of the first century BCE.[23] Moreover, the argument that the use of ossuaries attests to a belief in resurrection is no longer accepted, for several reasons. First, the emergence of ossuaries is dated only to the end of the first century BCE, while the Jewish belief in resurrection evolved at least a century earlier. Furthermore, some ossuaries contained the bones of several members of a family and in other cases the collection of the bones was only partial.[24] Neither of those situations sits well with the notion of enabling the resurrection of the individual. It is also very probable that the Sadducees, who rejected the belief in resurrection and the afterlife, also engaged in this burial practice.[25] As for the use of stone vessels—this should probably be traced to the development of a stone industry in Jerusalem alongside Herod's construction of the Temple; this might also explain the use of ossuaries in secondary burial.[26] There is also room for doubt concerning the notion that, as Deines claims, the Pharisees' political power was in fact at its zenith during the reign of Herod.[27]

To my mind, there is no indication that the Pharisees tried to live like priests. But, as Schwartz points out,[28] one should differentiate between priesthood and holiness. There is no reason to assume that the Pharisees thought that holiness was mediated by priesthood:

---

[22] L.I. Levine, *The Ancient Synagogue* (New Haven and London, 2000), 38.

[23] See S. Gibson, "The Pool of Bethesda in Jerusalem and Jewish Purification Practices of the Second Temple Period," *Proche-Orient Chrétien* 55 (2005): 278–79; A.M. Berlin, "Jewish Life before the Revolt: The Archaeological Evidence," *JSJ* 36 (2005): 452–53. Admittedly, however, it was only in the second half of the first century BCE that *mikva'ot* became widespread.

[24] See A. Kloner, "Burial Caves and Ossuaries from the Second Temple Period on Mount Scopus," in *Jews and Judaism in the Second Temple, Mishna and Talmud Period—Studies in Honor of Shmuel Safrai* (ed. I.M. Gafni et al.; Jerusalem, 1993), 105 (in Hebrew).

[25] See E. Regev, "The Individual Meaning of Jewish Ossuaries," *PEQ* 133 (2001): 41.

[26] See S. Fine, "A Note on Ossuary Burial and the Resurrection of the Dead in First-Century Jerusalem," *JJS* 51 (2000): 69–76. The development of a stone industry in Jerusalem does not explain the motivation for the use of stone vessels and ossuaries. It only means that these vessels could not have been produced before the reign of Herod.

[27] See Deines, *Steingefässe*, 10 n. 19, regarding Josephus' descriptions of the Pharisees.

[28] Schwartz, "Kingdom," 63–64.

> In the polemic context normally assumed, would it not be a better strat-
> egy for non-priests to insist that all, priests and non-priests alike, have
> to answer to a common standard of holiness...than to admit that stan-
> dards were set for the priests and non-priests were outsiders who could
> try to meet them?[29]

Indeed, this is the main thesis of several scholars, such as Eyal Regev,
who rejects Neusner's theory and argues that the desire to achieve personal sanctity was widespread within Jewish society (not only among
a minority of pietists) from the beginning of the second century BCE.[30]
Thus, certain routine actions which had become an integral part of
any Jew's everyday life were seen at this time as expressive of sanctity,
and therefore as possessing religious significance; for that reason, they
had to be performed in a condition of ritual purity, because purity is
necessary in order to achieve holiness.[31] Regev claims that "those who
voluntarily observed purity in order to eat, pray, and read Scripture
were seeking holiness in their everyday life, outside the realm of the
Temple...holiness occurs, without doubt, in the reading of the Shema,
reading in the Torah, and praying."[32] He explains that the act of cleansing is a transition from a profane status to a status of sanctity.[33]

I cannot, however, accept this explanation, which is not supported
by the sources. There is no evidence that a ritually impure person did
not read Scripture. On the contrary, t. Ber. 2:12 states that he may.[34]
Similarly, although it is true that, as Regev notes, it was a common
practice to immerse before praying, this was not necessarily connected to ritual purity.[35] Moreover, the supposed connection between

---

[29] Ibid., 64.

[30] E. Regev, "Pure Individualism: The Idea of Non-Priestly Purity in Ancient Judaism," JSJ 31 (2000): 186–87. See also Hengel and Deines, "Judaism," 46, concerning
the motivation behind the Pharisees' aspirations towards purity: "This lies in the oft-
repeated summons of God to his people, 'be holy, for I am holy.'"

[31] Regev, "Pure Individualism," 187.

[32] Ibid. See also Hengel and Deines, "Judaism," 46 n. 116: "Life in the presence of
God also requires a holiness which comes to expression in ritual purity...wherever
one prayed, studied the Torah, or was in any way involved in worship...there was a
demand for purity." See also J.C. Poirier, "Purity beyond the Temple in the Second
Temple Era," JBL 122 (2003): 254.

[33] Regev, "Pure Individualism," 187.

[34] Except one who had a nocturnal emission.

[35] "It may well be that these halakhot, which ordain immersion or washing of the
hands for prayer, are not based on the suspicion of actual defilement, but on the fact
that the service of the heart is likened to the Temple service, which requires washing
of the hands and immersion even by those who are clean" (G. Alon, "The Bounds
of the Laws of Levitical Cleanness," in idem, Jews, Judaism and the Classical World
[Jerusalem, 1977], 202).

routine actions (such as eating) and holiness is not very clear.[36] Actually, the only definite expression of observance of ritual purity outside the Temple precincts was the eating of ordinary food in a state of ritual purity, and the purpose of using stone vessels and of immersing in *miqva'ot* (ritual baths) was to assure ritual purity at mealtime.

That practice, however, did not stem from a desire to achieve holiness, but rather from different reasons:[37] Mary Douglas has argued that in any society, special emphasis on matters of ritual purity usually represents the desire of certain sectors of that society to segregate themselves from other sectors, which they perceive as a threat. Thus, the fear of contact with non-Jews, which was an outcome of the threatening encounter between the Jewish minority and the Gentile majority in the Babylonian Diaspora and under Persian rule, was symbolically expressed in strict observance of bodily purity.[38] Moreover, life in the Diaspora (and later the encounter with Hellenism in the Land of Israel itself) aroused a desire for national segregation among certain circles of the returnees to Zion, and even hostility toward non-Jews, which was expressed in the treatment of them as ritually impure. The fear of defilement created a feeling of revulsion towards anything that had been in contact with a defiling agent; so that people refrained, for example, from eating food that had been prepared by non-Jews or had been in contact with physical impurity.

Both motives—the care to eat food in a pure state, and the view of non-Jews as ritually impure—are expressed in literary works of the Persian and Hellenistic periods. The practice of eating nonsacred food in a condition of ritual purity was not exclusive to a minority, such as the priests (who ate the priestly gifts only when pure) or the Qumran sectarians; it was in fact the accepted practice among many circles, as implied by the wide distribution of the stone vessels. To my mind, rabbinic literature implies that such was the practice of the Pharisees,[39]

---

[36] See Hengel and Deines, "Judaism," 46 n. 116: "The rabbis' confidence 'of God's presence and accessibility'...also required an extension of the purity halakhah to daily life." But why then restrict the demand for purity to praying, studying and eating? According to this reasoning, every routine action should be performed in a state of ritual purity!

[37] See H. Birenboim, "Observance of the Laws of Bodily Purity in Jewish Society in the Land of Israel during the Second Temple Period" (Ph.D. diss., The Hebrew University of Jerusalem, 2006), 83–108 (in Hebrew).

[38] See M. Douglas, *Purity and Danger: An Analysis of Concepts of Pollution and Taboo* (London, 1966), 124.

[39] See Birenboim, "Observance," 46–59.

and their considerable influence can explain the popularity of this practice already in the Hasmonean Period.

To sum up, Martin Hengel and Deines are probably right when they claim that "this demand for holiness does not apply to the Temple area and its personnel alone, but in descending degrees also to...the entire people."[40] But to my mind, the practical applications of this demand for holiness are not clear. The Pharisees did not try to live like priests in the Temple even while outside the Temple; and there is no evidence that the reason for observing purity outside the Temple was the quest for holiness in everyday life. In place of the general notion of the demand for holiness, I want to point out a more specific characteristic of the Pharisees, which was one of the causes of their conflict with the Sadducees/priests.

Ya'akov Sussmann has already observed that "the Pharisees' primary goal was to enable the general public to participate as extensively as possible in Temple life and religious worship."[41] The Pharisees were accordingly extremely lenient on questions of purity related to Jerusalem and the Temple, especially during the periods of the Festivals and pilgrimages; they relied on the presumption that the commoners (עמי הארץ) purified themselves before coming to Jerusalem at those times.[42] Occasionally, the desire for popular participation in the life of the Temple led to its defilement. Thus, the Pharisees held that the Temple court and the Temple vessels were to be purified after a pilgrimage festival, for fear that they had been defiled by the commoners.[43] Apparently, the Pharisees permitted the display of the Temple vessels to the pilgrims.[44] They might also have permitted the masses to enter the sacred precinct (בין האולם למזבח) on the festival of Sukkot.[45] These

---

[40] Hengel and Deines, "Judaism," 47.

[41] Y. Sussmann, "The History of the Halakha and the Dead Sea Scrolls: Preliminary Talmudic Observations on Miqṣat Maʿaśe Ha-Torah (4QMMT)," in E. Qimron and J. Strugnell, eds., Qumran Cave 4.V: Miqṣat Maʿaśe ha-Torah (DJD 10; Oxford, 1994), 198. See also E.E. Urbach, The Sages: Their Concepts and Beliefs (Jerusalem, 1971), 519–20 (in Hebrew).

[42] See, e.g., m. Ḥag. 3:6; y. Ḥag. 3:6 (79d); y. B. Qam. 7:7 (6a); b. Ḥag. 26a.

[43] See m. Ḥag. 3:7–8; t. Ḥag. 3:35 (ed. Lieberman, 394).

[44] See y. Ḥag. 3:8 (79d); b. Ḥag. 26b. See also Sussmann, "History of the Halakha," 199; I. Knohl, "Participation of the People in the Temple Worship—Second Temple Sectarian Conflict and the Biblical Tradition," Tarbiz 60 (1991): 140 (in Hebrew); G.A. Anderson, "Towards a Theology of the Tabernacle and its Furniture," in Text, Thought, and Practice in Qumran and Early Christianity (ed. R.A. Clements and D.R. Schwartz; Leiden, 2009), 161–94, esp. 168–83.

[45] Knohl, "Participation," 141.

practices aroused the opposition of the Sadducees, who regarded them as sacrilegious.[46] According to *t. Sukkah* 3:1 (ed. Lieberman, 266), the commoners supported the Pharisees. Sussmann notes that most of the authentic traditions that pertain to the Sadducees/Boethusians and concern halakhic matters derive from the public, ritual sphere; this public aspect of the dispute is indicated, and even emphasized, in the sources. He mentions, inter alia, the traditions concerning the reaping of the sheaf of barley (*'omer*); the burning of incense on the Day of Atonement; the water libation and the circuits of the altar with willow branches on the Festival of Sukkot; the funding of public sacrifices; and the determination of the calendar.[47]

I would like to add another example of this Pharisaic drive to enable popular participation in the Temple rite: the controversy between the Pharisees, on the one hand, and the Sadducees and the members of the Qumran sect, on the other, regarding the preparation of the ashes of the red heifer and the purification water.[48] According to *m. Parah* 3:7, the Sadducees insisted that those who prepared these substances must themselves be completely pure, having themselves been purified and awaited sundown, while the Pharisees asserted the eligibility of one who had bathed but not waited for evening (*ṭevul yom*). This disagreement was of the greatest practical significance, since one who had acquired corpse impurity could not enter the Temple, and this impurity could not be expunged without resort to the ashes of the red heifer. The publication of 4QMMT revealed that, in this matter, the sectarian halakhah was identical with that of the Sadducees.[49] Joseph Baumgarten observed that "the Pharisees insisted that since the red cow was not a Temple sacrifice, the *ṭevul yom* was considered adequately pure, just as he was eligible to consume nonsacramental purities."[50] We may conclude, then, that the Pharisees and their opponents fundamentally

---

[46] Sussmann, "History of the Halakha," 199; Knohl, "Participation," 141–42.

[47] See Y. Sussmann, "The History of the Halakha and the Dead Sea Scrolls—Preliminary Observations on *Miqṣat Maʿaśe Ha-Torah* (4QMMT)," *Tarbiz* 59 (1990): 67 n. 220 (in Hebrew).

[48] See H. Birenboim, "*Tevul Yom* and the Red Heifer: Pharisaic and Sadducean Halakhah," *DSD* 16 (2009): 254–73. For a nonpolemical construal of the Qumran texts, see M. Himmelfarb, "The Polemic Against the *Ṭevul Yom*: A Reexamination," in *New Perspectives on Old Texts* (ed. E.G. Chazon, B. Halpern-Amaru, and R.A. Clements; Leiden, 2010), 199–214.

[49] 4QMMT B:13–17. See also 4Q277 1 ii 2.

[50] J.M. Baumgarten, "The Red Cow Purification Rites in Qumran Texts," *JJS* 46 (1995): 112.

disagreed regarding the standing of the red heifer: the Sadducees (and the Qumran sect) maintained that it was a sacrifice, while the Pharisees rejected that position.

It seems that by determining that the red heifer is not a sacrifice, the Pharisees also opened the way for nonpriests to take an active part in the ritual of preparing its ashes, and even in the sprinkling of the water of purification on the impure. This is also expressed in traditions preserved in the Mishnah that indicate the important role of children in the sanctification of the water.[51] True, the Mishnah implies that this practice derived from an insistence upon stringency concerning the purity of the water.[52] It should be noted, however, that the use of children also highlights the ceremony's popular nature[53]—a point that may explain why the texts from Qumran opposed this practice and demanded that only adult priests officiate at each stage in the purification process.

It seems, to be the case, then, that the Pharisees neither tried to live like priests nor tried to undermine the priests' authority by founding an alternative religious ritual. Rather, they clearly recognized the fundamental role of the Temple and the priests in worshiping God, and hence tried to ensure that the Temple worship would be conducted as fully and properly as possible.[54] But they did want the people to be involved as extensively as possible in Temple life, and to be active players in the Temple ritual rather than passive spectators. Their main purpose, accordingly, was to provide the common people with a temporal separation from everyday life and a religious experience of closeness to God (that is, holiness). Perhaps that was the primary reason for their great popularity among the people[55] and for the hostility between them and the Sadducees/priests.

---

[51] *M. Parah* 3:2–3.

[52] *M. Parah* 3:2. It seems that the children put the ashes in the water, and even sprinkled the purification water on the impure, as is indicated by 4Q277 1 ii 7 and by the *Epistle of Barnabas*; see Baumgarten, "Red Cow," 119 n. 9.

[53] Children are also mentioned in *m. Sukkah* 4:7, which notes their participation in the circuits of the altar with willow branches, a practice which the Boethusians did not recognize. See *t. Sukkah* 3:1 (ed. Lieberman, 266).

[54] See, for example, Josephus, *Ant.* 13.408. In the Herodian period, the question as to who was controlling the Temple became quite a complicated one. See E. Regev, *The Sadducees and their Halakhah: Religion and Society in the Second Temple Period* (Jerusalem, 2005), 348–377 (in Hebrew).

[55] See Josephus, *Ant.* 13.296; 18.17.

SECTARIANISM BEFORE AND AFTER 70 CE

Jodi Magness

> With the destruction of the Temple the primary focal point of Jewish sectarianism disappeared.... For most Jews...sectarian self-definition ceased to make sense after 70.[1]

> The standard assumption that these Jewish groups disappeared soon after 70 is therefore no more than an assumption. Furthermore, the presuppositions which have encouraged the assumption are so theologically loaded that historians' suspicions should be instinctive.... My hypothesis is that groups and philosophies known from pre-70 Judaism continued for years, perhaps centuries, after the destruction of the Temple.[2]

Notwithstanding Martin Goodman's cautionary note, Shaye Cohen's statement reflects a widely held view that the sectarian divisions that characterized the late Second Temple period disappeared soon after the Temple's destruction. This view is based mainly on the silence of rabbinic writings, which provide little indication that Essenes and Pharisees or Sadducees and Pharisees (for example) continued to debate halakhic issues after 70.[3] As David Instone-Brewer remarks,

> A good case can be made that all the rival groups simply lost their distinctiveness and impetus with the destruction of the Temple. The Sadducees lost their locus of activity, the Essenes lost the reason for their rebellion, and the Pharisees' attempt to replicate Temple activities in

---

[1] S.J.D. Cohen, "The Significance of Yavneh: Pharisees, Rabbis, and the End of Jewish Sectarianism," *HUCA* 55 (1985): 45.

[2] M. Goodman, "Sadducees and Essenes after 70 CE," in *Crossing the Boundaries: Essays in Biblical Interpretation in Honour of Michael D. Goulder* (ed. S.E. Porter, P. Joyce, and D.E. Orton; Leiden, 1994), 348, 355.

[3] The editors of the Mishnah and other rabbinic documents sought to represent Yavneh as the end of sectarianism; see C. Hezser, *The Social Structure of the Rabbinic Movement in Roman Palestine* (Tübingen, 1997), 64. For the claim that Essenes should be identified as one group among others that the early rabbis condemned as *minim*, see J.E. Burns, "Essene Sectarianism and Social Differentiation in Judea after 70 C.E.," *HTR* 99 (2006): 247–74. Burns rejects the argument from silence: "But just as the absence of the title 'Christian' in rabbinic texts does not mean that Christians were absent from the social world of the early rabbis, the lack of explicit testimony to the Essenes does not mean that the sect had ceased to exist" (p. 268).

the home, synagogue, and schoolhouse became the only way to express Jewish rites.[4]

A number of passages in the Mishnah reflect the rabbis' struggle to adapt legal observance to the new reality. Thus, for example:

[Laws concerning] sheqel dues and firstfruits apply only in the time of the Temple. But those concerning tithe of grain, tithe of cattle, and of firstlings apply both in the time of the Temple and not in the time of the Temple. He who [nowadays] declares sheqels and firstfruits to be holy—lo, this is deemed holy. R. Simeon says, "He who says, 'Firstfruit is holy,'—they do not enter the status of Holy Things." (m. Sheqalim 8:8)[5]

One who buys pieces of fruit [outside Jerusalem with money in the status of second tithe] pieces of fruit: unintentionally [not realizing the coins were consecrated]—let their payment be returned to its [former] place [to the purchaser who bought them by mistake]; on purpose—let [the pieces of fruit] be brought up and eaten in the [holy] place [Jerusalem]. And if the Temple does not exist, let [the pieces of fruit] rot.

One who buys [outside Jerusalem] a domesticated animal [with money in the status of second tithe]: intentionally—let its payment return to its [former] place; on purpose—let [the animal] be brought up and eaten in the [holy] place. And if the Temple does not exist, let it be buried with its hide. (m. Ma'aser Sheni 1:5–6)[6]

The result was that groups that were inclusive of all Israel and believed that the divine could be experienced anywhere—that is, the Pharisees

---

[4] D. Instone-Brewer, *Traditions of the Rabbis from the Era of the New Testament, Volume 1: Prayer and Agriculture* (Grand Rapids, 2004), 4; on p. 5 he notes that "the defining characteristic of Yavneh became inclusiveness rather than sectarian exclusiveness, which explains why those who continued after 70 C.E. to call themselves 'Pharisee' (*Perushim* in rabbinic literature) were regarded as sectarians."

[5] All of the quotes from the Mishnah and Tosefta are taken from Jacob Neusner's translations: *The Mishnah: A New Translation* (New Haven: Yale, 1988); and *The Tosefta: Translated from the Hebrew with a New Introduction, Vol. 1* (Peabody, MA: Hendrickson, 2002).

[6] B.M. Bokser ("*Ma'al* and Blessings over Food: Rabbinic Transformation of Cultic Terminology and Alternative Modes of Piety," *JBL* 100 [1981]: 567–68) points out that the Temple's destruction created special problems because Jews were obligated by biblical law to bring agricultural offerings and tithes to Jerusalem before the rest of the produce might be consumed. The rabbis adapted legal observance to the changed situation after 70 in various ways, including permitting the redemption of second tithes with money, allowing *terumah* to be given to any priest, and requiring blessings before all meals. Also see D. Amit and Y. Adler, "The Observance of Ritual Purity after 70 C.E.," in *"Follow the Wise" (B. Sanhedrin 32b): Studies in Jewish History and Culture in Honor of Lee I. Levine* (ed. O. Irshai, J. Magness, S. Schwartz, and Z. Weiss; Winona Lake, 2010), 121–43.

and Jesus' movement—survived (in some form) the Temple's destruction, whereas the exclusive priestly groups—the Sadducees and Essenes—vanished from view.[7]

The apparent disappearance of these sects after 70 does not mean that Jewish factionalism and debates over purity observance ceased.[8] To the contrary, rabbinic writings present a variety of rulings on purity issues relating to prayer and Torah study as well as the (now defunct) Temple cult.[9] However, whereas before 70 debates on halakhic issues divided Jews along sectarian lines, after 70 the rabbis tolerated and preserved different opinions.[10] Most scholars therefore view the rabbinic period as characterized by an inclusive and pluralistic attitude that contrasts with the period before 70.[11] As Instone-Brewer puts it, "This inclusivity is seen in the Mishnah, which was the first Jewish document to express rival views with equal authority, and which appears to 'agree to disagree' except when a clear decision was made by the voting of a majority."[12]

Still, rabbinic tolerance had its limits, with sages who refused to accept the majority opinion being condemned as heretics (often

---

[7] For the relationship between the Pharisees and the [later] rabbis see Burns, "Essene Sectarianism and Social Differentiation," 255–56, including n. 18: The early rabbis assumed the "ideological platform" and "religious tenets" of Pharisaism. For the rabbinic view that the divine presence is everywhere and not just in the Jerusalem Temple, see B.M. Bokser, "Ma'al and Blessings over Food," 567–68.

[8] As M. Himmelfarb, *A Kingdom of Priests: Ancestry and Merit in Ancient Judaism* (Philadelphia, 2006), 175, puts it, "even if the pre-70 sects did not survive long in the post-Temple era, it would not necessarily mean the end of sectarianism."

[9] See J.C. Poirier, "Purity beyond the Temple in the Second Temple Era," *JBL* 112 (2003): 264–65.

[10] Cohen, "The Significance of Yavneh," 29, 45, 48; Instone-Brewer, *Prayer and Agriculture*, 5. J. Milgrom, "The Scriptural Foundations and Deviations in the Laws of Purity of the *Temple Scroll*," in *Archaeology and History in the Dead Sea Scrolls: The New York University Conference in Memory of Yigael Yadin* (ed. L.H. Schiffman; Sheffield, 1990), 89, remarks that, although the Qumran sect and the rabbis were both heirs to the Bible's minimalist and maximalist traditions, "Qumran rejected the principle that the Rabbis had derived from Scripture: that even divergent interpretations can be the word of the living God."

[11] A.I. Baumgarten, *The Flourishing of Jewish Sects in the Maccabean Era* (Leiden, 1997), 134–35, suggests that sectarian divisiveness disappeared after 70 because of the "return to orality" in the era of the Mishnah, which enabled scholars to disagree.

[12] Instone-Brewer, *Prayer and Agriculture*, 5. Also see Cohen, "The Significance of Yavneh," 29. V. Noam, "Beit Shammai and the Sectarian Halakhah," *Jewish Studies (World Union of Jewish Studies)* 41 (2002): 47 (in Hebrew), makes the important distinction that after 70 disagreements and differences of opinion are confined to individuals rather than sects or "schools," and that these disagreements are on specific points of law rather than systemic approaches and attitudes.

denoted as *minim* [מינים] or as Sadducees), as a debate about resurrection in the Babylonian Talmud illustrates:

> A sectarian [*min*] said to R. Ammi: "Ye maintain that the dead will revive; but they turn to dust, and can dust come to life?"—He replied: I will tell thee a parable. This may be compared to a human king who commanded his servants to build him a great palace in a place where there was no water or earth [for making bricks]. So they went and built it. But after some time it collapsed, so he commanded them to rebuild it in a place where water and earth was to be found; but they replied, "We cannot." Thereupon he became angry with them and said, "If ye could build in a place containing no water or earth, surely ye can where there is!" "Yet," [continued R. Ammi], "If thou dost not believe, go forth in to the field and see a mouse, which to-day is but part flesh and part dust, and yet by to-morrow has developed and become all flesh. And shouldst thou say, 'That takes a long time,' go up to the mountains, where thou wilt see but one snail, whilst by to-morrow the rain has descended and it is covered with snails."
>
> A sectarian [*min*] said to Gebiha b. Pesisa, "Woe to you, ye wicked, who maintain that the dead will revive; if even the living die, shall the dead live?!" He replied, "Woe to you, ye wicked, who maintain that the dead will not revive: if what was not, [now] lives—surely what has lived, will live again!" "Thou hast called me wicked," said he, "If I stood up I could kick thee and strip thee of thy hump!" "If thou couldst do that," he retorted, "thou wouldst be called a great doctor, and command large fees." (*b. Sanhedrin* 91a; Soncino translation)[13]

In other words, whereas before 70 there were various groups, movements, or sects with different halakhic practices, after 70 mainstream (rabbinic) Judaism tolerated a plurality of views but only within certain limits.[14] Those who refused to conform were condemned as heretics, as Daniel Boyarin observes:

> I find in the fact that the Mishnaic text discussed above [*m. Niddah* 4:2–J.M.] opposed "Sadducees" and "Israel" not evidence for a tolerant, nonsectarian Judaism, but rather for a Catholic Israel, a former 'group' that has won the day, or at any rate, that so represents itself and defines all others as simply not in the fold at all.... Jewish sectarianism as a form

---

[13] For a discussion of this passage see M. Kister, "Law, Morality, and Rhetoric in Some Sayings of Jesus," in *Studies in Ancient Midrash* (ed. J.L. Kugel; Cambridge, Mass., 2001), 146–47.

[14] Even Cohen, "The Significance of Yavneh," 49, acknowledges the limits of rabbinic tolerance.

of decentralized pluralism by default had been replaced by the binary opposition of Jewish orthodox and Jewish heretics.[15]

Before 70 even the most extreme or marginal Jewish sects were not prohibited from participating in the sacrificial cult in the Jerusalem Temple (including the Essenes and the Jewish followers of Jesus after his death), whereas after 70, Jews who refused to accept the majority opinion were no longer considered Jews at all.[16] Boyarin views the creation of heresiological discourse as a rabbinic attempt to define and circumscribe Judaism in relation to Christianity.[17]

What happened to Jewish purity observance after the Jerusalem Temple—the place where God's presence dwelt—was destroyed?[18] Some scholars point out that purity issues continued to play a major role in Jewish religious life, as reflected by the centrality of purity laws in rabbinic debates.[19] As John Poirier says, "the relevance of purity was a debated issue for much, if not all, of the period between the destruction of the Temple and the late Gaonic period."[20] Other scholars assume that the observance of purity laws declined as time went on and hopes of a rebuilt Temple faded.[21] For example, Thomas Kazen observes that

---

[15] D. Boyarin, *Border Lines: The Partition of Judaeo-Christianity* (Philadelphia, 2004), 63, 65.

[16] For rabbinic self-definition in opposition to sectarianism see Burns, "Essene Sectarianism and Social Differentiation," especially 253–57.

[17] Boyarin, *Border Lines*, 63.

[18] Amit and Adler, "Observance of Ritual Purity," note that there is no comprehensive study of the observance of ritual purity laws after 70.

[19] See for example J. Neusner, *The Idea of Purity in Ancient Judaism* (Leiden, 1973), 130, who observes that in Talmudic Judaism the concern for purity continued and purity laws were greatly developed.

[20] Poirier, "Purity beyond the Temple in the Second Temple Era," 264; also see E. Regev, "Non-Priestly Purity and Its Religious Aspects According to Historical Sources and Archaeological Findings," in *Purity and Holiness: The Heritage of Leviticus* (ed. M.J.H.M. Poorthuis and J. Schwartz; Leiden, 2000), 243.

[21] A. Oppenheimer, *The 'Am Ha-aretz: A Study in the Social History of the Jewish People in the Hellenistic-Roman Period* (Leiden, 1977), 66, observes that after the ashes of the red heifer ran out, purification from corpse impurity was no longer possible. Also see Y. Adler, "The Observance of Ritual Purity in Agricultural Industry during the Second Temple and Mishnah Periods," *Jerusalem and Eretz-Israel* (Yehuda Feliks Memorial Volume) 4–5 (2007): 59 n. 3 (in Hebrew); Amit and Adler, "The Observance of Ritual Purity after 70 C.E.": "Indeed, the ability to achieve and maintain ritual purity was not dependent on the presence of the Jerusalem Temple, but rather on the continued supply of red-heifer ash...." Amit and Adler observe that there is no indication in Talmudic literature that purification using the ashes of a red heifer had been discontinued, and that the earliest evidence that purity observance had ceased dates to the Geonic period. Even then, menstruants and women who had given birth

the Talmudim contain no Gemara for any Mishnaic tractate belonging to the order of *Purities* except for *Niddah*.[22] Both points of view are correct, as rabbinic literature displays a concern with certain types of purity observance but ignores others.[23] Instone-Brewer provides a list summarizing which Temple practices continued to be debated by the rabbis after 70, which practices were continued in a limited way for a short period, and which ceased altogether after 70.[24] For the purpose of our discussion, I will consider evidence for sectarian practices after 70 by first focusing on (literary) controversies relating to the ingestion of creeping and swarming creatures and the consumption of the blood of fish and locusts, and then considering possible ties between the reported controversies and the archaeological record.

CREEPING AND SWARMING CREATURES

Matthew 23:13–36 attributes to Jesus a series of seven prophetic "woes" against the scribes and Pharisees. Jesus' criticism includes a halakhic point: "You blind guides! You strain out a gnat but swallow a camel!" (Matt 23:24).[25]

---

continued to immerse in *miqva'ot* for the purpose of maintaining marital relations. Also see S.S. Miller, "Stepped Pools and the Non-Existent Monolithic 'Miqveh,'" in *The Archaeology of Difference: Gender, Ethnicity, Class and the "Other" in Antiquity. Studies in Honor of Eric M. Meyers* (ed. D.R. Edwards and C.T. McCollough; Annual of the American Schools of Oriental Research 60/61; Boston, 2007), 222–24, 231 n. 58. Y. Elizur, "Miqva'ot for the Immersion of Hands," *Cathedra* 91 (1991): 172 (in Hebrew), states that the observance of purification for the consumption of *ḥullin* relaxed in the centuries following the destruction of the Temple.

[22] T. Kazen, *Jesus and Purity Halakhah: Was Jesus Indifferent to Impurity?* (Stockholm, 2002), 350.

[23] Adler, "Observance of Ritual Purity in Agricultural Industry," 71, notes that the demand for ritually pure agricultural produce (grain, wine, oil) declined dramatically after the Temple's destruction.

[24] Instone-Brewer, *Prayer and Agriculture*, 35–37.

[25] Jesus seems to be criticizing his opponents for being more concerned with minor points of law than with the more important issues of morality; see Instone-Brewer, *Prayer and Agriculture*, 292. Kister, "Law, Morality, and Rhetoric," 148–49, notes that Jesus uses the woes as a rhetorical device to turn a halakhic issue into a moral point; and A.J. Saldarini, *Matthew's Christian-Jewish Community* (Chicago, 1994), 141–42, 162, like others, considers Matt 23:24 a rhetorical reinforcement of Matthew's polemical stand against emphasis on the lesser (in his opinion) matters of the law. While several of the other "woes" are paralleled in Luke and may be attributed to Q, Matthew's pre-70 source, scholars have noted that v. 24 is without such a parallel and may reflect the concerns of Matthew's post-70 community. My thanks to Ruth Clements for drawing my attention to this point. The origin of this saying has engendered a wide

Biblical law prohibits the consumption of camels and gnats:

> But among those that chew the cud or have divided hoofs, you shall not eat the following: the camel, for even though it chews the cud, it does not have divided hoofs; it is unclean (*tamē*) for you. (Lev 11:4)

> All winged insects that walk upon all fours are detestable (*sheqetz*) to you. But among the winged insects that walk on all fours you may eat those that have jointed legs above their feet, with which to leap on the ground. Of these you may eat: the locust according to its kind, the bald locust according to its kind, the cricket according to its kind, and the grasshopper according to its kind. But all other winged insects that have four feet are detestable (*sheqetz*) to you. (Lev 11:20–23)

> These are unclean (*tamē*) for you among the creatures that swarm (*sheretz hashoretz*) upon the earth: the weasel, the mouse, the great lizard according to its kind, the gecko, the land crocodile, the lizard, the sand lizard, and the chameleon. These are unclean for you among all that swarm; whoever touches one of them when they are dead shall be unclean until the evening. (Lev 11:29–31)

These passages in Leviticus 11 distinguish between living creatures that are forbidden as food but do not cause impurity (described as שֶׁקֶץ; *sheqetz*), on the one hand, and swarming land creatures (שֶׁרֶץ; *sheretz*) that are forbidden as food and whose carcasses do convey impurity (and which are described as unclean [טָמֵא; *tamē*]), on the other.[26] The latter consist of the eight species listed in Lev 11:29–30: the weasel, mouse, great lizard, gecko, land crocodile, lizard, sand lizard, and chameleon. According to Lev 11:39, the carcass of a clean (permitted) animal also conveys impurity: "If an animal of which you may eat dies, anyone who touches its carcass shall be unclean until the evening."

---

range of opinion. See the discussion of this passage in W.D. Davies and D.C. Allison, *A Critical and Exegetical Commentary on the Gospel According to St. Matthew* (3 vols.; Edinburgh, 1988–1997), 3: 293–96, who note the Leviticus passages and some of the rabbinic discussion on straining out bugs.

[26] See J. Milgrom, *Leviticus 1–16: A New Translation with Introduction and Commentary* (New York, 1991), 656, 682; J. Milgrom, "Two Biblical Hebrew Priestly Terms: Šeqes and Tame'," *Maarav* 8 (1992): 107–9; H. Maccoby, *Ritual and Morality: The Ritual Purity System and its Place in Judaism* (Cambridge, 1999), 69; M. Douglas, "Impurity of Land Animals," in Poorthuis and Schwartz, *Purity and Holiness*, 33–46, p. 35; on p. 42 Douglas notes that the word *tamē* (impure) occurs mostly in Leviticus and is rare elsewhere in the Hebrew Bible.

Leviticus 11:41–44 complicates the picture, as it prohibits the consumption of all swarming things (*sheretz* and *sheqetz*) *and* associates them with impurity (*tum'ah*):[27]

> Any swarming creature (*sheretz*) that swarms upon the earth is detestable (*sheqetz*); it shall not be eaten. Whatever moves on its belly, and whatever moves on all fours, or whatever has many feet, all the creatures that swarm upon the earth, you shall not eat; for they are detestable. You shall not make yourself detestable with any creature that swarms; you shall not defile yourselves with them, and so become unclean. (אל־
> תשקצו את־נפשתיכם בכל־השרץ השרץ; ולא תטמאו בהם ונטמתם בם.).
> For I am the Lord your God; sanctify yourselves therefore, and be holy, for I am holy. You shall not defile yourselves with any swarming creature (*sheretz*) that moves [or creeps] (*haromes*) on the earth (כי אני
> יהוה אלהיכם, והתקדשתם והייתם קדשים, כי קדוש אני ולא תטמאו
> את־נפשתיכם בכל־השרץ הרמש על־הארץ).

Deuteronomy 14:19 further complicates matters by repeating the prohibition of Lev 11:20 but describes winged insects as unclean (*tamē*) rather than detestable (*sheqetz*): "And all winged insects (*sheretz ha'of*) are unclean (*tamē*) for you (וכל שרץ העוף, טמא הוא לכם); they shall not be eaten. You may eat any clean winged creature" (Deut 14:19–20).[28]

In light of the confusion created by Leviticus and Deuteronomy,[29] it is not surprising that Jewish groups in the late Second Temple period and later disagreed about which swarming creatures were not only forbidden but also impure. The rabbis understood Leviticus as meaning that only the eight species listed in Lev 11:29–30 were unclean and therefore did not consider insects to be a source of impurity.[30]

---

[27] See Milgrom, "Two Biblical Hebrew Priestly Terms," 108–10, who notes that these differences are due to the various sources of the biblical passages; also see Milgrom, *Leviticus 1–16*, 683–87. M. Douglas, *Purity and Danger: An Analysis of Concepts of Pollution and Taboo* (New York, 1966), 56, observes that the movements of creeping, crawling, and swarming creatures were thought to be contrary to God's order (holiness).

[28] Y. Yadin, *The Temple Scroll* (3 vols.; Jerusalem, 1983), 2:385, tentatively restored the relevant line in the *Temple Scroll* (48:1–2), which is missing, as, "All winged insects that go upon all fours are an abomination to you (?)."

[29] For the relationship between these passages in Leviticus and Deuteronomy see Milgrom, *Leviticus 1–16*, 698–704; Milgrom, "Two Biblical Hebrew Priestly Terms," 114; J.A. Kelhoffer, "Did John the Baptist Eat Like a Former Essene? Locust-Eating in the Ancient Near East and at Qumran," *DSD* 11 (2004): 304.

[30] See Milgrom, "Two Biblical Hebrew Priestly Terms," 110–14; Maccoby, *Ritual and Morality*, 70–71; Douglas, "Impurity of Land Animals," 35. Milgrom, ibid., 108–9, points out that according to the Priestly source a person is not punished for eating *sheqetz* accidentally or deliberately.

The *Damascus Document* indicates that the Qumran sect, in contrast, understood Leviticus and Deuteronomy as meaning that *all* swarming creatures were a source of impurity:

> Let no man pollute his soul with any living and swarming [or creeping] creatures (*remes*) by eating of them, whether it be the larvae of bees or any living thing which swarms [or creeps] (*tirmos*) in the water.... (So much for) the rule of the settlement of the towns in Israel in accordance with these precepts, to separate between the impure (*tamē*) and the pure (*tahor*) and to make known (the distinction) between the holy and the profane. (CD 12:12–13; 19–20)[31]

This legislation makes it clear that the Qumran sect viewed the consumption of all forbidden foods as a cause of defilement; it appears to be a polemic against those who (like the later rabbis) understood from Leviticus 11 that only the eight species listed there are unclean. The polemic is sharpened by the sectarians' use of the term *remes* to denote all swarming creatures as unclean, which contrasts with the rabbinic distinction between the eight unclean species (*sheretz*) and other forbidden but not unclean creeping and swarming creatures (*sheqetz*). The use of the term *remes* shows that the legislation in the *Damascus Document* is based on Lev 11:44. Furthermore, Lev 22:5 prohibits *priests* from even touching "any swarming thing by which he may be made unclean" (בכל־שרץ אשר יטמא־לו)—a point that will have impressed the Qumran sectarians, who had such pronounced priestly tendencies.[32]

Whereas Lev 11:41–44 prohibits the consumption of creatures that swarm *on the earth* ("You shall not defile yourselves with any swarming creature (*sheretz*) that moves [or creeps] (*haromes*) on

---

[31] Translation from J.M. Baumgarten and D.R. Schwartz, "The Damascus Document," in *The Dead Sea Scrolls: Hebrew, Aramaic, and Greek Texts with English Translations, Volume 2: Damascus Document, War Scroll, and Related Documents* (ed. J.H. Charlesworth; Tübingen, 1995), 51–53; see H.K. Harrington, *The Purity Texts* (London, 2004), 23. *Sheqetz* is used elsewhere in the Damascus Document (7:3–4) to denote the defilement of an individual's spirit; see M. Himmelfarb, "Impurity and Sin in 4QD, 1QS, and 4Q512," *DSD* 8 (2001): 13.

[32] Milgrom, "Two Biblical Hebrew Priestly Terms," 109, does not mention that this prohibition is directed specifically at priests, in contrast to the legislation in Leviticus 11. But Milgrom, *Leviticus 1–16*, 654, notes that Leviticus prohibits only priests from eating or touching all animal carcasses. Similarly the rabbis ruled that the prohibition against touching the carcasses of unclean animals (Lev 11:8) does not apply to Israel, as only priests are required to avoid corpse impurity; see V. Noam, "The Bounds of Non-Priestly Purity: A Reassessment," *Zion* 72 (2007): 136–37 (in Hebrew).

the earth"), the *Damascus Document* refers to swarming creatures *in water* ("...whether it be the larvae of bees or any living thing which swarms [or creeps] (*tirmos*) in the water"; CD 12:12–13). This seems to be a harmonization of the prohibitions in Lev 11:41–44 (involving swarming land creatures) and Lev 11:9–12 (involving swarming water creatures):

> These you may eat, of all that are in the waters. Everything in the waters that has fins and scales, whether in the seas or in the streams—you may eat. But anything in the seas or the streams that does not have fins and scales, of the swarming creatures in the waters and among all the other living creatures in the waters—they are detestable (*sheqetz*) to you and detestable they shall remain. Of their flesh you shall not eat, and their carcasses you shall regard as detestable. Everything in the waters that does not have fins and scales is detestable to you.

Apparently some Jewish groups of the late Second Temple period, including the Qumran sect, understood the legislation in Leviticus as prohibiting the consumption of all creatures that swarm in water—not just fish without fins and scales but land-based swarming creatures such as insects and larvae as well. Matthew 23:24 indicates, accordingly, that some Jews strained liquids to prevent the ingestion of these creatures. Rabbinic sources show that after 70 debates continued concerning whether biblical law prohibits the consumption of swarming land-based creatures found in water. The rabbis permitted the consumption of these creatures (see for example *b. Hullin* 66b–67a), and they even ruled that a person is not liable for ingesting insects and larvae generated inside fruits and vegetables because these had never crawled on the ground: "[If he ate] a mite which is [found] in lentils, or gnats that are [found] in pods, or worms that are [found] in dates and dried figs, he is exempt" (*t. Terumot* 7:11; also see *b. Hullin* 67b).[33] Ancient food remains discovered in the excavations at Masada were infested with insects and their larvae, which were found mainly in wheat, barley, and dates, as well as in figs and walnuts.[34]

Not only did the post-70 rabbis permit the ingestion of swarming land-based creatures found in water, but they condemned as heterodoxy

---

[33] I am indebted to Hanan Birenboim for bringing this to my attention.

[34] See M. Kislev and O. Simchoni, "Hygiene and Insect Damage of Crops and Foods at Masada," in *Masada VIII, The Yigael Yadin Excavations 1963–1965: Final Reports* (ed. J. Aviram et al.; Jerusalem, 2007), 133–70, who note that dates and figs became "severely infested" during the siege (p. 166).

the straining of wine and vinegar to remove these creatures, suggesting that some Jews continued this practice:

> [And as to] gnats which are [found] in wine and vinegar, lo, these are permitted. [If] he strained them [out of the wine or vinegar], lo, these are forbidden. R. Judah says, "One who strains wine and vinegar, and one who recites a blessing for the sun [*t. Berakhot* 6:6]—lo, this is heresy (דרך אחרת)" (*t. Terumot* 7:11).[35]

> R. Ḥisda said to R. Huna, There is [a baraita] taught that supports your contention: [The verse,] "And every creeping thing that creeps upon the earth [is a detestable thing; it shall not be eaten—Lev 11:41]," includes insects found in liquids that have been passed through a strainer. The reason [then that they are forbidden] is because they had passed through a strainer, but had they not passed through a strainer they would be permitted (*b. Ḥullin* 67a, Soncino translation).

Thus, Matt 23:24 alludes to a halakhic controversy that divided Jews before and after 70. Jesus' criticism seems to be aimed not at Pharisees but at other groups (designated as "scribes") who strained gnats out of liquids.[36] I believe that Matthew's Jesus refers here not to the Qumran sect (Essenes) but to Sadducees and other members of the Jerusalem elite who strictly observed biblical food laws yet consumed imported delicacies and exotic types of cuisine. Their lifestyle is reflected in the wealthy mansions of Jerusalem's Jewish Quarter, which were equipped with Hellenistic style dining rooms that provided a setting for lavish gatherings in which diners reclined on couches at individual tables and consumed delicacies served on fine dishes.[37] The finds from the mansions include luxury glass, expensive red-slipped ceramic table ware, and imported amphoras.[38] On the other hand, Nahman Avigad noted that the absence of figural decoration and the presence of numerous *miqva'ot* and stone vessels in these mansions indicates that the inhabitants observed Jewish purity laws.[39]

---

[35] See Kister, "Law, Morality, and Rhetoric," 148; I.C. Werrett, *Ritual Purity and the Dead Sea Scrolls* (Leiden, 2007), 34–35.

[36] The Aramaic word play on gnat and camel (*qalma* and *gamla*) suggests a relatively early date for Matt 23:24; see J.S. Hammett, "Camel," in *Eerdmans Dictionary of the Bible* (ed. D.N. Freedman; Grand Rapids, 2000), 212.

[37] See N. Avigad, *Discovering Jerusalem* (Nashville, 1983), 83; A.M. Berlin, *Gamla I: The Pottery of the Second Temple Period* (Jerusalem, 2006), 140; eadem, "Jewish Life before the Revolt: The Archaeological Evidence," *JSJ* 36 (2005): 448, 450.

[38] See Avigad, *Discovering Jerusalem*, 83–192.

[39] Ibid., 139–42, 174–83. Avigad's observations have been confirmed by more recent studies of the material from the Jewish Quarter excavations; see S. Rozenberg,

The *Assumption of Moses*, a pseudepigraphic work that probably was composed in the Herodian era, condemns the wealthy for their gluttonous habits and hypocrisy in the observance of purity:

> And these shall stir up the poison of their minds, being treacherous men, self-pleasers, dissemblers in all their own affairs and lovers of banquets at every hour of the day, gluttons, gourmands...Devourers of the goods of the (poor) saying that they do so on the ground of their justice, but in reality to destroy them, complainers, deceitful, concealing themselves lest they should be recognized, impious, filled with lawlessness and iniquity from sunrise to sunset, saying: "We shall have feastings and luxury, eating and drinking, and we shall esteem ourselves as princes." And though their hands and their minds touch unclean things, yet their mouth shall speak great things, and they shall say furthermore: "Do not touch me lest you should pollute me in the place (where I stand)." (*As. Mos.* 7:3–10).[40]

Thus, the complaint in Matt 23:24 seems to be directed against a practice associated with elite groups whose lifestyle before 70 is described in texts such as the *Assumption of Moses* and is known from archaeological remains such as those in Jerusalem's Jewish Quarter.

LOCUSTS AND FISH

The Qumran sectarians followed biblical law in permitting the consumption of certain types of winged insects such as locusts but required that they be cooked alive before being eaten:[41]

"Wall Painting Fragments from Area A," in *Jewish Quarter Excavations in the Old City of Jerusalem Conducted by Nahman Avigad, 1969–1982. Volume II: The Finds from Areas A, W and X-2, Final Report* (ed. H. Geva; Jerusalem, 2003), 302; S. Rozenberg, "The Absence of Figurative Motifs in Herodian Wall Painting," in *I temi figurativi nella pittura parietale antica; IV sec. a.C.–IV sec. d.C.: Atti del VI Convegno internazionale sulla pittura parietale antica* (ed. D. Scagliarini Corlàita; Bologna, 1997), 283–85, 415–16. The same is true of Jewish elite dwellings in Galilee and the Golan; see Z. Weiss, "Jewish Galilee in the First Century C.E.: An Archaeological View," in *Flavius Josephus, Vita: Introduction, Hebrew Translation, and Commentary* (ed. D.R. Schwartz; Jerusalem, 2007), 54 (in Hebrew).

[40] From R.H. Charles, *The Apocrypha and Pseudepigrapha of the Old Testament in English* (2 vols.; Oxford, 1913), 2:419–20. For a discussion of this work and its date see T.C. Vriezen and A.S. van der Woude, *Ancient Israelite and Early Jewish Literature* (trans. B. Doyle; Leiden, 2005), 605–9. For the consequences of the concentration of wealth in the hands of the Jerusalem elite, see J.D. Crossan, *The Historical Jesus: The Life of a Mediterranean Jewish Peasant* (New York, 1991), 222–23.

[41] Werrett, *Ritual Purity and the Dead Sea Scrolls*, 32–33, notes that Leviticus 11, which is the basis for this legislation, does not require locusts to be alive or cooked before being consumed.

[These among] the winged [insects] you may eat: the locust according to its kind, the ba[ld] locust according to its kind, the cri{c}ket according to its kind, and the grasshopper according to its kind. These among the winged insects you may eat: those that go on all fours which have legs above their feet, with which to leap from the earth and fly with their wings. You shall not eat the carcass of any winged thing or animal…(11QT 48:3–6).[42]

And all species of locusts shall be put into fire or water while still alive, for this is the precept of their creation (CD 12:14–15).

Whereas sectarian law prohibited the consumption of live locusts and locusts that were already dead (had died naturally), the rabbis ruled that live and dead locusts could be eaten: "[A man] may eat fish and locusts whether they are alive or dead and need not scruple" (t. Terumot 9:6).[43] The reference in this passage to fish followed by locusts suggests a polemical response to the sectarian position. The Damascus Document mentions these creatures in the same order (which differs from the order in Leviticus 11): "And they should not eat fish unless they were torn alive and their blood sh[e]d. And all species of locusts shall be put into fire or water while still alive…" (CD 12:13–15)

This means that sectarian law required the ritual slaughter of fish and locusts before they could be consumed.[44] True, the Hebrew Bible forbids the ingestion of blood, which must be drained during the ritual of slaughtering:

You must not eat any blood whatever, either of bird or of animal, in any of your settlements. Any one of you who eats any blood shall be cut off from your kin. (Lev 7:26–27)

Only be sure that you do not eat the blood; for the blood is the life, and you shall not eat the life with the meat. Do not eat it; you shall pour it on the ground like water. (Deut 12:23–24)

These biblical verses refer only to animals and birds in connection with the blood prohibition, but the Qumran sect extended this prohibition to include fish and locusts, thereby making necessary ritual

---

[42] For a recent discussion of this passage see Werrett, Ritual Purity and the Dead Sea Scrolls, 124–26.

[43] The Karaites, too, prohibited the consumption of locusts that died naturally; see Baumgarten and Schwartz, "The Damascus Document," 53 n. 187.

[44] Harrington, The Purity Texts, 23; Werrett, Ritual Purity and the Dead Sea Scrolls, 32–34.

slaughter.[45] In contrast, the rabbis allowed the consumption of live fish and condemned the slaughtering of fish as heterodoxy:[46]

> Jacob of Kefar Nibburaya gave a decision in Tyre that fish require ritual slaughtering. R. Haggai heard it and sent for him to come. He said to him: "Whence did you derive your decision?" The other replied, "From the following: *Let the waters swarm with swarms of living creatures, and let fowl fly* (Gen 1:20). As fowls, I argued, require ritual slaughter, so should fishes require ritual slaughter." Said R. Haggai to them [his assistants]: "Lay him down to be flagellated." The other objected: "Shall a man who has uttered words of Torah be flagellated?" "You have not given a fitting decision," said R. Haggai. "Whence do you say so?" asked the other. He answered him: "From the following: *If flocks and herds* BE SLAIN *for them...or if all the fish of the sea* BE GATHERED TOGETHER *for them*—this shows that the former have to be slaughtered and the latter have to be gathered." The other said: "Proceed with your beating, for there is a benefit in taking it." (*Num. Rab.* 19:3, Soncino translation)[47]

Jacob's appeal to Gen 1:20 as the basis for his ruling echoes the *Damascus Document*'s requirement to slaughter fish, which immediately follows a prohibition against eating living and swarming creatures: "Let no man pollute his soul with any living and swarming creatures by eating of them, whether it be the larvae of bees or any living thing which swarms in the water. And they should not eat fish unless they were torn alive and their blood sh[e]d" (CD 12:11–14).

Sectarian law also prohibited the consumption of any creatures that were already dead: "You shall not eat the carcass of any winged thing or animal...." (11QT 48:6).[48] The sectarian position derives from an injunction that prohibits *priests* from eating "of anything, whether bird or animal, that died of itself or was torn by animals" (Ezek 44:31).[49]

---

[45] See O. Irshai, "Yaakov of Naburaya: A Sage who Erred in Heterodoxy," *Jerusalem Studies in Jewish Thought* 2 (1982/83): 164–67 (in Hebrew), who discusses the strict observance of the blood prohibition among other groups including the Samaritans, Karaites, and Ebionites.

[46] M. Broshi, "Anti-Qumranic Polemics in the Talmud," in *The Madrid Qumran Congress: Proceedings of the International Congress on the Dead Sea Scrolls, Madrid 18–21 March, 1991* (ed. J. Trebolle Barrera and L. Vegas Montaner; 2 vols.; Leiden, 1992), 2: 599.

[47] For a discussion of this passage see Irshai, "Yaakov of Naburaya," 163–67.

[48] This prohibition is also mentioned in 4Q251; see E. Larson, M.R. Lehmann, and L. Schiffman, "4QHalakha A," in *Qumran Cave 4.XXV: Halakhic Texts* (ed. J. Baumgarten et al.; DJD 34; Oxford, 1999), 40.

[49] See Yadin, *The Temple Scroll*, 1:321; Milgrom, *Leviticus 1–16*, 654; R. Eisenman, *The New Testament Code: The Cup of the Lord, the Damascus Covenant, and the Blood of Christ* (London, 2006), 127; D.R. Schwartz, "Law and Truth: On Qumran-Sadducean

The sectarian prohibition against consuming fish blood means that popular Roman fish sauces would have been forbidden, even if prepared with biblically permitted species (fish with scales).[50] Roman fish sauces—*garum, muria, liquamen,* and *allec*—were used as seasonings and condiments in various dishes. They were made by fermenting fish such as anchovies or mackerel together with additional ingredients including fish intestines, gills, fish blood, and salt.[51] The discovery of amphoras and fish bones indicates that Herod imported high quality *garum* and *allec* from Spain to his palaces at Masada, Jericho, and Herodium.[52] Spanish amphoras for fish sauce have also been found in the area of Herod's palace in Jerusalem.[53] North African amphoras dating to the first century BCE that probably contained salted fish or fish sauce are published from Area E in Jerusalem's Jewish Quarter excavations.[54] Although no examples are published yet, Avigad's reference to amphora handles bearing Latin stamps leaves open the possibility that amphoras for fish sauce dating to the first century CE were found elsewhere in the Jewish Quarter excavations.[55]

'*Helek* or '*hilek* (הֶחִילָק; apparently *allec*) and *muries* (*muria*; מוּרְיָיס) are listed among the things belonging to Gentiles that the rabbis prohibited (*m. 'Avodah Zarah* 2:4; 2:6).[56] In the Palestinian Talmud (*y. 'Avodah Zarah* 32a) and Babylonian Talmud (*b. 'Avodah Zarah* 39a), this prohibition was attributed to the possibility that Gentile products

---

and Rabbinic Views of Law," in *The Dead Sea Scrolls: Forty Years of Research* (ed. D. Dimant and U. Rappaport; Leiden, 1992), 231.

[50] For kosher fish sauces see H.M. Cotton, O. Lernau, and Y. Goren, "Fish Sauces from Herodian Masada," *Journal of Roman Archaeology* 9 (1996): 236–37.

[51] See Cotton, Lernau, and Goren, "Fish Sauces from Masada," 230–31; S. Grainger, *Cooking Apicius: Roman Recipes for Today* (Devon, 2006), 27–28.

[52] Cotton, Lernau, and Goren, "Fish Sauces from Masada"; R. Bar-Nathan, *Masada VII, The Yigael Yadin Excavations 1963–1965, Final Reports: The Pottery of Masada* (Jerusalem, 2006), 314, 336–39, Types M-AM 12–14 (with a reference on p. 338 to an unpublished example from Cyprus); R. Bar-Nathan, *Hasmonean and Herodian Palaces at Jericho: Final Reports of the 1973–1987 Excavations, Volume III: The Pottery* (Jerusalem, 2002), 132–33, 136–37, Types J-AM 4–6; R. Bar-Nathan, "Pottery and Stone Vessels of the Herodian Period (1st century BC–1st century AD)," in *Greater Herodium* (ed. E. Netzer; Jerusalem, 1981), 66; 117, Pl. 4:4–6; 127, Pl. 10:2.

[53] See A.D. Tushingham, *Excavations in Jerusalem 1961–1967* (5 vols.; Toronto, 1985–), 1:55; 373 fig. 21:42; 374 fig. 22:1; also see Bar-Nathan, *Masada VII,* 337.

[54] G. Finkielsztejn, "Imported Amphoras," in *Jewish Quarter Excavations in the Old City of Jerusalem Conducted by Nahman Avigad, 1969–1982. Volume III: Area E and Other Studies, Final Report* (ed. H. Geva; Jerusalem, 2006), 175.

[55] Avigad, *Discovering Jerusalem,* 202–3, no. 249 (stamped *ex figlin*[*is*] *Caesaris* ["from the Imperial potteries"]).

[56] See Cotton, Lernau, and Goren, "Fish Sauces from Masada," 237.

might contain nonkosher species of fish:[57] "What is the meaning of ḤELEK—R. Nahman b. Abba said in the name of Rab: It is the *sultanith*. Why is it prohibited? Because other species [of fish] of a similar kind [but prohibited] are caught together with it" (*b. ʿAvodah Zarah* 39a; Soncino edition). The rabbinic discussions suggest that after 70 fish sauce was popular among Jews, some of whom may have continued indulging in imported Gentile products.

Fish and locusts are mentioned together in a debate between the houses of Hillel and Shammai about the biblical prohibition against boiling a kid in its mother's milk (Exod 23:19; 34:27; Deut 14:21).[58] This is a rare case in which the house of Shammai ruled more leniently, allowing fowl and cheese to be served (but not eaten) together:

> It is prohibited to cook every [kind of] flesh [of cattle, wild beast, and fowl] in milk, except for the flesh of fish and locusts. And it is prohibited to serve it up onto the table with cheese, except for the flesh of fish and locusts. He who vows [to abstain] from flesh is permitted [to make use of] the flesh of fish and locusts. "Fowl goes up onto the table with cheese, but it is not eaten"—the words of the House of Shammai. And the House of Hillel say, "It does not go up, and it is not eaten." Said R. Yose, "This is one of the lenient rulings of the House of Shammai and the strict rulings of the House of Hillel." Concerning what sort of table did they speak of? Concerning a table on which one lays out cooking, one puts this beside that and does not scruple. (*m. Ḥullin* 8:1; based on Neusner's translation)[59]

There is no mention of this prohibition in sectarian literature from Qumran, although Sanders is probably correct in concluding that "many people would not cook meat or cheese together" even before 70.[60] However, the ruling of the house of Shammai indicates that some Jews served meat and poultry together with cheese. In my opinion these were likely Sadducees, as this would be consistent with other evidence suggesting that they limited their observance of purity laws to the Temple cult, and because the elite could afford the luxury of serving different types of food, including meat, at a single meal. On the other hand, the house of Shammai was more stringent in ruling that

---

[57] Ibid.

[58] For a discussion see Milgrom, *Leviticus 1–16*, 737–42.

[59] For a discussion see Kelhoffer, "Did John the Baptist Eat like a Former Essene?" 309.

[60] E.P. Sanders, *Judaism: Practice and Belief, 63 BCE–66 CE* (London, 1992), 217.

fish become susceptible to impurity when they are caught, whereas according to the house of Hillel fish become susceptible only when they die (*m. ʿUqtzin* 3:8).[61]

ARCHAEOLOGICAL EVIDENCE FOR SECTARIAN PRACTICES AND PURITY OBSERVANCE AFTER 70

Archaeology sheds valuable light on purity observance and sectarian practices in the decades and centuries following the Temple's destruction. Objects and installations associated with purity observance, especially *miqvaʾot* and stone vessels, continue to be attested after 70, although they are not as common and widespread as before.[62] These features are concentrated in regions and sites where remnants of the Jewish elite—among them priestly families—settled after 70, mostly in Lower Galilee (such as at Sepphoris, Tiberias, and Beth Sheʿarim) and southern Judea's periphery.[63] Recent excavations at Shuʿafat on Jerusalem's northern outskirts have brought to light a Jewish settlement that dates to the period between the two revolts (70–135), the first ever discovered in the city's vicinity.[64] The settlement consists of large,

---

[61] Similarly, Werrett, *Ritual Purity and the Dead Sea Scrolls*, 32–33 notes that the author of the *Damascus Document* seems to suggest that that individual could become impure by eating an uncooked locust.

[62] The same is true of ossilegia, although in my opinion the use of ossuaries is not connected with purity observance but instead reflects fashions that were adopted by the Jewish elite. This is demonstrated by the fact that by the third or fourth century stone sarcophagi largely replaced ossuaries in the catacombs at Beth Sheʿarim, reflecting the influence of contemporary Roman funerary customs.

[63] Amit and Adler, "The Observance of Ritual Purity after 70 C.E.," suggest that the large numbers of post-70 *miqvaʾot* found at Sepphoris and Susiya are connected with priestly groups and therefore might not reflect purity observance among the general population. However Miller, "Stepped Pools and the Non-Existent Monolithic 'Miqveh,'" 221, rejects a connection between priests and *miqvaʾot* at Sepphoris.

[64] The settlement is located four kilometers north of Jerusalem, along the early Roman road to Nablus. The excavated remains consist of a ca. 500 m.-long narrow strip. For preliminary reports see R. Bar-Nathan and D.A. Sklar-Parnes, "A Jewish Settlement in Orine between the Two Revolts," in *New Studies in the Archaeology of Jerusalem and its Region* (ed. J. Patrich and D. Amit; Jerusalem, 2007), 57–64 (in Hebrew); D.A. Sklar-Parnes, "Jerusalem, Shuʿfat, Ramallah Road," *Ḥadashot Arkheologiyot* 117 (2005): http://www.hadashot-esi.org.il/report_detail_eng.asp?id=179&mag_id=110; D.A. Sklar-Parnes, "Jerusalem, Shuʿfat, Ramallah Road," *Ḥadashot Arkheologiyot* 118 (2006): http://www.hadashot esi.org.il/report_detail_eng.asp?id=347&mag_id=111; R. Bar-Nathan and D.A. Sklar-Parnes, "A Jewish Settlement Revealed in the Shuʿafat Neighborhood of Jerusalem," *ASOR 2007 Annual Meeting Abstract Book* (2007): 13 (http://www.asor.org/AM/abstracts07[final].pdf).

well-built village-type houses and public buildings laid out along a regular network of streets and alleys. Some of the buildings are equipped
with *miqva'ot*.[65] The excavators report finding a large number and variety of lathe-turned and hand-carved stone vessels.[66] Among the buildings are Roman-style bath houses with wall paintings and hypocaust
systems, and the finds include pottery manufactured in the kiln works
of the Tenth Roman Legion in Jerusalem.[67] Five mold-made ceramic
inkwells, apparently products of the legionary kiln works, were discovered on the floor of one of the rooms.[68] The evidence of a relatively
prosperous, Romanized lifestyle combined with Jewish purity observance suggests that this was a settlement of elite families including
priests who remained as close as possible to Jerusalem after 70, perhaps awaiting the rebuilding of the Temple.[69]

Nevertheless, evidence for the use of objects and installations associated with purity observance—most notably *miqva'ot* and stone vessels—declines gradually after 70, largely disappearing in the course
of the third to fourth centuries.[70] The kiln works at Kfar Hananya in

---

[65] Bar-Nathan and Sklar-Parnes, "A Jewish Settlement in Orine," 59, 60 (including
a *miqveh* in a bath house), 63; Bar-Nathan and Sklar-Parnes, "A Jewish Settlement
Revealed in the Shuʿafat Neighborhood of Jerusalem."

[66] Bar-Nathan and Sklar-Parnes, "A Jewish Settlement in Orine," 63; Sklar-Parnes,
"Jerusalem, Shuʿfat, Ramallah Road," (2005).

[67] Bar-Nathan and Sklar-Parnes, "A Jewish Settlement in Orine," 60; Sklar-Parnes,
"Jerusalem, Shuʿfat, Ramallah Road," (2005). For pottery from the legionary kiln
works in Jerusalem, see J. Magness, "The Roman Legionary Pottery," in *Excavations
on the Site of the Jerusalem International Convention Center (Binyanei Haʾuma): A
Settlement of the Late First to Second Temple Period, the Tenth Legion's Kilnworks, and
a Byzantine Monastic Complex—The Pottery and Other Small Finds* (ed. B. Arubas and
H. Goldfus; Portsmouth, R.I., 2005), 69–191. Perhaps pottery produced in the legionary
kiln works is the "Hadrianic earthenware" prohibited by the rabbis among the "things
belonging to Gentiles" (*m. ʿAvodah Zarah* 2:3). In the Babylonian Talmud (*b. ʿAvodah
Zarah* 32a), this prohibition is derived from the possibility that Hadrianic earthenware
could absorb wine and when subsequently wetted would release the wine, which was
prohibited for Jewish consumption.

[68] Bar-Nathan and Sklar-Parnes, "A Jewish Settlement in Orine," 60 (from Insula 8);
Sklar-Parnes, "Jerusalem, Shuʿfat, Ramallah Road," (2005). For an inkwell of this type
from the kiln works see Magness, "The Roman Legionary Pottery," 156 fig. 33:3.

[69] See Bar-Nathan and Sklar-Parnes, "A Jewish Settlement in Orine," 63, who suggest that the villagers were aristocratic Jewish refugees. The village at Shuʿafat brings
to mind Josephus' reference to a settlement called Gophna which Titus allotted to
members of the Jewish elite (*J.W.* 6.115). For Gophna see H.M. Cotton, "The Administrative Background to the New Settlement Recently Discovered near Givʿat Shaul,
Ramallah-Shuʿafat Road," in Patrich and Amit, *New Studies*, 12*–14* (in Hebrew).

[70] For *miqva'ot* and stone vessels dating to after 70 see Amit and Adler, "The
Observance of Ritual Purity after 70 C.E." Nearly all of the post-70 *miqva'ot* that they

Galilee, which produced pottery that may have been marketed to a Jewish population concerned with purity (although small quantities are attested at non-Jewish sites), also ceased operating by the end of the fourth century or early in the fifth.[71]

Whereas the issue of purity observance was at the heart of many of the sectarian debates that deeply divided Palestinian Jewish society of the late Second Temple period, with the exception of Paul's claim to be a Pharisee (Acts 23:6; 26:5; Phil 3:6), we have no evidence of sectarianism among Diaspora Jews before 70 and correspondingly, no objects or installations associated with purity practices in the Diaspora before 70.[72] As Jacob Neusner concludes, "nearness to the Temple cult yields concrete and socially significant interpretations of purity, while distance from the Temple (both spatially and temporally) generally results in a metaphorical interpretation of purity laws."[73] He notes

document are no later than the fourth century, and the "Byzantine" examples that they cite are unpublished or not securely dated. Also see Weiss, "Jewish Galilee in the First Century C.E.," 47 n. 101; S. Gibson, "Stone Vessels of the Early Roman Period from Jerusalem and Palestine: A Reassessment," in *One Land—Many Cultures: Archaeological Studies in Honour of Stanislao Loffreda* (ed. G.C. Bottini, L. Di Segni, and L.D. Chrupcała; Jerusalem, 2003), 302; R. Reich, "Miqva'ot (Jewish Ritual Immersion Baths) in Eretz-Israel in the Second Temple and the Mishnah and Talmud Periods" (Ph.D. diss.; The Hebrew University of Jerusalem, 1990), 142–44 (in Hebrew).

[71] See D. Adan-Bayewitz, *Common Pottery in Roman Galilee: A Study of Local Trade* (Ramat- Gan, 1993), 231–32, 239–43, who attributes the cessation of production at Kefar Hananya to the decline of Jewish settlement in Galilee during the mid-fourth to early fifth centuries. According to Adan-Bayewitz, "However, considering that Kefar Hananya accounted for the large majority of the common cooking vessels in use in the Galilee in the Roman and early Byzantine periods, it seems likely that ritually pure vessels were also supplied to observant customers by trustworthy potters of that center" (p. 231). For a pottery workshop at Shikhin see J.F. Strange, D.E. Groh, and T.R.W. Longstaff, "Excavations at Sepphoris: The Location and Identification of Shikhin, Part I," *IEJ* 44 (1994): 216–27; J.F. Strange, D.E. Groh, and T.R.W. Longstaff, "Excavations at Sepphoris: The Location and Identification of Shikhin, Part II," *IEJ* 45 (1995): 171–87.

[72] J.D. Lawrence, *Washing in Water: Trajectories of Ritual Bathing in the Hebrew Bible and Second Temple Literature* (Atlanta, 2006), 168 notes that, "There is no physical evidence for ritual bathing in the Diaspora during the Second Temple period"; but see pp. 57–59 for the possibility that hand-washing before prayer was practiced by the Jews of Egypt in the Second Temple period. I agree with L. Matassa, "Unravelling the Myth of the Synagogue on Delos," *BAIAS* 25 (2007): 81–115, that the archaeological and inscriptional evidence does not support the identification of a Hellenistic period building on Delos as a synagogue.

[73] Neusner, *The Idea of Purity in Ancient Judaism*, 108–9. M. Douglas, "Critique and Commentary," in Neusner, *The Idea of Purity in Ancient Judaism*, 141, suggests that it is distance from membership in a sectarian group that turns purity rules into metaphors of spiritual good instead of regulations for admission, exclusion, and rankings.

that after 70 (and especially after 135) the rabbis came to believe that
the Temple's purity and holiness could only be replicated in a diminished way.[74]

Since purity observance was a focus of sectarian debate before 70, the
fact that these objects and installations are attested until the third to
fourth centuries lends indirect support to Goodman's suggestion that
such groups survived in some form long after the Temple's destruction.[75] Therefore we should consider the possibility that sources such
as rabbinic writings and the New Testament contain nuggets of information that reflect their own contemporary historical reality, however
distorted they may be due to the motivations and biases of the authors
and editors. In this case some of the practices that the rabbis condemned as heresy (*minut*) might attest to continuing sectarianism in
the period after 70.[76] Perhaps the numerous and generally hostile references to Pharisees in the canonical gospels are not entirely anachronistic or inaccurate but reflect the continuing existence and influence
of this group after the Temple's destruction.[77]

The final blow to Jewish expectations of a rebuilt Temple occurred
under Julian the Apostate. It is probably not a coincidence that installations and objects associated with purity practices relating to the
Temple disappeared by the second half of the fourth century.[78] At the
same time, however, the first monumental synagogue buildings were

---

[74] J. Neusner, *A History of the Mishnaic Law of Purities, Part Twenty-Two: The Mishnaic System of Uncleanness, Context and History* (Leiden, 1977), 254–56, discusses changes in rabbinic purity laws after the Bar Kokhba revolt, as hopes of a
rebuilt Temple faded.

[75] Goodman, "Sadducees and Essenes after 70 C.E." Also see Burns, "Essene Sectarianism and Social Differentiation," who places the final demise of Jewish sectarianism—and in particular the Essene movement—in the third to fourth centuries (272
n. 61).

[76] For a similar argument with regard to the Essenes see Burns, "Essene Sectarianism and Social Differentiation." It is not clear whether this evidence attests to the
continued existence of sectarian groups (in whatever form) or only to isolated sectarian practices among individual members of the population.

[77] See, for example, E. Schürer, *The History of the Jewish People in the Age of Jesus
Christ (175 BCE–135 CE)* (ed. G. Vermes et al.; 3 vols.; rev. English ed.; Edinburgh,
1973–1986), 2:400.

[78] Bokser, "*Maʿal* and Blessings over Food," 557, 570–71, notes that during the third
and fourth centuries the rabbis distanced themselves from the Temple and consciously
accepted its loss.

erected in Palestine, such as the so-called Synagogue of Severus at Hammath Tiberias.[79] The rich Temple imagery and liturgical furniture of these buildings enabled Jews to preserve the memory of the Temple and sacrificial cult while awaiting their future reestablishment.

---

[79] See M. Dothan, *Hammath Tiberias, I: Early Synagogues and the Hellenistic and Roman Remains* (Jerusalem, 1983); J. Magness, "Heaven on Earth: Helios and the Zodiac Cycle in Ancient Palestinian Synagogues," *DOP* 59 (2005): 1–52. For the chronology of monumental synagogue buildings in Palestine see J. Magness, "The Question of the Synagogue: The Problem of Typology," in *Judaism in Late Antiquity, Part Three: Where We Stand: Issues and Debates in Ancient Judaism. Volume Four: The Special Problem of the Synagogue* (ed. A.J. Avery-Peck and J. Neusner; Leiden, 2001), 1–48.

WERE PRIESTS COMMUNAL LEADERS IN LATE ANTIQUE PALESTINE? THE ARCHAEOLOGICAL EVIDENCE

Zeev Weiss

The priests ran the Temple and its sacrificial cult according to divine law, and they were also politically influential in Jerusalem during the Second Temple period. Archaeological excavations in the city have uncovered their luxurious homes, with ritual baths and household vessels that demonstrate the priests' punctiliousness in maintaining ritual purity.[1] After the destruction of the Temple in 70 CE, the sacrificial cult was terminated, and the priesthood, especially the high priests, lost their religious and political power in Jewish society. Despite their bereft status in the new configuration of post-Destruction society, however, the priests did not entirely disappear.[2] They were given special roles in the synagogue service, and we know of several priests who were also rabbis. Theoretically, it is possible to connect the ritual baths or stone vessels found at various sites in the Galilee with priests who resided in those locales after 70 CE. However, we also know that, in the

---

[1] N. Avigad, "Jerusalem," *NEAEHL* 2:729–35; L.I. Levine, *Jerusalem: Portrait of the City in the Second Temple Period 538 B.C.E.–70 C.E.* (Philadelphia, 2002), 260–61, 358–61. On the *miqva'ot* found in Jerusalem's Upper City, see R. Reich, "*Miqwa'ot* (Jewish Ritual Immersion Baths) in Eretz-Israel in the Second Temple and the Mishnah and Talmud Periods" (Ph.D. diss., The Hebrew University of Jerusalem, 1990), 94–102 (in Hebrew). For the use of *miqva'ot* by priests and Pharisees in the Second Temple period, see E.P. Sanders, *Judaism: Practice and Belief, 63 BCE–66 CE* (London and Philadelphia, 1992), 224–29; E. Regev, "Pure Individualism: The Idea of Non-Priestly Purity in Ancient Judaism," *JSJ* 31 (2000): 176–202.

[2] S.D. Fraade, *From Tradition to Commentary: Torah and Its Interpretation in the Midrash Sifre to Deuteronomy* (Albany, 1991), 72–74; M. Himmelfarb, *A Kingdom of Priests: Ancestry and Merit in Ancient Judaism* (Philadelphia, 2006), 160–70; P.S. Alexander, "What Happened to the Jewish Priesthood after 70?" in *A Wandering Galilean: Essays in Honour of Seán Freyne* (ed. Z. Rodgers et al.; Leiden, 2009), 5–33. According to Alexander, the priests survived the destruction of the Temple and continued to transmit and develop their distinct tradition, but it remains difficult to distinguish them in late antique Judaism or to tell priests and rabbis apart. On the priests, their migration to the Galilee, and their role in Galilean society in the mishnaic and talmudic periods, see R. Kimelman, "The Conflict between the Priestly Oligarchy and the Sages in the Talmudic Period (on Explication of PT *Shabbat* 12:3, 13C = *Horayot* 3:4, 48C)," *Zion* 48 (1983): 135–47 (in Hebrew); L.I. Levine, *The Rabbinic Class of Roman Palestine in Late Antiquity* (Jerusalem, 1989), 171–73.

post-Temple era, the maintenance of a certain level of religious purity was observed by other segments of society, as well as the priests.[3] Thus, notwithstanding this evidence, it is still quite conceivable that the priests had been pushed aside and now played only minor roles, if any, in the life of the Jewish community.[4]

The status of the priests in Jewish society of fifth- and sixth-century CE Palestine has been a recent subject of discussion in modern research. It is assumed that the priestly class paved its way to communal leadership in the Galilee following the void created by the disappearance of the pedigreed cadre of the Patriarchate and the waning of the intellectual elite known as the rabbinic class. At approximately the same time, the focus of religious life shifted from the *bet midrash* to the synagogue, from a framework of pure study to one of engagement in synagogue liturgy.[5] The reference in several letters of the church fathers to priests who represented the community; an allusion to priests in imperial legislation; the forging of the tradition of the twenty-four priestly courses that resided in the towns of the Galilee; the intensive preoccupation with the Temple and its cult on the part of liturgical poets, or *paytanim*,[6] some of whom hailed from priestly

---

[3] Several ritual baths were excavated in Sepphoris, see K. Galor, "The Stepped Water Installations of the Sepphoris Acropolis," in *The Archaeology of Difference: Gender, Ethnicity, Class and the "Other" in Antiquity: Studies in Honor of Eric M. Meyers* (ed. D.R. Edwards and C.T. McCollough; Boston, 2007), 201–13; S.S. Miller, "Stepped Pools and the Non-Existent Monolithic 'Miqveh,'" in Edwards and McCollough, *Archaeology of Difference*, 215–34. Stone vessels were also found at Sepphoris and in other locales throughout the Galilee; see, for example, L.V. Rutgers, "Some Reflections on the Archaeological Finds from the Domestic Quarter on the Acropolis of Sepphoris," in *Religious and Ethnic Communities in Later Roman Palestine* (ed. H. Lapin; Bethesda, Md., 1998), 179–95, and the literature there; Z. Weiss, *The Sepphoris Synagogue: Deciphering an Ancient Message through Its Archaeological and Socio-Historical Contexts* (Jerusalem, 2005), 310; S.S. Miller, "Some Observations on Stone Vessel Finds and Ritual Purity in Light of Talmudic Sources," in *Zeichen aus Text und Stein: Studien auf dem Weg zu einer Archäologie des Neuen Testaments* (ed. S. Alkier and J. Zangenberg; Tübingen, 2003), 402–19.

[4] P. Schäfer, "Rabbis and Priests, or: How to Do Away with the Glorious Past of the Sons of Aaron," in *Antiquity in Antiquity: Jewish and Christian Pasts in the Greco-Roman World* (ed. G. Gardner and K.L. Osterloh; Tübingen, 2008), 155–72.

[5] O. Irshai, "Confronting a Christian Empire: Jewish Culture in the World of Byzantium," in *Cultures of the Jews: A New History* (ed. D. Biale; New York, 2002), 193–98; idem, "The Priesthood in Jewish Society of Late Antiquity," in *Continuity and Renewal: Jews and Judaism in Byzantine-Christian Palestine* (ed. L.I. Levine; Jerusalem, 2004), 67–106 (in Hebrew).

[6] J. Yahalom, *Poetry and Society in Jewish Galilee of Late Antiquity* (Tel-Aviv, 1999), 107–16 (in Hebrew). According to M.D. Swartz, the poet, who composes *piyyutim* to commemorate the Temple and the sacrificial cult for the realm of the synagogue,

circles; the linking of *targum* to the priestly class;[7] and even the *Hekhalot* literature which, according to some scholars, originated with the priests[8]—all these attest to the plausibility of the notion of the restoration of priestly status in Jewish society of the late Roman era.

Archaeology, too, has provided information that further supports this theory regarding the priests. According to Amit, the main entrance to Judean synagogues in the Byzantine period was located on the eastern wall, in imitation of the layout of the Temple; the holy ark was shaped to resemble the Temple façade; a three-dimensional menorah was placed inside the sacred space; and even the sabbatical year, which was not employed outside of the Land of Israel, was used in inscriptions for dating purposes. In Amit's opinion, all of these points attest to the increased influence of priestly circles in these locales.[9] Magness argues that the zodiac appearing in several ancient synagogues evokes the solar calendar and, like other images occurring in synagogue mosaics, recalls the Temple cult, pointing to what she believes to be the increased involvement of the priestly class in the synagogue of late antiquity.[10] Depictions of the Tabernacle and the Temple in various synagogue mosaics also bolster emerging trends in the historical-social-textual study of the priests and their place in the Jewish community of fifth- and sixth-century CE Palestine.[11] The

---

perpetuates the role of the sage and priest who functioned in that sacred space; see M.D. Swartz, "Sage, Priest, and Poet: Typologies of Religious Leadership in the Ancient Synagogue," in *Jews, Christians, and Polytheists in the Ancient Synagogue: Cultural Interaction during the Greco-Roman Period* (ed. S. Fine; London and New York, 1999), 101–17. See also his contribution to the present volume.

[7] P.V.M. Flesher, "The Literary Legacy of the Priests? The Pentateuchal Targums of Israel in Their Social and Linguistic Context," in *The Ancient Synagogue: From Its Origins until 200 C.E.* (ed. B. Olsson and M. Zetterholm; Stockholm, 2003), 467–508.

[8] For the argument that *Hekhalot* literature was influenced by priests who wished to preserve the Temple cult, see R. Elior, "From Earthly Temple to Heavenly Shrines: Prayer and Sacred Song in the Hekhalot Literature and Its Relation to Temple Traditions," *JSQ* 4 (1997): 217–67; see also I. Gruenwald, "The Impact of Priestly Traditions on the Creation of *Merkabah* Mysticism and the *Shiur Qomah*," *Jerusalem Studies in Jewish Thought* 6 (1987): 65–120 (in Hebrew).

[9] D. Amit, "Priests and the Memory of the Temple in the Synagogues of Southern Judaea," in Levine, *Continuity and Renewal*, 143–54 (in Hebrew).

[10] J. Magness, "Heaven on Earth: Helios and the Zodiac Cycle in Ancient Palestinian Synagogues," *DOP* 59 (2007): 1–52, esp. 21–28.

[11] See, for example, Yahalom's conclusion regarding the Sepphoris mosaic: J. Yahalom, "The Sepphoris Synagogue Mosaic and Its Story," in *From Dura to Sepphoris: Studies in Jewish Art and Society in Late Antiquity* (ed. L.I. Levine and Z. Weiss; Portsmouth, R.I., 2000), 83–91. Priests were a significant social element in Sepphoris generally, and appear to have influenced the content of the synagogue's mosaic floor

selection of Temple motifs in the synagogue was influenced, accordingly, by the priests, who sought to use visual art to establish their
status in the local Jewish community. The intent of the many depictions and their location in the floor's layout was intended—it is now
urged—to bring to mind not only the sacrificial cult that had taken
place in the Temple but, indirectly, the historical role of the priests
in the destroyed Temple and, subsequently, in the future one. At the
same time, these motifs may have served the priests in conveying
another message: that is, that those of the old priestly class are worthy
of occupying their places anew, not only in the synagogue but as leaders of the entire Jewish community.

By analyzing the archaeological finds pertaining to the ancient synagogue, the institution in which the priests purportedly reclaimed their
status and became communal leaders, I will question the plausibility
of the recent theory—one which, whatever archaeological evidence has
been adduced in its support, nonetheless depends largely on historical
sources concerning the leadership of the Jewish community of late
antique Palestine.[12] I will examine to what extent, if any, the archaeological evidence attests to a rise in power and strengthening of the
priestly class within the synagogue in particular, and in the Jewish
community in general. Apart from a priori questions, such as the one
posed by the notion that an elite group whose status had been suppressed for such a long time (about 300 years or more) might regain a
prominent role in community leadership, I shall argue that, method-
ologically, there is no way to prove that the architectural appearance
or artistic decorations of the synagogue originated in priestly circles,
or even that priestly traditions somehow shaped the internal space or
decorative medium inside the synagogue.

The emergence of various features associated with the Temple cult
in ancient Palestinian synagogues—the architecture, internal furnishings, inscriptions, and art—cannot be denied. They appear not only

---

in particular; see L.I. Levine, "Contextualizing Jewish Art: The Synagogues at Hammat
Tiberias and Sepphoris," in *Jewish Culture and Society in the Christian Roman Empire*
(ed. R. Kalmin and S. Schwartz; Leuven, 2003), 115–30. Rutgers makes an unconvincing attempt to connect the incense shovels from Sepphoris and the depictions of such
vessels elsewhere in Jewish art with the priestly population, some of whom resided in
Sepphoris; see: L.V. Rutgers, "Incense Shovels at Sepphoris?" in *Galilee through the
Centuries: Confluence of Cultures* (ed. E.M. Meyers; Winona Lake, 1999), 177–98.

[12] Irshai, "Priesthood in Jewish Society," 70; Amit, "Priests and the Memory of the
Temple," 154.

in the Judean synagogues, as claimed by Amit, but were occasionally found in other regions as well. The synagogue in some places was oriented toward Jerusalem, in others the main entrance to the building faced eastward (Yafia, Horvat Sumaqa)—as in the Temple.[13] The holy ark in some synagogues imitated the Temple façade (Nabratein, Umm el-Qanatir).[14] Sometimes three-dimensional *menorot* were even positioned in conjunction with it (Merot, Sepphoris);[15] we also have evidence that an eternal light (*ner tamid*) burned within the synagogue (Nabratein), as it did in the Temple.[16] Inscriptions listing the twenty-four priestly courses were installed in several synagogues (Caesarea, Nazareth, Rehov, and Ashkelon);[17] beyond that, priestly influence is

---

[13] E.L. Sukenik, "The Ancient Synagogue at Yafa near Nazareth—Preliminary Report," *Louis M. Rabinowitz Fund Bulletin* 2 (1951): 6–24; S. Dar, *Sumaqa: A Roman and Byzantine Jewish Village on Mount Carmel, Israel* (Oxford, 1999), 17–32.

[14] S. Fine, *Art and Judaism in the Greco-Roman World: Toward a New Jewish Archaeology* (Cambridge and New York, 2005), 189–94; H. Ben David, I. Gonen, and J. Drei, "Umm el-Qanatir: The First Excavation Season," *Qadmoniot* 39 (2006): 110–20 (in Hebrew).

[15] Z. Ilan and E. Damati, *Meroth: The Ancient Jewish Village* (Tel-Aviv, 1987), 50 (in Hebrew). One fragment from the arm of a three-dimensional marble menorah was found in the Sepphoris synagogue (unpublished). Similar freestanding *menorot* were found elsewhere in the region; see D. Amit, "A Marble *Menorah* from the Ancient Synagogue at Ma'on," *Judea and Samaria Research Studies* 7 (1998): 155–68 (in Hebrew); M. Fischer, I. Taxel, and D. Amit, "Rural Settlement in the Vicinity of Yavneh in the Byzantine Period: A Religio-Archaeological Perspective," *BASOR* 350 (2008): 15–16 (menorah fragment from Khirbet ed-Duheisha). Freestanding seven-branches *menorot* also stood in some Diaspora synagogues: one was found in Sardis in Caria and an inscription from Side in Pamphylia mentions two others; see G.M.A. Hanfmann, "The Sixth Campaign in Sardis," *BASOR* 174 (1964): 36–38; J.H. Kroll, "The Greek Inscriptions of the Sardis Synagogue," *HTR* 94 (2001): 42, no. 69; B. Lifshitz, *Donateurs et fondateurs dans les synagogues juives* (Paris, 1967), no. 36. Remains of soot found on the *menorot* in Hammat Tiberias and Ma'on clearly indicate that they were not merely decorative, but were in actual use to illuminate the prayer hall; see D. Amit, "The Synagogues of Hurbat Ma'on and Hurbat 'Anim and the Jewish Settlement in Southern Hebron Hills" (Ph.D. diss., The Hebrew University of Jerusalem, 2003), 154–65 (in Hebrew).

[16] C.L. Meyers, and E.M. Meyers, "The Ark in Art: A Ceramic Rendering of the Torah Shrine from Nabratein," *ErIsr* 16 (1982): 176*–85*; E.M. Meyers, "The Current State of Galilean Synagogue Studies," in *The Synagogue in Late Antiquity* (ed. L.I. Levine; Philadelphia, 1987), 131–32.

[17] L.I. Levine, *The Ancient Synagogue: The First Thousand Years* (2d ed.; New Haven, 2005), 524, with references to earlier studies. The list of priestly courses indicates the scope of priestly settlement throughout the Galilee; see S. Klein, *The Galilee* (Jerusalem, 1946), 62–68, 177–92 (in Hebrew); E.E. Urbach, "Mishmarot and Ma'amadot," *Tarbiz* 42 (1973): 304–27 (in Hebrew); T. Kahane, "The Priestly Courses and Their Geographical Settlements," *Tarbiz* 48 (1979): 9–29 (in Hebrew); D. Trifon, "Did the Priestly Courses (*Mishmarot*) Transfer from Judaea to Galilee after the Bar Kokhba Revolt?" *Tarbiz* 59 (1989): 77–93 (in Hebrew).

thought to be indicated in particular by some of the artistic depictions incorporated in the mosaic floors of several synagogues: the architectural façade, menorah, four species, sacrifices, and other Temple scenes.[18] In some locales, some of these architectural or artistic features were deliberately installed in the forefront of the synagogue's prayer hall to attract the attention of the synagogue-goers and to emphasize the importance of these features in the sacred space. However, it is questionable whether these finds that shaped the sacred space were created or commissioned by priests or allude in any way to the social-religious-political changes in the Jewish community of late antique Palestine.

I will begin by questioning several methodological assumptions that, according to some scholars, demonstrate priestly endeavors to reinstate their historical role. These reservations must be seriously considered, especially when using archaeological finds to assess the role of the priests in the synagogue, the main Jewish communal institution in late antique Palestine.

1) Members of the Priestly Class had the Strongest Interest in Promoting the Temple Cult

The role of the priests in the Tabernacle and, later on, in the Temple, is a fact, but the hope for the restoration of the destroyed building and the reinstatement of the sacrificial service within it was not exclusive to the priests. It was, rather, a shared yearning of all the Jewish people in both Palestine and the Diaspora, expressed in prayers recited thrice daily and commemorated in the sermons of the sages and later in *piyyutim*.[19] True, a number of *payetanim*, such as Shimon

---

[18] Z. Weiss, "The Tabernacle, Temple, and Sacrificial Service in Ancient Synagogue Art and in Light of the Judeo-Christian Controversy," in *Image and Sound: Art, Music and History* (ed. R.I. Cohen; Jerusalem, 2007), 65–85 (in Hebrew).

[19] J. Yahalom, "The Temple and the City in Hebrew Liturgical Poetry," in *The History of Jerusalem: The Early Islamic Period (638–1099)* (ed. J. Prawer; Jerusalem, 1996), 215–35 (in Hebrew). The remembered Temple, according to Himmelfarb, "was the place of all Jews equally, laypeople and priests alike"; see Himmelfarb, *Kingdom of Priests*, 170–73; and, for a similar view: S.S. Miller, "Priests, Purities, and the Jews of Galilee," in *Religion, Ethnicity, and Identity in Ancient Galilee: A Region in Transition* (ed. J. Zangenberg, H.W. Attridge, and D.B. Martin; Tübingen, 2007), 375–402.

ben Megas, Yose ben Yose, and Pinḥas Ha-Cohen, were of priestly lineage. However, although their *piyyutim* lament the destruction of Jerusalem and the Temple, or, alternatively, yearn for the rebuilding of the Temple and the imminent redemption, such expressions by no means ascribe to priests a special status within the community that would have allowed them to decide which motifs would adorn the synagogue's floors.[20]

2) The architecture of the synagogue relates to the destroyed Temple

The orientation of the synagogue toward Jerusalem, whether by placing the main façade or *bema* in that direction or by building the main entrance to face eastward, as in the Temple, is known from several locales (see above). Similarly, designing the Torah shrine, the focal point inside the synagogue, to resemble the Temple façade, or placing a freestanding menorah beside it, finds expression, as mentioned, in several synagogues (fig. 1). Nevertheless, when reviewing the various synagogues constructed in ancient Palestine during the Byzantine period, the overall picture points rather to diversity and complexity than to a uniformity that could have been brought about by the influence of a specific group.[21] Although various rabbis discussed the question of synagogue orientation, as well as that of the direction of prayer toward Jerusalem and the destroyed Temple, nowhere do we find any special statements of priestly involvement in such issues.

---

[20] Irshai ("Confronting a Christian Empire," 198) reaches a similar conclusion: "Preoccupation with the oppressive subjugation of the Christian world and concern with the approaching redemption were not limited to a few individuals. The poets expressed the deepest, most existential aspirations of the entire community." Yahalom, who has studied the *Avodah* service for the Day of Atonement, notes that the priests found "some consolation in the memories and testimonies regarding customs of the service that no longer exist...." Thus, these poems seem also to reflect the sentiments of the public to whom the *piyyutim* were recited; see J. Yahalom, *'Az be-'En Kol: Seder ha-'Avodah ha-Ereṣ-Yisraeli ha-Qadum le-Yom ha-Kippurim* (Jerusalem, 1996), 56–58; and also note the observations by Swartz in his contribution to this volume.

[21] Levine, *Ancient Synagogue*, 313–80; Weiss, *Sepphoris Synagogue*, 40–50; Y. Sappir, "The Ancient Synagogue in Israel in the Light of the Talmudic Sources" (Ph.D. diss., The Hebrew University of Jerusalem, 2007), 290–310 (in Hebrew).

3) The use of Temple motifs in synagogue art

Various Tabernacle and Temple scenes appear in synagogue art. In the early fifth-century synagogue at Sepphoris, for instance, the mosaic is composed of several such interrelated depictions, whereas the synagogues of Ḥammat Tiberias (fig. 2) or Bet Alpha, for example, exhibit only an abbreviated form of an architectural façade, together with other sacred motifs.[22] Are we to assume, then, that the distribution of the symbols of the Tabernacle or Temple originated in priestly circles who wished to convey specific visual messages to members of the community? Does every place decorated with an architectural façade, menorah, incense shovel, shofar, or the four species—symbolizing, according to many scholars, the hope of rebuilding the Temple—actually indicate the presence of an authoritative group of priests in the synagogue? The existence of such themes in a variety of synagogues, even in places devoid of all priestly involvement, raises doubts about the plausibility of such a theory.

4) The use of Temple motifs in other Jewish contexts

One of the most frequently recurring compositions in ancient Jewish art is the architectural façade accompanied by Temple objects. This model, in its entirety or in part, is found not only in the synagogue but also in catacombs throughout Palestine and the Diaspora, as well as on glass, pottery vessels, and small objects in daily use (fig. 3).[23] Was the widespread use of such a composition inspired by priests in particular, or did it merely express the desire shared by all to rebuild the Temple? Its appearance in various media and its relatively wide distribution throughout ancient Palestine and the Diaspora indicate

---

[22] Sepphoris: Weiss, *Sepphoris Synagogue*, 65–104. Compare with Ḥammat Tiberias or Bet Alpha: M. Dothan, *Hammath Tiberias*, 33–39; E.L. Sukenik, *The Ancient Synagogue of Beth Alpha* (Jerusalem, 1932), 22–34.

[23] S. Appelbaum, "The Minor Arts of the Talmudic Period," in *Jewish Art: An Illustrated History* (ed. C. Roth; Tel-Aviv, 1961), 225–46; D. Barag, "The Menorah as a Messianic Symbol in Antiquity," in *In the Light of the Menorah: Story of a Symbol* (ed. Y. Israeli; Jerusalem, 1999), 71–75; E.R. Goodenough, *Jewish Symbols in the Greco-Roman Period* (13 vols.; New York, 1953–1968), 1: 164–77. For a discussion of the finds from ancient Rome, see H.J. Leon, *The Jews of Ancient Rome* (Philadelphia, 1960), 195–228; L.V. Rutgers, *The Jews in Late Ancient Rome: Evidence of Cultural Interaction in the Roman Diaspora* (Leiden, 1995), 73–92.

that this combination of motifs may have been used to express the ethno-religious and cultural identity of the Jewish people in the face of the rising power of Christianity, but these were not necessarily or exclusively priestly aspirations.

5) CHRONOLOGY

The Sepphoris mosaic, with its Tabernacle and Temple scenes, is dated slightly earlier than the changes from patriarchal to priestly authority proposed by modern scholarship, although, in principle, the mosaic could still support the theory concerning a renaissance of the priest-hood. It is important to stress, however, that the depiction of the archi-tectural façade with accompanying Temple motifs was not conceived in the Byzantine period. Rather, as finds at other sites show, albeit in a more limited scope, this representation had most probably already developed in the course of the third and fourth centuries CE, when the Patriarch and the rabbinic class played a more significant role in the Jewish society of ancient Palestine (fig. 4).[24]

The existence of Temple motifs in reliefs or in the mosaic floors of various Byzantine synagogues, or the installation of a freestanding menorah beside the holy ark, certainly reflect the importance that the local community ascribed to the Temple and its cult. Were the priests responsible for incorporating these motifs into synagogue design as a means of promoting their own agendas; or were these architectural and artistic expressions merely a reflection of the will and interests of the patrons and local community, who wanted to venerate the Temple cult while, at the same time, expressing their hopes for reinstating the destroyed building? The plausible role of the priests in introducing such themes into the sacred realm can be assessed, if only indirectly, from the level of their involvement in synagogue leadership both as benefactors and officials.

---

[24] B. Mazar, *Beth She'arim* (New Brunswick, N.J., 1973), 1: 112–13; 176–80; N. Avi-gad, *Beth She'arim* (New Brunswick, N.J., 1976), 3: 173–74. On the crystallization of the menorah into a symbol of ethnic religious identity in the early Byzantine period, see L.I. Levine, "The History and Significance of the Menorah in Antiquity," in *From Dura to Sepphoris*, 131–53.

Admittedly, it would not unreasonable to find that priests had played a major role in choosing the motifs incorporated into the mosaic floors, like those at Sepphoris (fig. 5), and, if this were indeed the case, it would also be logical to infer that in doing so they hoped to restore their old-new status within the community. However, the many dedicatory inscriptions reveal a different reality. Over two hundred dedicatory inscriptions found in the synagogues of ancient Palestine refer to donors and officials acting within the community, but they hardly indicate marked priestly involvement in giving donations toward making synagogue mosaics.[25] At Sepphoris, the dedicatory inscriptions inserted in almost every panel of the central carpet clearly indicate that the donation was made to create "this whole panel."[26] This phrase, appearing less frequently in other synagogues, makes a direct link between the donor or donors and the panel for which they contributed money, along the top of which runs a dedicatory inscription telling of their deeds. Of the twenty dedicatory inscriptions preserved in the Sepphoris synagogue mosaics, only one mentions a priest: "Remembered be for good Yudan son of Isaac the priest and Parigri his daughter. Amen Amen."[27] This inscription is incorporated into the geometric mosaic in the aisle (fig. 6) and has no connection whatsoever to the Tabernacle and Temple scenes appearing in the mosaic in the main hall. In other synagogues, only three dedicatory inscriptions in Aramaic specify donations made by priests. Rabbi Isi the priest and Rabbi Yoḥanan the priest are mentioned in one inscription found in the southern corridor of the Susiya synagogue; Lazar the priest and his sons in are mentioned at Eshtemoa, and Pinḥas the priest son of Justus in Naʿaran.[28] None of the Greek inscriptions specifies the names of any other priest, apart from "Theodotos the son of Vettenos, priest and

---

[25] H. Lapin, "Palestinian Inscriptions and Jewish Ethnicity in Late Antiquity," in *Galilee through the Centuries: Confluence of Cultures* (ed. E.M. Meyers; Winona Lake, 1999), 239–68, esp. 265. On the means of funding the synagogues and the types of donations made for their construction, see Z. Safrai, "Financing Synagogue Construction in the Period of the Mishna and the Talmud," in *Synagogues in Antiquity* (ed. A. Kasher, A. Oppenheimer, and U. Rappaport; Jerusalem, 1987), 77–95 (in Hebrew).

[26] Weiss, *Sepphoris Synagogue*, 216–17.

[27] Ibid., 203–4, no. 3.

[28] J. Naveh, *On Stone and Mosaic: The Aramaic and Hebrew Inscriptions from Ancient Synagogues* (Jerusalem, 1978), 58, 74, 75 (in Hebrew).

archisynagogos," mentioned in a Jerusalem inscription that predates the destruction of the Temple.[29]

The Levites' involvement in the synagogue was similar to that of the priests. One Levite named Reuven donated a certain sum toward the creation of the mosaic in Sepphoris, and this same name is also incorporated in the geometric mosaic in the aisle.[30] Three other Levites are known from other synagogues: the name of Yosi the Levite son of Levi is incised on a door lintel from Bar'am, Tanḥum the Levite son of Ḥalafta is mentioned among other donors in Ḥammat Gader, and Yudan the Levite son of Simeon appears twice in the inscriptions from Susiya.[31]

The number of inscriptions, their locations in the synagogues, and their conjunction with certain artistic representations clearly indicate that the donations of the priests and Levites have no connection whatsoever to the various Tabernacle or Temple scenes. These inscriptions were sometimes placed in the courtyard, entrance area, or aisle, or were carved on an entrance door; except for the inscription of Yudan the Levite son of Simeon, which is incised on the chancel screen in Susiya, none of them appears inside the main prayer hall.[32] This silent testimony is invaluable and would seem to indicate that the donors contributed funds for the sake of the synagogue and not to enhance their personal status, and that priests and Levites were not among the main donors to the synagogues. Now, since we may assume that in late antiquity, as in modern times, the well-to-do were able to choose and influence the way in which their donations would be used based on their role in the synagogue and their social status, it is difficult to imagine that a priest, like any other donor, would have held sway in

---

[29] L. Roth-Gerson, *The Greek Inscriptions from the Synagogues in Eretz Israel* (Jerusalem, 1987), 76–86 (in Hebrew); J.S. Kloppenborg Verbin, "Dating Theodotos (CIJ II 1404)," *JJS* 51 (2000): 243–280.

[30] Weiss, *Sepphoris Synagogue*, 205–6.

[31] Naveh, *On Stone and Mosaic*, nos. 1, 14, 33, 80, 82; see also: Z. Yeivin, "Inscribed Marble Fragments from the Khirbet Sûsiya Synagogue," *IEJ* 24 (1974): 201–209, nos. 1 and 17

[32] Pinḥas the priest son of Justus, from Na'aran, paid for the panel in which a menorah is depicted (Naveh, *On Stone and Mosaic*, no. 58); however, the location of menorah beside the entrance to the prayer hall, its features, as well as its appearance without any other cultic symbols indicate that it was neither significantly connected with the priests nor an expression of priestly aspirations, but rather a more general symbol testifying to the nature and purpose of the building.

selecting the depictions, and perhaps even in determining their location in the floor's layout, without contributing from his own pocket.

Of course, one might speculate that priests did play an important
role in the synagogue even though they did not, for the most part,
contribute toward the building and decoration of the prayer house;
consequently, their names rarely appear in the dedicatory inscriptions.
However, the fact is that several synagogue officials—the *archisynagogos, parnas,* and *hazzan*—are indeed mentioned among other donors
in the Greek and Aramaic inscriptions; while, except for the above-
mentioned Theodotos, who is too early to interest us here, none of
them was identified as a priest.[33] Similarly, a broader examination of
the known Greek and Aramaic inscriptions found in various burial
catacombs in ancient Palestine indicates that those who held positions
in the synagogue in the late Roman period were not priests either.[34]
A handful of priests are mentioned in several inscriptions from Bet
She'arim, Jaffa, and Caesarea, for example, but none of them held an
official title, either in the synagogue or elsewhere.[35]

Moreover, since some scholars attribute a rise in the authority of the
priesthood to a similar trend among the Christian clergy, it is important
to emphasize that the role of the priests in the contemporary churches
was entirely different. The many dedicatory inscriptions discovered in
the churches of Byzantine Palestine attest that the local bishop, priests,
and deacons often actively contributed funds for the construction of
churches or the making of mosaics.[36] If Jewish priests indeed had a role

---

[33] Naveh, *On Stone and Mosaic,* nos. 20 and 28 (*hazzan*); no. 63 (*parnas*); Roth-
Gerson, *Greek Inscriptions,* nos. 24, 27, II, V (*archisynagogos*); 16, 18 (*parnas*); IV
(someone in charge of furnishings) [the Roman numerals refer to the inscriptions in
Roth-Gerson's Appendix]. The *archisynagogos* is the official most commonly associated with the synagogue; together with him, other officials performed additional chores
for the benefit of the synagogue community in ancient Palestine and the Diaspora; see
Levine, *Ancient Synagogue,* 412–53.

[34] M. Schwabe and B. Lifshitz, *Beth-Shearim* (Jerusalem, 1974), 2: nos. 164, 203;
J.-B. Frey, *CIJ* (Rome, 1952), 1: nos. 918, 919, 931, 949.

[35] Beth She'arim: Mazar, *Beth She'arim,* 1:137; Schwabe and Lifshitz, *Beth Shearim,*
2: nos. 148, 181; Jaffa: Frey, *CIJ,* 1: nos. 900, 930 (priests); 902, 911, 917 (Levites);
Caesarea: B. Lifshitz, "Inscriptions de Césarée," *RB* 74 (1967): 50–51; C.M. Lehmann
and K.G. Holum, *The Greek and Latin Inscriptions of Caesarea Maritima* (Boston,
2000), no. 167.

[36] L. Di Segni, "The Involvement of Local, Municipal, and Provincial Authorities
in Urban Building in Late Antique Palestine and Arabia," in *The Roman and Byzantine Near East: Some Recent Archaeological Research* (ed. J.H. Humphrey; Ann Arbor,
1995), 312–17. On the role of the bishop and his involvement in the urban life of
Byzantine Palestine, see Y. Dan, *The City in Eretz Israel during the Late Roman and*

resembling that of the bishops in the church leadership—an interesting comparison raised in modern scholarship[37]—one would expect to find wider expression of their involvement in the dedicatory inscriptions in synagogues. The inventory from the synagogues in our region, even if haphazard and limited, indicates rather clearly, however, that priests, unlike bishops, neither played an extraordinary role nor were in a position that empowered them to influence the artistic design of the prayer hall.[38] While priests bore the appropriate title (ha-kohen), which recognized their lineage, the title did not guarantee that they assumed any definitive role within the synagogue.[39]

Furthermore, priests were virtually ignored in later imperial legislation concerning the Jews, Judaism, and synagogues, thus indicating that this group did not have any real communal leadership role in the Byzantine period. The priests are indeed mentioned in the second version of the law instituted by Constantine in 330 CE, to exempt from liturgies those holding positions of leadership, but "priests" in this law seems, as the context shows, merely to be a way to refer those holding positions in the synagogue and the community and there is no reason to think it applies specifically to kohanim, descendants of Aaron.[40]

Byzantine Periods (Jerusalem, 1984), 93–102 (in Hebrew). The finds from Byzantine Palestine are essentially similar to those that have been found in the other cities of the Byzantine East; see C. Roueché, *Aphrodisias in Late Antiquity* (London, 1989), 75–79.

[37] Irshai, "Priesthood in Jewish Society," 99–104.

[38] Levine, *Ancient Synagogue*, 524–29. Priests are mentioned in a number of dedicatory inscriptions from Diaspora synagogues, but these inscriptions do not indicate that they held important positions of leadership in the synagogue or community; see P.W. van der Horst, *Ancient Jewish Epitaphs* (Kampen, 1991), 96; L. Roth-Gerson, *The Jews of Syria as Reflected in the Greek Inscriptions* (Jerusalem, 2001), 291–93 (in Hebrew).

[39] According to Burtchaell, priests were given religious privileges because of their lineage; other than this, they had no official status whatsoever in the functioning of the synagogue; see J.T. Burtchaell, *From Synagogue to Church: Public Services and Offices in the Earliest Christian Communities* (Cambridge, 1992), 253–56. In his comprehensive survey of officers in the synagogue, which is based on epigraphical, historical, and talmudic evidence, Levine does not include the priests among its functionaries; see Levine, *Ancient Synagogue*, 412–53. The silence of the sources, therefore, is not coincidental, as the priests indeed had no substantive leadership role in the synagogue.

[40] *Cod. Theod.* 16.8.2, 4. On the various formulations of the law and the relationship between them, see A. Linder, *The Jews in Roman Imperial Legislation* (Detroit, 1987), 132–35. For further discussion of this law and its historical implications, see idem, "The Roman Imperial Government and the Jews under Constantine," *Tarbiz* 44 (1974/75): 106–26 (in Hebrew).

In conclusion, it appears that the architecture of the synagogue, internal furnishings, and especially the mosaic depictions of the Tabernacle and Temple were not designed by the priestly circles and in all probability were not conceived or commissioned by them either. Neither the introduction of architectural elements nor the inclusion of artistic motifs in a mosaic such as the one from Sepphoris lends support for the notion of a rise in the status of the priests, who, with the abolition of the Patriarchate and the waning of the rabbinic class, strove to be the leaders of the community. In all events, even if we were to assume that priests held a specific role in the leadership of the synagogue and contributed to the liturgy performed inside it, it was not because they wanted to restore their ancient status, but rather because they were on a par with the *archisynagogoi, hazzanim, parnasim,* and other men of means who functioned within the community. The priests were only one sector within the larger multifaceted congregation, which included also the wealthy, *payetanim,* people associated somehow with the rabbinic class, and mystics, as well as other communal groups that cannot be identified with any degree of accuracy. We may assume that each group brought to the synagogue its own traditions, thoughts, and ideas, all of which contributed to formulating synagogue liturgy, art, and architecture; but none of these groups had any unique position or special privileges to promote an individual agenda.[41]

Increased interest in the Temple and its cult in late antiquity therefore should not be ascribed to the motivations of the priestly class, but to the new religio-political configuration resulting from the rise of Christianity in the fourth century CE.[42] The various expressions found in the ancient synagogue evoking memories of the Temple, especially

---

[41] Himmelfarb, *Kingdom of Priests,* 170–73; see also Ehrlich's conclusions regarding the influence of mystics on shaping the synagogue's liturgical texts: U. Ehrlich, "Prayer as an Arena for Constructing Cultural Power: On the Influence of Mystic Groups on the Siddur," in *Spiritual Authority: Struggles Over Cultural Power in Jewish Thought* (ed. B. Huss, H. Kreisel, and U. Ehrlich; Beer-Sheva, 2010), 35–45. I would like to thank Prof. Ehrlich for discussing the subject with me and for sharing his paper prior to its publication. Trifon, who discusses the few literary sources pertaining to priests in the fifth and sixth centuries CE, also reached a similar conclusion; that is, that the Jewish leadership in Tiberias at that time included sages and other communal segments, in addition to significant priestly representatives; see D. Trifon, "The Jewish Priests from the Destruction of the Second Temple to the Rise of Christianity," (Ph.D. diss, Tel-Aviv University, 1985), 257–76 (in Hebrew).

[42] R.L. Wilken, *The Land Called Holy: Palestine in Christian History and Thought* (New Haven, 1992), 82–100; L. Perrone, "'The Mystery of Judaea' (Jerome, *Ep.* 46): The Holy City of Jerusalem between History and Symbol in Early Christian Thought,"

those embedded in the colorful tesserae gracing the prayer hall, mark the Jewish claim—contrary to Christian doctrine and its depictions of the end of days—that the restoration passages regarding the rebuilding of the Temple were still expected to be fulfilled. Yearning for the restoration of the destroyed Temple and its sacrificial cult was not the exclusive domain of priests, but rather a reflection of the common hope of the entire Jewish community, which believed that the priests would be reinstated in their historical role in the future, with the rebuilding of the Temple.[43]

Ideas and hopes embedded in synagogue art and architecture say practically nothing about the political or religious leadership of the Jewish community in late antique Palestine, nor do they demonstrate any priestly attempt to pave the way toward communal leadership. The archaeological finds emerging from the late antique synagogue, the major communal institution of Jewish society in fifth- and sixth-century CE Palestine, thus cast doubts upon the historical-social conclusions drawn in recent research. Rather, it seems that the priests who ran Temple affairs and held political power in Jerusalem lost their influence with its destruction and did not recapture it in the synagogue, the institution that replaced the lost sacred building. For the priests—returning to the question posed by this conference—the traumatic events of 70 CE signified a true watershed; their status was diminished in the post-Temple period and would again blossom, as expected, in the messianic era in the days to come.

---

in *Jerusalem: Its Sanctity and Centrality to Judaism, Christianity, and Islam* (ed. L.I. Levine; New York, 1999), 221–39.

[43] Weiss, *Sepphoris Synagogue*, 225–62; see also H.L. Kessler, "The Sepphoris Mosaic and Christian Art," in Levine and Weiss, *From Dura to Sepphoris*, 65–72; B. Kühnel, "Jewish Art in its Pagan–Christian Context: Questions of Identity," in *Continuity and Renewal: Jews and Judaism in Byzantine–Christian Palestine* (ed. L.I. Levine; Jerusalem, 2004), 49–64; R. Talgam, "Comments on the Judeo–Christian Dialogue in the Mosaic Floor of the Sepphoris Synagogue," in *And Let Them Make Me a Sanctuary: Synagogues from Ancient Times to the Present Day*, (ed. Y. Eshel et al.; Ariel, 2004), 77–86 (in Hebrew). For Jewish and Christian usage of biblical imagery to illustrate the tenets of their faith, see A. Grabar, *Christian Iconography: A Study of its Origins* (Princeton, 1968), 141–46; H.L. Kessler, "Pictures as Scripture in Fifth-Century Churches," in *Expansion of Narrative Illustrations* (ed. S. Kimura et al.; Toyonaka, 1985), 17–31. Fine, in contrast, argues that increased interest in the Temple, sacrifices, and priests is connected with the liturgy and the sanctification of the synagogue as a "holy place," modeled—if only metaphorically—after the Temple in Jerusalem; see S. Fine, "Between Liturgy and Social History: Priestly Power in Late Antique Palestinian Synagogues?" *JJS* 56 (2005): 1–9.

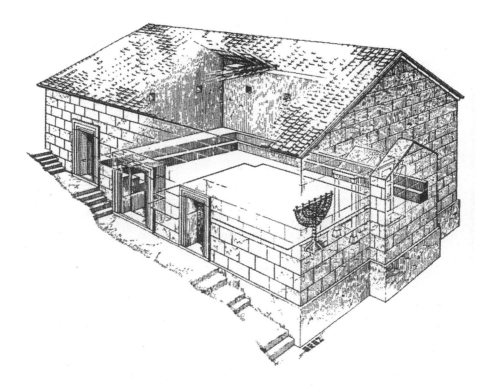

Fig. 1: Ma'on, suggested reconstruction of the synagogue; a freestanding menorah located beside the holy ark indicated the direction of prayer toward Jerusalem (courtesy of David Amit).

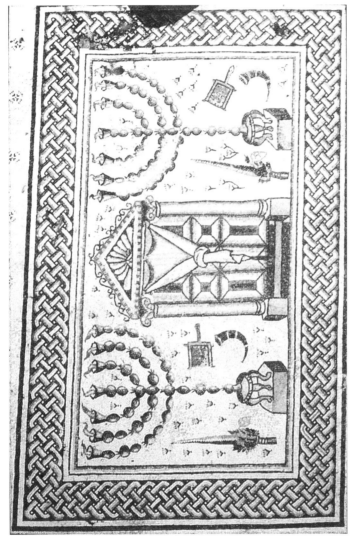

Fig. 2: Hammat Tiberias, architectural façade decorated with two menorot and other Jewish symbols (after M. Dothan, *Hammath Tiberias* [Jerusalem, 1983], Plate 27:1).

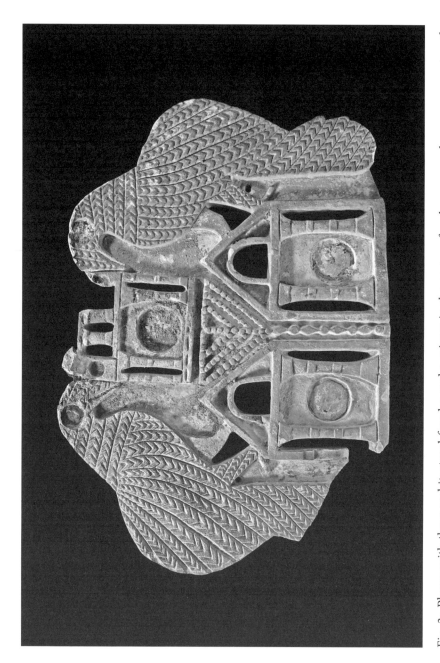

Fig. 3: Plaque with three architectural façades and a mirror in the center of each; a menorah appears prominently in the center of the plaque; and two birds appear on either side (courtesy of the Institute of Archaeology, Hebrew University of Jerusalem).

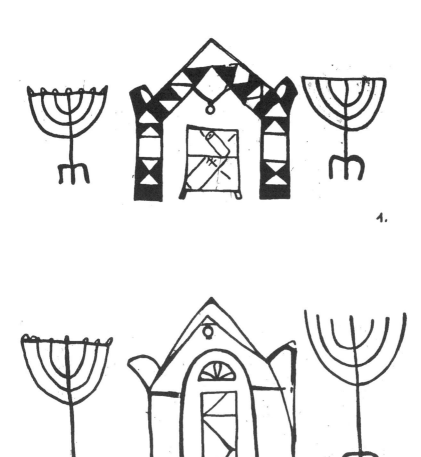

Fig. 5 : Two representations of the Ark of the Law flanked by candlesticks.

Fig. 4: Representations of a holy ark inside a niche flanked by two menorot, painted on two sealing stones at the entrance of Catacomb 1, Bet She'arim. The eternal light hanging above the ark symbolizes the one that was lit daily in the Temple (after B. Mazar, *Bet She'arim* [New Brunswick, 1973], 113 fig. 11).

Fig. 5: Sepphoris, Bands 3 and 4 of the synagogue mosaic, which includes various depictions related to the service of the Tabernacle and Temple (photo by G. Laron).

Fig. 6: Sepphoris, the central section of the mosaic preserved in the aisle. The names of Yudan son of Isaac the Priest and his daughter Parigri appear in the uppermost inscription (photo by G. Laron).

PART II

"THE PLACE" AND OTHER PLACES

PLACE BEYOND PLACE: ON ARTIFACTS, RELIGIOUS TECHNOLOGIES, AND THE MEDIATION OF SACRED PLACE

Ori Schwarz

Temple, a sacred place—what is it good for? Of course, declaring a place sacred may be a good way to claim ownership of it, or to incorporate former traditions concerning its sacredness, but apart from such relatively rare and much discussed strategic usages, sacred places and temples may be conceived of as material infrastructure for at least two main sorts of religious functions. First, for those present at a temple, it is a stage, crowded with material props—thus well-equipped for certain kinds of performances[1] which enable certain religious techniques: communication with gods, fulfillment of commitments towards them, and achieving their cooperation in worldly matters; performance in front of the community; also what Michel Foucault called "*Techniques de soi*": the ways people manipulate themselves, transforming their bodies, souls and thought in order "to attain a certain state of perfection, of happiness, of purity, of supernatural power...."[2] These techniques or technologies are products of historically and culturally specific evolution, yet material infrastructures do allow for some techniques while precluding others.

Secondly, for those not present at the temple it functions as a continuity mechanism: a constant material expression of the relationship between worshippers, their community, and their gods, especially at times when they are not performing worship. Scholars of interpersonal relationships have recognized sundry temporal continuity mechanisms which make interpersonal relationship exist beyond interaction: both discursive mechanisms, like making plans and reminiscing; and materially aided mechanisms, like gifts and photos.[3] Sociologist Bruno

---

[1] S. Coleman and J. Elsner, "Performing Pilgrimage: Walsingham and the Ritual Construction of Irony," in *Ritual, Performance, Media* (ed. F. Hughes-Freeland; London, 1998), 46–65.

[2] M. Foucault, "About the Beginning of the Hermeneutics of the Self," *Political Theory* 21 (1993): 198–227.

[3] S. Sigman, "Handling the Discontinuous Aspects of Continuous Social Relationships: Toward Research on the Persistence of Social Forms," *Communication Theory* 2 (1991): 106–27.

Latour makes a good case that any cultural continuity relies on materiality.[4] The Second Temple did just this: it functioned as a physical residence for the *Shekhinah*, where the people's representatives constantly interacted with it. Its continuity-enhancing function was not unlike that of photos, family homes, or wedding rings.

Changes in religious stage props, or material infrastructure—such as occurred in 70 CE—pose a constitutive practical problem: The religious group as a discursive construct or imagined community may continue to exist, but it must invent new religious practices, new technologies for communication and negotiation with God and for constant representation of this relationship; in brief, it must reinvent itself. One good example of such an alternative technology is the *Siddur* (prayer book), which (while supported by other time-gauging technologies) enables people in different places to pray the same prayer at the same time, compensating for the lost co-presence once provided by the central Temple.

My paper is dedicated to a religious transformation in contemporary Judaism, which is also the product of a material change—not the destruction of a building, but the penetration of new photographic technologies, particularly the video camera phone. This transformation will be explicated while focusing on the changing religious roles of two sacred places of contemporary Judaism: the Western Wall, a remnant of the Temple that still functions, synecdochically, in some Temple rituals, including the Priestly Blessing (*Birkat Kohanim*) to be discussed later; and the gravesite of Rabbi Nachman of Breslov in Uman, Ukraine—an emerging pilgrimage destination for tens of thousands of Israeli Jews, the access to which poses a financial challenge for thousands of nonaffluent pilgrims. In addition, I will refer to places of temporary sacredness, such as a football stadium turned into a one night synagogue, or a synagogue rotating among the houses of community members.

The religious reform I will portray below represents a blind spot, since it involves no transformation of Jewish sacred texts or sacred symbols, does not challenge the juridical textual corpus called "halakhic literature," and involves artifacts not usually conceived of as sacred, i.e., it does not concern any of the traditional *foci* of the study of Judaism. However, social studies and religious studies have gone through an

---

[4] B. Latour, "On Interobjectivity," *Mind, Culture and Activity* 3 (1996): 228–45.

important shift during the last two decades. Briefly put, this is a shift from the exegesis of texts, and the interpretation of human activity as if *it* were a text that tells something about society, to meticulously and seriously looking at whatever people do and say in order to manipulate the world and themselves. For contemporary sociologists, following Pierre Bourdieu and Bruno Latour, what members of cultural groups share, the source of cultural unity and continuity, is not a symbolic code to be interpreted and translated, but rather practices—patterns of routine action, which once acquired are embodied and become second nature.[5] These are always affected by material arrangements: our walk is affected by our shoes;[6] you can't sacrifice without an altar; and as Horowitz demonstrated, nocturnal devotion (*Tiqqun*) is much more likely to become popular when coffee is available.[7] The physicality of ritual is now recognized as bodily movement which enables a certain responsiveness, certain sensitivities and emotions,[8] as manipulations of artifacts that are affected by their affordances, i.e., what they seem to allow or preclude. Not only do artifacts enable us to achieve objectives, but the possibilities of usage we recognize in them produce new desires. Following in this vein, religion is no longer seen as a system of metaphysical beliefs, but rather as a system of acquired skills, practical knowledge, and disciplinary patterns.[9] In all cases described below, the material world (in this case, camera phones) enables the transformation of old rituals and the introduction of new ones which relate differently to place, thus re-forming religion: Techno-cultural practices offer new ways to cope with (permanent or temporary) lack of access to the sacred places and to transgress the boundaries of sacred temporality, forming new technologies of self—new ways for people to manipulate themselves and their religiosity.

As a sociologist of photography and internet culture in Israel, I have encountered a massive trend of documentation of Jewish rituals by a

---

[5] P. Bourdieu, *Outline of a Theory of Practice* (Cambridge, 1977); Latour, "Interobjectivity"; A. Reckwitz, "Toward a Theory of Social Practices: A Development in Culturalist Theorizing," *European Journal of Social Theory* 5:2 (2002): 243–63.

[6] M. Mauss, "Techniques of the Body," *Economy and Society* 2/1 (1973): 70–88.

[7] E. Horowitz, "Coffee, Coffeehouses, and the Nocturnal Rituals of Early Modern Jewry," *AJS Review* 14/1 (1989): 17–46.

[8] K.L. LaMothe, "Why Dance? Towards a Theory of Religion as Practice and Performance," *Method and Theory in the Study of Religion* 17 (2005): 101–33.

[9] T. Asad, *Genealogies of Religion: Disciplines and Reasons of Power in Christianity and Islam* (Baltimore, 1993).

growing number of worshippers. This is undoubtedly due to the fact that mobile phones are carried everywhere and digital cameras have become a default gadget in mobiles: photography no longer necessitates planning in advance (bringing a camera) or expenditure of money on film and development. Yet technology has no deterministic effect: people choose to document certain rituals, while avoiding the documentation of others. Among the most heavily documented religious events are mass events in sacred places and/or on sacred occasions, including the Priestly Blessing at the Western Wall on Passover and Sukkot, the *Tiqqun Klali* prayer in Uman before Rosh Hashanah, and penitential prayers (*Seliḥot*) before Yom Kippur. These are usually videotaped by hundreds of worshippers, whereas daily prayers of individuals or small groups in local synagogues or at home usually remain undocumented. Within each mass ritual there are certain moments and phases that invite photography, while at others photography would be inappropriate; occasionally, the question of the appropriateness of photography at a particular moment provokes a debate among those attending the ritual.[10]

The focus on documentation of unusual rituals in sacred places and times is telling: it shows that it is the boundaries of co-presence, in the sacred places and times, that the participants are attempting to manipulate by documentation. Co-presence, that is, the association of worshipers with each other and with a particular ritual time and space, plays a dominant role in Judaism. Most Jewish prayers require a *minyan*—a quorum of at least ten male Jews adhering to the unities of time and place. Compared with other religions, Judaism is relatively strict in this regard: the Methodist Church of Britain, in contrast, has operated websites where real ordained ministers hold services that include the real prayers of online worshippers. Its first website was designed as an internet-game-like, 3D "virtual church," where each worshipper was represented by an avatar. Some other internet sites have gone further, offering individualized, multimedia online versions of Holy Communion. Similarly, Catholics in the Philippines were given the sacrament of penance via e-mail (before the Vatican declared the procedure invalid in 2005). Neopagan e-worshippers use

---

[10] Rituals taking place on Shabbat and many holidays are not documented due to halakhic prohibitions concerning the use of electronic devices.

online images of candles to substitute for real candles.[11] Compared with the cases mentioned above, the Jewish halakhah is rather conservative: Halakhic rulings given by rabbis of different movements are in agreement that participation in a *minyan* through telephone or internet mediation is impossible, and that recorded blessings are not valid. Many also argue that blessings heard via electronic mediation (e.g., via broadcast, telephone, or even amplification) are invalid. Prayers may be e-mailed to the Western Wall, but they are actually printed out and placed between the stones.[12] By insisting on co-presence as a prerequisite for traditional rituals, the halakhic framework thus constrains the potential transformation of the place of place within Jewish ritual.

Nevertheless, technologies of digital photography do lead, for Jews and others, to the introduction of new rituals (albeit of lesser importance than traditional rituals, occupying a position closer to the middle of the sacred/profane continuum). These new rituals are centered around the consumption of videotaped primary rituals; while they are not indifferent to physical place and co-presence, they do manipulate the place of place within ritual in an inventive manner, which I discuss below. The camera phone is a technology which enables the translation of a concrete prayer event, occurring in a particular time and place, into an artifact, a product to be consumed in different times and places, and shared with different people. Photography not only endows the event with a status of unusual importance and "televisual" aura;[13] it also opens possibilities for new practices of religious video consumption, three of which I would like to briefly introduce.

---

[11] G. Bell, "No More SMS from Jesus," in *Ubicomp 2006* (ed. P. Dourish and A. Friday; Berlin and Heidelberg, 2006), 141–58; C.A. Casey, "Virtual Ritual, Real Faith: The Revirtualization of Religious Ritual in Cyberspace," *Online—Heidelberg Journal of Religions on the Internet* 2/1 (2006): n.p. Online: http://online.uni-hd.de/; R. Kluver and Y. Chen, "The Church of Fools: Virtual Ritual and Material Faith," *Online—Heidelberg Journal of Religions on the Internet* 3/1 (2008), n.p. Online: http://online .uni-hd.de/; S.D. O'Leary, "Cyberspace as Sacred Space: Communicating Religion on Computer Networks," in *Religion Online: Finding Faith on the Internet* (ed. L.L. Dawson and D.E. Cowan; New York, 2004). For Evangelical online Holy Communion see http://www.alphachurch.org/holycomm.htm.

[12] http://www.aish.com/wallcam/Place_a_Note_in_the_Wall.asp, consulted 6.11.2008.

[13] Cf. M. van de Port, "Visualizing the Sacred: Video Technology, 'Televisual' Style, and the Religious Imagination in Bahian Candomblé," *American Ethnologist* 33 (2006): 444–61.

First I will discuss the notion of *secondary ritual*. In secondary rituals, worshippers watch the documentation of primary rituals which they themselves both participated in and documented. This is sometime practiced while murmuring the sacred text recited during the primary ritual (though many avoid recitation for halakhic reasons). The consumption of documented rituals is usually described as evoking great spiritual excitement, enlightenment of the soul. Even identifying himself in a *commercial* video from Uman made a Hasid tremble and cry, "*Back there again.*"[14] Here, the experience of the sacred is detached from the sacred time and place, and may be evoked at will—like the consumption of music in order to manipulate one's spirituality and mood. However, this detachment is only *prima facie*: the efficacy of the secondary ritual as a spiritual technique relies strongly upon the identity between producer and consumer, his *having been there*.

To start with, watching the videos evokes a feeling of unity: "*Watching twenty thousand people shouting 'God is the Lord,'*" creates a huge, unified ad hoc ritual congregation made of people who usually don't feel they belong together; e.g., ultra-Orthodox and moderately orthopractic traditionalist Jews. This feeling is described by participants as highly unique to events like mass *Seliḥot* services and Uman's *Kibbutz* (assembly of pilgrims). This rare feeling of Jewish unity may now be consumed at will, relived through the secondary ritual without physically revisiting the holy place. Videos often stress the volume of the crowd, by slow pan movements of the camera back and forth from one side of the site to the other. Thus, although secondary rituals are often performed in solitude, videos are efficacious in creating ritual in the classic terms proposed by Emil Durkheim, who defined ritual as worship of the group by the group—that is, a mechanism for the (re)production of society through collective consciousness and emotions.[15] However, now we depart from Durkheim to discuss techniques where collectivity plays no major role in manipulations of the self and the sacred.

An ultra-Orthodox Breslover Hasid told me of two alternative techniques which he and his fellow Hasidim use for self-energizing and interaction with the sacred in times of spiritual "descent" and *hitraḥakut* (being distant from God): the first is imagining the pilgrim-

---

[14] All quotations not otherwise attributed are taken from interviews conducted with practicing Jews.

[15] E. Durkheim, *The Elementary Forms of the Religious Life* (New York, 1969).

age to the Rabbi Nachman's grave at Uman while in solitude, which is a privileged spiritual technique in Breslov hasidut. The second method is watching videos from Uman that document the Rosh Hashanah *Kibbutz*. The interviewee described both techniques as equal alternatives for coping with the same practical problem: the inaccessibility of the sacred place due to the lack of financial resources for more frequent pilgrimages.

A poor craftsman, who travelled on pilgrimage to Uman for Rosh Hashanah, taped and published online a video of the peak moment of the pilgrimage, a moment of personal conversion—the *Tiqqun Klali* prayer. *"I haven't ceased praying, the Tiqqun Klali in one hand and in the other hand, held high above my head, the camera."* He watches the film to get rid of "bad thoughts" and "the evil inclination" (*yetzer hara*): whenever he struggles with financial or other distresses and improper coping methods pop into his head, he watches the films from Uman and the bad thoughts are replaced with an *"indescribable happiness."* Watching also helps him cope with his "longing for the Rebbe," yet it also fosters this longing. It makes longing bearable, yet it does not extinguish it but rather fans it: "Watching is like, how should I explain it, like, an addict who needs his drug is dope-sick, and when he gets it he's high, but with me it's the other way around, I'm always dope-sick for the Rebbe, even when I watch, so yes, it increases the longing." Similar techniques of longing management are practiced by other ultra-Orthodox Breslovers, who watch videos to cope with longing both when they are unable to make the pilgrimage and as a spiritual buildup in the last weeks before the pilgrimage.

While asked whether the videos are sacred, the craftsman answered, "But of course, our Rebbe is in there." Just as the Rebbe is physically present in Uman, and the spatial proximity brings his followers spiritual merit, so is the video of the *Tiqqun Klali* a physical presence of the Rebbe brought back to Israel (even if somehow depleted): the Rebbe is simply "there."

What is described above encompasses a wide range of religious technologies of self. Videos are used for self-disciplining, moral reformation, coping with financial and moral difficulties, and manipulation of religious emotions: the fostering and domestication of religious longing, the evocation of happiness and self-contentment. All of these are intensive, mediated effects of physically distant holy places. The practical problem of inaccessibility is solved through inventive usage of available material aids. The film's efficacy is derived both from its being anchored in a personal memory of the primary ritual, and also from the connection with the Rebbe that it offers: it perpetuates the moment of spatial closeness between the worshipper and the Rebbe's tomb, thus opening a channel of constant communication.

This communication channel may be used by others in addition to the worshipper/photographer: usually, worshipper/photographers share the documentation with their relatives and friends, and sometimes with wider audiences, via internet publications. This brings us to the second practice of religious videoconsumption which I'd like to discuss: The *surrogate ritual*, in which worshippers reuse the spiritual work of others for their own spiritual benefits, often through the mediation of objects and texts. Such religious techniques were developed long before the invention of the camera phone—accounts of pilgrimages to Jerusalem from fifteenth-century Germany being only one example. Some of these accounts were written as contemplation aids to be read by nuns, so as to substitute for the hard and dangerous pilgrimage which many women refrained from making.[16] A very similar practice exists among Uman pilgrims: One Hasid told me that his wife always asks him to take his camera to Uman and film it for her. Women, who are not allowed to join the *Kibbutz* in Rosh Hashanah, and often lack money to journey at other times, may thus experience the place through videos taken by their husbands or other pilgrims.

However, the surrogate ritual which the camera enables is not textual, but audiovisual. Video is not a text, written in retrospect in order to textually reconstruct the event, but rather an object of indexical value—electronic vestiges of the sacred event, the sacred temporality and spatiality, on the camera's memory card. As such, its functionality resembles not only that of pilgrims' accounts, but also that of objects brought from sacred places, such as holy water and holy soil. Like the secondary ritual, the surrogate ritual's power is also derived from the physical presence in the sacred place and time, but unlike it, here the producer and consumer diverge. The participation of someone in the primary ritual (preferably someone close to the viewer or at least similar to him, an ordinary worshipper rather than a professional

---

[16] E.g. Felix Faber's, "Sionpilgerin." See K. Hannemann, "Fabri, Felix," in *Die deutsche Literatur des Mittelalters: Verfasserlexicon* (Berlin and New York, 1980), 2:682–89. Another form of surrogate-pilgrimage common at Faber's time were the professional paid pilgrims who went on pilgrimage on behalf of others and for the other's salvation: L. Schmugge, "Der falsche Pilger," in *Fälschungen im Mittelalter* (6 vols.; Hannover, 1988–1990), 5: 475–84, esp. 479–81.

photographer, who may support the images with an enthusiastic first-person narrative), suffices to endow the surrogate ritual with some efficacy.

In the ultra-Orthodox Hasidic world, video documentation is also a way to go beyond the religious community's boundaries, that is, the norm demanding that every Hasid, especially in small "courts" (communities centering on a particular rebbe), celebrate holidays with his rebbe. A young Hasid told me he always obeys this norm, although he occasionally wants to attend impressive events conducted by rebbes of larger courts. The strongest temptation is the desire to visit Uman on Rosh Hashanah, which he yet resists. Instead, he watches videos and imagine himself there. Watching, he says, "helps you feel and experience what has been there. Because you know how you feel at prayer, and the whole outpouring of the heart (…) you take this… this experience, close your eyes, watch the video and say, 'Wow, me among twenty-five thousand, how would I conduct myself?' It's… it's an experience." This unusual style of watching deserves careful attention: it is watching which involves *closing* one's eyes, the very opposite of "watching" in the usual sense. It is not the passive act of beholding the sight of a past event attended by others, but rather a body technique, which affords disengagement from the physical environment and transcending into another spatiality (that of Uman). Here, watching (which is rather listening and imagining) allows devotees to overcome the inaccessibility of holy places which is grounded in norms rather than in financial or technical difficulties.

Photography reifies the religious experience for future consumption (by the documentation producer himself or by others) as an aid for rituals oriented toward the holy place, but detached in time and space from the primary ritual. Thus, as I have indicated, Breslover Hasidim use videos to cope with their physical distance from their rebbe's tomb, whereas others use it to experience sacredness, religious power and unity in seemingly profane contexts, outside of sacred time, hybridizing situations as different as *Seliḥot* on the night before Yom Kippur and a free moment at work.

The third and last phenomenon I would like to refer to is the *virtualization of the sacred place*. To exemplify what I mean by this term, I'll share with you the story of a small Israeli community that I'll call "Bamidbar" to avoid identification. The story takes place in a new, middle class neighborhood with a high percentage of nationalist-religious residents, but with no synagogues. The residents have organized themselves into a few religious communities that are engaged in an ongoing struggle with the municipal authorities for the establishment of synagogues. The Bamidbar community meets regularly: every Shabbat or holiday it assembles in the house of a different family, which is turned into a synagogue *pro tempore*. The group also organizes weekly prayers for their children and occasional family trips, and they celebrate civic holidays (e.g., Independence Day) together. Nevertheless, at the time of the interview the community's chairman felt that creating a community without a synagogue was a difficult challenge, for when prayer is over, the "synagogue" turns back into a family residence, and the religious community thus remains without any physical representation in the world. It is without a place.

But why do community members consider this a problem? Partly because they considered praying without a synagogue disrespectful. More important, however, is the fact that this neighborhood is not highly communal. Most members moved in during the last few years and work out of town; architecture is suburban, so residents do not live in apartment houses; and nothing unites them, apart from the synagogue project. When we recall the degree to which the relationship between the Jew and his/her God is mediated by the religious community, it becomes clear that Bamidbar faces a real problem: How can a religious community be given existence also on weekdays, beyond their interactions on holy days? The lack of a synagogue building required alternative mechanisms of continuity.

The strategy adopted by Bamidbar's chairman was to partially replace the physical site with a virtual site—a community internet site with photos and a discussion forum, along with a community YouTube page featuring videos of communal prayers and events, filmed in part by the chairman himself and in part by other members of the community. This was done consciously and instrumentally:

> For now, the photos I upload are to connect the community, which doesn't have enough place for it.... A community with no place, and no building, that works each Shabbat from a different place, and I send them a link—not only of a message, the Shabbat prayer will be here or there, but I send them "Dear members, enter this Youtube link," or I send them this or that photo, and they enter, and get connected, and they see themselves; it makes the community—though virtually—into something a bit more tangible.

Nonverbal communication is especially important considering the high percentage of immigrants in the community, i.e., people who have difficulties reading long Hebrew texts.

However, it must be admitted that halakhic constraints have made this mechanism less efficient: since most community meetings are on Shabbat, they remain undocumented. The uploaded videos have been warmly received, yet tracking their view counts proves that people have watched them only once, upon receiving the links. In other words: the community does have a site continuous in time, including a virtual "chapel" where the videos are presented, and community members visit the site for coordination of prayers and other reasons. Yet, the chapel remains unchanged, and hence is visited only seldom: evidently, to whatever extent it provides continuity, it still produces less communality than hoped for by the chairman.

Conclusions

The camera phone is responsible for an expansion of the traditional repertoire of rituals, opening up new channels to the sacredness of places (e.g., Uman and the Western Wall), persons (live and dead rebbes), and times (various holidays). These channels are not limited to a collective experience in predetermined holy times and places, but are at the devotees' disposal for private consumption, occasionally in highly mundane contexts and in a posture similar to the one of mobile phone texting.

The two first phenomena I portrayed above, the secondary ritual and the surrogate ritual, are mediations of the holy place as construed in the first sense I mentioned at the opening of this paper; that is, the holy place functions as a well-equipped stage for actions directed towards the world, God, and the self. These "second hand" ritual techniques enable the use of the holy place for such activity even when not physically there, and even by people who have *never* been there. The video enables the viewer/worshipper to experience the unity of mass events when alone, via privatized consumption. Uman and the Western Wall become more available, helping Jews communicate with their rebbe or the *Shekhinah* and transform their own souls. The video offers a mediated sacred place, which does not substitute for the physical one but supports it, offering different embodied ways of manipulating the sacred.

Yet it should be underlined that videos are not the only means that mediate sacred places. Imagining the sacred place during ritual seclusion offers an alternative technique. That is, mediated religious techniques oriented towards holy places are nothing particularly modern. It may, therefore, be interesting to ask whether the phenomenon of Diaspora, both before and after the destruction of the Second Temple, led to the development of mediated Temple-oriented techniques of observance.

The third phenomenon I portrayed, the virtualization of sacred place, relates to the Temple's second functionality as a continuity mechanism in the relationship between individuals, community and God. After the destruction of the Temple of Jerusalem, the synagogue was gradually transformed into a Temple substitute, *miqdash-me'at*: they hosted a few of the former Temple-based rituals—besides new religious techniques, the most important of which was prayer—and were gradually awarded sacred status.[17] Yet, as we have seen, this substitute can also be substituted for.

Under circumstances which render a sacred place less accessible (financial, physical, normative; due to its destruction or to its adherents being at a distance), it may keep functioning in religious practices through different mediators: persons to whom it still *is* accessible, synecdoches (like the Western Wall, or imported holy water and holy soil), representations (like videos), or bodily techniques of imagination. All of these mediators require the development of new techniques of observance. Such mediators do not nullify the place of place altogether, but rather manipulate it—and they may be found alongside other emerging religious techniques that are not oriented around places. Though I am no expert on ancient Judaism, I would like to close this paper with two humble suggestions: 1) that we consider the Temple as an element in the whole fabric of religious practice within ancient Palestine and abroad, and that, 2) accordingly, we examine the alterations and transformations of these practices on the basis of the premise that sacred place should not be regarded in terms of a dichotomy of existence and absence, but rather as part of a continuum, a whole spectrum of techniques that offer indirect and mediated relations to its spatiality. It may be that this suggestion, based on my study of modern experience, will make a worthwhile, if humble, contribution to reframing the discussion of the destruction of the Second Temple.

---

[17] S. Fine, *This Holy Place: On the Sanctity of the Synagogue during the Greco-Roman Period* (Notre Dame, 1997).

PRIESTS AND PRIESTHOOD IN PHILO:
COULD HE HAVE DONE WITHOUT THEM?

Jutta Leonhardt-Balzer

1. Introduction

In an earlier paper I demonstrated that for Philo, there is no rivalry between the Temple and the synagogue, as they serve completely different functions.[1] Furthermore, far from being dispensable, the Temple is the focus of Philo's idea of worship. Philo's spiritual interpretation of worship hinges on its connection with a material place, and there is no evidence whatsoever that he could easily have done without the existence of the Temple in Jerusalem. Indeed, his depiction (in *Legat.* 186–198) of his reaction to Gaius's threat against the Temple is ample proof that attachment to the Temple and the worship performed there was for him a matter, not only of intellectual obligation to tradition, but also of deep emotion. Philo's conception of Jewish worship is twofold and combines particular and universal aspects.

Building on this earlier study, I will look here at the place of the priesthood in Philo's thought. This will show in greater detail the actual role of the Second Temple and its cult for Philo's own perception of what Judaism really was, and thus will fill out our notion of the way the cessation of that cult—which came within a few decades of his death—would have affected his thought.

2. The Priests

2.1 *The Worship Conducted by the Priests in the Temple*

Philo depicts the priests as performing the sacrifices in the Temple and receiving the offerings of the people as commanded by the Torah. In *Mos.* 2.141–146 the election of the priests is described. Their main task

---

[1] "Jewish Worship and Universal Identity in Philo of Alexandria," in *Jewish Identity in the Greco-Roman World* (ed. J. Frey, S. Gripentrog, and D.R. Schwartz; Leiden, 2007), 29–53.

is "offering the sacrifices and performing the sacred rites" (τὰς θυσίας
ἀνάγειν τε καὶ ἱερουργεῖν, 141).[2] Moses purifies and clothes them
(143); he then anoints the priests, the Temple furniture, and "everything else that is necessary and useful for the sacrifices" (τὰ ἄλλα ὅσα
πρὸς θυσίας ἀναγκαῖα καὶ χρήσιμα), culminating with the high priest
himself (146). This is only one of the many examples of Philo's references to the priests that appear in the context of his exposition of the
biblical text and Israel's history—and not all of them can be discussed
here. In the present context, only those texts will be studied that refer
to Philo's idea of the priesthood, especially in his own day.

In *Spec.* 1.167, Philo points out that the priests must be pure in body
as well as in soul "whenever they approach the altar to pray or to give
thanks" (ὁπότε προσέρχοντο βωμοῖς ἢ εὐχόμενοι ἢ εὐχαριστήσοντες).
The passage does not refer to prayer and sacrifice as two individual elements of worship, but as designations for the priestly service as a whole.
The priestly service is summed up as service at the altar (sacrifice)
accompanied by prayer as communication with God, which is charac-
terised more specifically as communication in a spirit of gratitude.

In his allegorical commentary, Philo emphasises the good reason
and high intellect behind the individual regulations for the Temple
service (*Leg.* 3.118–128);[3] consequently, reason and intellect are also
the special attributes of "those consecrating and sacrificing in purity"
(τῆς ἱερωμένης καὶ θυούσης καθαρῶς [ἐστι φέρειν ταῦτα]). But the
priests are only purely rational beings when they serve in the Temple,
and even the high priest is only completely focused on God when he
enters into the presence of God in the Holy of Holies (125). Outside
the performance of their duties, the priests have no special status. This
description of the priests expresses Philo's esteem for them, but it does
not give an impression of any internal knowledge about them. In none
of Philo's accounts of the priests and their conduct of the cult is there
any evidence that Philo himself was a priest.[4]

---

[2] The Greek is based on the LCL edition, the translation is my own. Even where the
Greek is only quoted elliptically, care is taken to maintain the original meaning.
[3] On the priestly service, see J. Leonhardt, *Jewish Worship in Philo of Alexandria*
(Tübingen, 2001), 228–30.
[4] Against D.R. Schwartz, "Philo's Priestly Descent," in *Nourished with Peace:
Studies in Hellenistic Judaism in Memory of Samuel Sandmel* (ed. F.E. Greenspahn,
E. Hilgert, and B.L. Mack; Denver, 1984), 155–71.

The priestly service has not only spiritual benefits, but material ones as well. As commanded by Deut 18:4, the priests receive a share of all agricultural produce "as tithes" (ἀπαρχαί); one part of this share is "for sacrifices" (εἰς…θυσίας), and the other is given to the priests (*Spec.* 4.98). The shoulder and the fat of the "sacrificial victims" (θυσιαί), as symbols of strength and mildness, are to be given to the priests (*Spec.* 1.145–146). As for "the animals sacrificed away from the altar" (ἀπὸ…τῶν ἔξω τοῦ βωμοῦ θυομένων, 147), from these the priests receive, according to Deut 18:3, the shoulder, the jaws and the stomach: the first symbolises strength; the second, the mouth and the *Logos*; and the third, contempt for desire and greed (*Spec.* 1.147–150).

The material benefits given to the priests lead to spiritual benefits for the people. In *Leg.* 3.133–137, Philo interprets Lev 7:34, which refers both to the thank-offering of the people and the donation of the victim's shoulder to the priests. Philo explains the significance of the priestly share taken "from the sacrifices of salvation" (ἀπὸ τῶν θυσιῶν τοῦ σωτηρίου, 133), identifying the two offerings.[5] Discussing the prescription that Aaron and the priests are to take the breast with the shoulder (134–136), Philo explains that the breast and shoulder belong to the "sacrifice of salvation" because the salvation of the soul results only when reason, the *Logos*, has taken up residence: the *Logos* controls the passions, and "toil has created the willingness to yield to the benefactor, God" (ὁ πόνος…ἐγκατασκευάσῃ…παραχώρησιν τῷ εὐεργέτῃ θεῷ, 137). The act of the priests' receiving of the shoulder symbolises the taking up of residence by reason in the body. By providing the sacrificial animal, the people express their willingness to leave control to the divine Logos, represented by the priests, who take over the preparation of the sacrifice from them. Thus the priests appear as partners with the people in the worship of God, performing the rites in purity and in turn receiving a share of the sacrifice.

The proper state of the priest is important for the validity of the rite. In *Spec.* 1.117, Philo refers to the laws in Lev 21:17–18 that forbid "any priest" (τις…τῶν ἱερέων) physically or spiritually unfit for duty to participate in the sacrificial meal or in the sacrifices. He summarises the passage as being "about those who deal with the offerings" (περὶ τῶν χρησομένων ταῖς ἀπαρχαῖς), using a phrase not contained in the biblical text. For Philo this phrase summarises the duties of the priests.

---

[5] On the income of priests, see J. Leonhardt, *Jewish Worship*, 202–5.

In §120 Philo continues that from the "special offerings" (ἀπαρχαί), only the pure priests may eat, "so that one does not give away any of the consecrated foods by misusing untimely humane feeling as an excuse for impiety" (μὴ προῆταί τις τὰ καθιερωθέντα προφάσει καταχρησάμενος εἰς ἀσέβειαν ἀκαίρῳ φιλανθρωπίᾳ). The holiness of the offering thus depends on the person who receives it; if a lay person were to eat from the offering, it would be desecrated (122). This reflects the fundamental fact of Jewish worship that laypeople everywhere—not only in the Diaspora—had to rely on the priests to perform the sacrifices for them, and they had to trust them to do so correctly. While Lev 22:10 forbids neighbors (122), hired servants (123), and foreigners (124) to eat from these offerings, Lev 22:11 permits the slaves of priests to eat "from the special offerings" (ἐκ τῶν ἀπαρχῶν), because they belong to the household of the priest and must be maintained (126–127). Philo explains that in this case the holiness of the offerings (ἀπαρχαί) is still guaranteed through the sanctity of their masters, who make sure that the slaves conduct themselves properly (128). Philo himself seems to imply that this is an ideal when he comments that the slaves would steal their share of the offerings if they were not given it honestly (126–127). Philo adds, following Lev 22:13, that the married daughter of a priest may return to her father's household and eat from the offerings, if she has no children and is either widowed or divorced (129). None of these details, however, changes or obscures the fundamental fact that for Philo it is necessary, in order for the offering to be valid, that it is offered and consumed by a priestly recipient in a proper state of purity.

The same point is made with regard to the sin-offering, which is eaten in the Temple precinct. According to Philo (not the Bible) the meat must be eaten within one day; it is not to be eaten by the person offering it, but rather by the priests (*Spec.* 1.240).[6] When the priests eat "the sacrifice" (ἡ θυσία) this honors their service and therefore those who provide the sacrifice. The fact that the priests eat the sacrificial

---

[6] I. Heinemann, *Philons griechische und jüdische Bildung: Kulturvergleichende Untersuchungen zu Philons Darstellung der jüdischen Gesetze* (Breslau, 1932), 21, remarks that the Bible commands only that the thank-offering be eaten on the same day (Lev 7:15); but he finds confirmation for the same practice concerning the sin-offering in *Sifra* ad loc., and in Josephus, *Ant.* 3.231. Cf. also S. Belkin, *Philo and the Oral Law: The Philonic Interpretation of Biblical Law in Relation to the Palestinian Halakha* (Cambridge, Mass., 1940), 58–59.

meat shows that the sacrifice was successful and the sins have truly been forgiven. As the priests can only "perform the rites" (λειτουργεῖν), i.e., receive the sacrifice, if every single priest is "completely pure" (ὁλόκληρος, 242), the fact that the priests in their purity receive the sacrifice emphasises its honourable status and that of everyone connected with it. The repentant person offering the sacrifice is shown to be of purity equal to that of the priests (243). It has been suggested that this indicates the conferring of a quasi-priestly status and even the concept of a common priesthood;[7] but, although the people participate in the pure status of the priests, it is quite clear that they do *not* have the right to perform the sacrifices themselves and are utterly dependent on the priests.

When the priests eat the sacrificial meat, their purity links them with God and provides intercession for the sinner. This is why the sacrifices on behalf of the high priest and the nation must be burnt completely: "For nobody is greater than the high priest or than the nation, so that he could become an intercessor for the sinners" (κρείττων γὰρ οὐδεὶς ἀρχιερέως ἢ τοῦ ἔθνους ἐστίν, ὃς ἁμαρτησάντων γενήσεται παραιτητής, 244). Therefore, their sacrifice is offered not for themselves but in honor of the nation (246).

For Philo, the purity of the priests requires them "to purify the soul and the body first" (πρότερον ὥσπερ τὴν ψυχὴν καὶ τὸ σῶμα καθαρεῦσαι) before performing the Temple rites (*Mos.* 2.68), and the purification of the soul is mentioned repeatedly in discussions of the Temple personnel (*Det.* 170; *Her.* 182–185; *Somn.* 1.81).[8]

The priests' right to eat not only from the sacrifices, but also from the produce offerings given to the Temple, is mentioned in Philo's interpretation of the first-fruit offering of wheat, fifty days after the bringing of the Sheaf (*Spec.* 2.176–187, esp. 183), on "the Festival of First Produce" (ἑορτὴ πρωτογεννημάτων).[9] Once again, the priests not only receive the offerings of the people, but also help them with their

---

[7] H. Wenschkewitz, "Die Spiritualisierung der Kultusbegriffe Tempel, Priester und Opfer im Neuen Testament," *Angelos* 4 (1932): 138–40.

[8] Philo does not describe many actual rites for priestly purification, he only specifically mentions the rite of the red heifer and the sprinkling of the High Priest with water and ashes on the day of Atonement; cf. Leonhardt, *Jewish Worship*, 264–66. On the importance of ritual purity for Philo, see Leonhardt, *Jewish Worship*, 256–72.

[9] Cf. Leonhardt, *Jewish Worship*, 192–97.

offerings. Thus in connection with the "Basket" (κάρταλος),[10] which later in §215 he calls not a festival but an occasion with "a festive character" (ἑορτώδη τύπον), every farmowner[11] offers baskets filled with a "first-fruit offering of the good harvest" (ἀπαρχὴ τῆς εὐκαρπίας), which is brought to the Temple as commanded by Deut 26:1–11 (216). This offering is accompanied by the recital of a "canticle" (ᾆσμα, 217), Deut 26:5–11, which Philo summarises in §§217–219: the song commemorates the metamorphosis of the Israelites from homeless nomads to owners of rich land, and celebrates the bringing of the "first-fruit offering" (ἀπαρχή) to God their "benefactor" (εὐεργέτης). Philo points out that if the donor himself cannot recite this song the priest does it for him. In *m. Bikkurim* 3:7 this practice is also mentioned: although at first the priest recited the passage only for those who could not do so, there was a change in the law, after which the priest recited the song for everyone; before the change, some people had shied away from bringing their offerings, because of their shame at not being able to recite the text.[12] Philo thus refers here to an actual practice, not mentioned in the Bible, from the time before the change in protocol.

The offerings are consumed by the priests, and Philo mentions the reason for this: "The first-fruit offerings of the nation are their inheritance in return for the acts of their ministry, which are left with them by day and by night" (κλῆροι δ᾽ εἰσὶν αὐτοῖς αἱ παρὰ τοῦ ἔθνους ἀπαρχαὶ ἀντὶ τῶν λειτουργιῶν, ἃς μεθ᾽ ἡμέραν καὶ νύκτωρ ὑπομένουσι, 222). The offerings to the Temple are not the payment for the priests, but their "inheritance"; they are the priestly share in the land of Israel. Philo emphasises that the first-fruits are due to the priests because of their service to the Temple.

The same idea is expressed in *Spec.* 4.96–99, in connection with Deut 18:4: the Jews are commanded to offer "first-fruits" (ἀπαρχαί) from their fields and flocks "as a thanksgiving to God" (ἕνεκα εὐχαριστίας τῆς πρὸς θεόν), as a lesson of "temperance" (σωφροσύνη, 96), and

---

[10] On the "Basket" festival see Heinemann, *Philons Bildung*, 17–18; H. Graetz, "Das Korbfest der Erstlinge bei Philo," *MGWJ* n. F. 9 (1877): 433–42; S. Safrai, *Die Wallfahrt im Zeitalter des Zweiten Tempels* (Neukirchen-Vluyn, 1981), 280–85.

[11] Philo does not mention that this offering is only required of landowners in the Land of Israel.

[12] Reasons given for why some people could not recite the passage: the people could not *read* (J. Neusner, *The Mishnah: A New Translation* [New Haven, 1988], 173–74); the people could not remember the words (Philo); the people did not know Hebrew (so could not recite the midrash). See Heinemann, *Philons Bildung*, 18–19.

in order to achieve "self-restraint, humanity and, most of all, piety" (πρὸς ἐγκράτειαν καὶ πρὸς φιλανθρωπίαν καὶ—τὸ μέγιστον—πρὸς εὐσέβειαν, 97). They are given to the priests "for the sake of their ministry to the Temple, so that they may receive a reward for their service in the holy rites" (τοὺς δ' ἕνεκα τῆς περὶ τὸ ἱερὸν ἁγιστείας, μισθὸν ληψομένους τῶν περὶ τὰς ἱερουργίας ὑπηρεσιῶν, 98).

2.2 The Priests and the Levites

Yet Philo does not describe clearly how the offerings are given and to whom. According to *Virt.* 95, the "tithes" (δεκάται) of all agricultural produce—of grain, wine, oil, wool, and the flocks—are set apart by law "to be offered as first-fruits" (ἀπάρχεσθαι). These offerings are brought "in baskets" (ἐν ταλάροις), and they are handed over "with hymns, composed in honour of God, which are preserved in written records in the sacred books" (σὺν ᾠδαῖς εἰς τὸν θεὸν πεποιημέναις, ἃς ἀναγράπτους στηλιτεύουσιν αἱ ἱερώταται βίβλοι). This is probably another reference to the recital of Deut 26:1–11 at the "Basket" ceremony, already described in *Spec.* 2.215–220.[13] However, in *Virt.* 95, Philo explicitly mentions that the offering must be "given to the officiating clergy" (ἀπάρχεσθαι τοῖς ἱερωμένοις), a reference to texts such as Deut 26:12–15 and Num 18:25–32 on the offering of the tithe to the Levites.[14] By contrast, *Spec.* 2.216 explicitly mentions that the person offering the "Basket" "gives it to the priest" (δίδωσι τῷ ἱερεῖ). Thus, Philo does not distinguish between the different laws for the priests and the Levites.[15]

---

[13] F.H. Colson, in *Philo of Alexandria* (ed. F.H. Colson, G.H. Whitaker, and R. Marcus; 10 vols. and 2 supplements; Cambridge Mass, 1929–1962), 7: 221.

[14] While the LXX uses terms which emphasise the "tenth" (δεκάτη) which is given, Philo almost without differentiation employs terms which emphasise the "gift of the first produce" (ἀπαρχή), which emphasises not the quantity but the quality of the offering, cf. J. Leonhardt, *Jewish Worship*, 190–214, esp. 190–192.

[15] Against S. Belkin, *Philo*, 68–69, who thinks it "highly improbable that Philo is here using the term δεκάτη as synonym for ἀπαρχή" (68), but does not give any reason for that conclusion. Belkin also finds a difference between Philo's reference to the offering and biblical or rabbinic traditions. On the other hand, Belkin points out that Josephus, Tobit, and Judith, like Philo, do not differentiate between the priests and Levites as recipients of the offerings (69–70), which indicates a lack of a "unified system" (70). Many Tannaitic references to the priestly and Levitical dues do not correspond to the biblical text either, but represent the historical development of the first-fruit and tithe laws; thus, Philo is historically accurate for his time (71–76).

The reason for this is that for Philo there is no difference between the priests, as members of the tribe of Levi, and the Levites. The people of Israel are commanded to offer their first fruits (Exod 25:1–2) and dedicate their firstborn (Exod 13:1–2) to God (*Her.* 113–119), and Philo emphasises here that "first" means "best."[16] In *Sacr.* 117–118, Philo points out that the fact that human beings are mortal, a combination of soul and body, makes it necessary to offer a "ransom" (λύτρα, the half-shekel offering according to Exod 30:12) for the soul, "with first-offerings and honors" (ἀπαρχαῖς καὶ τιμαῖς, 117). And in accordance with Num 3:12–13, the Levites are also regarded as a "ransom" (λύτρα), who "in the place of the firstborn" (ἀντὶ τῶν πρωτοτόκων) are selected "as worshippers" (θεραπευτές) of God (118). Thus the Levites represent the dedication of the firstborn of Israel. Note moreover, that since Levi was not Jacob's firstborn, Philo here must again have applied his identification of "first and best" and read the firstborn as the *prime* of Israel, who are given to the service of God. A similar point is made in Philo's discussion of the tithe laws of Leviticus in *Congr.* 89–99. Commenting on Lev 27:30, 32 and the commandment to offer the tithe of all produce to God, Philo reads the offerings of wood and other materials as representing the body (96), and the dedication of the Levites as representing the mind (97–99).[17]

The special status of the priests is also derived from the concept of the land as Israel's shared inheritance. All the other tribes have a share in the land; according to Deut 18:1–2; however, "for the priests" (τοῖς ἱερεῦσι), "God is their inheritance" (τὸν θεὸν…κλῆρον αὐτῶν εἶναι). Following the biblical text, Philo sees the evidence of this in the fact that they may use the first-fruits,[18] which is the "thank-offering" (εὐχαριστία), and in the fact that they perform God's rites (*Spec.* 1.131). The first part of the offering is the gift of the first loaf of bread as mentioned in Num 15:18–20; the first-fruit offerings are the expression of piety (132). This food-offering is performed "as an indelible recollection of God" (τὴν θεοῦ μνήμην ἄλησον, 133) and, due to the great number of Jews bringing the offering, there is no shortage of food among the priests (133).

---

[16] Cf. Leonhardt, *Jewish Worship*, 198–202. In Philo's account of the first-fruit offerings he frequently identifies the first with the best (cf. also *Post.* 96–97).

[17] Cf. Leonhardt, *Jewish Worship*, 201–2.

[18] On the "first-fruits" (ἀπαρχαί) as the Levites' true inheritance, see *Spec.* 2.120 (in connection with the Levitical cities of Lev 25:32–34).

To increase the comfort of the priests, however, the Jews also offer "portions of every other possession" (ἀπὸ τῆς ἄλλης ἁπάσης κτήσεως ἀπάρχεσθαι), a general designation which appears to encompass other offerings, such as those mentioned in Exod 22:29, 34:26; Num 18:13; and Deut 18:4; 26:2-15. Philo's emphasis on the priests' right to enjoy comparative wealth (134) is not derived from the biblical texts about the offerings that are due to them. For Philo their income shows the goodness of God's provision for them, the quality of their lot. The offerings from the people bestow on the priests the status of kings (142),[19] but unlike kings, who have to force their subjects to pay taxes (143), the Jews gladly make these offerings (144):

> Thinking that they are not giving but receiving, they make their contributions at each of the yearly seasons with benedictions and thankfulness, men and women alike, with unbidden zeal, readiness and haste, which is greater than words.

> λαμβάνειν ἀλλ᾽ οὐ διδόναι νομίζοντες, μετ᾽ εὐφημίας καὶ εὐχαριστίας καθ᾽ ἑκάστην τῶν ἐτησίων ὡρῶν ποιοῦνται τὰς εἰσφοράς, ἄνδρες ὁμοῦ καὶ γυναῖκες, αὐτοκελεύστῳ προθυμίᾳ καὶ ἑτοιμότητι καὶ σπουδῇ παντὸς λόγου κρείττονι.

Thus all the offerings to the Temple and its personnel are above all gifts to God, the donor of everything, and ensure the honor of the Temple, while God passes on the benefits of this gift to those who serve Him. Their honor and His honor are linked.

On the basis of Num 18:8-19, Philo emphasises in *Spec.* 1.152 that the priests do not receive the offerings directly, to avoid disrespectful behavior toward the priests who are supported by these offerings:[20]

> But so that none of the givers should reproach the recipients, he commands that the special portions should be brought into the Temple first and that then the priests should take them from there.

> ὑπὲρ δὲ τοῦ μηδένα τῶν διδόντων ὀνειδίζειν τοῖς λαμβάνουσι, κελεύει τὰς ἀπαρχὰς εἰς τὸ ἱερὸν κομίζεσθαι πρότερον, εἶτ᾽ ἐνθένδε τοὺς ἱερεῖς λαμβάνειν.

---

[19] Heinemann, *Philons Bildung*, 36–39, points out the difference between the rabbinic idea of offerings and Philo's view, which comes close to the idea of an income tax, although it is based on the biblical passages concerning the first-fruit offerings and other taxes. Philo does not distinguish between the different offerings, and in the Diaspora the payment of the required sum may *de facto* have seemed like an income tax.

[20] On the reception of the offerings, see J. Leonhardt, *Jewish Worship*, 205–9.

The practice of bringing the offerings to the Temple's storage rooms is mentioned in Mal 3:10 and especially Neh 10:35–39. However, Philo's interpretation of the custom does not correspond to that of the biblical texts.[21] According to Philo, the priests must be kept apart from the people who are offering in order to protect them from the people's contempt. This indicates an attitude of disrespect among some people, because of the clergy's dependence on the contributions of the people.[22] Philo's emphasis on God as both the "inheritance" of the priests (131) and the first recipient of the offerings (152) is a defense of their dignity:

> For it was right that those who had received benefactions in every aspect of their lives offer special portions as thank-offerings, and then that the one who himself does not need anything gave it charitably to those serving and ministering around the Temple with all dignity and honor; for to take the gift coming apparently not from men but from the benefactor of all does not carry shame.

> ἥρμοττε γὰρ θεῷ μὲν τοὺς εὐεργετουμένους ἐν ἅπασι τοῖς κατὰ τὸν βίον χαριστηρίους ἀνάγειν ἀπαρχάς, τὸν δὲ ἅτε μηδενὸς ἐπιδεᾶ τοῖς ἀμφὶ τὸ ἱερὸν ὑπερέταις καὶ λειτουργοῖς χαρίζεσθαι μετὰ σεμνότητος καὶ τιμῆς τῆς ἁπάσης· τὸ γὰρ μὴ παρ' ἀνθρώπων ἀλλὰ παρὰ τοῦ πάντων εὐεργέτου δοκεῖν λαμβάνειν ἀδυσώπητον ἔχει δωρεάν (152).

In light of Josephus' references to malpractice among certain priests, who sent their servants for the tithes directly and thus starved the lower levels of priests (*Ant.* 20.179–181, *Vita* 63, 80), and in light of biblical evidence about priestly improprieties (cf. 1 Sam 8:1–3; Mal 1:6–14), Philo's remarks are plausible despite his repeated emphasis on the offering being voluntary.

To counter potential instances of disrespect, Philo emphasises in *Spec.* 1.153 that the priests could be much wealthier, "if we obeyed the commandments and offered the special portions" (εἰ…ἐπειθαρχοῦμεν

---

[21] O. Eissfeldt, *Erstlinge und Zehnten im Alten Testament: Ein Beitrag zur Geschichte des israelitisch-jüdischen Kultus* (Leipzig, 1917), 136; W. Bunte, *Die Mischna: Maaserot/ Maaser Scheni* (ed. G. Beer et al.; Berlin, 1962), 33–34, mentions 2 Chr 31:5–6 as support for this passage in Philo. However, the biblical text mentions only that the offering was deposited in heaps, and says nothing about the presence or absence of priests.

[22] Belkin, *Philo*, 71, refers in this context to *m. Gittin* 3:7, which says that a layman can withhold a share of his Temple tithes to cancel the debts of individual priests or Levites to him. It is possible that Philo argues against such practices on the grounds that the offerings belong to God in the first place.

τοῖς κελευσθεῖσι καὶ τὰς ἀπαρχὰς ἐποιούμεθα); this appears to indicate that not every Jew offered what was due. But the emphasis that Philo puts on the offerings throughout the whole passage shows that in spite of this potential for conflict, the priests were very popular and well-respected (cf. also *Spec.* 1.78).[23] This respect towards the priests and the importance of the Temple offerings is also shown in *Spec.* 1.279, where Philo claims that even people who break the law offer the set portions of their income—which he therefore condemns as "unholy offerings" (ἀπαρχαὶ...ἀνόσιοι).

The whole people offers the tithes, and those who serve in the Temple offer them in their turn. Commenting on the tithe laws for the Levites (Num 18:26) in *Mut.* 2 and 192, and in greater detail in *Spec.* 1.156–157, in a discussion of the priests' income, Philo does not name the Levites explicitly, but mentions instead second-class priests, Temple attendants (νεωκόροι), who receive the taxes from the people (156). The practice so described reflects the biblical laws concerning the tithe for the Levites in Num 18:21–24, 26–28.[24] Like the nation, the Levites themselves must also "offer portions...to the priests of a higher class" (ἀπάρξασθαι...τοῖς τῆς ἀμείνονος τάξεως ἱερεῦσι) before they may use their own income (157). Philo distinguishes between the offerings to the Levites and the offerings to the priests not by assigning a specific term to each, but by mentioning the recipient, and he never uses the nomenclature of "second" or "third" tithe.[25] Thus Philo is closer to the biblical laws than to later practice, for which the evidence is mixed: Josephus refers to direct (*Ant.* 4.205) and indirect (*Ant.* 4.68) payments to the priests; and in Jdt 11:13–15, Tob 1:6–8, and *Jub.* 13:25–27 and 32:15 the Levites are not referred to at all.[26] Thus here Philo appears to refer to the biblical ideal that was no longer always followed in reality. The fact that in the passages discussed above he does not normally differentiate between priests and Levites

---

[23] For rabbinic accounts of the people's eagerness to pay the tithes, see E.P. Sanders, *Jewish Law from Jesus to the Mishnah* (London, 1990), 303–5.

[24] Cf. M. del Verme, "La 'prima decima' nel Giudaismo del Secondo Tempio," *Henoch* 9 (1987): 5–38, esp. 25–26.

[25] Eissfeldt, *Erstlinge*, 137–38; Bunte, *Maaserot/Maaser Scheni*, 34. Del Verme, "La 'prima decima,'" 26, also comments on the considerably more detailed distinctions mentioned in Josephus, which appear to go beyond mere reference to the biblical passages (27–34).

[26] Cf. W. Horbury, "The Aaronic Priesthood in the Epistle to the Hebrews," *JSNT* 19 (1983): 43–71, 50–51.

when discussing the recipients of the Temple offerings shows that he is aware of contemporary practice.

But not only must the Levites bring an offering. According to *Spec.* 1.255–256,

> the priests also have to offer some special portions to the altar, so that they should not think that they find immunity on account of the services and observances to which they were appointed.

> ἔδει δὲ καὶ τοὺς ἱερεῖς ἀπάρξασθαί τι τῷ βωμῷ, μὴ νομίσαντες ἀσυλίαν εὑρῆσθαι τὰς ὑπηρεσίας καὶ λειτουργίας ἐφ᾽ ὧν ἐτάχθησαν.

Their offering consists of fine flour, presented twice daily and not eaten by anyone (*Spec.* 1.256 on Lev 6:20–22). Thus the priests, like the people, are to offer a share of their income to God, because tithes and offerings are fundamental expressions of the worship tendered by the whole people, priests and laymen alike, not just a means of maintaining the cult.

2.3   *The Priests outside the Temple*

In one of the few passages that depict Sabbath activities in the *proseuchai*,[27] *Hypoth.* 7.13–14, Philo describes the Bible reading as follows: "Some priest who is present, or one of the elders, reads the holy laws to them and interprets them at each point" (τῶν ἱερέων δέ τις ὁ παρὼν ἢ τῶν γερόντων εἷς ἀναγινώσκει τοὺς ἱεροὺς νόμους αὐτοῖς καὶ καθ᾽ ἕκαστον ἐξηγεῖται). This shows that even outside the Temple the priests were respected, and were expected to be able not only to read the Torah (Philo uses the term ἱεροὶ νόμοι for the text, a term which he reserves for the Pentateuch), but also to expound it in a qualified manner. The method of teaching is a monologue, rather than a discussion or disputation, for the audience remains silent (13). The exposition follows the biblical text "point by point" (καθ᾽ ἕκαστον ἐξηγεῖται). True, the priests do not have any particular function reserved for them alone within the Sabbath assemblies. When there is a priest present in the *proseuche*, however, he is given the prominent and fundamental role as reader and interpreter of the Torah.

Thus the priests are depicted here, too, as perfect paradigms of the Jewish people as a whole, for the Sabbath teaching enables every Jew

---

[27] On these activities in general, which mainly comprised Torah reading and exposition, see Leonhardt, *Jewish Worship*, 74–100.

to account for their traditions to outsiders and to teach their families about them (*Hypoth.* 7.14).[28] Again, the priests are the elite representatives of the whole nation.

3. The High Priest[29]

For Philo, the high priest is a particular symbol of the essence of Jewish worship. In *Her.* 82, Philo emphasises that the high priest is defined by his love for God and follows the laws and duties even when he is "outside the area of purification (ἔξω τῶν περιρραντηρίων). Thanksgiving is a fundamental concept that summarises the cult in general, and the duties of the high priest in particular.[30] Thus, in *Ebr.* 129, Philo describes the main duty of the officiating high priest in the Temple as "approaching the altar, to offer sacrifices of thanksgiving for himself or for the public" (τῷ βωμῷ προσιόντα θυσίας ὑπέρ τε τῶν ἰδίων καὶ κοινῶν χαριστηρίους ἀναγαγεῖν). The fact that Philo does not include in this summary statement the high-priestly task of pleading for forgiveness on behalf of the people shows that his emphasis is on the aspect of gratitude, and not on contrition or petition. This summary of high-priestly worship as prayer and thanksgiving is identical to the description of the service of the priests in *Spec.* 1.167. Thus for Philo the high priest represents the entirety of the worship in the Jerusalem Temple.

The high priest's first duty is to pray for the nation, and for Philo this is such a matter of course that he refers to it only in passing. Thus someone who has accidentally caused another's death must remain in the city of refuge only until the death of the high priest, because the high priest is the one "who performs prayers and sacrifices" (εὐχὰς...καὶ θυσίας τελῶν) for the nation and who alone has the power of vengeance for each member thereof (*Spec.* 3.131–132). Josephus describes the office of the high priest in precisely the same terms as the regular priestly service; i.e., the priests serve "for the sacrifices and the prayers on our behalf" (ταῖς θυσίαις καὶ ταῖς ὑπὲρ ἡμῶν

---

[28] Cf. also ibid., 84–86.

[29] Cf. also ibid., 230–33.

[30] Cf. J. Laporte, "Philonic Models of Eucharistia in the Eucharist of Origen," *LTP* 42 (1986): 71–91, esp. 81–83. On the cosmic religion in Philo, see idem, *La doctrine eucharistique chez Philon d'Alexandrie* (Paris, 1972), 150, 153–57.

εὐχαῖς, *Ant.* 3.189).[31] Whether prayers or sacrifices are mentioned first does not indicate a difference in esteem but depends on the context, for in *Ebr.* 129–131 Philo also lists the sacrifices first as one of the two main duties of Aaron, and thus of every high priest:

> For it is his duty either, while serving, to enter the Tabernacle to accomplish the unseen mysteries, or to approach the altar to offer sacrifices for the thanksgiving for private or public blessings.
>
> ἀνάγκη γάρ ἐστιν ἢ ἀρρηφοροῦντα αὐτὸν εἰς τὸν σκηνὴν εἰσιέναι τὰς ἀοράτους ἐπιτελέσοντα τελετὰς ἢ τῷ βωμῷ προσιόντα θυσίας ὑπέρ τε τῶν ἰδίων καὶ κοινῶν χαριστηρίους ἀναγαγεῖν.

The special honor shown to the high priest is awarded not to his person, but to his office as representative of the people. For it is important "that the high priest is thought worthy of the same privilege as the people" (τὸν δ᾽ ἀρχιερέα τῷ ἔθνει τῆς αὐτῆς ἠξιῶσθαί). He is of the same dignity as they are, but conversely they are of the same dignity as he is. His dignity depends on his service to them, because he serves the people in his performance of the rites (*Spec.* 1.229).

In this context it is necessary that the high priest (as holder of the office) be free from sin (*Spec.* 1.189).[32] The high priest's mediating position has long been studied under the aspect of Philo's spiritualization of Jewish rites and offices.[33] Philo, interpreting Lev 16:17, which forbids any human being to be present in the Tent of Meeting when the high priest enters on the Day of Atonement, emphasises that the high priest himself is more than human when entering the holy of holies on that day (*Spec.* 1.116).[34] In the context of explaining the sin-offering, Philo points out that the sin-offering of the high priest does not pertain to himself but is offered, "because he is the servant of the people, giving thanks in common for all in the most holy prayers and in the purest sacrifices" (ἢ διότι τοῦ ἔθνους ὑπηρέτης ἐστὶ τὰς κοινὰς

---

[31] Cf. Horbury, "Aaronic Priesthood," esp. 64–65.

[32] Cf. Wenschkewitz, "Spiritualisierung," 135; Heinemann, *Philons Bildung*, 60.

[33] Wenschkewitz, "Spiritualisierung," 136–38, links the mediating position of the high priest and the Logos with the Stoic ideal of the sage, while J. Laporte, "The High Priest in Philo of Alexandria," *SPhA* 3 (1991): 71–82, esp. 75, connects Philo's interpretation with mysticism: the aim of the mediation is ultimate union with God, "mystical" and not "cosmic."

[34] Philo interprets the biblical passage in the same way in *Her.* 84 and *Somn.* 2.189, 231.

ὑπὲρ ἁπάντων ποιούμενος εὐχαριστίας ἐν ταῖς ἱερωτάταις εὐχαῖς καὶ ἐν ταῖς εὐαγεστάταις θυσίαις, 229).

The high priest represents the people when he performs the Temple service, the ultimate purpose of which is the expression of gratitude to God (Lev 4:3). According to the biblical text, the involuntary sin of the high priest casts the whole nation into sin. Philo inverts the meaning, however: the true high priest does not sin himself; rather, sin is transferred on him through an act of the nation.[35] The Torah, however, offers a "remedy" (θεραπεία)[36] in the sin-offerings (230).

Because of the seriousness of his office, purity is important for the high priest. In *Spec.* 2.163, the high priest represents the nation before God, "when he carries out all the purificatory rites and obeys the divine Laws in body and soul" (ἅπασι τοῖς ἁγνευτικοῖς καθαρσίοις χρώμενον καὶ κατὰ σῶμα καὶ κατὰ ψυχὴν ὑφηγήσεσι νόμων θείων), by overcoming the sensual "pleasures" (ἡδοναί). In this context, Philo mentions the purificatory sprinkling of the high priest with water and ashes on the Day of Atonement before the performance of "the service" (λειτουργία, *Somn.* 1.214).[37] The high priest's immersion in water before the service on the Day of Atonement is mentioned in Lev 16:4, but there is no reference to ashes there. The addition of ashes and the change from immersion to sprinkling was probably customary at Philo's time and may have resulted from the influence of the rite of the red heifer, which purified one before entry into the sanctuary after contracting corpse impurity (Numbers 19), and which was particularly important for people from the Diaspora.[38]

The ashes are important for Philo's argument. For Philo, the ashes represent the mortal human being and balance the tunic of the high priest, which represents the universe (214). This reflects the basic structure of the visible and invisible creation, in which the high priest is the representative of the true human being, who in turn represents the Logos (215). Thus the ashes and the garb remind the high priest

---

[35] On the sinlessness of the high priest, see R.A. Stewart, "The Sinless High-Priest," *NTS* 14 (1967–1968): 126–35, esp. 115; Heinemann, *Philons Bildung*, 60; Belkin, *Philo*, 79–80.

[36] θεραπεία is a *Wortspiel*; referring to the *healing* of an illness: here it is both the cure for sin, and the *act of worship*—the rite which frees from sin.

[37] On this rite in Philo, see Leonhardt, *Jewish Worship*, 264–66.

[38] See F.H. Colson, *Philo*, V, 410–411 and 604 on the basis of Heb 9:13 and Num 19:9; W. Horbury, "The Aaronic Priesthood," 51, on the basis of *m. Yoma* 1:1 and *m. Parah* 3:1, which refer to the rite of the red heifer, in which ashes are involved.

that he is the mediator between humankind and the invisible, immaterial and ideal creation, in the service of the Creator. Philo's whole argument would have collapsed if he had merely invented the addition of the ashes and his readers had not recognised the rite.[39]

The high priest's prayers for the nation occur especially on the Day of Atonement, when he enters the inner sanctum of the Temple. In Philo's version of Agrippa's letter to Gaius, the petitionary aspect is emphasised, and and the prayer itself is expanded into a universal petition (*Legat.* 306). Agrippa pleads against the plan to set up Gaius' statue in the inner sanctum,

> into which the high priest enters once a year only, on the event called the Fast, offering incense and praying according to the ancestral custom for a crop of blessings, prosperity and peace for all human beings.
>
> εἰς ἃ ἅπαξ τοῦ ἐνιαυτοῦ ὁ μέγας ἱερεὺς εἰσέρχεται τῇ νηστείᾳ λεγομένῃ μόνον ἐπιθυμιάσων καὶ κατὰ τὰ πάτρια εὐξόμενος φορὰν ἀγαθῶν εὐετηρίαν τε καὶ εἰρήνην ἅπασιν ἀνθρώποις.

But it is not only in an apologetic context that Philo sees the high priest as representative of humankind before God. The importance of the figure of the high priest lends itself to allegorical interpretation. In *Somn.* 1.214–15, Philo describes and interprets the high priest's breastplate:

> For there are, as it seems, two Temples of God: the one is this cosmos, in which the firstborn divine Logos is also high priest; the other is the rational soul, whose priest is the true man, whose perceptible image is the one who offers the traditional prayers and sacrifices.
>
> δύο γάρ, ὡς ἔοικεν, ἱερὰ θεοῦ, ἓν μὲν ὅδε ὁ κόσμος, ἐν ᾧ καὶ ἀρχιερεὺς ὁ πρωτόγονος αὐτοῦ θεῖος λόγος, ἕτερον δὲ λογικὴ ψυχή, ἧς ἱερεὺς ὁ πρὸς ἀλήθειαν ἄνθρωπος, οὗ μίμημα αἰσθητὸν ὁ τὰς πατρίους εὐχὰς καὶ θυσίας ἐπιτελῶν ἐστιν.[40]

The prayers and sacrifices conducted by the earthly high priest symbolise human worship, the rational soul's veneration of the true God. Thus these rites carry humanity's prayers before the transcendent God and they mirror the immaterial world of ideas to the visible world. The high priest can do this because he is the visible

---

[39] Against Heinemann, *Philons Bildung*, 25–26, who calls this just one of the "Ungenauigkeiten einer hübschen Deutung zuliebe."

[40] On the details of the two Temples, see Leonhardt, *Jewish Worship*, 230–33.

representative of the "true man," while the heavenly Logos is the invisible representative of the material world. Thus the high priest is the earthly counterpart of the heavenly Logos, the one representing the idea of the true man to the material world, the other representing the material world in the world of ideas.

A slightly different approach is taken in *Mos.* 2.133. Here it is the high priest who represents creation vis-à-vis its maker: the high priest's robes symbolise the whole created universe, "when he enters to offer the ancestral prayers and sacrifices" (ὅταν εἰσίη τὰς πατρίους εὐχάς τε καὶ θυσίας ποιησόμενος). These prayers and sacrifices are the core of the high priest's worship. Not even the death of a relative is allowed to interfere with this crucial duty, so that the high priest is exempt from mourning in order to be able to offer "the prayers and sacrifices" (εὐχαὶ καὶ θυσίαι) for the nation at the proper times (*Spec.* 1.113).

In the same way the dress of the high priest symbolises all of creation in *Spec.* 1.97 (93–96). The other nations' priests perform rites only for their own people:

> The high priest of the Jews, however, does not only offer prayers and thanksgiving for the whole human race, but also for the parts of nature, earth, water, air and fire, because he regards the world, as in truth it is, as his home country, for which he is accustomed to propitiate the Sovereign with supplications and entreaties, imploring Him to give His creature a share of his good and merciful nature.

> ὁ δὲ τῶν Ἰουδαίων ἀρχιερεὺς οὐ μόνον ὑπὲρ ἅπαντος ἀνθρώπων γένους ἀλλὰ καὶ ὑπὲρ τῶν τῆς φύσεως μερῶν, γῆς, ὕδατος, ἀέρος, πυρός, τάς τε εὐχὰς καὶ τὰς εὐχαριστίας ποιεῖται, τὸν κόσμον, ὅπερ ἐστὶ ταῖς ἀληθείαις, ἑαυτοῦ πατρίδα εἶναι νομίζων, ὑπὲρ ἧς ἱκεσίας καὶ λιταῖς εἴωθεν ἐξευμενίζεσθαι τὸν ἡγεμόνα ποτνιώμενος τῆς ἐπιεικοῦς καὶ ἵλεω φύσεως αὐτοῦ μεταδιδόναι τῷ γεγομένῳ.

Here, the service of the high priest is summarised as a plea to God to perfect His creation in goodness and mercy. The same ideal, of the attainment of virtue by all the nations, is expressed as the goal of the Jews' prayers in *Virt.* 120. In *Spec.* 1.97, the universal relevance of the high priest's office lies in the fact that the Jewish God is not just a national God but the Creator of the universe, symbolised by the four elements.

The content of these prayers is expressed in a different way in *Praem.* 56. In a description of Moses' "position as chief priest" (ἀρχιεροσύνη) Philo writes that as the duty of this office:

he will worship the Being, and offer up thanksgiving for those subjects who do well; and if they have gone astray, conciliating, he offers prayers and supplications.

θεραπεύσει τὸ ὂν καὶ τὰς ὑπὲρ τῶν ὑπηκόων κατορθούντων μὲν εὐχαριστίας, εἰ δὲ διαμαρτάνοιεν, εὐχὰς καὶ ἱκεσίας ἱλασκόμενος ποιήσεται.

Here, thanksgiving and supplication are seen as the two duties of the high priest; they are the two different sides of his speech to God. On the basis of *Spec.* 1.97 and *Virt.* 120, it may be assumed that for Philo the success or failure of the people's progress *in virtue* is the object of the high-priestly prayer.

Altogether the high priest is the link between the people and God not only in the performance of sacrificial worship but also as representative, guide, and guardian of their virtue.

4. The People as Priests

4.1 *Passover*

Philo's peculiar mixture of universal and particular interpretations of Jewish rites leads him to develop in explicit ways the notion of the priestly status of the Jewish people in its relationship with God, not as a general principle (Exod 19:6), but rather in the interpretation of specific rites. Thus in the cultic calendar in *Spec.* 2.41, discussing the fourth "festival" (ἑορτή), the "Crossing-festival" (τὰ διαβατήρια),[41] or "Passover" (Πάσχα, 145–148), he emphasises that, on this occasion, the lay-people have the status and purity of priests and can offer "sacrifices" (θυσίαι) in the priests' stead (145). The reason is that the festival celebrates the Exodus, and during the Exodus, in Philo's reading, the people were so exhilarated by their freedom from animal worship and captivity that they could not wait for the appointment of priests for their sacrifices. This practice was sanctioned and institutionalised later through the laws regulating the annual celebration of the event (146). It is noteworthy that the people's priestly status is not permanent; the Passover may be a recurring ritual but it only gives the people a tem-

---

[41] On the Greek senses of this term and alternative Greek translations for the Passover, see Heinemann, *Philons Bildung*, 120. On Passover in Philo, see Leonhardt, *Jewish Worship*, 29–36.

porary priestly status—it does not turn them into priests. The difference is never dissolved completely.[42]

The people's priestly status depends on their spiritual participation in priestly purity. Basing himself on the Greek term τὰ διαβατήρια, which is the customary sacrifice offered when crossing borders (41), Philo adds an "allegorical" (πρὸς ἀλληγορίαν) interpretation of the Passover, calling it "the purification of the soul" (ψυχῆς κάθαρσις) and "the crossing from the passions" (τῶν παθῶν διάβασις, 147).[43]

This internal purification has external consequences: For on the day of the Passover, every house "is invested with the appearance and semblance of a temple" (σχῆμα ἱεροῦ καὶ σεμνότητα περιβέβληται): as in the Temple, "the victim is slaughtered and prepared for the feast fitting for the occasion" (τοῦ σφαγιασθέντος ἱερείου πρὸς τὴν ἁρμόττουσαν εὐωχίαν εὐτρεπιζομένου), the guests are cleansed "by purificatory lustrations" (ἁγνευτικοῖς περιρραντηρίοις) and the rites are performed "with prayers and hymns" (μετ᾽ εὐχῶν τε καὶ ὕμνων, Spec. 2.148). These hymns in connection with the Passover (also mentioned, for example, in Matt 26:30 and Mark 14:26) could refer to the recitation of the Hallel.[44] But even if Philo's language does not imply a specific liturgy for the day, the term ὕμνοι is commonly used by Philo for the Psalms,[45] the use of which in the context of sacrifice constitutes another parallel to the practices of the Temple.

Passover was celebrated among the Jews everywhere, but the question remains as to whether Philo attests to a practice of Passover sacrifices outside the Temple. Philo is adamant that there is only one place where God allows sacrifices (e.g. Somn. 1.61–67). There can be little doubt that Philo's Passover account proves the practice of slaughtering and eating lamb in the Diaspora on the Passover, but even in this passage with its direct parallel between the house and the Temple he

---

[42] This distinction is important in the context of conceptions of zeal and priesthood. Cf. G. Aran's contribution to this volume.

[43] The same psychological interpretation can be found in Leg. 3.165.

[44] Cf. S. Stein, "The Influence of Symposia Literature on the Literary Form of the Pesah Haggadah," in Essays in Greco-Roman and Related Talmudic Literature (ed. H.A. Fischel; New York, 1977), 198–229, esp. 206; repr. of JJS 8 (1957): 13–44; S. Safrai, "Jerusalem in the Halacha of the Second Temple Period," in The Centrality of Jerusalem: Historical Perspectives (ed. M. Poorthuis and C. Safrai; Kampen, 1996), 94–113, esp. 96–97; D.K. Falk, Daily, Sabbath and Festival Prayers in the Dead Sea Scrolls (Leiden, 1998), esp. 195–97.

[45] Cf. Leonhardt, Jewish Worship, 142–47.

refrains from using the term θυσία for this practice,[46] except in his general introduction and description of the time of the Exodus itself in *Spec. Leg.* 2.145–146. In every reference to contemporary practice Philo takes great pains not to introduce the term "sacrifice." This corresponds to what is known from rabbinic sources: As if by way of extension of the Temple precinct, it was permitted to eat the Passover lamb in the private houses of Jerusalem;[47] according to *m. Pesaḥim* 4:4 it was permissible to eat the Passover lamb roasted even outside Jerusalem, if that was the local custom;[48] so Philo's account is still within the limits of these stipulations. In contrast, *m. Beṣa* 2:7 and other rabbinic texts attest to the fact that the rabbinic tradition objected to those local customs which made the Passover lamb outside Jerusalem appear too much like the Passover sacrifice in the Temple and blurred the difference between a meal and a sacrifice.[49] Philo thus seems a borderline case, avoiding the precise terminology but nevertheless using the metaphor of sacrifice.

The same interpretation is given to the Passover in *Mos.* 2.222–233: the "Pascha" (Πάσχα), the "crossing, a public festival" (τὰ διαβατήρια, δημοφανὴς ἑορτή),

> on which the laymen do not bring the victims to the altar while the priests sacrifice them, but the law commands that the whole nation officiate, each person bringing the sacrifices for himself according to his part and dealing with them with his own hands.

> ἐν ᾗ οὐχ οἱ μὲν ἰδῶται προσάγουσι τῷ βωμῷ τὰ ἱερεῖα, θύουσι δ᾽ οἱ ἱερεῖς, ἀλλὰ νόμου προστάξει σύμπαν τὸ ἔθνος ἱερᾶται, τῶν κατὰ μέρος ἑκάστου τὰς ὑπὲρ αὑτοῦ θυσίας ἀνάγοντός τε καὶ χειρουργοῦντος.

The custom is so popular that those who cannot perform the sacrifices because of corpse impurity complain because they are not allowed "to

---

[46] Against E.P. Sanders, *Judaism: Practice and Belief, 63 BCE–55 CE* (London, 1992), 133–34. For a criticism of Sanders, see A. Mendelson, "'Did Philo Say the Shema?' and Other Reflections on E.P. Sanders' *Judaism: Practice and Belief*," *SPhA* 6 (1994): 160–70, esp. 163–65. The Diaspora practice of assembling for Passover meals is also attested by Josephus *Ant.* 14.216, cf. E. Schürer, *The History of the Jewish People in the Age of Jesus Christ (175 BCE–135 CE)* (ed. G. Vermes et al.; 3 vols.; rev. English ed.; Edinburgh, 1973–1986), 3.1: 144–45.

[47] Safrai, "Jerusalem in the Halacha of the Second Temple Period," 94–113, esp. 97. Cf. also idem, *Wallfahrt*, 220–21.

[48] G.F. Moore, *Judaism in the First Centuries of the Christian Era: The Age of the Tannaim* (Cambridge, Mass., 1927–1930), 2: 41.

[49] Ibid.

purify and to besprinkle" themselves (καθάρασθαι καὶ περιρράνασθαι, 225) and participate in the sacrifices. As in *Spec.* 2.145–148, the layman's priestly status on that day is determined by his ability to purify himself and perform the sacrifice. While this passage, too, could imply the conducting of sacrifices in the Diaspora, Philo nowhere says explicitly that the said sacrifices occur outside the Temple.[50] Philo is here rendering the biblical texts on Passover in the context of a biography of Moses. He refers to the time of the Exodus—when the Temple did not yet exist and the whole nation could settle in the vicinity of the Tabernacle.[51] At the end of the passage Philo applies the Numbers text to the pilgrimage of his time (*Mos.* 232–233),[52] but the point here is precisely that those who live too far away and miss the Passover date are allowed to celebrate one month later *in Jerusalem*.

There is even more explicit evidence that Philo is aware of the difference between the situation as described in the Pentateuch and that of his time: In his interpretation of Exod 12:6b in *QE* 1.10, Philo points out that the people sacrifice because the Levites and the priests had not yet been elected, and there was no Temple. Thus, his emphatic claim that the Passover transfers responsibility for worship to every Jew does not provide evidence for sacrifices outside the Temple.

When Philo describes the Passover he uses the term "priest" as a metaphor, based on the purity, virtue and religious zeal common both to the people celebrating the Passover and to the priests who served in the Temple. In the celebration of the festival rites the people can participate in the perfection of the priests, but he does not identify the two in actual practice.

4.2 Dedication

There is a way for the layperson to dedicate his or her life fully to the divine service in a manner similar to the priests, and this is the Nazirite vow, ἡ μεγάλη εὐχή. As the Nazirite vow was normally not

---

[50] Cf. Heinemann, *Philons Bildung*, 33–34; A. Mendelson, *Philo's Jewish Identity* (Atlanta, 1988), 64; E.P. Sanders, *Judaism: Practice and Belief*, 137.

[51] Cf. especially L. Treitel, "Der Nomos, insonderheit Sabbat und Feste, in philonischer Beleuchtung, an der Hand von Philos Schrift De Septenario," in *MGWJ* 47/n. F. 11 (1903): 214–31, 317–21, 390–417, 490–514, esp. 415, but also B.M. Bokser, *The Origins of the Seder: The Passover Rite and Early Rabbinic Judaism* (Berkeley, 1984), 23.

[52] B.M. Bokser, *The Origins of the Seder*, 23–24.

taken for a lifetime, this act of dedication is temporary—similar to the celebration of the Passover, but longer lasting.

Those who take this vow give themselves as offerings to God (*Somn.* 1.252–253).[53] The priestly parallels are obvious in Philo's long discussion of the "great vow" (εὐχὴ μεγάλη) in *Spec.* 1.247–254 on Num 6:1–12. Philo does not count the Nazarite vow among the other oaths and vows, but among the sacrifices (247), because the people who make this vow "dedicate and consecrate themselves, showing indescribable piety and superiority of god-loving intention" (αὐτοὺς ἀνατιθέασι καὶ καθιεροῦσιν, ἄλεκτον ἐπιδεικνύμενοι ὁσιότητα καὶ ὑπερβολήν τινα γνώμης φιλοθέου, 248).[54] They must not drink wine and intoxicating drinks (Num 6:3–4) "because of the demolition of reason" (ἐπὶ καθαιρέσει λογισμοῦ, 249). By not cutting their hair they express the purity of their intentions (Num 6:5), "giving a visible symbol to those who watch that he does not cheat against the custom of the vow" (σύμβολον ἐναργὲς τοῖς ὁρῶσιν παρέχοντα τοῦ μὴ παρακόπτειν τὸ νόμισμα τῆς εὐχῆς); and they have no contact with the dead, not even those of their family (Num 6:6–7), in order to demonstrate visibly the superior strength of their "piety" (εὐσέβεια), cherishing their relationship with God above all others (250). Thus—apart from the cutting of the hair—all aspects of the vow have parallels in Philo's description of priestly service: purity, abstention, the giving of sacrifices (in the vow, this is the sacrifice of the self), and exclusive relationship with God (cf. Philo's description of the zeal of the Levites). The idea of the Nazirite vow as a self-offering can also be found in Josephus *Ant.* 4.72, and the priestly reading of the Nazirite vow can be traced back even to the biblical text.[55]

Apart from categorizing the Nazirite vow as a sacrifice, as mentioned above, Philo also calls the Nazirite vow the "first-fruit offering" (ἀπαρχή) of the laity. Here, laypersons can dedicate themselves to God

---

[53] Leonhardt, *Jewish Worship*, 117–21.

[54] On the contrast between Philo's enthusiasm for the Nazirite vow as self-offering and the rabbis' sceptical attitude towards it, see Heinemann *Philons Bildung*, 91.

[55] Cf. Heinemann, *Philons Bildung*, 92. On the solid support for these ideas of self-offering and the priestly status of the Nazir from biblical sources, see M. Boertien, *Die Mischna...Berakot* (ed. G. Beer et al.; Gießen, 1912), 16, 21–25; for an overview of the interpretation of the vow as self-offering and the priestly status of the Nazir from the biblical texts to the destruction of the Temple, see E. Diamond, "An Israelite Self-Offering in the Priestly Code: A New Perspective of the Nazirite," *JQR* 88 (1997): 1–18.

and become like priests. Consequently, after the Nazirite vow, Philo describes the first-fruit offerings of the priests (255), of which a share was offered as "sacrifice" (θυσία) by burning it completely so that it could not be eaten, for "every sacrifice of the priests must be wholly burnt" (πᾶσαν θυσίαν ἱερέως ὁλόκαυτον εἶναι, 256). Thus, as in the celebration of the Passover, the performance of a certain rite, combined with the practice of abstention and virtue, endows the people with a temporary priestly status. Again, priesthood is used as a metaphor for the purity and perfection of the worshipper. This can also be seen in the allegorical interpretation of the Nazirite vow. The fact that the Nazir (Num 6:2) and the priest on duty (Lev 10:9) both abstain from wine is emphasised in *Ebr.* 2, where both are praised as unusual examples of moderation.

A stronger link between moderation and priesthood is made in *Ebr.* 125–126 in Philo's interpretation of Exod 32:19, which forbids the priests to drink wine altogether. Philo begins with the admonition: "Pray to God, never to become a leader in wine" (εὔχου . . . τῷ θεῷ μηδέποτε ἔξαρχος οἴνου γενέσθαι, 125). The lack of moderation in excessive consumption of wine is seen as idolatry, leading to "stupidity and folly" (ἀπαιδευσία καὶ ἀφροσύνη, 125). Yet if someone does pray for moderation in wine drinking in the above-mentioned way this enables even an ordinary layman to receive the "priesthood" (ἱερουσύνην, 126). In a slightly un-Aristotelian piece of logic Philo concludes that, since priests abstain from wine, someone who abstains from wine is a priest. This skewed way of arguing clearly shows the metaphorical weight of "priesthood" in this context. In this allegorical interpretation of the Torah, Philo finds that by practicing those virtues towards which the rite is aiming—moderation and self-control—the truth behind the rite is also attainable: i.e., moral priesthood. As this interpretation is found in Philo's allegorical commentary and not in his exposition of the Special Laws, it does not imply that Philo abrogates the ritual difference between the priests and the laypeople; but it does show that the wise person also has access to the allegorical benefits of priesthood. It is even likely that *Ebr.* 125 must be read in the context of *Ebr.* 2, and that Philo had the Nazirite vow in mind when writing about moderation and priesthood in this way, so that the said priestly status is once more tied to the observance of a rite.

Thus for Philo the actual observance of certain Jewish rites confers a temporary priestly status on the worshipper. "Priesthood" here is a metaphor for the worshipper's zeal, virtue and purity, but that does not mean that the ordinary Jew could ever take a priest's place in the Temple service.

4.3   The Jews as Priests of the World

But not even a specific act of dedication is needed for the Jewish people to have the function of priests. In *Spec.* 2.162–175 Philo describes the Sheaf-offering as follows (162):[56]

> for this [the Sheaf] is brought to the altar as a first-fruit offering of the land, which has been given to the people to dwell in, and of the whole world, so that it should be the first-fruit offering of the people in particular and of the whole human race in general.

> τοῦτο γὰρ ἀπαρχὴ προσάγεται τῷ βωμῷ καὶ τῆς χώρας, ἣν ἔλαχε τὸ ἔθνος οἰκεῖν, καὶ τῆς συμπάσης γῆς, ὡς εἶναι τὴν ἀπαρχὴν καὶ τοῦ ἔθνους ἰδίαν καὶ ὑπὲρ ἅπαντος ἀνθρώπων γένους κοινήν.

The Jewish nation acts as the "priest" (ἱερεύς) of humankind, checking the excesses of body and soul (163). Again the aspect of virtue is important for the function of a priest: the Jews are priests because they read the Torah, which guides them in a life of virtue and keeps them to the veneration of the one God (164–165). They undo the mistakes of the other nations as they focus on "the worship of the Uncreated and Eternal only" (τοῦ δ' ἀγενήτου καὶ αἰδίου μόνον τὴν θεραπείαν,[57] 166). Philo therefore cannot imagine why the Jews are accused of being inhumane, when they serve humanity by "offering their prayers, festivals and first-fruit offerings for the whole human race" (εὐχὰς καὶ ἑορτὰς καὶ ἀπαρχὰς ὑπὲρ τοῦ κοινοῦ γένος τῶν ἀνθρώπων ἐπιτελεῖν, 167).

On this festival the Jews "give thanks" (εὐχαριστοῦσι) for the whole human race (*Spec.* 2.168) and for themselves. Like the service of the priests and the high priest, their worship is summarised as thanksgiving. The land and the possessions which they have been able to acquire in many countries and from which they can offer these "first-fruits" (ἀπαρχαί, 168) are only the outward signs of their blessing. The Jews also celebrate the first-fruits out of gratitude for their good and fertile

---

[56] On the Sheaf, see Leonhardt, *Jewish Worship*, 38–39.

[57] The more general term θεραπεία is chosen, instead of the specific Jewish term λατρεία, because Jewish worship is compared here with the worship of the nations.

land (169) and in obedience to the lesson which they learned from the negative fate of their predecessors in the land (170).[58]

Referring to the nation as a whole, not to individual commitments, Philo calls the Jews as a whole "priests" only in relation to humankind. This general idea of the priesthood of the people is the application of Exod 19:6 with its idea of Israel as a "priestly kingdom and a holy nation" versus the other nations. He uses the metaphor of the priesthood in a way similar to that of the biblical passage as an expression of the election of the Jews from among the nations, and of their special privilege and responsibility. The idea contained in this verse, however, does not level the distinction between priesthood and laity within the Jewish people.

5. Conclusion

Thus the high priest is at the top of Philo's human hierarchy in standing before God: he represents the nation and the creation before God. The priests are the first of the nation in the service of the one God, their share is the Temple service, and nobody can ever replace them in this context. They serve the people by offering sacrifices for and on behalf of them. The people can advance in the service of God, but they can only do so by performing their particular religious duties. They do *not* have a share in the Temple service, but if they are dedicated to the service of God, they can become metaphorical priests, aiming to be first in the service of God. By being the chosen nation of God, striving to do God's will, and practising virtue, the Jewish people as a whole serve as priests for the world, representing the virtue of God to the nations and bringing to God the offerings due to the Creator of all, offerings that the pagans do not bring. Thus, the priestly office of the Jewish people is tied to the observance of the Torah. Like the priests, the Jews are born

---

[58] Y.F. Baer has argued that Philo's description of the harvest of the *Omer* sheaves and their universal importance has strong parallels to the universal relevance attributed to similar rites in the Eleusinian mysteries. If Baer is correct— and Philo's responses to pagan accusations in the passage certainly indicate that he is presenting apologetic arguments for Judaism—Philo consciously presents Judaism as an alternative to one of the most popular pagan cults of his time. Cf. Y.F. Baer, "Harvesting the Omer," *Zion* 44 = *Yitzhak F. Baer Memorial Volume* (1979): 1–13, esp. 8–11 (in Hebrew).

to their inheritance. By doing their duty in their particular place each serves God's will.

The priests thus play an essential part in Philo's understanding of Jewish worship. They are present at every level, even in the synagogue. They represent the best of the Jewish people, dedicated to the service of the one true God. Nowhere does Philo separate the universal relevance of the Temple from the actual worship in it. However, he can also read the priesthood in a metaphorical way: if the priests represent the people at their purest, the people, if they are pure, can be priests. And as the recipients of God's particular revelation, the Torah, His intention for human behavior, the Jewish people is particularly well-equipped to be virtuous. Philo may use the metaphor of the priests and their service extensively in his allegories, but he never loses sight of literal observance. Although he can interpret the Jewish people as priests, their priesthood is tied to their perfect worship in mind and body, in allegory and actual practice, and this is tied to the physical Temple.[59] To borrow the terminology of Ori Schwarz in his contribution to this volume, for Philo the Temple serves as a "continuity mechanism: a constant material expression"[60] which guarantees the continuity of the people and their relationship with their community and with God. In this sense the Passover celebration, the Nazirite vow, and coming together in the synagogue all served, in a way similar to the techniques described by Schwarz, to bridge the distance to the Temple and create a "continuum," not a "dichotomy of existence and absence" in and apart from the Temple, but "a whole spectrum of techniques that offer indirect and mediated relations to its spatiality."[61] There are no additional rites or customs invented to turn laypeople

---

[59] On the importance of the physical Temple, see my above-mentioned article, "Jewish Worship and Universal Identity in Philo." *Cher.* 99–100, which rejects the idea of a material temple as worthy of containing God, cannot be taken as indicating that Philo rejected the physical Temple: The passage is in the allegorical commentary on the Bible, which does not concern itself with external practices but with the virtue of the soul. In the overall context of *Cher.* 94–100, Philo does *not* write about the Jerusalem Temple; he does not even write about the Jews, but rather about pagan festivals, their debauchery, and their failure to improve of the soul. This failure he contrasts to the progress of the soul of the virtuous person, who does not build rich temples and offer expensive sacrifices, but focuses instead on virtue and purity. Thus, here he echoes the prophetic criticism of pagan temples and does not imply any criticism of the Jewish sanctuary.

[60] See above, "Place beyond Place," 115.

[61] Ibid., 126.

into priests. They themselves serve as such by observing the Torah and practising virtue.

Thus, the evidence and examples supplied by Philo indicate that the Temple was a focal point of his religion. For Philo, the Temple and the worship conducted there was for Judaism what the heart is for the human body: its beating is what keeps the blood flowing and the person alive, even if one does not check on it every day. Accordingly, the loss of the Temple would have shaken Philo's conception of Jewish worship to the same extent that it did for those who witnessed it.

SANCTITY AND THE ATTITUDE TOWARDS THE TEMPLE IN HELLENISTIC JUDAISM

Noah Hacham

Diaspora Jews differed from the Jews of the Land of Israel in their affinity to the Temple. While the latter were more closely connected to the Temple, Diaspora Jews, physically distanced from it, expanded and stressed other manifestations of religiosity, apart from those linked with the site of the Temple; whether we consider this an imitation or a substitute, they consolidated other patterns of religiosity and worship of God.

In the following, I will discuss one limited aspect of this extensive topic—the manifestations of sanctity in the Second and Third Books of Maccabees and the attitudes towards the Temple that emerge from these two books. I will strive to demonstrate that though both books were largely or completely authored in the Diaspora, a significant difference between them is apparent in their respective treatments of the concept of sanctity and their attitudes to the Temple. I will also seek to show that 3 Maccabees presents, in this context, an emphatically critical diasporan position regarding the Jerusalem Temple—a position that has not been recognized by and thus has not been fully accepted in scholarly research—while 2 Maccabees presents a substantially more moderate position. The article is therefore divided into two parts: in the first part I will examine the occurrence of the concepts of sanctity in the two books, and in the second I will examine 3 Maccabees' viewpoints concerning the Temple and compare them with those of 2 Maccabees.

I

An examination of the occurrences of the word ἅγιος in 2 and 3 Maccabees produces interesting results.[1] An obvious difference between

---

[1] Occurrences of ἅγιος in 2 Maccabees relating to a place: 1:7, 12, 29; 2:18; 3:1; 5:15; 8:17; 9:14, 16; 13:10; 14:3, 31; 15:14, 32 (note that the word ἁγιωσύνη, too,

the objects described as sacred in the two books is apparent. In 3 Maccabees, the majority of uses of the word "sacred" refer to God: of fourteen occurrences nine relate to God while the remaining five refer to sacred vestments, the people, or any sacred site. In contrast, in 2 Maccabees, of twenty-two occurrences of the word, fourteen relate to a place: the Holy Land, the Holy City, or the Temple itself and its furnishings (and once to the sacrifices as well). Only twice is God referred to as holy, and only once are the people described as a Holy People by the use of the term ἅγιος.

A review of the occurrences of ἅγιος in a number of other contemporary books is useful in illustrating the significance of this difference. The word appears many times in 1 Maccabees, almost always in relation to the Temple. In Judith use of the word is minimal, but it seems that the context of all the occurrences is supplied by the Temple and its sacrificial cult. In contrast, in the *Letter of Aristeas* the word appears three times: to characterize the Torah (45), the letters with which the name of God was inscribed on the headplate (98), and the Temple's vessels and its furnishings (99).

The picture is more ambiguous with regard to cognate verbs related to ἅγιος. The verb ἁγιάζω appears in 2 Maccabees once in relation to the sanctity of the Patriarchs (1:25), and three times in 3 Maccabees: twice referring to a site (2:9, 16) and the third time referring to the people (6:3). The verb καθαγιάζω appears three times in 2 Maccabees: twice in relation to a site (2:8; 15:18), and once in relation to the people (1:26). This verb does not appear at all in 3 Maccabees. These small and apparently haphazard figures make no contribution to our understanding of the concepts of sanctity in the two books.

It does seem, however, that the data concerning ἅγιος allow a clearer picture to emerge: in the eyes of the author of 2 Maccabees sanctity is attributable to a place—that place being the Land of Israel, mainly Jerusalem and the Temple. In contrast, the author of 3 Maccabees attaches little importance to place-related sanctity; the city is described as holy only once (6:5), and the location of the Temple is referred to as holy only in the prayer of the high priest in Jerusalem (2:14). Sanctity pertains primarily to God and is not restricted to a physical location.

---

which appears once in 2 Maccabees, relates to a place [3:12]); relating to the people: 15:24; relating to God: 6:30; 14:36; to time: 5:25; to the Torah: 6:23, 28; to an object: 15:16, 17. Occurrences of ἅγιος in 3 Maccabees relating to God: 2:2, 13, 21; 5:13; 6:1, 18, 29; 7:10, 16; relating to the people: 2:6; 6:9 (mss); to a place: 2:14; 6:5; to an object: 1:16 (mss).

Moreover, although God's sanctity is mentioned three times in the part of the story occurring in Jerusalem—twice in Simon's prayer (2:2, 13) and once more in the verse following the prayer (2:21), which depicts God as listening to the prayer—it is not said that the sanctity was manifested in Jerusalem. In Egypt, in contrast, where it was manifested, God's sanctity is mentioned four or five times.

What is the cause of the dissimilarity between the two books? One hypothesis might suggest that it is simply the difference between the topics of the narratives of the two books that accounts for the disparity in the treatment of the concept of sanctity. In other words: 2 Maccabees describes the events surrounding the Hasmonean revolt, the desecration of the Temple and its subsequent reconsecration, and the wars of Judas Maccabeus, thereby rendering the multiplicity of references to the Temple and its description as sacred nearly inevitable, while the main locus of the events described in 3 Maccabees, on the other hand, is Egypt. That allows the author to dispense with multiple references to the Temple and thus he is not compelled to describe its sanctity. According to that hypothesis, this matter should be viewed merely as a technical detail and not as an expression of an essential difference between the two authors.

This explanation, however, appears overly simplistic and unpersuasive, for several reasons. First, 3 Maccabees, too, describes an attempt to inflict severe damage on the Temple, but nevertheless its description of that episode does not emphasize the sanctity of the Temple. Second, a comparison with other books demonstrates that emphasis upon the holiness of the Temple is not dependent on the recounted content. This works both ways. On the one hand, although the story of Judith, for example, does not deal with a direct threat to the Temple, the author deemed it appropriate to incorporate references to the Temple's sanctity several times throughout the book (Jdt 4:12, 13; 8:21, 24; 9:8; 16:20). On the other hand, although the *Letter of Aristeas* discusses the Temple and its rites and the high priest at length (83–99), it places no special emphasis on their sanctity. So it appears that even an author who focuses on the Temple is not required to stress its sanctity, just as emphasis on the sanctity of the Temple site can be incorporated into narratives not themselves centered on the Temple. Authors have a large measure of sovereignty. We must not content ourselves, therefore, with a "technical" explanation maintaining that it is only the difference between the stories they had to tell that led the author of 2 Maccabees to elaborate on the sanctity of the site while the author of 3 Maccabees did not.

It seems to me that the premise underlying the question of the source of the difference between these two diasporan books should be reevaluated. At the crux of this question is the assumption that a diasporan author cannot be expected to attach tremendous value to place-related institutions or values, since he himself is detached from the said place. As I stated at the onset, it is logical that a Diaspora Jew seek out substitutes or imitations and stress other aspects of religiosity that are not necessarily temple-related. And indeed, in his commentary on 2 Maccabees, Daniel Schwartz emphasized these aspects of diasporan Jewish perceptions of the institutions of the Land of Israel (such as the focus upon the Holy City as opposed to the Temple at the beginning of 2 Maccabees 3), and demonstrated in several places the lack of interest of Diaspora Jewry in the Temple and temple-based worship.[2] And yet, though one has to agree with these suppositions, it is incumbent upon us to map out the complete picture, with all its complexities, to differentiate between the various diasporan authors, and to point out the conceptual spectrum then extant among Diaspora Jewry.

The figures presented above concerning the word ἅγιος clearly establish that 2 Maccabees and 3 Maccabees are distinct from one another in their perceptions of place-related sanctity. While 3 Maccabees ascribes very little importance to the sanctity of place, it seems that the author of 2 Maccabees attributes great weight to the sacred site; although he is in the Diaspora, in Cyrene (the author, Jason), or in Ptolemaic Egypt (the epitomator/author of the shortened version), he does not reject the concept of the sanctity of a place. Indeed, the list offered in n. 1 of occurrences of the word in 2 Maccabees shows that the sanctity of place is not mentioned exclusively in those portions believed to be of Judean provenance; rather, positive treatment of the concept of place-related sanctity is found in the chapters composed by Jason or the epitomator as well. So it appears that, although "God did not choose the people on account of the Place; rather he chose the Place on account of the people" (2 Macc 5:20), His choice of the Place nevertheless endowed it with undeniable sanctity. In short: even diasporan Hellenistic Jewish thought might concede the centrality of the concept of location in connection with sanctity and God.

---

[2] D.R. Schwartz, *The Second Book of Maccabees* (Berlin and New York, 2008), esp. 45–56.

The disparity in the perceptions of the authors of the two books is also apparent with regard to additional points: the use of epiphanies, and the number and nature of references to the Temple epiphanies, are an important phenomenon in 2 and 3 Maccabees, as in the Hellenistic world in general. In both books, epiphanies indicate God's assistance and providential care for His devotees and His chosen ones. Yet the objects and location of epiphanies vary between the two books. In 2 Maccabees, divine epiphany occurs in a variety of contexts: within the Temple and outside of it; on behalf of the people; and to save the Temple. The principle guiding 2 Maccabees regarding epiphany is that God "by apparition always succors His own portion" (14:15)—meaning, both within the Temple and outside of it, in the context of any misfortune befalling the people.[3] In 3 Maccabees, in contrast, most epiphanies occur on behalf of the people, and nowhere in the narrative does an epiphany occur on behalf of the Temple. Though God had indeed graced the Temple with an epiphany on the occasion of its establishment (2:9), this occurred in the very distant past; in the present of the narrative, in contrast, the high priest's request that God reveal His mercy in His Temple is not fulfilled. Epiphanies in 3 Maccabees occur on behalf of the *people*, but in the *place* where we would expect to find epiphany—it is entirely absent. The importance of epiphany in 3 Maccabees is further accentuated in light of the fact that it brackets the second part of the prayer of Simon, the Jerusalemite high priest (2:9, 19); yet despite this centrality, and despite the fact that both those references indeed refer to Jerusalem, no epiphany is manifested *in* Jerusalem. Thus, this topic too confirms the low value conferred on the Temple by the author of 3 Maccabees, in contrast to the perceptions of the author of 2 Maccabees.

A further matter worth noting are the sheer number and nature of references to the Temple itself in both books. Indeed, while 2 Maccabees contains numerous references to the Temple (ἱερός/ἱερόν), with frequently superlative descriptions—"the biggest" (2:19), "the Temple…honored throughout the entire world" (3:12), "the holiest" (5:15)—there are but sparse references to the Temple in 3 Maccabees. Only once is it described in the superlative—depicted as "the highest" (1:20)—apparently in a purely technical description. This feature, too,

---

[3] And indeed in this very verse it is written: "…had constituted His own people forever."

conveys the difference between the supportive, positive attitude of 2
Maccabees to the Temple and the alienated approach of 3 Maccabees
to the same institution.

I will adduce a further example that in my opinion clearly elucidates the distinction between the two authors. In the depiction of
the priests' pleas to prevent the Gentile official from breaking into
the Temple (3 Maccabees) or its treasury (2 Maccabees), both books
recount how the priests, clad in their vestments, prostrated themselves and appealed for salvation. In 2 Maccabees (3:15) we read: οἱ
δὲ ἱερεῖς πρὸ τοῦ θυσιαστηρίου... ῥίψαντες ἑαυτοὺς ἐπεκαλοῦντο εἰς
οὐρανόν ("the priests, throwing themselves before the altar... called
to heaven")—despite their calls to heaven, they fell facing the altar.
In contrast, the parallel verse in 3 Maccabees (1:16) states: τῶν δὲ
ἱερέων... προσπεσόντων δεομένων τοῦ μεγίστου θεοῦ ("the priests
prostrated... and asked the Highest God..."). Although here, too, the
priests are said to have prostrated themselves, no reference is made to
the sacred object in front of which they did so. This distinction seems
to reflect the different attitudes of the two authors toward the Temple
and its furnishings: although they both portray the appeal as directed
to the Most High, to heaven, the author of 2 Maccabees points out that
there are also symbols or holy things on earth and that the acts of the
priests relate to them as well, in a particular place; while the author of
3 Maccabees does not direct any attention to such things. True, 3 Maccabees does continue by describing how the high priest bends his knees
while facing the inner sanctum (3 Macc 2:1, in some manuscripts); but
even here this act greatly downplays the significance of the Temple
in comparison with 2 Maccabees, where Onias, the high priest of its
story, offers a sacrifice for Heliodorus's salvation. Here too, although
it is clear to the author of 2 Maccabees that the sacrifice is a form of
prayer (vv. 31–33), the prayer is nevertheless enacted through a flesh
and blood ceremony and not (exclusively) through verbal means. In
3 Maccabees, in contrast, there are no sacrifices—only prayers.

The discrepancy between the two books in the conclusions reached
by the Gentiles concerning the object of God's protection should be
understood in a similar fashion. Heliodorus reports to the king that
"He, though He has His residence in heaven, watches over and aids
that *place*" (2 Macc 3:39), but Philopator declares roundly that "the
heavenly God has surely shielded the *Jews*" (3 Macc 7:6).

To conclude this part of our study, it seems reasonable to claim that
the Hellenistic Jewish Diaspora's conceptions of sanctity are diverse,

particularly with regard to the Temple and sacred places. Distance from Jerusalem does not engender one uniform reaction, and within this broad spectrum one can find both positive and negative attitudes towards the sacredness of place in Hellenistic Judaism.

II

In light of the information hitherto presented, we can now embark on a presentation of the full scope of 3 Maccabees' own conception of the sanctity of place. This presentation is based on three elements: the narrative and the structure of the two parts of 3 Maccabees; a comparison of the two prayers in 3 Maccabees—one recited at the Temple of Jerusalem and the other at the hippodrome in Alexandria; and a comparison of the whole book of 3 Maccabees to the account of Heliodorus' attempt to break into the Temple as it appears in 2 Maccabees 3.

3 Maccabees recounts two clashes between Ptolemy IV Philopator and the Jews. The first occurs when the king attempts to enter the Holy of Holies in Jerusalem; the second occurs in Egypt, when the king endeavors to annihilate all of Egyptian Jewry by having them trampled by drunken elephants in the hippodrome. Though the king fails in both attempts, there is a vast difference between the two failures: While in Jerusalem the king is smitten but does not repent, and indeed continues to persecute the Jews after returning to Egypt, in the hippodrome he feels contrition, repents, and becomes the defender of the Jews. Thus, the final salvation takes place in an unexpected location, the hippodrome in Alexandria, and not in the ostensibly suitable place—the Temple of Jerusalem. Moreover, as noted above, God reveals Himself in Egypt, rather than in the Temple—not for the sake of His desecrated place but on behalf of His endangered people.

The superiority of Egyptian Jewry over the Jerusalemite Temple is established by many additional details. In his prayer, the Jerusalemite high priest Simon requests (2:19) "manifest Your mercy at this hour" (ἐπίφανον τὸ ἔλεός σου κατὰ τὴν ὥραν ταύτην); but although God does indeed save His Temple there is no hint that this request has been fulfilled there. These words, however, do appear in the description of the deliverance in Egypt (6:38–39): "three days, during which...the Ruler of all did with great glory manifest His mercy" (ἡμέραις τρισίν, ἐν αἷς καὶ...ἐπιφάνας τὸ ἔλεος αὐτοῦ). In other words, the manifestation of compassion that Simon requested "at this hour" is actually fulfilled

in a different place, within a different time frame—"three days"—and
for a different purpose. God's mercy, not apparent in the Temple in
Jerusalem, is actually manifested in the hippodrome in Egypt in order
to rescue the Jews, who are in immediate mortal danger.[4]

This superiority of the hippodrome over the Temple as the locus of
deliverance is further confirmed by the use of the word peace (εἰρήνη).
The high priest Simon's prayer concludes with a request that the Jews
be able to praise God after they are granted peace (ποιήσας ἡμῖν
εἰρήνην, 2:20). The Jews, however, are not granted peace throughout
the events in Jerusalem. The word εἰρήνη, in contrast, appears twice in
the account of the deliverance of the Egyptian Jews: (1) Following the
divine epiphany in the hippodrome, the king orders all the bound Jews
released and sent back to their homes in peace (6:27: μετ' εἰρήνης), and
the Jews are indeed released and brought home in peace (μετ' εἰρήνης,
7:19); and (2) At 6:32, the book states that the Jews celebrated and
thereby expressed a peaceful joy (6:32: εἰρηνικός)—again, not in Jerusalem but rather by virtue of the deliverance of the Jews in Egypt.

Similarly, or in consequence, the response by the Jews of blessings
and praise for their deliverance—absent from the story of Philopator
in Jerusalem—appears in the story of the Jews' deliverance in the hippodrome in Egypt. Immediately following their release, the Jews bless
their God (6:29); later they add many more blessings and thanks (6:32,
35; 7:12, 16, 19, 20).

The description of God and His relationship with His people further
emphasizes this superiority. The manifestation of God's holiness in
Egypt is discussed above. In Egypt, moreover, the relationship between
God and the Jews is portrayed five times as that of a father and son
(5:7; 6:3, 8, 28; 7:6), while with reference to Jerusalem a fatherly name
for God appears only once (προπάτωρ, 2:21).[5] Even then, this uncom-

---

[4] Similar language also appears in the prayer of Eleazar the priest (6:4), which states
that God revealed the light of His mercy to the people of Israel (φέγγος ἐπιφάνας
ἐλέους Ἰσραηλ γένει) in Egypt. This epiphany is the precedent for the epiphany that
saved the Jews in the hippodrome, which is mentioned at the end of the chapter. The
fact that the epiphany is for the benefit of the people of Israel (Ἰσραηλ γένει) emphasizes the difference between the deliverance of *the people of Israel* in Egypt and the
high priest Simon's plea to save the *Temple*.

[5] Most manuscripts have this or a slightly different construction. Some manuscripts
read πρὸ πάντων, a phrasing intended, according to C.L.W. Grimm (*Kurzgefasstes
exegetisches Handbuch zu den Apokryphen des Alten Testamentes* [Leipzig, 1857],
4:238), to create a heightened exaggeration of the juxtaposed holy names of God.

mon appellation[6] does not imply fatherly protection but rather the authority of primeval greatness.[7] This means that, in contrast to the description of the intimate relationship in Egypt, in Jerusalem this appellation does not denote a close relationship between father and son but actually implies a measure of distance: paternal relations exist, though the father in question is a remote ancestor and not a direct father. Thus, while in Egypt a close relationship between God and His people is apparent, in Jerusalem it is almost nonexistent.

In a similar fashion one should interpret the appellation ἀληθινός. Simon asks that God keep his promise regarding the Temple, since he is "faithful and true" (πιστὸς ... καὶ ἀληθινός, 2:11). Although God hears the plea (2:21), His attribute of truth is not mentioned in relation to God's response in Jerusalem. Rather, this attribute is reserved for the description of the epiphany in Egypt (6:18): ... καὶ ἀληθινὸς θεός. Thus, God's truth is made manifest, not where the prayer invoking this quality is uttered, but in a different place and for a different purpose.

The appellation ὁ μέγιστος θεός, which appears a number of times in 3 Maccabees, should probably be interpreted in a similar manner. This appellation designates the God to whom Philopator sacrifices (1:9) and to whom the priests pray to save the Temple (1:16). However, in the description of the deliverance in Jerusalem, the greatest God is not mentioned, and Philopator later continues to rebel against Him (3:11; 4:16). The Egyptian Jews pray to Him, too (5:25), and at the end the king himself acknowledges His power (7:2: μέγα θεός); all those who had seized Jewish property return it out of fear of the greatest God, savior of the Jews (7:22). In other words, at the onset of the book, before the crisis in the Temple, the king acknowledges the greatest God but nevertheless acts and rebels against him. Only in Egypt, after the epiphany, does the king acknowledge God again, and

---

According to that reading the first part of 3 Maccabees makes no mention at all of God as Father.

[6] This divine epithet also appears in Jewish Hellenistic literature in Wis 2:16. See R. Marcus, "Divine Names and Attributes in Hellenistic Jewish Literature," *PAAJR* 3 (1931–1932): 106. Concerning its appearances in Philo and their significance, see G. Schrenk and G. Quell, "πατήρ," *TDNT* 5:956–58.

[7] In other sources, this appellation is sometimes used of God, with the meaning of a primal Deity. The word is also used to indicate an ancient ancestor of a tribe or of a town, in contrast to a biological father (cf. LSJ, s.v. προπάτωρ). According to both of these meanings, the dimension of closeness in fatherhood is not the most salient component of the word, and, therefore, one should not view it as an expression of extreme closeness between God and His people.

do all the Jews' enemies come to fear Him. If this analysis is accurate, this passage, too, may be read in contrast to the narrative in 2 Maccabees, where this particular designation of God is mentioned only once, at the point when Heliodorus recounts the deeds of the greatest God that were performed in the Temple in Jerusalem (3:36). According to 3 Maccabees, by contrast, Philopator and the Jews' other enemies recognize this greatest God not in Jerusalem but in Egypt.

The nature of the place where the epiphany in Egypt actually occurs—the hippodrome, a large space within which horse races and athletic competitions are run—supplements my point. Such institutions of entertainment were also used for large scale assemblies or for mass arrests, as they were able to contain thousands of people. However, it seems that the capacity of the hippodrome was not the only thing the author of 3 Maccabees had in mind when he chose this place as the arena for this important stage of the narrative; rather, he was certainly aware of its religious and cultural quality as well. This characteristic Greek institution is hardly the quintessential symbol of divine holiness: it is a place where pagan rituals were held, before and during the games. Nonetheless, this is where God's epiphany occurs. Thus, the religious nature of a place or its sanctity neither causes nor inhibits God's epiphany or His holiness. It is only the nature of those in need of God's grace and holiness that does so.

Who is the cause for all these persecutions? According to 3 Maccabees the king originally persecutes the Egyptian Jews on account of the Jews of Jerusalem (2:24ff.). Later, the king threatens to wage a campaign against Judea after annihilating Egyptian Jewry (5:42–43), but because the Egyptian Jews are saved, his scheme is foiled. Thus, the diasporan Jews, far away from the Temple, not only suffer on account of the Jews of the homeland, but eventually rescue them, too.

According to Simon's prayer, the Temple is the place where "if, coming to this place, we should pray, you will hear our prayer" (2:10). However, only Simon's prayer is heard (2:21), while all the prayers of the Jerusalem Jews mentioned in chapter 1 (16–21, 23–24, 27–28) remain unanswered. In contrast, God assists the Diaspora Jews after each prayer (5:7–12, 25–35, 50–51; 6:1–15)—indeed, even before they actually pray (4:21). Moreover, some Jerusalemites, unconvinced that prayer will be effective, advocate taking up arms against the king, and it is only with difficulty that they revert to prayer (1:22–23). In Egypt, however, even in the most difficult moment an instant before their impending death, the Jews do not lose their confidence that God will hear their prayer (5:50). One should add that prayer—as opposed to sacrifice—may be performed anywhere, rendering irrelevant any claims of exclusivity or primacy on behalf of the Temple. Once again, the place appointed for prayer neither facilitates its acceptance nor convinces the people of its power, while the efficacy of prayer is actually demonstrated in a place remote from the Temple.

A comparison of the two prayers in 3 Maccabees reinforces this perception. Who is the person that prays? In Jerusalem, Simon the high priest is the one who recites the prayer properly (2:1, 21: ἔνθεσμος λιτανεία), but no details of his personality are offered. In Egypt, Eleazar, also a priest, prays; but here we are informed about his character and personality. He is from the *chora*, and the author describes him as a "distinguished person...who had attained an advanced age and throughout his life had been adorned with every virtue" (6:1). He also succeeds in imposing order on the elders around him, providing evidence of his leadership. Thus, although Simon is officially the world's leading priest, a simple provincial Jewish priest in Egypt possesses all the virtues that Simon apparently lacks. One may thus conclude that it is not the role one fills in the Temple that fashions the person but vice versa—the person's qualities are the determinant of his role: it is by virtue of his character that the Egyptian priest's prayer is better received.

Comparison with 2 Maccabees underlines this point. 2 Maccabees credits Onias, whose qualities and leadership are described in detail (2 Macc 3:1, and throughout Ch. 3; see also 15:12), with the rescue of the Temple. Moreover, Onias is involved in the crisis at the Temple from its onset, whereas Simon appears only at the critical moment. Thus 2 Maccabees shows that high priests may be allowed quite a central role, and the fact that the author of 3 Maccabees downplays the high priest's role clarifies his view of the office.

In the list of precedents cited in his prayer, Simon includes the punishment of Pharaoh, incurred due to his enslavement of the Israelites, the holy people (2:6). However, in his request, Simon pleas for the rescue of the holy place (14), and does not mention the holiness of the people. Indeed, Anna Passoni Dell'Acqua argues that this reference to the holy people is more appropriate in the context of the events in Egypt described later on in the book than in the context of the attempt to enter the Temple in Jerusalem. Note, indeed, that verse 6 of Simon's prayer refers to the enslavement of the Israelites in Egypt, which calls to mind the situation of the Egyptian Jews following Philopator's decree.[8] In any case it seems that the reference to the importance of the people of Israel in this part of the prayer hints at the primacy of the people of Israel over the Temple.

The manifestation of God's power is the solution to both predicaments. The fact that Simon asks God to save the Temple but does not call upon Him to manifest Himself (hoping at best only for a revelation of His mercy—2:19) reveals that Simon is relating to the symptom but not to the source of the problem. In contrast, Eleazar asks God to manifest Himself (6:9), correctly diagnosing the problem, and requesting the appropriate response. Eleazar's prayer is thus preferable to Simon's from this standpoint.

The last verse of Simon's prayer also seems to be relevant to our subject. The first words of this verse are an exact quote of the Septuagint of Ps 79(78):8: ταχὺ προκαταλαβέτωσαν οἱ οἰκτιρμοί σου ("Let Your compassion speedily overtake [us]"). This psalm expresses the Israelites' prayer following a severe national calamity that had befallen them. Judith Newman points out that the reference to this psalm cannot be merely coincidental, and indicates, in her view, a strong link between this psalm and Simon's prayer.[9] The context of Simon's prayer, a request for divine intervention to avert the desecration of the Temple by Philopator, resembles that of the psalm, which opens as follows: "O God, heathens have entered your domain, defiled your holy temple, and turned Jerusalem into ruins." Further on in the text, the psalmist requests divine intervention in the wake of the Temple's desecration. Newman notes several additional similarities between the two prayers. In both, the supplicant pledges that God's acceptance of the prayer will cause Him to be praised by the people of Israel.[10] Avoidance of the blasphemy engendered by the heathens' arrogant words provides further encouragement for God's acceptance of the prayer.[11] In addition

---

[8] A. Passoni Dell'Acqua, "Le preghiere del III libro dei Maccabei: Genere letterario e tematica," *RivB* 43 (1995): 173.

[9] J.H. Newman, *Praying by the Book: The Scripturalization of Prayer in Second Temple Judaism* (Atlanta, 1999), 196–98.

[10] Ps 79:13: "Then we, Your people, the flock You shepherd, shall glorify You forever; for all time we shall tell your praises." Note also the similarity between the LXX: "Your praise" = αἴνεσιν σου; and 3 Macc 2:20: καὶ δὸς αἰνέσεις ἐν τῷ στόματι...

[11] Ps 79:10: "Let the nations not say, 'Where is their God?' Before our eyes let it be known among the nations that You avenge the spilled blood of Your servants." Verses 4, 6, 9, 12 also allude to or explicitly mention this matter. 3 Macc 2:17–18: "...ἵνα μὴ καθχήσωνται οἱ παράνομοι ἐν θυμῷ αὐτῶν μηδὲ ἀγαλλιάσωνται ἐν ὑπερηφανίᾳ

to Newman's observations, one should add that both prayers request that the Israelites' past sins be disregarded.[12] A clear literary link therefore exists between both prayers: the author of 3 Maccabees carefully and deliberately integrated Psalm 79 into Simon's prayer, reinforcing the later prayer with a suitable biblical precedent involving desecration of the Temple.

There is, accordingly, quite a convincing connection between Simon's prayer and Psalm 79. However, although Psalm 79 commences with the destruction of Jerusalem and the desecration of the Temple (v. 1),[13] the main section deals not with this disaster but with calamities befalling the people of Israel themselves and the spilling of their blood. Verses 2–3 offer a shocking description of the unburied dead Israelites, and the continuation of the psalm (v. 10) explicitly mentions the spilling of Israelite blood again. The words "for they have devoured Jacob" (v. 7), signifying the injury and destruction of the children of Jacob, also indicate this bloodshed. In another verse, the supplicant asks to be saved from the nations' plan to kill him and his people and to be liberated from prison: "Let the groans of the prisoners reach You; reprieve those condemned to death, as befits Your great strength" (11). The supplicant pleads primarily for revenge upon the Gentiles and the deliverance of the people of Israel,[14] *and among all these supplications, the Temple is not mentioned even once.* This point distinguishes the psalm from Simon's prayer, where the second section

---

[12] γλώσσης αὐτῶν λέγοντες. Ἡμεῖς κατεπατήσαμεν τὸν οἶκον τοῦ ἁγιασμοῦ, ὡς…οἱ οἶκοι τῶν προσοχθισμάτων" ("…lest the transgressors boast in their wrath or exult in their arrogance of tongue, saying, 'We have trodden down the house of the Sanctuary as the houses of the abominations are trodden down'").

[12] Ps 79:9: "Do not hold our former iniquities against us"; 3 Macc 2:19: "ἀπάλειψον τὰς ἁμαρτίας ἡμῶν καὶ διασκέλασον τὰς ἀμβλακίας ἡμῶν" ("Blot out our sins and scatter abroad our offenses").

[13] To be more precise, profanation of the sacred is only mentioned in one of the three segments of the verse: "defiled Your holy Temple." The other segments of the verse deal with "Your domain" (נחלתך) (perhaps the entire land of Israel?) and "Jerusalem." In other words, the desecration of the Temple is one expression of the calamities that have transpired. V. 7b may also allude to this desecration of the Temple: "and desolated his home." (Note that the word "home" is translated as τόπος, which is the term 3 Maccabees employs for the Temple.) Still, "*his* home" (נוהו) refers to Jacob, not God, and it should therefore indicate Jacob's dwelling-places; that is, the land of Israel and its cities. If so, the people of Israel and not the Temple form the focus of the calamities depicted in all the segments of this verse.

[14] Verses 6, 10, 12—revenge upon the Gentiles; verses 8, 9—deliverance of the Israelites. The Gentiles' abuses are also directed against the people of Israel, and through them against God, but not against the Temple; see vv. 4, 12.

focuses on the Temple—especially in its request that the desecration
of the Temple be averted (17) and in its reference to the blasphemy
of the Gentiles through their acts against the Temple (18). Since the
author of 3 Maccabees evidently wished to allude to the original biblical context of the verse, "Let Thy compassion speedily overtake us," we
must determine whether the centrality of the violation of the people of
Israel in Psalm 79 is somehow taken over in Simon's prayer.

The focus of Psalm 79 corresponds to the second half of 3 Maccabees, where an account is given of the persecution of the Egyptian
Jews. Moreover, Ps 79:11 might easily be applied to the predicament
of the Egyptian Jews, imprisoned in the hippodrome and condemned
to be trampled to death by elephants: "Let the groans of the prisoners
reach You; reprieve those condemned to death, as befits your great
strength."[15] The allusion to Psalm 79 in the prayer is equally or even
more appropriate to the situation of the Egyptian Jews in danger of
annihilation, than to that of the threatened Temple.[16]

It seems then, that this verse too supports my view regarding the
Temple and the people: even when he requests that the Temple be
saved, the high priest Simon bases his prayer upon an ancient biblical entreaty of which the main topic is the deliverance of the people
of Israel rather than that of the Temple itself. The biblical quotation,
while serving as a rather good justification for saving the Temple from
desecration, provides an even better reason for saving the people of
Israel from annihilation. Being well-versed in the Bible, and expect-
ing similar proficiency from his readers, the author of 3 Maccabees
ascribes to the high priest Simon the opinion that though the Temple
is indeed important, the importance of the people of Israel is of greater
magnitude.

Several other points reinforce this interpretation. In both incidents
in 3 Maccabees, the priests and the people ask God to have mercy on
them (3 Macc 2:19–20; 5:51; 6:12). Only in Egypt, however, are God's
attributes of mercy and loving-kindness mentioned: God is described as
"merciful" (5:7: ἐλεήμων); "readily appeased" (5:13: εὐκατάλλακτος);
"rich in mercy" (6:9: πολυέλεος); one who "governs all creation with

---

[15] According to 3 Maccabees, the Jews were indeed imprisoned; the author endeavors to describe the Jews being bound (5:5) and their release (6:27, 29).

[16] That this psalm is understood as concerned with the slaughter of the people of
Israel can be seen also in 1 Macc 7:16–17, which cites two verses from Psalm 79 in
lamenting the murdered Ασιδαῖοι.

loving-kindness" (6:2: ἐν οἰκτιρμοῖς); and the "protector of all" (6:9: τῶν ὅλων σκεπαστά). In the first two cases, the epithets apply to God's relationship with the people of Israel and thereby augment the story's emphasis on the special relationship between God and His people. The other attributes mentioned do not actually involve the people of Israel. However, inasmuch as Eleazar depicts the heathens as arrogant and worthy of hatred (v. 9), God's mercy and protection clearly applies to those who are not arrogant, in other words—the people of Israel. Such divine epithets are absent from the Jerusalem narrative. Thus it seems, again, that God's mercy and closeness to those who call upon Him are more potent and manifest in Egypt than in Jerusalem.

Both prayers point out God's love for the people of Israel. Simon's prayer states that because of His love for the House of Israel (καὶ ἀγαπῶν τὸν οἶκον τοῦ Ισραηλ), God promises to hearken to the prayer recited in the Temple (2:10),[17] and Eleazar's prayer terms Israel "those beloved of Thee" (6:11: τῶν ἠγαπημένων σου). But the significance assigned to this love differs in each prayer. In Simon's prayer, this love does not justify the present plea; rather, it elucidates the basis for the general promise to hearken to a prayer recited in the Temple. The obligation to fulfill this promise is the main argument presented by the supplicant. In contrast, God's love forms the basis for Eleazar's claim, which contends that the destruction of God's beloved will result in the desecration of His name. Love consequently plays a more essential role in Eleazar's prayer than in Simon's.

Similarly, both prayers emphasize concern for the profanation of God's name. Simon's asks God to spare the Temple from desecration, "lest the transgressors boast in their wrath or exult in their arrogance of tongue, saying, 'We have trodden down the House of the Sanctuary as the houses of the abominations are trodden down'" (2:17–18). Eleazar proposes a similar rationale in his request to save the people of Israel: "Let not those whose thoughts are vanity bless their vanities for the destruction of those beloved of Thee, saying, 'Neither did their God deliver them'" (6:11). Both prayers present similar arguments by juxtaposing the God of the Jews with the heathen gods and citing the mockery of the heathens for the God of Israel. However, while Simon

---

[17] Note that Israel is called here "the House of Israel." This probably implies that the real house is not the Temple but Israel, and only if *they* are threatened is the house in danger. If so, this constitutes a further expression of the superiority of the people of Israel over the Temple.

compares the Temple to the houses of abominations, Eleazar contrasts the gods of vanity with the God of the Jews. In other words, Simon is concerned with the desecration of the honor of the holy Sanctuary while Eleazar fears the desecration of the honor of the God of Israel. Moreover, Simon's prayer expresses apprehension over a potential parallel being drawn between the Temple and the houses of abominations, whereas Eleazar is anxious about the potential victory of pagan gods over a God who does not save His people. Simon is troubled by the heathens boasting and glorying but does not mention any praise of their gods; Eleazar is distressed by the praise bestowed on the pagan gods, which implies an increase in their prestige. Hence, 3 Maccabees is not concerned to argue that damaging the Temple would involve a direct attack upon the God of Israel, but it does emphasize that injury to God's beloved people would directly jeopardize God's good name.[18]

Both prayers address the sins of the people of Israel. Simon's prayer mentions these sins several times. He attributes the difficult situation of the people to its numerous transgressions (2:13) and asks that their sins be forgiven and scattered to the winds (19). Eleazar, in contrast, is unsure if there were sins, and he requests that if indeed the people are guilty, God should punish them Himself after saving them from the Gentiles (6:10).[19] True, stipulations concerning sins do appear in Simon's prayer as well (2:10);[20] but they refer to God's promise to Solomon. Simon, on his part, is sure that the people have sinned, and requests forgiveness.[21]

The absence of a confession of sins in Eleazar's prayer is not surprising. Not all prayers from the Second Temple period refer to or acknowledge sins.[22] Still, it is implausible that mere coincidence accounts for

---

[18] The fear of profaning God's name appears is other works as well. The profanation of God's name in Judith 9 is comprised of the desecration of the Temple (8, 13), injury to the people of Israel, and the heathen nations' arrogance (13–14). So too, the prayer of Esther (Additions to Esther, C: 19–21) speaks of injury to both the Temple and the people of Israel as components of the desecration of God's name.

[19] For a similar approach see 2 Macc 10:4.

[20] On the meaning of ἐὰν γένηται ἡμῶν ἀποστροφή as "if we sin," see Grimm, *Kurzgefasstes*, 236–37; Newman, *Praying by the Book*, 193.

[21] Unlike Passoni Dell'Acqua, "Le preghiere del III libro dei Maccabei," 176, who views these conditional statements as similar; and D. Flusser, "Psalms, Hymns and Prayers," in *Jewish Writings of the Second Temple Period* (ed. M.E. Stone; Assen and Philadelphia, 1984), 572, who argues that the request for the forgiveness of sins is common to both prayers in 3 Maccabees.

[22] For example, see Mordechai's prayer in Additions to Esther (addition C) and Judith's prayer (9:2–14).

the fact that the two parallel prayers in 3 Maccabees are differentiated from one another concerning the confession of sins. This distinction may convey the author's assessment of the relationship between the Jews of Jerusalem and those of Egypt. As regards the latter, it is doubtful, for our author, whether they had sinned,[23] while it is evident that the former did, and that this is the source of their predicament. In other words, while sin was definitely extant in Jerusalem, it is doubtful whether it existed in Egypt.

To conclude this part, comparing the two prayers clearly demonstrates that in many aspects, and to a great extent, the prayer recited in the hippodrome of Alexandria is preferable to the one uttered in the Temple in Jerusalem. Such a comparison reveals the superiority of the Jewish people in Egypt over their Judean brethren despite their closer link to the Temple in Jerusalem. Thus the Temple does not bring the Jews closer to God, and this proves that the cult carried out there is not such an efficacious means of divine worship.

Let us turn now to the comparison of 3 Maccabees and 2 Maccabees 3. As is well known, the story of Heliodorus' attempt to confiscate funds from the treasury of the Jerusalem Temple (2 Maccabees 3) is replete with thematic and linguistic parallels to the story of Philopator's attempt to break into the Sanctuary (3 Macc 1–2:24).[24] Both stories contain the following themes in common: the foreign king initially relates positively to the Temple (2 Macc 3:2–3; 3 Macc 1:9; 3:16); both Gentile visitors have traveled widely in Κοίλη Συρία καὶ Φοινίκη before visiting Jerusalem (2 Macc 3:8; 3 Macc 1:6–7; 3:15); both are warmly

---

[23] At the beginning of the prayer (6:3) Eleazar describes the Jews in the hippodrome as perishing "unjustly" (ἀδίκως). This can be interpreted as meaning, unjust insofar as the Jews did not injure those who wanted to kill them. Yet U. Mittmann-Richert, *Einführung zu den historischen und legendarischen Erzählungen* (Gütersloh, 2000), 69–70, interprets this term in a theological context—there is no justification for God to injure the people of Israel in such a manner. According to that analysis, although Eleazar explicitly declares the absence of any sin, v. 10 may be viewed, to a certain degree, as a retraction of this declaration.

[24] On the linguistic aspect see the lists of C.W. Emmet, "The Third Book of Maccabees," in *The Apocrypha and Pseudepigrapha of the Old Testament* (ed. R.H. Charles; Oxford, 1913), 1:156; and my supplements ("The Third Book of Maccabees: Literature, History and Ideology" [Ph.D. diss., The Hebrew University of Jerusalem, 2002], 104–6 [in Hebrew]); see also M.Z. Kopidakes, *Το Γ' Μακκαβαιων και ο Αισχυλος: Αισχυλειες μνημες στο λεκτιτο και στη θεματογραφια του Γ' Μακκαβαιων* (Herakleion, 1987), 26–27. The literature on the thematic level is vast; I will mention several items in the following discussion.

received in Jerusalem (2 Macc 3:9; 3 Macc 1:8); both try to harm or
desecrate the Temple; and both encounter fierce opposition. Nevertheless both Heliodorus and Philopator persist and neither will yield.
The accounts of the reactions induced by the characters' intentions to
execute their plans are analogous in both structure and content. Struc-
turally, the first reactions described are those of the priests (2 Macc
3:15; 3 Macc 1:16), followed by those of the townspeople (2 Macc 3:18;
3 Macc 1:17);[25] both books also reserve a special place for the women's
reactions (2 Macc 3:19; 3 Macc 1:18-20).[26] Following this description,
there is reference to a prayer (2 Macc 3:20; 3 Macc 1:21).[27]

The only deviation in these structural similarities is in the high
priest's reaction to the events and its place in the narrative. Though
both books recount this reaction, in 2 Maccabees the account appears
following the description of the priests' prayer (3:16-17), whereas in
3 Maccabees it is only when the suspense is at its peak, and Philopator
is about to execute his plan, that Simon the high priest intervenes—
moving to center stage and praying to save the Temple (2:1-20).[28] That
prayer, however, corresponds to Onias's prayer (to save Heliodorus's
life—2 Macc 3:31-33). The structural similarities between these two
prayers should be underlined: in both cases, the high priest prays and
his prayer is accepted; and in both cases it is written explicitly that
it was the high priest's prayer that was responsible for effecting the
desired change (2 Macc 3:33; 3 Macc 2:21). The fact that there is no
parallel in 3 Maccabees to the appearance of the high priest Onias in
the description of the tumult and the prayer in 2 Maccabees, and the
other differences between the two stories in terms of the high priest's
figure and function, should be accounted for as deriving from the high
priest's role in each story, as discussed above.[29]

---

[25] In both cases the rare verb ἐκπηδάω is used.

[26] The maidens are described in both stories as normally sequestered: κατάκλειστοι
παρθένοι (3 Macc 1:18); κατάκλειστοι τῶν παρθένων (2 Macc 3:19).

[27] In both prayers, people prostrate themselves (2 Macc 3:15, 21; 3 Macc 1:16; 2:1)
and there are those who stretch their arms forth (προτείνω τὰς χεῖρας) while praying:
the women in 2 Maccabees (3:20) and the high priest Simon in 3 Maccabees (2:1).

[28] The argument that Simon is the person who prays is based on the Lucianic manuscripts and on the Syriac version. On the preferability of this reading, see Hacham,
"Third Book of Maccabees," 69 n. 22.

[29] In 2 Maccabees Onias III represents the moderate Jewish leadership that advo-
cates for peaceful coexistence and a relationship of mutual respect with the foreign
regime. In 3 Maccabees the high priest represents the king's rival: he is the only
human being on earth who is allowed entrance into the place the king would forcibly

Eventually, the plot fails. God responds, and the offender is flogged: in 2 Maccabees, two young men thrash Heliodorus, while in 3 Maccabees, God does the beating. Very similar verbs are used in both stories: μαστιγόω in 2 Maccabees (3:26, 34, 38); and the comparable verb with the identical meaning, μαστίζω, in 3 Maccabees (2:21). As a result of the beating, the intruder falls to the ground (2 Macc 3:27; 3 Macc 2:22), rendered helpless and mute (2 Macc 3:29; 3 Macc 2:22). The lack of voice is similarly described in both stories: "voiceless" (ἄφωνος) in 2 Maccabees, and "unable to make a sound" (μηδὲ φωνῆσαι δύνασθαι) in 3 Maccabees. Both books remark on the suddenness (2 Macc 3:27) or sharpness (3 Macc 2:23) with which the man falls, and on the haste of his companions' reactions. 2 Maccabees relates that some of those with Heliodorus speedily (ταχύ) turn to the high priest asking him to pray for Heliodorus (31); and in 3 Maccabees, Philopator's friends and bodyguards speedily (ταχέως) draw him away (2:23). In both stories the companions drag out their smitten friend (2 Macc 3:27–28; 3 Macc 2:23), and in both cases, the authors refer to the man's life (τὸ ζῆν). 2 Maccabees describes God as giving life to Heliodorus (2 Macc 3:31, 33, 35) and 3 Maccabees states that Philopator was about to "yield up his life" (2:23). The thematic affinity is also apparent in that both stories contain descriptions of fear and terror (2 Macc 3:17, 24, 25, 30; 3 Macc 2:23), and the final result of the conflict is that those who threaten the Temple leave Jerusalem and return to their original places (2 Macc 3:35; 3 Macc 2:24–25).

Is there, finally, a happy ending to this episode? It depends. For 2 Maccabees the answer is definitely in the affirmative. In 3 Maccabees, however, since no epiphany occurs in the Temple and the king does not repent, continuing instead to persecute the [Egyptian] Jews, the answer is a definite no. Yet four chapters later, in Egypt, the happy ending does indeed transpire, when Philopator repents, after a miraculous epiphany.

The comparison of the two stories reveals differences in addition to the similarities noted above. The main difference, broadly speaking, is that the confrontation in 3 Maccabees is more acute: while in 2 Maccabees the miscreant is Heliodorus, in 3 Maccabees it is the king himself. Philopator desires to enter the sanctuary, whereas Heliodorus "only"

---

enter (1:11), and the fact that it is the power of his prayer that prevents the king from executing his plan expresses the Jews' victory and the king's defeat.

acts to confiscate the Temple treasury; in 2 Maccabees the act is initiated by a Jew (3:5–7, 11) whereas in 3 Maccabees the king's pursuit
of honor is his motivation (3 Macc 1:12, 15). Philopator's arrogance is
also a salient factor, in that others repeatedly try to prevent him from
executing his plans in various ways but he is not dissuaded (3 Macc
1:11–15; 25–26); whereas only one attempt is made (by the high priest)
to dissuade Heliodorus (2 Macc 3:10–12). As Philopator advances
towards the Temple, his arrogance reaches such heights that even his
own men join the Jews' prayer to save the Temple (3 Macc 1:27). In
2 Maccabees, on the other hand, there is no account of Heliodorus'
men acting against him; on the contrary—his bodyguards are auda-
cious enough to enter together with him (2 Macc 2:24, 28).

Comparison of the people's reactions in the two books displays similar characteristics. 2 Maccabees devotes only one verse to a description of the women's reaction (3:19), while 3 Maccabees, which devotes
three verses to this issue (1:18–20), distinguishes in detail between different categories of women who could not leave their home but who
nevertheless join the crowd. The difference is substantive as well as stylistic. In 2 Maccabees, only some of the secluded maidens leave their
homes, while others are content to peer out from inside (19); whereas
3 Maccabees relates that the secluded maidens left their chambers, and
makes no mention of maidens who stayed inside. The fact that in 3
Maccabees the mothers, not mentioned in 2 Maccabees, abandon their
young children and assemble at the Temple reinforces the impression
that in 3 Maccabees all the women partake in the prayer and in the
assembly, whereas in 2 Maccabees, only a part of the women participate in these activities. These differences create the sense that the danger to the Temple in 3 Maccabees was extremely grave whereas the
danger to the Temple in 2 Maccabees was of a lesser degree.

The stark contrast between the positive ending of the Heliodorus
story and the negative conclusion of the story of Philopator in 3 Maccabees is particularly significant in light of the opening narratives of
both stories. The Heliodorus story begins with Heliodorus' iniquitous
intentions (2 Macc 3:7), whereas Philopator comes to Jerusalem in
order to honor the place (3 Macc 1:8–9). Thus, the Heliodorus story
evolves from a conflict to the recognition of God's power and peace
with the Jews. In 3 Maccabees, by contrast, the reader at first finds a
high degree of mutual respect between the king and the Jews, only to
encounter a severe head-on confrontation between them by the end.

The situation described above generates expectations of redemption
and dramatic salvation, befitting the grave danger recounted in 3 Mac-

cabees. The absence of such an end to the events in Jerusalem seems, therefore, strange and remarkable. The fact that no epiphany, repentance, and recognition of God's power come about, whereas these do occur vis-à-vis the relatively minor danger incurred in the parallel story of 2 Maccabees, calls for explanation.

It seems, however, that once we adjust the boundaries of the comparison, beyond 3 Macc 1–2, this conundrum is resolved. A close reading of the remainder of 3 Maccabees reveals additional parallels, both thematic and linguistic, between the latter and the story of Heliodorus. A divine epiphany occurs in the hippodrome in Egypt, rescuing the Jews on the verge of being trampled by the elephants, saving them from imminent death. The similarity to 2 Maccabees is apparent at several points. In both books God appears; both accounts utilize the stem ἐπιφαίνω: in 2 Maccabees ἐπιφάνειαν...ἐποίησεν (3:24), ἐπιφανέντος (3:30); and in 3 Maccabees ἐπιφάνας (6:18, 39).[30] Both books recount the appearance of two figures, glorious in appearance:[31] young men (νεανίαι) in 2 Maccabees (3:26, 33); and in 3 Maccabees, angels (ἄγγελοι; 6:18).

Following this epiphany, the king acknowledges God's power (6:28; 7:9) and also thanks Him (6:33), in the same way that Heliodorus testifies to God's deeds (3:36) and thanks Him by offering sacrifices (3:35). In common with the Heliodorus story, Philopator's recognition of the God of Israel is accompanied by reconciliation with the Jews (6:25; 7:7); the king even grants to the Jews royal protection of their rights (3 Macc 7:8; 20). Moreover, Philopator bestows generous gifts upon the Jews (3 Macc 6:30, 40; 7:18)—similarly to Heliodorus, who sacrifices to God and makes grand vows to the preserver of his life (2 Macc 3:35). Furthermore, in both stories the enemy declares that the God in heaven (ἐπουράνιον)[32] protects the Temple (2 Macc 3:39) or the Jews, his children (3 Macc 7:6), and therefore, the kingdom should not get into trouble with Him. As in 2 Maccabees, so here, blame for

---

[30] Although the appellation παντοκράτωρ is quite common (see: C. Zimmermann, *Die Namen des Vaters: Studien zu ausgewählten neutestamentlichen Gottesbezeichnungen vor ihrem frühjüdischen und paganen Sprachhorizont* [Leiden, 2007], 240–56), it is interesting to note that the term appears in both of these verses (2 Macc 3:30; 3 Macc 6:18).

[31] Both writers also express this using the words δόξα (2 Macc 3:26), δεδοξασμένοι (3 Macc 6:18).

[32] This appellation also appears in other Egyptian Jewish books (see Marcus, "Divine Names," 74), so this common phrase does not constitute unequivocal proof of a connection between 2 Maccabees and 3 Maccabees.

provoking the Jews is attributed not to the king himself but to rebellious and evil-natured officials (3 Macc 6:24; 7:3–5).

The Jews' reaction to their salvation in the hippodrome is similar to their reaction in the Heliodorus story. In 3 Maccabees they bless God (6:29), and later they add many more blessings and thanks (6:32, 35; 7:12; 16, 19, 20); in 2 Maccabees, the Jews bless God, who glorified His place (3:30).[33]

How should all these data be interpreted? The resemblance between the Heliodorus story and 3 Maccabees suggests that the books are interconnected; the discrepancies between the Heliodorus/Philopator stories and the conclusion of the second part of 3 Maccabees probably reveal the direction of that influence and its purpose. Johannes Tromp has already proposed that some elements of the Heliodorus story were incorporated into the second part of 3 Maccabees.[34] I have here identified additional imported elements. When we factor in the linguistic similarities between the books, this corroborates Tromp's view that the author of 3 Maccabees was conversant with the Heliodorus story in 2 Maccabees; in fact, he used it by splitting this story between the two parts of 3 Maccabees.

In light of the above, it seems therefore that Daniel R. Schwartz's view of the Heliodorus story as a "floating" legend should be rejected.[35] The recently-published inscription concerning the probable appointment of Olympiodorus to supervise the temples of Coele Syria and Phoenicia in 178 BCE, and the role of Heliodorus in this dossier of letters[36] reinforces the historicity of the Heliodorus story or at least reveals its originality and historic kernel, demonstrating that this story should not be regarded as a floating legend.[37] Moreover, Schwartz's

---

[33] In both verses (2 Macc 3:30; 3 Macc 6:29) the verb used is εὐλογέω, in the identical form: εὐλόγουν. Another linguistic similarity is the combination of joy and gladness appearing in 2 Macc 2:30 (χαρᾶς καὶ εὐφροσύνης) and 3 Macc 7:15 (εὐφροσύνην μετὰ χαρᾶς).

[34] J. Tromp, "The Formation of the Third Book of Maccabees," *Henoch* 17 (1995): 311–28, esp. 319, 321.

[35] Schwartz, *Second Maccabees*, 185; see also his uncertainty on p. 87, on the connections between the Heliodorus story and 3 Maccabees.

[36] H.M. Cotton and M. Wörrle, "Seleukos IV to Heliodoros: A New Dossier of Royal Correspondence from Israel," *ZPE* 159 (2007): 191–203; D. Gera, "Olympiodoros, Heliodoros and the Temples of Koile Syria and Phoinike," *ZPE* 169 (2009): 125–55.

[37] But see Schwartz's solution (*Second Maccabees*, 185–86) to this problem.

view[38] that 2 Maccabees was completed by 143/2 BCE weakens the "floating legend" hypothesis, since 3 Maccabees was written no earlier than about 100 BCE.[39] It is, therefore, unlikely that the account in 3 Maccabees is either independent or the original story.[40] The above substantiates the contrary theory: that 2 Maccabees conveys the earlier form of the story, while 3 Maccabees revises it for its own purposes.

What are those purposes? According to Tromp the author's purpose is to justify and "elevate the festival legend" of 3 Maccabees "to a higher, theological plane."[41] However, these features—that the story is depicted in graver terms; that it is split into two different parts; and that the happy ending occurs in the hippodrome in Egypt—indicate a different purpose. Namely, the revised story demonstrates that in contrast to the Heliodorus story, God does not reveal himself in His Temple, even when it is endangered; yet He does reveal himself when His people are persecuted in Egypt, far away from the Temple. While at 2 Macc 3:39, Heliodorus declares that "He, though He has His residence in heaven (ὁ τὴν κατοικίαν ἐπουράνιον ἔχων), watches over (ἐπόπτης ἐστί) and aids that place and…destroys those who come there to do evil," in 3 Maccabees 7:6 the king writes that "the heavenly God (τὸν ἐπουράνιον θεόν) has surely shielded the Jews as a father always (διὰ παντός)…on behalf of his children." In the events in Jerusalem (3 Macc 2:21), God is described as "the God who is the watcher over all" (ὁ πάντων ἐπόπτης θεός); while in 2 Maccabees, although in heaven, He watches over the Temple (3:39). In 3 Maccabees, however, when the Temple is endangered He watches over *all*, and when the people are endangered, although He is in heaven, He shields the Jews. Moreover, although it is stated that God "always" acts on behalf of

---

[38] Schwartz, *Second Maccabees*, 11–15.

[39] See summary in my "Third Maccabees," 221–43.

[40] For this view see Schwartz, *Second Maccabees*, 87; A. Kasher, *The Jews in Hellenistic and Roman Egypt: The Struggle for Equal Rights* (Tübingen, 1985), 212–13 n. 16; S.R. Johnson, *Historical Fictions and Hellenistic Jewish Identity: Third Maccabees in its Cultural Context* (Berkeley, 2004), 136. N. Stokholm, "Zur Überlieferung von Heliodor, Kuturnahhunte und anderen missglückten Tempelräuben," *ST* 22 (1968): 1–28, believes that the relationship between the two stories (and between them and 4 Maccabees 4) is mainly one of oral traditions that were recounted and redacted in different places and that were eventually put in writing. However, Stokholm deals only with the thematic similarities between Temple-invasion stories, and does not take into account the apparent linguistic affinity between them, which is a major consideration for understanding the relationship between the two stories.

[41] Tromp, "Formation of Third Maccabees," 322.

his children (3 Macc 7:6), He does not do so to the same degree in Jerusalem and in Egypt.

SUMMARY AND CONCLUSIONS

Fourteen years ago David S. Williams published an innovative article in which he suggested that 3 Maccabees should also be regarded as an apologetic by Egyptian Jewry directed at the Jews of the Land of Israel; he argued that it conveys the contention that the divine presence is to be found among diasporan Jews just as it is in the Land of Israel, thus legitimizing Diaspora Judaism. According to Williams, Palestinian Jews considered diasporan Jews inferior; therefore, the diasporan author of 3 Maccabees stresses God's presence with them, as well as the kinship of both groups.[42] This view was criticized by many scholars, such as Erich Gruen, John Collins, Sara Johnson and J.R.C. Cousland. Gruen asserts that "there is no evidence for criticism of Diaspora Jewry by those in Palestine"; Cousland holds that in 3 Maccabees, "Jerusalem is not linked to the victory (of the Jews in Egypt): the triumph remains purely diasporan," and doubts "how successful as an apologetic this implicit derogation of Jerusalem would have been to a Palestinian audience."[43] Or, as Collins writes: "[T]here is little to indicate Palestinian Jews as the primary audience, or indeed that such a defense would have been necessary."[44]

However, in light of the discussion above, it appears undeniable that Williams' hypothesis is basically correct, and that 3 Maccabees attempts to bolster the legitimacy of Diaspora Jewry. Moreover, it seems that Williams was overly cautious in claiming that according to 3 Maccabees God is "also" with diasporan Jews; indeed the author's view is that God's revelation in the hippodrome in Egypt, to save His people, surpasses His manifestation in His Temple in Jerusalem. 3 Maccabees, a work of the first century BCE, expresses a decisive opinion on the inconsequentiality of the Temple in Jerusalem and on the preferred

---

[42] D.S. Williams, "3 Maccabees: A Defense of Diaspora Judaism?" *JSP* 13 (1995): 17–29.

[43] E.S. Gruen, *Heritage and Hellenism: The Reinvention of Jewish Tradition* (Berkeley, 1998), 233 n. 192; J.R.C. Cousland, "Reversal, Recidivism and Reward in *3 Maccabees*: Structure and Purpose," *JSJ* 34 (2003): 40–41.

[44] J.J. Collins, *Between Athens and Jerusalem: Jewish Identity in the Hellenistic Diaspora* (2d ed.; Grand Rapids, 2000), 129 n. 88.

status of the chosen people over the chosen place. In other words, the Lord is preeminently with the people, to a greater degree than within the Temple. Consequentially, it is obvious that the intended audience cannot be the Jews of the Land of Israel, but rather the diasporan-Egyptian Jews, who were bothered by their alleged inferior status and needed encouragement in relation to their religious status and their closeness to their God.

What does this reveal about Diaspora Judaism in general? Schwartz, in many studies, and Michael Tuval in his paper in this volume, try to characterize Diaspora Judaism in the Second Temple period as uninterested in temples, including the one in Jerusalem. Tuval shows that Hellenistic Judaism does not ascribe importance to the Jerusalemite Temple. Although I also believe that we should endeavor to define the uniqueness of Diaspora Judaism and the ways in which it differs from the center, especially with the Temple in Jerusalem still *in situ* and functional, we should not view Diaspora Judaism as monolithic. Even Jews of the same period, living in close proximity to each other, and probably even sharing a common cultural milieu like the authors of 2 and 3 Maccabees, are liable to differ radically in their views about sanctity and the Temple. As demonstrated above, a huge difference indeed exists between these two books: according to 2 Maccabees the Temple was saved, a place can indeed be holy, and that place, the Temple, has sanctity. Therefore sacrifices are meaningful and important, although one has to regard them as a form of prayer. On the other hand, 3 Maccabees ascribes little importance to place-related sanctity, does not mention sacrifices as a means by which the Jews might address God (even in the Temple), and views prayer as the main way of worshiping God.

Our discussion thus demonstrates that although it is necessary to discuss diasporan conceptions of worship and religion, conceptions that bespeak the necessity of dealing with the diasporan situation of distance from the Temple and the national religious center, it is important to bear in mind that we are not speaking of a single perception. A range of perceptions of the Temple and Jerusalem obtained among the Hellenistic Jewish Diaspora, and it is our task to refine and hone these various definitions and perceptions.

DOING WITHOUT THE TEMPLE: PARADIGMS IN JUDAIC LITERATURE OF THE DIASPORA

Michael Tuval

I. The Problem: How Can a Diaspora Jew Worship a God Whose Temple is Far Away?

The question of the role of the Jerusalem Temple and its cult in Diaspora literature, and that of the attitudes of Diaspora authors towards them, cannot be explored outside of the broader contexts of Jewish religious worldviews, practices and identities in the Diaspora communities of the Greco-Roman world. The Diaspora Jews' predicament vis-à-vis the Temple and its cult could be succinctly delineated as follows.[1]

According to the pentateuchal tradition, which is usually considered to have taken its final shape by the end of the Persian and the beginning of the Hellenistic periods, the Temple, its sacrificial cult and its priesthood stood at the center of the Judean religion.[2] Most of the legal materials contained in the Torah of Moses, on diverse levels, in numerous ways, and in different measures are related to the Temple and the sacrificial cult carried out in it. Various sacrifices (as well as other cultic acts performed in the Temple such as, for example, libations, the burning of incense and the like) were the main rituals of Mosaic religion as conceived by the authors-redactors of the Torah, and as the writer of the Letter to the Hebrews pithily put it at the end

---

[1] This paper, a shortened version of one of the chapters of my doctoral dissertation, which I am preparing under the supervision of Prof. Daniel R. Schwartz, was written while I was a member of the Scholion research group that sponsored the conference that this volume represents.

[2] Although the pentateuchal traditions refer to the Tabernacle as the center of Israel's sacrificial cult, it is clear that their *Sitz im Leben* was the Temple in Jerusalem; see H. Liss, "The Imaginary Sanctuary: The Priestly Code as an Example of Fictional Literature in the Hebrew Bible," in *Judah and Judeans in the Persian Period* (ed. O. Lipshits and M. Oeming; Winona Lake, 2006), 663–89. On the formation of the Pentateuch see J. Blenkinsopp, *The Pentateuch: An Introduction to the First Five Books of the Bible* (New York, 1992). On the centrality of the Temple in ancient Jewish religious practice and thought, see M.D. Herr, "Jerusalem, the Temple and Its Cult— Reality and Concepts in Second Temple Times," in *Jerusalem in the Second Temple Period* (ed. A. Oppenheimer et al.; Jerusalem, 1981), 166–77 (in Hebrew).

of the Second Temple period, "without the shedding of blood there [was] no pardon."[3] The ritual purity system, which played such an important role in the Mosaic legislation, mainly answered the questions: "Who can and who cannot participate in the Temple cult, when and how?"[4] Major biblical festivals were defined, basically or broadly, as those of the pilgrimage to the Temple, and the activities of the celebrants were to take place in it or in its vicinity.[5] All this should not surprise us since the majority of the pentateuchal legal materials are most likely to have originated with the priestly and levitical circles based in the Temple or at least connected to it—circles which were eager to promote the Temple as the center, indeed, the embodiment, of the Judean religious expression.[6] So much for the *written* tradition authoritative in the period under review.

From the historical point of view, correspondingly, at the very beginning of the Persian period Judea was reconstituted as a "Temple-state," at the head of which stood the high priest.[7] This situation endured in the early Hellenistic period, until the beginning of the Maccabean revolt, of which the apogee was the rededication of the Temple and the

---

[3] Hebrews 9:22. See L.L. Grabbe, *Judaism from Cyrus to Hadrian* (2 vols.; Minneapolis, 1992), 2:607–8; for a more detailed discussion, see idem, *Judaic Religion in the Second Temple Period: Belief and Practice from the Exile to Yavneh* (London, 2000), 129–49.

[4] The theme of purity seems to enjoy much popularity in recent research on ancient Judaism. See J. Klawans, *Impurity and Sin in Ancient Judaism* (New York, 2000); and idem, *Purity, Sacrifice, and the Temple: Symbolism and Supersessionism in the Study of Ancient Judaism* (New York, 2006).

[5] See Leviticus 23. For the analysis of these traditions, see J. Milgrom, *Leviticus 23–27* (New York, 2001), ad loc.

[6] On the role of the priestly circles in the creation of the Pentateuch and its establishment as "the Law of the Land," see M. Smith, *Palestinian Parties and Politics That Shaped the Old Testament* (New York, 1971), 170–87. Cf. L.L. Grabbe, *A History of the Jews and Judaism in the Second Temple Period, Vol. 1: Yehud: A History of the Persian Province of Judah* (London, 2004), 331–43, for an evaluation of the role of Ezra *the priest* in the development of "the Law" and "Scripture" in the early Persian period. Ezra's crucial role in the promulgation of the Torah has been recognized at least since the Talmudic period; see *b. Sukkah* 20a.

[7] On the history of the Restoration era, see S. Japhet, "The Temple in the Restoration Period: Reality and Ideology," *USQR* 44/3–4 (1991): 195–251; Grabbe, *History, Vol. 1*; P.R. Bedford, *Temple Restoration in Early Achaemenid Judah* (Leiden, 2006). On the high priests in the first half of the Second Temple period, see M. Brutti, *The Development of the High Priesthood during the Pre-Hasmonean Period: History, Ideology, Theology* (Leiden, 2006). On the religious developments of the Persian period, see M. Smith, "Jewish Religious Life in the Persian Period," in *The Cambridge History of Judaism, Vol. 1, Introduction: The Persian Period* (ed. W.D. Davies and L. Finkelstein; Cambridge: 1984), 219–78.

reinstitution of the sacrificial cult there. The Hasmoneans rose to rule over the Judeans first of all as high priests, only several decades later adding the royal diadem to the high priestly turban.[8] Most of the political and religious controversies of this period seem to have centered on the issue of the Hasmonean usurpation of the high-priestly office.[9]

When Herod the Great was appointed to the Judean throne by the Romans, he carefully took two major steps to buttress his rule, in addition to the elimination of the Hasmonean high priests and the appointment of his own obscure but loyal candidates to the position. On the one hand, in order to show his Roman overlords that he was their faithful friend and ally, and that his kingdom was an integral part of their Empire, he built Caesarea Maritima as a major administrative center, port, and Roman religious center. On the other hand, to prove his loyalty to Judaism he magnificently rebuilt the Jerusalem Temple on an unprecedented scale.[10] After the Romans abolished the client kingdom of Judea, it was again the high priests who stood at the head of as much as remained of the Judean autonomy and who represented the Judeans before the imperial authorities.[11] When Gaius Caligula decided to Romanize the Jerusalem Temple by erecting his statue in it, in all probability it was only his assassination that forestalled a wholesale Judean rebellion.[12] The Great Revolt against Rome took off with the termination of the customary sacrifice on behalf of the Emperor,[13] and crashed with the destruction of the Temple and the concomitant cessation of the sacrificial cult.

Such examples of the centrality of the Temple in the religious and political life of Judea could easily be multiplied, but these should suffice

---

[8] The first to proclaim himself a king was Aristobulus I (104–103 BCE). On priesthood and monarchy in the Hasmonean period, see D.R. Schwartz, "Priesthood and Monarchy in the Hasmonean Period," in *Kehal Yisrael: Jewish Self-Rule Through the Ages, I: The Ancient Period* (ed. I.M. Gafni; Jerusalem, 2001), 13–25 (in Hebrew).

[9] See J. Sievers, *The Hasmoneans and Their Supporters from Mattathias to the Death of John Hyrcanus I* (Atlanta, 1990); H. Eshel, *The Dead Sea Scrolls and the Hasmonean State* (Grand Rapids-Jerusalem, 2008); E.P. Sanders, *Judaism: Practice and Belief. 63 BCE–66 CE* (London, 1992), 13–29. Cf. A.I. Baumgarten, *The Flourishing of Jewish Sects in the Maccabean Era: An Interpretation* (Leiden, 1997).

[10] On Herod's politics, see M. Stern, "The Reign of Herod and the Herodian Dynasty," in *The Jewish People in the First Century* (ed. S. Safrai and M. Stern; 2 vols.; Assen, 1974–1976), 1: 216–307.

[11] This is abundantly clear both from Josephus and the Gospels.

[12] P. Bilde, "The Roman Emperor Gaius (Caligula)'s Attempt to Erect His Statue in the Temple of Jerusalem," *Studia Theologica* 32 (1978): 67–93.

[13] *J.W.* 2.409.

to illustrate that this institution, its rituals and personnel were paramount both in the religious and political history of Judea throughout the Second Temple period.[14] Quite predictably, accordingly, the Jerusalem Temple, its cult, and its priesthood play central roles in the Jewish literature written in the Land of Israel in the Second Temple period and in the decades immediately following it.[15]

On the other hand, however, one should not ignore the fact that in the Second Temple period most Jews resided outside of the Land of Israel, far away from Jerusalem and its cultic center. So far I have been describing the situation in Judea,[16] but the fact is that sheer geographical remoteness prevented the Diaspora Jews, for most of their lives, from regular active participating in the life of the Temple.[17] So, here are the questions: How could one meaningfully live a Jewish "religious" life in the Diaspora, if the basis and center of that life were located hundreds and thousands of miles away, all but inaccessible? How could anybody maintain a vibrant Jewish identity for generations in the midst of the engulfing sea of competing cults, worldviews, and

[14] On Temple piety as the main constituent of "common Judaism" in the Land of Israel in the early Roman Period, see Sanders, *Judaism: Practice and Belief*. On the extent of the participation of Diaspora Jews in this "common Judaism," cf. A. Mendelson, "'Did Philo Say the Shema?' and Other Reflections on E.P. Sanders' *Judaism: Practice and Belief*," *SPhA* 6 (1994): 160–70. On the history of the high priesthood in the Second Temple period, see J.C. VanderKam, *From Joshua to Caiaphas: High Priests after the Exile* (Minneapolis, 2004); Brutti, *The Development of the High Priesthood*.

[15] As conspicuous examples of Palestinian writings preoccupied with Temple- and cult-related issues and composed in the period under review, one may adduce 1 Esdras, *Aramaic Levi Document (ALD)*, Baruch, Sirach, Daniel 7–12, *Jubilees*, 1 Maccabees, *Psalms of Solomon*, *1 Enoch*, *Testament of Moses*, Pseudo-Philo's *Liber Antiquitatum Biblicarum*, *4 Ezra*, *2 Baruch*, *Ladder of Jacob*, and the *Apocalypse of Abraham*.

[16] Although the Qumran Scrolls and early rabbinic literature, too, were primarily composed and edited in the Land of Israel, they present special cases and have to be discussed separately. On Qumran as basically an "exilic" community, see N. Hacham, "Exile and Self-Identity in the Qumran Sect and in Hellenistic Judaism," in *New Perspectives on Old Texts: Proceedings of the Tenth International Symposium of the Orion Center for the Study of the Dead Sea Scrolls and Associated Literature, 9–11 January, 2005* (ed. E.G. Chazon, B. Halpern-Amaru, and R.A. Clements; Leiden, 2010), 3–21; on the comparison between Diaspora, Qumranic, and rabbinic conceptions of the location of Divine presence, see idem, "Where Does the Shekhina Dwell? Between the Dead Sea Sect, Diaspora Judaism and Rabbinic Literature," in *The Dead Sea Scrolls in Context: Integrating the Dead Sea Scrolls in the Study of Ancient Texts, Languages, and Cultures* (ed. A. Lange, E. Tov, M. Weigold; Leiden, 2011), 399–412.

[17] Cf. E.S. Gruen, *Diaspora: Jews amidst Greeks and Romans* (Cambridge, Mass., 2002), 234: "Hellenistic Jews did not have to face the eradication of the Temple. It was there—but they were not."

philosophies, and at the same time hold fast to the belief that the only true worship, indeed, the one revealed by God Himself to His covenant people, was being conducted in a remote place stuck away among the mountains of Judea?[18]

The answer that I would propose to these questions would be considered controversial by some. In my view the Jews of the Greco-Roman Diaspora did not, by and large, hold fast to that belief, but rather gradually developed coherent Judaic religious systems of belief and practice that did not require a focus on the Temple and its sacrificial cult. Indeed, one might say that if Diaspora Jews wanted to preserve and perpetuate their religious and cultural identities, they did not have any other choice.[19]

This is not to say that the Jews of the Diaspora generally and consistently exhibited anti-Temple, anti-cultic or anti-priestly attitudes, openly criticized the Jerusalem Temple and its cult, regularly emphasized their own estrangement from these institutions, or called for their abolishment.[20] Indeed, until recently it was a common view, at least in some scholarly circles, that the attitude of Diaspora Jews towards the Temple and its sacrifices was not much different from that of their coreligionists in Judea.[21] In fairness to the scholars who held that view

---

[18] This question was already posed in D.R. Schwartz, "Temple or City: What did Hellenistic Jews See in Jerusalem?" in *The Centrality of Jerusalem* (ed. M. Poorthuis and C. Safrai; Kampen, 1996), 114–27. Cf. M.J. Martin, "The School of Virtue and the Tent of Zion" (Ph.D. diss., University of Melbourne, 2000), discussed and quoted below.

[19] Cf. J.N. Lightstone, "Roman Diaspora Judaism," in *A Companion to Roman Religion* (ed. J. Rüpke; Oxford, 2007), 367–68: "I do not wish to understate the importance of physical distance from Jerusalem and the biblical interdiction against sacrificing elsewhere in describing transformations of biblical Judaism devised and/or adopted in the Diaspora—in particular, the emergence of the synagogue, and a cult of scriptural readings and scriptural lessons, and of prayer—as normative alternatives to the sacrificial cult in the Jerusalem Temple. Indeed, with the destruction of the Temple, and with the realization that the opportunity to reestablish that Temple was a remote eventuality (confirmed by the failure of the Bar Kochba rebellion), these normative institutions of the Diaspora became the norm for Palestinian Jews as well."

[20] Among those who did were the author of *Sibylline Oracle* 4 and the figure of Stephen in Acts 7. On these, see below. Cf. M. Simon, *St Stephen and the Hellenists in the Primitive Church* (London, 1958); Schwartz, "Temple or City"; and M. Tuval, "The 4th *Sibylline Oracle* and the Popularity of Judaism among the Pagans after the Destruction of the Second Temple," *Vestnik Yevreyskogo Universiteta* 10 (28) (2005): 23–54 (in Russian).

[21] S. Safrai, *The Pilgrimage in the Second Temple Period* (Tel-Aviv, 1965) (in Hebrew); idem, "Relations between the Diaspora and the Land of Israel," in Safrai and Stern, *The Jewish People in the First Century*, 1: 184–215; M. Stern, "The Diaspora:

it should be said that some of the writings produced in the Diaspora do witness to the respect of their authors towards the Temple, its cult, and its priests. But the question I want to ask is not about elementary respect and honor towards the institutes of divine service sanctioned by the Holy Writ.[22] Rather, my question is whether the contemporary Jerusalem Temple and its cult provided—indeed, could have provided—a meaningful basis for the religious identity and practice of the myriads of North African, Egyptian, Syrian, Mesopotamian, Asian, Mediterranean and Roman Jews in the course of their lives lived in the Temple-less Diaspora; the question is about how the Temple and cult practically functioned in their Judaism. I claim that the analysis of Jewish literature produced in the Graeco-Roman Diaspora shows that these institutions did not have such a practical function; on the basis of this analysis I argue, rather, that Diaspora Jews devised types of Judaism different from that centered on the Jerusalem Temple and its cult.[23]

It has been a commonplace to speak about the "loyalty" of Diaspora Judaism to the Jerusalem Temple, this "loyalty" mainly being understood as the recognition by Diaspora Jews of that institution's centrality for Judaism, and their practices of the payment of the half-shekel tax, and pilgrimage to Jerusalem. However, in my view, it has also been convincingly demonstrated that this kind of terminology does not really describe or explain anything in the religious views and practices of Diaspora Jews. In comparing the relative importance of the Jerusalem Temple and Diaspora synagogue for the life of the Diaspora communities of the early Roman period, M.J. Martin wrote:

> Those Jews who dwelt in Jerusalem or its immediate environs and had reasonable access to the Temple may well have counted the Jerusalem and its Temple a significant part of their religious experience. But what of the Jewish communities who dwelt in the Graeco-Roman Diaspora?

General Outline," in *The Diaspora in the Hellenistic-Roman World* (ed. M. Stern and Z. Baras; Jerusalem, 1983), esp. 11–20 (in Hebrew).

[22] Respect and honor might come especially easy if, among many other things, one does not have to wage bloody wars with the pagans for the Temple, to be persecuted by a Judean High Priest, to be too closely familiar with the officiating priests, or to think too much about the differences between one's own *halakhah* and that of the Sadducean Temple establishment. That is, it might be easier to respect and honor the Temple and its personnel if one is not too closely involved and familiar with them—in other words, if one lives in the Diaspora.

[23] See Schwartz, "Temple or City."

> The realities of their situation were such that, in all likelihood, very few of these Jews ever had the opportunity to see the Temple. On the contrary, it was the institution of the synagogue which formed the fundamental focus of their religious life and experience. Whatever significance the Temple may have possessed, it must have been largely restricted to the field of the notional.[24]

In other words, the fact that one does not routinely find hard evidence of opposition to, or criticism and negation of, the Temple and its cult in Diaspora literature does not automatically mean that Diaspora Jews were "loyal" to the Temple in any immediate way, or that this institution was "central" to their Judaism. Even if one could say, generally, that they were "loyal," this would convey very little about their religious worldview, practices, and identity. In other words, such statements are essentially meaningless as far as the description and analysis of Diaspora faith and practice are concerned.[25]

In my view, it is not entirely surprising that several Diaspora compositions should ascribe some importance to the Temple and its cult; after all, as we have seen, they were at the center of Judaism as conceived by the Torah of Moses. Although the Diaspora Jews used Greek translations of the Torah, it is difficult to deny that they read basically the same book as the Jews in Judea, and it would be nothing short of astonishing had they decided to consign the Temple and its cult to oblivion. Rather, what is indeed remarkable about the Diaspora authors is that, despite the centrality of the Temple and its cult in the Torah and its importance in the religious and political life of Judea in the Second Temple period, so many of them did marginalize it in most of their writings.

In this study, I will analyze some prominent Diaspora writings and try to describe the various components of their religious constructs, in some cases contrasting them with the Temple-centered worldviews of Judean texts. I am not just looking for the absence of the Temple and its cult. Rather, I am looking for different religious paradigms. I am looking for coherent Judaisms which do well without the Temple and sacrifices.

At the outset, several caveats are in order. First, this is not a full-scale and comprehensive study of Temple, cult, and priesthood in all

---

[24] Martin, "School of Virtue," 25–26.
[25] Martin's influence on my study and his analysis of Philo's attitude to the Temple are discussed below.

of Diaspora literature. That corpus is simply too vast to be exhaustively treated in one article. Indeed, several studies have already been written on Philo of Alexandria's views of the Temple and Jewish worship alone.[26] Neither will I attempt to comprehensively analyze and describe the various religious systems designed by Diaspora Jews, or the identity paradigms that emerge from literary and archaeological remains. Fortunately, this has also been successfully attempted a number of times in recent years.[27] Rather, I will limit my treatment to the analysis of the evidence demonstrating that most Diaspora writers, in contrast to contemporary Palestinian authors, routinely and naturally transferred their emphasis from Temple-and-cult-related issues to other aspects of Jewish practice and belief. In many cases this emphasis was novel and unprecedented, or at least brought into prominence issues underemphasized in the literature produced in the Land of Israel.

II. Previous Studies of Diaspora Jewish Religion

In some respects, this study has been anticipated, and inspired, by the work of earlier scholars. Among those whose work on religious aspects

---

[26] Martin, "School of Virtue"; J. Leonhardt-Balzer, *Jewish Worship in Philo of Alexandria* (Tübingen, 2001). In addition to these, see E.R. Goodenough, *By Light, Light: The Mystic Gospel of Hellenistic Judaism* (New Haven, 1935), 95–120; idem, *Jewish Symbols in the Greco-Roman Period* (13 vols.; New York, 1953–68), vol. 4 (on symbols from the Jewish cult); I. Heinemann, *Philons griechische und jüdische Bildung* (Breslau, 1932), 16–82; V. Nikiprowetzky, "La spiritualisation des sacrifices et le culte sacrificiel au Temple de Jérusalem chez Philon d'Alexandrie," *Semitica* 17 (1967): 97–116; J. Laporte, "Sacrifice and Forgiveness in Philo of Alexandria," *SPhA* 1 (1989): 34–42; idem, "The High Priest in Philo of Alexandria," *SPhA* 3 (1991): 71–82; A. Lieber, "Between Motherland and Fatherland: Diaspora, Pilgrimage, and the Spiritualization of Sacrifice in Philo of Alexandria," in *The Heavenly Tablets: Interpretation, Identity, and Tradition in Ancient Judaism* (ed. L. LiDonnici and A. Lieber; Leiden, 2007), 193–210.

[27] See Stern and Baras, *The Diaspora in the Hellenistic-Roman World*; P.R. Trebilco, *Jewish Communities in Asia Minor* (Cambridge, 1991); W.C. van Unnik, *Das Selbstverständnis der jüdischen Diaspora in der hellenistisch-römischer Zeit* (Leiden, 1993); J.M.G. Barclay, *Jews in the Mediterranean Diaspora from Alexander to Trajan* (Edinburgh, 1996); I.M. Gafni, *Land, Center and Diaspora: Jewish Constructs in Late Antiquity* (Sheffield, 1997); L.V. Rutgers, *The Hidden Heritage of Diaspora Judaism* (Leuven, 1998); J.J. Collins, *Between Athens and Jerusalem: Jewish Identity in the Hellenistic Diaspora* (2d ed.; Grand Rapids, 2000); E.S. Gruen, *Heritage and Hellenism: The Reinvention of Jewish Tradition* (Berkley, 1998); idem, *Diaspora*, 2002; I.M. Gafni, ed., *Center and Diaspora: The Land of Israel and the Diaspora in the Second Temple, Mishnah and Talmud Periods* (Jerusalem, 2004) (in Hebrew); T. Rajak, *Translation and Survival: The Greek Bible of the Ancient Jewish Diaspora* (Oxford, 2009).

of Diaspora Judaism has had much influence on my understanding of the question, I should single out E.R. Goodenough, M. Smith, D. Georgi, J.N. Lightstone, D.R. Schwartz, J.J. Collins, and M.J. Martin.[28] However, for reasons of space I will concentrate here on the work of just two of them: J.N. Lightstone and M.J. Martin.

Lightstone's *Commerce of the Sacred* is not a full-scale textual study of the literary heritage of Diaspora Judaism(s), but many of his conclusions are similar to my own. Lightstone's main achievement consists of his success in demonstrating that the Temple-oriented Judaism of Judea and the Temple-less Judaisms of the Diaspora basically represent different paradigms for configuring access to the sacred and the divine. He presents his provocative thesis concerning the difference between "the Judaic universe...centered in the Jerusalem Temple of the Second Commonwealth" and Diaspora Judaism as follows:

> I shall argue that Judaism of the Graeco-Roman Diaspora reflects a different configuration in appropriating and mediating the sacred, a shamanistic model in many respects. Removed first by distance (before 70 CE), and later (after 70) by the cult's demise, from the "socio-systemic" sacred order of the Temple, the Yahwehists [sic] of the Graeco-Roman world depended upon various and varied loci at which the sacred could be had—this to effect health, order and prosperity in this lower realm.[29]

As is clear from this passage as well as from the subtitle of Lightstone's book, his study is mainly concerned with the "mediation of the divine among Jews in the Graeco-Roman Diaspora." I agree that the question concerning the "loci at which the sacred could be had" is of paramount importance as far as the basic and paradigmatic difference between pre-70 Palestinian and Diaspora Judaisms is concerned. However, in addition to "the commerce of the sacred" I would also like to emphasize the question of coherent religious and cultural identities of Diaspora Jews—identities mainly constructed without recourse to the Temple and sacrifices, and able to provide meaning and cohesion to Jews in Diaspora conditions—both as individuals and as whole

---

[28] Goodenough, *By Light, Light*; Goodenough, *Jewish Symbols*; M. Smith, *Studies in the Cult of Yahweh* (ed. S.J.D. Cohen; 2 vols.; Leiden, 1996); D. Georgi, *The Opponents of Paul in Second Corinthians* (Philadelphia, 1986); J.N. Lightstone, *The Commerce of the Sacred: Mediation of the Divine among the Jews in the Graeco-Roman Diaspora* (2d ed.; New York, 2006 [1st ed., 1984]); idem, "Roman Diaspora Judaism"; Schwartz, "Temple or City"; Collins, *Between Athens and Jerusalem*; Martin, "School of Virtue."

[29] Lightstone, *Commerce of the Sacred*, 5.

communities. I do not think that identity was at all times necessarily concerned with the "mediation of the divine."

Moreover, as will become clear from the following discussion, although I do recognize the importance of "holy men," semidivinized patriarchs, and martyrs' atoning deaths, for some of the Diaspora Judaic systems, I do not necessarily agree with Lightstone that *all* of these systems were axiomatically more "shamanistic" than those current in Palestine. We know that there were "holy men" and "magicians" in the Jerusalem Temple precincts.[30] We will also see that the Diaspora identity paradigms reflected in the fragmentary Hellenistic Jewish authors focus on Torah-study, and those in the *Testament of Abraham, Pseudo-Phocylides* and the *Sibylline Oracles* are preoccupied with ethics.[31] In other words, I take Lightstone's "shamanistic" paradigm as only one of a whole series of multifaceted Diaspora Judaism configurations.

This study has also been inspired by the doctoral dissertation of M.J. Martin, which was quoted above and which unfortunately, remains unpublished.[32] As the dissertation's subtitle states, it is "an investigation into the relationship between the institutions of the Graeco-Roman Diaspora synagogue and the Jerusalem Temple in late Second Temple Judaism: Philo of Alexandria—a case-study." Martin sets out to thoroughly analyze the place and function of these two institutions in the worldview and practice of Philo of Alexandria. After presenting the data concerning pre-70 CE Diaspora synagogues, he discusses, first, the place of the Alexandrian synagogue, and then, that of the Jerusalem Temple, in the thought of Philo. Next, Martin analyzes Philo's description of the sect of the Therapeutae, which Philo presents as the ideal Jewish community and the embodiment of the virtues taught by Moses; and finally, he treats Philo's eschatological views.

Martin argues convincingly that the Temple is conspicuously absent both from Philo's description of the ideal Jewish community, and from his eschatological vision of the ideal future. According to Martin,

---

[30] Indeed, it seems that most of those we actually hear of were active in Palestine. See M. Smith, *Jesus the Magician* (New York, 1978); R. Gray, *Prophetic Figures in Late Second Temple Palestine: The Evidence from Josephus* (Oxford, 1993); D.C. Duling, "Solomon, Exorcism, and the Son of David," *HTR* 68 (1975): 235–52; G. Bohak, *Ancient Jewish Magic: A History* (Cambridge, 2008). On an expert exorcist who is described as "a Syrian from Palestine," see Lucian, *Philopseudes,* 16 (in *GLA* 3:222 [no. 372]).

[31] See the analysis below.

[32] Martin, "School of Virtue."

the Temple was important to Philo mainly on the political and communal level. It symbolized the Roman recognition and protection of Judaism, and served as a convenient point of reference for common Jewish piety.

Philo was not only an ivory tower intellectual, but also a communal leader, and he realized that not all Jews were as sophisticated and "spiritual" as himself:

> At one level Philo attributes to the Temple a role as guide for those Jews who lack the intellectual sophistication of men like Philo himself to apprehend the true nature of the worship of God in the Temple of the rational soul. Philo construes two types of people in the world—the sages (like himself) and the mob (ὁ ὄχλος); those who love God, and those who fear Him. The Temple is for the benefit of the latter. The former have no need of it. Thus we find revealed an aspect of Philo as a leader of the Jewish community of Alexandria—in the guise of what we might call pastoral concerns.[33]

Martin goes on to explain that as a communal leader, Philo realized all too well that "if the Roman state may freely and openly attack the Temple of the Jewish *metropolis*, then a signal is given that any Jewish community, anywhere in the world, may be readily made the target of oppression."[34] The Temple was thus important for Philo since—and insofar as—it symbolized Roman recognition and protection of Judaism.

In my view, Martin's achievement is mainly his success in explaining convincingly, on the one hand, the factors from which the positive attitude to the Temple in Philo's thinking stemmed; and on the other, the reasons for the negligible role it played in his personal faith and practice. Martin claims that the synagogue played a much more important and immediate role than the Temple in Diaspora Judaism (as represented by Philo), to the point that Diasporan religious life can be described as "the life of the synagogue." As will become clear from the following analysis of Diaspora writings, I accept Martin's conclusions as valid. However, granting that "the synagogue" was the main *communal institution* of Diaspora Judaism, I tend to see it as only one of a whole array of new ideas and paradigms, devised by Diaspora Jews

---

[33] Martin, "School of Virtue," 250.
[34] Ibid., 250–51.

in the course of their search for suitable replacements for the "life of the Temple."[35]

As has been stated above, no full-scale study and comprehensive analysis of all features of Diaspora literature will be attempted here. I will first provide some introductory material concerning the corpus of literature to be discussed. Then I will concentrate on the analysis of what these particular compositions say about the Temple and the cult, if they say anything about them at all. On the basis of this analysis I will also try to document the development of religious ideas and identity paradigms created to provide coherence outside of the system of the Temple and its cult.

III. The Literary Corpus to be Considered

The extant corpus of Diaspora Jewish literature is a heterogeneous collection of disparate compositions and fragments written by many authors over a long period, originating in various locations,[36] and belonging to different genres. One thinks of the fragmentary collection of excerpts from the "Hellenistic Jewish Authors" (mostly of Egyptian provenance) on the one hand, and of the voluminous works of Philo (also Egyptian) and Josephus (Roman), on the other. The writings include works of historiography, like 2 Maccabees; expansions and rewritings of biblical stories or postbiblical tales (*Prayer of Joseph, Joseph and Aseneth*, Tobit,[37] *Letter of Aristeas*, 3 Maccabees); wisdom and philosophical literature (Wisdom of Solomon, 4 Maccabees, *Sentences of Pseudo-Phocylides*); testamentary writings (*Testament of Job, Testament of Abraham*); apocalyptic and other revelatory literature

---

[35] Moreover, Martin makes clear in his introduction that he thinks that, in contrast to Philo, Josephus' writings cannot be used as the basis for a comparable study. Josephus, in his view, "was not a Diaspora Jew. On the contrary, Josephus' experience of Judaism is firmly centered in Judaea, more specifically, in Jerusalem" (p. 32). It seems to me that Martin's characterization of Josephus' religious experience is only valid in respect to his earliest writing, namely, the *Jewish War*. As far as his later writings are concerned, I would argue that they were written from the position of a mature Diasporan intellectual. The present study is intended to provide the context for a much fuller treatment of Josephus' views on the Temple and cult—which I am undertaking in my doctoral dissertation.

[36] Although the vast majority of what has survived originated in Ptolemaic and Roman Egypt.

[37] Although Tobit, with its emphasis on the righteous deeds, angelic protection, and exorcism, would be a good witness to Diasporan concerns, it is not discussed here.

(*2 Enoch, Sibylline Oracles*), exegetical works (Philo); prayers (*Hellenistic Synagogal Prayers*); and much more. It is extremely difficult to speak of any features common to all of these compositions. Even if one tried to do so, the results would seem artificial and forced. Therefore, instead of trying to distill from this motley collection any common denominator of attitudes towards the Temple and its cult, I will attempt to describe each text on its own terms, paying attention to a number of pertinent factors, as described below.

First, I will discuss a number of Diaspora documents which in my view exhibit coherent Judaic worldviews without assigning any role to the Jerusalem Temple and its cult, or which at least downplay them. In the course of this discussion I will occasionally compare what Diaspora authors say on the Temple-and-sacrifice-related topics with parallel Palestinian material, indicating differences, novelties, and alternatives in light of what has been stated above. I will try to isolate new and religiously important ideas and phenomena that are not documented or are merely marginal in Palestinian literature but are prominent in Diaspora writings; I will then try to imagine how these ideas and phenomena functioned in the religious worldview of Diaspora Jews, and whether they provided them with working alternatives to the Temple-centered system regnant in the Land of Israel. Finally, I will try to account for the Diaspora compositions that seem to emphasize the importance of the Temple and its cult—whether in the here and now or in their eschatological scenarios.

IV. Fragments of Hellenistic Jewish Authors

One may begin the discussion with the group of writings known as "Fragments of Hellenistic Jewish Authors."[38] As D.R. Schwartz noticed, the Temple and its cult are not mentioned in this corpus apart from

---

[38] Specifics are given below. These texts have been recently reedited, with introductions, notes and commentaries, by C.R. Holladay, *Fragments from Hellenistic Jewish Authors* (4 vols.; Chico and Atlanta, 1983–96). See also the introductions to the annotated translations in *OTP* 2:775–918. The classic study of these authors is J. Freudenthal, *Hellenistische Studien, 1–2: Alexander Polyhistor und die von ihm erhaltenen Reste jüdischer und samaritanischer Geschichtswerke* (Breslau, 1875). For an analysis of these fragments in their broader contexts, see P.M. Fraser, *Ptolemaic Alexandria* (3 vols.; Oxford, 1972), 1:687–716 (text); 2:955–1003 (notes). Cf. Collins, *Between Athens and Jerusalem*; and Y. Gutman, *The Beginnings of Jewish-Hellenistic Literature* (2 vols.; Jerusalem, 1958) (in Hebrew).

the excerpts from the writings of Eupolemus—who was not a Diaspora Jew at all, but rather a Judean priest.[39] Another exception to this rule is Ps.-Hecataeus, whose fragment, preserved in Josephus's *Against Apion* 1:183–204, contains an idealized description of the Temple precincts and priestly activities.[40] One could of course object by saying that these "Fragments" are just that, fragments—and so it is risky to form an opinion concerning anything that is not mentioned in them, since it might have been mentioned in those parts which have not survived. Moreover, they have mostly been preserved in later Christian compositions, and may have been arbitrarily taken out of their context to prove points quite contrary to their original authors' intentions.

However, it should be said that we are dealing with more than a dozen authors, some of whom are represented in extensive excerpts. And it has actually been demonstrated that most of these excerpts, albeit fragmentary, develop coherent topics and exhibit consistent worldviews. In many cases it is possible to ascertain the authors' overall agendas and even to describe the identity paradigms they represent.[41]

These identity (re-)constructions are mainly centered on the explaining, reworking, reinterpreting, reenacting, and embellishing of inherited sacred biblical traditions, mainly of the "historical" genre.[42] Thus, for example, we find a preoccupation with exegesis, biblical chronology, and genealogy in Demetrius and Aristeas the Exegete. In the writings of Artapanus, Philo the Epic Poet[43] and Ezekiel the Tragedian we see various creative attempts to rewrite, reinterpret, and actualize diverse biblical stories. In addition to this, Ezekiel the Tragedian, in his portrayal of Moses, seems to witness to a tradition of the apotheosis of

---

[39] Schwartz, "Temple or City," 119. Schwartz is correct, if he considers only the "Fragmentary authors" preserved in Eusebius and Clement.

[40] This passage is discussed below.

[41] See, above all, Collins, *Between Athens and Jerusalem*. Cf. Barclay, *Jews in the Mediterranean Diaspora*; Gruen, *Heritage and Hellenism*, and idem, *Diaspora*.

[42] Collins, *Between Athens and Jerusalem*, 29–60; 224–30. On the praxis of biblical interpretation in these texts, see P.W. van der Horst, "The Interpretation of the Bible by the Minor Hellenistic Jewish Authors," in *Mikra: Text, Translation, Reading and Interpretation of the Hebrew Bible in Ancient Judaism and Early Christianity* (ed. M.J. Mulder; Leiden, 1988; Assen and Philadelphia, 1990), 519–46.

[43] Philo the Epic Poet wrote a work *On Jerusalem*, but no mention of the Temple is preserved among the surviving fragments. He seems to have been fascinated by Jerusalem's water system, and the only mention of "high priest" is in the context of the description of various hydraulic installations. See H.W. Attridge, "Philo the Epic Poet," in *OTP* 2:784.

biblical heroes, which will be discussed below.[44] In the case of the fragmentary "Pseudo-Greek" authors we find attempts to ascribe biblical messages to pagan worthies and in this way to add authority to Jewish sacred tradition and Jewish values, or even to preach these traditions and values out of the mouths of pagans themselves. In these cases no biblical history is retold, since that would compromise the pseudepigrapher.[45] The fragments from the writings of Aristobulus are our earliest example of the attempt to reconcile the teachings of Moses with Greek thought, and to claim primacy and superiority for the former.[46]

As noted above, the only "fragmentary" Diaspora author from whom any mention of the Jerusalem Temple survives is Ps.-Hecataeus.[47] However, it should be noted that the relevant fragment seems to be more interested in the Temple as the most interesting edifice in Jerusalem than in its function.[48] It is worth mentioning that Ps.-Hecataeus states that there was "not a single statue or votive offering, no trace of a plant, in the form of a sacred grove or the like" in the Temple precincts, thus contrasting the Jewish Temple with pagan shrines. This contrast seems to be an important element in this passage, since throughout his fragments the author repeatedly emphasized the Jewish

---

[44] See now P. Lanfranchi, *L'Exagoge d'Ezéchiel le Tragique: Introduction, texte, traduction et commentaire* (Leiden, 2006). On the traditions of Moses' exaltation see W. Meeks, "Moses as God and King," in *Religions in Antiquity: Essays in Memory of E. R. Goodenough* (ed. J. Neusner; Leiden, 1968), 354–59; B.L. Mack, "Imitatio Mosis: Patterns of Cosmology and Soteriology in the Hellenistic Synagogue," *SPhilo* 1 (1972): 27–55. The "divinity" of Moses has also been recently discussed by L.H. Feldman, *Philo's Portrayal of Moses in the Context of Ancient Judaism* (Notre Dame, 2007), 331–57.

[45] However, the authors of the Jewish *Sibylline Oracles* seem not to have thought that there was a tension between presenting their oracles as pagan prophecies and praising the Jewish people and their Law—and sometimes even their sacrificial cult. In addition to the texts collected in Holladay, one should add Ps.-Phocylides to this category. The *Sibylline Oracles* and Ps.-Phoc. are treated below.

[46] See the classic study by N. Walter, *Der Thoraausleger Aristobulus* (Berlin, 1964); Holladay, *Fragments*, vol. III: *Aristobulus*. On Aristobulus' interpretation of the Bible, see F. Siegert, "Early Jewish Interpretation in a Hellenistic Style," in *Hebrew Bible/Old Testament: The History of Its Interpretation, Vol. 1: From the Beginnings to the Middle Ages (Until 1300)* (ed. M. Sæbø; Göttingen, 1996), 154–62.

[47] On Ps.-Hecataeus, see especially B. Bar-Kochva, *Pseudo-Hecataeus, "On the Jews": Legitimizing the Jewish Diaspora* (Berkeley, 1996).

[48] No sacrifices are mentioned, just a crude stone altar, and another golden altar and lampstand, upon which the light is never extinguished (§§198–199). Curiously, in his description of the priests he does not think it is important enough to discuss their main activity, sacrifices, but only to say that they "pass their nights and days performing certain rites of purification, and abstaining altogether from wine while in the Temple" (§199). Translations of Ps.-Hecataeus are taken from Holladay, *Fragments*, 1:309–13.

abhorrence of idolatry and pagan superstitions, along with their willingness to suffer "tortures and death in its most terrible form, rather than repudiate the faith of their forefathers" (§191). As will become clear from the following discussion, the valorization of martyrdom for the sake of the Law was an important theme in Diaspora literature.

In other words, the written Torah (broadly defined) with its messages, meanings and conundrums—and faithfulness to that text—is what occupies the central place in these fragmentary writings. Most of these works could be—albeit anachronistically—placed in the category described by the later rabbinic concept of "talmud Torah," i.e., Torah study, the only activity worthy of a pious Jewish man, and the main act of worship. The profile of Judaism that can be discerned in these compositions reflects the fact that its proponents highly valued the biblical narrative, venerated their national heroes, and believed that it was extremely important to observe the commandments of the Torah, which some of them considered to be universal truths revealed by God to all humanity. However, with one exception, none of these fragments indicates that its author evinced any interest in the Jerusalem Temple, its cult, or its ritual.

V. Mysteries and Revelations

The authors surveyed above could be said to represent text-oriented Diaspora paradigms. There were also more mystic authors. The main representative of this group, of course, is Philo of Alexandria, but since—because of their volume and scope—his writings constitute a special case, he will be discussed separately in a broader study. Here, I will examine three representatives of mystic Diaspora compositions— a romance (*Joseph and Aseneth*), an enigmatic, fragmentary *Prayer of Joseph*, and an apocalypse known as *2 Enoch*. These compositions are notoriously difficult to date, and we can only speculate concerning their precise geographical provenance and *Sitz im Leben*.[49]

1) *Joseph and Aseneth*

This text is a riddle, confronting its interpreters with a number of difficulties, both with regard to both its exact provenance and its

---

[49] However, their general Diaspora provenance is taken for granted by most scholars.

message.[50] However, because the story is set in Egypt, deals with questions that were likely to have been faced by Egyptian Jews, and is full of criticism of Egyptian cults, the majority of scholars tend to posit an Egyptian origin.[51]

The romance is based on the biblical story of Joseph and his marriage to Aseneth, a daughter of a pagan Egyptian priest. At the center of the plot is the narrative of her conversion from idolatry to the worship of the one true God of the Jews. This conversion is accompanied by deep repentance and the recognition of the vapidity of idolatry, and sealed by arcane and esoteric rites, which have perplexed generations of scholars. Following her transformation, Aseneth becomes a paradigmatic convert, a city of refuge for all those who will recognize the futility of idol worship and see the true light of the one God of the Jews.[52] It is important to note that the only sacrifices and temples mentioned in the story are those of the dead and dumb pagan gods (e.g., 11:8–9). In contrast to what is known about the admittedly later rabbinic conversion ceremony, Aseneth's conversion is not accompanied by any sacrifice.[53] One is led to conclude that the God of the Jews is truly and sufficiently worshipped by acts of repentance, ascetic practices, and continual supplications. Throughout the story, much importance is ascribed to the virginity and chastity of both Aseneth and Joseph, and it is clear that for the author of the romance, austere sexual morality is one of the prime virtues of Judaism. Questions of food purity are also prominent.[54] Thus, the Diaspora author of *Joseph and Aseneth* managed to create the description of a paradigmatic conversion from

---

[50] See E.M. Humphrey, *Joseph and Aseneth* (Sheffield, 2000), for an introduction and further bibliography. Cf. Collins, *Between Athens and Jerusalem*, 103–10; 230–39. R.S. Kraemer, *When Aseneth Met Joseph* (New York, 1998) prefers a third- or fourth-century date and remains agnostic as far as the provenance of the work is concerned. For another introduction, along with an English translation, see C. Burchard, "Joseph and Aseneth," in *OTP* 2:177–247. Burchard has also produced an exemplary critical edition of the Greek text: *Joseph und Aseneth* (Leiden, 2003).

[51] An ingenious interpretation has been advanced by G. Bohak, who links this composition to the circles around the Temple of Onias in Leontopolis in Egypt; see his *Joseph and Aseneth and the Jewish Temple in Heliopolis* (Atlanta, 1996). This suggestion, however interesting, seems to have failed to convince the majority of scholars, and I believe this work may still be understood without linking it to Onias' temple.

[52] On conversion in Joseph and Aseneth, see R.D. Chesnutt, *From Death to Life: Conversion in Joseph and Aseneth* (Sheffield, 1995).

[53] On the rabbinic conversion ritual, see S.J.D. Cohen, *The Beginnings of Jewishness: Boundaries, Varieties, Uncertainties* (Berkeley 1999), 198–238.

[54] See R.D. Chesnutt, "Joseph and Aseneth: Food as an Identity Marker," in *The Historical Jesus in Context* (ed. A.-J. Levine et al.; Princeton, 2006), 357–65.

idolatry to the only true divine worship without mentioning the center and content of the Jewish sacrificial cult even once. Apparently, for him real worship consisted of something totally different.

2) *Prayer of Joseph*

Our next example is the no less enigmatic *Prayer of Joseph*, which is preserved in two short but extremely fascinating fragments, and was thoroughly analyzed by J.Z. Smith in an article appropriately published in the memorial volume dedicated to E.R. Goodenough.[55] As is well-known, Goodenough dedicated most of his career to the analysis of the literary and archaeological remains of what he considered to be a Hellenistic Jewish mystery religion. Leaving aside the problematic aspects of Goodenough's overarching thesis, it is possible to concede that the *Prayer of Joseph* is a prime example of the kind of Hellenistic Jewish theology that he reconstructed: heavenly mediators, the patriarchs as incarnations of divine Law and as savior figures, mystical heavenly ascents and descents. The work offers a speech by the Patriarch Jacob who presents himself as "Israel, an angel of God and a ruling spirit...Israel, i.e., a man seeing God, because I am the firstborn of every living thing to whom God gives life....I, Israel, *the archangel of power of the Lord* and the *chief captain* among the sons of God." Jacob also declares that "*Abraham* and Isaac *were created before any work*," and claims to have "*descended to earth* and...tabernacled (κατεσκήνωσα)[56] among men" (Fragment A).[57]

Of course, at first glance the mere fact that Temple and cult are not mentioned in this fragment does not mean much. However, if this fragment is considered in the broader context of other Hellenistic Jewish literature, primarily the materials studied by Goodenough (and later, Lightstone), it does look like a coherent piece of Hellenistic Jewish theology centered on semi-divinized biblical heroes as living incarnations of divine powers and mediators of salvation both in this

---

[55] "The Prayer of Joseph," in *Religions in Antiquity: Essays in Memory of E.R. Goodenough* (ed. J. Neusner; Leiden, 1968), 253-94. See also idem, "The Prayer of Joseph," in *OTP* 2:699–714; The document has also been recently discussed in P.W. van der Horst and J.H. Newman, *Early Jewish Prayers in Greek* (Berlin and New York, 2008), 247–58.

[56] Cf. John 1:14 on the incarnation of the preexistent Logos-Jesus: ἐσκήνωσεν ἐν ἡμῖν. See Goodenough, *By Light, Light*, 155, where he suggests that Christian copyists might have suppressed Philonic tractates *On Isaac* and *On Jacob*, precisely because of the parallels with Jesus that they may have offered.

[57] Translation is taken from Smith, "The Prayer of Joseph," in *OTP* 2:713 (italics in the original).

world and in the hereafter. The preexistent, supernatural patriarchs were available and ever-present in every part of the *oikoumene*, and could serve as conduits of heavenly boons and truths to anybody willing to delve into the deeper meanings of the Law. Even if this does not mean that in such a case the Temple and sacrifices necessarily became entirely irrelevant, it is very likely that in the Temple-less Diaspora context the omnipresent patriarchs and other heavenly figures, who had *tabernacled* (!) among men, had a much better chance of being considered as first choices when a Diaspora Jew asked the question: "Via whom, where, and by what means might I find *Shekhinah?*"[58]

3) 2 (Slavonic) Enoch

The apocalypse known as *2 Enoch* has been preserved only in mediaeval Slavonic manuscripts; some recent preliminary reports indicate that a few fragments are attested in Coptic.[59] Although the text is not cited in any earlier sources, most scholars incline in favor of a Jewish original, written in Greek in the Diaspora of the Second Temple period, probably in Egypt.[60] As is well known, the authors of most apocalypses,

---

[58] σκηνόω, κατασκηνόω = שׁכן. The role of the patriarchs and other biblical figures as the embodiments of divine law and conduits of salvation and other heavenly gifts is discussed at length in Goodenough, *By Light, Light*. For another document, in which Jacob is an (earthly) angel (ὡς ἄγγελον ἐπ[ίγ]ειον), see the "Prayer of Jacob." The Greek text was published by K.L. Preisendanz, *Papyri Graecae Magicae: Die griechischen Zauberpapyri* (2 ed. Stuttgart: 1973–74) (2:148–150=PGM XXII.b). Translation: PGM XXIIb: 1–26, "Prayer of Jacob," translated by D.E. Aune, in *The Greek Magical Papyri in Translation including the Demotic Spells* (ed. H.D. Betz; Chicago, 1986), 261. Translation and commentary also in: van der Horst and Newman, *Early Jewish Prayers*, 215–46.

[59] Two recensions of this apocalypse exist. See the discussions of the textual problems in F.I. Andersen, "2 (Slavonic Apocalypse of) Enoch," in *OTP* 1:92–94; and C. Böttrich, *Weltweisheit, Menschheitsethik, Urkult: Studien zum slavischen Henochbuch* (Tübingen, 1992), 59–144. For the long recension of the Slavonic text (with Latin translation) see M.I. Sokoloff, *The Slavonic Book of Enoch the Righteous* (Moscow, 1910); for the short recension, see A. Vaillant, *Le livre des secrets d'Hénoch* (Paris, 1952). On the Coptic fragments, see J.L. Haagen, "No Longer Slavonic Only: 2 Enoch Attested in Coptic from Nubia," in *Enoch, Adam, Melchizedek: Mediatorial Figures in 2 Enoch and Second Temple Judaism* (ed. G. Boccaccini; forthcoming). Quotations are taken from Andersen, "2 (Slavonic Apocalypse of) Enoch."

[60] Collins, *Between Athens and Jerusalem*, 252 n. 175; G.W.E. Nickelsburg, *Jewish Literature between the Bible and the Mishnah: A Historical and Literary Introduction* (2d ed.; Minneapolis, 2005), 225; C. Böttrich, *Das slavische Henochbuch* (Gütersloh, 1996), 812. Andersen, "2 (Slavonic Apocalypse of) Enoch," 95–97 is more cautious concerning geographical provenance. M. Goodman, "Jewish Literature of Which the Original Language Is Uncertain," in E. Schürer, *The History of the Jewish People in the*

including those produced in the Land of Israel, exhibit much more interest in the heavenly Temple, its appurtenances, cult, and ministers, than in their earthly counterparts in Jerusalem. The question of the sources of and reasons for these speculations has been discussed many times in recent research, and it would be superfluous to review this discussion here.[61] Suffice it to say that most scholars agree that the disproportionate interest of the writers of apocalypses in the heavenly Temple and cult, as opposed to the physical Temple on earth, reflects at least to some degree their dissatisfaction with and even estrangement from the earthly Temple, its cult, and its contemporary ministers.[62] The dissatisfaction and estrangement does not necessarily need to have been based on any coherent or ideological anti-Temple views. Rather, they might have stemmed from such worldly issues as power struggles between various groups of priests. The losing and disenfranchised party would then retreat and try to find comfort in the visions and revelations of the true heavenly Temple, where angelic ministers bring pure offerings right before the Throne of Glory.[63]

However, most apocalypses written in the Land of Israel still exhibit at least some measure of interest in and concern for the historical Jerusalem Temple, even if, like *1 Enoch*, they purport to describe antediluvian antiquity. Thus, parts of *1 Enoch* contain "historical" sections, in which the Jerusalem Temple plays a role,[64] and such compositions as *4 Ezra* and *2 Baruch* reflect the anguish in their authors' souls over the destruction of the Temple in 70 CE.[65] Although the authors of those last two apocalypses finally find consolation through other aspects of

---

Age of Jesus Christ (ed. G. Vermes, F. Millar, and M. Goodman; Edinburgh, 1987), 3.2:748, thinks that "it is safer to conclude that elements belonging to *2 Enoch* existed both in Greek and in Hebrew." For the bibliography on *2 Enoch*, see A. Orlov, *From Apocalypticism to Merkabah Mysticism* (Leiden, 2007), 19–35.

[61] See M. Himmelfarb, *Ascent to Heaven in Jewish and Christian Apocalypses* (New York, 1993).

[62] E.g., D.W. Suter, "Fallen Angel, Fallen Priest: The Problem of Family Purity in *1 Enoch* 6–16," *HUCA* 50 (1979): 115–35.

[63] The prime example of such a group is, of course, Qumran.

[64] M.A. Knibb, "Temple and Cult in Apocryphal and Pseudepigraphical Writings from Before the Common Era," in *Temple and Worship in Biblical Israel* (ed. J. Day; London, 2005), 404–8.

[65] Nickelsburg, *Jewish Literature*, 270–85; On *4 Ezra*, see M.E. Stone, *Fourth Ezra* (Minneapolis, 1990), 35; On *2 Baruch*, see G.B. Sayler, *Have the Promises Failed? A Literary Analysis of 2 Baruch* (Atlanta, 1984); and A.F.J. Klijn, "2 (Syriac Apocalypse of) Baruch," in *OTP* 1:615–52.

Judaism,[66] which in their view are able to compensate for the loss of the Temple, it is clear that for them the Temple's destruction was a tragedy of monumental proportions.[67]

In contrast to these apocalypses, the author of *2 Enoch* seems not at all to have been interested in the contemporary Jerusalem cult and its priesthood. This is especially noteworthy since he is usually considered to have been thoroughly familiar with *1 Enoch*, and to have used it as a source.[68] However, he omitted all the indirect references to the Temple contained in that source. True, no one would suggest that this author was not interested in "cultic" and "priestly" matters at all, since they form the subject matter of several chapters of his work.[69] However, these passages are limited to the description of either the antediluvian cult, or of such non-Aaronite priests as Enoch, Methusalam, Noah's otherwise unknown brother Nir, and especially his miraculously-born son Melchizedek (later taken to Paradise for permanent residence).[70]

The narrative dealing with Melchizedek is repetitive and somewhat obscure, and its interpretation is even more complicated by serious textual problems. In 71:33–36 (J version) a future Melchizedek is mentioned. This figure will be considered the head of the thirteen priests who preceded him, as well as the first of the twelve priests who will serve in the future—of whom the last will be "the Word and Power of God, who will perform miracles, greater and more glorious than all the previous ones." This story is repeated in 72:6–7 (J), where it is said that

---

[66] Thus, for example, the author of *2 Bar.* 85:3 states clearly that, even without Land and Temple, the Jews still have the Torah: "Also we have left our land, and Zion has been taken away from us, and we have nothing now apart from the Mighty One and his Law."

[67] On various reactions to the destruction of the Temple, see M.E. Stone, "Reactions to the Destruction of the Second Temple: Theology, Perception, Conversion," *JSJ* 12 (1981): 195–204; J. Neusner, "Judaism in Time of Crisis: Four Responses to the Destruction of the Second Temple," *Judaism* 21 (1972): 313–27.

[68] Nickelsburg, *Jewish Literature*, 221–25.

[69] E.g., *2 En.* 2:2 (A); 45; 59.

[70] It should be noticed that "Achuzan," where Methusalam, his brothers, and Enoch's sons construct an altar (68:5), is routinely identified with Jerusalem; this is the spot from which Enoch had earlier been taken up into heaven. See Böttrich, *Weltweisheit, Menschheitsethik, Urkult,* 196 n. 216; A. Orlov, "Melchizedek Legend of 2 (Slavonic) Enoch," *JSJ* 31 (2000): 27 n. 18. It is also mentioned in 71:35 (J) as the place where Melchizedek will serve as priest and king. This is the place of Adam's creation and of his final grave.

after the Deluge, Noah will find on the mountain of Ararat "another
Melchizedek," who "will be the first priest and king in the city of Salim
in the style of this Melchizedek [presumably, the one who is in Eden]."
After him there will be twelve priests until the "great Igumen, that is
to say, Leader, will bring out everything visible and invisible."[71] The
book contains no hint whatsoever of any matters related to the real
Jerusalem Temple cult or its flesh-and-blood Aaronite priesthood.
The sacrificial *halakhah* commanded by Enoch to his sons in 59:1–4 is
markedly different from that commonly believed to have been in force
at the Jerusalem Temple.[72] Even if one could say that the author of
2 Enoch was indeed interested in antiquarian cultic and priestly matters, what can be said concerning the relevance of these antediluvian
fantasies to the real Jerusalem Temple, its sacrifices, and its Aaronite
priests? Would any author who was familiar with the Bible (as the
author of *2 Enoch* surely was), and who assigned any relevance to the
present Jerusalem Temple establishment, invent stories of Enochic and
Melchizedekian priesthood and then claim that these priests had been
transferred to heaven forever?[73] What kind of sacrificial cultic *Sitz im
Leben* could possibly be envisaged for a community responsible for the
composition of these fantastic myths? I can think of none.[74]

---

[71] The long (J) and the short (A) texts differ at this point. The short text at 71:33–34
says only "And Melkisedek will be the head of the priests in another generation"
(speaking, presumably, only of the first, miraculously-born Melchizedek) and the parallel section dealing with this other Melchizedek in 72:6–7 is missing from J. In other
words, in the longer version two Melchizedeks are envisaged, while in the shorter
version, only one.

[72] Cf. *m. Tamid* 4:1; *b. Tamid* 31b. For the discussion of the sectarian nature of the
sacrificial *halakhah* in *2 Enoch*, see A. Orlov, "'Noah's Younger Brother': The Anti-
Noachic Polemics in *2 Enoch*," *Henoch* 22 (2000): 210–12.

[73] Cf. Andersen, "2 (Slavonic Apocalypse of) Enoch," 96–97: "The Melchizedek legend constitutes a special problem. The fantastic details about this priest conflict…with
the Jewish idea that the descendants of Aaron (or Zadok) are God's sole legitimate
priests on earth."

[74] *Mutatis mutandis*, the emphasis of the author of *2 Enoch* on the Melchizedekian
priesthood and the direction of his discussion of cultic matters could be compared
with another composition, whose author also dealt with some very similar subjects.
As is well known, the anonymous author of the Letter to the Hebrews developed at
length his own views concerning the superiority of the Melchizedekian priesthood
and the cult of the heavenly Tabernacle over the Aaronite priesthood and the earthly
Tabernacle/Temple with its cult, prescribed by the Torah. At first glance, one might
imagine that since the author of Hebrews discussed these matters in such detail and
with such a measure of sophistication, the Temple, its cult, and its priesthood must
have been very important to him. However, virtually all scholars agree that what really
mattered to the author was the metaphysical status and role of Jesus, who in his view

In the light of the previous discussion of glorified patriarchs, it should also be pointed out that the author of this Diaspora apocalypse continued and amplified the tradition of glorification of Enoch which was begun in *1 Enoch*.[75] Some scholars would even claim that in this scenario Enoch takes a place superior to Moses, and in some ways his status is similar to that of Jesus in the Christian tradition.[76] Is it just a coincidence that in *2 Enoch* Melchizedek, the originator of the priests, is said to have been miraculously born without a human father? To summarize, it seems that for the author of *2 Enoch* the traditions elevating Enoch to a semidivine status and making him into the revealer of divine lore (including cultic matters), as well as traditions of transcendental Melchizedekian priesthood formed the center of his religious outlook and interests. At the same time the Jerusalem Temple and its Aaronite priesthood did not even merit a mention.

---

was above angels, greater than Abraham, and more perfect than Aaron. Therefore, he appropriated Jewish cultic and priestly traditions by transferring them onto the exalted heavenly Jesus, who sat at the right hand of the Almighty in Heaven. In other words, the cult he was promoting was wholly invisible and metaphysical, while the real Temple, with its sacrificial cult and obsolete priesthood, was devoid of any meaning and useless. The author squeezed them dry of their significance in the process of creating an even higher and more exalted Christology. On the attitude of Hebrews towards the Temple and cult, see Klawans, *Purity, Sacrifice, and the Temple*. For another illuminating discussion of the place of Hebrews in the development of Christianity as something different from Judaism, see B. Chilton and J. Neusner, *Judaism in the New Testament: Practices and Beliefs* (London, 1995), 160–88. For a comparison of the function of Melchizedek in *2 Enoch* and Hebrews, see A. Orlov, "The Heir of Righteousness and the King of Righteousness: The Priestly Noachic Polemics in *2 Enoch* and the Letter to the Hebrews," *JTS* 58 (2007): 45–65.

[75] Many scholars admit that the glorification of the patriarchs and other biblical figures served as an antecedent for later developments in the glorification of Jesus, and that many of the features of these glorified figures were transferred to him by the early Christians. In this sense it seems that, just as the exalted Christ eventually became the sole conduit of divine blessings to his followers, rendering the Temple cult redundant, so similarly exalted patriarchs might have competed for the attention of the faithful in the Diaspora long before Jesus. On the exalted biblical figures in Hellenistic Judaism, see Goodenough, *By Light, Light*, 121–234. On the various "agents of God's activity," including Enoch and Melchizedek, and their adaptation in early Christianity, see G.W.E. Nickelsburg, *Ancient Judaism and Christian Origins: Diversity, Continuity, and Transformation* (Minneapolis, 2003), 90–117.

[76] Nickelsburg, *Jewish Literature*, 224–25; P.S. Alexander, "From Son of Adam to Second God: Transformations of the Biblical Enoch," in *Biblical Figures Outside the Bible* (ed. M.E. Stone et al.; Harrisburg, 1998), 87–122. See *2 En.* 22:8–10.

VI. Prayer as Sacrifice: Hellenistic Synagogal Prayers
and the Wisdom of Solomon

1) *Hellenistic Synagogal Prayers*

The "unorthodox" line of priests attested in *2 Enoch* appears with
some variations in one of the *Hellenistic Synagogal Prayers*.[77] In 8.5.3
it is stated that "You [God] are the one who foreordained from the
beginning priests (ἱερεῖς) for the oversight of your people: Abel first,
Seth and Enos and Enoch and Noah and Melchizedek and Job." In
his analysis of these compositions, Goodenough claimed that these
characters could have only been considered *priests* by initiates of the
"Hellenistic-Jewish mysteries," traces of which he strove to identify in
Jewish documents and archaeological remains of the Diaspora.[78] The
debates concerning whether mysteries such as those reconstructed by
Goodenough actually existed have continued ever since,[79] but what
is clear is that for the author(s) of the prayer the meaning of "priesthood" apparently was not coterminous with the Aaronite ministers of
the Temple in Jerusalem.

The prayers under discussion have been preserved in the *Apostolic
Constitutions*, a Christian legal and liturgical compilation of the late
fourth century. Although in their present form the prayers contain
extensive Christian interpolations, since the early twentieth century
most scholars have considered them originally to have been Jewish liturgical compositions which were used in Diaspora synagogue services.[80]
Their date and exact geographical provenance remain disputable, but
their Diasporan character is taken for granted by most scholars.[81]

---

[77] For the introduction, Greek text, translation and analysis, see D.A. Fiensy,
Prayers Alleged to Be Jewish: An Examination of the Constitutiones Apostolorum (BJS
65; Chico, Calif., 1985). Most recently, see van der Horst and Newman, *Early Jewish
Prayers in Greek*, 1–93. Among earlier studies, see Goodenough, *By Light, Light*, 306–
58, who considered these prayers to have been the liturgy of the "Hellenistic-Jewish
Mysteries." Quotations are taken from Fiensy, *Prayers Alleged to Be Jewish*.

[78] Goodenough, ibid., 331, 355.

[79] G. Lease, "Jewish Mystery Cults since Goodenough," *ANRW* 20.2 (1987), 858–80.

[80] This has been recognized since W. Bousset, "Eine jüdische Gebetssamlung im
siebenten Buch der apostolische Konstitutionen," *Nachrichten von der Königlichen
Gesellschaft der Wissenschaften zu Göttingen: Philologisch-historische Klasse* (Göttingen, 1915), 438–85.

[81] Various dates have been proposed for the composition of the Prayers. Thus, on the
one hand, Fiensy, *Prayers Alleged to Be Jewish*, writes, "We shall not date the original
composition of the prayers of AC 7.33–38, since the prayers circulated orally at first"

The authors of these prayers seem to have equated the sacrificial cult described in the Bible and the bloodless prayer service of their fellow congregants. Thus at 7.37.1–5, the author asks God to accept the entreaties from the lips of his people just as he accepted the "gifts (τὰ δῶρα) of the righteous in their generations." Then follows a long list of these righteous persons, which includes Abel, Noah, Abraham, Isaac, Jacob, Moses, and others who offered sacrifices, as well as gifts of "Daniel in the den of lions, of Jonah in the whale's belly, of the three youths in the furnace of fire, of Hannah in the tent before the ark…, of Mattathias and of his sons in (their) zeal, of Jael in blessings." The prayer then concludes with the request: "And now, therefore, accept the prayers of your people which are offered (προσφερομένας) in the spirit and with knowledge to you…" (7.37.1–5).[82] In 7.33.2 the author says that "…in every region of the inhabited earth incense is sent to you through prayer and words (τὸ διὰ προσευχῆς καὶ λόγων ἀναπέμπεταί σοι θυμίαμα)."

In other words, for the authors of these prayers, "prayer and words" offered "in the spirit and with knowledge" could take the place of sacrifices and incense. As God accepted both bloody sacrifices and earnest prayers in the days of old, in the same way now he accepts the prayers from the lips of his people. The authors do not seem to exhibit any tension over the question of the many obvious differences between sacrifice and prayer, which seems to imply that by the time these prayers took shape, this equation had become a commonplace— at least in some Diaspora circles.[83]

(p. 223); on the other hand, he considers them to be "post-first century AD" (p. 223), preferring a date around 250 CE (p. 227). Van der Horst, *Early Jewish Prayers*, 26, writes: "it is highly probable that the Greek text of the prayers was produced at some time in the third century CE, or otherwise at any rate between 150 and 350 CE."

[82] The words "in the spirit" are marked as a Christian interpolation in Goodenough, *By Light, Light*, 313.

[83] A striking parallel to these ideas, which is openly polemical towards the Jerusalem-based sacrificial cult, is preserved in Justin Martyr's *Dialogue with Trypho*, which was written circa 160 CE. In chapter 117, Justin says to Trypho, "Yet even now, in your love of contention, you assert that God does not accept the sacrifices of those who dwelt then in Jerusalem, and were called Israelites; but says that He is pleased with the prayers of the individuals of that nation then dispersed, and calls their prayers sacrifices" (καὶ μέχρι νῦν φιλονεικοῦντες λέγετε, ὅτι τὰς μὲν ἐν Ἰερουσαλὴμ ἐπὶ τῶν ἐκεῖ τότε οἰκούντων Ἰσραηλιτῶν καλουμένων θυσίας οὐ προσδέχεται ὁ θεός, τὰς δὲ διὰ τῶν ἐν τῇ διασπορᾷ τότε δὴ ὄντων ἀπὸ τοῦ γένους ἐκείνου ἀνθρώπων εὐχὰς προσίεσθαι αὐτὸν εἰρηκέναι, καὶ τὰς εὐχὰς αὐτῶν θυσίας καλεῖν). Quotation follows *The Apostolic Fathers with Justin Martyr and Irenaeus* (ed. A. Roberts; Grand Rapids, 2001),

2) *The Wisdom of Solomon*

Prayer as a crucial part of the divine service and as a means of expiation is also prominent in the Wisdom of Solomon, which most probably, was written in Egypt.[84] The second part of this book retells the story of the Exodus and the Wilderness wanderings. When the author rewrites the episode dealing with the rebellion of Korah, and the subsequent plague with which God smote the Israelites, he changes the biblical story and adds several significant details.[85] I will present the two passages synoptically:

Numbers 17:11–13, NJPS	*Wisdom 18:20–25*
	But the righteous, too, were touched by an experience of death, and a mass slaughter took place in the wilderness, though the divine wrath
Then Moses said to Aaron, "Take the fire pan, and put on it fire from the altar. Add incense and take it quickly to the community and make expiation for them. For wrath has gone forth from the Lord: the plague has begun!" Aaron took it, as Moses had ordered, and ran to the midst of the congregation, where the plague had begun among the people. He put on incense	did not long abide. For a blameless man (ἀνὴρ ἄμεμπτος) pressed forward to fight as their champion, introducing the armor of his ministry (λειτουργίας), prayer and atoning incense. He withstood the wrath and set a limit to the disaster, showing that it was you whom he served. He overcame the divine anger not by bodily strength, nor by force of

---

257. The question of Justin's knowledge of contemporary Judaism has been discussed many times—see, e.g., E.R. Goodenough, *The Theology of Justin Martyr* (Jena, 1923), 92–96; L.W. Barnard, "The Old Testament and Judaism in the Writings of Justin Martyr," *VT* 14 (1964): 400–406; P. Sigal, "An Inquiry into Aspects of Judaism in Justin's *Dialogue with Trypho*," *Abr-Nahrain* 18 (1978–1979): 82–94. W. Horbury, "Jewish-Christian Relations in Barnabas and Justin Martyr," in J.D.G. Dunn (ed.), *Jews and Christians: The Parting of the Ways AD 70 to 135* (Grand Rapids, 1999), 341: "His Palestinian and Jewish knowledge should not be exaggerated, but it is not negligible." In the context of the materials considered above, this statement sounds like a plausible piece of radical Diaspora Jewish theology, albeit somewhat bizarre or even "heretical" by Palestinian standards. See Schwartz, "Temple or City," 118 n. 15.

[84] On this text, see D. Winston, *The Wisdom of Solomon* (New York, 1979); and H. Hübner, *Die Weisheit Salomons* (Göttingen, 1999); both scholars argue that the book was composed in Egypt. D. Georgi, *Weisheit Salomos* (Gütersloh, 1980), 396, thinks that Syria is a better candidate; in my view, however, his arguments fail to demonstrate that this is a more likely place of origin than Egypt. Translations of this text are drawn from Winston, *Wisdom*.

[85] These passages were brought to my attention by D.R. Schwartz.

and made expiation for the people; he stood between the dead and the living until the plague was checked.

arms, but by word he subdued the chastiser, by recalling the oaths and covenants of the fathers. For when the dead already lay fallen upon one another in heaps, he interposed and checked the divine anger, cutting off its line of advance toward the living. On his full-length robe there was a representation of the entire cosmos, and the glories of the fathers upon his four rows of carved stones, and your splendor on the diadem upon his head. To these the destroyer gave way, these he feared; for the single taste of his wrath was enough.

According to the biblical passage, God was propitiated by the cultic act of the high priest—incense placed on the fire pan was sufficient for the expiation. For the Diaspora author of Wisdom this was definitely not enough. He significantly altered the story by introducing several important elements. According to the passage in Wisdom, in contrast to the Bible, the plague was stopped, not by the burning of incense but because of the prayer of the "blameless man," who reminded God of His oaths and covenants with the fathers. This is not surprising, since in the Diaspora context prayer should have been thought of as a more effective—because more available—means to worship and propitiate God, than incense and sacrifices.[86] Another detail that should be mentioned is the representation of the high-priestly vestments as symbolizing the entire cosmos. This seems to have been an important motif in the Jewish literature of the Second Temple period.[87]

In a similar vein, real and God-pleasing sacrifice is something totally different from slaughtered and smoking bulls and goats—it is *the life of a virtuous man*. The author allots much space to the discussion of the

---

[86] Cf. Philo, *De Vita Mosis* 2.24, on the role of prayer in the context of the Day of Atonement.

[87] J. Daniélou, "La symbolique du temple de Jérusalem chez Philon et Josèphe," in *Le symbolisme cosmique des monuments religieux* (Rome, 1957), 83–90. I will discuss this issue separately in a study dealing with cosmic symbolism in Philo and Josephus. Schwartz, "Temple or City," 119 has emphasized that the Temple is mentioned twice in *Wisdom*: in 3:14, where he "actually emphasizes that 'the Temple of God' is something other and better than the Temple of Jerusalem," and in 9:8, where the author "demonstratively avoids the notion that God resides in [the Temple]."

sufferings of the righteous. The wicked who persecuted the righteous until death (because of his righteousness) thought that they themselves had had the upper hand. However, the souls of the righteous have survived and are with God forever, since "[a]s gold in a blast furnace he tested them, and as a whole burnt offering he accepted them (ὡς ὁλοκάρπωμα θυσίας προσεδέξατο αὐτούς)" (3:6). In other words, the death of a virtuous martyr is considered by the author to be a sacrifice pleasing to God.[88]

VII. Martyrs vs. Freedom-Fighters, Holy People vs. Holy Place: The Diaspora Maccabean Books

1) *2 Maccabees as Compared to 1 Maccabees*

The valorization of martyrdom as equivalent to sacrifice seems to play a prominent role in several Diaspora documents. Anyone who compares 1 Maccabees with 2 Maccabees will see that these books share much in common as far as the historical events described are concerned.[89] Both narrate the history of the Hasmonean revolt, the events immediately preceding it, and the wars of Judas Maccabaeus.[90] However, there also are many differences, which in my opinion stem from the fact that 1 Maccabees is a Judean composition, and 2 Maccabees is basically a product of the Diaspora.[91] One of the major differences in the outlook

---

[88] See Nickelsburg, *Ancient Judaism*, 106–7; also 66–67 on 2 and 4 Maccabees.

[89] On 1 Maccabees, see J.C. Dancy, *1 Maccabees: A Commentary* (Oxford, 1954); J. Goldstein, *1 Maccabees* (Garden City, N.Y., 1976); U. Rappaport, *The First Book of Maccabees: Introduction, Hebrew Translation, and Commentary* (Jerusalem, 2004) (in Hebrew). On 2 Maccabees, see C. Habicht, *2. Makkabäerbuch* (Gütersloh, 1976); J. Goldstein, *2 Maccabees* (Garden City, N.Y., 1983); D.R. Schwartz, *2 Maccabees* (Berlin, 2008). On both books, see F.M. Abel, *Les Livres des Maccabées* (Paris, 1949).

[90] 1 Maccabees continues its account through the reign of Hyrcanus I. For a synopsis, see J. Sievers, *Synopsis of the Greek Sources for the Hasmonean Period: 1–2 Maccabees and Josephus, War 1 and Antiquities 12–14* (Rome, 2001).

[91] 2 Macc 1:1–2:18 (the two letters to the Jews in Egypt) and 10:1–8 (the Hanukkah story) are Hasmonean additions to this Diaspora work. See Schwartz, *2 Maccabees*, 3–37. On the differences in outlook between these two works, see D.R. Schwartz, "What's the Difference Between I Maccabees and II Maccabees? or: The Challenging Hyphen in Such Combinations as 'State-Religious,' 'Religious-National,' and 'Zionist-Religious,'" in *Jewish Tradition in a Changing Educational World* (ed. M. Barlev; Jerusalem, 2005), 11–20 (in Hebrew); and idem, "On Something Biblical About 2 Maccabees," in *Biblical Perspectives: Early Use and Interpretation of the Bible in Light of the Dead Sea Scrolls* (ed. M.E. Stone and E.G. Chazon; Leiden: Brill, 1998), 223–32.

of these two authors is in their treatment of martyrs. For the author of 1 Maccabees the faithful martyrs, those who die in the wilderness because of their unwillingness to fight on the Sabbath, are misled, even if innocent and pious. Their example of noble death in the face of persecution is not to be followed:

> When the news reached Mattathias and his friends, they were deeply grieved over the victims' fate. They said to one another, "If we all do as our brothers have done and do not fight against the gentiles for our lives and our laws, they will now quickly wipe us off the face of the earth." On that day they came to a decision: "If any man comes against us in battle on the Sabbath day, we shall fight against him and not all die as our brothers died in their hiding places." (2:39–41)[92]

And so they fought, and won religious and political freedom for their people. The author's "theology" is plain and straightforward: the wicked Gentiles overstepped the boundaries of their authority by persecuting the Jews, and provoked God's anger. The Hasmonean clan led the armed struggle against them for the sake of their families, the Law, and the Sanctuary; they were assisted from Heaven; and they won a glorious victory and eternal renown. In the eyes of the author of 1 Maccabees, they were "that family of men to whom it had been granted to be agents of Israel's deliverance" (5:62).[93]

The author of 2 Maccabees offers a totally different interpretation: the Gentiles persecuted the Jews because the sins of the latter provoked God's righteous anger. In his view it was the blood of the righteous martyrs, tortured for their faithfulness to the Law—to the Judean way of life, Ἰουδαϊσμός (2:21)—which propitiated God. The deaths of the martyrs are the turning point in the story: the last of the seven martyred brothers says before his death:

> As for me, just as my brothers I give up both body and soul for the ancestral laws, calling upon God that He speedily become merciful to the people; and that you, after afflictions and scourging, will therefore admit that He alone is God; and that, with me and my brothers, shall be stayed the anger of the All-Ruler which was justly loosed against our entire nation. (7:37–38)[94]

---

[92] Translations of 1 Maccabees follow Goldstein, *1 Maccabees*.

[93] ἐκ τοῦ σπέρματος τῶν ἀνδρῶν ἐκείνων, οἷς ἐδόθη σωτηρία Ισραηλ διὰ χειρὸς αὐτῶν.

[94] Translations of 2 Maccabees follow Schwartz, *2 Maccabees*.

Several verses later the author brings Judas Maccabaeus onto the scene with the following introduction: "As soon as Maccabaeus got his corps together he could not be withstood by the Gentiles, the Lord's anger having turned into mercy" (8:5). So, it is the martyrs' blood that expiated the sins of the nation and moved God to forgive his people, have mercy on them, and make Judas Maccabaeus invincible.[95]

Until recently, it was commonly held that the author of 2 Maccabees had an entirely positive attitude towards the Temple. Indeed, some scholars described the purpose and character of the book as "Temple propaganda."[96] However, a closer look at the Temple passages reveals a more complex picture, as has been convincingly demonstrated by Schwartz. When the author of 2 Maccabees explains how it was possible for Antiochus IV to rob the Temple, he supplies a key passage:

> Had it not happened that they had been caught up in many sins, he too—just as Heliodorus, who had been sent by King Seleucus to audit the treasury—immediately upon moving forward (into the Temple) would have been flogged and overturned from his insolence. But God did not choose the people on account of the Place; rather, He chose the Place on account of the people. Therefore the Place itself, having shared in the disasters which befell the people, later shared also in the benefactions, and that which had been abandoned in the anger of the All-Ruler was again reestablished with full honor when the great Sovereign was reconciled. (5:18–20)

So the Holy Place is subordinate to the holy people, and its fate is dependent on their righteous or unrighteous conduct. Schwartz adduces several instances of the author's lack of interest in sacrifices or cultic vessels, or in Judean-Samaritan temple polemics. At the same time, he also demonstrates that the author repeatedly emphasizes the power of prayer, the transcendent and heavenly nature of God, God's providential care for His covenant people, and the redemptive value of the martyrs' deaths. In Schwartz's view, these ideas are exactly what one should expect from a Diaspora writer like the author of 2 Maccabees.[97]

---

[95] For the full treatment of the role of martyrdom in 2 and 4 Maccabees, see J.W. van Henten, *The Maccabean Martyrs as Saviours of the Jewish People: A Study of 2 and 4 Maccabees* (Leiden, 1997).

[96] R. Doran, *Temple Propaganda: The Purpose and Character of 2 Maccabees* (Washington, D.C., 1981); J. Zsengellér, "Maccabees and Temple Propaganda," in *The Books of the Maccabees: History, Theology, Ideology* (ed. G.G. Xeravits and J. Zsengellér; Leiden, 2007), 181–95.

[97] Schwartz, *2 Maccabees*, 45–48.

2) 4 Maccabees

Even if 2 Maccabees does not stress Judas Maccabaeus' valor and heroism as much as 1 Maccabees, he is still a major character in its plot. When we turn to 4 Maccabees, however, a book that builds upon 2 Maccabees, we discover that for its author the only real heroes and saviors are the martyrs.[98] Their steadfastness in the face of torture is used to exemplify the main thesis of the author, which is that the "reason is absolute master over the passions (αὐτοκράτωρ ἐστὶν τῶν παθῶν ὁ λογισμός)" (1:13).[99] It is the martyrs, and not the Hasmonean freedom-fighters, who saved the Jewish people; it is their mode of piety that must be followed as an example. The author unequivocally states this in the following passage:

> It would be in fact appropriate to inscribe upon their tomb itself, as a memorial to those members of our nation, the following words: "Here lie buried an aged priest,[100] an old woman, and her seven sons through the violence of the tyrant bent on destroying the polity of the Hebrews. They vindicated (ἐξεδίκησαν) their race, looking unto God and enduring torments even unto death." (17:8–10)

In another passage the atoning and purifying value of their sacrificial deaths is made even more apparent:

> These then, having consecrated themselves for the sake of God, are now honored not only with this distinction but also by the fact that through them our enemies did not prevail against our nation, and the tyrant was punished and our land purified (καθαρισθῆναι), since they became, as it were, a ransom for the sin of our nation (ὥσπερ ἀντίψυχον γεγονότας τῆς τοῦ ἔθνους ἁμαρτίας). Through the blood of these righteous ones and through the propitiation (ἱλαστηρίου) of their death the divine providence rescued Israel, which had been shamefully treated.... O offspring of the seed of Abraham, children of Israel, obey this Law and be altogether true to your religion, knowing that devout reason is master over

---

[98] On 4 Maccabees, see H.-J. Klauck, *4. Makkabäerbuch* (Gütersloh, 1989); van Henten, *The Maccabean Martyrs*; D.A. DeSilva, *4 Maccabees* (Sheffield, 2006); idem, *4 Maccabees: Introduction and Commentary on the Greek Text in Codex Sinaiticus* (Leiden, 2006).

[99] αὐτοδέσποτός ἐστιν τῶν παθῶν ὁ εὐσεβὴς λογισμός in 1:1. Translations of 4 Maccabees follow H. Andersen, "4 Maccabees," in *OTP* 2:531–64. The Temple is mentioned in chapter 4, in a paraphrase of the Heliodorus affair which originally appeared in 2 Maccabees 3; however it does not play any role in the subsequent narrative. The paraphrase serves as a background to the martyrs' story.

[100] Eleazar is not described as a priest in 2 Maccabees; this is an innovation of the author of 4 Maccabees.

the passions, and not only over pains from within, but also from outside ourselves. (17:20–22, 18:1–2)[101]

The exact provenance and date of this Diaspora work are debatable.[102] Not a few scholars tend to locate it in Syrian Antioch because of the witnesses indicating that at a later period (third century CE) there existed in Antioch the "Synagogue of the Maccabean Martyrs," where their cult flourished.[103] However, whether or not there was any connection between the traditions embedded in 4 Maccabees and a later "Maccabean Martyrs" cult, it is clear that the author of this work was concerned neither with the military exploits of the Hasmonean brothers, nor with their political-religious achievements, including the rededication of the Temple and the reinstitution of the sacrificial cult. For him, it was the martyrs, who through their sacrificial death for the laws of the Torah had brought vindication and deliverance to the Jewish people.[104]

3) 3 Maccabees

I will complete my discussion of the Maccabean corpus with a brief treatment of 3 Maccabees. Despite its title, this work deals neither with the Maccabean wars nor with the martyrs of the Seleucid persecutions. Rather, the events described in 3 Maccabees are set in the reign of Ptolemy IV Philopator (221–204 BCE). According to the story, the king wanted to enter the Jerusalem Temple, which caused a great dis-

---

[101] Cf. Nickelsburg, *Ancient Judaism,* 66–67.

[102] E.J. Bickerman, *Studies in Jewish and Christian History: A New Edition in English, Including The God of The Maccabees* (2 vols.; Leiden, 2007), 1:266–71, dates it "between 18 and 55 CE, that is about 35 CE with a scope of fifteen years or so in either direction" (p. 271). Van Henten, *The Maccabean Martyrs,* 73–82 argues for one of the cities in Asia Minor as a probable place of composition, and a date around 100 CE or slightly later.

[103] Klauck, *4. Makkabäerbuch,* 666–67; Andersen, "4 Maccabees," 535. Nothing in the book requires a date later than the first century CE; see Klauck, *4. Makkabäerbuch,* 669; Andersen, "4 Maccabees," 533–34. On the tradition locating the Maccabean martyrs' grave in Antioch, see Bickerman, *Studies,* 465–82. For Lightstone's integration of these data into his bold conception of the roles of saints' tombs, martyrs' bones, and other relics in Diaspora Judaism, see *The Commerce of the Sacred,* 84.

[104] D.R. Schwartz, "From the Maccabees to Masada: On Diasporan Historiography of the Second Temple Period," in *Jüdische Geschichte in hellenistisch-römischer Zeit. Wege der Forschung: Vom alten zum neuen Schürer* (ed. A. Oppenheimer; Munich, 1999), 33, sees the emphasis on martyrdom as a distinctly Diasporan development: "Dying for their religion is something Jews can do anywhere; fighting is something which goes hand in hand with a Jewish state."

turbance in the city. When he persisted in his desire, he was struck by
God in answer to the high priest's prayer, and consequently decided to
take revenge on the Jews. After his return to Alexandria, he deprived
the Egyptian Jews of their civil rights, forced them to participate in
pagan cults, end eventually confined them in the city's hippodrome
and ordered that they be trampled to death by elephants. This plan was
providentially frustrated several times, and when it was finally on the
brink of being executed, a Jewish priest named Eleazar asked God to
intervene. In response, God turned the elephants back upon the king
and his troops. The king, who finally realized his mistakes, released
the Jews and even financed, out of his own pocket, a seven-day festival
instituted to commemorate the occasion.

Whether any of this reflects real historical events is debatable, to say
the least.[105] However, as is usually the case, when there is not much
history, there will be lots of theology. And according to the theology
of the author of 3 Maccabees, God is no more present in the Jerusalem Temple than in the Alexandrian hippodrome. Here I will quote
N. Hacham:

> As far as the causes of this difficult situation are concerned, it seems
> that from the point of view of the author of 3 Maccabees, the situation
> originated in the Land of Israel but was resolved in Alexandria. There-
> fore, the Jews of Alexandria take precedence over the Jews of the Land of
> Israel and Jerusalem. As for the place where God is found, the author of
> 3 Maccabees does not consider the Jerusalem Temple to take precedence
> over the hippodrome in Alexandria—the opposite is the case. At the
> Egyptian hippodrome God revealed His holy face and fatherly attitude
> to His children, neither of which were revealed in Jerusalem.[106]

In other words, here we again witness the idea that the Chosen People
takes precedence over the Holy Place; moreover—any place, where
the Holy People are found, becomes "holy." God is omnipresent, and
wherever His people call upon Him in righteousness, He is ready to
come to their help. The interesting point, however, is that in the case
of 3 Maccabees the prayer offered to God by the Jews in Alexandria
prompted Him to deliver them from their predicament, while the one
offered by the Jews in the Temple of Jerusalem did not. So it seems

---

[105] On 3 Maccabees as basically a fiction, see S.R. Johnson, *Historical Fictions and
Hellenistic Jewish Identity: Third Maccabees in Its Cultural Context* (Berkeley, 2004).

[106] N. Hacham, "The Third Book of Maccabees: Literature, History and Ideology"
(Ph.D. diss., Jerusalem, 2002), 101 (in Hebrew); translation my own.

that in the author's view those who worship God at the Jerusalem
Temple—indeed, the high priest himself!—are no closer to Him than
those who worship Him at the Alexandrian hippodrome.

VIII. "You Shall Pursue the Right Cause Righteously so that You May Live" (LXX Deut 16:20): The *Testaments of Job* and of *Abraham*, The *Sentences of Pseudo-Phocylides*, and *Sibylline Oracles* 1–2

1) *The Testament of Job*

The will to persevere and sacrifice oneself for righteousness which
we encountered in 2 and 4 Maccabees is also among the main virtues emphasized in the *Testament of Job*.[107] This text was most likely
composed in Egypt, and some scholars even think it likely that it was
produced in circles similar to the Jewish ascetic conclave of the Therapeutae, described by Philo in *De Vita Contemplativa*.[108] In *Testament
of Job*, Job is described as one of the sons of Esau (here this connection is viewed positively), is married to Jacob's daughter Dinah,[109]
and is therefore fully integrated into Israel's sacred history. The most
important of Job's virtues, which are recounted in excruciating detail,
include hatred of idolatry, charity, generosity, hospitality, care for the
poor and the needy, and the staunch belief in divine justice and the
reality of heavenly recompense.

Although the author follows the biblical account in saying that Job
offered sacrifices on behalf of his children (Job 1:5; *T. Job* 15:4–5),
the main point of the story is that he donated to the poor everything
that remained after the sacrifices. Moreover, note that while according to the biblical version, Job offered burnt offerings on behalf of his
children, thinking "Perhaps my children have sinned and blasphemed
God in their thoughts," according to the *Testament* he distributed the
sacrificial leftovers to the poor, saying: "Take these things remaining
after the rites, *so that you may pray on behalf of my children*. Pos-

---

[107] On *T. Job*, see B. Schaller, *Das Testament Hiobs* (Gütersloh, 1979); R.P. Spit-
tler, "Testament of Job," in *OTP* 1:829–68; M.A. Knibb and P.W. van der Horst, eds.,
Studies on the Testament of Job (Cambridge, 1989). For the Greek text, see S.P. Brock,
Testamentum Iobi. PVTG II (Leiden, 1967), 1–60.

[108] See Spittler, "Testament of Job," 834.

[109] Cf. *L.A.B.* 8:8.

sibly, my sons may have sinned before the Lord through boasting…"
(*T. Job* 15:5–6, italics mine).[110] In other words, sacrifices alone are not
enough to effect atonement; prayers offered by the poor are considered
to be more effective than burnt offerings. It is true that in the same
passage, the author adds that Job also "offered up a select calf on the
altar of God, lest my sons may have thought evil things in their heart
towards God" (*T. Job* 15:9), and later rewrites the biblical passage, in
which Job's friends were commanded by God to ask him to sacrifice
on their behalf (Job 42:7–10; *T. Job* 42:4–8). Nevertheless, it is clear
that sacrifice itself is nearly inconsequential for his view of what constitutes genuine piety.

Satan's attack on Job is precipitated by his resolute destruction of
an idol's shrine, and, in contrast to his biblical prototype, here Job
perfectly realizes the reason for his sufferings, his eternal destiny, and
his future (as well as present) heavenly rewards. Job, who is presented
as a king who lost his earthly throne because of the Satanic assault,
does not tire of emphasizing before his friends/opponents that his *real*
throne is in heaven, and that his true life is in the unseen world:

> My throne is in the upper world (ἐν τῷ ὑπερκοσμίῳ), and its splendor
> and majesty come from the right hand of the Father. The whole world (ὁ
> κόσμος) shall pass away and its splendor will fade. And those who heed
> it shall share in its overthrow. But my throne is in the holy land (ἐμοὶ δὲ
> ὁ θρόνος ὑπάρχει ἐν τῇ ἁγίᾳ γῇ), and its splendor is in the world of the
> changeless one (ἐν τῷ αἰῶνί ἐστιν τοῦ ἀπαραλλάκτου). (*T. Job* 33:3–5)

That is, for the author of the *Testament of Job* (as for Paul)[111] the "Holy
Land" turns out to be in heaven, not in the Land of Israel. Accordingly, and similarly to 2 and 4 Maccabees, this *Testament* is preoccupied with eternal life and heavenly recompense for suffering, at the
same time emphasizing the transience of this physical world and its
circumstances.[112] Another fascinating feature of this document, relevant to the present discussion, is the emphasis put on miraculous
amulets. After Job distributes his estate among his seven sons, and, in
contradiction to the biblical account, does not bestow any inheritance
upon his three daughters, the latter wonder why. Job answers them: "I

---

[110] Translations of *T. Job* are taken from Spittler, "Testament of Job."
[111] Phil 3:20: ἡμῶν γὰρ τὸ πολίτευμα ἐν οὐρανοῖς ὑπάρχει.
[112] In this sense, *T. Job* could have been included with the "mystical" materials
discussed above.

have already designated for you *an inheritance* better than that of *your seven brothers*" (*T. Job* 46:1–4, italics in the translation).

This better inheritance turns out to be miraculous heavenly cords, which "will lead you into the better world, to live in heavens" (*T. Job* 47:3). Job discloses to his daughters that the Lord bestowed these cords upon him, and that the moment he had put them on, the worms which had infested him before had disappeared from his body, as did also the plagues. "And the Lord spoke to me in power, showing me things present and things to come" (*T. Job* 47:4–9). When his daughters put the cords on themselves, they underwent miraculous transformation: the first one "took on another heart—no longer minded toward earthly things (τὰ τῆς γῆς)—but she spoke ecstatically in the angelic dialect, sending up a hymn to God in accord with the hymnic style of the angels. And as she spoke ecstatically, she allowed 'The Spirit' to be inscribed on her garment" (*T. Job* 48). The second daughter's heart

> changed so that she no longer regarded worldly things (τὰ κοσμικά). And her mouth took on the dialect of the archons and she praised God for the creation of the heights (ἐδοξολόγησεν δὲ τοῦ ὑψηλοῦ τόπου τὸ ποίημα).[113] Accordingly, if anyone wishes to know "The Creation of the Heavens" (τὸ ποίημα τῶν οὐρανῶν),[114] he will be able to find it in "The Hymns of Kasia." (*T. Job* 49)

The third daughter's mouth "spoke ecstatically in the dialect of those on high, since her heart also was changed, keeping aloof from the worldly things (τῶν κοσμικῶν). For she spoke in the dialect of the cherubim, glorifying the Master of virtues by exhibiting their splendor" (*T. Job* 50:1–2). Not surprisingly, the author says that the Lord and the holy angel were present on this occasion (*T. Job* 51:1–2).

To summarize: in this composition Job is made into the embodiment of virtues common to all humanity such as charity, generosity, and care for the poor, and is presented as a staunch believer in supernatural realities and the world to come. After his suffering and restoration, he also serves as the mediator of divine blessings and pow-

---

[113] Schaller, *Das Testament Hiobs*, 370, translates this phrase as "das Werk des erhabenen Ortes" and thinks that ὁ τόπος here "serves as a circumscription of the Divine name." In other words, in his view, the phrase refers to the heavenly cult.

[114] R. Thornhill, "The Testament of Job," in *The Apocryphal Old Testament* (ed. H.D.F. Sparks; Oxford, 1984), 646, translates these phrases as "heavenly sanctuary" and "the worship that goes on in heaven," respectively.

ers by bestowing miraculous amulets on his daughters. Throughout the book, the author uses his main character to emphasize the virtues of righteous conduct, mainly expressed in Job's care for other human beings, and the importance of faith in the heavenly realities. Job lives a righteous life on earth, but his spirituality is not of this world; his "Holy Land" is in heaven—and sacrifices play a role that is marginal and relatively insignificant.

2) *The Testament of Abraham*

The themes of "common piety" that we encountered in the *Testament of Job* are also prominent in another Diaspora work, whose author did not make any mention of the Temple and sacrifices at all: the *Testament of Abraham*.[115] Despite its title, the *Testament of Abraham* is not formally a testament, since Abraham neither makes his final wishes known, nor gives an ethical accounting anywhere in the course of the narrative.[116] However, similarly to other testamentary writings, the events described in the book transpire on the eve of its hero's death. When Abraham's appointed hour arrives, God sends the archangel Michael to tell the patriarch to make his testament, and to convey him to heaven. However, Abraham refuses to follow, and requests God to take him instead on a tour of the inhabited world. In the course of this tour Abraham witnesses all kinds of sins perpetrated on the face of the earth, and calls down lethal curses upon the people engaged in these sins. Lest he destroy all humanity, God transfers Abraham to heaven to witness the process of judgment, which is then described in detail. Abraham realizes he was too severe in his judgment, and asks God to reverse the curses he pronounced on the sinners. He is taken back to earth, but still refuses to follow Michael to heaven. Then God sends

---

[115] This book has been preserved in two recensions—the long (A) and the short (B). Some scholars used to assume that B went back to a Hebrew original (and thus was possibly of Palestinian provenance). However this assumption no longer holds, for the "Hebraisms" of B (which was the better candidate for a Hebrew original) have all been satisfactorily explained as attempts to imitate "biblical Greek"; therefore, in all probability, the *Testament* is a Diaspora composition, likely written in Egypt at the end of the first century CE. See the discussions in E.P. Sanders, "Testament of Abraham," in *OTP* 1:873–74; Nickelsburg, *Jewish Literature*, 327. The fullest recent treatment is D.C. Allison, *Testament of Abraham* (Berlin, 2003), 12–27; 34–35, who argues for a Greek original, of Egyptian provenance. For the Greek text, see F. Schmidt, *Le Testament grec d'Abraham* (Tübingen, 1986).

[116] Sanders, "Testament of Abraham," 879.

Death to Abraham, who manages to deceive him and finally takes his soul to God.

At the first glance one may wonder how serious the author of *Testament of Abraham* really was, and whether the book is not actually a parody on the biblical patriarch.[117] Even though Abraham is still the paradigm of piety and virtue, he is presented as the opposite of the biblical hero, who was considered righteous because of his obedience to God, which stemmed from his absolute faith. The book abounds in satirical and humorous details, some of which verge on indecency— thus, when Archangel Michael disguises himself as a guest and sleeps in Abraham's house, he goes outside "as if he needed to urinate." In fact, he ascends to God in the twinkling of an eye for a consultation with the Creator (5:5–6).

However, at a deeper level, the author seems to be trying to make several important points, of which the main one is the inevitability of death and the reality of God's postmortem judgment. People must live their lives righteously, since their eternal destiny depends on their earthly conduct. Nevertheless, God is merciful, and His followers are exhorted to be merciful to other human beings.

Although the *Testament of Abraham* shares many parallels with other Jewish Diaspora writings of the period,[118] it is in many ways a unique and therefore extremely important piece of work. In the words of E.P. Sanders:

> The Torah and the covenant of Israel seem to play no role. The Testa-
> ment of Abraham is one of the few witnesses, and thus a very important
> one, to the existence in Egypt of a form of Judaism that stressed neither
> the philosophical interpretation of Judaism, as did Philo, nor the need
> to retain strictly the commandments that set Jews apart from gentiles, as
> did the author of Joseph and Asenath. Judaism is depicted here as a reli-
> gion of commonplace moral values, which nevertheless insists both on
> the strictness of God's judgment and on his mercy and compassion.[119]

It is needless to elaborate on the obvious fact that in this type of Judaism, Jerusalem Temple, its sacrifices, and its laws of impurity did

---

[117] See A.Y. Reed, "The Construction and Subversion of Patriarchal Perfection: Abraham and Exemplarity in Philo, Josephus, and the Testament of Abraham," *JSJ* 40 (2009): 185–212.

[118] See the discussion in Sanders, "Testament of Abraham," 875.

[119] Sanders, "Testament of Abraham," 876–77 (cf. his discussion there of "Theologi-cal Importance," 877–78).

not play any role at all; "the only means of atonement mentioned are repentance and premature death."[120] It is also important to note that, in the matters of human righteousness and God's judgment, the author seems to ascribe no importance to the question of descent: Jews and Gentiles alike are judged exclusively on the basis of their right or wrong behavior. This, of course, undercuts the importance of the Jewish priesthood as well.

3) The Sentences of Pseudo-Phocylides

Even if the *Testament of Abraham* is in many ways unique, it is not alone in presenting a Judaic worldview lacking most of the particularly Jewish traits (including a focus on the Jerusalem Temple and its cult) and putting exclusive emphasis on ethics. The *Sentences of Pseudo-Phocylides* and *Sibylline Oracles* 1, 2 and 4 can also be placed in this category.[121] One might of course claim that the author of the first of these documents was masquerading as a pagan poet-sage, and the authors of the other three, as a pagan prophetess; these poses will have prevented them from touching on the Jewish Temple and its cult. However, the authors of *Sibylline Oracles* 3, 4 and 5 do mention the Temple several times, the latter two even prophesying that Rome would suffer punishment for destroying it. Similarly, *Sibylline Oracles* 1–2 and 4 and also Ps.-Phocylides speak about resurrection from the dead and monotheism,[122] which in this period were clearly Jewish

---

[120] Sanders, "Testament of Abraham," 877.

[121] On Ps.-Phocylides, see most recently W.T. Wilson, *The Sentences of Pseudo-Phocylides* (Berlin, 2005); J.J. Collins, *Jewish Wisdom in the Hellenistic Age* (Louisville, 1997), 158–77; P.W. van der Horst, *The Sentences of Pseudo-Phocylides* (Leiden, 1978). On the Jewish Sibyllines see J.J. Collins, *The Sibylline Oracles of Egyptian Judaism* (Missoula, Mont., 1974); idem, "Sibylline Oracles," in *OTP* 1:317–472; idem, "The Sibylline Oracles," in *Jewish Writings of the Second Temple Period* (ed. M.E. Stone; Assen and Philadelphia, 1984), 357–82; idem, "The Development of the Sibylline Tradition," in *ANRW* 20.1 (1987), 421–59; idem, "Sibylline Oracles," *ABD* 6:2–6; idem, "The Jewish Adaptation of the Sibylline Oracles," in idem, *Seers, Sibyls and Sages in Hellenistic-Roman Judaism* (Leiden, 1997), 181–97; idem, *Between Athens and Jerusalem,* 160–67; idem, "The Third Sibyl Revisited," in *Things Revealed: Studies in Early Jewish and Christian Literature in Honor of Michael E. Stone* (ed. E.G. Chazon, D. Satran, and R.A. Clements; Leiden, 2004), 3–19; H. Merkel, *Sibyllinen* (Gütersloh, 1998).

[122] Ps.-Phoc. 103–4 and 54, respectively. Note also 8 and 106, for other clearly biblical ideas. Monotheism in *Sibylline Oracles* 1–2: *passim*; resurrection: 1:355; 4:180–182. When Paul speaks to the Athenian philosophers about Jesus and the "Resurrection," they think that he proclaims to them "foreign divinities" (Acts 17:18).

ideas, foreign to the Greek mind.[123] Ps.-Phocylides even paraphrases such a characteristically Jewish precept as not taking a mother bird together with her fledglings (84–85; see Deut 22:6–7).

Despite the author's pagan mask, the most convincing theory of his identity seems to be the suggestion that Ps.-Phocylides was a Jew aiming to show his fellow Jews that the best of pagan minds found Jewish ethics attractive. That is, he probably wrote his poem in order to strengthen inner Jewish morale and bolster the self-confidence of a Jewish community living in the midst of culturally and intellectually challenging pagan surroundings.[124] The author could easily have said something about Jewish sacrificial worship, had he considered it an important constituent of his understanding of Judaism—after all, even some pagan authors were not always unanimously critical of the Jewish Temple cult.[125] However, he did not. Although his vision of Judaism was based on ethics that were more recognizably Jewish than those emphasized in the *Testament of Abraham*, still no mention is made of anything connected to the Jewish ritual and cult. Fittingly, Ps.-Phocylides sums up his poem by stating that "Purifications (καθαρμοί) are for the purity of the soul, not of the body. These are the mysteries of righteousness (δικαιοσύνης μυστήρια); living thus may you live out (your) life well to the threshold of old age" (228–230).[126] It is clear that the author intends his ethical teaching, expounded in the poem, to comprise the "mysteries of righteousness."[127] Concerning "purifications," van der Horst observes, "For Ps-Phoc. the purity of the soul expresses itself in the good deeds inculcated by him in all the previous lines of the poem."[128] An extensive portion of the text (lines 5–79) also

---

[123] Ps.-Phocylides is usually dated to the second half of the first century BCE–beginning of the first century CE. Egypt is the most probable place of composition of his work. See Wilson, *The Sentences of Pseudo-Phocylides*, 12–13; Collins, *Jewish Wisdom*, 164.

[124] G. Alon, "The Halakha in the Teaching of the Twelve Apostles," in idem, *Studies in Jewish History* (Tel-Aviv, 1957), 274–94 (in Hebrew); Cf. V.A. Tcherikover, "Jewish Apologetic Literature Reconsidered," *Eos* 48 (1956): 169–93.

[125] See Hecataeus of Abdera, *Aegyptiaca*, in Diodorus Siculus, *Bibliotheca Historica* 40.3.4–7 (*GLA* 1:26–35 [no. 11]). True, this passage may be a Jewish forgery; see D.R. Schwartz, "Diodorus Siculus 40.3—Hecataeus or Pseudo-Hecataeus?" in M. Mor et al., eds., *Jews and Gentiles in the Holy Land* (Jerusalem, 2003), 181–97. But even if it is, it demonstrates that a Jew did not think it unnatural for a pagan author to say good things about the Jewish cult.

[126] Translation follows P.W. van der Horst, "Pseudo-Phocylides," *OTP* 2:582.

[127] See W.T. Wilson, *The Mysteries of Righteousness: The Literary Composition and Genre of the Sentences of Pseudo-Phocylides* (Tübingen, 1994).

[128] Van der Horst, *The Sentences of Pseudo-Phocylides*, 260.

appears as part of *Sibylline Oracles* 2 (lines 55–149) with some changes and additions[129]—and it is to that document that we now turn.

4) *Sibylline Oracles 1 and 2*

In the manuscript tradition, *Sibylline Oracles* 2 is not separated from *Sibylline Oracles* 1; rather, they appear to form two parts of a single composition.[130] In its present form both texts, but especially *Sibylline Oracles* 2, contain Christian interpolations, and they are universally held to have undergone extensive Christian redaction. However, it is also beyond doubt that most of the material in these two books comes from Jewish sources; they may have been composed in Phrygia between 30 BCE and 70 CE.[131] It is difficult to know for sure at what stage of composition/redaction the passage from Ps.-Phocylides was inserted into the oracle, and when additional interpolations were introduced into it. In my view, there is no reason to assume that the passage was inserted into the text of *Sibylline Oracles* 2 only at the Christian stage of redaction. It seems to fit well with the surrounding Jewish context, and none of the additions to it contains any Christian elements. In other words, it was part of the original Jewish work, taken over from the *Sentences* and slightly reworked.[132]

If this indeed is the case, then one of the Sibylline additions to the text of Ps.-Phocylides might be an important witness to the attitude of the author(s) of the Jewish substratum of these two Sibylline books to the Temple and sacrifices. After Ps.-Phocylides 22 (*Sibylline Oracle* 2.78) we read:

> With perspiring hand give a portion of corn to one who is in need. Whoever gives alms knows that he is lending to God. Mercy saves from death when judgment comes. God wants not sacrifice but mercy instead of

---

[129] See ibid., 84–85.

[130] On *Sibylline Oracles* 1–2, see most recently J.L. Lightfoot, *The Sibylline Oracles: With Introduction, Translation, and Commentary on the First and Second Books* (Oxford, 2007). However, Lightfoot does not seem to be very interested in separating the Jewish substratum from the Christian redaction. The Greek text of the *Sibylline Oracles* was published by J. Geffcken, *Die Oracula Sibyllina* (Leipzig, 1902).

[131] See Collins, "Sibylline Oracles," *OTP* 1:332; Trebilco, *Jewish Communities*, 95–99. Phrygian provenance had already been advocated by J. Geffcken, *Komposition und Enstehungszeit der Oracula Sibyllina* (Leipzig, 1902), 50.

[132] Collins, "Sibylline Oracles," *OTP* 1:330: "Nothing in these verses is necessarily Christian."

sacrifice (οὐ θυσίην, ἔλεος δὲ θέλει θεὸς ἀντὶ θυσίης). Therefore clothe the naked. Give the hungry a share of your bread.[133]

The passage receives additional significance if we take into account the fact that in all of the Jewish parts of this oracle, filled as they are with ethical teaching, summonses to repentance, promises of doom for disobedience to divine will, and eschatological teaching, this is the only place in which anything related to the Temple and cult is mentioned.

The message of the Jewish author(s) of *Sibylline Oracles* 1 and 2 is fairly straightforward: they convict sinners of such common trespasses as violence, deceit, fornication, adultery, slander, pride, insolence, idolatry, sorcery, godlessness and the like.[134] The sinners are called to repentance and supplication—mainly by Noah in *Sibylline Oracle* 1 and by the Sibyl herself in *Sibylline Oracle* 2. If the sinners do not repent, they will face the terror of divine retribution—first in the Deluge, and at the end of time (which, of course, is near) in Gehenna and Tartarus. Those who did not commit such sins, but "were concerned with justice and noble deeds, and piety and most righteous thoughts—angels will lift them through the blazing river and bring them to light and to life without care" (2.313–16). These righteous ones will experience eternal bliss in the hereafter.

IX. Diaspora Radicals: *Sibylline Oracles* 4 and Stephen "the Hellenist"

1) *Sibylline Oracles* 4

The message of condemnation and call to repentance in *Sibylline Oracles* 1 and 2 is similar in many ways to that of *Sibylline Oracles* 4, which is arguably the most anti-Temple-and-cult composition written in the Diaspora.[135] This rather short oracle is conventionally and convinc-

---

[133] Translations of *Sibylline Oracles* are taken from Collins, "Sibylline Oracles," in *OTP*.

[134] The excerpt from Ps.-Phocylides contains the most detailed list of ethical commandments—both positive and negative—in the whole of *Sibylline Oracles* 1–2.

[135] On this, see J.J. Collins, "The Place of the Fourth Sibylline Oracle in the Development of the Jewish Sibyllina." *JJS* 25 (1974): 365–80; idem, "Sibylline Oracles," *OTP* 1:381–89. On *Sibylline Oracle* 4 in general, see H.C.O. Lanchester, "The Sibylline Oracles," in *The Apocrypha and Pseudepigrapha of the Old Testament, Vol. 2: Pseudepigrapha* (ed. R.H. Charles; Oxford, 1913), 368–406; V. Nikiprowezky, "Reflexions sur

ingly dated to around 80 CE, although no consensus has been reached as to its exact place of origin.[136] *Sibylline Oracles* 4 is clearly a Jewish missionary pamphlet, and, unlike most of the other Jewish Sibyllines, it has not undergone any Christian redaction and does not contain any Christian interpolations.

The author of *Sibylline Oracles* 4 calls upon pagans to renounce idolatry and various sins similar to those denounced in *Sibylline Oracles* 1 and 2, repent, and praise God. At the very beginning of the oracle they are assured that this God is different from false gods because "he does not have a house, a stone set up as a temple (Ms group ψ: ναὸν λίθον ἱδρυθέντα)" (8);[137] rather, His temple is in fact "one which it is not possible to see from earth nor to measure with mortal eyes, since it was not fashioned by mortal hand" (10–11). It is clear that the author's vision of piety is absolutely irreconcilable with any kind of sacrificial worship:

> Happy will be those of mankind on earth who will love the great God, blessing him before drinking and eating, putting their trust in piety. They will reject all temples when they see them, altars, too, useless foundations of dumb stones defiled with blood of animate creatures, and sacrifices of four-footed animals (οἳ νηοὺς μὲν ἅπαντας ἀπαρνήσονται ἰδόντες καὶ βωμούς, εἰκαῖα λίθων ἀφιδρύματα κωφῶν, αἵμασιν ἐμψύχων μεμιασμένα καὶ θυσίῃσιν τετραπόδων·).[138] They will look to the great glory of the one God and commit no wicked murder, nor deal in dishonest gain, which are most horrible things. Neither have they disgraceful desire for another's spouse or for hateful and repulsive abuse of a male. (24–34)

---

quelques problemes du quatrième et du cinquième livre des Oracles Sibyllins," *HUCA* 43 (1972): 29–76; Schürer, *History*, 3:641–43.

[136] E.g., Nikiprowezky, "Reflexions sur quelques problemes," 29–30, dates it to between 79 and 88 CE.

[137] Translations of *Sibylline Oracle* 4 are from Collins, "Sibylline Oracles," *OTP* 1: 381–19. The text of this line is discussed in Tuval, "The 4th *Sibylline Oracle*," 36–37.

[138] Even scholars who think that *Sibylline Oracle* 4 criticizes only pagan sacrificial worship agree that its author did not have much use for the Jewish Temple either. See A. Chester, "The Sibyl and the Temple," in *Templum Amicitiae: Essays on the Second Temple Presented to Ernst Bammel* (ed. W. Horbury; Sheffield, 1991), 66: "On balance, therefore, although the main thrust of both 4–11 and 27–30 is polemic against idolatry, they allow no positive place for the form and practice of the Jerusalem Temple either." Collins, "Sibylline Oracles," *OTP* 1:383 writes "While these passages are not specifically an attack on the Jewish Temple (which no longer existed), they undermine the very idea of temple worship and make no allowance for the possibility of an acceptable temple."

In lines 162–170, which form the climax of the composition, the author exhorts the pagans to abandon their sins, repent, and turn to God. No sacrifices are needed in order to propitiate God; words of praise will atone for "bitter impiety":

> Ah, wretched mortals, change these things, and do not lead the great God to all sorts of anger, but abandon daggers and groanings, murders and outrages, and wash your whole bodies in perennial rivers. Stretch out your hands to heaven and ask forgiveness for your previous deeds and make propitiation for bitter impiety with words of praise (καὶ εὐλογίαις ἀσέβειαν πικρὰν ἱλάσκεσθε); God will grant repentance and will not destroy. He will stop His wrath if you all practice honorable piety in your hearts.[139]

True, lines 115–118 and 125–127, referring to the Roman destruction of the Jerusalem Temple, term it "great." However, several important points should be taken into account. First, the destruction of the Temple is mentioned in the context of the *vaticinium ex eventu* concerning the last days. By any standard, this was a momentous event which had to be mentioned in such a context. Second, the author asserts that the Temple will be sacked "whenever they [i.e., the people of Jerusalem] put their trust in folly and cast off piety and commit repulsive murders in front of the Temple" (116–118).[140] Third, the mention of the Destruction allows the author to pour additional abuse upon the hated Romans and to promise divine punishment. Fourth, no restoration of the Temple is envisaged in the detailed eschatological scenario presented in lines 171–192. One has to admit that it is rather striking to find such an attitude to the Temple and its cult in a Jewish writing from a mere decade after its demise. And it is, of course, even more striking when compared with the attitude of contemporary Jewish authors from the Land of Israel, such as those of *4 Ezra* and *2 Baruch*.

---

[139] Collins, "The Place of the Fourth Sibylline Oracle," 377–78: "The placing of this passage [vv. 63–169] in Sib IV elevates baptism and repentance as the only key to salvation." Cf. H. Hartman, "*Teste Sibylla*: Construction and Message in the Fourth Book of the Sibylline Oracles," in idem, *Text-Centered New Testament Studies: Text-Theoretical Essays on Early Jewish and Early Christian Literature* (ed. D. Hellholm; Tübingen, 1997), 160: "[H]ere is the heart of the text."

[140] It is intriguing to speculate on what constituted the "folly" of Jerusalemites in our author's view. Given the author's description of genuine piety, quoted above, would it be rash to suppose that, for him, the "folly" consisted of their excessive trust in the Temple and its sacrificial cult, which he denounced in lines 27–30?

2) *Stephen's Speech*

The closest parallel to the anti-cultic attitude of the author of *4 Sibylline Oracle* is found in what is known as Stephen's speech in Acts 7.[141] Although in its present context the speech is put on the lips of a Christian martyr and is supposed to convey a Christian message, most scholars tend to consider it originally to have been a Diaspora Jewish sermon.[142] Although the speech is presented as the answer to the question of the high priest, it does not answer the question. Moreover, as H. Conzelmann succinctly phrased it, "this is not a martyr's speech."[143] The speech has been frequently examined, and I will limit my treatment here to discussion of the most pertinent points.

First of all, in Stephen's retelling of biblical history, all divine epiphanies, miracles, and key events in Jewish history take place beyond the borders of the Land of Israel. Indeed, Stephen is so bold as to state that God had "exiled (μετῴκισεν) Abraham from Haran into this land in which you are now living" (7:4);[144] and most of the heroes active in the Land of Israel, such as judges, prophets, righteous kings, Ezra, Nehemiah, Simon the Just, or the Hasmoneans, are not mentioned in his narrative (excluding direct quotations from the prophets). The climax is reached with the story of the Golden Calf. The Sons of Israel spurn Moses and worship the idol (39–41), and God hands them over to idolatry (42). Stephen quotes from the prophecy of Amos, which speaks about idolatry in the wilderness (42–43; cf. Amos 5:25–27). Immediately after this he declares: "Our fathers had the tent of witness in the wilderness, even as he who spoke to Moses directed him to make it, according to the pattern that he had seen" (44). The tent is brought into the Promised Land, but David decides to find "a habitation" for

---

[141] Simon, *St Stephen*; Collins, "Sibylline Oracles," *OTP* 1:383.

[142] See the discussion in D.R. Schwartz, "Residents and Exiles, Jerusalemites and Judaeans (Acts 7:4; 2:5, 14): On Stephen, Pentecost and the Structure of Acts," in idem, *Studies in the Jewish Background of Christianity* (Tübingen, 1992), 117–27; and C.K. Barrett, *A Critical and Exegetical Commentary on the Acts of the Apostles* (2 vols.; Edinburgh, 1994–1998), 1:335–40. The latter writes: "Luke gives us, in outline, a 'Hellenist' sermon; the sort of sermon that might be preached in a 'Hellenist,' Diaspora, synagogue, and could easily be taken over and used when Hellenist Jews became Hellenist Jewish Christians.... The speech of Acts 7, which can hardly have been spoken by Stephen in the circumstances described, recovers great historical value as a document of that sector of Judaism from which Stephen and his colleagues are said to have come" (338–39).

[143] H. Conzelmann, *Acts of the Apostles* (Philadelphia, 1987), 57.

[144] Schwartz, "Residents and Exiles," 117–22.

the God of Jacob (or "House of Jacob").[145] His son Solomon builds a house for Him. Here Stephen explodes: "But the Most High does not dwell in things made with hands (ἀλλ᾽ οὐχ ὁ ὕψιστος ἐν χειροποιήτοις κατοικεῖ)![146] As the prophet says: 'Heaven is my throne and the earth is the footstool for my feet. What kind of house will you build for me, says the Lord, and what is the place of my rest?'" (48–50, quoting Isa 66:1–2). Stephen then proceeds to a verbal assault on his listeners. The parallel between the idolatrous practices in the wilderness and the "perverse cult" of Stephen's opponents could not be emphasized more clearly.

As has been noted above, the author of Acts probably utilized here a Hellenistic-Jewish source. This judgment is based on the general absence of specifically Christian material in this speech and on the use of the first person to refer to Jews and Jewish traditions until v. 51, where the specifically Christian part of the speech begins. The Diaspora Jewish homilist behind the speech apparently wanted to say that any place on earth was just as holy as the Temple. God is not limited by any territory; He manifests himself in various places, and does not dwell in any particular location.

X. The Temple Plays a Role: *Letter of Aristeas,* *Sibylline Oracles* 3 and 5

Finally, I would like to discuss three Diaspora compositions in which, in contrast to the writings treated above, the Temple and the cult do seem to play a prominent role. These are the *Letter of Aristeas* and *Sibylline Oracles* 3 and 5, all of which are most likely to have been written in Egypt.[147] The interest of these authors in the Temple, cult, and priesthood has attracted some attention in the history of research, and some even have noticed this as atypical in comparison to the other

---

[145] See the apparatus in B. and K. Aland et al. (eds.), *Nestle-Aland Novum Testamentum Graece* (27th ed.; Stuttgart, 2006) ad loc.; and B. Metzger, *A Textual Commentary on the Greek New Testament* (2d ed.; Stuttgart, 1994), 308–9.

[146] 7:48. When χειροποίητος appears in cultic contexts in Hellenistic Jewish literature, it might have idolatrous connotations. Cf. *Sib. Or.* 3.606, 618, 722; *Sib. Or.* 4.28A. Whenever there is a Hebrew original for the LXX χειροποίητος, it is always אֱלִיל.

[147] See the discussion of each of these documents below.

literary products of the Jewish Diaspora.[148] As I will suggest in the following discussion, this interest may be ascribed to the specific political and cultural circumstances in which these compositions seem to have been produced.

1) *The Letter of Aristeas*

The *Letter of Aristeas*, which is usually dated to the second half of the second century BCE,[149] purports to relate the story of the translation of the Torah into Greek under the auspices of Ptolemy II Philadelphus (283–247 BCE). Although it is universally admitted that the work is a pseudepigraphon, it is not ascribed to a biblical hero but rather to a certain Aristeas, who is presented as a high-ranking pagan official at the Ptolemaic court.[150]

According to the story, after the translation of the Torah into Greek was proposed to the king by his librarian, he sent envoys with a letter (accompanied by generous gifts) to the Judean high priest Eleazar, requesting him to provide seventy-two translators well-suited for the work of translation. The envoys, of whom Aristeas was one, arrived in Jerusalem, and were enormously impressed by the country, the city of Jerusalem, its Temple complex, its sacrificial cult and the appearance of the high priest. Paragraphs 83–99 of the work contain detailed and laudatory descriptions of these matters.[151] The description of the

---

[148] E.g., Schwartz, "Temple or City," 119 on *Aristeas*; Collins, "Sibylline Oracles," in *OTP* 1:356 on *Sibylline Oracles* 3; ibid., 392 on *Sibylline Oracles* 5.

[149] Bickerman, *Studies*, 129–33; M. Hadas, *Aristeas to Philocrates* (New York, 1951), 54; J. Goldstein, "The Message of Aristeas to Philocrates in the Second Century BCE: Obey the Torah, Venerate the Temple of Jerusalem, but Speak Greek, and Put Your Hopes in the Ptolemaic Dynasty," in *Eretz Israel, Israel and the Jewish Diaspora: Mutual Relations* (ed. M. Mor; London, 1991), 8–18; Collins, *Between Athens and Jerusalem*, 98–101; Nickelsburg, *Jewish Literature*, 198. For a discussion of earlier scholarship on dating the *Letter*, see S. Jellicoe, *The Septuagint and Modern Study* (Oxford, 1968), 47–52; he dates it before 168 BCE. For a full list of dating proposals, see G. Dorival, "Les origines de la Septante: La traduction en grec des cinq livres de la Torah," in *La Bible grecque des Septante* (ed. M. Harl et al.; Paris, 1994), 41–42. Most recently, see Rajak, *Translation and Survival*, 24–63.

[150] In addition to the studies listed in the previous note, see A. Pelletier, *Lettre d' Aristée à Philocrate* (Paris, 1962); Schürer, *History*, 3:677–87. H.St.J. Thackeray, "The Letter of Aristeas," in H.B. Swete, *An Introduction to the Old Testament in Greek* (Cambridge, 1902), 533–606, provides an introduction to the textual history and an edition of the Greek text.

[151] For a commentary on this passage, see C.T.R. Hayward, *The Jewish Temple: A Non-Biblical Sourcebook* (London, 1996), 26–37. J.-G. Février, *La date, la composition*

country of Judea and the qualities of the translators, chosen by Eleazar, is followed by an allegorical exposition in defense of the Law, delivered by the high priest. Upon their arrival in Alexandria the translators were immediately introduced to the king, who treated them to a lavish week-long symposium, in the course of which they repeatedly astonished him with their philosophical answers to his riddles. Then they were taken to the island of Pharos, where in the course of seventy-two days they completed the translation of the Torah into Greek. The translation was read first to the Jewish community, and then to the king, to the utter satisfaction of both. After the affirmation of the perfection and unalterable status of the Greek version by the Jews, and expression of compliments from the king, the translators were sent home with additional gifts.

The *Letter* is usually considered to be one of the most universalistic compositions produced by Jews in the Greco-Roman Diaspora, in which "[d]ifferences between Jews and Gentiles are reduced to a minimum."[152] Thus, the translation of the Torah is ordered by the Ptolemaic monarch, who manumits all Jewish slaves in his realm, sends gifts to the Jerusalem Temple, admires the wisdom of the Jewish translators-sages, and acknowledges the sublimity of Torah's contents. It is also generally agreed that, apart from its defense of the Alexandrian translation of the Torah into Greek, the *Letter* also functions apologetically to present Judaism and its origins to sympathetic Gentiles in the best possible light. Thus, it is presented as the work of an educated pagan, who is immensely impressed by all aspects of Jewish life: the Jewish Law and theology; the Jerusalem Temple, its cult and priesthood; the country of the Jews; and Jewish philosophical wisdom. However, it is clear that the real author is an Alexandrian Jew, interested, above all, in the respectful coexistence of his own local Jewish community and the pagan rulers of the land. Therefore, the passage devoted to the Jerusalem Temple has to be interpreted in this context.

---

et les sources de la Lettre d'Aristée à Philocrate (Paris, 1924), 26–27; and Schwartz, "Temple or City," 119, think that this passage might be secondary. However there seems to be no convincing proof for this. The author might have used a source here, but as it is, the passage fits neatly with the rest of the narrative. It is true that this whole section is omitted by Josephus from his fairly close paraphrase of the *Letter* in *Ant.* 12.11–118, but in my view this fact does not prove that he did not find it in his source. He might have had other reasons for omitting it, which I will discuss elsewhere.

[152] Nickelsburg, *Jewish Literature*, 198.

It should be noticed that the descriptions of the Temple and the ministrations of its priests are highly idealized and might not be based upon the personal experience or knowledge of the author. The whole picture presented in the *Letter* is aimed at conveying the impression of a highly spectacular performance, astonishing the observer with its order, sublimity and "otherworldliness" (e.g., in the description of the high priest in 96–99). The author seems to embellish the narrative even to the point of contradicting reality: thus, an oft-discussed feature of his account is the maintenance of *total silence* in the Temple notwithstanding the performance there of manual tasks by *seven hundred* priests (92–95). The main message conveyed by the author is that the Temple, the service of the priests, and the appearance of the high priest are aesthetically appealing, awe-inspiring, and dignified.[153] In the words of Collins:

> The *Letter* as a whole is not characterized by any polemic against Judea, but it does not present a view of Judaism centered on Jerusalem either. It is rather a manifesto of the self-sufficiency of Diaspora Judaism, which respects Jerusalem as its source, but speaks of an idealized biblical Judea rather than of the actual state of the Hasmoneans.... Judaism is not defined in national terms. The law is the vehicle of a philosophy which is potentially universal.[154]

So although the Temple, cult, and priests are seemingly prominent in the *Letter*, the main question concerning their role is the same one I asked earlier concerning Philo: What is the place and function of these institutions in the author's conception of Judaism? Are they vital and indispensable foundations of Jewish life wherever Jews are found, and do they function as the primary medium of communication between the human and the divine spheres? The answer seems to be in the negative, since the overall impression, from the existential point of view, is that the Temple is even less important in the *Letter* than in Philo. For if Philo at least saw the Temple as the symbol of Roman recognition of Jewish political and religious rights, as well as an important physical symbol of invisible divine realities intended for the simple-minded

---

[153] Cf. Nickelsburg, *Jewish Literature*, 196–97: "His idealized description of the country is marked by utopian elements that characterize travelogues in classical and Hellenistic literature." See Hadas, *Aristeas to Philocrates*, 48–50.

[154] Collins, *Between Athens and Jerusalem*, 103.

Jews, for the author of the *Letter*, it functions almost exclusively as an impressive show.[155]

To summarize the above discussion, it should be said that the *Letter* is in no sense a polemic against the Jerusalem Temple and its priests. The opposite is true: they are idealized and embellished, even to the point of creating a utopian and fantastic account. However, they do not function in any immediate and profound way in the Judaism of the *Letter*, but rather as a nice and aesthetic decoration. The author's real concern is with the Greek Torah, congenial relations within the pagan environment of his community, and Gentile respect for Judaism and its philosophical worldview.

2) *Sibylline Oracles 3*

The work I will discuss next is admittedly one of the most interesting and unusual products of Hellenistic Judaism. *Sibylline Oracles* 3 is considered by most scholars to be composite in nature, and was probably created over a substantial period of time. Various theories have been proposed as to its geographical provenance, but the location of the bulk of the work in Ptolemaic Egypt still seems to be the best-argued and most convincing proposal.[156] According to the analysis of Collins,[157] which I accept, three main parts can be discerned in the current book, reflecting various stages of composition: a) the main

---

[155] For this point, see esp. Collins, *Between Athens and Jerusalem*, 195: "No mention is made of the efficacy of the sacrifices or their effect on the relations between human beings and God. The liturgy is considered a *spectacle* and is admired for its emotional effect on the onlookers.... The concern is not with the mechanism of the atonement but with the public impression of Judaism that is conveyed."

[156] Most recently, R. Buitenwerf has proposed Asia Minor, on the basis of the prominence of topographical references to Asian locations in the Oracle; see his *Book III of the Sibylline Oracles and its Social Setting: With an Introduction, Translation and Commentary* (Leiden, 2003), 124–34. However, he seems to ignore the fact that it is the Egyptian (Ptolemaic) king who is referred to by the author in messianic terms. Why should an Asian Jew consider an Egyptian king a universal deliverer? Palestinian provenance for *Sibylline Oracles* 3 was considered an option by F. Millar, "Review of V. Nikiprowetzky, *La Troisième Sibylle*," *JTS* 23 (1972): 223–24; however he did not prove it. V. Nikiprowezky, *La Troisième Sibylle* (Paris, 1970), 206–17 argued for the unity of the work, and dated it to the first century BCE, in the reign of Cleopatra. Gruen, *Heritage and Hellenism*, 269–88, sees the work as a compilation of oracles from different periods. I follow Collins, "Third Sibyl Revisited," where he responds to these criticisms.

[157] Collins, "Sibylline Oracles," *OTP* 1:354–61; reaffirmed in Collins, "Third Sibyl Revisited."

corpus (97–349 and 489–829); b) oracles against nations (350–488); and c) lines 1–96, which may have formed the conclusion of a different book.[158] Since these segments are in turn comprised of various oracles with distinct subtopics and characteristics, no full analysis will be attempted here. Instead, I will briefly discuss the main themes and concerns of *Sibylline Oracles* 3, discuss the possible historical context in which it was created, and address the question of the importance of the Temple in its author's thought.

Similarly to the other *Sibylline Oracles*, the main corpus contains a periodization of world history, condemnations of various sins, and descriptions of divine punishments. The unusual feature of the book is that the end-time deliverer, who in the Jewish writings of the period is usually a Jewish Messiah or some other supernatural agent of divine salvation like Enoch, Melchizedek, or the archangel Michael, is here none other than a (pagan) Ptolemaic king.[159] He is described in messianic terms: "Every kind of deceit will be found among them until the seventh reign, when a king of Egypt, who will be of the Greeks by race, will rule. And then the people of the great God will again be strong, who will be guides in life for all mortals."[160] In verses 652–56 he is also described as the "king from the sun." On the basis of this reference and the prominence of the Romans in verses 175–190, the main corpus of *Sibylline Oracles* 3 is dated by Collins to between the sixties and the forties of the second century BCE.[161]

Two other major sections of the text, verses 1–96 and 350–488, are of composite nature, and are dated to various periods. Some of the material incorporated into them may actually be pagan and stem from the early Hellenistic period; other parts were composed late in the first century BCE, while still others may come from the late first century CE. Verses 1–96 contain a sublime vision of a transcendent, metaphysical, and omnipresent God, not unlike that contained in the *Sibylline Oracles* 4, which was discussed above. The rest of the section is a vision of history with prophecies of doom. In verses 350–488, as many as four distinct oracles have been identified, which almost exclusively contain

---

[158] Collins, "Sibylline Oracles," *OTP* 1:354.

[159] This, of course, has a precedent in Isa 44:28, where Cyrus is called by God "My anointed."

[160] *Sib. Or.* 3.191–195.

[161] Collins, "Sibylline Oracles," *OTP* 1:354–355.

prophecies of impending destruction without any ethical exhortation. However, the striking fact is that *neither Temple nor sacrifices are mentioned even once* in these two remaining sections of *Sibylline Oracles* 3.[162] In this feature, they conform to other Diaspora compositions, in which the Temple plays no role. It seems that the authors-redactors of the later additions to the main corpus of the book were not interested in these matters, and therefore, I will concentrate my attention here on verses 97–349 and 489–829 and their putative *Sitz im Leben*. In my view, if the historical reconstruction proposed by J.J. Collins is correct, it may account for the centrality of the Temple in this core of the composition.

It is obvious, and has been noted by all scholars, that the Temple and sacrifices play an important role in the outlook of the author of the main corpus of *Sibylline Oracles* 3, to an extent "which is unparalleled in any document from Egyptian Judaism."[163] The Temple and sacrifices to God are mentioned in 286–294, 564–579, 624–629, 657–659, and 715–718, and it is clear that they are central to the author's view of piety and the end-time triumph of Judaism. He repeatedly exhorts the pagans to forsake idolatry and moral depravity and worship the one true God with sacrifices and offerings: "But you, devious mortal, do not tarry in hesitation but turn back, converted, and propitiate God. Sacrifice to God hundreds of bulls, and firstborn lambs, and goats at the recurring times" (624–627). The end-time Jews are described in the following terms:

> There will again be a sacred race of pious men who attend to the councils and intention of the Most High, who fully honor the Temple of the great God with drink offering and burnt offering and sacred hecatombs, sacrifices of well-fed bulls, unblemished rams, and firstborn sheep, offering as holocausts fat flocks of lambs on a great altar, in holy manner. (573–579)

As has been stated above, with regard to what it says about the Temple, the *Sibylline Oracles* 3 is an unusual Diaspora work. I have suggested that the interest exhibited by its author in cultic matters might possibly be explained on the basis of the theory proposed by Collins

---

[162] If Collins (ibid., 469) is right in considering Fragments 1–3 to be part of the same work as *Sib. Or.* 3.1–45, then sacrifices are mentioned in Fragment 1:21. (The fragments are translated in Collins, ibid., 469–72).

[163] Collins, ibid., 356.

concerning its provenance. He thinks that the promotion of the seventh Ptolemaic king to the rank of the savior of the world should be seen as the key to the most probable context for the writing of the book. He also notices that the down-to-earth fascination of the author with military and political matters is not a feature one would expect from the more spiritually-minded Jewish authors of Alexandria, but it might rather obtain among the circles of the Jewish military colony in Leontopolis, which is known for its close connections with the Ptolemies. From Josephus we know of the very close interaction between the circles associated with Onias and his descendants and the Ptolemaic house, to the point that at a slightly later period Onias' sons Chelkias and Ananias were in command of the entire Ptolemaic army.[164] Although this conception of the community responsible for creating the bulk of *Sibylline Oracles* 3 must remain hypothetical, there is nothing implausible about it. On the contrary, it has the benefit of accounting for some of the unusual features of the composition, including the prominence of the Temple-and-cult related matters.

Moreover, although the temple of Onias in Leontopolis is usually considered to be schismatic and even "heretical" by Deuteronomistic standards, we do not find much evidence for tension between the authorities of the Jerusalem Temple (or Alexandrian Jews) and those of the temple of Onias, or vice versa, even though this Egyptian temple coexisted with its Jerusalem counterpart for more than two hundred (!) years.[165] We also know from Josephus that Onias' son Ananias played a crucial role in the preservation of the independence of Alexander Yannai's kingdom at a later date.[166] In other words, it would not be unnatural to expect such praise of the Jerusalem Temple as we now find in the main corpus of *Sibylline Oracles* 3 in a work written by a follower (or descendant?) of the Zadokite high priest, Onias.

---

[164] In *Ag. Ap.* 2.49–50 Onias himself is said to have been one of the two Jewish commanders of Ptolemy Philometor's and Cleopatra's entire army. However, the reference is somewhat problematic. See J.M.G. Barclay, *Flavius Josephus: Translation and Commentary, Vol. 10: Against Apion* (Leiden, 2007), 196 n. 167; Bohak, *Joseph and Aseneth and the Jewish Temple*, 24–25. On Chelkias and Ananias, see *Ant.* 13.285–287; 348–355. Cf. Bohak, *Joseph and Aseneth and the Jewish Temple*, 32–34. On the Oniads, see Collins, *Between Athens and Jerusalem*, 69–78.

[165] See D.R. Schwartz, "The Jews of Egypt between the Temple of Onias, the Temple of Jerusalem, and Heaven," in Gafni, *Center and Diaspora*, 37–55 (in Hebrew; English summary: vi–vii).

[166] *Ant.* 13.352–355.

3) *Sibylline Oracles 5*

The last Diaspora composition I would like to consider is *Sibylline Oracles* 5, which was written in Egypt in the first third of the second century CE. The discussion of this work must take into account the great changes which took place in the position of Egyptian Jewry vis-à-vis its Gentile environment early in that century. If earlier Jewish Egyptian authors of the Ptolemaic and early Roman period had entertained various hopes for peaceful and fruitful coexistence between the Jewish community and the surrounding Gentile culture, these hopes had been brutally shattered beginning with the late thirties of the first century CE.[167]

Already in Philo's times we hear of escalating tensions between the pagans of Alexandria and their Jewish neighbors, which resulted in the desecration of synagogues and physical violence directed against the Jews. Both from Philo and from Josephus we know of the increase in anti-Jewish pagan propaganda, slander, and political activity aimed at dispossessing local Jewish communities from what they perceived as their inalienable rights. The situation deteriorated even more with the outbreak of the Great Revolt in Judea, resulting in Jewish disturbances in Alexandria and their subsequent suppression at the price of tens of thousands of Jewish casualties. Although the sources at our disposal that deal with this period are scanty and fragmentary,[168] it seems safe to suppose that in the second half of the first century CE and the early years of the second, the earlier hopes of peaceful coexistence of Jews and pagans in Egypt were swiftly evaporating. This disillusionment is usually considered to be the hotbed that nurtured the seeds of the bloody, and—as it eventually turned out—catastrophic, revolt of the Diaspora late in the days of Trajan.

Although here I cannot discuss that revolt in any detail, it is clear from all sources at our disposal that it was characterized by an unusu-

---

[167] See V.A. Tcherikover, "Prolegomena," *CPJ* 1:55–86, on the deterioration of the relationships between the Jews and pagans in Egypt. Cf. the more recent treatment in Barclay, *Jews in the Mediterranean Diaspora*, 72–78; on pp. 226–28 he adduces *Sibylline Oracle* 5 as an extreme example of "cultural antagonism."

[168] We hear of continuing quarrels between pagans and Jews in the time of Trajan; see H. Musurillo, *Acts of the Pagan Martyrs* (Oxford, 1954), 44–48; 161–78; *CPJ* 2:82–87 (no. 157).

ally high level of hatred, ferocity and violence on both sides.[169] Even if we might doubt the horrible picture of the atrocities perpetrated by the Jews on their pagan enemies as presented in the pagan sources (e.g., Cassius Dio, *Roman History* 68:32), most scholars agree that it was a fierce and brutal war, which claimed hundreds of thousands of victims. For the Jewish community of Egypt it marked a calamitous watershed.[170]

In the context of my discussion of *Sibylline Oracles* 5, it seems that the most salient feature of this revolt, which is recognized by most scholars, is its messianic character. Apart from the fact that the revolt was led by royal (and therefore, messianic) pretenders, we know that it was systematically directed at the total eradication of paganism. Not a few scholars consider it to have been conceived by the rebels as a kind of "new Exodus," the final goal of which would have been the retrieval of the Land of Israel from the Romans and the creation of an independent Jewish state with Jerusalem as its capital.[171] If this was indeed the case, as seems very likely, one should not be surprised to find, in a document roughly contemporary with these events, the abandonment of the paradigms which had been created in a different atmosphere of peaceful coexistence between the Jews and their pagan neighbors in the Diaspora. These paradigms mostly became obsolete in the new situation, in which the Jews came to realize that peaceful coexistence was a thing of the past, and became convinced that their hopes for a happy life in the Diaspora had been shattered. In the atmosphere of the emergence of fierce anti-pagan ideology and the hope of the liberation of the Land of Israel from pagan rule, it is not surprising to find the abandonment of earlier Diasporan conceptions of Judaism, and a return to nationalistic ideologies centered on the Land of Israel, Jerusalem, and its Temple.

---

[169] For the most recent comprehensive treatment of the literary and archaeological evidence, as well as an interpretation, see M. Pucci Ben Zeev, *Diaspora Judaism in Turmoil, 116–117 C.E.: Ancient Sources and Modern Insights* (Leuven, 2005).

[170] Tcherikover, "Prolegomena," 93: "The tragic events of AD 115–17 stamp the early Roman period as having seen an almost total annihilation of Egyptian Jewry; strictly speaking, with this period the history of the Egyptian Jews in the Hellenistic-Roman age comes to an end, and the next period marks the beginning of a new development."

[171] See Tcherikover, "Prolegomena," 85–93, esp. 90 n. 84.

That said, however, one should not exaggerate the centrality of the Temple and its cult in the worldview of the author of *Sibylline Oracles* 5. It is true that these institutions do form part of his vision for the end-time restoration. Thus, he writes that God will yet be honored with sacrifices and prayers (!) (266–268), and prophesies that the savior-figure will rebuild the Temple (420–433), even as he laments the destruction of the Second Temple by the Romans (397–413). But the space devoted to the building of a temple to God in Egypt seems to be just as important, and the Ethiopians who destroyed it are singled out for severe divine punishment (501–511). In the final analysis, it seems that the main message that the author wanted to deliver was more negative than positive: it is not chiefly about the future bliss of the pious, but rather about the total annihilation of the wicked. To find such a hope in a book written shortly after the shattering of Jerusalem-centered messianic hopes and the brutal repression of the Jewish uprising is not a surprise. As J.M.G. Barclay remarks, "It is somehow fitting that the violent propaganda of this Sibylline Book concludes with the bleak prospect of a starless sky."[172]

XI. Summary and Conclusions

As noted above, M.J. Martin's work on Philo, which emphasized the Alexandrian's greater attachment to the synagogue and relative lack of attachment to the Temple of Jerusalem, served as a major inspiration for this study. In the present article I have conducted a similar analysis of many other works of the Hellenistic and early Roman Diaspora.

The literary heritage which I have surveyed here represents different genres, and witnesses to the multifaceted religious conceptions and worldviews of its authors, pointing to the extraordinary breadth and vitality of Diaspora Jewish religious expression. At the outset, I proposed that, in my view, it would be unnatural to expect ancient Diaspora Jews to see the Jerusalem Temple, its sacrificial cult, and its priests as the axis of their religious systems. Rather, I suggested that the Jews of the Diaspora, who spent most of their lives without the possibility of access to the Jerusalem Temple, had to develop alterna-

---

[172] Barclay, *Jews in the Mediterranean Diaspora*, 228.

tives to Temple-centered views of Jewish worship, as well as, more generally, different means of access to the divine.

In the course of this investigation, we discovered that the vast majority of these writings indeed evinced, in comparison to contemporary Palestinian literature, much less interest in the Temple and its cult, if any. And this is not only an argument from silence (however impressive that may often be). Rather, most of these writings offer something in place of the Temple and its cult: along with not mentioning the latter, they propagate coherent Judaic worldviews and identities and deal with such essential matters as worship,[173] ethics,[174] atonement for sin,[175] mediation of the divine powers,[176] God's presence,[177] salvation,[178] conversion,[179] eschatology and life after death.[180] In some cases we saw the emerging ideal of Torah study as central, which in later rabbinic Judaism was to achieve its full supremacy as the focal act of divine worship.[181] In others we saw that prayer (whether individual or communal) took the place of sacrifice, either being considered equal to it, or even totally replacing it.[182] In several compositions we witnessed the emphasis on martyrdom for the Law as the ultimate act of piety, indeed, as the ultimate sacrifice, which atoned for the sins of the entire Jewish nation and earned their salvation.[183] The notion of the Holy People as more important than the Holy Place, and the concomitant idea that it is the Holy People that makes any place "holy," have also been documented.[184] In other compositions we pointed to mystical trends, including speculations concerning the heavenly cult, exalted patriarchs and transcendental high priests, who might have seemed

---

[173] This and the following notes are not intended to provide an exhaustive list, but only to remind of some examples. Worship without the temple is illustrated in *Joseph and Aseneth*, *4 Sibylline Oracle*, 4 Maccabees.

[174] *Ps.-Phocylides, Sibylline Oracles, Testament of Job.*

[175] 2 and 4 Maccabees, Wisdom of Solomon.

[176] *Testament of Job, Prayer of Joseph.*

[177] 3 Maccabees.

[178] *2 Enoch, Testament of Job, Joseph and Aseneth*, 2 and 4 Maccabees.

[179] *Joseph and Aseneth, 4 Sibylline Oracle.*

[180] *2 Enoch*, 2 and 4 Maccabees, Wisdom of Solomon, *1, 2*, and *4 Sibylline Oracles, Testament of Job, Testament of Abraham.*

[181] See the section above on "Fragmentary Hellenistic Jewish Authors." As I noted earlier, Philo is, of course a prime example of this trend. Josephus's *Jewish Antiquities* also illustrate this tendency.

[182] *Hellenistic Synagogal Prayers*, Wisdom of Solomon.

[183] 2 Maccabees, and, esp., 4 Maccabees.

[184] 2 and 3 Maccabees.

much closer and more available to the Diaspora Jews than the real cult and priests in Jerusalem.[185] Above all, we saw an overwhelming emphasis on ethics—and even if sometimes they were presented under Gentile pseudonyms, these were always recognizably Jewish ethics, taught in the Torah of Moses.[186]

Apart from two radical Diaspora writings that took the lack of interest in the Temple and preference for more spiritual worship to a polemical extreme,[187] we have not detected any categorical rejection of the Temple and its cult. As stated in the introduction, this is not surprising. The Jews of the Diaspora read and venerated basically the same Torah as their brethren in the Land of Israel, the Torah which held the Temple, its cult and its priests in great esteem. They had no need to argue about these things. However, I believe that the above survey has demonstrated that the Temple and the cult did not function in any immediate and meaningful way in the Judaisms of the authors who produced the literature under review. Even in the *Letter of Aristeas*, which treated the Temple at length and with sympathy, the Temple was shown to be secondary to the author's view of Judaism, and its ritual mainly an impressive performance—not really the only way to God. These findings correspond, broadly, with Martin's conclusions in regard to Philo.

In other words, even before the destruction of the Temple in 70 CE and the cessation of its sacrificial cult, the Jews of the Greco-Roman Diaspora had successfully created alternative Judaic systems in which the Temple did not play a crucial role. These systems provided them with meaning and order as far as they looked at the world around them, and with a coherent sense of identity and purpose as far as they looked at themselves—both individually and communally. They also provided Diaspora Jews with alternative mediums of access to the divine, apart from the Temple rituals and away from Jerusalem. Although it is reasonable to assume that the destruction of the Jerusalem Temple caused a certain amount of anxiety on the part of the Diaspora Jews, especially as events in Palestine gave rise to *uncertainty* concerning the status of Jewish communities elsewhere in the Roman Empire, it might not be too bold to suppose that for the religious life

---

[185] *2 Enoch, Prayer of Joseph, Ezekiel the Tragedian, Testament of Job.*
[186] *Sibylline Oracles, Ps.-Phocylides, Testament of Job, Testament of Abraham.*
[187] *4 Sibylline Oracle* and Stephen's speech in Acts 7.

of the average Diaspora Jew, nothing much changed on the morning of the tenth of Ab in 70 CE.[188]

---

[188] Contrast M. Goodman, "Diaspora Reactions to the Destruction of the Temple," in *Jews and Christians: The Parting of the Ways A.D. 70 to 135* (ed. J.D.G. Dunn; Tübingen, 1992), 27, who claims that "[t]here is...every reason to suppose that the rasing of the Temple horrified the Diaspora Jews as much as their Judaean compatriots. Jews outside Palestine seem to have presumed the central importance of the Temple in Jewish worship despite the physical obstacles to their frequent attendance at the cult." The only evidence he adduces to support this statement are the *Letter of Aristeas*, which he dates to the second century BCE, and which I discussed above, and Josephus' description of the Temple cult in *Against Apion*. I deal with Josephus' views of the Temple and cult in my doctoral dissertation. Goodman is unwilling to seriously consider *Sibylline Oracle* 4, since "the complex psychology of the author of such oracles, whose success depended on his (or her?) ability to achieve the tone of a pagan prophetess, preclude use of such material as reliable evidence of Jewish self-perception in this period" (p. 29). It seems, however, that if this rule were applied to the Jewish literature of the Second Temple period generally, we would have to exclude from consideration many other compositions, not least the *Letter of Aristeas*, which is also placed in the mouth of a non-Jew.

PART III

ART AND MAGIC

THE RISING POWER OF THE IMAGE:
ON JEWISH MAGIC ART FROM THE SECOND TEMPLE
PERIOD TO LATE ANTIQUITY*

Naama Vilozny

From different types of evidence, textual and material, we learn that just as they were popular among pagans, magic activity and the belief in superstition played a major role in the Jewish world as well. In the Bible itself we find references to magical practices, among which we may include the copper serpent (Num 21:8), the Urim and Thummim (Lev 8:8), and the Witch of Ein Dor (1 Sam 28:3–25). It seems, that is, that belief in demons and angels was a natural phenomenon and an integral part of the ancient world among both pagans and Jews. Jews, like their neighbors, believed that the world is populated by supernatural entities, some of whom can harm people and some of whom have the ability to protect; human beings have the power to control these beings—to mobilize them for personal benefit, either by carrying out, unaided, certain practices that must be learnt thoroughly and implemented with care and precision; or by seeking the assistance of professional practitioners—i.e., sorcerers.

Archaeological evidence uncovered over the years has supplied, and continues to supply, evidence that as early as the First Temple period the Israelites made use of written amulets. Such amulets were either made of various kinds of metal or of perishable materials. After they were written, the amulets were rolled up and hidden in the walls of houses or in graves. Sometimes they were worn by living people, hung on various parts of the body. On the slope of the Hinnom Valley in Jerusalem, the archaeologist Gabriel Barkay discovered a Hebrew amulet, written on a metal sheet and dated to the seventh century BCE, in which the Priestly Blessing (known to us from Numbers 5) functions as part of the magical text.[1] This evidence shows us that, already

---

* This article is based on my doctoral dissertation, which focuses on the artistic aspects of magical artifacts. See N. Vilozny, "Figure and Image on Magic and Popular Art: Between Babylonia and Palestine, during the Roman and Byzantine Periods" (Ph.D. diss., Jerusalem, 2010) (in Hebrew).

[1] G. Barkay, "Excavations on the Slope of the Hinnom Valley, Jerusalem," *Qadmoniot* 68 (1984): 94–108 (in Hebrew).

in that early period, the contents of this blessing served as a protective element against demons and other evil powers.

During the Hellenistic period these beliefs among the Jews found broader textual expression. We know of several books written in that period, in which the writers try to discover the origins of evil in the world. Such, for example, are the works of the Enochic corpus, preserved in larger or smaller fragments in different languages, primarily Aramaic, Greek, and Ge'ez.[2] The earliest work of this Enochic literature is the Book of the Watchers (preserved in *1 Enoch*), composed no later than the third century BCE. Here we find the main Enochic discussions of the origin of evil spirits (*1 En.* 6:1–6, 7:1–4). According to one version, the evil spirits or demons were the descendants of the "sons of God" (= "Watchers") and the "daughters of men" (Gen 6:1–6); according to this version, those descendants were termed *nephalim*—"evil spirits" or "demons."[3]

The *Book of Jubilees* likewise explains the genesis of evil spirits as a result of the mating of the "Watchers" and the "daughters of men." It also mentions these spirits in the story of Noah: when Noah's children were oppressed by evil demons, which caused many afflictions, Noah prayed to God and God sent his angels to bind the demons.[4] Noah asks God to eliminate the spirits and the demons, but a spiritual being named Mastema asks God to spare some of them so as to allow them to aid Him in controlling humanity.

Protective prayers against demons, such as the prayers of Noah and Abraham mentioned in the *Book of Jubilees* (10:3–6, 12:19–20), are in evidence in texts from the latter part of the Second Temple period, as well; for examples from Qumran, note Levi's prayer in the *Aramaic Levi Document* (4Q213a 1 10–18), and some protective prayers against demons in the "Plea for Deliverance" and Psalm 155, which were included in the Qumran Psalms Scroll (11QPs[a] 19:14–16; 24:12–13).[5] Josephus, who reports that King Solomon was blessed with the knowledge necessary to combat evil spirits,[6] adds that he himself saw

---

[2] E. Eshel, "Demonology in Palestine during the Second Temple Period," *Maḥanaim* 14 (2002): 11–18 (in Hebrew).

[3] According to another version, the offspring of those matches were called—as in the Masoretic text (Gen 6:4)—*nephilim*, "giants." See Eshel, ibid., 12.

[4] G. Bohak, *Ancient Jewish Magic: A History* (Cambridge, 2008), 82.

[5] Eshel, "Demonology in Palestine," 16; eadem, "Apotropaic Prayers in the Second Temple Period," in *Liturgical Perspectives: Prayer and Poetry in Light of the Dead Sea Scrolls* (ed. E.G. Chazon, R.A. Clements, A. Pinnick; Leiden, 2003), 69–88.

[6] I.M. Gafni, *The Jews of Babylonia in the Talmudic Era* (Jerusalem, 1990), 168 (in Hebrew).

someone named Eleazar exorcize demons from a human being.[7] The New Testament also witnesses to belief in evil spirits and demons—usually in contexts in which Jesus is responsible for the miraculous exorcism of spirits.[8]

Thus, magic is broadly attested among the Jews of antiquity, from the earliest times until the end of Second Temple period. What is striking, however, and will supply the focus of our attention here, is the total absence of any artistic expression, whether figurative or otherwise, as well as the almost total absence of *objects* used for magical purposes, or even of an allusion to such in the texts. Everything is so very textual, as though words could do it all. Although we cannot discount the possibility that Jews practiced magic rituals that employed ritual objects or perhaps "special instruments" that were never documented nor preserved, it nevertheless seems that most activity was accomplished using texts. Of this we may be confident not only due to the survival of a large number of Jewish texts which make no reference to such objects, but also by comparison with the manifold evidence for the use of magical art and objects among pagans of the same region: we find so many amulets, gems, curse tablets, and related figurative decoration widespread throughout the pagan population of Palestine and the surrounding region, that, had the same practices obtained among the Jews, the evidence should have survived just as well.

In order to understand the force of this argument, we must recall that all sorts of magical objects both passed through Palestine during the Second Temple period and were produced there, first by the Greek population and later by the Roman settlers. From this point of view, Palestine was no different from the rest of the Greco-Roman world. Thus, for example, various magical items, including magical papyri written in Greek and illustrated, were found in Egypt; the papyri are dated from the second century BCE through the fifth century CE.[9] Similarly, curse tablets made of lead or other metals were very popular in the Greek world (ca. 1500 tablets are known today);[10] they have

---

[7] Josephus, *Ant.* 8.46.

[8] See, for example, Mark 1:21–28. In the story of the healing of the Gadarene demoniacs (Mark 5:1–20//Matt 8:28–34//Luke 8:26–39), Jesus expels the demons *into* a herd of swine.

[9] These have been published by several scholars, among them H.D. Betz, *The Greek Magical Papyri in Translation, Including the Demotic Spells* (2d ed.; Chicago, 1992).

[10] J.G. Gager, *Curse Tablets and Binding Spells from the Ancient World* (New York, 1992), 3.

been found in widely-distributed sites all over the Middle East, Greece, and Italy.[11]

Returning to Palestine, we first note the female figurines made of lead, wax, or mud—similar to exemplars known from Egypt[12]—found in the southern city of Maresha.[13] Their legs and hands are bound by ropes, and in some cases they are pierced by needles. These figurines are dated to the third century BCE and were probably used in supplementary procedures meant to reinforce the prescriptions found in magical texts.[14] The figurines served the non-Jewish population, probably of Greek origin, that settled in Palestine during this period. In Egypt this phenomenon had already appeared in the second millennium BCE,[15] and so it is likely that the relative lateness of the figures found at Maresha is only a matter of happenstance.

Again, we may note that amulets of various kinds—pendants, gems and jewels—were very common among the pagan population, beginning in the first century BCE and increasing in use in the succeeding centuries. Quite a lot of amulets have been unearthed in archaeological excavations throughout Palestine, especially in cities that served as centers for non-Jewish communities, such as Caesarea and Dor.[16] In Caesarea an impressive first-century collection of gems was discovered, probably products of a local workshop. The collection also includes magical gems, meant to prevent diseases and to hold evil beings at bay.[17] In this context we should also mention an amulet found at Kibbutz Mazzuvah, in the Upper Galilee.[18]

---

[11] David Jordan has published many of them; for instance see his "Defixiones from a Well near the Southwest Corner of the Athenian Agora," *Hesperia* 54 (1985): 205–55; idem, "New Defixiones from Carthage," in *The Circus and a Byzantine Cemetery at Carthage* (ed. J.H. Humphrey; Ann Arbor, 1988), 117–49, pls. 1–4; idem, "Inscribed Lead Tablets from the Isthmian Sanctuary," *Hesperia* 63 (1994): 111–26. Lead tablets of a similar nature were also discovered in Palestine, although they are somewhat later (not before the 5th century CE). See, inter alia, H.C. Youtie and C. Bonner, "Two Curse Tablets from Beisan," *Transactions and Proceedings of the American Philological Association* 68 (1937): 43–128.

[12] Gager, *Curse Tablets*, 97–100.

[13] Bliss and Macalister, *Excavations*, 85, 154.

[14] C. Clermont-Ganneau supported this assumption, arguing that the figurines were connected to magic tablets found in the site (noted in F.J. Bliss and R.A.S. Macalister, *Excavations in Palestine during the Years 1898–1900* [London, 1902], 154). Bohak (*Ancient Jewish Magic*, 125 n. 163), in contrast, argues that those tablets are not magical, and are, therefore, not connected in any way to the figurines, which definitely *are* magical.

[15] Gager, *Curse Tablets*, 15.

[16] G. Bohak, "A Note on the Chnoubis Gem from Tel Dor," *IEJ* 47 (1997): 255–56.

[17] A. Hamburger, "Gems from Caesarea Maritima," *Atiqot* 8 (1968): 1–38.

[18] C. Dauphin, "A Graeco-Egyptian Magical Amulet from Mazzuvah," *Atiqot* 22 (1993): 145–47.

Finally, in underlining the lack of figurative art in Jewish magic during the Second Temple period, we may note that while there is a good bit of evidence for mutual influence between Jewish and non-Jewish magical practice in the period, figurative art was left out of the exchange. Namely, on the one hand, many of the pagan magical texts on amulets and papyri, whether dated to the Second Temple period or later, show traces of Jewish influence—but only of such textual elements as the use of the name of the Jewish God or of Jewish names for angels. It is possible that those names were considered by the sorcerers to be powerful names that could assist the efficacy of the magical activity.[19] Similarly, on the other hand, we see influence in the other direction as well; namely, we can track the Greek and Iranian elements adapted by the Jewish writers for their magical texts.[20] But as for figurative art for use in magic—the Jews were neither lenders nor borrowers.[21]

True, it might be thought that the lack of figures in Jewish magic art is simply an aspect of the general absence of figurative art among Jews in this period. However, while that general absence derived from Jewish piety, in light of the Second Commandment, the use of amulets was anything but pious; if already a Jew was getting involved with demons, as his neighbors were, why not do it the way they did it? Here, we might suggest that as long as the Temple still stood, the Jewish population, whether in Palestine, Syria, or even in the further-flung Diaspora, was fully occupied by the divine service and the Temple rituals, whether firsthand (by pilgrimage) or via long-distance prayers. It seems, that is, that as long as the Temple existed the belief in magic was only a relatively minor additional element in the spiritual religious life of the Jewish people. The rituals and activities around the Temple, which included sacrifice, were perhaps satisfying enough as an appeasing activity directed towards God, to ask his help in preventing the arrival of all kinds of evils into the people's lives. Also, the ceremonies around the Temple rituals, with their colorful decorations, smells, and sounds, probably filled the aesthetic needs of the people.[22] When the

---

[19] G. Bohak, "Inter-cultural Encounters in Ancient Magic," *Zmanim* (2008): 8–11 (in Hebrew).

[20] S. Shaked, "Popular Religion in Sasanian Babylonia," *Jerusalem Studies in Arabic and Islam* 21 (1997): 103–17; Bohak, "Inter-cultural Encounters," 8–11.

[21] Bohak, "Inter-cultural Encounters," 11.

[22] A. Glucklich, *The Road to Qumran* (Tel-Aviv, 2006), 46–50 (in Hebrew).

rituals were gone, those needs had to be satisfied some other way, and the addition of figurative art to magical items may have been one of the results.

If this were not the case, we would need some other explanation for the large number of magical objects in use among the pagans surrounding the Jewish communities in Palestine, Syria and Egypt; while the Jews, although they, too, sought to communicate with demons, are represented by words alone. But there is no evidence for such an alternate explanation.

*   *   *

During the first four centuries after the destruction of the Second Temple, Jewish belief in magic underwent an essential transformation, as did other aspects of religious and spiritual life. Concerning magic, this change is characterized by the growth and flourishing of magic activity (rituals) involving the use of magical objects, not only magical texts. Some scholars of the history of ancient Judaism have argued that the changing nature of Judaism in late antiquity is a result of processes of change that had already begun towards the end of the Second Temple period; both internal and external cultural influences played a role in such processes. Among these scholars is Shaul Shaked, whose work has focused upon the Iranian cultural orbit as a source of influence on Judaism.[23] His studies demonstrate how certain changes in the Jewish *Weltanschauung* are already testified to by various extracanonical books, some of which had been written by the end of Second Temple period. According to Shaked, such a cultural transformation is expressed, for example, in the movement from a religiosity concentrated around a Temple and its rituals to one that focuses upon inner and private beliefs; in the new interest in the struggle between two forces, God and the devil; and in the addition of good and evil angels or powers alongside God, who until this point had been the only power in the world.[24]

Shaked finds the origins of these conceptions in Iranian culture, mainly in the Zoroastrian religion. This opinion will be more relevant to our discussion later on, when we see that Iranian magical influ-

---

[23] S. Shaked, "The Influence of Iranian Religion on Judaism," in *The Restoration: The Persian Period* (ed. H. Tadmor; Jerusalem, 1982), 236–51 (in Hebrew). See also G. Bohak's contribution to this volume.

[24] Shaked, "The Influence of Iranian Religion," 245.

ences, too, which began to enter into Jewish awareness during the Second Temple period,[25] continued to make their presence felt during the Talmudic period as well, as Shaked shows in his research on the incantation bowls.[26] Yaakov Elman also sees quite a few meeting points between rabbinic and Iranian culture.[27]

Judging by the large amount of Jewish evidence from late antiquity, in contrast to the Second Temple period, it would seem that magical practices involving the use of objects, and not limited to texts alone, increased quite significantly in this period. This increase is to be seen both in Palestine and Babylonia. If during the Second Temple period our knowledge of popular beliefs was limited to textual evidence alone (although again we should recall the possibility that evidence for amulets or nondocumented rituals may simply not have been preserved), once we get to late antiquity we are confronted by a plethora of magical objects, some of them ornamented, which are broadly disseminated and quite popular among the Jews.

Now it is an interesting fact, and one that will be of relevance for our own specific topic, that this same period, late antiquity, was also the setting for one of the most significant changes in the Jewish world: the extensive utilization of figurative art.[28] This phenomenon appears in architectural decorations as well as in the decoration of small objects—in contexts both public and private. This turnabout, in stark contrast to what was common during the Second Temple period, is to be seen both in official art and popular art.

From the end of the second century and the beginning of the third century CE, figurative art bearing a symbolic meaning flourished among Jews. This art eventually led to Jewish iconic art, inspired by

---

[25] For example, the book of Tobit first mentions Ashmedai as the king of demons; the name's origin is in that of the Zoroastrian "prince" of anger and wrath, Ishma Diva). See Shaked, ibid., 247.

[26] J. Naveh and S. Shaked, *Amulets and Magic Bowls: Aramaic Incantations of Late Antiquity* (Jerusalem, 1985); J. Naveh and S. Shaked, *Magic Spells and Formulae: Aramaic Incantations of Late Antiquity* (Jerusalem, 1993).

[27] Y. Elman, "Middle Persian Culture and Babylonian Sages: Accommodation and Resistance in the Shaping of Rabbinic Legal Tradition," in *The Cambridge Companion to the Talmud and Rabbinic Literature* (ed. C.E. Fonrobert and M.S. Jaffee; Cambridge, 2007), 167–97.

[28] L.I. Levine and Z. Weiss, eds., *From Dura to Sepphoris: Studies in Jewish Art and Society in Late Antiquity* (Portsmouth, R.I., 2000), 40. See also Levine's contribution to the present volume.

Christian models.[29] On the other hand, the Jews of the period became more open-minded concerning the cultures that surrounded them, a fact which brought them face-to-face with local artistic tendencies—especially with the move into the fourth century, when Christian religious buildings would become more and more impressive, including ornamentation that featured massive figurative art. Bit by bit the Jews began to develop a figurative art of their own, using both pagan and Christian models for human and animal images.[30] In the same way as their Christian neighbors, the Jews' art represented religious symbols and narrative scenes (which were usually borrowed from the Bible or from midrashic legends).[31] One of the earliest instances of such art is the synagogue in Dura Europos,[32] dated to the middle of the third century CE.

By the end of the fourth century CE, the richness of figurative decoration had found its way into the synagogue buildings of Palestine. This art has primarily been preserved for us in floor mosaics. But it also appears on such small objects as oil lamps and glass flasks; the latter are in the style of Christian pilgrimage culture. The small objects were usually decorated with clearly Jewish symbols such as the menorah and the Torah shrine, while on the synagogue floors we see much more varied decorative motifs, including the aforementioned symbols, but also the "four species" (Lev 23:39–42) and certain biblical scenes. This repertoire seems to have been chosen for its ability to transmit certain symbolic meanings—the images make a religious statement, which can be encoded or plainly understood, just as was the case in Christian churches.

To revert now to our discussion of Jewish magical art in late antiquity, which will focus upon the two large Jewish communities of late antiquity, I would suggest that the history of this phenomenon, and the way it changed during this period in comparison to that which preceded it, has everything to do with the history of figurative art among the Jews. Although the popularity of magic increased significantly in

---

[29] R. Hachlili, *Ancient Jewish Art and Archaeology in the Land of Israel* (Leiden, 1998), 285–86.

[30] E.R. Goodenough, *Jewish Symbols in the Greco-Roman Period* (13 vols.; New York, 1953–1968).

[31] Hachlili, *Ancient Jewish Art*, 285–86.

[32] J. Gutmann, ed., *The Dura-Europos Synagogue: A Re-Evaluation* (rev. ed.; Atlanta, 1992); M.I. Rostovtzeff, *Dura-Europos and Its Art* (Oxford, 1938); C.H. Kraeling, *The Excavations at Dura Europos: The Synagogue* (aug. ed.; New Haven, 1956).

the Jewish communities of both Palestine and Babylonia during this period, an intensive examination of the magical activity characteristic of each community shows that they took completely different directions. These differences between the communities are emphasized by both the nature of their magical objects and their decorations. Such differences enable us to study the differences between the attitudes towards magic prevalent in each community and also to understand the diverse cultural resources upon which each of the communities drew.

Within the limited scope of this discussion, I intend to survey the artistic expressions of Jewish magic in Palestine and Babylonia; to understand their nature and their artistic and iconographic meaning; and to clarify the cultural background from and within which they grew. I will also examine the differences and similarities between the respective corpora of art, in order to place in view both the connections between the two communities and, within each community, the relationship between magic art and public figurative art of the Jewish world.

It is well known that there were many differences between the Jews of Babylonia and those of Palestine, in many different fields. These gaps resulted from the development of local traditions preserved in each place, which, quite naturally, frequently did not agree.[33] One such field that scholars have identified concerns openness toward non-Jews, which in the Talmudic period seems to have been much more prevalent—but the non-Jews surrounding Jews in Babylonia were not, by and large, the same as those who surrounded their cousins in Palestine.[34] Rather, if in Palestine the neighbors were more and more Christian, in Babylonia they were Iranian. With regard to magic, this distinction made a further difference. In Palestine, Jewish popular beliefs functioned in various arenas and are also reflected in a diversity of magical objects, such as mirror plaques against the evil eye, amulet pendants and incised amulet tablets of various metals or other materials, which have survived to us. In Babylonia we are familiar so far with only one kind of magical object that carries a clear Jewish character: incantation bowls; and these artifacts reflect fundamental influences of Iranian culture.

---

[33] M. Margalioth, ed., *The Distinctions between the People of the East and the Sons of the Land of Israel* (Jerusalem, 1937/1938), 15 (in Hebrew).

[34] J. Neusner, "How Much Iranian in Jewish Babylonia?" *JAOS* 95 (1975): 184–90.

PALESTINIAN RITUAL OBJECTS

Mirrors

Mirrors of various sizes, including mirror plaques, were among the popular tools used for protection against the evil eye. Most of the mirror plaques that have been discovered in archaeological sites in Syria-Palestine were found in graves dated to the end of the Roman period or to the Byzantine period.[35] These mirror plaques probably served their owners during their lives and were buried with them after their deaths. The plaques are made of stucco, stone, or clay, and were meant to be hung on walls. Round mirrors, one or more, were set in sockets all over the plaque, arranged in various designs. A relief or painted decoration was added around the mirrors, consisting of geometric or architectonic patterns, but also using figurative images (animals and human beings).[36] It seems that these plaques were common among pagan, Jewish and Christian contemporaries at the same time, as is indicated by the decorative features on some of them, which include obvious religious symbols. Thus, along with plaques featuring pagan goddesses (fig. 1) we can also find Jewish ones showing menorahs or an architectonic façade with lions, apparently representing the Torah shrine (fig. 2); along with yet other plaques identified as Christian by their crosses, peacocks, and human figures in the *orans* position (fig. 3).

The relationship of this figurative art to its artistic environment can be illustrated by comparing the various motifs to those found in contemporary Palestinian art. The frontal and motionless posture in which the figures are represented is one of the characteristics of eastern art.[37] Moreover, it is known that the menorah, as well as the cross, had some apotropaic features,[38] and thus we may assume that, quite frequently, these symbols were added as a decoration in order to express that other symbolic, magical meaning, in addition to the nonapotropaic religious meaning. In this way we can understand the

---

[35] L.Y. Rahmani, "Mirror-Plaques from a Fifth-Century A.D. Tomb," *IEJ* 14 (1964): 50–60.

[36] For details, see Rahmani, ibid.

[37] M. Avi-Yonah, *Art in Ancient Palestine: Selected Studies* (Jerusalem, 1981).

[38] L. Habas, "Identity and Hope: The Menorah in the Jewish Catacombs in Rome," in *In the Light of the Menorah: Story of a Symbol* (ed. Y. Israeli; Jerusalem, 1999), 76–80; M. Gough, *The Origin of Christian Art* (London, 1973), 18–48.

appearance of the menorah in Jewish art, as part of the decorative arrangement of synagogues, as an apotropaic symbol. After all, since it decorates a synagogue, a building which is naturally identified with Judaism, the menorah's function as a religious symbol alone is trivial. If, however, we accept the assumption that the menorah served as a symbol of salvation and hope, national but also private, it becomes simpler to recognize that the menorah, even as part of synagogal art, had a magical-apotropaic function just as it did in mirror plaques. The apotropaic aspect of the menorah is indicated by its widespread appearance on a large number of glass pendants[39] and jewels[40] from Syria-Palestine, dated to the fourth and fifth centuries CE (some of which were probably hung around the neck as amulets),[41] as well as on the above-mentioned glass flasks, which served as objects bearing the sanctity of the Holy Land.[42] In the same way we can see the use of the cross as an apotropaic, decorative symbol on glass flasks and pendants; this, too, was very common throughout Palestine during our period.[43]

Influences from the surroundings can also be noted in the decorative arrangement of the plaques. The composition of some of the plaques, in which two menorahs surround a Torah shrine with a shell-like niche above it, is not so rare; indeed it is quite similar to the design of some synagogue mosaics (Hammath Tiberia, Susiya, Sepphoris, Beth Shean, Usaffia, Beth Alpha, and Naaran).[44] The same composition is seen on a stone lintel from the Golan Heights[45] and on the Torah shrine from Dura Europos;[46] in the latter case the menorah is designed the same way it is on the plaques.

---

[39] J.H. Iliffe, "Rock-Cut Tomb at Tarshiha," *QDAP* 3 (1934): 12; see Israeli, *In the Light of the Menorah*, 136.

[40] Goodenough, *Jewish Symbols*, 2:217; 3:fig. 1009.

[41] Goodenough, *Jewish Symbols*, 2:218–22; 3:figs. 1022–24, 1026–27, 1032–34. Since my discussion focuses on figurative art, I mention the menorah amulets here solely as evidence for the menorah as a magical symbol; an extensive discussion of the wider use and significance of this symbol is beyond the scope of this article.

[42] D. Barag, "Glass Pilgrim Vessels from Jerusalem," *Journal of Glass Studies* 12 (1970): 35–63; 13 (1971): 45–63.

[43] Y. Israeli and D. Mevorah, eds., *Cradle of Christianity* (Jerusalem, 2000), 140–43.

[44] R. Hachlili, *The Menorah: The Ancient Seven-Armed Candelabrum* (Leiden, 2001), 58. While on such mosaics the menorah is usually surrounded by other ritual objects, like a *shofar, lulab* and/or incense shovel, they are absent from the plaques, perhaps because either there was not enough space for them or they were not held to be effective in magical acts.

[45] Ibid., 58, fig. II–15.

[46] Ibid., pl. II–37.

To summarize: There is no doubt that the artists who decorated the mirror plaques were inspired by the local art of Palestine—both Jewish and non-Jewish. Since it is obvious that the plaques were products of Palestinian origin, such a similarity is not at all surprising. On the mirror plaques, in contrast to other magical objects, no text is written. Therefore, our ability to recognize their function as magical derives from their small size (too small to be of any practical use) and their decorative features.[47] An artist engaged in producing such plaques will have borrowed artistic elements that were common in his region, and which seemed to him to be sufficiently relevant to his purposes to give the object effective magical force. It was to this end that such an artist will have brought together the different elements on his plaque.

Metal Sheet Amulets

I now turn to rolled metal sheet amulets, most of which have been discovered in Palestine.[48] Most of the amulets were made from flattened sheets of copper, silver, or gold. The writing was incised into them using a small nail and written in small, nonregular letters, which join together into a magical text. After the text was written, the sheet was folded and rolled. The texts of the spells are usually in Aramaic or in Hebrew, and sometimes include quotations from Jewish literature.[49] Various scholars, such as Naveh and Shaked, have already pointed to the literary associations between these Palestinian magical texts of late antiquity, on the one hand, and the Hekhalot literature, on the other— since fragments of the latter are included in the former. It is possible that both traditions, the mystic and the magic, find their origins in one literary tradition, whose origins are to be dated to the end of the Second Temple period, or even earlier.[50]

In some cases, the amulets were placed in a leather pouch which was carried or attached to one's clothing or body. Sometimes they were deposited in the walls of synagogues (as at Nirim, Meroth,[51] Kanaf,

---

[47] Rahmani, "Mirror-Plaques."

[48] I should mention that a few similar amulets, non-Jewish, were also discovered in Mesopotamia. See for example C. Müller-Kessler, "A Mandaic Gold Amulet in the British Museum," *BASOR* 311 (1998): 83–88.

[49] Naveh and Shaked, *Magic Spells*, 22–31.

[50] J. Naveh, *On Sherd and Papyrus: Aramaic and Hebrew Inscriptions from the Second Temple, Mishnaic, and Talmudic Periods* (Jerusalem, 1992), 171 (in Hebrew).

[51] Naveh and Shaked, *Magic Spells*, 43–50.

and Maʿon),[52] in the same way the Greek curse tablets, written against athletic competitors, were hidden in the walls of hippodromes;[53] they might also be left in any place which had some significance concerning the particular magical text.

In contrast to the pagan amulets, which were in use as early as the third century BCE, the Jewish amulets are later and do not include any decorations, except for a few magical signs called *charaktēres*. These signs have a special place in the symbolic world of amulet and tablet texts in several languages (Greek, Coptic, Aramaic, Hebrew and Arabic), and no doubt they were taken to be mysterious and powerful—but their real origin is still not understood.[54] Until today only two Jewish amulet sheets incised with a figurative decoration have been found in Palestine: the first one is from Emmaus, republished by Naveh and Shaked,[55] and contains an *ouroboros* pattern (a snake eating his own tail), along with two probably demonic figures (fig. 4); the other is a folded amulet from Sepphoris, which has yet to be published. The *ouroboros* motif is very common on amulets and magical objects found elsewhere in the region;[56] it is of Egyptian origin, but was diffused throughout the Mediterranean world and in Mesopotamia as well, on pagan objects.[57] In Jewish contexts we find the *ouroboros* on the amulet from Emmaus and on Babylonian incantation bowls (fig. 5).

BABYLONIAN INCANTATION BOWLS

The fact that Greco-Roman culture, and the Jews and Christians of that western part of the ancient world, made great use of medallions and gems in amulets, contrasts starkly with the rarity of such use of medallions and gems in the Mesopotamian region. Mesopotamia had its own ancient magical tradition, colorful and rich, which was expressed by numerous incantations intended for different demons, and by visual, artistic representations of these demons. Among the

---

[52] Naveh and Shaked, *Amulets and Magic Bowls*, 16.

[53] D. Jordan, "Inscribed Lead Tablet from the Games in the Sanctuary of Poseidon," *Hesperia* 63 (1994): 111–26.

[54] Gager, *Curse Tablets*, 10–11.

[55] Naveh and Shaked, *Amulets and Magic Bowls*, 61–63.

[56] C. Bonner, *Studies in Magical Amulets* (Ann Arbor, 1950), pl. XIII: 271, 279–81, 284; pl. XIX: 356–57.

[57] W. Deonna, "Ouroboros," *Artibus Asiae* 15 (1952): 163–70; R.K. Ritner, "A Uterine Amulet in the Oriental Institute Collection," *JNES* 43 (1984): 219.

more famous ones we should mention Pazuzu and Lamashtu,[58] who are visible on numerous amulet pendants and amulet tablets and stat-uettes, starting at the end of the first millennium BCE.[59]

In late antiquity a Jewish magical tradition developed in Mesopo-tamia, of which the main activity was the writing of incantations on terracotta bowls (fig. 6). Such bowls have been discovered in archae-ological excavations all around Mesopotamia and western Iran, but many are also known via dealers of antiquities, and are therefore often unprovenanced. The bowls are simple in design, written mostly in a spiral arrangement in ink; sometimes an image was added at the cen-ter or on the inside.[60] Almost two thousand such bowls are known, and approximately two-thirds of them are inscribed in Jewish Aramaic and include an abundance of texts that show an intensive knowledge of Jewish culture.[61] Such familiarity with the Bible and other Jewish literature proves that only someone who belongs to the Jewish world could have written these texts. Similar bowls, written in Syriac and Mandaic, were produced by neighboring communities in Babylonia.[62]

Although the texts on these bowls have been the object of intense study, the artistic features of the bowls have been rather neglected. My own work strives to fill this gap, focusing upon the artistic aspects of these incantation bowls. I have catalogued 122 bowls bearing figura-tive images that will be presented for the first time as the focus of study, and examined on the basis of their artistic and iconographic significance.[63] In general, we can interpret the meaning of a decoration

---

[58] Lamashtu is a dreaded Babylonian female demon, the daughter of the great god Anu, who harms pregnant women and steals babies from their mothers. Pazuzu is a male demon, the son of Harpu, king of the evil spirits of the air. For further reading see E.A.W. Budge, *Amulets and Talismans* (New York, 1961).

[59] M.E.L. Mallowan, *Nimrud and Its Remains* (London, 1966), 1:117–18, fig. 60.

[60] The first scholar who studied the bowls seriously was J.A. Montgomery, whose book, *Aramaic Incantation Texts from Nippur* (Philadelphia, 1913), is still relevant today. He was followed by his student C.H. Gordon, who also published some bowls: C.H. Gordon, "Aramaic Incantation Bowls in the Istanbul and Baghdad Museums," *Archiv Orientální* 6 (1934): 319–34; idem, "Aramaic and Mandaic Magical Bowls," *Orientalia* 20 (1951): 88–92.

[61] S. Shaked, "Magical Bowls and Incantation Texts: How to Get Rid of Demons and Pests," *Qadmoniot* 38/129 (2005): 2–13 (in Hebrew).

[62] W.S. McCullough, *Jewish and Mandaean Incantation Bowls in the Royal Ontario Museum* (Toronto, 1967); E.M. Yamauchi, "A Mandaic Magic Bowl from the Babylo-nian Collection," *Berytus* 17 (1967): 49–63.

[63] The majority of the bowls belong to the Schøyen collection. Some of the remain-ing bowls are from Nippur, published in Montgomery, *Aramaic Incantation Texts*, and some are from other publications.

in conjunction with the demonic world towards which the incantation text is also directed. However, only rarely can a direct connection be established between the text and the drawing attached to it.

Artistic analysis of these bowls must proceed on two fronts. First, the individual drawings must be analyzed; only thereafter may we attempt to characterize the art of the corpus as a whole.

On a few bowls the sorcerer himself is presented in the drawing. This identification may be established on the basis of some characteristic features to be discussed; the majority of the drawings, however, represent demonic entities, be they male or female. Almost all of these demons are depicted as bound by chains or shackles, a fact that makes obvious their identification as demonic images. It can be more challenging to achieve a more specific identification—something at times facilitated by anatomical elements or additional accessories that allow us to suggest that a certain image is a particular familiar demon.

Moving beyond the individual bowl to the larger art historical context, we may observe that many of the iconographic motifs employed by Jews made their way to Jewish magical art from the cultural and artistic world of Mesopotamia and Iran—from both ancient and contemporary times, namely, the fifth and sixth centuries CE. Various scholars have noted the affinities between the Babylonian Jewish community and the local populations, including their Iranian neighbors. As I mentioned before, the influence of Persian culture upon Judaism began already in the Second Temple period;[64] and later too, in the Talmudic period, it seems that the rabbis of Babylonia tended to have a more positive attitude toward the Persians than toward other nations.[65]

Although belief in entire systems of evil spirits and demons was widespread all over the eastern world, it seems that the Babylonian Jewish community particularly adopted those views that were current in the Iranian world. The Zoroastrian religion posits a long list of demons, originally known in the early Indian-Iranian religion as gods; after the Iranian religion split off from the Indian, they were demoted to the rank of demons. The Avesta describes struggles between the demons and human beings: as it shows, the demons were defeated by

[64] Shaked, "The Influence of Iranian Religion," 245.
[65] Neusner, "How Much Iranian?" 184.

Iranian gods and heroes, but the prayers, sacrifices, and magical incantations of ordinary folk could also overpower them.[66] Indeed, some of
these demons figure frequently in the Babylonian Talmud,[67] and—as
Shaked has shown—can also be recognized in incantation bowl texts,
where linguistic similarities between Aramaic and Persian texts testify
to syncretism, including the use of Iranian names for demons and
people. That the Jews were influenced by their surroundings may also
be seen in various elements composing the figures on the bowls, some
of which will be presented in the next pages.

First, however, we must realize that, in general, all of the drawings
are quite rude, of low artistic quality. Almost all of the figures are in
a frontal pose and look very static. Such representation is one of the
basic elements that characterize eastern art, and in this respect we can
see a fundamental similarity between the bowls and the mirror plaques
discussed earlier.

Having said that, let us turn to some of the elements that compose
the figures on the bowls:

1) It is not always possible to identify the demon's sexual identity
(fig. 7), because of its bisexual or asexual features. Uncertainty of sexual
identity is very common in Mesopotamian art representing gods and
demons, and may be seen as early as the Luristan plaques of the first
millennium BCE, which probably show the female demon Lamashtu.[68]
On some of the bowls, the incantation is phrased so as to appeal to
both male and female demons. We might conjecture that the author
of the text was not really sure as to the sexual identity of the entity he
was addressing, and thus made sure to cover all the possibilities, for
example: "...and magic words and envoy-spirits and male and female
liliths, and all harmful male and female entities, vows, dreams..." Similarly, we might guess that the artist/painter's interest in drawing the
figures, especially if the bowl was to contain only a single figure, was
to represent all possibilities in one body; therefore the figures were
made deliberately indeterminate, sexually. A text that well illustrates
the motivations for such a practice appears on a bowl published by
Montgomery, on which the description of the demons is as follows:

---

[66] Shaked, "The Influence of Iranian Religion," 245.
[67] Gafni, *The Jews of Babylonia*, 169.
[68] B. Goldman, "The Asiatic Ancestry of the Greek Gorgon," *Berytus* 14 (1961):
1–25.

...who appear to mankind, to men in the likeness of women (13) and to women in the likeness of men, and with mankind they lie by night and by day...[69]

2) On one of the bowls a male figure is drawn (fig. 8). It is quite realistic, dressed in Iranian style, bound around its legs; it holds a long, large blade in one hand and, in the other a spear, affixed to the ground. The image represents any embodiment of evil power that holds a weapon. Montgomery and Isbell both recognize the figure as the angel of death, whose name is written on the bowl as *Zefasek* (צפעסק).[70] The incantation on the bowl describes the demon as one "who kills the man from beside his wife and the wife from beside her husband and sons and daughters from their father and from their mother—by day and by night."

If we look elsewhere for images of figures holding weapons, we find, in Parthian art, a representation of the god of the netherworld, Hades-Nergal-Ahriman, shown in a full-front pose, dressed in Parthian-Iranian style, with his legs bound and a sword in his hand.[71] This image is part of the temple decoration in Hatra, from the second century CE. Similarly, reference to a demonic entity that holds a weapon in its hands may be found in a Palestinian text, one of the minor tractates of the Talmud, which connects this weapon to the rod of Moses: "What did Samael, the angel of death do? He pulled his sword out of its scabbard and immediately stood before Moses. Moses arose in great wrath and, taking in his hand the staff of God, upon which is inscribed the Tetragrammaton, and which he had used to split the (Red) Sea and do great miracles, he rebuked him and fumed at him until he fled from him."[72] On the basis of these parallels we may infer that the figure on the bowl in fact represents the angel of death, probably Samael, who is here given a nonfamiliar name that combines sequential letters.

3) Quite a large number of figures are presented as hybrids; that is, their appearance combines human elements with animal-like features. Among these features are goat horns,[73] which are used to convey a

---

[69] Montgomery, *Aramaic Incantation Texts*, 118.

[70] Montgomery, ibid., 127–32; C.D. Isbell, *Corpus of the Aramaic Incantation Texts* (Missoula, Mont., 1975), 36–37. The five Hebrew letters are adjacent in the alphabet but written, here, in reverse order and "rounded off" by the placement of the last of the five before the others (à la the *ouroboros*?).

[71] R. Ghirshman, *Iran: Parthians and Sasanians* (London, 1962), 87, pl. 98.

[72] Addendum B to *Abot de Rabbi Nathan A* (ed. Schechter), 156.

[73] The description of demons as ugly creatures with horns on their heads is well known already in one of the Qumran magical texts (11QPsApᵃ, lines 6, 7), where the

demonic appearance in literary descriptions as well (fig. 9), both
on the bowls and in the Talmud;[74] and bird claws and chicken legs,
which appear in the Talmud, in the story of Ashmedai.[75] The figures of
Lamashtu and Pazuzu, as portrayed in visual art or described in incantations, emphasize the imagery of birds of prey. A similar description
is known from the Sumerian description of Lamashtu:

> She is wild, she is violent, she is the goddess,
> She is terrible, and she is like a tiger, the daughter of Anu,
> Her feet are like Zu, her hands are dirty,
> Her face is like that of a lion...
> Her hair is disheveled, her breast is exposed...[76]

As such evidence indicates, it seems that the characteristic elements of
these figures are of Mesopotamian origin, and were only later adopted
by Jewish magic.

4) One may distinguish the representations of sorcerers first of all by
the fact that they are not bound (fig. 10). Furthermore, in most cases
the sorcerer appears holding a weapon in his hands—a sword, spear,
or palm branch which he is brandishing above his head. Turning first
to the use of weapons, we find earlier evidence for their use against
demons in amulets against Lamashtu, dated to the first millennium
BCE.[77] Textual evidence for the use of sharp weapons as part of magical activity directed against demons may be found in several incantations. Thus, for example, a Manichaean magical text, which consists of
spells for freeing a man's body from fever, includes the description of
the ritual executed by the sorcerer.[78] Again, note that Frēdōn, the first

---

description is very similar to that on the bowls: "Your face is a face of delusion and
your horns are horns of illusion..." (translation and discussion in H. Lichtenberger,
"Demonology in the Scrolls and the New Testament," in *Text, Thought, and Practice
in Qumran and Early Christianity* [ed. R.A. Clements and D.R. Schwartz; Leiden,
2009], 6).

[74] *B. Pesaḥim* 111b: "That the afternoon is called *Keteb Yashud Zaharaim*; it looks
like a goat's horn, and wings compass it about."

[75] *B. Gittin* 68b.

[76] E.A.W. Budge's translation in his *Amulets and Superstitions* (London, 1930), 109,
after the French version by F. Thureau-Dangin, "Rituel et amulettes contre Labartu,"
RA 18 (1921): 170.

[77] P.O. Harper, P.O. Skjaeruo, and L. Gorelick, "A Seal-Amulet of the Sasanian
Era," *BAI* 6 (1992): 43–58.

[78] W.B. Henning, "Two Manichaean Magical Texts with an Excursus on the Parthian Ending—*endeh*," *BSOAS* 12 (1947): 39–66.

Iranian physician, who is regularly mentioned in Manichaean prayers and incantations, as well as in Zoroastrian amulets, is described as follows:

> Three forms are in me, and a belly (?) of fire. In my hands I hold a sharp and stirring hatchet, I am girt with whetted sword and dagger of pure adamant, and have with me the whip of speech and hearing of the angels...The seven daggers (of) hard steel that I have grasped with my hand...in great...the hard one...[79]

An incantation text on one of the bowls in my catalogue mentions the use of a spear as an effective weapon against the demons:

> I adjure you, this Halbas Lilita, granddaughter of Zaranai Lilita, that you should be smitten at the pericardium of your heart by the spear of Qita-ros the mighty; (you,) who dwell over Diča (?) daughter of Aramdukh (?), (you, who are) the daughter of Lilita...[80]

As for brandishing the weapons above the head: It is known that the Babylonians employed palm branches as magical instruments, raising the branches above the head during certain rituals in an attempt to push the devils aside and place them under the ban.[81] The Persians, too, made use of palm branches for the same reasons.[82] Likewise in Judaism, the raising of a palm branch was incorporated into magical practices, mainly in connection with expelling demons. As evidence for this we may point to the practice of "taking the palm branch" (*lulab*) on the festival of Tabernacles, during which the participant is supposed to shake the palm branch above his head and toward all four winds. The reasons for this practice are described by the Babylonian Talmud (*Sukkah* 37b) as follows: "Rabbi Yossi the son of Rabbi Hanina said: wave the *lulab* back and forth so as to prevent evil spirits, raise and lower it so as to prevent bad dew...." True, the "*taking*" of "the four species" was a custom already known in the biblical period, but all we hear of is that they were taken to the Temple for the holiday celebrations (Lev 23:39–42). The practice of *shaking* the *lulab* seems to have become popular only in the Talmudic period, and it came together, as we just saw, with an understanding of the practice as a

---

[79] Henning, "Two Manichaean Magical Texts," 40.
[80] Translation by S. Shaked, unpublished.
[81] R.C. Thompson, *The Devils and Evil Spirits of Babylonia and Assyria* (London, 1904), xlix.
[82] Ibid., 23.

means of keeping evil spirits at bay. Thus, it seems that the Jews of Babylonia were influenced by their close surroundings, where it was common to use palm branches (which are plentiful in this area) in magic rituals. As happened with other adaptations from local culture, so, too, this one became an integral part of Jewish religious ritual.

5) Iranian parallels to the drawings on the Jewish incantation bowls may also be seen in the clothing style of the figures and in their head-coverings. On most of the bowls, the figures' clothing is rather non-descript, but one can recognize the massive influence of Iranian style of the Parthian and Sasanian periods. Thus we can understand the straight lines on the limbs of the figures as schematic representations of long-sleeved tunics, decorated with stripes, and of wide pants, made of a large piece of material that, when falling down along the legs, creates numerous folds (fig. 11). Over these elements a heavy tunic or armor was worn. Figures dressed in this style are found in various artistic media and periods, from the huge Parthian rock relief statues[83] of the second–third centuries CE to the silver Sasanian bowls with delicate incised or relief decorations[84] dated to the sixth century.

Similar representations of clothing appear in the Parthian and Sasanian miniature art of the third to sixth centuries CE—on coins, amulets and seals.[85] On these objects, the clothing is depicted as straight narrow lines drawn over the arms and legs (fig. 12). We might assume, from the use of such representations on high quality pieces of art, that the origin of these stripes is in the artist's attempt to illustrate the folds of the clothing. On small-scale everyday items, like seals and coins, the folds are very stylized, and look like straight stripes along the clothing. I assume that the painters of the bowls, for whom these small items were an integral part of everyday life, adopted their motifs from their contemporaries and used it for their own needs in some of the figures they painted on their bowls.

---

[83] R. Ghirshman, *Iran: Parthians and Sasanians*, 56, fig. 70.

[84] Ghirshman, ibid., 125–30; P.O. Harper and P. Meyers, *Silver Vessels of the Sasanian Period, Vol. 1: Royal Imagery* (New York, 1981).

[85] F.D.J. Paruck, *Sasanian Coins* (Bombay, 1924), tab. XXI, XXII; Harper and Meyers, *Silver Vessels*, 44 fig. 13.

CONCLUSIONS

For centuries before the destruction of the Temple we find a widespread expression of the popular belief in magic among the Jews, but only one type of expression of such belief is known to us—textual expression. The absence of any evidence for figurative representation presents a striking contrast to the evidence of ritual practice found among the Jews' neighbors. Only some few centuries after the Destruction do we begin to see the use of magical "tools" as a norm in Jewish magical practice, a trend which signals a profound change in the Jewish attitude towards magic. So from this point of view we may say that yes, the Destruction was something of a turning point. It is not clear, however, whether this change began immediately after the Destruction, or in actual consequence of it.

Comparison to surrounding local cultures and art might assist us in identifying some of the figures found among Jewish magical artifacts, and even bolster the assumption that the Jews were influenced by their surroundings. This phenomenon has long been recognized on the basis of textual evidence, and in this study it receives support from the world of art as well. Indeed, Jewish art was quite connected to its environment, which served to nurture its development, both in Palestine (where the Eastern Hellenistic tradition was preserved in large measure by Christian art) and in Mesopotamia—where not only the artistic traditions of contemporary Mesopotamia and Iran, but also those of the ancient cultures, were still quite alive and well.

We may assume that the Jews were considered to be efficient practitioners of magic and, as such, also served the non-Jewish population, even providing something of their own to the pagan magical texts, although it does not seem that they enriched the pagans' magical iconography. The parallels between Jewish magic art and local art show us that the Jews adapted their non-Jewish neighbors' iconography; and that Jewish drawings, both in Palestine and Mesopotamia, were neither a creation *ex nihilo* nor the product of the Jewish painters' creative imagination alone; rather, the Jews participated in the cultures of their geographical region. Nondescript as the drawings might be, nevertheless they contain clear and culturally recognized codes which enable us—like those who saw and used them in antiquity—to identify the figures and their powers. And for efficient magic art, that, indeed, is what was needed. Like iconic art, so, too, the magic art I have presented in this study was meant to deliver a quick and clear message.

In such paintings, attention is not focused upon the aesthetic aspects; rather, it is focused upon the representation of the precise icono-graphic features that are needed in order to understand the scene. The bowls' drawings and the mirror plaques definitely belong to this class of functional art.

In examining the various aspects of Jewish figurative art from this period, we come to realize the deep gap between official art—that is, public art—and hidden art, art made for private needs, usually for use in a private ritual. The latter type appears to have been of low artistic quality, naïve and simple; in fact, it is difficult to compare these rep-resentations with what we usually term art. A chasm separates such private art, both in Palestine and in Babylonia, from official Jewish art and from pagan magic art, particularly that which employed gems.

One of the fundamental differences between Palestine and Babylo-nia is the appearance of Jewish and Christian religious symbols on the Palestinian items, while these are completely absent from the Baby-lonian incantation bowls. Even on those objects inscribed with *texts* that show a clear Jewish character, the *drawings* are not at all of Jew-ish inspiration. This phenomenon may be explained in a few ways. Is it perhaps the case that, although the bowls are influenced by local tradition, nevertheless the Hebrew writing upon them was enough to identify them as Jewish; so that those who made and/or used them saw no need to establish that identity via their art as well? Or is it rather the case that, although these magical objects featured Hebrew texts, the religious orientation of their art was simply not so important to their users: if it works, it works. In any case, we must remember that that incantation bowls were made in order to be buried under the floor; what was important about the artwork on them was not so much how it looked, since it would not be seen, but, rather, the pro-cess of being painted. That process itself—accomplished according to the specific needs of the individual consumer, featuring the meticulous portrayal of the magical procedure which he or she needed—consti-tuted an integral part of the magic ritual. This is, on both counts, in diametrical contrast to the situation concerning plaques and pendants, which were mass-produced for use as amulets, to be hung on walls or on people's bodies. As such, the art upon them was made to be seen, and the process that produced them was not part of any specific magi-cal ritual, but more generally apotropaic.

Fig. 1: A mirror plaque showing a fertility goddess. Clark Collection, no. 75 (YMCA, Jerusalem); after Y. Israeli, "A Mirror Plaque from the Clark Collection, Jerusalem," *IEJ* 24 (1974): 228–31, pl. 50B. Photo © The Israel Museum, Jerusalem.

Fig. 2: A mirror plaque showing menorahs and an architectonic façade.
Courtesy of the Hebrew University Institute of Archaeology, Archive
no. 88.85/1. Photo by Gabi Laron.

Fig. 3: A mirror plaque showing a figure in *orans* prayer posture. Rockefeller Museum 40.306. Today in the Israel Museum. Photo courtesy of the Israel Museum.

Fig. 4: An amulet from Emmaus showing the *ouroboros* motif. After J. Naveh and S. Shaked, *Amulets and Magic Bowls: Aramaic Incantations of Late Antiquity* (Jerusalem, 1985), 40.

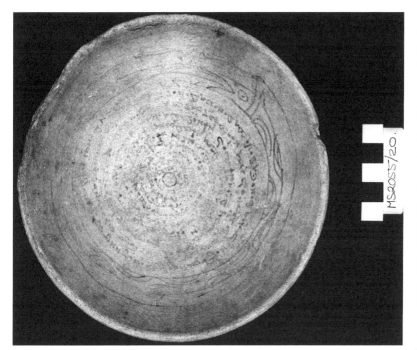

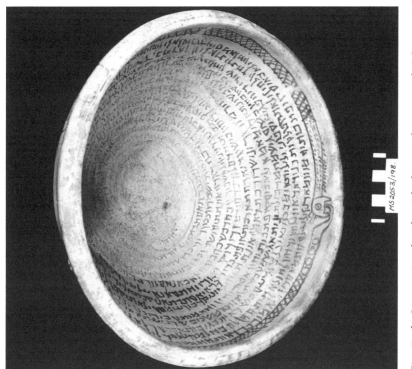

Fig. 5a–b: Incantation bowls with the *ouroboros* motif. Schøyen Collection, 2053–198; 2055–20. Photo by the Schøyen Collection, Oslo & London.

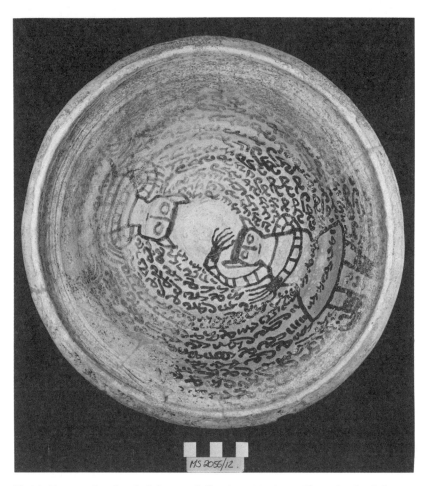

Fig. 6: Incantation bowl. Schøyen Collection, 2056–12. Photo by the Schøyen
Collection, Oslo & London.

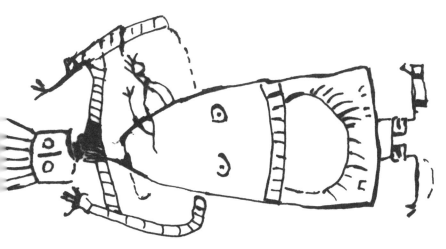

Fig. 7a–b: Two incantation bowls (Schøyen Collection, 1911–3; 2053–237). Photo by the Schøyen Collection, Oslo & London. Drawing by Naama Vilozny.

Fig. 8: Incantation bowl. After J.A. Montgomery, *Aramaic Incantation Texts from Nippur* (Philadelphia, 1913), Bowl 3, pl. IV.

Fig. 9a–b: Two incantation bowls showing bestial elements in the figures' appearance (Schøyen Collection, 1928–31; 2056–10). Drawings by Naama Vilozny.

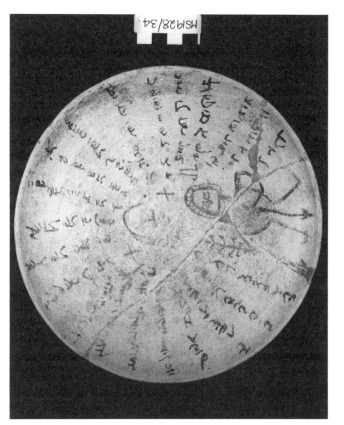

Fig. 10a–b: An incantation bowl showing the sorcerer (Schøyen Collection, 1928–34). Photo by the Schøyen Collection, Oslo & London. Drawing by Naama Vilozny.

Fig. 11a–b: A Sasanian style of clothing on an incantation bowl (Moussaieff Collection) and on a Kushano-Sasanian gold coin. Bowl: Drawing by Naama Vilozny, from a photograph by Matthew Morgenstern. Coin: P.O. Harper and P. Meyers, *Silver Vessels of the Sasanian Period, Volume One: Royal Imagery* (New York, 1981; Photograph © Trustees of the British Museum), 44, fig. 13.

Fig. 12a–b: A Sasanian coin and an incantation bowl (Schøyen Collection,
1911–3). Coin: P. Gignoux, *Catalogue des sceaux, camees, et bulles sasanides
de la Bibliothèque nationale et du Musée du Louvre* (Paris, 1978; photograph
© Bibliothèque nationale de France), pl. X:4.33. Bowl: Drawing by Naama
Vilozny.

JEWISH EXORCISM BEFORE AND AFTER THE DESTRUCTION OF THE SECOND TEMPLE

Gideon Bohak

In the *Testament of Solomon*, an ancient Christian demonological compendium with much data on the pernicious activities of demons and on the different manners in which they may be thwarted, there is a clear connection between the Jerusalem Temple and the war on demons. On the one hand, the *Testament* recounts the story—which is well known from many other late antique sources—of how Solomon subdued various demons and used them for the construction of his Temple. On the other hand, it also relates how Solomon subsequently locked the demons up below the Temple's foundations, and how, many centuries later, when the Babylonians destroyed the Temple they inadvertently let loose a hoard of wild demons who caused much affliction to the humans they encountered. But if we take the *Testament of Solomon* seriously—although it is extremely difficult for a modern reader to take the *Testament* seriously—we should also note that when it comes to the destruction of the Second Temple (as against the First), we find no hair-raising stories about the release of pent-up demons. For the author of the *Testament*, the real watershed event in the history of demonology had come some forty years before the Destruction with the appearance of the Jewish Messiah, the Emanuel, the Savior who was crucified and rose to heaven, and at whose name(s) all the demons tremble. For the author of the *Testament*, Nebuchadnezzar's destruction of the First Jewish Temple was an important event in the history of humanity's fight against the demons, but Titus' destruction of the Second Jewish Temple made no difference to the demons or those who fought them. Accordingly, it is not even mentioned in the entire work.

Leaving such *Heilsgeschichte* behind and turning to more secular—and hopefully more objective—history, we may ask whether Jewish demonology and Jewish exorcism underwent any major changes in the period after the destruction of the Temple, the failure of the Diaspora revolt, and the crushing of the Bar Kokhba revolt, and whether such changes may be attributed to the direct or indirect influences of these events. But before turning to the question itself, we may ponder its wider nature. A first point to consider is that whereas some aspects of Jewish culture were directly influenced by the destruction of the Temple—most notably, all sacrificial activity and all Temple-related cultic activity either ceased completely or were entirely transformed— the belief in demons and the use of special techniques to fight them does not seem like something that *had* to change after 70 CE. That is: although the three Jewish revolts brought many changes to Jewish society, including the destruction of much of the priestly class and its most important powerbase, the decimation of Diaspora Jewry, the shift of the centers of the Jewish population in Palestine from Judea to the coastal plain and to the Galilee, and the gradual rise of a rival Jewish center in Babylonia, such major transformations need not have had a strong impact on the exorcistic practices of those Jewish exorcists who survived the revolts or on the transmission and actual use of the oral and written knowledge relating to demons and the war against them. Thus, asking whether 70 or 135 CE are meaningful dates in the history of Jewish exorcism is one way of asking whether these events entirely transformed all aspects of Jewish society and culture; or rather, whether their impact was greatly felt in some spheres, but was more, or even mostly, imperceptible in others.

A second preliminary observation has to do with the sources at our disposal. One obvious change that took place after 70, and especially after 117 and 135 CE, has to do with the nature of the sources available for historians studying the periods before and after these events. For whereas the Second Temple period, and especially its later centuries, is well endowed with a variety of literary sources—including the writings of Josephus and Philo, the Apocrypha and Pseudepigrapha, the Dead Sea Scrolls and most of the New Testament—for the period after 135 CE we must rely mostly on rabbinic literature, which is a much more unidimensional, and much less historian-friendly, body of texts. Thus, it is much easier to write a history of the Jewish people, or of most aspects of Jewish society and culture, in the Second Temple period than to write a similar history for the period from the end of the Bar Kokhba revolt to the Muslim conquest, and this imbalance in our sources often makes it hard to say what changed after 70 or 135 CE and what did not.

Nevertheless, when it comes to Jewish exorcism we happen to be blessed with quite a few sources, and—what is even more important— with a great variety of different types of sources that supplement and complement each other, both from the Second Temple period and from the post-Destruction period. So while a survey of Jewish medicine, astrology, or aggressive or erotic magic before and after the Destruction would soon have to confront the paucity and uneven nature of the available sources, a similar survey of Jewish exorcism may benefit from a variety of independent but mutually illuminating bodies of ancient evidence.

Thus, from the Second Temple period we have interesting discussions of demons and their activities in such works as *1 Enoch*, *Jubilees*, and the Dead Sea Scrolls, and detailed descriptions of Jewish exorcists in action provided by the New Testament, by Josephus, by Tobit and by the Pseudo-Philonic *Book of Biblical Antiquities*. We even have some exorcistic hymns and prayers found among the Dead Sea Scrolls or cited in such texts as *Jubilees* or the *Book of Biblical Antiquities*. For the later period, we have the extensive discussion of demons, including the quotation of antidemonic spells, in rabbinic literature; the citation and use of Jewish exorcistic formulae in the Greek magical papyri (the PGM); and numerous Jewish magical texts from late antique Palestine and Babylonia, or copies thereof which were preserved in the Cairo Genizah. Thus, when trying to compare Jewish exorcism in the Second Temple period with that of a subsequent period, we may be less worried that a single source, or one specific type of evidence, might entirely skew the two historical images we wish to reconstruct and compare.

With these two points in mind, we may turn to the question of Jewish exorcism before and after 70 or 135 CE. In order to present the data in a coherent and systematic manner, I shall begin with a broad survey of Jewish demonology and exorcism in the Second Temple period, basing myself on two recent studies that cover all the primary sources. Then I shall turn to a close examination of Jewish demonology and exorcism in the post-Destruction period (a topic which still awaits a more thorough treatment), in an attempt to find continuities, discontinuities, and innovations in comparison with the earlier period, and to assess their relative significance. I shall then end with some broader conclusions on the impact of the Destruction on the Jewish handling of demons—or on the lack thereof.

⋆   ⋆   ⋆

Exorcism—by which I refer to any practice aimed at keeping demons or ghosts away or expelling them from the persons, animals, or inanimate objects in which they have chosen to dwell—is always seen by its users as a very practical set of techniques. Their common premises are

the convictions that demons and/or ghosts do exist, that they are ubiquitous, and that they can be extremely harmful—and therefore must
be detected, subdued, and driven away. The pervasiveness of such
beliefs in the Second Temple period is manifest in numerous ancient
Jewish texts, from *1 Enoch* and *Jubilees* to the Dead Sea Scrolls, Josephus, the New Testament, and virtually every strand of ancient Jewish
literature.[1] Moreover, Jewish demonology became so developed during
the Second Temple period that we find it branching off into numerous
subfields and distinct bodies of knowledge—including:

- the granting of personal names to some demons (most notably
  Ashmedai, who first appears in the book of Tobit and who is still
  with us to this very day);
- the endless discussion of their ultimate origins and the sources of
  their aggressiveness (with much attention given to the story of the
  Fallen Angels and the demonic offspring of their union with the
  daughters of men [Gen 6:1–4], and with other etiologies, such as
  the view of demons as the ghosts of evil people or as a part of God's
  creation of the universe, trailing not too far behind);
- the enumeration of their evil activities (from killing the many husbands of Sarah in the book of Tobit to leading the Sons of Light
  astray in some of the Dead Sea Scrolls, not to mention the causing
  of numerous illnesses);
- and the recounting of the numerous stories of people who had met
  them, or had to face their onslaught (including the retelling of biblical stories which thereby acquire a much stronger demonological
  character, such as the story of David's exorcism of the evil spirit that
  had pestered King Saul).

Even writers who seem to us far more rational and much less prone
to "superstition" had no doubt that demons did in fact exist, as may
be seen from Josephus' explanation of what demons are, or from his
proud description of a Jewish exorcist of his own day demonstrating

---

[1] In what follows, I have made much use of E. Eshel, "Demonology in Palestine
during the Second Temple Period" (Ph.D. diss., The Hebrew University of Jerusalem,
1999 [Hebrew]); and of my own *Ancient Jewish Magic: A History* (Cambridge, 2008),
88–114. As those books offer quite a thorough coverage of the primary sources, I shall
provide here only a bird's-eye survey of the entire field without entering into a detailed
discussion of each specific source.

his abilities to the (future) Emperor Vespasian. Thus, even a Jewish writer who was deeply involved in Jewish apologetics, and therefore very careful about what he said about his fellow Jews, did not refrain from highlighting this aspect of Jewish culture, not least because he knew that the fear of demons of one sort or another was pervasive among many of his non-Jewish readers as well.

Such fear of demons, and such extensive speculation about their origins, their nature, and their activities, led to the development of a large set of antidemonic techniques, which seem to have been known to, and even practiced by, quite a few Jews in the Second Temple period. Surveying the entire body of the available evidence, we may discern three different types of exorcism practiced by Jews at the time: exorcism through the use of naturally exorcistic substances; exorcism by means of prayers and adjurations; and exorcism performed by holy men by means of their innate powers. In what follows, I shall briefly summarize what is currently known about the application of each of these techniques in the Second Temple period.

1) Exorcism Through the Use of Naturally Exorcistic Substances

Throughout the ancient world, much knowledge was in circulation about the occult powers of different mineral, vegetable, animal, or human substances, and such knowledge was often incorporated into wider theories of sympathy and antipathy and other hidden powers that were thought to govern everything from the ocean's tides to the ability of sealskin to fend off lightning. Jews, too, shared the pervasive belief that some materials were naturally endowed with great powers, and one such power was that of driving demons away. In the book of Tobit (6:8, 17), the protagonist is taught by the angel Raphael (in human disguise) that when fire is applied to the heart and liver of a certain fish from the Tigris the smoke will drive away the demon Ashmedai, and actual use proves the soundness of this advice. In Josephus' *Jewish War* (7.180–185), we learn of the root *baaras*, which grows in one specific location across the Jordan River—a root which is extremely dangerous to procure yet well worth the trouble, since it is quite powerful for expelling demons. And in his *Jewish Antiquities* (8.45–49), we hear that one Eleazar, a Jewish exorcist whom Josephus saw in action before Vespasian, his two sons, and numerous Roman

soldiers, used to place a ring and a certain root—prescribed by King
Solomon himself—near the demoniac's nose, and then forcefully pull
the demon out with the help of a powerful adjuration that Solomon
had once composed. Josephus also tells us (*War* 2.136) that the Essenes were extremely interested in the healing powers of roots and
stones, and it would not be too wild a guess to suspect that some of
this knowledge was antidemonic in nature. Unfortunately, none of the
ancient Jewish texts in which such specialized knowledge was transmitted has been preserved, but the diffusion of such knowledge among
the Jews of the Second Temple period—in oral or written forms—may
hardly be doubted, for it was in frequent use in the daily war against
the demons.

Given the nature of such practices—which involved placing or
carrying various materials near one's body (or applying fire to them
so as to release smoke, thus annihilating them during the exorcistic
process)—one is not likely to find too many archaeological remains
which could securely be identified as the products of these practices.
And yet, Yigael Yadin's excavations in the Cave of Letters came up
with a most remarkable T-shirt, clearly made for a small child, the
cloth of which was tied by cords in two places, creating small pouches
that were stuffed with various items—including some shells, salt crys-
tals, seeds, and other unidentified materials.[2] Since this item was found
together with the other objects and documents left behind by the Jewish refugees who fled to the Cave of Letters during the Bar Kokhba
revolt, it provides an unexpected confirmation of the widespread use
of amuletic substances by Jews in the early second century CE. And
although we cannot tell how many Jewish mothers made their children
run around in such uncomfortable T-shirts, with pouches full of small
hard objects dangling all around them, we shall soon see that such
apotropaic mixtures remained popular in later periods as well, and
were warmly recommended by the Babylonian Talmud.

2) Exorcism by Means of Prayers and Adjurations

A second means of keeping demons at bay, or driving them away, in
common use in the Second Temple period, was the recitation of anti-

---

[2] See Y. Yadin, *The Finds from the Bar-Kokhba Period in the Cave of Letters* (Jerusalem, 1963), 257–58 and Plate 89; idem, *Bar-Kokhba* (London, 1971), 79–82.

demonic prayers, spells, and adjurations. These could range from the humble request directed to God ("…and do not let any demon rule over me…"), to complex psalms and adjurations, often attributed to biblical protagonists like King David or King Solomon. The former must have circulated widely among ordinary Jews at the time, and may be found in such works as the *Aramaic Levi Document* or the book of *Jubilees*; the latter were apparently recited from written copies by professional, or at least experienced, exorcists. As noted above, Josephus describes Eleazar as using magical substances (a root) and implements (a ring) as well as magical spells (attributed to King Solomon, of whose wisdom Josephus is speaking in that part of his narrative). Unfortunately, he does not provide a description or citation of the spells themselves, but we may reconstruct the appearance of such texts both from literary sources (including, for example, the *Book of Biblical Antiquities'* detailed reproduction [in ch. 60] of the exorcistic psalm supposedly recited by David when he drove the evil spirit out of King Saul), and from the remains of exorcistic psalms found among the Dead Sea Scrolls. Some of these psalms are of a demonstrably sectarian origin, while others must have been used by nonsectarian Jews as well; the latter include some exorcistic psalms which were attributed to King David and perhaps also to Solomon. We even have a Greek exorcistic text which seems to be entirely Jewish and which was palaeographically dated to ca. 100 CE;[3] it, too, fits well within the general patterns of Jewish exorcistic formulae that emerge from the other sources.

3) Exorcism Performed by Holy Men by Means of their Innate Powers

A third method of exorcising demons which was widely known and used in Second Temple period Jewish society was the appeal to a "man of God," a holy man whose great innate powers, or whose intimate relationship with God, make the demons shudder and flee when he commands them to do so. Such men did not use any exorcistic

---

[3] See P. Fouad 203, published by P. Benoit, "Fragments d'une prière contre les esprits impurs?" *RB* 58 (1951): 549–65; it is listed by J. van Haelst, *Catalogue des Papyrus littéraires juifs et chrétiens* (Paris, 1976), as no. 911. For a recent analysis of this text, see P.W. van der Horst and J.H. Newman, *Early Jewish Prayers in Greek* (Berlin, 2008), 123–34.

substances, nor did they employ any elaborate spells ascribed to an ancient forefather. In fact, they made no use of any specialized exorcistic technologies, because the use of such technologies would entirely obviate the demonstrative power of the exorcistic acts, which served to prove the innate power and "chosenness" of the holy man himself and often won him prestige, disciples, and material support. Moreover, for the holy man exorcism was just one deed out of many, since he could also perform many other miracles, including healing the sick, quelling storms, procuring rain, and harming those who offended him. The best example of such a figure is Jesus of Nazareth, whose many miracles, including several different exorcisms, are extensively described in the Gospels, as are the exorcistic exploits of his disciples.

Our understanding of such figures and their exorcistic activities is amplified by the story of Abraham as an exorcist, found in the so-called *Genesis Apocryphon*, as well as reports in the writings of Josephus, and especially in rabbinic literature, of the many miracle-working holy men who roamed the streets of Judea in the last two centuries BCE and in the period up to ca. 150 CE. Honi the Circle Maker, Hanina ben Dosa, Shimeon bar Yohai and others are credited with numerous miracles; the latter two actively participated in the war on demons. Usually, such holy men exorcised demons merely by ordering them to shut up and leave, but occasionally they made use of simple gestures (such as laying their hands on the demoniac), a brief prayer, or a more complex process of negotiation with the demons themselves. And while the demons were expected to give the holy man a real fight by refusing to leave, by issuing various taunts and threats, and by haggling over the conditions of their departure, by the end of the duel the demons were on the run, the patient was exhausted, and the holy man was being congratulated and cheered by the patient's family and (in most cases) by a crowd of onlookers.

Much more could be said about exorcistic techniques utilized by Jews in the Second Temple period, as well as the personal, social, and religious implications of each of these techniques for the demoniacs, for the exorcists, and for the audiences who often observed the entire process. The above survey should suffice, however, for our attempt to answer the question that interests us in the present paper: Did Jewish exorcism undergo a major transformation after the events of 70, 117, or 135 CE, or was this aspect of Jewish culture mostly uninfluenced by external events? To answer this question, we must next examine what remained the same, and what changed, in Jewish exorcistic practice of late antiquity.

* * *

Leaving the Second Temple period, and turning to the period from 70 or 135 CE to the Muslim conquest, we may now ask what evidence we have of the unhindered continuity of the Jewish exorcistic beliefs and practices surveyed in the previous section; and conversely, what evidence we have of the demise of some of these beliefs and practices or of the rise of others. Moreover, when looking at the changes, we must also try to explain their possible historical causes, and see whether these are in any way connected with the destruction of the Second Temple or the collapse of the three Jewish revolts.[4]

Perhaps the most important preliminary observation is that Jewish belief in the pervasiveness of demons and the dangers posed by them remained as strong in late antiquity as ever before. Reading the Mishnah, which is relatively free of demon- and magic-related discussions, and probably deliberately so, we nevertheless learn that, "If someone extinguishes the Sabbath candle because he is afraid of Gentiles, of robbers, of an evil spirit... he is exempt"—a casual indication that fear of demons was common in the daily lives of ordinary Jews and could influence their behavior in very perceptible ways.[5] We also find the Mishnah taking it for granted that many people would walk around with amuletic substances and pouches fastened to their bodies, a fact of life that engendered debates both as to whether such materials were halakhically unacceptable (because they were classified as *Darkhei*

---

[4] Unfortunately, I am not aware of any systematic studies of late antique Jewish demonology and exorcism, but useful starting points may be found in E. Yassif, *The Hebrew Folktale* (Bloomington, Ind., 1999), 144–66; M. Bar-Ilan, "Exorcisms Performed by Rabbis: Something on the Talmudic Sages' Dealings with Magic," *Daat* 34 (1995): 17–31 (in Hebrew); R. Lesses, "Exe(o)rcising Power: Women as Sorceresses, Exorcists, and Demonesses in Babylonian Jewish Society of Late Antiquity," *JAAR* 69 (2001): 343–75; J. Seidel, "Possession and Exorcism in the Magical Texts of the Cairo Geniza," in *Spirit Possession in Judaism: Cases and Contexts from the Middle Ages to the Present* (ed. M. Goldish; Detroit, 2003), 73–95; R. Knoll, "Demonology in the Literature of the Sages: The Demons and their Characteristics" (M.A. thesis, Tel-Aviv University, 2005 [in Hebrew]); Y. Harari, "The Sages and the Occult," in *The Literature of the Sages* (ed. S. Safrai et al.; 2 vols.; Assen, 1987–2006), 2: 521–64, esp. 536–41. For what follows, see also Bohak, *Ancient Jewish Magic*, 298–305.

[5] See *m. Shabbat* 2:5; for other tannaitic references to demons, see *m. Eruvin* 4:1; *m. Avot* 5:6; *Sifre Deut.* 318 (ed. Finkelstein, p. 364: "What is the way [of action] of a demon? It enters a man and makes him epileptic"); *Sifre Deut.* 321 (p. 368: "By the way, you learn that whoever is possessed by a demon drools spittle").

ha-Emori, "the Ways of the Amorites"), and as to whether one might keep them on on the Sabbath, when one is only allowed to wear one's essential clothes outside of the home (see below). And when we turn to the Talmudim and the midrashic compilations, we find numerous discussions of demons, amulets, and exorcisms, and—at least in the Babylonian Talmud—even a whole set of antidemonic spells and recipes. This pervasive, not to say obsessive, fear of demons is also manifest in the numerous Jewish magical artifacts which have come to light over the last century and a half, including dozens of Jewish metal-plate amulets from Byzantine Palestine and elsewhere and hundreds of incantation bowls from Sassanian Babylonia, which were meant to manipulate, and especially to thwart, demons of every conceivable type.

Concerning these materials, it is quite easy to point to many continuities from the older practice, including the names of some demons (Ashmedai being the clearest example); speculations about their origins (including the story of the Fallen Angels, still echoed in some Jewish magical texts of late antiquity and the early Middle Ages); and—most of all—the conviction that many illnesses, as well as numerous physical and psychological calamities and disorders, are caused by the demons that surround us all. In this regard, it is tempting to point to some regional diversity among late antique Jews; the Jews of Babylonia were clearly influenced by some local Mesopotamian and Iranian beliefs about demons which were quite unknown to the Jews of Palestine.[6] But such observations do not shed much light on the impact of the destruction of the Second Temple on Jewish demonology, beyond the fact that it clearly facilitated the rise of the Babylonian Jewish center in the first few centuries CE, and thus exposed more Jews to Mesopotamian and Iranian influences. Thus, whereas we probably could point to some developments in Jewish demonology in late antiquity which were not yet present in the Second Temple period, such developments must be attributed more to the passage of time, and to shifts in regional influences, than to the destruction of the Temple or the failure of the three Jewish revolts.

Turning from demonology to exorcism, we find ourselves facing a slightly more complex picture, characterized by an exponential rise in

---

[6] See esp. S. Shaked, "Popular Religion in Sasanian Babylonia," *Jerusalem Studies in Arabic and Islam* 21 (1997): 103–17.

the quantity and quality of sources at our disposal due to the emergence of the above-mentioned metal-plate amulets and incantation bowls. These are regionally conditioned phenomena, with the Aramaic incantation bowls found exclusively in Babylonia (or, in modern terms, in Iraq and Western Iran), while the Aramaic and Hebrew metal-plate amulets come from as far afield as Italy in the West and Georgia in the East, with a large concentration in Palestine itself while only very few, and perhaps none, come from Babylonia.[7] These are, moreover, chronologically conditioned phenomena, with both types of magical artifacts unattested before the fourth or fifth century, becoming very common afterwards, and apparently tapering off soon after the Muslim conquests. But the rise of these new magical technologies seems to be related, not to any wider historical processes (and certainly not to the destruction of the Temple a few centuries earlier!), but rather to changing fashions and the adoption of non-Jewish practices. Thus, the scribalization of Jewish magic—that is, the rise of new modes of transmission and application of magical practices, involving a much higher incidence of writing down magical spells instead of or in addition to their oral recitation (which seems to have been the norm in earlier periods)—provides modern historians with a much wider body of evidence for the study of late antique Jewish magic, including the war on demons.

With these observations in mind, we may turn to the question that interests us here: To what extent is late antique Jewish exorcistic technology a continuation of what went on in the Second Temple period?[8] To answer this question, I will follow up each of the exorcistic practices outlined in the previous section and analyze its occurrence in the Jewish world of late antiquity, and then search for exorcistic practices which were prevalent in late antiquity but had not yet been in use in the Second Temple period.

---

[7] For a possible exception, see the amulet published by M.J. Geller, "More Magic Spells and Formulae," *BSOAS* 60 (1997): 327–35, the authenticity of which is uncertain. But given the diffusion of Mandaic and Syriac metal-plate amulets, the existence of such Aramaic amulets in late antique Mesopotamia would seem quite likely.

[8] For this formulation of the question, see also M.D. Swartz, "The Dead Sea Scrolls and Later Jewish Magic and Mysticism," *DSD* 8 (2001): 182–93.

1) Exorcism Through the Use of Naturally Exorcistic Substances

When we look at the late antique sources for the exorcistic materials mentioned in our discussion of Second Temple period exorcism—for example, the heart and liver of a certain fish or the wondrous root *baaras*—we are quickly disappointed, for such substances do not make an appearance in the later Jewish sources. This, however, is hardly surprising, since these are very specific substances, and since even in the Second Temple period there must have been many more such materials that were known to possess exorcistic powers and were used in the war on demons. Thus, instead of looking for these specific items, we should look for the continuous use of naturally exorcistic substances, and here the evidence is more readily available. As one example, we may take the famous story, found in a late rabbinic compilation, of how Rabban Yohanan ben Zakkai was asked by a Gentile about the red heifer; he answered the question by comparing this ritual (ordained in Numbers 19) to an exorcism, in which one burns roots so as to release their smoke under the demoniac, and then pours water over the demon until it runs away.[9] Whether this late anecdote may be used as evidence for the views of a first-century rabbi is a matter of some debate, but there is no doubt that the example assumes that its late antique audience would be quite familiar with the ritual that the rabbi and the Gentile were describing: namely, the exorcising of demons by releasing the smoke of special roots under the demoniac. The assumption behind such a ritual, namely, that the smoke of a certain natural substance will drive demons away, is the same assumption that guided the book of Tobit many centuries earlier, when it described the burning of fish parts to achieve a similar aim.

Side by side with this explicit reference to an exorcistic procedure based on the manipulation of antidemonic substances, we may also note the long list of amuletic substances mentioned by the rabbis. As noted above, the Mishnah discusses the permissibility of setting out on the Sabbath with various amulets tied to one's body, including "knots" (presumably, herbs, roots and cords tied into knots), bells, the egg of a locust, the tooth of a fox, and a nail from a crucifixion. Unfortunately, the Mishnah does not explain what these amuletic objects were sup-

---

[9] *Pesikta de-Rav Kahana, Parah* 7 (ed. Mandelbaum, p. 74).

posed to heal or ward off. But a comparison with other ancient texts suggests that bells, for example, were seen as excellent antidemonic *apotropaia*, and their ubiquity in late antique graves demonstrates their widespread use.[10] In a similar vein, we may note that the list of forbidden "Amorite" practices in *t. Shabbat* 6-7 includes several references to the magical uses of iron, including the practice of tying a piece of iron to the bed of a woman in labor (*t. Shabbat* 6:4). Given the extensive evidence for the antidemonic uses of iron throughout antiquity, including such references in rabbinic literature itself, it seems quite certain that here, too, the iron bar was supposed to keep the demons away from the parturient woman and her newborn infant at a time when they were most vulnerable to demonic attacks.[11]

To end this survey of apotropaic substances with one more specific example, we may cite a talmudic recipe which prescribes the preparation of an amulet against tertian fever:

> Rav Huna said: For a tertian fever, one should take seven thorns from seven palm trees, seven chips from seven beams, seven pegs from seven bridges, seven (lumps) of ashes from seven ovens, seven (clods) of earth from under seven door sockets, seven (chunks) of bitumen from seven boats, seven handfuls of cumin, and seven hairs from the beard of an old dog, and tie them around the nape of the neck with a white twisted cord. (*b. Shabbat* 67a)

Without going into the details of all the substances mentioned here, and of the recurrence of the number seven, we may note that the end result of the procedure recommended here would be an amuletic pouch quite similar to those on the amuletic T-shirt from the Cave of Letters. The T-shirt dates from before the Bar Kokhba revolt, the recipe is found in the Babylonian Talmud, compiled ca. 500 CE, and is attributed there to Rav Huna, a Babylonian rabbi of the third century CE. In this time span of several centuries, very little seems to have changed in the Jewish use of amuletic substances, placed in little

---

[10] For the apotropaic and antidemonic uses of bells (as in *m. Shabbat* 6:9), and their ubiquity in late antique sites, see J. Russell, "The Archaeological Context of Magic in the Early Byzantine Period," in *Byzantine Magic* (ed. H. Maguire; Washington, DC, 1995), 35-50, esp. 42; O. Saar, "Superstitions in Israel during the Roman and Early-Byzantine Periods" (M.A. thesis, Tel-Aviv University, 2003 [in Hebrew]), 87-90.

[11] See *t. Shabbat* 6:4, with S. Lieberman, *Tosefta Ki-feshuta*, 3 (2d ed.; Jerusalem, 1992), 84 (in Hebrew). For the antidemonic powers of iron, see also the lovely story of Abba Yosi of Tzaitor in *Leviticus Rabbah* 24:3 (ed. Margalioth, 553-55).

pouches, carried around one's body, and conceived of as useful *apotropaia* against demons, diseases, and the evil eye.

2) Exorcism by Means of Prayers and Adjurations

In late antiquity, as in the Second Temple period, exorcistic substances were not the only means of driving demons away. Another common method involved the recitation of either apotropaic, antidemonic prayers addressed to God, or threatening psalms and adjurations against the demons themselves. Since, as I have already noted, by this time Jews had begun writing down these prayers and spells—and sometimes were kind enough to the modern historian to write them on durable writing surfaces—we now have a large, and constantly growing, body of ancient Jewish magical texts, including dozens of amulets from Byzantine Palestine, Egypt, and elsewhere, and hundreds of incantation bowls from Sassanian Babylonia. We also have indirect access to some of the magical recipe books utilized by the Jewish practitioners of late antiquity. Although the original texts were written on papyrus and parchment and therefore perished long ago, they continued to be copied in later times as well, and some of these copies may still be read among the magical texts preserved in the Cairo Genizah and in other collections of medieval Jewish manuscripts.[12] Reading all these texts, one may note not only the numerous antidemonic spells and adjurations, but also some striking continuities from the exorcistic hymns and spells of the Second Temple period. Perhaps the clearest example is the continuous use of Psalm 91, which was used as an antidemonic psalm in the Second Temple period and became extremely popular (in its Greek version, i.e., LXX Psalm 90) in early Christian amulets and exorcisms; it remained quite popular (in the Hebrew original) among the Jews of late antiquity and the Middle Ages and continues so to our own day.[13]

---

[12] For a fuller survey of these sources see Bohak, *Ancient Jewish Magic*, 143–226.

[13] See, for example, 11Q11; *y. Shabbat* 6:2 (8b) and *y. Eruvin* 10:12 (26c); *b. Shev.* 15b; M. Benayahu, *Maʿamadot and Moshavot* [= *Studies in Memory of the Rishon Le-Zion R. Yitzhak Nissim* 6] (Jerusalem, 1985), 65–80 (in Hebrew); for the Christian/Greek evidence, see T.J. Kraus, "Septuaginta-Psalm 90 in apotropäischer Verwendung: Vorüberlegungen für eine kritische Edition und (bisheriges) Datenmaterial," *BN* 125 (2005): 39–73.

To Psalm 91 we may add other biblical verses and stories that remained popular in the Jewish exorcistic tradition from the Second Temple period through late antiquity, including Zechariah 3:2 ("May God rebuke you, Satan") and the story of David driving the evil spirit out of Saul (1 Sam 16:14–23). But the evidence of textual continuity extends to nonbiblical texts as well. Thus, in one amulet found in Egypt we read a long set of Aramaic and Greek adjurations in which is embedded a short exorcistic psalm in Hebrew, attributed to King David himself. Similarly, one of the incantation bowls from Mesopotamia includes a different exorcistic psalm, also in Hebrew, which is again attributed to the same biblical figure.[14] Both psalms show no overlap with the "Davidic" psalms of the Second Temple period which happen to have reached us, but they may nonetheless be copies of copies of Second Temple period Jewish compositions. Moreover, even if we assume they are new compositions of the fourth or fifth century CE, they at the very least show, first, that the "pseudepigraphic habit," and the tendency to ascribe exorcistic psalms to such figures as David and Solomon, were alive and well in late antiquity just as in the earlier period; second, that such psalms circulated, or were composed, both in Byzantine Palestine and Egypt and in Sassanian Babylonia; and third, that they were incorporated into different types of antidemonic artifacts.

But we may go even further. In a fragment of a magical recipe book from the Cairo Genizah (T-S K 1.123) which probably dates to the eleventh century, we find an antidemonic spell which bears an unmistakable resemblance to an exorcistic formula ("If it [the demon] comes to you by night, you should say to it, 'Who are you, of the seed of man and of the Holy Ones? Your face is the face of nothingness and your horns are the horns of a dream!'"), which is also attested in one of the exorcistic psalms found among the Dead Sea Scrolls (11Q11). As these two sources are separated by more than a full millennium of Jewish history, such a resemblance provides striking evidence of the long-term continuity of the transmission and recitation of this formula. Moreover, a very similar formula is found on several Jewish incantation bowls from Mesopotamia, which are chronologically

---

[14] See R. Kotansky, J. Naveh and S. Shaked, "A Greek-Aramaic Silver Amulet from Egypt in the Ashmolean Museum," *Le Muséon* 105 (1992): 9; D. Levene, *A Corpus of Magic Bowls: Incantation Texts in Jewish Aramaic from Late Antiquity* (London, 2003), 77 (Bowl M117).

halfway between the Qumran texts and the Genizah fragments and geographically remote from the Palestine–Egypt trajectory of the Qumran to Genizah transmission, thus proving that this formula was known to and used by Jews in many different times and places (and was not, for example, reborrowed in the Middle Ages from some Christian or Muslim source).[15] Thus, while we should not necessarily assume that copies of the exorcistic texts of the Second Temple period were still in circulation in the Middle Ages (although this too is not entirely impossible), we now know for certain that some spells and adjurations were continuously transmitted from one Jewish exorcist to another for over a thousand years—notwithstanding the destruction of the Second Temple, the Christianization of the Roman Empire, and the Muslim conquests of the entire Middle East. The demons were still around, the danger was the same, and some of the means for handling them remained the same in the days of Maimonides as in the days of Josephus.

Thus far, we have focused solely on Jewish exorcistic texts in Hebrew and Aramaic. A search for Jewish exorcistic texts in Greek reveals a similar pattern, but here we must note that the evidence points to the continuous circulation of Jewish exorcistic spells through "pagan" and Christian hands, a process which might be of less interest in the present context. Nevertheless, I may cite at least one example which is of some relevance here. It is found in the Great Magical Papyrus of Paris (PGM IV), an extremely long "pagan" magical compendium of the fourth century, and forms a part of an exorcistic spell which is attributed to the Egyptian Pibechis but which is clearly of Jewish origin. The spell itself consists of eight consecutive adjurations of the demon—by "the God of the Jews, Jesus," by "the one who appeared to Osrael (sic) in a shiny pillar and a cloud," by "the great God Sabaoth, through whom the Jordan River drew back," and so on. Of particular interest is the last adjuration, "by the one in holy Jerusalem, before whom the unquenchable fire burns for all time"—a clear reference to the eternal lamp burning in the Temple, that is, the lamp which used to burn in the Temple more than three centuries before this recipe

---

[15] For a detailed analysis of this example, see G. Bohak, "From Qumran to Cairo: The Lives and Times of a Jewish Exorcistic Formula (with an Appendix by Shaul Shaked)," in *Ritual Healing in Antiquity and the Middle Ages* (ed. C. Burnett and I. Cepregi; London, forthcoming).

was copied into PGM IV.[16] Regardless of whether we see this magical text as Jewish (as it surely once was), as Christian (as the reference to Jesus might perhaps indicate), or as "pagan" (and its inclusion in PGM IV surely demonstrates its appeal to the "pagan" copyist and users of this magical handbook), we should note that here too the fact that the Jerusalem Temple was no longer there, and that its eternal lamp had proved less than unquenchable, made no difference whatsoever. The exorcistic text passed from exorcists of one generation to those of the next, and from one cultural context to another, with no apparent break in the lines of transmission.

3) Exorcism Performed by Holy Men by Means of their Innate Powers

Whereas the use of amuletic substances seems to have remained the same in late antiquity, and the continuous use of psalms and adjurations can be documented with even greater precision, exorcisms performed by men of God appear far less frequently in the period after 135 CE. This is part of a wider phenomenon, namely, the virtual disappearance of Jewish holy men (or, at least, the disappearance of stories about them) after the middle of the second century CE, with Rabbis Shimeon bar Yohai and Pinhas ben Yair as the last great miracle workers whose exploits were celebrated in rabbinic literature. It must be stressed, however, that the dearth of Jewish charismatic figures in late antiquity probably is due less to the destruction of the Temple than to the spread of Christianity, which was based to a large extent on the missionary activities of such miracle workers (whose exploits are recounted in almost every early Christian text, from the Gospels onwards). With this mode of miracle working so heavily exploited by the Christians, and given the inherent inability to control the messages imparted by such men of God to the admirers of their charismatic powers, the rabbis were quick to develop alternative narratives of miraculous powers, in which the rabbis themselves, by virtue of

---

[16] See PGM IV.3007–86 (= K.L. Preisendanz, *Papyri Graecae Magicae* [rev. by A. Heinrichs; Stuttgart, 1973–74]). My translation follows that of W.C. Grese in H.D. Betz, ed., *The Greek Magical Papyri in Translation, Including the Demotic Spells* (2nd ed.; Chicago, 1992), 96–97. For another reference to the Jerusalem Temple and its eternal flame, see PGM IV.1219.

their mastery of Torah, acquired some of the powers formerly associated with the charismatics. In this respect, at least, the *Testament of Solomon* probably is right in stressing the impact of the life and death of Jesus on the Jewish exorcistic tradition, but it was not the demons who vanished from sight as a result of the rise of Christianity, only the charismatic Jewish exorcists.[17]

Even here, however, the transformation was not complete, and in rabbinic literature we find several different types of Jewish exorcists and demon-handlers. At one extreme we find the story of Rav Yaakov, who unwittingly entered a demon-infested *beit midrash* (*b. Qiddushin* 29b). When attacked by a seven-headed demon who dwelt there, he recited a prayer, and for each of his blessings one of the demon's heads fell off, in a manner quite reminiscent of the Christian saints and their many miracles. As this rabbi is not usually mentioned as a great halakhic authority, we may see here a remnant of the older style of Jewish miracle workers, a man whose virtues and proximity to God make him immune to demons and an effective warrior against them. At the other pole, in contrast, we may note the talmudic stories of how Abbaye was convinced of Rav Papa's (temporary?) immunity to demons (*b. Pesaḥim* 111b), and of how Rabbi Hanina was entirely immune to magic (*b. Sanhedrin* 67b; *b. Ḥullin* 7b); both of these stories depict eminent rabbis as protected by their sagacity and their mastery of Torah from the onslaught of the powers of evil. This is a new pattern, since a power that once was attributed to charismatic miracle workers is now attributed to some of the greatest halakhic authorities of the Babylonian Talmud. Perhaps the most telling demonstration of this transformation is the tradition (*b. Pesaḥim* 112b) which claims that Agrath bat Mahlath, the Queen of evil demons, used to roam the world all nights of the week, escorted by her evil cohort, and inflict harm upon those she encountered on her way. But then she met Rabbi Hanina ben Dosa, who not only was immune to her actions but also forced her not to perambulate in inhabited places, except on the nights of Saturdays and Wednesdays. On another occasion, she met Abbaye; he, too, was immune to her efforts, and ordered her not to set out in

---

[17] Such exorcists would reemerge only a millennium later, in the world of the Safed Kabbalists and of Eastern European Hassidism, for which see esp. J.H. Chajes, *Between Worlds: Dybbuks, Exorcists, and Early Modern Judaism* (Philadelphia, 2003), and M. Goldish, ed., *Spirit Possession in Judaism: Cases and Contexts from the Middle Ages to the Present* (Detroit, 2003).

inhabited places even on those two nights. According to this tradition, the first person to tame the evil demoness was Hanina ben Dosa, the charismatic miracle worker of the Second Temple period, but the second person to do so was Abbaye, the fourth-century rabbi who is one of the most important halakhic figures in the entire Babylonian Talmud. Thus, in a single tradition we may see the rabbis' efforts to convince their hearers and readers that what was once done by the likes of Jesus, and is now done by some of his followers, is done with even greater success by the learned rabbis themselves.

The rabbis' power over the demons, a result not of their charismatic abilities but of their learning, is reflected in other stories too, such as the story of a demon who was forced by a rabbinic judge to pay for a barrel he had broken (*b. Ḥullin* 105b). Moreover, the rabbis' conviction that various magical practices, including the exorcism of demons, represented an art that could be learned, is most eloquently demonstrated by the long list of spells and recipes provided by the Babylonian Talmud. To cite just one example, we may note the following suggestion:

> For a demon of the privy, one should say: On the skulls of lions and on the snouts of lion cubs I found the demon Bar Shirika Panda; in a bed of leeks I struck it, with the jawbone of an ass I hit it. (*b. Shabbat* 67a)

Much could be said about this interesting spell, its possible Babylonian and biblical precedents and its obvious similarities with some of the spells found on the Babylonian incantation bowls.[18] However, for the purpose of the current inquiry suffice it to note that rather than insisting that only a holy man or a learned expert could drive a demon away, the editors of the Babylonian Talmud give away this knowledge to all their hearers and readers. One implication of this "do it yourself" approach to exorcism is that no specialized exorcists are necessary, and at least some demons could be thwarted by means of widely known exorcistic substances or by means of prayers and adjurations whose contents the rabbis are happy to give away for free. But other specialized knowledge remained in the rabbis' own hands, as may be seen from the numerous stories in which a rabbi "said what he said" (i.e., uttered a magic spell, of which the contents are not provided) and

---

[18] For a fuller treatment of this point, see G. Bohak, "Babylonian Incantation Bowls— Past, Present and Future," *Peʿamim* 105–6 (2005–2006): 253–65 (in Hebrew).

performed great deeds, or from the story of the rabbinic disciples who
first wrote the wrong amulet (aimed against a single demon rather
than sixty demons, as it should have been) and then wrote the right
one, which indeed proved very successful (*b. Pesaḥḥim* 111b). Here
too, the details of what exactly was written in the amulet are not provided, and remain the rabbis' own prerogative.

4) The Antidemonic Benefits of Halakhic Observance and Rabbinic Advice

Having considered the rabbis' conviction—and their attempts to convince their audience—that some rabbis are immune to demons and
even have powers over them, we may now note that the same rabbis repeatedly hammer home the point that observance of both the
halakhic commandments, as interpreted by the rabbis themselves, and
of more general rules of conduct, again suggested by the rabbis themselves, has great power over the demons. Such a practice can prevent
the demons from tormenting the religiously observant (à la "a *mitz-
vah* a day keeps the demons away"). This concept seems to have been
something of an innovation, which is not yet attested in the Second
Temple period (although I suspect that the priests would have insisted
that the Temple rituals had a strong antidemonic efficacy, in addition
to all their other benefits).[19] Thus, reciting the *Shema* on the bed before
going to sleep is an excellent means for keeping demons at bay, and
the recitation of the *Shema* at other times is equally useful for driving away fearful apparitions in general. Affixing a *mezuzah* to one's
doorpost helps keep the demons out of the house, and washing one's
hands every morning, avoiding water which was poured out in the
evening but only drunk in the morning, and refraining from sitting
under water drains, will save you from demonic attacks.[20] In providing such long lists of apotropaic and antidemonic practices, the rabbis
were assuring both themselves and their followers that the observance
of their *halakhot* had its useful benefits even here on earth (beyond

---

[19] For an interesting example, see the discussion in *b. Sukkah* 37b of the antidemonic powers of some Temple sacrifices, and the rabbis' attribution of similar powers
to the waving of the *lulav*. I owe this reference to Naama Vilozny; see her contribution
to the present volume, p. 261.
[20] For a fuller discussion of this point, see Bohak, *Ancient Jewish Magic*, 366–68.

its great advantages in the World to Come), and that in matters of demons and how to fight them they had much useful practical knowledge. Some of this knowledge was made public and available for all to use, but if you wanted to know more you probably should infer that consulting a rabbi might be a good idea. Here too, in other words, we see the rabbis themselves as the new experts on matters of demons and exorcism, but probably not the only experts around.

5) New Exorcistic Technologies

Looking at the metal-plate amulets and clay incantation bowls, one is struck by their testimony to many magical practices and techniques which apparently were not yet in use in the Second Temple period. In both corpora, one finds a plethora of meaningless "magic words" (which also are quite common in the spells prescribed by the Babylonian Talmud), special signs and symbols, *Hekhalot*-related materials, and (at least in the incantation bowls) a rich iconographic representation of the demons and of other creatures. As far as we currently know, none of these resources was used by Jewish exorcists and magicians in the Second Temple period, and they should therefore be considered late antique innovations in the history of Jewish magic. But such changes were mostly due to the borrowing and adaptation of non-Jewish magical technologies or to gradual developments within Jewish culture itself, and do not seem to have been shaped, or even influenced, by the destruction of the Second Temple. Moreover, most of these developments seem to postdate that event by several centuries. Thus, we may safely state that like all other aspects of Jewish culture, Jewish magical and exorcistic practices did not remain frozen in time. But the changes seem to have been gradual, and the emergence of new magical technologies did not spell the demise of the old ones, only their supplementation by the newer forms. Moreover, the entire trajectory does not seem to have been greatly influenced by any specific historical event, but by the slower rhythms of cultural changes; it was an evolution rather than a revolution.

* * *

What, then, was the impact of the events of 70, 117, or 135 CE on Jewish demonology and the Jewish exorcistic tradition? As far as I can see, the answer to this question is that the destruction of the Temple, the decimation or weakening of the priestly class, the annihilation of much of the Greek-speaking Jewish Diaspora, and the move of the Jewish centers of gravity away from Judea all had a very limited impact on the way in which Jews dealt with demons; perhaps none at all. One by-product of these events, namely, the growth of rabbinic Judaism, had some impact on the Jewish exorcistic tradition, because the rabbis sometimes represented themselves as the performers of spontaneous exorcisms and the producers of apotropaic amulets, and advocated the observance of their own halakhic injunctions as the best means to keep demons away. Another by-product of the Destruction, namely, the rise of a major center of Jewish cultural activity and creativity in Parthian and Sassanian Babylonia, had some impact on Jewish demonology because it involved a greater Jewish exposure (or perhaps we should say reexposure, since the Jews had already been deeply influenced by Babylonian culture in the sixth to third centuries BCE) to Babylonian and Iranian demonology and demon-thwarting technologies. Some of the results of this exposure may be seen in the Babylonian Talmud and in the Jewish incantation bowls from late antique Mesopotamia, but even here there is very little that is entirely unprecedented in the earlier Jewish sources or that constitutes a complete break with the past.[21] And the two major changes which can be discerned in the history of Jewish exorcism in late antiquity—the disappearance, around the mid-second century CE, of the figure of the holy man who could also exorcise demons by his innate powers, and the rise, in the fourth or fifth centuries, of a more scribal form of magic in which exorcistic aims too were served by spells written on metal-plate amulets or clay bowls—seem to be quite unrelated to the destruction of the Jerusalem Temple. Thus, unlike Jewish sacrificial or liturgical habits, which underwent major changes in the post-Destruction world, the Jewish exorcistic tradition seems to have sailed on quite undisturbed.

In accounting for this striking continuity, three explanations come to mind, the one quite obvious, the others much less so. On the one hand, I note that, apart from the *Testament of Solomon*'s reference to the demons supposedly imprisoned beneath Solomon's Temple, or the Greek magical papyri's reference to the Jerusalem Temple in an anti-

---

[21] Moreover, note that even prior to the Destruction there was a large Jewish diaspora in Parthia. It is largely undocumented, and so we simply do not know how much of the magical and exorcistic practice we later find documented in the Babylonian Talmud was already widespread in that community much earlier.

demonic adjuration, there is very little evidence in the ancient sources for a necessary connection between the world of the Temple and that of demons and exorcism; and there is little reason to think that such a connection would have existed (except, perhaps, the priestly use of the powers inherent in Temple-related objects and rituals to scare demons away). Thus, there really is no *a priori* reason to assume that the destruction of the Temple would have made much of a difference to those Jewish exorcists who survived it, or to the firm belief of many Jews that demons could and should be driven away with the help of exorcistic materials or exorcistic prayers and spells, or even by the innate powers of Jewish holy men. In this respect, our conclusion would not seem too unexpected.

A second reason for the continuity of the Jewish exorcistic tradition is its highly diffuse nature. As we noted throughout the present survey, exorcism never was the proprietary domain of a small group of experts who kept all their knowledge stored inside a few human brains or in a small group of manuscripts, all of which would easily have perished in any of the cataclysmic events of the first two centuries CE. Jewish exorcism was an extremely popular affair, practiced by professionals and laypersons alike, transmitted in oral and in written forms, available in Hebrew, Aramaic and Greek, and passed on from masters to disciples, from parents to children, from rabbis to their followers. Thus, while the events of 70 or 135 probably brought about the destruction of much exorcistic knowledge, and much of the exorcistic literature of the Second Temple period, some of it survived, and the continuous demand assured a continuous supply, in an unbroken chain of tradition.

There is, however, a third factor which may have abetted the continuity of the Jewish exorcistic practices even in times of great upheavals, and this is the constant exchange of demonological information and exorcistic technologies between Jews and non-Jews throughout antiquity. Whether we look at Josephus' description of the exorcist Eleazar demonstrating his abilities to a Roman audience; at the rabbinic stories of Rabban Yohanan Ben Zakkai and a Gentile discussing standard exorcistic practices; at the Jewish exorcistic spells and recipes which were incorporated into the Greek magical papyri; at the Babylonian-sounding antidemonic spells recommended by the Babylonian Talmud; or at the Greek "magic words" and magic signs strewn throughout the Jewish amulets of late antique Palestine, we repeatedly find Jews who are teaching their non-Jewish neighbors, learning from them, or merely comparing notes. Accordingly, I would argue that the remarkable cultural openness which is visible in the magical practices of many cultures, including ancient Jewish magic, played an important role in the seamless flow of Jewish exorcism of the Second Temple to its late antique successors. True, in late antiquity many Jews no longer had access to Tobit, Josephus, the *Book of Biblical Antiquities* and many other products of the vibrant Jewish culture of the Second Temple period. But they had some access to the older Jewish exorcistic texts, and they had a good deal of access to non-Jewish exorcistic technologies, many of which were quite like those used by Jews at an earlier time as well, and some of which were directly borrowed from the Jews themselves.[22] True, whereas some late antique Jews could have had access to the above-mentioned books (copies of which were available even in the Origen's library in Caesarea), most Jews apparently did not display much interest in their lost written heritage, and the rabbis simply ignored it altogether. But when it came to exorcism, which was considered a vital means of fighting the ubiquitous demons, there was a greater interest, and a greater willingness among Jews to turn to their non-Jewish neighbors for advice—and perhaps also for a glimpse at the Jews' own long lost techniques. Thus, the pervasiveness of the Jewish exorcistic practices, and the willingness to learn at least some things from non-Jews, contributed to turning the cumulative Destructions of 70, 117, and 135 CE into relatively meaningless events in the history of Jewish exorcism.

---

[22] One striking example is the recurrence of Y'W in Jewish magical texts, clearly a reborrowing of Iaô, the Greek name of the Jewish God, as noted, for example, by D. Sperber, *Magic and Folklore in Rabbinic Literature* (Ramat Gan, 1994), 86–91.

THE EMERGENCE OF A NEW JEWISH ART
IN LATE ANTIQUITY

Lee I. Levine

It is widely recognized that Jewish art in the pre-70 era, whatever its variety and levels of sophistication, was severely limited, in part owing to its popular and scattered contexts in the First Temple era and in part owing to the prevailing aniconic policy in Jewish society toward the end of the Second Temple period.[1] By late antiquity, however, the nature and content of Jewish art had changed dramatically as Jews began to use figural representations of animals, humans, and even pagan mythological characters, biblical scenes, and a variety of religious symbols in their synagogues and cemeteries.

To explain this phenomenon, it has often been posited that the appearance of this new type of Jewish art was inextricably intertwined with the triumph of Christianity. Since the overwhelming majority of sites with Jewish artistic remains dates from the fourth century onward, it has been assumed that the challenges and threats presented by the new *Verus Israel* gave impetus to Jewish artistic creativity that found expression in the synagogues, cemeteries, and private homes of the period. Modern scholars' efforts to compare and contrast various aspects of Jewish and Christian art from this era have often yielded interesting and illuminating insights.[2]

But what about earlier instances of similar Jewish art from the century before the ascendancy of Christianity? The well-known Dura Europos synagogue and the impressive *necropoleis* of Bet Sheʿarim and Rome all date to the third century, the latter two continuing to function into the fourth and perhaps fifth centuries as well. These three

---

[1] On Jewish art in the First and Second Temple periods, see L.I. Levine, *Visual Judaism: History, Art and Identity in Late Antiquity* (New Haven, forthcoming).

[2] F. Vitto, "The Interior Decoration of Palestinian Churches and Synagogues," *ByzF* 21 (1995): 283–300; R. Hachlili, "Aspects of Similarity and Diversity in the Architecture and Art of Ancient Synagogues and Churches in the Land of Israel," *ZDPV* 113 (1997): 92–122; R. Talgam, "Similarities and Differences between Synagogue and Church Mosaics in Palestine during the Byzantine and Umayyad Periods," in *From Dura to Sepphoris: Studies in Jewish Art and Society in Late Antiquity* (ed. L.I. Levine and Z. Weiss; Portsmouth, R.I., 2000), 93–110.

sites offer a remarkable display of artistic expression unknown in earlier Israelite-Jewish history. What factors predating the rise of Christianity might have led to this significant spurt of creativity in Jewish art that stretched from Rome, through Palestine, to the eastern frontiers of the Roman Empire?

The answer, I would suggest, lies in a series of religious and cultural developments occurring throughout the Empire, though primarily in the East, during the first three centuries CE, which can explain the reinvention of Jewish artistic expression in dramatically new ways in the third century. Each of the three above-mentioned locales, widely separated throughout the Empire, was influenced by a different cultural context. We will begin our discussion by indicating the unique cultural context that contributed to the singularity of each and then turn to the finds from the sites themselves.

THE DURA EUROPOS SYNAGOGUE IN ITS URBAN RELIGIOUS CONTEXT

The religious ferment originating in the eastern provinces swept through the Roman Empire in the first three centuries CE; wave after wave of cults, many often referred to as mystery religions, succeeded in capturing the hearts and minds of countless individuals. Dura provides a rare look into the interaction between the forces at play in this city, which found expression, inter alia, in the local synagogue.[3]

Ironically, while Rome was pushing eastward, with one emperor after another (from Trajan to Gallienus, and later Julian) seeking to expand the empire's territories in eastern Syria, Mesopotamia, and Babylonia, and while attempts were being made to spread the imperial cult and thus unite the various provinces religiously as well, a large number

---

[3] These three centuries CE indeed witnessed the greatest penetration of eastern cults into the Empire, although Greek and Egyptian deities, as well as those from Asia Minor, appeared in Rome and Italy much earlier; see R. Turcan, *The Gods of Ancient Rome: Religion in Everyday Life from Archaic to Imperial Times* (New York, 2001), 105–54; B. Metzger, "Considerations of Methodology in the Study of the Mystery Religions and Early Christianity," *HTR* 48 (1955): 1–20; and the comments of J.Z. Smith, *Drudgery Divine: On the Comparison of Early Christianities and the Religions of Late Antiquity* (Chicago, 1990), passim, and esp. pp. 99–115. A corollary of this development is the decline of the civic model of religion that had held sway for centuries, and with it the steady disappearance of social and political control over religion. For an enlightening example of this process with regard to Carthage, see J.B. Rives, *Religion and Authority in Roman Carthage from Augustus to Constantine* (Oxford and New York, 1995).

of eastern cults began moving westward, eventually penetrating virtually all regions of the empire as far as Spain, Germany, and Britain.[4]
Thus, while a veneer of homogeneity was being created throughout the
provinces by the imperial cult,[5] it was counterbalanced by the rapid
dissemination of a wide range of eastern cults and the transformation
of older local ones throughout the Roman Empire.[6]

The second and early third centuries were indeed a time of religious
vitality. It has been noted that "the interest of many educated men in
secret learning from the East, from Egypt, India, Babylonia, Israel, Persia...seems to have become increasingly fashionable in the second and
third centuries AD."[7] With the ascendance of the African and Syrian
emperors (and empresses) of the Severan dynasty, Dionysos, Mithras,
Helios, and the Syrian gods, not to mention Christianity in all its early
forms, made significant inroads into Rome and other parts of the
Empire. For instance, both Septimius Severus and his son Caracalla
were devoted to Egyptian deities, especially the cult of Serapis; the

---

[4] Adherents of these cults were at first foreigners who mingled freely with the local
populations. Some were soldiers returning from military duty in the East, and others
were slaves who brought their local cults with them and continued to worship accordingly, while slaves and then as freedmen. Free laborers, merchants, and artisans from
the East were also agents in the propagation of these cults, opening shops in the cities
and near army camps or becoming ensconced as servants in the homes of the aristocracy and wealthy as well as in the imperial bureaucracy. As a result, inroads made
into the Roman aristocracy, and even the imperial court, were far from uncommon.
Although Augustus and Tiberius attempted to repress these new cults, later emperors
were often attracted to one or more of them—Caligula to Isis, Claudius to Phrygian-
ism, Nero to Syrian gods and the doctrines of the magi, Vespasian to Serapis, and
Titus to Isis (R. Turcan, *The Cults of the Roman Empire* [Oxford and Cambridge,
Mass., 1996], 14; C. Edwards and G. Woolf, "Cosmopolis: Rome as World City," in
Rome the Cosmopolis [ed. eidem; Cambridge and New York, 2003], 9). On earlier
appropriations of foreign cults by leaders of the Republic, see A. Momigliano, *On
Pagans, Jews, and Christians* (Middletown, Conn, 1987), 180–81.
[5] The imperial cult was the exception; other than that, no Roman cult had successfully implanted itself in the East; see R.L. Gordon, "Mithraism and Roman Society:
Social Factors in the Explanation of Religious Change in the Roman Empire," *Religion*
2 (1972): 111.
[6] Much like Rome's early contacts with the Hellenistic world, when its political and
military feats were countered by a significant degree of reverse infiltration and the
adoption of Greek culture, so, too, under the Roman Empire; a new wave of Eastern
influences permeated Roman society, as evidenced by Horace's statement (*Epistles*
2.1.156), written in the time of Augustus, that conquered Greece had taken Rome
captive by educating the Romans in her arts. Had such a statement been made in the
second or third centuries CE, it would have included other Eastern religions, to wit,
Juvenal's comment that "the Orontes has poured into the Tiber" (*Satires* 3.62).
[7] Gordon, "Mithraism and Roman Society," 110.

emperor Elagabalus imported into Rome the Syrian god Elagabal of Emesa, depicted as a conical black stone that presumably represented the sun;[8] and Alexander Severus reportedly had a room with busts of gods and heroes, including those of Apollonius of Tyana, Abraham, and Jesus. The success of the eastern cults reached new heights, and the "orientalization" of the Roman Empire reached its culmination, when Aurelian made Sol Invictus the supreme god of the Empire and when Constantine introduced Christianity as the official religion in the fourth century.

Several scholarly assessments assert that these centuries were indeed a period of tremendous religious and cultural ferment. As Case noted some eighty years ago: "At no period before or since in the history of civilization as known to us have so many separate religious movements flourished at one time within a single area so thoroughly unified culturally and politically as was the Roman Empire."[9] Rives described this phenomenon about a decade ago as follows: "The period from Augustus to Constantine was in terms of religious developments one of the richest, perhaps the richest, in the history of Europe and the Mediterranean world."[10] Jewish communities at this time were not immune to such developments.

The synagogue at Dura is unusually well preserved, as is the city generally, since after its destruction in 256 CE it was never resettled. The city boasted fifteen religious buildings, but the synagogue is by far the most impressive; all four of its walls were once covered from floor to ceiling with frescoes of biblical scenes and figures, and those remaining intact constitute about half the synagogue's original paintings. The western wall is the best preserved one and was also the focus of the sanctuary, having the Torah shrine at its center (fig. 1). The synagogue scenes span the entire biblical period, from the book of Genesis to the exodus from Egypt and the Wilderness sojourn, and down to the story of Esther in the Persian era. The attempt to decode this art and discover its overriding theme(s) has engaged scholars for over seventy-five years; however, no consensus has yet been reached. Until recently, it was generally assumed that this art could not have been produced by a small and remote community such as the one at Dura, and it

---

[8] Herodian describes this cult as having a large temple and attracting many pilgrims, satraps, and barbarian princes from a wide area in Syria (*Roman History* 5.3.4–5).

[9] S.J. Case, "Popular Competitors of Early Christianity," *JR* 10 (1930): 55.

[10] Rives, *Religion and Authority*, 2.

was thus surmised that what was found there was but the tip of the ice-berg and that any artistic creativity of the Jews at this time must have originated in one or more of the large urban centers of the empire.[11] However, with the passing of almost eight decades and the discovery of many more synagogues, none even begins to compare with Dura. Accordingly, scholars have now begun to focus on the unique set-ting of this city and its Mesopotamian context in order to explain the synagogue's art.

A number of studies have demonstrated that virtually all aspects of the synagogue building, its architecture, art, and inscriptions can best be explained as an outgrowth of the regnant styles and practices in Mesopotamia in general, and at Dura in particular.[12] To date, however, most of these comparisons address only the externalities of the build-ings in question. What we are particularly interested in here is the art itself, the *pièce de résistance* of the synagogue and, indeed, of Dura generally. Remains of the artistic expression in most Duran temples are generally fragmentary. What is clear, however, is that religious art existed in this region in the service of the traditional cults (e.g., Zeus Theos and the Palmyrene deities) as well as those now newly invigo-rated ones (e.g., Isis). It is in Dura that we can catch an early glimpse of how art was harnessed to promote a cult, first and foremost to its adherents, but perhaps to others as well. Rostovtzeff formulated this phenomenon as follows: "The excavations of Dura have shown for the first time that the revival of Semitic religions in the Near East, the cre-ation there of a Semitic religious κοινή, the concentration of the reli-gious thought and feeling on one leading god and one leading goddess, found among other modes of expression that of a new religious art."[13]

---

[11] See, for example, C.H. Kraeling, *The Excavations at Dura Europos, 8.1: The Syna-gogue* (New Haven, 1956; repr. New York, 1979), 382–84; R. Brilliant, "Painting at Dura-Europos and Roman Art," in *The Dura-Europos Synagogue: A Re-Evaluation (1932–1972)* (ed. J. Gutmann; Missoula, Mont., 1973), 23–30; M.L. Thompson, "Hypo-thetical Models of the Dura Paintings," in ibid., 31–52; K. Weitzmann, "The Individual Panels and Their Christian Parallels," in K. Weitzmann and H.L. Kessler, *The Frescoes of the Dura Synagogue and Christian Art* (Washington, D.C., 1990), 143–50.

[12] M.I. Rostovtzeff, *Dura-Europos and Its Art* (Oxford, 1938), 57–134; A. Perkins, *The Art of Dura-Europos* (Oxford, 1973), 55–65, 114–26; M.H. Gates, "Dura-Europos: A Fortress of Syro-Mesopotamian Art," *BA* (1984): 166–81. On the shared char-acteristics of Mesopotamian temples and the unique aspects of those in Dura, see S.B. Downey, *Mesopotamian Religious Architecture: Alexander through the Parthians* (Princeton, 1988), 124–29, 175–80.

[13] Rostovtzeff, *Dura-Europos and Its Art*, 67.

What makes this geographical context so fascinating and crucial is that there are very few places in the Roman world other than Dura that have preserved so much material evidence of religious diversity at one specific time.[14] Indeed, Rostovtzeff suggested over seventy years ago that this art be called Mesopotamian art, "though we might as well call it the artistic κοινή of the Parthian Empire."[15] Dura's temple art was overwhelmingly pagan in the traditional sense; only three relative latecomers—the synagogue, church, and Mithraeum—deviated from this norm.[16]

Perhaps a key to the enigma of Dura's Jewish art may be found in the timing of its appearance. The community decorated the synagogue lavishly when the building and the sanctuary were enlarged (Stage II, ca. 244–45). Earlier, in Stage I, its decoration had been limited to imitation marble incrustation work (e.g., dados and moldings), multicolored geometric patterns such as diamonds and triangles, and some floral designs.[17] It is only in Stage II that we have the stunning display of figural biblical scenes, the likes of which are unattested in any other ancient synagogue. However, what is significant is that this art work was executed at the same time that two nearby houses of worship, the church and Mithraeum, were likewise being decorated (some time in the 240s)—the former for the first time, the latter with an expanded decorative scheme largely replacing what had existed in previous decades.[18] Was this merely a coincidental development, or were there common stimuli affecting these three religious communities that

---

[14] See, most recently, L.R. Brody and G.L. Hoffman (eds.), *Dura Europos: Cross-roads of Antiquity* (Boston, 2011).

[15] Rostovtzeff, *Dura-Europos and Its Art*, 90.

[16] On the pagan gods of Dura, see C.B. Welles, "The Gods of Dura-Europos," in *Beiträge zur alten Geschichte und deren Nachleben: Festschrift für Franz Altheim*, (ed. R. Stiehl and J.E. Stier; Berlin, 1970), 50–65.

[17] Kraeling, *Excavations at Dura Europos: Synagogue*, 26–38: "The decorations of the earlier building...contrast sharply with those of the later edifice. They are much simpler and contain no representations of animate beings. Whether this reflects merely the limited financial and artistic resources of the local Jewish community in its earlier days, or whether it reflects also a point of view hostile to the use of such representations, is unknown. What is evident is that the decorations do not rise above the conventional, and restrict themselves to designs that had become common-place by the second century of our era" (p. 36).

[18] *Church*: Kraeling, *The Excavations at Dura-Europos, 8.2: The Christian Building* (New Haven, 1967), 34–39; *Mithraeum*: M.I. Rostovtzeff et al., *The Excavations at Dura-Europos: Preliminary Report of the Seventh and Eighth Seasons of Work—1933–1934 and 1934–1935* (New Haven, 1939), 64–80, and esp. pp. 76–80. See also Perkins, *Art of Dura-Europos*, 49–55.

found expression in the art forms of their respective buildings?[19] A number of scholars have pointed to similar stylistic elements in each of the buildings, strongly suggesting a common artisan or workshop.[20]

It is important to note that the decorative schemes of these three institutions differ from anything else found in Dura. In other local sanctuaries, the art invariably consisted of worshippers bringing gifts to a god, or priests in the act of sacrificing or offering incense (*supplicatio*).[21] The most extensive remains of this motif were found in the temples of Bel, Zeus Theos, and Adonis (fig. 2). In contrast, the synagogue, church, and Mithraeum each emphasize something of its adherents' own unique historical or mythological heritage.

The art of the church, for example, featuring scenes from the Hebrew Bible and New Testament, was concentrated in its baptistery (fig. 3); depictions of Adam and Eve along with David and Goliath appear beside representations of the Good Shepherd, the Samaritan woman at the well, two miracles of Jesus (walking on the water and healing the paralytic), and the women approaching the empty tomb.[22] In the Mithraeum, numerous scenes from the life of Mithras are shown on its walls alongside episodes of the Mithraic cosmogony on the arch of

---

[19] Gates cites features such as mudbrick construction, the overall plan of the sanctuary, the presence of a cult niche or *aedicula*, at times accompanied by programs of painted decoration, the focus along the back wall with the figure (or statue) of a deity, frontality in depictions, a series of registers along the wall featuring cultic ceremonies, and more, as was characteristic of Mesopotamian art from earlier periods that had roots as much as a millennium earlier ("Dura-Europos," 169). Perkins had already noted many of these points (*Art of Dura-Europos*, 55–65) without, however, reaching the conclusions regarding the synagogue's overall provenance, as Gates has. Also of interest is the fact that the religious orientation of all three sanctuaries was to the west. In the synagogue, the *aedicula* with its Torah shrine faced in that direction, as did the primary depictions relating to Mithras in the Mithraeum and the baptismal font and its decorations in the church.

[20] R.M. Jensen, "The Dura Europos Synagogue, Early Christian Art, and Religious Life in Dura Europos," in *Jews, Christians, and Polytheists in the Ancient Synagogue* (ed. S. Fine; London and New York, 1999), 180–87, and esp. p. 184: "In any case, it seems likely that both Jews and Christians availed themselves of the same atelier to decorate their houses of worship, a workshop that had already produced murals for pagan temples and other public buildings in the area." In the same vein, see also A.J. Wharton, *Refiguring the Post Classical City: Dura Europos, Jerash, Jerusalem and Ravenna* (Cambridge, 1995), 60–61; J. Elsner, "Reflections on Late Antique Jewish Art and Early Christian Art," *JRS* 93 (2003): 119.

[21] Perkins, *Art of Dura-Europos*, 33–49; Downey, *Mesopotamian Religious Architecture*, 88–130; Wharton, *Refiguring the Post Classical City*, 33–38.

[22] For a suggestion as to the role of this art, at least in part, in the liturgy of the baptistery, see T.F. Mathews, *The Clash of the Gods: A Reinterpretation of Early Christian Art* (Princeton, 1993), 152–53.

the niche at the western end of the room (fig. 4). Flanking this arch are two large figures of Mithraic prophets or magi, and on the side walls are hunting scenes, in one of which Mithras, with a flowing cloak and bow in hand, is shown astride a galloping horse. The sacred banquet of Mithras and his ally Sol, and various symbols including the zodiac signs, are also displayed here. The focus in the Mithraeum is the altar, where Mithras appears slaying the bull (*Mithras Tauroctony*).

Thus, these three religious communities—all relative newcomers to Dura, appearing there only under Roman rule (after 165 CE)—built or refurbished their buildings at the same time, each using a decorative scheme that highlighted its *Heilsgeschichte*, its sacred icons or symbols (the synagogue and Mithraeum), its god and his *aretai*, or its sacred possessions. It is thus difficult to avoid the conclusion that there must have been significant connections between these contemporary communities and their initiatives.[23]

Some scholars have suggested that a competitive atmosphere permeated Dura, with some religious groups struggling for survival and expansion at the expense of others.[24] However, no compelling case has been made for a milieu of conflict or competition among these three religions or vis-à-vis other cults in the city.[25] On the contrary, in a number of instances several gods were recognized in the same temple and priests of different cults were represented in the same place.[26] It would therefore seem that Dura was a city of many commonalities and interactions, resulting in mutual influences among these three communities. It is impossible to assess which of them influenced the others or whether the emergence of religious art was a simultaneous response among them to some other forces at work. It is probably not too far off the mark to surmise that such parallel creativity permeated many cities throughout the Roman world where the eastern cults were then flourishing, and that Dura is simply an unusually rich visual

---

[23] See Kraeling, *Excavations at Dura-Europos: Christian Building*, 218–20.

[24] See Weitzmann and Kessler, *Frescoes*; J. Elsner, "Cultural Resistance and the Visual Image: The Case of Dura Europos," *CP* 96 (2001): 269–304.

[25] See the well-argued case presented by L. Dirven, "Religious Competition and the Decoration of Sanctuaries: The Case of Dura-Europos," *Eastern Christian Art* 1 (2004): 1–19. See also, however, J. North, "The Development of Religious Pluralism," in *The Jews among Pagans and Christians in the Roman Empire* (ed. J. Lieu, J. North, and T. Rajak; London and New York, 1994), 174–93.

[26] Dirven, "Religious Competition," 13. P.V.M. Flesher, "Conflict or Co-operation? Non-Jews in the Dura Synagogue Paintings," in *Hellenic and Jewish Arts: Interaction, Tradition and Renewal* (ed. A. Ovadiah; Tel-Aviv, 1998), 199–221.

expression of a widespread phenomenon. Thus, in the absence of hard evidence, there is little justification to invent a hypothetical situation of competition, struggle, and polemic to account for this development. Self-assertion and communal religious pride, as well as the creation of institutional (and artistic) boundary markers, are not necessarily to be confused with situations of tension and confrontation.

Whatever the case, we may conclude that the rather unique configuration of the variety of religious cults and their preserved artistic expression in Dura must have provided the local Jewish community with enough impetus to create the quintessential example of synagogue art in antiquity, distinguishing the Dura synagogue from anything that preceded or followed it—indeed to this very day.[27]

Bet She'arim in Its Greco-Roman Setting

A second instance of third-century CE Jewish art is set in a very different cultural and social milieu. Many of those interred in the Bet She'arim necropolis—people from the urban Jewish elites, synagogue officials, and others who functioned under Patriarchal auspices—chose to do so out of their identification with and respect for that office (fig. 5).

The confluence here of two developments impacted upon early third-century Palestine, especially, though not exclusively, with respect to the Patriarch, R. Judah I—a most extraordinary individual whose wealth, political stature, and religious-intellectual achievements[28] distinguished him from all other sages in his generation. The first of these developments was the political and cultural rapprochement between many Jews and the Severan government, the second was the renaissance of Greek culture in the East during the first to third centuries.[29] Their impact on R. Judah and his circle, as well as on other parts of

---

[27] See in this regard A. Grabar, *Christian Iconography: A Study of Its Origins* (Princeton, 1968), 19–30, esp. p. 30.

[28] Foremost among which was the compilation of the Mishnah, a work that quickly became a standard sacred text among the rabbis.

[29] On the oftentimes close relationship between Severan culture and the culture of the East, particularly with reference to art, see Z. Newby, "Art at the Crossroads? Themes and Styles in Severan Art," in *Severan Culture* (ed. S. Swain, S. Harrison, and J. Elsner; Cambridge and New York, 2007), 249: "In many ways we can see the Severan period as the culmination of the cultural philhellenism which had dominated the second century."

Jewish society, was considerable and found expression, inter alia, in the Patriarchal necropolis of Bet She'arim.

The Roman architectural features of Bet She'arim are pronounced. The façades of the two main catacombs (14 and 20), where most, if not all, members of the Patriarchal family were interred for generations, are typically Roman, with small side arches flanking a larger middle one. In addition, there were typically Roman bases, pilasters, capitals, architraves, cornices, and friezes, all influenced primarily by the regnant style in Roman Syria.[30] The mausoleum of Catacomb 11 is likewise typical of Roman funerary monuments (fig. 6), and the widespread use of sarcophagi, especially in Catacomb 20, follows the practice of primary burials recently introduced in second-century Rome. Of the 200 burials in Catacomb 20, 125 were in sarcophagi.[31]

An additional indication of the cultural orientation of those buried in Bet She'arim is the language of the approximately 300 inscriptions; almost 80 percent are in Greek, and this number jumps to almost 90 percent if we exclude the two Patriarchal catacombs, 14 and 20, where Hebrew was more widely used.[32]

Finally, the art found in the Bet She'arim necropolis combines a Hellenistic dimension, including many mythological depictions, and a heretofore unattested emphasis on Jewish symbols. Thus, the representation of Leda and the swan and scenes featuring Amazons[33] are found together with depictions of the menorah (fig. 7). The appearance of clearly pagan motifs alongside uniquely Jewish symbols in Bet She'arim characterizes Jewish artistic representations at several other Palestinian sites throughout late antiquity.

Yet the Bet She'arim necropolis differs from other Jewish burial sites, both in Second Temple Jerusalem and the contemporary Galilee and Diaspora. Sarcophagi are extremely scarce in Jerusalem, where only some 37 percent of the inscriptions found are in Greek. More-

---

[30] N. Avigad, *Beth She'arim: Report on the Excavations during 1953–1958, 3: Catacombs 12–23* (New Brunswick, 1976), 86–93.

[31] Ibid., 136–83.

[32] To be precise, there are 279 published inscriptions, but according to Jonathan Price (personal communication), about 20 additional inscriptions from the site, almost all in Greek, have yet to be published. See a forthcoming volume of *Corpus Inscriptionum Iudaeae/Palestinae: A Multi-lingual Corpus of the Inscriptions from Alexander to Muhammad* (Berlin).

[33] On the popularity of mythological scenes in Roman art at this time, see Newby, "Art at the Crossroads?" 233–40.

over, Jerusalem's art is almost entirely aniconic, and there are certainly no instances of pagan mythological representations. The use of Greek or any kind of figural art in contemporary Galilean burial sites is marginal, and while symbols and Greek were used in the Diaspora at this time, figural representations were studiously avoided (see below).

Why, then, was Bet She'arim so unique? The answer lies in the Severan historical context, which had a significant impact both on Palestine generally and on the Patriarchal house and other Jewish aristocratic circles in particular.

The Severan Political Dimension

Jewish affinities toward Rome at this time included the following:[34]

1) Jewish political support of Septimius Severus in his early wars of accession;
2) R. Judah's attempt (foiled by other sages) to abolish the fasts of the 17th of Tammuz and the 9th of Av, days commemorating the destruction of the Temple;
3) The purportedly close relationship between R. Judah and a Roman emperor named Antoninus noted in many rabbinic traditions, most of which are clearly legendary.[35] The earlier tannaitic accounts are somewhat more plausible, as they speak of conversations and consultations between R. Judah and the emperor;[36]

---

[34] The following issues, as well as references to the relevant primary sources, are discussed by G. Alon, *The Jews in Their Land in the Talmudic Age* (2 vols.; Jerusalem, 1980), 2: 681–737; M. Avi-Yonah, *The Jews of Palestine* (New York, 1976), 54–88; A. Büchler, *Studies in Jewish History* (London, 1956), 179–244; A. Tropper, *Wisdom, Politics, and Historiography: Tractate Avot in the Context of the Graeco-Roman Near East* (Oxford, 2004), passim; L.I. Levine, "The Age of R. Judah I," in *Eretz-Israel from the Destruction of the Second Temple to the Muslim Conquest* (ed. Z. Baras et al.; 2 vols.; Jerusalem, 1982), 1: 93–118 (in Hebrew); A. Oppenheimer, "The Severan Emperors, Rabbi Judah ha-Nasi and the Cities of Palestine," in *"The Words of a Wise Man's Mouth are Gracious" (Qoh 10, 12): Festschrift for Günter Stemberger on the Occasion of his 65th Birthday* (ed. M. Perani; Berlin, 2005), 171–81.

[35] On the contacts between sophists and Rome, see G. Bowersock, *Greek Sophists in the Roman Empire* (Oxford, 1969), passim, but esp. pp. 43–58.

[36] Even if these rabbinic traditions do not reflect much of the historical reality, the Jews' (or rabbis') desire to invent such images is an indication of their wish for cultural–social–political recognition (given their political inferiority?), which permeated other parts of the Greek world as well. See S. Swain, *Hellenism and Empire: Language, Classicism, and Power in the Greek World: AD 50–250* (Oxford and New York, 1996), 196–97.

4) R. Judah's encouragement of Jews to move to the large non-Jewish cities of Palestine. He exempted these cities from the requirements associated with halakhic agricultural laws in the Holy Land (e.g., tithes, sabbatical year laws), while at the same time declaring these cities "pure," as if they were part of the Land of Israel. Such decrees might have been intended to coincide with (and support) Rome's policy of urbanization in Palestine, with an eye toward insuring Jewish economic prosperity while fostering the increased integration of Jews within the larger society;[37]

5) R. Judah's move from Bet She'arim to Sepphoris, one of the two major Jewish cities of the Galilee. The move undoubtedly reflects, inter alia, his desire to be more closely involved in the larger political and social decisions of the day. Residence in Sepphoris would have offered R. Judah a greater opportunity to shape policy and facilitate his contact with the Roman authorities and the non-Jewish population of the province.

The rapprochement with Rome, however, was not confined to Patriarchal circles alone, but also had a wider resonance among the Jews of Palestine. Two examples, both *sui generis* and thus indicative of a radically new attitude toward Rome, will suffice to highlight this reality:

1) An inscription discovered in the village of Qatzion in the Upper Galilee, dated to 197 CE, reads: "For the welfare of our lords, the ruling emperors Lucius Septimius Severus the pious, Pertinex, Caesar, and Marcus Aurelius Antoninus (i.e., Caracalla—*L.L.*) and Lucius Septimius Geta, his sons, on the basis of a vow, the Jews (dedicated this—*L.L.*)."[38] In a wreath to the side we read: "and Julia Domna the empress."[39] While the reason for this particular dedication remains unknown, this evidence makes it patently clear that a pro-Roman posture was not limited to ruling circles.

---

[37] In addition to Büchler, *Studies*, 179–244 ("The Patriarch Judah I and the Graeco-Roman Cities of Palestine"), see also Oppenheimer, "Severan Emperors," 171–81.

[38] L. Roth-Gerson, *The Greek Inscriptions from the Synagogues in Eretz-Israel* (Jerusalem, 1987), 125–29 (in Hebrew).

[39] For a suggestion that the depiction of Esther in the Dura Europos synagogue was influenced by an iconography associated with Julia Domna, see D. Levit-Tawil, "Queen Esther at Dura: Her Imagery in Light of Third-Century C.E. Oriental Syncretism," in *Irano-Judaica* (ed. S. Shaked and A. Netzer; vol. 4; Jerusalem, 1999), 274–97, esp. pp. 287–97.

2) The city of Sepphoris issued several series of coins in the early third century during the reign of the emperor Caracalla, acknowledging a special relationship between this city and Rome. The legends on some of these coins read:

    a. "Diocaesarea the Holy, City of Shelter, Autonomous, Loyal (a treaty of) friendship and alliance with the Romans"

    b. "Diocaesarea the Holy, City of Shelter, Autonomous, Loyal (a treaty of) friendship and alliance between the Holy Council and the people of Rome."

How this Sepphorean evidence relates to R. Judah, then a resident of the city, remains unknown, but his pro-Roman proclivity was clearly shared by the city's leaders.

On the Roman side as well, the evidence for a similar kind of rapprochement is no less striking:

1) The following law (either a new one or a reaffirmation of an already existing privilege) from the early third century allowed Jews to participate in municipal councils while protecting them from liturgies that might disrupt their religious practices.

> The Divine Severus and Antoninus permitted those that follow the Jewish religion to enter offices (probably a reference to the municipal rather than the imperial government—*L.L.*) but also imposed upon them such liturgies such as should not (cause them to—*L.L.*) transgress their religion.[40]

2) Furthermore, the *Scriptores Historiae Augustae* (late fourth century), a historically problematic source, notes ongoing imperial contacts with Jews and/or Judaism from Caracalla to Alexander Severus, the latter being unflatteringly referred to on one occasion by an Antiochene mob as a "Syrian *archisynagogos*."[41] As mentioned above, this same emperor reputedly included busts of Abraham, Apollonius of Tyana, Jesus, and Orpheus in his palace shrine.[42]

---

[40] A. Linder, *The Jews in Roman Imperial Legislation* (Detroit, 1987), no. 2. While the *Constitutio Antoniniana* of 212 upgraded Jewish status in the Empire, it of course was not directed specifically toward Jews, but rather toward virtually all inhabitants of the realm.

[41] *SHA, Alexander Severus* 28.7.

[42] Ibid., 29.2. In addition, this emperor claimed to be following a Jewish and Christian practice when he ordered that the names of candidates for public office be announced prior to their appointment (ibid., 45.6–7); and once he cited the Golden

3) Origen refers to the status of the Patriarch (here referred to as the "ethnarch") around the year 240 CE as follows:

> Now that the Romans rule and the Jews pay them two drachmae, we, who have experience in this, know how much authority the ethnarch among them has, and that he differs only slightly from being a king of the people. He conducts legal proceedings secretly and some are even sentenced to death. And even though there is not total recognition for this, nevertheless these things are done with the knowledge of the ruler.[43]

Such a status was clearly recognized by Rome, *de facto* if not *de iure*, as indicated by Origen, and was undoubtedly extended to the Patriarch in the time of Judah I.

In sum, the above sources offer clear-cut evidence of a positive Jewish attitude toward Rome, and this is matched by a number of traditions attesting to Rome's supportive and sympathetic attitude toward the Jews. Indeed, much had changed politically and socially in Jewish life in Palestinian at the outset of the third century.

The Greek Cultural Dimension

Integration into the Severan world included a cultural element as well. R. Judah I embraced many practices, attitudes, and values that were current throughout the Greek East, which was then undergoing, as noted, a cultural renaissance. This more general phenomenon is often referred to as the Second Sophistic, a term that focuses, in its narrow sense, on the sophists or orators of this age, although the renaissance it represented included many other areas as well—philosophy, music, sculpture, architecture, athletics and more.[44] It is thus often used as a

---

Rule, which he supposedly heard from Jews and Christians (ibid., 51.6–8). Among the most enigmatic and problematic statements in *SHA* regarding the relationship between the Jews and the Severan rulers are the following: (1) Septimius Severus supposedly forbade conversion to Judaism (as well as Christianity) and exacted heavy penalties from violators (*Severus* 17.1); (2) Elagabalus purportedly transferred the "religions" (?) of Jews and Samaritans as well as the "rites" (?) of the Christians to the palace he had built for the god Elagabal: "in order that the priesthood of Elagabal might include the mysteries of every form of worship" (*Antoninus Elagabalus* 3.5).

[43] *Letter to Africanus* 14.

[44] The term "Second Sophistic" stems from the third-century sophist Philostratus, who describes several scores of intellectuals living from the late first through the mid-third centuries in his book, *Lives of the Sophists (Vitae Sophistarum)*. On Philostratus, see G. Anderson, *Philostratus: Biography and Belles Lettres in the Third Century A.D.* (London, 1986); C.P. Jones, "The Reliability of Philostratus," in *Approaches to*

shorthand for the cultural dimension of the period as a whole.[45] Sophists served as prominent cultural representatives, civic leaders (at times actively involved in resolving crises), participants in the life of their eastern cites and beyond, major benefactors, and public entertainers,[46] and came to represent the most visible element in the revival of Hellenic culture in the Roman East.[47] According to Edwards, the cultural norm created affected the contemporary Christian world as well: "it remains true in the Severan as in the Antonine age that the orator was the model for the writer, and that even at their most academic, Christian theologians are hortatory, homiletic, even strident in their desire to persuade the reader."[48]

Second Sophistic culture found expression in Palestine as well. The province produced a number of local sophists and others who

---

the Second Sophistic (ed. G. Bowersock; University Park, Pa., 1974), 11–16. Philostratus called these intellectuals the Second Sophistic (rather than the New Sophistic) to emphasize their continuity with earlier generations in Greece, and, indeed, one of their priorities was to reinstate Greek Atticism as the favored language of their discourse; see G. Anderson, *The Second Sophistic: A Cultural Phenomenon in the Roman Empire* (London, 1993), 86–100; Swain, *Hellenism and Empire*, 17–64; T. Whitmarsh, *The Second Sophistic* (Oxford, 2005), 41–56.

[45] According to E.L. Bowie ("Greeks and Their Past in the Second Sophistic," *Past and Present* 46 [1970]: 4): "The most characteristic and influential figures of the age, not least in their own eyes, were the sophists. Oratory had always been important in Greek society, before even it had been developed as an art to help the individual to survive or succeed in the fifth-century democracies of Sicily and Athens. Training in rhetoric became a major part of Greek higher education and was for many synonymous with it, contesting the rôle of educator with philosophy." See also Swain, *Hellenism and Empire*, passim; Whitmarsh, *Second Sophistic*, 3–22; Tropper, *Wisdom, Politics, and Historiography*, 136–46.

[46] Philostratus (*Vitae Sophistarum* 613) offers an example of the benefits accruing from the presence and activities of a successful sophist: "So, then, (Heraclides) filled Smyrna with a brilliant company, and helped her too in even more ways besides, as I shall show. A city with a large influx of foreigners, particularly if they are lovers of wisdom, will be prudent in its councils, and prudent too in its assemblies, since it will naturally be wary of being convicted of acting wrongfully in the presence of so many distinguished people; and it will take care of its temples, gymnasia, fountains, and porticoes, so as to appear to offer such facilities for such a throng."

[47] See especially G. Anderson, "The *Pepaideumenos* in Action: Sophists and Their Outlook in the Early Empire," *ANRW* 33.1 (1989), 80–208. Such an assertion usually involves the inclusion in the Sophistic movement of second-century figures such as Galen, Plutarch, Pausanias, Sextus Empiricus, and others. See Swain, *Hellenism and Empire*, passim, esp. pp. 1–13, 409–22; B.P. Reardon, "The Second Sophistic and the Novel," in Bowersock, *Approaches*, 23–29. For a more reserved evaluation of the scope and significance of the Second Sophistic phenomenon, see P.A. Brunt, "The Bubble of the Second Sophistic," *Bulletin of the Institute of Classical Studies* 39 (1994): 25–52.

[48] M. Edwards, "Severan Christianity," in Swain, Harrison, and Elsner, *Severan Culture*, 401.

hailed from Palestine but lived elsewhere in the Empire. The cities of
Gadara and Ashkelon were especially prominent in nurturing such
intellectuals,[49] and in the second and third centuries CE alone 28 local
figures are identified with the Sophistic movement.[50]

The Second Sophistic highlights a number of cultural foci that have
a bearing on our subject: (1) it emphasized Atticism and the return to
the classical Greek world, which included the use of classical Greek
and the treatment of subjects connected with the Greek past (especially the period before Alexander);[51] (2) by embracing an allegiance
to Roman imperial domination, it fostered a desire to become integrated into that world and its civic order; contacts with Roman offi-
cialdom, from the municipal to the provincial and imperial—not to
speak of the imperial family itself—were considered desirable; for
many, receiving imperial honors was the quintessence of recognition;[52]
(3) it endorsed a deep commitment to Hellenism as a universal culture;[53]
and (4) sophists were, first and foremost, teachers, and the inculca-
tion of their values and skills was a desideratum of prime importance;

---

[49] J. Geiger, "Athens in Syria: Greek Intellectuals of Gadara," *Cathedra* 35 (1985):
3–16 (in Hebrew), mentions six well-known figures from Gadara (Menippos, Melea-
gros, Philodemos, Theodoros, Oenomaos, and Apsines), spanning the third century
BCE to the third century CE. From Ashkelon we know of ten figures, eight of whom
were noted by Stephanus of Byzantium and who included philosophers, historians,
and grammarians. Geiger adds two more: Aristus, a philosopher, and Euenus, a poet.
All the above were active in the first centuries BCE and CE.

[50] Geiger, "Athens in Syria"; idem, "Greek Intellectuals of Ascalon," *Cathedra* 60
(1991): 5–16 (in Hebrew); idem, "Notes on the Second Sophistic in Palestine," *Illinois
Classical Studies* 19 (1994): 221–30; idem, "Local Patriotism in the Hellenistic Cities
of Palestine," in *Greece and Rome in Eretz Israel: Collected Essays* (ed. A. Kasher,
U. Rappaport, and G. Fuks; Jerusalem, 1990), 141–50. For this era, Geiger lists Hadrian of Tyre, Theodoros and Apsines of Gadara, Heliodorus of Arabia, Genethius (of
Petra?), as well as Gaius and his son Callinicus, and Gessius, all from Petra. One tradition mentions a sophist by the name of Epiphanius, also a native of Petra. Two other
intellectuals from Arabia were Diophantus and Gaudentius; one Flavius Gaudentius
may have been a descendant of the latter. From Gerasa, Stephanus of Byzantium notes
three orators: Ariston, Plato, and Cerycus. Many more are known from the fourth
century and thereafter. From the renowned school of Gaza, we know of Aeneas, Procopius, Choricius, and John, as well as Procopius, Acacius, Thespesius, Priscio and
Panegyrius, and perhaps Orion at Caesarea. Several rhetors are also recorded from
Neapolis—Andromachus, and perhaps Siricius as well as Ulpian. Finally, one Zosi-
mus, a philologist, Julian, an architect, and Eutocius of Ashkelon, a mathematician,
flourished in late antiquity. All in all, therefore, Palestine had an abundance of Greek
scholars, especially in the second and third centuries CE.

[51] Anderson, *Second Sophistic*, 86–132; Swain, *Hellenism and Empire*, 17–100.

[52] See Bowersock, *Greek Sophists, passim.*

[53] Anderson, *Second Sophistic*, 69–85, 234–46.

nurturing students and creating educational frameworks were part and parcel of this tradition.[54]

In light of the above-noted features of the Second Sophistic, many activities and religio-cultural innovations of R. Judah and his circle gain an extra dimension of significance. While R. Judah I was not a "sophist," many traditions associated with him reflect concerns and behavior similar to those of intellectuals of his era. Evidence for the adoption of such Hellenistic-Roman patterns by R. Judah is far from negligible:

1) Tantamount to the supreme importance of Attic Greek for sophists,[55] Hebrew also enjoyed a golden age among the rabbis of the third century, beginning with R. Judah's redaction of the Mishnah and including the Tosefta and Tannaitic *midrashim*, likewise edited in the third century; this is in contrast to the use of Aramaic, which became the predominant language in the Yerushalmi and early amoraic aggadic *midrashim* only in subsequent centuries.[56] In fact, R. Judah is quoted, albeit in the Bavli, as preferring either Greek or Hebrew, considering Aramaic to be of marginal importance.[57]

2) R. Judah embraced the Jewish past wholeheartedly, much as the sophists focused on the era of classical Greece. In R. Judah's case, however, it was the Temple and its rituals, and indirectly Jerusalem, that occupied a large part of his Mishnah; together with related traditions, these topics constitute almost half of the material therein.[58]

3) R. Judah compiled the Mishnah at about the same time that Ulpian of Tyre undertook the compilation, organization, and systematization of Roman law. Whether there may be some connection, either direct or indirect (for example, as part of an imperial *Zeitgeist* regarding standardization of law), between these two occurrences, merits further consideration.[59]

---

[54] Ibid., 13–46.

[55] Bowie, "Greeks and Their Past," 17–64.

[56] See N. de Lange, "The Revival of the Hebrew Language in the Third Century CE," *JSQ* 3 (1996): 342–58.

[57] *B. Bava Qamma* 82b–83a.

[58] See J. Geiger, "Sophists and Rabbis: Jews and their Past in the Severan Age," in Swain, Harrison, and Elsner, *Severan Culture*, 440–48.

[59] See the comments of A. Tropper, *Wisdom, Politics, and Historiography*, 196; as well as J. Neusner, "The Mishnah in Roman and Christian Contexts," in *The Mishnah*

4) The fourth section of the Mishnah, the "Ethics of the Fathers" (*Pirqei Avot*), commences with a validation of tradition by tracing lines of succession and authority from Moses through the early third century. This parallels similar lines of tradition that were being created by philosophers and church fathers in the second and third centuries.[60]

5) R. Judah's Mishnah contains the earliest-known proto-*seder* in the post 70 era. In some respects this bears a striking resemblance to the Roman symposium, as has been pointed out by scholars on numerous occasions.[61]

6) Three "foreign" practices, singled out in rabbinic literature, are associated with R. Judah—the use of mirrors, fancy hairdos, and Greek.[62]

7) R. Judah made a point of including in his Mishnah an account of the visit of his grandfather, Rabban Gamaliel II, to the bath of Aphrodite in Acco. The latter defended his actions to a non-Jewish philosopher who questioned his presence there.[63] Clearly, the quintessential Greco-Roman practice of visiting a bathhouse was deemed legitimate by R. Judah, in all probability because he found this story to be in line with his own cultural proclivities and therefore appropriate for inclusion in the Mishnah.

8) It has recently been suggested that the palatial residence in Sepphoris, which contains a remarkable mosaic depicting Dionysiac mythology ("The House of Dionysos"), may have belonged to R. Judah—indeed a stunning, though still speculative, theory. If, in fact, this were his residence, then the degree of his hellenization would be far more extensive than previously thought possible.[64]

---

in *Contemporary Perspective: Part 1* (ed. A.J. Avery-Peck and J. Neusner; Leiden, 2002), 121–34; S.A. Stertz, "Roman Legal Codification," in ibid., 149–64.

[60] See in this regard the important study of Tropper, *Wisdom, Politics, and Historiography*, passim.

[61] See especially the seminal study of S. Stein, "The Influence of Symposia Literature on the Literary Form of the Pesaḥ Haggadah," *JJS* 8 (1957): 13–44; L.I. Levine, *Judaism and Hellenism in Antiquity: Conflict or Confluence?* (Seattle, 1998), 119–24. See, however, the comments of B. Bokser (*The Origins of the Seder: The Passover Rite and Early Rabbinic Judaism* [Berkeley, 1984], 50–66), who emphasizes, rather, the diachronic trajectory from earlier times.

[62] *Y. Shabbat* 6:1, 7d.

[63] *M. ʿAvodah Zarah* 3:4.

[64] This suggestion was first raised by Z. Weiss; see R. Talgam and Z. Weiss, *The Mosaics of the House of Dionysos at Sepphoris* (Jerusalem, 2004), 125–31.

Having established R. Judah's predilection for many aspects of Hellenistic culture, we can safely say that the art at Bet She'arim fits comfortably into the wider Severan/Sophistic world. It certainly would account for the use of blatantly Hellenistic motifs as well as the fact that 80 percent of the inscriptions were written in Greek. However, the wider context of the Roman East would also help to explain the first appearance of symbols, particularly the menorah. In the second and third centuries, the use of symbols and icons (for example, statues, statuettes, coins, and gems depicting Artemis of Ephesos and Mithras Tauroctony) became ubiquitous throughout the contemporary Greek world.[65] Another instance of the prominence of symbolic representation at this time is the Sacred Stone brought by the emperor Elagabalus to Rome.[66]

Moreover, even the appearance side by side of Hellenistic and local motifs, as in the art of Bet She'arim, was far from uncommon at this time. A combination of Roman and local Palmyran/Eastern motifs appears on sarcophagi from Palmyra; in one case, the lid depicts the person interred as an Eastern caravan leader while the chest itself shows the same person in Roman dress. In the architectural sphere, the upper half of the façade of one Palmyran temple bears an eastern appearance—a flat roof, deep wall niches, and several stories—while the lower half exhibits typically Roman features.[67]

Therefore, one important stimulus for the representation of Jewish symbols, arguably for the first time in Judea-Palestine, was the growing tendency toward the use of comparable symbols throughout the East.[68] Such a change does not seem to have emerged from internal Jewish

---

[65] J. Elsner, "The Origins of the Icon: Pilgrimage, Religion, and Visual Culture in the Roman East as 'Resistance' to the Centre," in *The Early Roman Empire in the East* (ed. S. Alcock; Oxford, 1997), 184–91.

[66] Herodian, *Roman History* 5.3.4–5.

[67] A. Schmidt-Colinet, "Aspects of 'Romanisation': The Tomb Architecture at Palmyra and Its Decoration," in Alcock, *Early Roman Empire*, 164–70. For aspects of Romanization and its limits in respect to the burial practices of Asia Minor, see S. Cormack, "Funerary Monuments and Mortuary Practice in Roman Asia Minor," in Alcock, *Early Roman Empire*, 137–56. By way of comparison, see Z. Newby, "Art and Identity in Asia Minor," in *Roman Imperialism and Provincial Art* (ed. S. Scott and J. Webster; Cambridge and New York, 2003), 192–213, for a description of the integration of Roman, Hellenic, and local components in the art of second- and early third-century Asia Minor.

[68] See Elsner, "Origins of the Icon," 196: "The icons of pagan polytheism in the east were used during and after the second century AD...as a prime means for ethnic and religious self-assertion.... The particular feature of this use of sacred art for eastern

developments; there is virtually no precedent for displaying the menorah alone, as had been done beforehand only in a Temple/priestly context in late Second Temple Jerusalem, on some lamps from southern
Judea, and on the Arch of Titus. However, in light of the widespread
use of icons in the Roman East, the emergence of the menorah and
other religious artifacts as symbols is more readily explicable (fig. 8).
What we have here may indeed be an instance of Romanization, with
some or many Jews, now, after 212, as citizens of the Empire, responding more favorably to regnant cultural trends and practices than they
had in the past.[69]

We have focused on the Bet She'arim necropolis and its intimate
association with the Patriarchal dynasty, as well as with elements of
the urban elite, synagogue officials, Diaspora leadership, and others.
Nevertheless, as important as these circles may have been, they do not
reflect the whole of third-century Jewish Palestine; the extensive use
of Greek and the art forms discovered there, both pagan and Jewish,
remain for the present largely unattested elsewhere in contemporary
Galilee.

THE ROMAN CATACOMBS: BETWEEN JUDAISM AND CHRISTIANITY

The third factor behind this Jewish artistic renaissance was the spread
of Christianity, which by the third century was beginning to constitute
a noticeable, if not formidable, religious and communal framework in
many places throughout the Roman world.

While our information regarding the Jews in third-century Rome,
aside from the archaeological material, is virtually nil, we are somewhat better informed as regards the Christian community.[70] The Severan era was reportedly a favorable time for Christians, as land was
already being acquired by the church. At this time, Callistus (awarded

---

self-assertion was that it never denied the logic of empire: it never argued for nationalism or separatism."

[69] See Hecataeus on the tendency of Jews to adopt foreign burial and marital practices (*GLA*, 1:29).

[70] See P. Lampe, *From Paul to Valentinus: Christians at Rome in the First Two
Centuries* (Minneapolis, 2003), 35–41; J.R. Curran, *Pagan City and Christian Capital:
Rome in the Fourth Century* (Oxford, 2000), 35–41; J. Elsner, "Inventing Christian
Rome: The Role of Early Christian Art," in Edwards and Woolf, *Rome the Cosmopolis*,
73–74.

the title *pontifex maximus* when he became bishop of Rome)[71] was appointed to organize a Christian cemetery on the Via Appia.

The third century was also a time of periodic persecutions aimed at Christians, both in Rome and elsewhere, the best known being those initiated by Decius and Diocletian. While the severity of these crises is difficult to assess (Christian authors tended to exaggerate such events), they were generally of relatively short duration. Already in the middle of that century, the bishop of Rome, Cornelius, noted that his church included 46 presbyters, 7 deacons, 7 subdeacons, 42 acolytes, 52 exorcists, readers, and doorkeepers, and assisted more than 1500 widows and poor through its charity.[72]

Nevertheless, the Christians remained a relatively small minority of the Roman population at the turn of the fourth century, perhaps 10 percent of the city's inhabitants (often estimated to have numbered about 800,000, although these are very speculative figures). The physical, demographic, and institutional Christianization of the city was a gradual process, even after the "conversion" of Constantine, and it is only from the turn of the fifth century onward that one can speak of *Roma Cristiana*.[73]

In the third century, and even beyond, Jews and Christians shared a common text and similar rituals (especially when compared to their pagan neighbors). Furthermore, their catacombs (and perhaps areas of residence as well) were found in the same locations. It is therefore not hard to imagine that these phenomena played a major role in shaping the nature of the Jewish catacombs in Rome, including their epigraphical and artistic evidence.

These catacombs consisted of passageways or galleries lined with layers of horizontal burial niches (*loculi*) and painted burial chambers (*cubicula*) containing both *arcosolia* (arched recesses) and *loculi*, in addition to sarcophagi (fig. 9). The artistic remains in these catacombs are far

---

[71] This is the interpretation often given to a comment of Tertullian, *On Modesty* 1.
[72] *Eccles. Hist.* 6.43.11.
[73] Throughout almost the entire fourth century, a traditional pagan urban framework maintained the temples, priesthoods, festivals, rites, and games. As formulated by Krautheimer: "The Church, though backed by the imperial court and by the urban masses inside the city, had a hard time asserting her position. The struggle, at times bitter, ended early in the fifth century with the triumph of the Church, no longer contested. Only from then on does the map of Rome increasingly reflect the city's Christian character, and this remains so unto 1970" (R. Krautheimer, *Rome: Profile of a City, 312–1308* [Princeton, 1980], 33).

more plentiful than those from other Jewish burial sites of late antiquity. Relatively few utilize Hellenistic motifs (e.g., Nike, Tyche, or the seasons of the year); many depictions are neutral (floral and geometric designs, with some fish and animals); and a considerable number have Jewish symbols. Leon counted 144 representations of the menorah, with representations of other Jewish symbols ranked as follows: *lulav* (34), *ethrog* (27), flask (27), *shofar* (14), and Torah shrine or *aron* (6) (fig. 10).[74] These Jewish symbols are concentrated mainly in two types of objects: on the plaster of slabs and bricks that seal the *loculi* along the galleries where most of the burials are found, and on fragments of gold glass.[75]

The valuable artistic evidence from the catacombs is surpassed only by the treasure trove of some 600 inscriptions found there. Greek appears in approximately 74 percent of the inscriptions, and together with Latin in another 6 percent; Latin is used alone in 17 percent of the inscriptions, and 3 percent are in either Hebrew or Aramaic.[76]

What, then, are the implications of these finds? First and foremost, we must examine the context. The Jewish catacombs resemble the Christian ones in many respects: they are underground burial places with similar chronologies, plans, artistic designs, gold glass, painted rooms, sarcophagi, and inscriptions. It is not unlikely that in many cases Christians and Jews used the same workshops.[77] As noted, there was also geographical propinquity between the catacombs of these two groups, as both the Jewish and Christian communities were scattered and fragmented throughout the first centuries CE. Finally, the use of art as a vehicle for symbolic expression surfaces at this time in Jewish, Christian, and contemporary pagan contexts.[78]

At the same time, however, there are also significant differences. The plaques used for sealing the *loculi* in Christian settings are usually plain with almost no decoration or artistic representation. The more

---

[74] See H.J. Leon, *The Jews of Ancient Rome* (Philadelphia, 1960), 196. New material has been identified since 1960; however no new statistics have yet been published.

[75] Gold glass is made by adhering gold leaf to the base of a glass vessel, etching a design and inscription in the gold, and then overlaying it with a thin layer of colorless glass.

[76] D. Noy, *Foreigners at Rome: Citizens and Strangers* (London, 2000), 264. In another publication from the same year, Noy mentions slightly different numbers: Greek—73 percent; together with Latin—7 percent; Latin—17 percent; and Hebrew or Aramaic—3 percent ("The Jews in Italy in the First to Sixth Centuries C.E.," in *The Jews of Italy: Memory and Identity*, [ed. B.D. Cooperman and B. Garvin; Bethesda, Md., 2000], 56).

[77] L.V. Rutgers, "Archaeological Evidence for the Interaction of Jews and Non-Jews in Late Antiquity," *AJA* 96 (1992): 101–18.

[78] See Newby, "Art at the Crossroads?" 233–49.

elaborate ones are usually reserved for the individual *cubicula* of the more wealthy classes. Christian inscriptions are frequently personal in content, while the Jewish ones repeatedly note synagogue or communal titles. The use of gold-glass cups is far from uncommon in pagan and Christian Rome, but when the Jews adopted this widespread practice they decorated their cups with Jewish motifs (fig. 11).

In the realm of art, Christians were far freer in their use of both pagan motifs and biblical scenes. Intriguingly, it has been shown that Christians used four times as many scenes from the Hebrew Bible as from the New Testament.[79] In contrast, the Jews used neither human figural art nor biblical scenes in the decoration of their catacombs.

While the evidence of the language of the inscriptions and names appearing therein seems to indicate a high degree of acculturation,[80] other aspects of the Jewish epigraphical material point in a very different direction. Whereas inscriptions from other Jewish communities, such as Sardis and Aphrodisias, highlight Jewish involvement in civic and imperial political institutions, as well as the participation of non-Jews in the Jewish community,[81] the inscriptions from Rome ignore the civic dimension entirely (if it even existed there) and focus solely on the Jewish institution par excellence, i.e., the synagogue. Synagogue officials are mentioned some 40 times in the approximately 130 synagogue-related inscriptions, the latter number constituting more than 20 percent of all catacomb inscriptions. The remaining inscriptions often highlight, inter alia, many members of the community who were specifically identified as being affiliated with this central institution. This evidence clearly points to the more insular framework of the Jews residing in the imperial capital.

The Roman material may also be relevant to a wider issue that has recently commanded scholarly attention, i.e., the relationship between Jews and Christians prior to the triumph of Christianity in the fourth

---

[79] R.M. Jensen, *Understanding Early Christian Art* (London, 2000), 68–69.

[80] Jewish onomastic practices followed those of Roman society: "By comparing the Latin names in third and fourth century C.E. Jewish funerary inscriptions with contemporary onomastic data in non-Jewish inscriptions, it can be shown that in this respect the Jewish epitaphs reflect remarkably closely onomastic trends that are general in late antiquity. The gradual disintegration of the traditional *duo* and *tria nomina* system, formal changes in the traditional Roman naming system, as well as the preference of specific *gentilicia* and *cognomina* over others are all typically Late Ancient developments" (L.V. Rutgers, *The Jews in Late Ancient Rome: Evidence of Cultural Interaction in the Roman Diaspora* [Leiden, 1995], 163).

[81] See W. Ameling, *Inscriptiones Judaicae Orientis, 2: Kleinasien* (Tübingen, 2004), 70–123, 224–97.

century and thereafter; or, phrasing the issue in contemporary parlance, when did Judaism and Christianity "part ways"?[82]

The implications of the catacomb material in this regard are complex. On the one hand, the many similarities between Christian and Jewish burials during the third and fourth centuries (and most often, as noted, they were located in the same general locale in the city's suburbs) would lead us to assume a great deal of communication, parallel developments, and perhaps even cooperation, between these groups. There is no way of assessing whether other groups in the city shared these same practices (and if so, to what degree). No catacomb, for example, has been discovered that might relate to a well-defined pagan community.[83] Jews and Christians clearly acted in tandem, no matter how we might define the nature and extent of this parallel activity. From this perspective, it would be difficult to conclude that there was any serious enmity or hostility between these communities.

On the other hand, the archaeological remains preclude any assumption that the boundary lines between the two groups were largely blurred, if not entirely non-existent. As noted, many aspects of the Jewish remains reflect an exclusiveness and insularity that bespeaks the *mentalité* of a very distinct ethnic-religious group seeking to preserve its unique identity and culture. Jewish art differed strikingly from that of the local Christians, both in what it emphasized (Jewish symbols) and in what it ignored or perhaps rejected (i.e., figural scenes, biblical and otherwise). Moreover, the exclusive focus in many inscriptions on the synagogue and its officials further highlights the insular world of the local community.

Indeed, the ways seem to have parted, as the differences between Jews and Christians in Rome are many and of primary importance to each group. But even with the apparent parting, a not insignificant degree of similarity and commonality remained. Hostility does not seem to have been the order of the day between Jew and Christian in Rome, although, admittedly, it would be rather unusual for archaeological material to reflect such a dynamic. Within the larger pagan

---

[82] For a collection of recent studies relating to a late date for the "parting of the ways," see A.H. Becker and A.Y. Reed, eds., *The Ways that Never Parted: Jews and Christians in Late Antiquity and the Early Middle Ages* (Tübingen, 2003).

[83] The presence of some pagan motifs within both Jewish and Christian contexts, to which we have made reference above, is irrelevant. Such art now appears in a plethora of nonpagan contexts and was clearly accepted by at least some Jews and Christians.

surroundings of Rome's sprawling metropolis (sometimes referred to as a cosmopolis)[84] of the third and early fourth centuries, both groups probably were regarded by the "mainstream" as the "other" and perhaps they even saw themselves as outsiders, thereby minimizing whatever tensions might have otherwise surfaced between them.[85]

CONCLUSION

We have seen that a renewed and reinvigorated expression of art emerged among Jews in the third century at geographically disparate sites across the Empire. From Dura in the East through Bet She'arim in the Galilee and westward to Rome, each Jewish community—reacting to different stimuli in vastly differing historical contexts—turned to a heretofore unutilized repertoire of symbols and images to express its beliefs and reinforce its identity as a community and as individuals. The one identifiable commonality between these places, in addition to their being part of the Empire, is that each was associated with a city or setting[86] in which the interaction between Jew and non-Jew may well have constituted a significant factor in the above-noted process. Nevertheless, in the end, there was no single all-embracing cause for the emergence of this art among Jews, but rather a series of cultural and religious developments in the Roman world that impacted various Jewish communities in different ways.[87] As a result, the art of each was quite diverse—the use of symbols, but very limited figural art (Rome); the use of Jewish symbols and figural art (though no biblical scenes)

---

[84] Edwards and Woolf, "Cosmopolis," 1–20.

[85] Over the course of the fourth and fifth centuries, anti-Jewish and anti-Judaic sentiment became far more public and ubiquitous in both imperial and ecclesiastical circles, as well as on the street; see J. Parkes, *The Conflict of the Church and the Synagogue: A Study in the Origins of Antisemitism* (Cleveland, 1961), 151–95.

[86] Although Bet She'arim itself was probably not in the category of city, the fact remains that starting from the Patriarchs themselves, the people brought there for burial, undoubtedly a significant majority, hailed from the cities of Palestine and Syria.

[87] On the differences in Christian art between Dura and Rome, see Grabar, *Christian Iconography*, 19–30; Perkins, *Art of Dura-Europos*, 55. The art produced in the Severan era was likewise multifaceted: "It is impossible to characterize Severan art as having any one style or theme. Instead, each object or monument forms part of a bigger picture showing the crucial role that art continued to play in expressing the identities of, and relationships between, people, emperors, and gods across the Roman world" (Newby, "Art at the Crossroads?" 249).

together with a series of blatantly pagan images (Bet She'arim); and a wide-ranging use of figural and biblical art with little "pagan" imagery (except for destroyed Philistine idols), but with the absence of Jewish symbols *per se* (Dura).[88]

Having said this, two caveats are called for. First, one should remember that there is a difference between a public display of art in a synagogue such as Dura (a public venue par excellence) and the type of art appearing in the *necropoleis* of Rome and Bet She'arim, be they more communally organized, as the former, or more individually (or familially) oriented, as the latter. In other words, are we running the risk of mixing the proverbial "apples and oranges"? Thus, the richness of Dura stands in striking contrast to the far more modest representation of the burial areas where few people entered and where the lighting was minimal. Nevertheless, having taken note of this difference, the fact remains that the art emerging at this time, whatever its location, was new to the Jewish scene generally and continued to function with similar diversity, both in synagogues and cemeteries, for centuries to come. Whatever the differences in third-century settings, the art that appears now served as a basis for further expansion and development until the very end of antiquity.

Secondly, were these artistic expressions a completely synchronic phenomenon, solely dependent upon the immediate contextual setting? To what degree might these communities have been influenced by one another or by some as yet unidentifiable and untapped reservoir of Jewish artistic tradition already existing in the third century? In a word, was there some sort of common Judaism at the time that might have contributed, actively or passively, to the emergence of this art?[89] For example, in considering the two *necropoleis*, we see the following artistic similarities: the use of the menorah as a symbol (in contrast to its status in Dura as representative of the Temple); the use of other symbols such as the *shofar, lulav,* and *ethrog*; and the appearance of some pagan themes, especially on sarcophagi and in several *cubicula* paintings. The use of pagan themes on marble sarcophagi in Rome and Bet She'arim may attest to the reliance on workshops

---

[88] At Dura, the menorah appears on several occasions not as a symbol, but as a representation of a specific object closely linked to the Tabernacle and Temple.

[89] See L.I. Levine, "'Common Judaism': The Contribution of the Ancient Synagogue," in *Common Judaism: Explorations in Second-Temple Judaism* (ed. W.O. McCready and A. Reinhartz; Minneapolis, 2008), 27–46, 232–37.

that were frequented by people from all sectors of society, where Jews could have acquired such items while adapting them to meet their specific needs. Finally, in noting the commonalities between all three sites discussed above, we should mention the motif of the façade of the Temple or a Torah shrine flanked by one or two *menorot*. These simultaneous appearances, especially at such an early stage of Jewish artistic development in late antiquity, may well be a product of a common artistic tradition, but such an assumption remains unsubstantiated for the present.

With regard to the subject of this volume, we may ask whether the year 70 made a difference with respect to the Jews' use of art. Any response to such a query, however, must remain somewhat ambiguous. On the one hand, as we have seen above, there was a change, but it took place much later and transpired in very different contextual situations that had nothing whatsoever to do with the year 70. Thus, from this perspective, the answer to the above question should be negative. Nevertheless, it is important to point out that certain kinds of changes regarding art, albeit of a very different nature than what we have been discussing, seem to have occurred already in early second-century CE Palestine and may well have been connected to the destruction of Jerusalem and the absence of its Temple and traditional leadership groups.

Two instances stand out in this respect. One is the aforementioned mishnaic tradition of R. Gamaliel's visit to the Acco bathhouse dedicated to Aphrodite, and his pronouncement, in response to the question posed by one Proclus, that such behavior is perfectly acceptable if the statues in question are not intended for worship purposes.[90] The second instance is the appearance of pagan deities and temples on the coins of two Jewish cities, Tiberias and Sepphoris; in the pre-70 era, these same cities refrained from depicting any figural images, much less ones with explicitly pagan motifs, on their coins. Explanations have been offered for each of these two rather surprising occurrences, usually in the nature of extenuating circumstances or as reflecting an attitude that such art is to be considered merely decorative. However, if indeed one were to accept the Gamaliel account as historical (and not merely later literary fiction), and the coins as reflecting a change in Jewish attitudes toward art, in large part as an accommodation to

---

[90] See above, *m. 'Avodah Zarah* 3:4.

second-century Galilean political and economic realities,[91] then these changes might well have been, at least in part, a result of the events of 70 CE and the relaxation of earlier prohibitions and inhibitions. These considerations nevertheless remain quite speculative for the present, representing rather isolated *sui generis* occurrences, and have been dealt with more extensively elsewhere.[92] If the above-noted evidence is indeed less than compelling and the events of 70 CE in themselves had only a marginal impact on Jewish artistic expression, then—as argued above—the dramatic change in Jewish art first surfaced in the early third century owing to the unusual circumstances that coalesced only at that time.

---

[91] For a far more radical interpretation of such evidence, see S. Schwartz, *Imperialism and Jewish Society* (Princeton, 2001), 129–61.
[92] See my forthcoming *Visual Judaism*, Chapter 3.

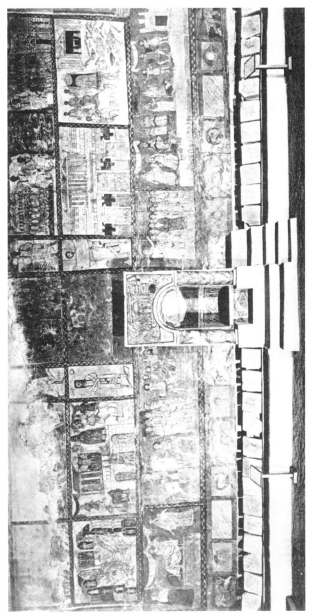

Fig. 1: Dura Europos synagogue, western wall. Courtesy of the Hebrew University Institute of Archaeology, Slide Archive, no. 9378.

Fig. 2: Dura Europos, temple of Zeus Theos. Courtesy of the Hebrew University Institute of Archaeology, Slide Archive, no. 24564.

Fig. 3: Dura Europos, baptistery in Christian building. Courtesy of the Hebrew University Institute of Archaeology, Slide Archive, no. 26354.

Fig. 4: Dura Europos, mithraeum altar. After "Mithraeum at Dura Europos." Online at: http://www.mithraeum.eu/monumenta/mithraeum_dura_europos&pid=120.

Fig. 5: Bet She'arim, catacombs 14 and 20. After E. Stern (ed.), *New Encyclopedia of Archaeological Excavations in the Holy Land* (Jerusalem, 1993), 1:236.

Fig. 6: Bet She'arim, mausoleum over catacomb 11. After E. Stern (ed.), *New Encyclopedia of Archaeological Excavations in the Holy Land* (Jerusalem, 1993), 1:244.

Fig. 7: Bet She'arim, sarcophagus fragment of Leda and the swan. After
E. Stern (ed.), *New Encyclopedia of Archaeological Excavations in the Holy
Land* (Jerusalem, 1993), 1:247.

Fig. 8: Bet Sheʿarim, menorah relief in catacomb 3. After E. Stern (ed.), *New Encyclopedia of Archaeological Excavations in the Holy Land* (Jerusalem, 1993), 1:243.

Fig. 9: Vigna Randanini, catacomb gallery. After H.J. Leon, *The Jews of Ancient Rome* (Philadelphia, 1960), Plate VI/8.

Fig. 10: Monteverde, plaque for sealing loculi. Courtesy of Hebrew University Institute of Archaeology, Slide Archive, no. 22426.

Fig. 11: Gold glass with Jewish symbols, probably from catacombs in Rome. After C.L. Avery, "Early Christian Gold Glass," *Bulletin of the Metropolitan Museum of Art* 16 (1921): 171, fig. 1.

PART IV

SACRED TEXTS: EXEGESIS AND LITURGY

LEGAL MIDRASH BETWEEN HILLEL AND RABBI AKIVA: DID 70 CE MAKE A DIFFERENCE?

Paul Mandel

Introduction

The Second Temple period has been called by James Kugel an "age of interpretation."[1] During this period, he writes, "the interpreters of Scripture enjoyed an increasing prominence and authority.... They were, first of all, the guardians of writings preserved from Israel's ancient past. With their bookman's skills, they could explain what that past was, what had been set down in writing...they could likewise look deeply into the words of ancient lore and traditions.... Clearly, interpreting such ancient texts was a matter of more than merely antiquarian interest: *the interpretation of Scripture...determined...the significance of divine law and its application to daily life.*"[2]

According to this view, the process by which the scriptural text became the object of scrutiny, based upon a set of assumptions about the divine yet cryptic nature of that text,[3] was gradual and steady. That process is thought to have culminated near the end of the period in what would seem to be a natural development: the burgeoning of legal (as well as nonlegal) textual activity, through which the text of the Bible, and specifically that of the Torah, given by God to Moses on Mount Sinai, could be made to answer to new legal situations, and, through proper hermeneutic techniques, to generate new sets of laws. This view finds the roots of the exegetical activity we normally define as *midrash* planted deep in the soil of the Second Temple Judaic intellectual milieu: Scripture viewed as a book of instruction, as it undoubtedly

---

[1] J.L. Kugel, *Traditions of the Bible: A Guide to the Bible As It Was at the Start of the Common Era* (Cambridge and London, 1998), 2–3 (in Chapter 1: "The World of Ancient Biblical Interpreters").

[2] Ibid., 9 (my emphasis).

[3] See ibid., 14–19, concerning four assumptions which, according to Kugel, underlay the practice of scriptural interpretation during the Second Temple period. The first of these assumptions, "universally shared by ancient interpreters," is that the Bible is "a fundamentally cryptic document" (15). However, I doubt that this assumption was a common one in antiquity; see below.

was during this period, meant that not only biblical narrative, but also, and especially, biblical law, needed to be actively "searched out" and "divined" to bring forth its rich harvest of law and moral directives. This became especially significant with the disappearance, in postexilic times, of the prophet and his divinely inspired instruction.[4] Indeed, a central role in the legal textual study of Scripture has been ascribed to Ezra, named "scribe of the divine law."[5]

Ephraim E. Urbach, in his early study on the *soferim* (scribes),[6] also located the origins of midrashic activity—specifically legal midrashic activity—in the Second Temple period. Urbach, however, distinguished between the traditional institutional character of early halakhah, where laws were legislated not through textual exegesis but on the basis of the authority of the institutions and of those leading them, on the one hand; and the function of the scribes, whom he views as a group of biblical explicators whose initial activity was concerned with the preservation and elucidation of the biblical text, teaching and interpreting the text, and analyzing and solving the cruxes of interpretation inherent in the text, on the other. These scribes used standard text-oriented techniques in their interpretation of words and laws, including, for example, the comparison of parallel passages and the investigation of peculiarities of style. Although, according to Urbach, scribal activity originated *outside* the traditional purview of legal discussion (which was concentrated in the activity of the jurists comprising the Sanhedrin), the recognition of textual exegesis as a valid source of law slowly

---

[4] Thus Kugel: "[T]he Babylonian conquest...seems to mark the dawn of a new age with regard to Scripture and its interpretation" (ibid., 2); "[T]he interpreters of Scripture enjoyed an increasing prominence and authority in the period following the Babylonian exile" (ibid., 9).

[5] See Kugel, ibid.; W. Bacher, *Die exegetische Terminologie der jüdischen Traditionsliteratur* (2 vols.; Leipzig, 1905), 1: 25; J.N. Epstein, *Prolegomena to the Tannaitic Literature* (Tel-Aviv; Jerusalem, 1957), 502–3 (in Hebrew); M. Gertner, "Terms of Scriptural Interpretation: A Study in Hebrew Semantics," *BSOAS* 25 (1962): 5; M. Elon, *Jewish Law: History, Sources, Principles* (trans. B. Auerbach and M.J. Sykes; Jerusalem, 1994), 1: 275–76, 308–14; M. Fishbane, "From Scribalism to Rabbinism: Perspectives on the Emergence of Classical Judaism," in *The Sage in Israel and the Ancient Near East* (ed. J.G. Gammie and L.G. Perdue; Winona Lake, 1990), 441; J. Fraenkel, *Midrash veAggadah* (Tel-Aviv, 1997), 27; idem, *Darkei Ha-Aggadah veha-Midrash* (Givatayim, 1990), 11–15.

[6] E.E. Urbach, "The *Derashah* as the Basis for the *Halakhah* and the Problem of the *Soferim*," *Tarbiz* 27 (1958): 166–82 (in Hebrew). This study was later incorporated into, and expanded, in idem, *The Halakhah: Its Sources and Development* (trans. R. Posner; Jerusalem, 1986), 93–108 (Chapter 7: "Interpretation as the Source of *Halakhah*").

infiltrated the legal system, "until it became a source of law equal in status to all the others."[7] Referring to the famous instance of Hillel's answer to the "sons of Bathyra" who questioned him concerning the permissibility of offering the paschal sacrifice on the Sabbath during a year when the fourteenth of Nisan, the day of the sacrifice, happened to fall on a Saturday,[8] Urbach understands Hillel's answers— including both textual legal midrash (expounding the law from the text of the Torah) and an appeal to the authority of tradition (stating that the law was transmitted to him by his teachers, Shemaiah and Avtalyon)—as pointing to a time when textual legal exegesis was an acceptable approach, but did not yet enjoy full authority in itself for the establishment of a law. Thus, the time of Hillel (late first century BCE) may be seen as a turning point in the ascent of the relevance of exegetical techniques for the determination of law. These techniques became increasingly important in the period after the destruction of the Second Temple, ultimately providing a powerful set of hermeneutic tools for the explication of law from the text of the Torah.

The analyses of Kugel and Urbach represent two views concerning the origins of *midrash halakhah*—the textual analysis of Scripture for the purpose of drawing legal conclusions from it. The former view, of Kugel (and others), lays emphasis on the "need for interpretation"[9] as a catalyst for the development of law from the biblical text, existent already from earliest, postexilic times, while the latter opinion, Urbach's, locates the increasing dominance of legal textual interpretation near the end of the Second Temple period, as a pursuit parallel to that of the traditional, authoritative institutions of law, competing— and ultimately conquering—the more ancient development of law as transmission of traditional custom and decree. Both views see the Second Temple period as the locus for the pre-history of the *midrash halakhah* of the rabbinic period; and so for them, the destruction of the Temple in 70 CE would not seem to have played a significant role in the development of midrashic activity. Rather, the legal activity of the Tannaitic and Amoraic rabbinic periods is seen as a natural continuation of that of the Second Temple period, involving interesting

---

[7] Ibid., 100.
[8] *T. Pisḥa* 4:13–14; *y. Pesaḥim* 6, 1 (33a); *b. Pesaḥim* 66a.
[9] Kugel, *Traditions*, 3.

new developments and branching off into new areas, but having its roots firmly in the ground of Second Temple period Judaism.

Two related phenomena of the Second Temple period would seem to lend support to these views of the ancient roots of legal midrash. One is the nature of the activity of the "scribes" (*soferim*), already mentioned above, in the context of the interpretation of Scripture; many scholars view the activity of these "scribes" as connected to the development of legal midrash.[10] The other is the activity of the Pharisees as a precursor of later rabbinic legal textual exegesis—a view that would seem to be supported by Josephus' descriptions of the Pharisees as "*exegetai*" of the ancestral laws.[11]

In the present paper I will analyze several instructive passages lying at the intersection of law and text, cited in rabbinic literature in the names of Hillel and Rabbi Akiva. The passages are notable for their use of the verb *darash* to describe what seems to be the legal exegetical activity of these sages, and have been understood as examples of legal midrash, indicative of the centrality of textual interpretation in this activity. However, as I shall demonstrate, the verb *darash* and its cognate noun, *midrash*, as used in these passages, do not necessarily imply

---

[10] See S. Lieberman, "Rabbinic Interpretation of Scripture," in *Hellenism in Jewish Palestine* (New York, 1962), 47 ("[T]he Soferim were grammarians, and they engaged in the same activity which was pursued by the Alexandrian scholars. They elaborated the so called *Midrash* [interpretation] of the Bible"); Epstein, *Prolegomena to the Tannaitic Literature* ("The *soferim* after Ezra continued the activity of Ezra the scribe, explicated the *book* of the Torah and taught it to the people," 503 [emphasis in original]); Urbach, "The *Derasha* as Basis," ("In the circles of the *soferim*, the interpreters of the Torah and its explicators, the *derasha* was born," 173); I. Heinemann, "On the Development of Technical Terms for the Interpretation of Scripture: *Darash*," *Leshonenu* 14 (1946): 182–89 (in Hebrew); C. Albeck, "*Ha-halakhot veha-derashot*," in *Alexander Marx Jubilee Volume* (New York, 1950), Hebrew section, 1–8; M. Fishbane, "The Role of Scribes in the Transmission of Biblical Literature," in *Biblical Interpretation in Ancient Israel* (Oxford, 1985), 24–37; Kugel, *Traditions*, 2–3, 9–11; D. Weiss Halivni, *Midrash, Mishnah, and Gemara: The Jewish Predilection for Justified Law* (Cambridge, Mass., 1986), 18–19.

[11] See J.Z. Lauterbach, "The Pharisees and their Teachings," *HUCA* 6 (1929): 91–112; R. Travers Herford, *The Pharisees* (London, 1924), 63–70; Epstein, *Prolegomena to the Tannaitic Literature*, 512; Elon, *Jewish Law*, 314 ("The Pharisees...substantiated the validity of [Pharisaic] traditions through exegesis connecting the laws in the tradition to Biblical verses"), cf. 308–17. A third related phenomenon of the Second Temple period is the legal exegetical activity of the Qumran community, as exhibited in the writings of the sect. The nature of this activity and its relationship to later, rabbinic, exegesis and law is complex and cannot be dealt with here, although I will discuss it briefly below.

textual exegesis; indeed, a reconsideration of these passages as well as others of the Tannaitic period suggests that textual interpretation of Scripture, as a technique concentrating on the details of the scriptural text in its *written* form, becomes prominent only from the time of Rabbi Akiva. This requires a revision of the current understanding, set out above, of the activities of the "scribes" of the Second Temple period and the Pharisees' relationship to textual scriptural exegesis. Finally, I shall suggest various reasons for the appearance of the new approach of legal scriptural exegesis at this time; these may presuppose either a direct or an indirect influence of the dramatic events surrounding the destruction of the Temple, and its aftermath, on the development of legal midrash.

I. Hillel Expounds[12] Lay Language (doresh leshon hedyot)

The following passage has been cited as early as the geonic period as a demonstration of the clever, lawyerly use of midrash in making the technical wording of a document—here a marriage contract (*ketubbah*)—say something other than its "plain" meaning.

> דרש הלל הזקן לשון הדיוט: כשהיו בני אלכסנדריא מקדשין נשים, אחר
> בא וחוטפה מן השוק. ובא מעשה לפני חכמים, בקשו לעשות בניהן
> ממזרין. אמר להם הלל הזקן: "הוציאו לי כתובת אמותיכם." הוציאו לו
> וכתוב בה: "כשתכנסי לביתי תהוי לי לאנתו כדת משה וישראל."

> Hillel the Elder expounded lay language (*darash leshon hedyot*): When the Alexandrians would betroth a woman, someone else would come and abduct her from the street (lit., "the marketplace"). The incident came before the Sages who considered declaring the children [of the marriage

---

12 I have chosen to use the English word "expound" to translate *darash* in the passages cited in this paper. This verb is attested in English in two main definitions: 1) to set forth, declare, state in detail (doctrines, ideas, principles); 2) to explain (what is difficult or obscure), interpret, comment on (a passage or an author); see *The Oxford English Dictionary* (Oxford, 1961), 3:444–45 (and see also ibid., §3—to give a particular interpretation to, to construe in a specific manner). In my discussion here, I will argue that *darash*, as used in Tannaitic literature, should be understood primarily according to the first definition, which, in a legal context, means declaring a ruling in public. Indeed, in almost all passages using *darash* in Tannaitic literature it may be assumed that the "setting forth" and declaration of laws and principles takes place in a public setting. For a detailed discussion, see P. Mandel, "'*Darash Rabbi Peloni*': A New Study," *Dappim: Research in Literature* 16–17 (2008): 27–54 (in Hebrew). See also idem, "The Origins of *Midrash* in the Second Temple Period," in *Current Trends in the Study of Midrash* (ed. C. Bakhos; Leiden, 2006), 9–34.

with the abductor] to be illegitimate. Hillel the Elder said to them: Bring
me the marriage contract (*ketubbah* [that is, the document by which
they were betrothed to the first man]) of your mothers. They brought [it]
to him, and therein was written: "When you will enter my house, you
will be my wife in accord with the law of Moses and Israel."[13]

Consider the words of the tenth-century Babylonian scholar, Hai
Gaon:

> The essence of the matter is that Hillel the Elder…would examine in
> detail the language which laymen wrote in their documents and inter-
> pret it *in the same way that they [i.e., the rabbis] examined in detail and
> interpreted the words of the Torah, not by the simple meaning but by
> other interpretations.*[14]

Rav Hai views Hillel's approach to the text of the *ketubbah* as one of
midrash, understood as the detailed analysis and interpretation of the
text, leading to "other" interpretations that are not the "simple meaning" of that text. Such is the power of midrash that it can generate (or
discover) *other* meanings, through careful attention to textual idiosyn-
crasies.[15] The original domain for this method of interpretation is seen
to be Scripture; Hillel's contribution, accordingly, was to apply such

---

[13] *T. Ketubbot* 4:9–10, and see parallels in *y. Ketubbot* 4:9 (28d–29a); *b. Baba
Metziʿa* 104a. (All translations in this article are the author's [with the help of existing
translations] unless otherwise noted.) This is the first in a series of seven rulings cited
together in the Tosefta text, where the verb *darash* is used to describe legal activity in
relation to a specific use of language. It will be instructive to cite here also the second
ruling: "R. Meir expounded (*darash*): He who receives a field [as a tenant farmer] from
his fellow, and once acquiring it, neglects it—an estimate is made of how much [the
field] is potentially able to produce [and he, the lessee, pays that sum to him]; for so
he writes to him [in the leasing contract]: 'If I neglect and do not work [the land], I
shall pay you from the best produce.'"

[14] Citation in the name of Rav Hai by R. Judah al-Bargeloni, as quoted by Nahmanides in his *Novellae* to *b. Baba Metziʿa* 104a, and by R. Zechariah b. Judah Agmati,
Digest to Baba Metziʿa (facsimile edition, ed. J. Levin; London, 1961), 143 (in Hebrew;
my emphasis).

[15] Modern scholars have similarly understood the activity of *darash* in this passage
as implying a method of textual interpretation; see Urbach, *The Halakhah*, 101; Elon,
Jewish Law, 424–25. Elon emphasizes the importance of this definition of *midrash* for
the development of halakhah: "[T]his type of interpretation undoubtedly played a significant role in the development of the Jewish legal system" (ibid., 429). For an interpretation of Hillel's approach in this passage similar to the one that I am proposing
here, see A. Schremer, "'[T]he[y] Did Not Read in the Sealed Book': Qumran Halakhic
Revolution and the Emergence of Torah Study in Second Temple Judaism," in *Historical Perspectives: From the Hasmoneans to Bar Kokhba in Light of the Dead Sea Scrolls*
(ed. D.M. Goodblatt, A. Pinnick, and D.R. Schwartz; Leiden, 2001), 120–21.

methods, heretofore used for the interpretation of sacred texts, to the dynamic and creative interpretation of lay documents.

However, Hillel's interpretation of the text of the marriage document seems to be precisely the literal one, one that may indeed be seen as the "simple meaning" of the text. As Nahmanides, in a critique of Hai's approach, queries: "What 'midrash' is there here?!"[16] In his analysis of these passages, Nahmanides first suggests understanding Hillel's midrash as a more elaborate interpretation than one that might at first have been given to the words of the contract. According to that suggestion, the rejected interpretation imputed a more literal, constrained meaning to the words: the (first) husband's stipulation to the woman, "you shall become my wife when you enter my house," would be construed to imply that he intended to have her become *completely and finally* wedded to him "upon [her] entrance to [his] house," while prior to her entrance she was *only betrothed* to him (that betrothal nonetheless disallowing any other legal marital union on her part). On such a literal reading, her children by the second man would indeed be illegitimate (*mamzerim*). Hillel, according to this suggestion, would be then understood to have interpreted the phrase more flexibly, inferring from the phrase "you shall become my wife" that prior to her entrance to his house she was not the (first) man's wife *in any manner*.[17] However, as Nahmanides recognizes, it is precisely this latter "interpretation" that would seem to be the simple and literal

---

[16] See *Novellae* of Nahmanides to *b. Baba Metziʿa* 104a. This specific criticism is directed towards R. Meir's adjacent ruling, but Nahmanides' critique includes a similar discussion of Hillel's ruling. Cf. also Nahmanides' puzzlement regarding R. Meir's ruling, ibid. (cf. the wording as cited in n. 13 above): "This ruling [seems to be] trivial: do conditional clauses in monetary contracts require a special edict of the sages in order to be upheld?!"

[17] Regarding R. Meir's ruling, Nahmanides similarly suggests that the lessee's written stipulation, that he pay the owner of the land if he does not work on it, might be construed as obligating him to compensate the owner only for the *depreciation of the land* itself (i.e., for its reduced power to produce crops in the future due to having been left fallow for a period of time), and not for the total sum of damages (including the loss of potential usufruct during the time of the lease). The "*midrash*" of R. Meir would then interpret the stipulation in its more extensive context. But here, too, that is precisely the conclusion that any reader of the contract would have come to originally (without the need for R. Meir's "interpretation"). The strained nature of these suggestions is apparent. For a contemporary attempt at seeing Hillel's decision as based on "creative reading," see M. Kister, "'Kedat Moshe veyehudaei': Toldoteha shel nushah mishpatit-datit," in *Atara l'Ḥaim: Studies in the Talmud and Medieval Rabbinic Literature in Honor of Professor Haim Zalman Dimitrovsky* (ed. D. Boyarin et al.; Jerusalem, 2000), 202 n. 2.

meaning of the phrase, and should have been rightly recognized as
such by all jurists. Accordingly, Nahmanides offers another solution.
Namely, he suggests that in the case at hand there had actually been
no marriage document at all. Rather, Hillel had determined the general rule (that it is the woman's physical entrance into her husband's
house that creates her marital status) based upon local custom,[18] the
existence of which he learned from *other* marriage documents that he
had examined—ones that, although not drawn up according to the
rules of the Sages, did include such a phrase. As Nahmanides put it:

> They made the "custom of the laymen" (*leshon hedyot*) a precedent, and
> ruled according to it as if it had been instituted by the Sages. Although
> this custom had been initiated by the laymen not in accordance with the
> Sages, they made such stipulations a condition [of all similar contracts]:
> thus, even if [this stipulation] had not been [explicitly] written [in the
> contract], it was considered as having been written, since it had become
> the norm accepted by all.[19]

According to this interpretation, *doresh* attains the meaning of "pro-
nounce a (legal) ruling," and the phrase *doresh leshon hedyot* may
be translated, "make a normative ruling based on [the precedent of]
common custom."[20] This is in contrast to Rav Hai's understanding of
the verb, where *darash* is an *interpretive* mode of *textual* analysis that
yields new understandings, ones that overcome the "simple meaning"
of the words of the text. The difficulty with Nahmanides' approach,
however, is that the passage expressly states that Hillel ruled based on
a particular document's wording; it is, therefore, difficult to assume
that he was ruling precisely in cases where *no* document existed. This
is corroborated by the other cases following that of Hillel's ruling in the

---

[18] This suggestion by Nahmanides entails a novel understanding of the phrase
leshon hedyot as "language reflecting common (nonrabbinic) custom." See the following note.

[19] Nahmanides' *Novellae* to *b. Baba Metzi'a* 104a. See also Tosafot to *b. Baba Metzi'a*
104a, *s.v.* היה דורש לשון הדיוט. This understanding was taken up by Nahmanides'
disciple, R. Solomon ben Abraham Adret, who appeals to these Talmudic passages in
support of a ruling on the binding character of generally accepted local custom even
when not expressly stipulated in a contract; see his responsa, *Teshuvot ha-Rashba*, 3:17
and 3:433 (= 1:662). This was later codified in the authoritative *Tur Shulḥan Arukh*
and R. Joseph Karo's compendium, *Shulḥan Arukh*; see *Tur Ḥoshen Mishpat* 42:21;
Shulḥan Arukh, Ḥoshen Mishpat 42:15; also Elon, *Jewish Law*, 429–32. Cf. the similar
understanding of S. Lieberman, *Tosefta Ki-feshuta: Ketubbot* (New York, 1967), 6:
245–47 (in Hebrew), along with his short commentary ad loc. in *Tosefta Nashim:
Ketubbot* (New York, 1967), 3:68 (line 33).

[20] Cf. Rashi to *b. Baba Metzi'a* 104a, *s.v.* "דורש לשון הדיוט."

Tosefta (and parallels), where in each one the special ruling (*darash*) is justified by the phrase "for so he *writes* to him (in the contract)."

A simple and direct solution for this locution can be found, however, if we assume that the basic problem here is not semantic but legal. That is, I suggest that the words, "when you shall enter my house you shall be my wife," were themselves taken to be unambiguous and not open to reinterpretation. *The question was not what they meant, but whether they had legal force.* It should be emphasized that the locution *leshon hedyot* ("the language of a *hedyot*") does not refer to a particular textual wording; rather, it signifies a *style of language* that might be utilized in a document.[21] The word *hedyot* here means, as in Greek, "lay, unprofessional";[22] in legal documents, *leshon hedyot* is, accordingly, lay, unprofessional language. Now, one of the main problems in the legal interpretation of documents—any document—is the question of whether the words as written correctly express the intent of the author of the document. This is especially so if the document includes language which may not be that of a professional draftsman who is acutely aware of the exact meaning of every word he uses, but is rather that of the "man in the street" who may use colorful, expressive, but imprecise language—even exaggeration—to express his intent.[23] The question which came before Hillel was thus whether the phrase "when you will enter my house you shall be my (lawful) wife," written as a standard clause in the Alexandrian betrothal documents, is to be *expounded* (as law) literally, as if drafted by a lawyer intent on expressing his intentions through the precise use of words, or whether it is simply a colloquialism (= *leshon hedyot*), a turn of phrase not necessarily expressing the intent of the writer and therefore *not to be regarded as having legal force in its literal sense.* What Hillel did was nothing more than what has been understood by generations of jurists to be the proper procedure in the interpretation of

---

[21] The use of *leshon* in construct state implies a style of speech, and not the textual wording itself; cf. *leshon ḥokhmah* = "allusive, punning speech," in *b. Eruv.* 53b. See, however, *y. Sanh.* 7:12 (25d), where *leshon hedyot* is used to denote the vernacular tongue (= *lashon*) as opposed to Hebrew (*leshon qodesh*).

[22] See LSJ, 819, *s.v.* ἰδιώτης, III: "one who has no professional knowledge, layman," also ibid., *s.v.* ἰδιωτικός, II.

[23] The problem of *verba* (or *scriptum*) vs. *voluntas* is one of the major problems in the interpretation of legal documents in Roman law. See F. Schulz, *History of Roman Legal Science* (Oxford, 1946), 76–77, 133, 295; and cf. Cicero, *De inv.*, 1.38.68–69, 2.40.116–118; idem, *De or.* 1.57.244; Quintilian, *Inst.*, 3.6.61.

documents—"interpretation" here in the legal sense of the execution of their meaning and intent—as Sir Roland Burrows writes in his book on *Interpretation of Documents*:

> "The words of a will…are but the means of expressing the testator's intention, and where the intention is plain from the words themselves, it is then the duty of the Court to execute the intention however inartificially expressed." It may happen, however, that the writer has obviously set out with the intention of declaring one thing and has succeeded in saying quite plainly some other thing. If that is the case, then *effect must be given to his words*. It would not be the first time that a Balaam has set forth with his ass to make a solemn declaration and has found on the way that his intention has been defeated by the words of his ass.[24]

Doresh leshon hedyot, then, should be translated as, "to expound [= execute as law] [even] unprofessionally worded language (or language that might be construed as such)" as if it were drafted by a master draftsman.[25] What Hillel is noted for here is a wonderful wedding of perceptiveness, pragmatism, and sound legal sense: what promised to be an explosive problem of an abundance of bastard children, due to what appeared to the Palestinian authorities as lax moral behavior, was solved by Hillel through his attention to detail and his perceptive understanding of the need for simple, proper legal interpretation of the words of the engagement document. For the Palestinian rabbis, the betrothal ceremony, customarily (in Palestine) performed a significant time before the consummation of the marriage in a final ceremony,[26] constituted a complete bond between husband and wife,

---

[24] R. Burrows, *Interpretation of Documents* (2d ed.; London, 1946), 7 (my emphasis). The quotation at the beginning of the passage is from an 1888 court decision cited ibid., n. 2. Similarly, Hillel gives legal force to the plain meaning of the (written) words of the contract, even though they *may* plausibly be taken to reflect (only) the author's colloquial usage, and, if such authorial intention were to be considered in this case, would not be taken in their literal sense as a basis for the legal interpretation of the document.

[25] This is the consideration behind all the examples brought in the series in Tosefta *Ketubbot* containing the phrase *doresh leshon hedyot* (although explicitly only the first, that of Hillel and the betrothal document, is described as such; but see *y. Ketubbot* 4:9 [28b–29a]). So, for example, in R. Meir's case of the leased field, the lessee would find it advantageous to claim that the words, "I shall pay you from the best produce," should be construed as an exaggeration, used simply to lend rhetorical force to his promise to work the land, without implying an (actual) obligation on his part to compensate the owner in accordance with these precise words. Like Hillel, R. Meir takes this wording seriously as a basis for the lessee's obligation, and rules/expounds according to its simple, direct meaning.

[26] On the custom of a year-long engagement period, see *m. Ketubbot* 5:2.

one that could be severed only by divorce. Consequently, they could not perceive the Alexandrian betrothal in any other way. It was Hillel—the Babylonian!—who could see the possibility of a cultural difference that might, and should, be translated into legal procedure. Upon careful analysis of the betrothal document, he found evidence of such a cultural difference in the particular wording, which, when taken at face value, hints at the lower, nonbinding status of the prenuptial betrothal.[27]

Darash, *Midrash and Textual Interpretation*

This passage has two important ramifications in the present context: 1) Hillel's expertise in legal interpretation, while formidable and authoritative, is not related to creative *textual* interpretive skills, but rather involves the astute application of *legal acuity* and *common sense* in a problematic legal situation; and 2) the verb *darash* in these passages does not imply interpretation of a text, and certainly does not refer to any particular interpretive stance vis-à-vis a text, but rather should be translated "taught," "decided a law," "pronounced a ruling."

The first point has been the subject of a paper by Daniel Schwartz, "Hillel and Scripture: From Authority to Exegesis."[28] His analysis of legal rulings ascribed to Hillel leads to the conclusion that "Hillel is to be considered a sage of the oral tradition" and that his teachings "stand on his authority and that of his teachers in the Pharisaic tradition—but

---

[27] This may actually accord with Hellenistic Egyptian marital custom during the Roman period, when a separate legal contract to create a marriage (*engyēsis*, from ἐγγύη [lit., security, pledge], betrothal) was known; see: H. Wolff, *Written and Unwritten Marriages in Hellenistic and Post-Classical Roman Law* (Haverford, Penn., 1939), 46–47, 73–82 (and see n. 276); A. Büchler, "Das jüdische Verlöbnis und die Stellung der Verlobten eines Priesters im ersten und zweiten Jahrhundert," in *Festschrift zu Israel Lewy's siebzigstem Geburtstag* (ed. M. Brann and I. Elbogen; Breslau, 1911), 122–23; A. Gulak, "Deed of Betrothal and Oral Stipulations in Talmudic Law," *Tarbiz* 3 (1932): 365–66 (in Hebrew); idem, *Das Urkundenwesen im Talmud im Lichte der griechisch-aegyptischen Papyri und des griechischen und römischen Rechts* (Jerusalem, 1935), 40–41 (Hebrew translation: *Ha-shetarot Batalmud* [ed. R. Katzoff; Jerusalem, 1994], 46–56; but cf. Katzoff's notes there, esp. n. 24 and n. 26); B. Cohen, "Betrothal in Jewish and Roman Law," *PAAJR* 18 (1948/1949): 92–94; M. Friedman, *Jewish Marriage in Palestine: A Cairo Geniza Study* (Tel-Aviv and New York, 1981), vol. 2, no. 50:12–13, 376–83 (and cf. no. 2:6, 38); M. Kister, "From Philotas to Hillel: 'Betrothal' Contracts and Their Violation," *Tarbiz* 70 (2001): 631–32 (in Hebrew). Cf. Philo, *Special Laws* 3.72.

[28] In *Hillel and Jesus: Comparative Studies of Two Major Religious Leaders* (ed. J.H. Charlesworth and L.L. Johns; Minneapolis, 1997), 335–62.

not on that of Scripture."[29] Later reworkings of the early sources—in the Palestinian and Babylonian Talmudim as well as in the halakhic midrashim—replace the earlier picture of Hillel with one in which he applies recognized exegetical methods to Scripture in order to develop legal norms.[30] Concerning these later narrative traditions about Hillel, Schwartz writes, "it is most reasonable to conclude that the historical Hillel, who did what he did because he thought it should be done, has been domesticated into a rabbinic Hillel who did what he did because Scripture said it should be done,"[31] or, I may add, because Scripture may be made, by the use of appropriate exegetical techniques, to say it should be done.

As for the second point, the meaning of the verb *darash*, my studies of the use of this word in texts of the Second Temple period demonstrate that, during this time, *darash* principally indicates *instruction*, specifically the expounding of law in public, and is not used in the context of an interpretive stance towards a text, or in the context of a text at all.[32] Thus the person whose function is called *doresh ha-Torah*, as found in the literature of Qumran, was a *teacher* of the law and not an "interpreter" or "searcher" of the law.[33] Indeed, in the *pesher* on Num 21:18 cited in the *Damascus Document* (6:2–11), this function is taken as a gloss on מחוקק, a word denoting a lawgiver,[34] through whom God teaches the laws by which human beings are to live. This passage alludes to the importance of the *doresh ha-Torah* as the instructor of new laws to the chosen community. Similarly, the

---

[29] "Hillel and Scripture," 337 (emphasis in original).

[30] See Schwartz (ibid., 346–50), who proposes that Hillel's reasoning from Scripture, in the story of the paschal sacrifice that occurs on the Sabbath, would seem to be a later addition; the story originally included only Hillel's general *legal* argument (comparing the paschal sacrifice to the daily sacrifice) and an appeal to tradition ("I received from my teachers..."). If so, serious doubts may be raised concerning the authenticity of the passage in the Tosefta enumerating "seven methods of legal textual interpretation (*middot*) that Hillel the Elder expounded before the elders of Bathyra." On the gradual development of these interpretive methods, see M. Kahana, "Concerning the Historical Development of the Principle of *Kelal uFerat* in the Tannaitic Period," in *Studies in Talmudic and Midrashic Literature in Memory of Tirzah Lifshitz* (ed. M. Bar-Asher et al.; Jerusalem, 2005), 173–216 (in Hebrew); and see below.

[31] Schwartz, "Hillel and Scripture," 359.

[32] See Mandel, "'*Darash Rabbi Peloni*.'"

[33] See the *Damascus Document* 6:2–11; 7:12–21; 1QS (*Rule of the Community*) 6:6–7; 4Q174 (4QFlor) 1 i 10–13.

[34] On *meḥoqeq* as "lawgiver," "instructor in law," in texts of the Second Temple and rabbinic periods, see G. Vermes, *Scripture and Tradition in Judaism: Haggadic Studies* (Leiden, 1973), 49–55.

expression *midrash ha-Torah* does not denote the *study* of the law but rather the *teaching* of the law, compared in another *pesher* to the "way of God" of Isa 40:3:

ובהיות אלה ליחד בישראל,
יבדלו מתוך מושב הנשי [= אנשי] העול ללכת למדבר
לפנות שם את דרך הואהא, כאשר כתוב,
"במדבר פנו דרך ‥‥ ³⁵ ישרו בערבה מסלה לאלוהינו"
—הואה מדרש התורה אשר צוה ביד מושה לעשות ככול הנגלה עת
בעת, וכאשר גלו הנביאים ברוח קודשו.

> When these become the Community of Israel, they shall separate them-selves from the settlement of the men of deceit in order to go to the wilderness, to clear there the path of the Lord, as it is written: "In the wilderness clear a path of the Lord, make level in the desert a highway for our God" (Isa 40:3)—this is the instruction in the Law (*midrash ha-Torah*) which He commanded through Moses to observe, according to everything that has been revealed from time to time and according to that which the prophets revealed through His Holy Spirit.[36]

Midrash Torah is here made equivalent to "clearing the path (*derekh*)" for people to walk along (*derekh adonai* = the divine commandments) and to "observe" (*la'asot*), undoubtedly referring to instruction in the revealed laws (revealed through Moses and the prophets) themselves, and not to a method of derivation of these laws. It is not the study of the text (of the Torah) that is mandated here, but the *instruction in the laws* of Torah.

While it is a common view of scholars of Qumran texts that these describe a "study community" dedicated to the continuing deriva-tion of laws through analysis of the biblical text,[37] it has been noted

---

[35] The four dots appear here in the Qumran manuscript, and are a substitute for the Tetragrammaton.

[36] *Rule of the Community* (*Serekh ha-Yaḥad*), 1QS 8:12–16; cf. CD 20:6–7. On the phrase מדרש התורה האחרון at the conclusion of the *Damascus Document* (4Q266 [4QDᵃ] 11 18–21;4 Q270 [4QDᵉ] 7 ii 12–15;4 Q269 [4QDᵈ] 16 16–19), see P. Mandel, "*Inclusio*: On the Final Section of the *Damascus Document* and Its Literary Signifi-cance," *Meghillot: Studies in the Dead Sea Scrolls* 2 (2004): 64–66 (in Hebrew).

[37] For the consensus of scholarly understanding of these passages as referring to the *study* and *interpretation* of Scripture at Qumran, see S.D. Fraade, "Interpretive Author-ity in the Studying Community at Qumran," *JJS* 44 (1993): 46–69; idem, "Looking for Legal Midrash at Qumran," in *Biblical Perspectives: Early Use and Interpretation of the Bible in Light of the Dead Sea Scrolls* (ed. M.E. Stone and E.G. Chazon; Leiden, 1998), 59–79 (especially 63–68); L. Schiffman, *The Halakhah at Qumran* (Leiden, 1975), 57. See, too, D. Dimant, "Not Exile in the Desert but Exile in Spirit: The Pesher of Isa. 40:3 in the *Rule of the Community*," *Meghillot: Studies in the Dead Sea Scrolls* 2 (2004):

repeatedly that, although Scripture is cited and paraphrased frequently in the writings of the Qumran sect, there is little evidence for the type of conscious reinterpretation of biblical verses found in later rabbinic works.[38] When verses are cited as the basis for some rule, that rule is usually presented as a transparent reflection of the plain, surface meaning of the text.[39] Further study of the precise relationships to Scripture exhibited in the Qumran texts will, I believe, demonstrate that the use of textually-oriented techniques in the service of the interpretation of law in the writings of the Qumran sect was limited.

The nonhermeneutical sense of *darash* is also found in numerous texts of the early rabbinic period. A passage purportedly showing evidence of textual exegesis during the late Second Temple period appears in *b. Pesaḥim* 70b, where Hillel's teachers, Shemaiah and Avtalyon, are described as *darshanim gedolim*: the context of that passage clearly demonstrates that the word *darshan* was used specifically by the author of this *baraita* in the context of *public instruction in the law* ("they did not tell [the people] that the *ḥagigah* sacrifice [on the fourteenth day of Nisan] takes precedence over the Sabbath"), without any reference to Scripture.[40] Other contexts where the verb *darash* is used in Tannaitic

---

21–36 (in Hebrew). Even before the discovery of the Dead Sea Scrolls, I. Heinemann understood the activity of the *doresh ha-Torah* in the *Damascus Document* passage as reflecting the active interpretation of Scripture with intent to derive (new) practical legal pronouncements; see his "On the Development of Technical Terms for the Interpretation of Scripture: *darash*," *Leshonenu* 14 (1946): 184 (in Hebrew). For a view that is in accord with my conclusions proposed here, see J. Maier, "Early Jewish Biblical Interpretation in the Qumran Literature," in *Hebrew Bible/Old Testament: The History of Its Interpretation, vol. I: From the Beginnings to the Middle Ages (Until 1300)* (ed. M. Saebø; Göttingen, 1996), 108–29.

[38] See Fraade, "Looking for Legal Midrash at Qumran," 59–79 ("we find that there is relatively little legal midrash to be found at Qumran," 74); M. Kister, "A Common Heritage: Biblical Interpretation at Qumran and Its Implications," in Stone and Chazon, *Biblical Perspectives*, 101–11 ("we only find scattered examples of explicit interpretations of verses of the Law, and these are not presented in the form of hermeneutical compositions," 106); Schremer, "'[T]he[y] Did Not Read in the Sealed Book,'" 118–19 ("although the use of Scripture to justify halakha is evident, the conclusions drawn from the biblical text can usually be regarded as a plain meaning of the verse").

[39] See A. Shemesh, "Scriptural Interpretations in the *Damascus Document* and Their Parallels in Rabbinic Midrash," in *The Damascus Document: A Centennial of Discovery* (ed. J.M. Baumgarten, E.G. Chazon, and A. Pinnick; Leiden, 2000), 161–75; idem, "4Q251: *Midrash Mishpatim*," *DSD* 12 (2005): 280–302; and A. Shemesh and C. Werman, "Halakhah at Qumran: Genre and Authority," *DSD* 10 (2003): 104–29.

[40] On the possible Babylonian origin of this *baraita*, see S. Friedman, "Towards a Characterization of Babylonian *Baraitot*: Ben Tema and ben Dortai," in *Neti'ot leDavid: Jubilee Volume for David Weiss Halivni* (ed. Y. Elman, E.B. Halivni, and Z.A. Steinfeld; Jerusalem, 2004), 332–34 (in Hebrew). Scholars have cited this passage as

sources are similarly devoid of any reference to Scripture as the basis
for a legal rule, as in the following:

אמ' ר' אלעזר: והלא יודן ברבי היה דורש שאין רוצעין אלא במילת.

R. Eleazar said: Did not R. Yudan beRabbi expound that one pierces [an
indentured servant] only in the earlobe?[41]

זה אחד משלשה דברים שדרש שמיי הזקן: אין מפליגין את הספינה לים
הגדול אלא קודם לשבת שלשה ימים.

This is one of three things that Shammai the Elder would expound: One
may not set sail in a boat in the Great Sea (Mediterranean) less than
three days before the Sabbath. [42]

Similarly, in the following passage the term *midrash ḥakhamim* clearly
refers to *public instruction* by the sages (which can be "heard"), without any reference to derivation of law from Scripture:

"ואם לא תשמעו לי"—אם לא תשמעו למדרש חכמים. יכול למה שכתוב?
כשהוא אומר "ולא תעשו את כל המצות האלה"—הרי מה שכתוב בתורה
אמור. הא מה מה אני מקיים "אם לא תשמעו"? למדרש חכמים.

"But if you will not listen to me" (Lev 26:14)—(this means): 'if you will
not listen to the exposition of the sages (*midrash ḥakhamim*).' Might
one not suppose that [reference is made to not listening] to that which
is *written* [in the Torah]? [No, for] when the [Scripture] says "and will
not do all these commandments," it refers to that which is written in the

---

evidence for legal *midrash* in the mid-first century BCE; see Urbach, *The Halakhah*, 98;
Epstein, *Prolegomena to the Tannaitic Literature*, 511–12; C. Albeck, *Mavo la-Mishnah*
(Jerusalem and Tel-Aviv, 1959), 43; Fraenkel, *Darkei ha-Aggadah ve-Midrash*, 12–13.
However, the contexts of the words *darash* and *midrash* in this and following passages
of early rabbinic literature reflect an activity which seeks to impart *instruction* without
attempting to provide explanation for a text. In most of these cases it seems that this
instruction was imparted in a *public* setting; that is, the use of *darash* assumes the
existence of an audience who hears the instruction. Indeed, it has already been noted
that *darash* is used predominantly in the Babylonian Talmud to describe oral instruction in front of an audience; see Bacher, *Die exegetische Terminologie*, 2:41–43; and
cf. 1:26–27; Heinemann, "On the Development of Technical Terms," 188–89; Mandel,
"'Darash Rabbi Peloni,'" 29–31 and n. 17 there. Although considered anomalous by
some scholars (see Bacher, *Die exegetische Terminologie*, 2:43; and cf. O. Meir, "The
Meaning of 'Darash Rabbi X' in Rabbinic Midrashim," *Dappim: Research in Literature*
3 [1986]: 209–18 [in Hebrew]), it seems that this usage is simply a continuation of the
normal meaning of the verb as used in earlier times; see Mandel, ibid.

[41] *Sifre Deut.* 122 (ed. Finkelstein, 180). The context is the law of Deut 15:17, but
no effort is made to interpret its text.

[42] *Sifre Deut.* 203 (ed. Finkelstein, 239).

Torah. Then how shall I construe [the words] "If you will not listen to me"? [They refer] to exposition (*midrash*) of the sages.[43]

Another indication that the word *midrash* was understood in the early Tannaitic period as a straightforward instruction of laws and not as a method of textual interpretation is the use of the word as a gloss on the biblical word *ḥoq* in the following passages, all of which are taken from biblical passages that describe, explicitly or implicitly, the activity of *public legal instruction*:

"והודעתי את חוקי האלהים ואת תורתיו" (שמות יח, טז). "חקים"—אלו
המדרשות. "והתורת"—אילו ההוראות. דברי ר' יהושע.

"And I make known the statutes of God and His laws" (Exod 18:16). "Statutes"—these are the *midrashot*; "and His laws"—that is, the ordinances. So says R. Joshua.[44]

"והזהרת אתהם את החוקים"—אלו מדרשות. "והתורת"—אלו ההוריות.
דברי ר' יהושע.

"And you shall enjoin upon (lit., 'enlighten [for]') them the statutes" (Exod 18:20)—these are the *midrashot*. "and the laws"—these are the ordinances. These are the words of R. Joshua.[45]

"ולהבדיל בין הקדש ובין החל"—אילו הערכים. "ובין הטמא ובין הטהור"—
אילו הטמאות והטהרות. "ולהרות את בני ישראל"—אילו ההוריות. "את
כל החקים"—אילו המדרשות. "אשר דבר י"י אליהם"—אילו ההלכות.
"ביד משה"—זה המקרא. יכול אף התלמוד? תלמוד לומר "ולהורות". ר'
יוסה ביר' יהודה אומר: מניין אף התרגום? תלמוד לומר "ולהורות".

"To distinguish between the holy and the profane" (Lev 10:10–11)—these are the vows of valuation; "and between the impure and the pure"—these are impure and pure [categories]; "and to teach the children of Israel"—these are the ordinances; "and the statutes"—these are the *midrashot*; "which the Lord God has spoken"—these are the *halakhot*;[46] "by Moses"—this is Scripture. One might assume that even (theoretical) study is included? Scripture says, "and to teach." R. Jose b. R. Judah says:

---

[43] *Sifra Beḥuqotai, Parashah* 2.1.
[44] *Mekhilta Amalek* 4 (ed. Horowitz-Rabin, 196–97).
[45] *Mekhilta Amalek* 4 (ed. Horowitz-Rabin, 197–98).
[46] The term *halakhot* refers to the body of traditional law as transmitted from prior generations, as in the phrases *halakhah le-Moshe mi-Sinai* and *im halakhah neqabbel*. See A. Rosenthal, "Torah she-be'al peh," in *Meḥqerei Talmud* (Jerusalem, 1993), 2:456, n. 33 (in Hebrew).

From whence [do we know to include] also *targum*? Scripture says, "and to teach."[47]

In glossing these phrases, the rabbinic commentators correctly and aptly identify the biblical terms by their contemporary categories of religious instruction. Since the biblical phrases seem to indicate the general activity of instruction, the term *midrashot* should not be seen to be limited only to those laws derived from Scripture through exegetical means (which comprise only a small part of the range of religious instruction), but must indicate the laws in general (as indeed one might surmise from the word *ḥoq*),[48] as prescribed to the people by the sages.

But it is not only that the word *midrash*, in its occurrences in the literature of the early Tannaitic period, is devoid of any *lexical* implication of special textual techniques of biblical legal interpretation. It is also true that, as has been remarked by scholars, the *nature of legal exegesis* of Scripture by rabbinic figures of this period, such as Rabbi Ishmael, Rabbi Eliezer, Rabbi Joshua and Rabbi Tarfon, is generally of a simple, direct nature. This is especially true of Rabbi Ishmael:

> The exegetical interpretations (*midrashim*) from the school of R. Ishmael excel in their simplicity: they do not relate to the scriptural text in a circuitous fashion in order to derive the law (*halakhah*) from it at all costs, but rather attempt to bring the derived lesson near to the simple understanding of the verse, and do not gratuitously expound (seemingly) superfluous and redundant language.[49]

Although much has been written concerning the "canons of legal scriptural interpretation" (*middot she-ha-Torah nidreshet bahen*) and their relationship to recorded legal analyses of R. Ishmael and other Tannaitic scholars, it would seem that the actual enumeration of these principles and their conscious use in *textual analysis* is the result of later generations. Menahem Kahana has shown how some of these principles developed from simple legal rules into more formal scholastic principles; this development took place through the Tannaitic and Amoraic periods.[50] While an encompassing study of the legal derivations of the

---

[47] *Sifra Shemini, Parashah* 1.9. The text is according to MS Vatican Assemani 66. Cf. *b. Keritot* 13b, and Rashi there, *s.v. midrashot*.
[48] See n. 34 above concerning the word *meḥoqeq* as denoting "lawgiver."
[49] Epstein, *Prolegomena to the Tannaitic Literature*, 536.
[50] See Kahana, "Concerning the Historical Development."

early Tannaitic scholars based on a critical analysis of the texts is still a desideratum, I believe that the evidence points to the full development of these principles occurring only during the second half of the Tannaitic period, near the end of the second century CE.

II. Rabbi Akiva: Textual and Legal Interpretation and Scriptural Exegesis

Rabbi Ishmael's more direct analysis of scriptural language is at odds with the interpretive stance of his famous colleague, Rabbi Akiva. Indeed, Rabbi Akiva is reported to have provided legal derivations from Scripture that are based on "creative interpretation" of the text, as seems evident in the following two passages:

בו ביום דרש ר' עקיבה: "וכל כלי חרש אשר יפל מהם אל תוכו, כל
אשר בתוכו יטמא"—אינו אומר "טמא" אלא "יטמא": לטמא את אחירים,
וללמד על כיבר השיני שיטמא את השלישי. אמר ר' יהושע: מי יגלה
עפר מעיניך רבן יוחנן בן זכיי, שהייתה אומר: עתיד דור אחר לטהר את
הכיבר השלישי שאין לו מן התורה, והרי עקיבה תלמידך הביא לי מקרא
מן התורה שהוא טמא, שנאמר "כל אשר בתוכו יטמא."

That same day R. Akiva expounded: "And every earthen vessel into which any of them falls, whatsoever is in it *is unclean* (*yitma*)" (Lev 11:33)—it does not say "is unclean" (*tamē*) but "shall render unclean" (*yetamē* [so reading the consonantal text]), (that is,) *it imparts uncleanness to other [things]*, [this] teaches that a "second loaf" may impart impurity to a "third loaf." R. Joshua said: Might one take away the dust from your eyes, Rabban Yohanan ben Zakkai [= would that you were alive]! For you said: A latter generation shall come to rule the "third loaf" pure [although the halakhah rules that it is indeed liable to contract impurity from a "second loaf"], since [that halakhic rule] has no scriptural basis [and thus this rule will be forgotten]. But lo, Akiva your student has cited for me a scriptural verse [as proof] that it is unclean, as it says: "Whatsoever is in it *shall impart* uncleanness."[51]

בו ביום דרש ר' עקיבה: "אז ישיר משה ובני ישראל את השירה הזאת לי״י
ויאמרו לאמר"...ולמה נאמר "לאמר"? אלא שהיו ישראל עונין אחריו של
משה על כל דבר ודבר, כקוראין את הלל...ר' נחמיה אומר: כקורים את
שמע היו קורים, לא כקוראין את הלל.

---

[51] *M. Sotah* 5:2. In the final biblical citation of Lev 11:33 read again יטמא as if vocalized '*y'tamē*'.

That same day R. Akiva expounded: "Then sang Moses and the children of Israel this song unto the Lord, and *they said, saying*" (Exod 15:1)...Why does [Scripture] say, "saying"? Rather, [the superfluous use of the word "saying" teaches] that Israel responded after Moses upon every single sentence, as [in the] reciting [of] the *Hallel* (which is recited antiphonally in the synagogue)...R. Nehemiah said: They recited [the Song of the Sea] as [in the] reciting [of] the *Shema* (recited in unison in the synagogue), and not as [in the] reciting [of] the *Hallel*.[52]

These passages have been subjected to analysis in a recent paper by Ishay Rosen-Zvi,[53] who has shown that R. Akiva is expressly portrayed in this chapter of the Mishnah through a series of legal and nonlegal rulings as one who uses creative textual interpretation, based on seeming textual superfluities, contradictions and even "mis"-readings, to uphold traditional legal rulings (besides presenting creative readings in the service of nonlegal statements). This is evident also in the following passage:

דרש ר' עקיבה: מנין לקבלת דם שלא תהא אלא בכהן תמים ובכלי שרת?
תלמוד לומר: "והקריבו בני אהרן הכהנים את הדם וזרקו את הדם על
המזבח סביב"..."והקריבו"—[...] זו קבלה. מקיש קבלה לזריקה: מה
זריקה בכהן תמים ובכלי שרת, אף קבלה בכהן תמים ובכלי שרת. ולהלן
הוא אומר "[ואת בניו תקריב והלבשת אתם כתנת] ומשחת אתם...וכהנו
לי"—מה "כהן" האמור להלן בכהן תמים וכלי שרת, אף "כהן" האמור כאן
בכהן תמים וכלי שרת. אמר לו ר' טרפון: עקיבה! עד מתי אתה מגבב
ומביא עלינו? אקפח את בניי אם לא הפרש שמעתי בין קבלה לזריקה,
ואתה השויתה קבלה לזריקה! אמ' לו: תורשיני לומר לפניך מה שלמדתני.
אמר לו: אמור. אמר לו: קבלה—לא עשה בה מחשבה כמעשה, זריקה—
עשה בה מחשבה כמעשה.... אמ' לו: העבודה שלא היטיתה ימין ושמאל!
אני שמעתי ולא היה לי לפרש; ואתה דורש ומסכים להלכה! הא כל
הפורש ממך כפורש מחייו.

R. Akiva expounded: From whence do we know that the receiving of the blood should only be done by an unblemished priest and with priestly vestments [lit., "vestments for (divine) service"]? Scripture says, "And the sons of Aaron, the priests, shall offer the blood and they shall dash the blood around the altar" (Lev 1:5).... "Shall offer"—this is the receiving [of the blood by the priests]. Scripture (thus) draws an analogy between "receiving" and "dashing" [the blood]: Just as dashing [the blood around the altar] must be done by an unblemished priest and with priestly vestments, so must "receiving" [the blood] be done by

---

[52] *M. Sotah* 5:4 and parallel in *t. Sotah* 5:13; cf. *Sifre Num* 2:5.
[53] I. Rosen-Zvi, '"Who Will Uncover the Dust from Your Eyes?": Mishnah *Sota* 5 and R. Akiva's Midrash," *Tarbiz* 75 (2006): 95–127 (in Hebrew); see esp. 102–4, on R. Nehemiah's opinion as stated here.

an unblemished priest and with priestly vestments.... And elsewhere [Scripture] says, "[Then bring his (Aaron's) sons forward, put tunics on them,] and anoint them...that they may serve Me as priests (*vekhi-hanu li*)" (Exod 40:14–15): just as "priest" mentioned there [refers to] an unblemished priest and [his wearing of] priestly vestments, so "priest" mentioned here [refers to] an unblemished priest and [his wearing of] priestly vestments. R. Tarfon said to him: Akiva! How long are you going to pile up [scriptural verses] against us? May I lose (lit., "cut down") my sons if I have not heard a *distinction* between "receiving" [the blood] and "dashing" [the blood on the altar], whereas you have *equated* "receiving" [the blood] and "dashing" [it]! He [R. Akiva] said to him [R. Tarfon]: Will you permit me to say before you what you have taught me? He said to him: Say [it]. He said to him: [With respect to] "receiving" [the blood], [the law] does not treat intention as tantamount to action; but with respect to "dashing" [the blood] on the altar, [the law] treats intention as tantamount to action [i.e., improper *intention* while "receiving" the blood does not carry liability, unlike improper *actions* while "receiving" the blood that do carry liability; but improper intention during the "dashing" of the blood *does* create liability as do improper actions while "dashing" it].... He said to him: By the Temple service [= an oath], you have strayed neither right nor left! I had heard [the law concerning "receiving" and "dashing" the blood], but was unable to specify [the distinction between the two actions], but *you* expound and decisively formulate the law![54] Lo, whoever parts from you is like one who parts from his life."[55]

This passage begins with two derivations of law by R. Akiva, including an analogy drawn between two scriptural passages. First, the consecutive use of the two terms *vehiqrivu* (denoting the offering, or receiving, of the sacrificial blood by the priest) and *vezarqu* (denoting the dashing of the blood round the altar) in Lev 1:5 allows R. Akiva to apply the same law to both actions. Second, the seemingly superfluous word *ha-kohanim* ("the priests," following the equivalent term, "the sons of Aaron") in this verse, in comparison to its specific use (as a verb)

---

[54] On the meaning of the phrase *maskim le-halakhah* (in the parallel in *Sifra* the phrase is *maskim li-shemuah*) as "decisively formulate the law," in the sense of providing a final and definitive formulation of the law (that is, *sakkem* in the sense of summary and finalization, with the *lamed* as a preposition marking the direct object), see Z. Ben-Haim, "Ha-sakh veha-sekhum," *Leshonenu* 13 (1944–1945): 227–35, and especially 230–31 (and 230, n. 2). Thus, *doresh* and *maskim* describe here a two-part process of legal adjudication: *doresh* denotes the legal demonstration that leads to *maskim*, the final formulation of the law. (See the same usage in relation to Hillel in *y. Pesaḥim* 6:1, 32a.) See a similar discussion between R. Tarfon and R. Akiva, *Sifre Num.*, par. 75 (ed. Horowitz, 70) and the parallel in *b. Yoma* 66a.

[55] *T. Zevaḥim* 1:8; cf. *Sifra Nedavah, Parashah* 4.5; *b. Zevaḥim* 13a.

during the discussion of the clothing and anointing of Aaron's sons in Exod 40:14–15 ("put tunics on them…that they may serve me as priests," implying that all activity of the sons of Aaron performed in their capacity as priests require the wearing of the special priestly vestments), points to the requirement for both activities to be performed solely by *unblemished* priests wearing their *priestly vestments*. The strong objection to R. Akiva's derivation by R. Tarfon (a priest), specifically to the analogy drawn between *zeriqah* and *qabbalah*, is based on his recollection that there is some difference in law between *zeriqah* and *qabbalah*, although he cannot remember what that distinction is. His assumption is that this distinction must undermine the analogy that R. Akiva has drawn between the two activities. When R. Akiva reminds R. Tarfon of the distinction (one that he had learned from R. Tarfon himself) and explains its reasons, R. Tarfon praises him. Particularly significant is that R. Tarfon's praise *has nothing to do with R. Akiva's original textual derivation* (with which he neither agrees nor disagrees here). What impresses R. Tarfon is Akiva's ability to recreate the details of this forgotten legal distinction between the two categories of "receiving" and "dashing" despite the fact that he (Akiva) had not personally witnessed nor "heard" of the distinction.

What these and similar passages emphasize is R. Akiva's prowess and genius in *all* aspects of legal analysis: "pure" legal analysis of concepts and terms, as well as the textual analysis of Scripture. In the latter, especially, it seems that R. Akiva was famous. While R. Ishmael and others also cite Scripture in the context of legal rulings, these citations derive from a significantly different approach to the juristic declarations of the sages and their relationship to Scripture, one that preserves a profound distinction between rulings in Scripture and extrascriptural rulings, which are certainly accepted as authoritative even though they lack scriptural basis. R. Akiva, on the other hand, attempts to bridge the gap between law and text through a more creative and text-based approach. Although R. Akiva was undoubtedly an excellent jurist,[56] his textual virtuosity led his colleagues to complain that he was "piling up" verse upon verse without utility or sense: "Akiva! How long will you pile up verses and bring them to us?"[57] In a statement recorded

---

[56] His analyses of pure law are scattered throughout the rabbinic corpus.

[57] Special note should be taken of R. Tarfon's exclamation of disapproval in the passage above: ‏עד מתי אתה מגבב ומביא עלינו‎?. (Cf. also *Sifre Deut.* 1 [ed. Finkelstein, 7].) The verb ‏גבב‎ refers to the act of gathering together various objects (such as

in the Babylonian Talmud, R. Akiva is invited to be "just a jurist": to concentrate on the (dry and complicated) laws of purities and to leave the narrative text of Scripture and its interpretations alone.[58] Perhaps R. Akiva's nonscholastic background—there is ample evidence that he was not raised in professional juristic circles—led him, being endowed with creative genius, to forge new methods, transforming the ancient *midrash*, as legal instruction, into a new and powerful tool for both legal development and textual interpretation.

Thus, while the verb *darash* retains its earlier meaning of "instruction" in the passages cited above, in the context of Rabbi Akiva's propensity for textual analysis of Scripture it came to be used more frequently to denote a distinctive mode of instruction centering on those teachings derived from the particular lexical formulation of the scriptural text. This adumbrates the later Amoraic usage, wherein *darash* and *midrash* connote an interpretation of the biblical text.

III. Scriptural Interpretation in Second Temple Judaism

(1) *The Scribe (Sofer)*

The identity of the scribes in Second Temple Judaism has been an enigma for scholars. While the scribe as an inscriber and recorder of royal, military and sacral records is a well-known and ubiquitous figure in all societies of the ancient period, the term "scribe," appearing in the plural to designate a "company" of scribes as well as a referential title for specific individuals, is remarkably widespread in texts of Jewish provenance, or those related to Jewish provenance, of the Second Temple period.[59] The term appears (in the Aramaic *safar*, and, in Greek translation, as the word *grammateus*) as an appellation of such

---

dry leaves and plants) into a heap (see M. Moreshet, *A Lexicon of the New Verbs in Tannaitic Hebrew* [Ramat Gan, 1980], 115 [in Hebrew]); this is a precise (if caustic) description of R. Akiva's penchant for "gathering" verses of Scripture from disparate locations and comparing them one to another, as in the passage above.

[58] See *b. Ḥag.* 14a (and parallel in b. *Sanh.* 38b) and b. *Sanh.* 67b, where R. Eleazar b. Azariah registers the following complaint: "Akiva! What have you to do with *aggadah*? Go to [the laws of] *Negaʿim* and *Oholot!*"

[59] It is not insignificant that the title *"sofer"* is one of the most common titles, next to "priest" (*ha-kohen*), found on epitaphs of Second Temple graves and sarcophagi. See R. Hachlili, *Jewish Funerary Customs, Practices and Rites in the Second Temple Period* (Leiden, 2005), 215–16.

ancient figures as Enoch[60] and Aḥiqar;[61] in Ben Sira (38:24–39:11); in the books of Maccabees (1 Macc 7:12, 2 Macc 6:18); in numerous places in the New Testament in conjunction with priests and Pharisees (in legal discussions with Jesus, and at his trial);[62] and in the Aramaic targumic translation of particular uses of the word *navi* in *Targum Jonathan* to the books of the Prophets.[63] Indeed, of special significance is the designation of Ezra as "scribe" (and priest), named as such both by the author of the book of Ezra in Hebrew (first at Ezra 7:6 and 11), and in the Aramaic letter of Artaxerxes ("the 'scribe' of the law [= edict] of the God of the heavens," Ezra 7:12 and 21). The *divrei soferim* are also mentioned in rabbinic literature as the basis for rabbinically expounded laws, in opposition to *divrei Torah*.[64]

As mentioned above, most scholars connect the activity of some or all of these instances with *textual* activity involving the elucidation or teaching of the *text of Scripture*, as befitting a "scribal" profession. For

---

[60] *1 Enoch* 12:3–4, 15:1–2; and in the Enochic "Book of Giants" found at Qumran: 4Q203 8 1–4 (*The Books of Enoch, Aramaic Fragments of Qumran Cave 4* [ed. J.T. Milik; Oxford, 1976], 314–415); 4Q530 2:14 (ibid., 305). See also Enoch's appellation in *Testament of Abraham*, Recension B, 11:3 (ed. E.P. Sanders in *OTP* 1:900).

[61] In the Aramaic text Aḥiqar is given a title similar to Ezra's: *safar ḥakhim umahir* = "a wise and skillful scribe." See "The Words of Aḥiqar," in B. Porten and A. Yardeni, *Textbook of Aramaic Documents from Ancient Egypt, Vol. 3: Literature, Accounts, Lists* (Jerusalem, 1993), 22–53; see lines 1, 12, 18, 20, 27–28.

[62] See the following passages in the Synoptic Gospels and Acts: Matt 2:4; 5:20; 7:29; 8:19; 9:3; 12:38; 15:1; 16:21; 17:10; 20:18; 21:15; 23:2 and *passim*; 26:57; 27:41; Mark 1:22; 2:6, 16; 3:22; 7:1, 5; 8:31; 9:11, 14; 10:33; 11:18; 12:28; 14:1; 15:1; Luke 5:21, 30; 6:7; 9:22; 11:53; 15:2; 19:47; 20:1, 39, 46; 22:2, 66; 23:10; Acts 4:5; 6:12; 23:9.

[63] See A.J. Saldarini, "'Is Saul Also Among the Scribes?': Scribes and Prophets in Targum Jonathan," in *"Open Thou Mine Eyes…": Essays on Aggadah and Judaica Presented to Rabbi William G. Braude on His Eightieth Birthday and Dedicated to His Memory* (ed. H.J. Blumberg et. al.; Hoboken, N.J., 1992), 239–53; C.T.R. Hayward, "Some Notes on Scribes and Priests in the Targum of the Prophets," *JJS* 36 (1985): 210–21. The "prophets" that Saul meets (1 Sam 10:5–13; 19:20–24) are named ספריא, as are the diviners/seers that he consults (1 Sam 28:6). See also the translation of *navi* as *safar* when it is found in contextual proximity to the priest: Isa 28:7; Jer 6:13; 8:10; 23:11; Zech 7:3; and see especially Jer 18:18 and Ezek 7:26. The activity characteristic of those called *safar* is אולפן, instruction. The Aramaic *safar* is also found as the *targum* in passages where *navi* does not appear, but where the context requires the rendering "instructor"; see Hos 4:4, and cf. Isa 9:14; 29:10. From the fact that this Aramaic word was found by the targumists to be the most apt to describe the function of a diviner/instructor (when that was understood as such from the context), it may be concluded that at least during this period (first century BCE–third century CE), and most probably for a considerable time prior to it, the Aramaic word *safar* denoted an individual performing an *instructional* function; see below.

[64] See *m. Orlah* 3:9; *m. Yevamot* 2:4; *m. Sanhedrin* 11:3; *m. Kelim* 13:7; and *t. Miqvaot* 5:4.

many scholars, the activity of these scribes is, accordingly, connected with the development of the legal explication of Scripture (*midrash*).[65] However, I have demonstrated elsewhere that the term *sofer* is not connected with *textual* activity, but rather appears in texts within the Jewish milieu from the postexilic period onward as a calque of the Mesopotamian *tupšarru* (Akkadian)/*safar* (Aramaic), a common term (meaning "scribe") used specifically for experts in the interpretation of celestial omens (diviners), as well as expert "translators" of one language to another.[66] While both of these activities involve texts, it is not the textual element that is central to their professional activity, but rather their ability, based on authoritative knowledge of opaque messages (celestial omens, royal decrees, divine law), to be *guides* and *messengers*, "translating" these messages for those who are ignorant of them. In Jewish legal culture, similarly, the term *safar/sofer* became the prime title of an *instructor in divine law*. It is precisely for this reason that the Greek *grammateus* appears in parallel texts as *nomikos*, a legal guide—especially in the realm of unwritten custom and law.[67] Thus the Jewish "scribe" of the Second Temple period is a *legal consultant*, not a textual interpreter.

(2) *The Pharisees*

Primarily due to Josephus' description of the Pharisees as "accurate *exegetai* of the ancestral laws,"[68] scholars have viewed Pharisaic activity in the context of the *interpretation of Scripture*, as the precursor of the later exegetical activity of the Rabbis in legal *midrash*.[69] However, the term ἐξηγητής in the context of ancient Greek sources (including those within the Jewish Hellenistic milieu) does not imply textual interpretation. Rather, it denotes a consultant in the *categorical instruction in law*, especially in unwritten, traditional law (the *patrioi*

---

[65] See n. 10 above.

[66] See Mandel, "Origins of *Midrash*," 9–34.

[67] See Matt 22:35 (cf. Mark 12:28); Luke 7:30; 10:25; 11:45–54 (cf. Matt 23:4). Compare also 4 Macc 5:4 and 2 Macc 6:18. It is further significant that *safar* appears as the translation for *mehoqeq* in Gen 49:10; Num 21:18; Deut 33:21; Judg 5:9; and cf. the Greek translation of *mehoqeq* in Ben Sira 10:4. See above for the argument that the *mehoqeq* = *doresh ha-Torah*. A *nomikos* is a legal consultant who "explains...what are the usages in conformity with the law"; see Epictetus, *Discourses* 2.13.6–8.

[68] See *J.W.* 2:162 and 1:110; and cf. *J.W.* 1:648–649 and *Ant.* 17:149, 214–216; *Ant.* 18:81; *Ant.* 11:192.

[69] See above, n. 11.

nomoi)—just as Josephus similarly links the Pharisees to the ancestral laws, not the written ones. Thus, the ancient Greek *exegetai* were religious functionaries who were consulted by those in need of advice concerning the proper religious rites and rituals.[70] It is Apollo of the Delphic Oracle, according to Plato in his *Republic,* who is called "the ancestral *exēgētēs*," whose *instruction* concerns divine worship and rituals that cannot be fathomed by human beings unaided.[71] It is in this sense that the Septuagint uses this Greek root to render the term להורות in the description of the ritual guidance given by the priests in Lev 14:57. Moreover, there is little evidence in the writings of Josephus or Philo for the sustained public study and interpretation of the text of Scripture, except by special groups such as the Essenes and the Theraputae.[72] Rather, both authors emphasize public instruction in *laws.*[73]

It is thus clear that Josephus, in describing the Pharisees as "exegetes" of the *patrioi nomoi,* portrays them as the repositories of the ancient, unwritten laws that have been handed down by former generations, those whose authority was rejected by the Sadducees. Indeed, the Pharisees are never portrayed as "explaining" a text of Scripture, and their "exegesis" has nothing to do with a particular stance or interpretation of the *text* of the Bible. Whatever evidence we may have of prerabbinic interpretation of Scripture for legal or nonlegal purposes, there is no evidence from Josephus that the Pharisees, or those called the "sages" (*sophistai*),[74] derived their knowledge of the detailed laws from a special analysis of the text of Scripture (beyond the clear basis of laws apparent in the Bible), or that they utilized special techniques for scriptural (textual) interpretation.

---

[70] Cf. J.H. Oliver, *The Athenian Expounders of the Sacred and Ancestral Law* (Baltimore, 1950), 29–30, 47–52. For an extended discussion, see P. Mandel, "Scriptural Exegesis and the Pharisees in Josephus," *JJS* 58 (2007): 19–32.

[71] Plato, *Republic* 427B–C.

[72] See Mandel, "Origins of *Midrash*," 25–29. On the Essenes' textual scriptural activity, see Philo, *Prob.* 81–82; *Contempl.* 75–78.

[73] See the above-mentioned passages in Josephus, as well as *Ag. Ap.* 2.175–178 and Philo, *Hypoth.* 7.11–14 (*apud* Eusebius, *Praep. Evang.* 8.7). See also the emphasis on *laws* (*nomima*) in Josephus, *Ant.* 20.268 and elsewhere; including *Vita* 9, where Josephus boasts that as a youth of fourteen he was questioned by priests and elders on "precise information concerning the laws" (and cf. Luke 2:46–47). On Josephus' use of the plural, *laws* (*nomoi*), to designate the general collection of laws (and not necessarily the text of the Torah), see S. Mason, *Flavius Josephus on the Pharisees: A Composition-Critical Study* (Leiden, 1991), 96–106.

[74] See Josephus, *War* 1:648–649; *Ant.* 17:149, 214–216.

IV. SOME POSSIBLE REASONS FOR THE RISE OF TEXTUAL MIDRASHIC INTERPRETATION AFTER 70 CE

If, as I have argued, the activities of Hillel, the Pharisees and the Jewish "scribes" of the Second Temple period are hardly connected with textual interpretation of Scripture but rather with the interpretation (*viz.,* expounding) of law, especially the unwritten laws, it would seem futile to search in this period for the birth of special legal interpretation of the scriptural text, a genre that is attested in the collections that are known as *midreshei halakhah,* in passages in Mishnah and Tosefta and in the Babylonian and Palestinian Talmudim. In contrast, during the period of the early Tannaim, and especially in passages citing Rabbi Akiva's interpretation of law and Scripture, there appears a growing propensity to connect laws to Scripture, and to read Scripture in novel ways that provide proof for traditional legal positions, and also in ways that generate new aspects of law. The possibility thus exists that the dramatic events of the Great Revolt, viz., the destruction of the religious and legal center at Jerusalem in 70 CE, may have helped to effect this change. I conclude here with a brief list of possible causes for the rise of textual scriptural interpretation during the late first and early second century CE.

1. The sudden absence of a central law institution in Jerusalem, as well as the discontinuity of legal traditions due to the war, may have precipitated the need for a change towards the basing of law in Scripture.[75]
2. As mentioned above, the writings from the Dead Sea Scrolls, as well as descriptions by Philo and Josephus, reveal special preoccupation by the Essenes with scriptural interpretation. It is possible that later rabbinic legal interpretation was influenced to some degree by exegetical techniques utilized, for their own ends, by such communities.[76]

---

[75] See *t. Eduyyot* 1:1.

[76] See Schremer, "'[T]he[y] Did Not Read in the Sealed Book'"; V. Noam, "Traces of Sectarian Halakhah in the Rabbinic World," in *Rabbinic Perspectives: Rabbinic Literature and the Dead Sea Scrolls. Proceedings of the Eighth International Symposium of the Orion Center for the Study of the Dead Sea Scrolls and Associated Literature, 7–9 January, 2003* (ed. S.D. Fraade, A. Shemesh, and R.A. Clements; Leiden and Boston, 2006), 67–85.

3. The propensity for argumentation from Scripture is evident in the New Testament as well as in early Christian writings.[77] This may have also influenced similar activity within the rabbinic community, whether by way of imitation or of competition.

4. Rabbi Akiva, who is recorded as having attempted to bridge the gap between law and text through a creative and text-based approach, is represented in rabbinic literature as having been forceful, unusual, highly intelligent, and creative. It may be that, paradoxically, his approach to the special quality of Scripture as a "divine text" allowed for a more daring approach to interpreting the text, and thus the "revolution" in legal exegesis is largely due to this man.[78]

5. The primary role of the *ḥakham* of the late first and early second centuries CE as adjudicator and legal counsellor for the public can be seen in light of the activity of the Roman jurist of the same period.[79] Descriptions of the daily activities of the jurists bear a remarkable resemblance to those of the early *ḥakham*. These activities continued in Roman legal circles throughout the first and second centuries CE, but gradually came to be replaced by a growing reliance on written legal compilations (culminating in the great written

---

[77] See H. Hübner, "New Testament, OT Quotations in the," (trans. S.S. Schatzmann), *The Anchor Bible Dictionary* (ed. D.N. Freedman; New York and London, 1992), 4:1096–1104; J. Barr, "Scriptural Proof," in *The Encyclopedia of Christianity* (Grand Rapids, Cambridge UK, Leiden and Boston, 2005), 4:886–89.

[78] As M. Kahana has shown, the school of R. Akiva attained a dominant status near the end of the Tannaitic period; this is exemplified by the redaction of Rabbi Judah's Mishnah according to this school's principles and legal decisions, as well as by the central place of R. Akiva's exegetical methodology in the teachings of the Amoraim. See M. Kahana, *Sifre Zuta to Deuteronomy* (Jerusalem, 2003), 109–10 (in Hebrew); idem, "Concerning the Historical Development," 212–16, and ibid., n. 155 (in Hebrew).

[79] Concerning the Roman jurisconsult, see Schulz, *History of Roman Legal Science*; H.F. Jolowicz and B. Nicholas, *Historical Introduction to the Study of Roman Law* (3d ed.; Cambridge, 1972); W. Kunkel, *Die römischen Juristen: Herkunft und soziale Stellung* (Köln, 1967). For a comparison of the Roman jurists and rabbinical legal activity, see: P.S. Alexander, "Quid Athenis et Hierosolymis? Rabbinic Midrash and Hermeneutics in the Graeco-Roman World," in *A Tribute to Geza Vermes: Essays on Jewish and Christian Literature and History* (ed. P.R. Davies, R.T. White; Sheffield, 1990), 109–15; C. Hezser, "The Codification of Legal Knowledge in Late Antiquity: The Talmud Yerushalmi and Roman Law Codes," in *The Talmud Yerushalmi and Graeco-Roman Culture* (ed. P. Schafer; Tübingen, 1998), 581–95, especially 583–88; S.J.D. Cohen, "The Rabbi in Second-Century Jewish Society," in *The Cambridge History of Judaism, Volume 3: The Early Roman Period* (Cambridge, 1999), 976–77, and n. 241. See also E.S. Rosenthal, "Tradition and Innovation in the *Halakhah* of the Sages," *Tarbiz* 63 (1994): 321–74 (in Hebrew), esp. 321–22, where he hints at a philological connection between the Latin term *iuris prudens* and the Hebrew *ḥakham*.

compilation of Roman law in the sixth century, Justinian's *Digest*), with a concomitant emphasis on the interpretation of written law. A comparison between the development of the Roman and Jewish legal systems of this period may shed light on the parallel processes of evolution of textually dependent legal formulations.[80]

Some of these phenomena are directly related to the events of 70 CE, while others are only tangentially related to these events. Future research will be necessary in order to weigh these possibilities in writing the history of the development of textual legal interpretation of Scripture in rabbinic circles during the first and second centuries CE.

---

[80] See the studies by Alexander and Hezser cited in the preceding note.

LITURGY BEFORE AND AFTER THE TEMPLE'S
DESTRUCTION: CHANGE OR CONTINUITY?

Esther G. Chazon

The topic of this conference—"Was 70 CE Really a Watershed?"—goes to the heart of scholarly debate over the birth of Jewish liturgy. The question raised in the title of my paper gives voice to the opposing sides in the debate.

In his monumental 1990 article on "The Beginnings of Obligatory Jewish Prayer,"[1] Ezra Fleischer set forth the position that the Temple's destruction led directly to the innovation of fixed, obligatory, communal prayer with a binding *Urtext*, created *ex nihilo* under the direction of Rabban Gamaliel of Yavneh at the end of the first century CE. According to Fleischer, this was a completely new form of Jewish worship, instituted as a substitute for the sacrificial worship lost with the Temple's destruction, and nothing like it existed before 70 CE while the Temple cult was in operation. This historical model delineates a sea change and posits an essential *dis*continuity between pre-70 CE, private, voluntary, occasional, noncultic Jewish prayer and post-70 CE, fixed, obligatory, communal worship through institutionalized liturgy.

Fleischer's model of revolutionary change and liturgical creation *ex nihilo* is diametrically opposed to the model of continuity and gradual evolution put forward by Joseph Heinemann in 1964, which is widely accessible in the English translation of his seminal work, *Prayer in the Talmud: Forms and Patterns*.[2] Jewish liturgy, according to Heinemann, emerged gradually in an "organic process which sprung up among the people"[3] in various settings during the Second Temple period. The prayers from Qumran and in Ben Sira belong to this first stage of the

---

[1] *Tarbiz* 59 (1990): 397–441 (in Hebrew). See the review by R. Langer, "Revisiting Early Rabbinic Liturgy: The Recent Contributions of Ezra Fleischer," *Prooftexts* 19 (1999): 179–94; and the exchange between the two: Fleischer, "On the Origins of the ʿAmidah: Response to Ruth Langer"; and Langer, "Considerations of Method: A Response to Ezra Fleischer," *Prooftexts* 20 (2000): 380–87.

[2] Translated by R.S. Sarason (Berlin, 1977). The Hebrew original is: *Prayer in the Period of the Tannaʾim and the Amoraʾim: Its Nature and Patterns* (Jerusalem, 1964). Citations will follow the English translation.

[3] Heinemann, *Prayer*, 219.

process. The second stage was rabbinic systematization and imposition of norms on the originally diverse forms of prayer, which entailed setting the requisite time, number, order, and general content of the statutory prayers, but not their precise wording. The edition of the statutory prayers completed by the rabbis at Yavneh in the generation following the Temple's destruction is considered an important step in this middle stage of liturgical development, but neither Yavneh nor the Destruction is depicted as a watershed event. Rather, in this historical model the beginnings of Jewish liturgy stretch back at least two centuries before Yavneh to the time of Ben Sira and the oldest Dead Sea Scrolls, whereas the standardization of the liturgy is seen as continuing for centuries after Yavneh, reaching fruition with the first Jewish prayer books of the gaonic period (ninth–tenth centuries CE).

Heinemann and Fleischer formulated their respective positions on the origin of Jewish liturgy—evolution or revolution at Yavneh—when less than a fifth of the Dead Sea Scrolls were in the public domain. The nearly complete publication of the *Discoveries in the Judaean Desert* series, two volumes of which appeared just a few weeks before this "Watershed" conference, provides an unprecedented opportunity to reassess the issue.[4] It is from the vantage point of access to virtually the entire Scrolls corpus that I have reformulated the question for this paper in terms of the relationship between Jewish liturgy before and after 70 CE—change or continuity? The first part of the paper surveys the Qumran corpus and lays out the liturgical texts that are most relevant to the question. In the second and third parts, I examine two of the many examples of close correspondence between the pre-70 CE liturgies and post-70 CE Jewish liturgy. The implications for the question at hand are drawn out in the conclusion.

I. The Corpus

The corpus of texts discovered in the various Judean Desert sites now numbers approximately 1500 scrolls, of which about 930 are from the

---

[4] The two volumes released in December 2008 were DJD 37 and 40. The final volume—P.W. Flint and E. Ulrich, *Qumran Cave 1.II: The Isaiah Scrolls* (DJD 32)—was published in 2010. For the complete list of Dead Sea Scrolls and their DJD editions see E. Tov, *The Texts from the Judaean Desert: Indices and An Introduction to the Discoveries in the Judaean Desert Series* (DJD 39; Oxford, 2002) and *Revised Lists of the Texts from the Judaean Desert* (Leiden, 2010).

eleven caves at Qumran. The Qumran library contains works deriving from three very different points of origin. Biblical scrolls make up about a quarter of the library and signal the presence of nonsectarian works collected by the Qumran community. The distinctively Qumranic writings authored by members of the sect also represent only about a quarter of the library, revealing the corpus to be far less sectarian in origin than was imagined prior to the publication of most of the scrolls during the 1990s. The remaining texts, amounting to approximately 400 manuscripts, belong to a vast body of other, by and large previously unknown, Jewish literature that is not to be ascribed specifically to the Qumran community.[5]

The Qumran corpus preserves more than 300 discrete hymns, prayers, and psalms—including about one hundred biblical psalms. This tally counts as a separate entity each individual piece embedded in a collection and legal or narrative work, but each copy of the same prayer is counted only once. I have delineated seven major form-critical categories:[6]

1) Psalms collections: biblical manuscripts, noncanonical collections, and scrolls that juxtapose biblical and apocryphal psalms.
2) *Hodayot*: individual and communal sectarian thanksgiving hymns that typically open with the formula, "I thank you, Lord."

---

[5] For figures on the distribution of the Qumran library (based on a tally of 800 manuscripts) see P.R. Davies, G.J. Brooke, and P.R. Callaway, *The Complete World of The Dead Sea Scrolls* (London, 2002), 77; and D. Dimant, "The Qumran Manuscripts: Contents and Significance," in *Time to Prepare the Way in the Wilderness: Papers on the Qumran Scrolls by Fellows of the Institute for Advanced Studies of the Hebrew University, Jerusalem, 1989–1990* (ed. D. Dimant and L.H. Schiffman; Leiden, 1995), 23–58 (figures on pp. 31–32, 58). See also D. Dimant, "The Library of Qumran: Its Content and Character," in *The Dead Sea Scrolls: Fifty Years After Their Discovery 1947–1997, Proceedings of the Jerusalem Congress, July 20–25 1997* (ed. L.H. Schiffman, E. Tov, and J.C. VanderKam; Jerusalem, 2000), 170–76. In this paper, I use the term Qumran corpus/library to denote *all* texts *found* in the eleven caves near Qumran; the term Qumranic/sectarian denotes works *authored* by members of the Qumran community and, conversely, non-Qumranic/nonsectarian refers to works that were composed outside of the Qumran community even if they were copied and used at Qumran. For these categories see C.A. Newsom, "'Sectually Explicit' Literature in Qumran," in *The Hebrew Bible and Its Interpreters* (ed. W.H. Propp, B. Halpern, and D.N. Freedman; Winona Lake, 1990), 167–87.

[6] E.G. Chazon, "Prayers from Qumran and Their Historical Implications," *DSD* 1 (1994): 265–84; and "Hymns and Prayers in the Dead Sea Scrolls," in *The Dead Sea Scrolls After Fifty Years: A Comprehensive Assessment* (ed. P.W. Flint and J.C. VanderKam; 2 vols.; Leiden, 1998–1999), 1:258–68.

3) Prose prayers: prayers embedded in pseudepigraphic and other parabiblical works such as the *Aramaic Levi Document* and the *Apocryphon of Moses*.

4) Eschatological prayers: prayers requesting or depicting redemption (e.g., in 4Q521 *Messianic Apocalypse*) or for recitation in the eschaton such as the prayers in the *War Scroll*.

5) Magic incantations and apotropaic prayers: exorcisms (4Q560); apocryphal psalms with adjuration, curse, and incantation formulae (11QApPsa); *Songs of the Sage* (4Q510–511) to "frighten and terrify evil spirits"; etc.

6) Ceremonial liturgies: liturgies for periodic and ad hoc sectarian ceremonies such as the annual covenant renewal, initiation and expulsion of members, purification rites, and a marriage or old age ceremony.

7) Liturgies for fixed prayer times: liturgical collections, each containing a cycle of communal prayers for recitation at fixed times of the day, week, month or year.

Eileen Schuller recently surveyed the Qumran corpus and composed a list of the pre-Maccabean, and consequently also pre-Qumranic, prayers and psalms.[7] Only a handful of nonbiblical texts can be securely dated to the pre-Maccabean period based on the physical evidence of an archaic or early Hasmonean manuscript, most notably the weekly liturgy of 4Q504 *Words of the Luminaries* (see below). For this reason, Schuller expands her survey to include nonsectarian works, noting that: "It is generally assumed that nonsectarian prayers and psalms that were copied and preserved at Qumran are works composed before the formation of this distinctive group—that is, they could be accepted as coming from a received tradition and not from a contemporary

---

[7] E.M. Schuller, "Prayers and Psalms from the Pre-Maccabean Period," *DSD* 13 (2006): 306–18. Her initial survey was conducted for the 2004 SBL International Meeting, and there are only minor differences between the 2004 and 2006 versions. Schuller defines pre-Maccabean as "prior to the mid-second century BCE, before 160/150 BCE" (308). There is a scholarly consensus that the formation of the Qumran community took place during the second half of the second century BCE, based on both the earliest archaeological evidence for the sectarian settlement at Qumran (ca. 100 BCE) and the identification of the Wicked Priest with one of the Maccabean/Hasmonean high priests, the first of whom was Jonathan (152–143 BCE). For a review of the evidence see, for example, J.C. VanderKam, "Identity and History of the Community," in Flint and VanderKam, *Dead Sea Scrolls After Fifty Years*, 2:501–31.

rival."[8] Schuller was careful to include in her list only those texts that meet at least one of the hard criteria for non-Qumranic provenance, such as an early pre-Qumranic manuscript date, the use of the Tetragrammaton, or a calendar that diverges from the sectarian solar calendar.

The list has twenty-four items, eight of which are collections, yielding a total of at least 100 nonbiblical psalms; prayers embedded in narrative works such as the *Aramaic Levi Document*; and annual and daily liturgies. The latter, which are most relevant for the present inquiry, include the following liturgical cycles: benedictions praising God for the renewal of the heavenly lights at each evening and morning of the month in 4Q503 *Daily Prayers*; petitionary prayers for each day of the week and a hymn of praise for the Sabbath in the *Words of the Luminaries* (4Q504–506); *Festival Prayers* (1Q34[+bis], 4Q507–509) for the annual holidays, beginning with the New Year and Day of Atonement in Tishrei; and a cycle of thirteen Sabbath songs for the first quarter of the year, perhaps repeated quarterly throughout the whole year, in the *Songs of the Sabbath Sacrifice* (4Q400–407; 11Q17, Mas1k).[9]

---

[8] Schuller, "Prayers and Psalms," 312.

[9] In her list, Schuller italicizes "texts whose provenance is the subject of considerable uncertainty or disagreement" ("Prayers and Psalms," 313–16). However, a strong case for nonsectarian provenance can be made for the italicized texts that use the Tetragrammaton, such as the morning and evening prayers in 4Q408 *Apocryphon of Moses*, or texts whose calendar differs from the sectarian calendar, for example, the *Festival Prayers* (Newsom, "'Sectually Explicit,'" 177–78) and 4Q503 *Daily Prayers* (Chazon, "Prayers from Qumran," 282 n. 68; for the lunar and solar calculations in the *Daily Prayers* see n. 15 below). The *Songs of the Sabbath Sacrifice* are more vigorously debated. If they are Qumranic, these songs may be understood as a spiritual substitute for sacrifice in the defiled Temple, and they might point to a sectarian, apocalyptic context for the *merkabah* and *Qedushah* traditions to which they attest. For the first point, see A.S. van der Woude, "Fragmente einer Rolle der Leiden für das Sabbatopfer aus Höhle xi von Qumran," in *Von Kanaan bis Kerala: Festschrift für Prof. Mag. Dr. Dr. J.P.M. van der Ploeg O.P. zur Vollendung des siebzigsten Lebensjahres am 4. Juli 1979* (ed. W.C. Delsman et al.; Kevelaer, 1982), 311–37; and J. Maier, "*Shîrê 'Ôlat hash-Shabbat*: Some Observations on Their Calendric Implications and on Their Style," in *The Madrid Qumran Congress: Proceedings of the International Congress on the Dead Sea Scrolls, Madrid 18–21 March, 1991* (ed. J. Trebolle Barrera and L. Vegas Montaner; 2 vols.; Leiden, 1992), 2:543–70. For the second point see I. Gruenwald, *From Apocalypticism to Gnosticism* (Frankfurt, 1988), 145–70; R. Elior, "Mysticism, Magic, and Angelology—The Perception of Angels in Hekhalot Literature," *JSQ* 1 (1993): 3–53; and eadem, *The Three Temples: On the Emergence of Jewish Mysticism* (trans. D. Louvish; Oxford, Portland, 2004); P.S. Alexander, *The Mystical Texts* (London, 2006). If, however, the songs are non-Qumranic in origin, then another author, social context, and liturgical function should be sought. A few scholars have proposed roots in priestly circles connected to the Jerusalem Temple cult (see Alexander,

The non-Qumranic liturgical collections, with their set texts of communal prayers for fixed prayer times—annual festivals, Sabbaths, and regular weekdays—solidly attest regular, public prayer outside of Qumran during the two centuries prior to the destruction of the Second Temple.[10] Consequently, they radically alter the old view that the secessionist Qumran community was the only Jewish group that engaged in this type of liturgical practice in Palestine during the Second Temple period. They contribute to a growing awareness that not all fixed, communal prayer came into being as a substitute for sacrifice when the Temple was inaccessible—whether due to a sectarian boycott, geographical distance, or the Temple's destruction in 70 CE.[11]

Mystical Texts, 128–35; Elior, *Three Temples*, 11, 15–16; and Maier, "*Shîrê 'Ôlat hash-Shabbat*," 559–60, who suggested that the songs also may have been used by priests outside of Qumran and that similar compositions may have been recited by priests not "actually engaged in service" at the Jerusalem Temple). For the newer assessment by the text's editor, Carol Newsom, of the *Songs*' non-Qumranic authorship, see her article, "'Sectually Explicit,'" 179–85; cf. her first edition, *Songs of the Sabbath Sacrifice: A Critical Edition* (Atlanta, 1985).

[10] The venue for regular public prayer during the Second Temple period remains difficult to determine. As is well known, the burgeoning data for the early synagogue attest a variety of communal activities, including public Torah reading but not regular prayer services (see below, n. 25). Recently, some scholars have argued for regular, fixed liturgy in the Jerusalem Temple (see n. 9 above and J. Maier, "Zu Kult und Liturgie der Qumrangemeinde," *RevQ* 14 [1990]: 543–86; D.K. Falk, "Qumran Prayer Texts and the Temple," in *Sapiential, Liturgical, and Poetical Texts From Qumran: Proceedings of the Third Meeting of the International Organization for Qumran Studies* [ed. D.K. Falk, F. García Martínez, and E.M. Schuller; Leiden, 2000], 106–26; D.D. Binder, *Into the Temple Courts: The Place of the Synagogues in the Second Temple Period* [Atlanta, 1999]; E. Regev, "Temple Prayer as the Origin of Fixed Prayer [On the Evolution of Prayer during the Period of the Second Temple]," *Zion* 70 [2005]: 5–29 [in Hebrew]). Mustering the evidence against prayer in the "sanctuary of silence," Israel Knohl proposes that regular, fixed liturgies like those unearthed at Qumran were established by proto-Qumranic groups associated with such works as the books of *1 Enoch* and *Jubilees* (see his "Between Voice and Silence: The Relationship between Prayer and Temple Cult," *JBL* 115 [1996]: 17–30; and the updated Hebrew version in *Meḥqerei Talmud 2: Talmudic Studies Dedicated to the Memory of Professor Ephraim E. Urbach* [ed. Y. Sussman and D. Rosenthal; Jerusalem, 2005], 740–53; I thank Israel Knohl for sharing his view on *1 Enoch* in a personal communication). Clearly, we are in the midst of an intense scholarly debate over the geographical and social locations of early liturgy.

[11] Schuller ("Prayers and Psalms," 317) similarly concludes that "regular, set formulary prayer clearly was developing alongside of Temple worship." See also Falk, "Qumran Prayer Texts," 106–8, 124–26, and his discussion there of the classic model of prayer as a substitute for sacrifice.

II. The Pre- and Post-70 ce Liturgical Benediction— Continuity and/or Change?

In addition to their pathbreaking testimony to the very existence of fixed, communal prayer among some non-Qumranic groups in pre-70 ce Palestine, the Scrolls also reveal an impressive number of close correspondences with later Jewish liturgy for specific prayers, formulae, and practices. I will illustrate this liturgical continuity by two examples found in the important liturgical collections of non-Qumranic origin, taking care to also note points of divergence, in keeping with this study's agenda.[12]

The first case is the systematic use of blessing formulae to open and close liturgical prayers. This function comes to the fore in the daily,

---

[12] Beginning with the pioneering work of Shemaryahu Talmon, David Flusser, and Moshe Weinfeld, and in more recent studies by Johann Maier, Bilhah Nitzan, Daniel Falk, and others, dozens of suggestions have been made for identifying specific traditional Jewish prayers in the Dead Sea Scrolls and associated literature, most notably in Ben Sira and 1–2 Maccabees. See S. Talmon, "The 'Manual of Benedictions' of the Sect of the Judaean Desert," *RevQ* 2 (1960): 475–500; idem, "The Emergence of Institutionalized Prayer in Israel in the Light of the Qumran Literature," in his *The World of Qumran From Within: Collected Studies* (Jerusalem, 1989), 200–243; D. Flusser, "Sanktus und Gloria," in *Abraham unser Vater: Juden und Christen im Gespräch über die Bibel. Festschrift für Otto Michel zum 60. Geburtstag* (ed. O. Betz, M. Hengel, and P. Schmidt; Leiden, 1963), 128–52; idem, "Qumran and Jewish 'Apotropaic' Prayers," *IEJ* 16 (1966): 194–205; idem, "He Has Planted It [i.e., the Law] as Eternal Life in Our Midst," *Tarbiz* 58 (1989): 147–53 (in Hebrew); M. Weinfeld, "Traces of *Kedushat Yotzer* and *Pesukey De-Zimra* in the Qumran Literature and in Ben Sira," *Tarbiz* 45 (1976): 15–26 (in Hebrew); idem, "The Prayers for Knowledge, Repentance and Forgiveness in the 'Eighteen Benedictions'—Qumran Parallels, Biblical Antecedents, and Basic Characteristics," *Tarbiz* 45 (1979): 15–26 (in Hebrew); idem, "The Morning Prayers (*Birkhoth Hashachar*) in Qumran and in the Conventional Jewish Liturgy," *RevQ* 13 (1988): 481–94; idem, "Prayer and Liturgical Practice in the Qumran Sect," in *Dead Sea Scrolls: Forty Years of Research* (ed. D. Dimant and U. Rappaport; Leiden, 1992), 241–58; idem, "The Angelic Song Over the Luminaries in the Qumran Texts," in Dimant and Schiffman, *Time to Prepare*; see also L.H. Schiffman, "The Dead Sea Scrolls and the Early History of Jewish Liturgy," in *The Synagogue in Late Antiquity* (ed. L.I. Levine; Philadelphia, 1987), 33–48. The more recent studies include Maier, "Zu Kult"; B. Nitzan, *Qumran Prayer and Religious Poetry* (trans. J. Chipman; Leiden, 1994); eadem, "The Dead Sea Scrolls and the Jewish Liturgy," in *The Dead Sea Scrolls as Background to Postbiblical Judaism and Christianity* (ed. J.R. Davila; Leiden, 2003), 195–219; D.K. Falk, *Daily, Sabbath, and Festival Prayers in the Dead Sea Scrolls* (STDJ 27; Leiden, 1998); idem, "Qumran and the Synagogue Liturgy," in *The Ancient Synagogue, From Its Origins Until 200 CE: Papers Presented at an International Conference at Lund University, October 14–17, 2001* (ed. B. Olsson and M. Zetterholm; Stockholm, 2003), 404–33; and Chazon, "Prayers from Qumran"; see also the specific examples given below.

weekly, and annual liturgies unearthed at Qumran.[13] In 4Q503 *Daily Prayers* the formula, "Blessed is the God of Israel" (ברוך אל ישראל) opens each of these evening and morning prayers and closes many of them, occasionally adding "You" or "Your name" in the closing blessings that come right before this liturgy's standard concluding formula, "Peace unto you, Israel."[14] In these daily prayers, the blessing formula continues with a specific content clause formulated as a relative, participial, nominal, or prepositional clause that praises God primarily for the daily renewal of the luminaries' light, for instance: ברוך אל יש[ראל ...] ל דק(ג)לי או[ר...הוד[עתנו בתהלי כבודכה [...] בכול [...]מועדי לילה שלום עליכה [ישראל], "Blessed is the God of Is[rael...] flags of ligh[t ...]

---

[13] For the Qumran data see E.M. Schuller, "Some Observations on Blessings of God in Texts From Qumran," in *Of Scribes and Scrolls: Studies on the Hebrew Bible, Intertestamental Judaism and Christian Origins, Presented to John Strugnell on the Occasion of His Sixtieth Birthday* (ed. H.W. Attridge, J.J. Collins, and T.H. Tobin; Lanham, Md., 1990), 133–43; E.G. Chazon, "A Liturgical Document from Qumran and Its Implications: 'Words of the Luminaries' (4QDibHam)" (Ph.D. diss., The Hebrew University of Jerusalem, 1992), 100–101 (in Hebrew); Nitzan, *Qumran Prayer*, 72–80; and Falk, *Daily, Sabbath, and Festival Prayers*, 37–42, 79–84, 182–85. In addition to the three nonsectarian liturgies from Qumran cited here, several sectarian liturgical collections regularly employ opening blessing formulae (e.g., the purification rituals in 4Q512, 414, 284; 4Q502 *Marriage Ritual*; and many of the hymns in the *Hodayot*; see H. Stegemann, "The Number of Psalms in *1QHodayot*ᵃ and Some of Their Sections," in *Liturgical Perspectives: Prayer and Poetry in Light of the Dead Sea Scrolls, Proceedings of the Fifth International Symposium of the Orion Center for the Study of the Dead Sea Scrolls and Associated Literature, 19–23 January 2000* [ed. E.G. Chazon in collaboration with R. Clements and A. Pinnick; Leiden, 2003], 191–234), and at least two collections employ concluding blessings (*Songs of the Sage*, 4Q511 63 iv 1–3 and 1QHᵃ; for which see Chazon, "Liturgical Function in the Cave 1 *Hodayot* Collection," in *Qumran Cave 1 Revisited: Texts from Cave 1 Sixty Years after Their Discovery. Proceedings of the Sixth Meeting of the IOQS in Ljubljana* [ed. D.K. Falk, S. Metso, and E. Tigchelaar; Leiden, 2010], 135–149). The sectarian examples demonstrate that the Qumran community followed accepted liturgical conventions in writing its own prayers.

[14] Two examples of closing blessings in the second person are: ברו[ך אתה אל ישראל אשר העמדת בכול מועד[י] לילה [...] שלום עליכה ישראל] (4Q503 33 i–34 20–21); and ברוך ש[מכה אל ישרא[ל...שלום עלי]כה ישראל (frg. 66 2–3). Baillet (DJD 7, 116) reconstructed the second person pronoun in two of the opening blessings in frgs. 33 ii+35+36; however, in the first instance (ll. 1–2) there is absolutely no evidence for this and in the second (ll. 6–7) his reconstruction (א[תה א[ל...]ברוך]) is just one of several options (Falk's restoration, ברוך אל[י]שרא[ל אש]ר) fits the standard third person opening blessing formula but his reading of *yod* is difficult; see his *Daily, Sabbath, and Festival Prayers*, 37–40). The comparable morning and evening liturgy that is embedded in 4QapocMosesᶜ? (4Q408 3+3a 6–6a) has one extant opening blessing; in this case the original third person formula was corrected to a second person address by placing cancellation dots around the Tetragrammation and adding אתה אדני supralinearly: ברוך אתה אדני {יהוה} [ה]{צדיק בכל דרכיך ("Blessed are you, Adonay {Yahweh} who is righteous in all your ways"). For the growing tendency toward the second person address in blessings, see n. 18 below.

You have made [kno]wn to us in praises of Your glory [...in all] appointed times of night, peace unto you, [Israel]" (frgs. 51–55 6–10, see also ll. 12–15 and frgs. 29–32 7–11, 76 1–4).[15]

Each weekday prayer in the *Words of the Luminaries* and each of the *Festival Prayers* opens with the formula, "Remember, Lord" and, after a long petition, closes with a "Blessed is the Lord" formula completed by a content clause that briefly recapitulates the prayer's main theme, for example: ברוך אדוני אשר שמחנ[ו], "Blessed is the Lord who has made u[s] rejoice" (1Q34bis 1+2 4, the end of the prayer for the New Year); and ברוך], [אדוני אשר הודי[ענו, "Blessed is] the Lord who has made kno[wn to us...]" (4Q504 6 14, the end of the Sunday prayer).[16] The concluding benedictions in the weekday prayers are consistently formulated with a relative clause, whereas relative and participial clauses are used alternatively in the festival prayers (for a participial eulogy in the latter see 4Q509 4 4–5). An "Amen, Amen" response follows each concluding benediction in both of these liturgies.

The liturgical use of framing benedictions, particularly as closings, and the second person address to God as "You" in blessing formulae, are innovations vis-à-vis the classic biblical blessing, which opens a spontaneous personal expression of praise about God.[17] These innovations also

---

[15] For the phonetic *gimel/kaf* substitution see E. Qimron, *The Hebrew of the Dead Sea Scrolls* (Atlanta, 1986), 27. In this liturgy, the term דגלי אור, "flags of light," regularly denotes the half-day incremental change in lunar light between the previous evening's lunar phase and that of the next evening; the incremental daily change (0–14 portions of lunar light) is designated by the terms גורלות חושך, גורלות אור ("lots of darkness/light"). The number of שערי אור, "gates of light" equals the date of the lunar month but is counted at sunrise and refers to the rising and setting of the sun. The dating of the Sabbaths accords with the 364-day solar calendar. For this system see J.M. Baumgarten, "4Q503 (Daily Prayers) and the Lunar Calendar," *RevQ* 12 (1986): 399–407; see also E.G. Chazon, "The Function of the Qumran Prayer Texts: An Analysis of the Daily Prayers [4Q503]," in Schiffman, Tov, and Vanderkam, *The Dead Sea Scrolls: Fifty Years After*, 217–25.

[16] In the first example, the title for the "Prayer for the Day of Atonement" follows on line 6 after a full blank line (l. 5). In the second, the "Amen, Amen" response on the next line, followed by a *vacat*, indicates that this was a concluding benediction; compare especially the closing benediction and "Amen, Amen" response followed by a *vacat* in 4Q504 3 ii 2–3, where the title of the prayer for "the fourth d[ay]" is on the next inscribed line (l. 5). The Sunday and Thursday prayers are petitions for knowledge, repentance, and forgiveness; the Thursday prayer is discussed below in part III of this paper. For the reconstruction of the *Words of the Luminaries* see "4Q504 (4QDibHamᵃ)," ed. M. Baillet, DJD 7, and E.G. Chazon, in *The Dead Sea Scrolls Reader, Part 5: Poetic and Liturgical Texts* (ed. D.W. Parry and E. Tov; Leiden, 2005), 241–57.

[17] For instance, Jethro's blessing in Exod 18:10, ברוך יהוה אשר הציל אתכם מיד מצרים ומיד פרעה אשר הציל את העם מתחת יד מצרים "Blessed be the Lord who

have some, albeit limited and generally late, biblical roots;[18] however, they are essentially Second Temple period developments that serve as forerunners of the rabbinic liturgical benediction. In the latter, the rabbis imposed a rigid opening and closing blessing framework on the obligatory prayers, principally the *Shema* Benedictions and the daily Eighteen Benedictions, seven on Sabbaths and Festivals. The standard opening blessing with a relative clause for its specific content was kept distinct in rabbinic prayers from the concluding, participial eulogy, as, for example, in the Torah benediction: ברוך אתה ה' אלהינו מלך העולם אשר נתן לנו תורת אמת חיי עולם נטע(ה) בתוכנו. ברוך אתה ה' נותן התורה. ("Blessed are You, Lord, our God, King of the Universe, who gave us the true Torah [and] implanted it within us for eternal life. Blessed are You, Lord, who gives the Torah").[19] The participial pattern

---

[18] In the Bible, closing blessings are only used to mark the end of each book of Psalms (41:14, 72:18–19, 89:53, 106:48) and of three more hymns (Pss 66:20; 68:36; 135:21; for the late date of Psalm 135 and of the blessings that close the books of the Psalter see A. Hurvitz, *The Transition Period in Biblical Hebrew* [Jerusalem, 1972], 174). Note also the closing blessings in Tob 13:19; *Ps. Sol.* 2:37, 5:19, 6:6; and 3 Macc 7:23. The second person address to God in blessings is a feature of late biblical Hebrew, occurring only in Ps 119:12 and 1 Chr 29:10; see Hurvitz, ibid., 144–45. In addition to the daily prayers in 4Q503 and 4Q408 discussed above, blessings with a second person address to God are found in some apocryphal works (Tob 3:8, 15–17; LXX Dan 3:3, 29) and several of the distinctively sectarian liturgical collections cited above in n. 13, namely, the *Songs of the Sage, Purification Ritual*, and the *Hodayot*; tellingly, a supra-linear correction changes the typical *hodayot* formula, "I thank you, Lord" to "Blessed are You" in one hymn (1QH^a 13:2; for this emendation see H. Stegemann and E. Schuller, trans. of texts by C. Newsom, *1QHodayot^a*, DJD 40:167–68 and 173–74, and also Heinemann, *Prayer*, 80). The scrolls of both sectarian as well as non-Qumranic origin thus provide early evidence for a growing tendency toward the second person address to God in opening and closing blessings. For this tendency to "'personalize' prayer" in the rabbinic blessings see Heinemann, ibid., 89.

[19] Heinemann, *Prayer*, 77–103. The Torah benediction quoted here is one of Heinemann's examples (86, 97); its specific content and historical development are discussed below in section III of this paper. Heinemann showed that whereas the rabbinic opening blessing was based on the classic biblical pattern, the eulogy pattern was a "novel creation" of the Second Temple period that was used as the standard rabbinic closing and additionally came to function as an alternate opening formula (see the case of the first blessing before the *Shema* cited below). The new data from Qumran support these claims as well as Heinemann's observation about the later insertion of the second person address into the biblical pattern, but they call for a revision of certain details in his model of the blessing's development: 1) the frequent use of the second person address with the relative clause in many blessings from Qumran, on the one hand, and the many cases of an entirely third person participial blessing form, on the other, indicate (contra Heinemann, 87, 100) that the second person address to God

---

delivered you from the Egyptians and from Pharaoh, and who delivered the people from under the hand of the Egyptians." For the biblical pattern and numerous examples see M. Greenberg, *Biblical Prose Prayer* (Berkeley, 1983), 30–37; and Heinemann, *Prayer*, 82–89.

also served as an alternate opening formula as in the first of the two blessings before the *Shema*.[20] Both rabbinic patterns regularly combine second and third person addresses. The Scrolls now show that in the earlier period both the relative clause and the active participle were used interchangeably in closing as well as opening blessings, and that both patterns could be couched entirely either in the second or third person. The rabbinic liturgical benediction, which Heinemann dated no earlier than the second century CE,[21] thus exhibits some differences in detail and a greater degree of standardization than the pre-70 liturgies. But overall, a remarkable picture of continuity and gradual evolution emerges in the systematic, formal use of opening and closing benedictions in liturgical prayers. I venture to suggest that this formal function of the benediction is a tag that signals, and that can be used to trace, the rise of regular communal prayer during the Second Temple period, just as it later becomes the hallmark of the rabbinic fixed, statutory prayers.

III. Pre- and Post-70 ce Prayers for Knowledge: Continuity and/or Change?

As a second example of a close correspondence with post-70 CE Jewish liturgy, I have chosen the petition "to implant Your Torah in our heart" (לטעת תורתכה בלבנו) in the Thursday prayer of the *Words*

---

was not integral to the eulogy pattern, from which it entered the rabbinic opening blessing; rather, the general tendency toward the personalized second person address independently influenced both patterns, at first only sporadically; and 2) the classic biblical blessing pattern formulated with a relative clause was used not only in opening blessings, as Heinemann claimed (93, 97), but also in concluding benedictions. For these developments see also below.

[20] In the morning service the first blessing before the *Shema*, which is called the *Yotzer*, opens as follows: ברוך אתה ה' אלהינו מלך העולם יוצר אור ובורא חושך; "Blessed are You, Lord, King of the Universe who forms light and creates darkness." The specific content clause in the evening blessing begins thus: אשר בדברו מעריב ערבים, "who with his word brings on the evenings." See, for example, I. Davidson, S. Assaf, and I. Joel, eds., *Siddur R. Saadja Gaon* (Jerusalem, 1941), 13, 26, 36–37.

[21] Although Heinemann recognized the pre-70 CE origin of the eulogy form, he saw the rounded opening and closing framework of the rabbinic liturgical benediction as a development of the second century CE (*Prayer*, 95–96). He dated the motif of God's kingship in the opening benediction similarly, noting (94) that it is not reflected in the Eighteen Benedictions and that its requirement is first stated by a third-century sage (*b. Ber.* 12a, *y. Ber.* 9:1, 12d). Heinemann also drew attention (ibid., 80 and 87, n. 14) to the fact that leading third-century sages were still debating whether mentioning God's name or kingship, and addressing God as "You," were necessary in order to fulfill the requirement of reciting a benediction.

of the Luminaries.[22] This precise expression is not found in the Bible (cf. Isa 51:7; Jer 31:33), and therefore provides a particularly good test case.[23] The *Words of the Luminaries* documents this expression's liturgical use more than two centuries before it resurfaces in the early rabbinic period and first Christian centuries. David Flusser cited this scroll, along with an early rabbinic homily on Eccl 12:11 that likens the Torah's words to goads and implanted nails (*t. Sotah* 7:11), as evidence for the antiquity of the version of the Torah benediction that blesses God "who gave us the true Torah (and) implanted it (that is, the Torah) within us for eternal life," אשר נתן לנו תורת אמת חיי עולם נטעה בתוכנו.[24] The comparison between Thursday's petition in the *Words of the Luminaries* and this liturgical blessing recited after reading from the Torah unveils the continuity of a distinctive liturgical expression but a difference in liturgical function.[25]

---

[22] 4Q504 15:14 (frgs. 1+2 ii 13). The text is quoted from my edition in *DSSR* 5:250. The infinitive form of the verb לטעת is employed here in the context of a petitionary passage that opens six lines earlier with the word of entreaty and an imperative verb (אנא אדוני עשה נא). This passage has a counterpart in the Sunday prayer, in which the equivalent request is expressed by the imperative: [מולה עורלת, "Circumcise the foreskin of [our heart" (ibid., 244; compare the abbreviated form of the Eighteen Benedictions quoted in the name of the first-generation talmudic sage, Samuel, in *b. Ber.* 29a; the text is provided in the appendix).

[23] Jeremiah Unterman suggested, in response to this paper, that the *Words of the Luminaries* and the *Apostolic Constitutions* could have independently derived the expression for "implanting Torah/law in the heart" from Jer 31:33; 32:40–41. However, note that the metaphors of "placing the Torah/fear of God in Israel's heart" and "planting them in the Land" are separate in Jeremiah and that the *Words of the Luminaries* does not echo any of the other expressions in these Jeremian passages while it does have a cluster of parallels with the prayer of the catechumens in the *Apostolic Constitutions* (see below).

[24] David Flusser, "He has Planted It." For this ancient version, Flusser (152 nn. 25–27) quotes the old Yemenite rite and Maimonides' *Mishneh Torah, Sefer 'Ahavah* 12:5, in the section on "Laws of Prayer and the Priestly Blessing" (consult the edition by Y. Kapah [Jerusalem, 1985], 249). He sees an "echo" of this Torah benediction in John 5:38–40 ("He has Planted it," 152, n. 28), and "the full ancient version" in the *Qedushah de Sidra* prayer (151); he also cites (ibid.) a number of early Christian texts including *Apos. Con.* 7.26.3 (but not 8.6.5–7, which is discussed below) for the metaphor of implanting the Torah/*nomos* within a person's heart. See also Flusser's earlier discussion of this Torah benediction in "Sanktus und Gloria," 141–43. Another version of this benediction, used almost universally today, omits the feminine singular pronominal suffix on the verb for implanting, which refers to the Torah, and thus creates the impression that what is implanted is eternal life (for an early medieval example see *Siddur R. Saadja Gaon*, 359).

[25] I prefer the word "difference" to "change" in this case because both directions of influence are plausible: the Scrolls indicate the priority of a petition for implanting Torah whereas evidence of public Torah reading ceremonies during the Second

A later functional trajectory of the weekday petition to implant Torah in the worshippers' heart, together with a greater degree of thematic and contextual continuity, can be identified by factoring into the discussion a parallel passage in the prayer for the catechumens in *Apos. Con.* 8.6.5–8, as well as the rabbinic Eighteen Benedictions. In contrast to the purely laudatory rabbinic benediction recited after the public Torah reading ceremony, the early Christian prayer for the catechumens, like the second-century BCE *Words of the Luminaries*, uses the expression of implanting Torah/Law (*nomos*) to formulate a *petition* for knowledge.[26]

Furthermore, the context in the *Words of the Luminaries* and the prayer for the catechumens is the liturgical complex of petitions for knowledge, repentance, and forgiveness—the same complex institutionalized in the first three intermediary benedictions of the Eighteen

---

Temple period could support a claim that the benediction after the Torah reading was already recited pre-70 CE. This possibility was even entertained by Fleischer ("Beginnings," 408–9, 412–13), who vociferously denied any role to regular, communal prayer in the diasporan and Palestinian synagogues of the Second Temple period. For the centrality of public Torah reading and study in Second Temple synagogues and the possible role of communal prayer in some of the synagogues called *proseuchai* ("prayer houses"), see L.I. Levine, *The Ancient Synagogue: The First Thousand Years* (2d ed.; New Haven, 2005), 138–39, 162–73; idem, "The First Century CE Synagogue," in Olsson and Zetterholm, *The Ancient Synagogue From Its Origins Until 200 CE*, 1–24. A remarkably similar dialectic between linguistic continuity and functional differentiation can be observed in the rabbinic blessing recited *before* the Torah reading, whose content clause praising "He who has chosen us from all the nations" (R. Hamnuna, *b. Ber.* 11b) is now attested in a Sabbath blessing (4Q 503 *Daily Prayers* 24–25 4) and in a festival prayer (4Q508 4 2) from Qumran. For the latter occasions, a trajectory is found in rabbinic Sabbath and festival prayers (e.g., *b. Yoma* 87b). I discussed this example in Chazon, "Prayers from Qumran," 278.

[26] "Implant in them his pure and saving fear; open the ears of their hearts to engage in his Law day and night" (*Apos. Con.* 8.6.5). The direct object of the verb "implant" in *Apos. Con.* 8.6.5 is "fear" (*phobos*) of God, but it is significant that this verse immediately continues with the request to "open the ears of their hearts to engage in his Law (*nomos*) day and night," and that the phrase "You (God) implanted a law in our souls" occurs in *Apos. Con.* 7.26.3 (on the latter see n. 24 above). The translation is from D.A. Fiensy, *Prayers Alleged to Be Jewish: An Examination of the Constitutiones Apostolorum* (Chico, Calif., 1985), 47, 93, 95; see also his comment (p. 170) about the motif of "implanted law/knowledge"; in addition, see the comments by P.W. van der Horst and J.H. Newman, "The Hellenistic Synagogal Prayers in the *Apostolic Constitutions*," in *Early Jewish Prayers in Greek* (Berlin, 2008), 6, 42–43 (note the shift from the position taken earlier by van der Horst in "The Greek Synagogue Prayers in the Apostolic Constitutions, book VII," in *From Qumran to Cairo: Studies in the History of Prayer* [ed. J. Tabory; Jerusalem, 1999], 19–46, esp. 39, 43). For the motif of "fear of God" in a similar liturgical context, compare the petition for repentance in the Babylonian version of the abbreviated Eighteen Benedictions: ומול את לבבנו ליראתך (*b. Ber.* 29a).

Benedictions.[27] Both the *Words of the Luminaries* and the *Apostolic Constitutions* independently display parallels with the abbreviated and long forms of these three benedictions, for example: the language of granting understanding and forgiveness for sins in the prayer for the catechumens; "make us understand" and perhaps "[cause] us to [repe]nt" in the Thursday prayer; "forgive our sins" and "circumcise the foreskin of[our heart" in the Sunday prayer of the same weekly liturgy from Qumran.[28]

These parallels to the rabbinic liturgy are, however, of a more general and diffuse nature than the impressive set of correspondences between the Thursday prayer in the *Words of the Luminaries* and the prayer for the catechumens. Strikingly, the two nonrabbinic texts juxtapose the special request for implanting the Torah/Law with a distinctively phrased request to be saved from sin/impiety.[29] The two distinctive parallels, their juxtaposition in both prayers, and the relatively high

---

[27] See Weinfeld, "Prayers for Knowledge, Repentance, and Forgiveness." These are the fourth, fifth, and sixth of the Eighteen Benedictions. The prayer for the catechumens was a key text in Weinfeld's study (ibid., 194–95), informing his conclusion that prayers of this type sought "admission" to God's presence and were recited in a situation of repentance or conversion. He saw this *Sitz im Leben* reflected in the placement of the petitions for knowledge, repentance, and forgiveness before the other petitions in the daily Eighteen Benedictions. He mentions the *Words of the Luminaries* and the blessing after the Torah reading in a footnote on the language of implanting employed by the prayer for the catechumens (ibid., 194, n. 44). At the time of Weinfeld's 1979 study, only a partial, preliminary edition of the *Words of the Luminaries* had been published by M. Baillet, "Un recueil liturgique de Qumrân, grotte 4: 'Les paroles des luminaires," *RB* 68 (1961): 195–250; Baillet published the full edition in 1982 in DJD 7.

[28] For the first set compare חונן הדעת and סלח נא כי חטאנו in the long version of the Eighteen; for the second, compare הבינגו in the abbreviated Eighteen and השיבנו in the long version; for the third compare also מול את לבבנו ליראתך in the abbreviated Eighteen given in the Babylonian Talmud (*b. Ber.* 29a) and see n. 22 above. The texts are provided in the appendix.

[29] In contrast, neither the "implanting" metaphor nor the specific language of "saving from sin" occurs in the rabbinic complex or in petitions for knowledge and protection from sin that are more or less contemporary with the *Words of the Luminaries* (Pss 119, 155; 11QPs[a] *Plea for Deliverance*; see DJD 4:40, 76–79; Levi's prayer in 4Q213b Levi[b] ar frgs. 1+2, see DJD 22:27–32). The Thursday petition employs the infinitive חטוא, "sinning." The parallel in *Apos. Con.* 8.6.6 uses the noun *asebeia*; this Greek word is one of many translation equivalents for the Hebrew root חטא (see T. Muraoka, *Hebrew/Aramaic Index to the Septuagint Keyed to the Hatch–Redpath Concordance* [Grand Rapids, 1998], 49); the more common equivalent, *hamartia*, occurs in the exhortation to the catechumens that ends this section (*anamartētov*, *Apos. Con.* 8.6.8).

concentration of correspondences in a short passage[30] all suggest that the prayer for the catechumens made use of a Jewish liturgical source resembling the Thursday prayer, i.e., a petition for knowledge, repentance, and forgiveness that was more similar *linguistically* to the *Words of the Luminaries* than to the Eighteen Benedictions in any of its extant versions. It is important to note, however, that the *order* of the petitions in the *Apostolic Constitutions* agrees with that of the Eighteen Benedictions over against that of the *Words of the Luminaries*; specifically, the petition for forgiveness comes first in the *Words of the Luminaries* but last in the *Apostolic Constitutions* and in the rabbinic liturgy, both of which first request knowledge. Given the array of correspondences, it is plausible that the Jewish source behind the prayer for the catechumens would have been a version of the first three intermediary benedictions of the Eighteen.[31] I have suggested elsewhere that the fourth-century Christian compiler of the *Apostolic Constitutions* drew here, as he did in other places, upon contemporary synagogue liturgy in a form that preserves genuine Second Temple usage and that differs in its precise wording from the statutory liturgy as recorded in the Babylonian and Palestinian Talmuds and in the earliest Jewish prayer books (ninth–tenth centuries CE).[32]

---

[30] The cluster of parallels encompasses the more commonly phrased requests to grant understanding, instruction in God's laws, and forgiveness of sins as well as the distinctively phrased requests for "implanting" (see n. 26 above) and "saving from sin" (see n. 29 above).

[31] The literary relationship between this proposed source and the Eighteen Benedictions would then be comparable to that between the short and long versions of the Eighteen (compare, for example, הביננו, "make us understand," and חונן הדעת, "grant us understanding," in the latter with the alternate petition for knowledge, "implant Torah in our heart," in the proposed source). The original Hebrew source may well have been translated into Greek by the time it reached the compiler of the *Apostolic Constitutions*. For the suggestion that some of the prayers in the *Apostolic Constitutions* go back to a Hebrew original, see Fiensy, *Prayers Alleged to Be Jewish*, 209–22; and van der Horst and Newman, *Early Jewish Prayers*, 9–29.

[32] This state of affairs is consistent with the compiler's apparent use of the Sabbath *Amidah* in 7.33–38 and the *Shema* complex in 8.37–39. See E.G. Chazon, "A 'Prayer Alleged to be Jewish' in the *Apostolic Constitutions*," in *Things Revealed: Studies in Honor of Michael E. Stone* (ed. E.G. Chazon, D. Satran, and R.A. Clements; Brill, 2004), 261–77; on pp. 266–67 I give a comparative chart of the petitions for knowledge, repentance and forgiveness in the *Words of the Luminaries*, the prayer for the catechumens, and the abbreviated Eighteen Benedictions. In response to the critique by van der Horst and Newman (*Early Jewish Prayers*, 28), note my comment above that the order of the petitions in *Apos. Con.* 8.6.5–8 does in fact agree with the order of the petitions for knowledge, repentance, and forgiveness in the rabbinic Eighteen Benedictions.

To sum up thus far, the *Words of the Luminaries* in its own right displays thematic, contextual and functional, continuity with the trilogy of petitions for knowledge, repentance, and forgiveness in the rabbinic daily liturgy *par excellence*, the Eighteen Benedictions. In addition, linguistic continuity between pre-70 and post-70 formulations of this liturgical complex is unveiled by comparing this Second Temple period liturgy with the Christian prayer for the catechumens recorded in the fourth-century CE compilation of the *Apostolic Constitutions*. The comparison also seems to recover a missing link in early Jewish liturgical tradition.

At this juncture it is important to acknowledge not only the similarities but also how the *Words of the Luminaries* and the prayer for the catechumens *differ* from the Eighteen Benedictions in their distinctive formulations for "implanting Torah" and "saving from sin," as well as in their larger literary structure. Neither encompasses the full extent of the topics in the Eighteen nor is either structured as a series of short, single topic benedictions, even though each of the weekday petitionary prayers in the liturgy from Qumran does have a formal, concluding benediction.[33] These concomitant similarities *and* differences, continuities *and* changes, between the Eighteen Benedictions and the *Words of the Luminaries*, are representative of the larger picture of the relationship between the pre- and post-70 liturgies for fixed prayer times.[34]

---

[33] Compare Ben Sira 51, which has nearly the full range of topics found in the Eighteen Benedictions but is structured as a series of short doxologies each framed by a thanksgiving (*hodu*, cf. Ps 136) formula rather than as a benediction. Note that this hymn is not attested in the ancient versions: it is neither in LXX Sirach nor in the Hebrew fragments of Ben Sira found at Qumran and Masada. Nevertheless, on the basis of its thanksgiving for the election of the sons of Zadok as priests, some scholars suggest a pro-Zadokite priestly origin and an early second-century BCE date (see P.W. Skehan and A.A. Di Lella, *The Wisdom of Ben Sira* [New York, 1987], 568–71). The hymn might be an independent text that was later appended to Ben Sira in a fashion similar to the autobiographical hymn in the same chapter (51:13–30) for which another version has now been found in the large Cave 11 Psalms Scroll (see J.A. Sanders, *The Psalms Scroll of Qumrân Cave 11 [11QPsᵃ]*, DJD 4:79–85).

[34] Note also that the prayers vary from day to day in the *Words of the Luminaries* and 4Q503 *Daily Prayers*, whereas the same prayer is repeated daily in the rabbinic liturgy.

IV. Implications and Conclusion

In moving to assess liturgical continuity and/or change via the examples presented above, I aim to take a wider view of pre- and post-70 prayers and to draw some broad implications about liturgical composition and development. First and foremost, the examples are part of what now amounts to a critical mass of liturgical formulae, prayers, and practices with striking parallels to their counterparts in the statutory Jewish liturgy. This picture resembles what Heinemann described as "common liturgical property,"[35] from which the rabbis drew in composing the statutory prayers; a description that, in this limited source-material sense, could even fit Fleischer's historical model. However, the full publication of the Scrolls gives this "common liturgical property" a far grander scope and uncovers a sizeable, continuous liturgical tradition stretching from the second century BCE to the third century CE. Moreover, the Scrolls add the highly significant contribution of early, nonsectarian, liturgical collections. These results have implications for the early history of Jewish liturgy and for refining Fleischer's model of liturgical creation at Yavneh. They suggest that the establishment of the institution of fixed, obligatory, Jewish prayer by the rabbis after the Second Temple's destruction was not *ex nihilo* but rather took place against a rich background of considerable, well-rooted, liturgical precedent and tradition shared by several groups in different social and geographic locations, not only those who distanced themselves or were distanced from the Temple. This is a picture of continuity. But, it is continuity concurrent with change.

A desideratum of this study was to honestly investigate the possibilities of both change and continuity in pre- and post-70 Jewish liturgies. Within the continuous liturgical tradition outlined above, I detected two types of change: 1) functional differentiation in the liturgical uses of the distinctive expression, "implanting Torah"; and 2) stylistic variation in the formal opening and closing benedictions and in the petitions for knowledge, repentance, and forgiveness that were worded similarly in the *Words of the Luminaries* and the *Apostolic Constitutions*, on the one hand, but formulated differently in the rabbinic Eighteen Benedictions, on the other.

---

[35] Heinemann, *Prayer*, 56; see his chapter on "The Development of Prayers and the Problem of the 'Original Text,'" 37–76.

In fact, it is difficult and rather anachronistic to speak of the large
units of the statutory Jewish liturgy, particularly of the Eighteen Benedictions, before the second century CE. These begin to appear in a
recognizable form in the third century with the final edition of the
Mishnah and quotations of the specific wording of some statutory
prayers by first generation Amoraic sages, most notably Samuel's version of the abbreviated Eighteen Benedictions. Given this time frame,
it is likely that the Temple's destruction in 70 CE *was* a watershed of
sorts—although evidently not the ultimate continental divide—in the
development of the statutory Jewish liturgy. I see it as a defining event
whose impact was not realized immediately nor all at once but rather
in a slower, more complex process. I detect an evolutionary liturgical
process affected both by internal, literary factors and external stimuli, not the least of which will have been the loss of the Temple. My
answer to the question posed in the title of this paper, "Liturgy Before
and After the Temple's Destruction: Change or Continuity?" is, then,
not either/or but rather both change *and* continuity.

APPENDIX:
PRE- AND POST-70 CE PRAYERS FOR KNOWLEDGE

A. *The* Words of the Luminaries[36]

Sunday Prayer, 4Q504 Col. 5:5–15 = frg. 4 5–15 (Overlap: 4Q506 131–132 10–14)

[לפ(ניכ)ה̇ אלה ידענו (בא)שר (חנו)א̇ת̇](נו [רֹוח] ק̇](ודש רחמנו]	5
[(ואל (תז)כֹו(ר לנו עוונות)רשונים (בכו)ל̇ גמו(לם הר]ע ואשר]	6
[(ק)שו [בעורפם (אתה פ̇דֹינו וסלח[נא](לעוננו ולח)[טתנו]	7
)] [קיכה תורה̇ אשר צו̇]יתה [בֹ̇יד מושׁ]ה	8
[ ] [לל] [°[אשר °°] [בכ]ו[ל]	9
[ ] ממלכת [כֹוהנים וגוי קדוש [ ]°[ ]	10
[ ] א[שר בחֹרת מולה עורלת̇] לבנו	11
[ ] ע]וֹ̇ר[פֹ]נֹו עוד חזק לבנו לֹעֹשות]	12
[ ] ל[לכת בדרכיכה]	13
[ ] ברוך [אדוני אשר הודי]ענו	14
[ ] א̇מ̇ן אמן *vacat* [ ]	15

5. be[fore Y]ou. We know these things because You have graciously granted us [Your] h[oly] spirit. [Take pity on us,]

6. and ["*rem*]*ember not to hold against us the iniquities of our forebears*" (Ps 79:8) with all their wick[ed] deeds, [those]

7. who were stiff-necked. Redeem us, and [please] forgive our iniquities and si[ns.]

8. [   ] the Law that [You] commanded through Mos[es Your servant]

9. [   ] [   ] which [   ]in a[l]l[   ]

10. [*a dominion of*] *priests and a holy nation*" (Exod 19:6)[ ] [   ]

11. [w]hom you chose. Circumcise the foreskin of[our heart   ]

12. [   ] yet. Strengthen our heart to do[   ]

13. [to]walk in Your ways [   ]

14. [Blessed is]the Lord who made know[n to us   ]

15. [   ]Amen! Amen! *vacat* [   ]

Thursday Prayer, 4Q504 15:8–18 = frg. 1+2 ii 7–17

אנא א̇ד̇נ̇י עשה נא כמוֹכ̇ה כגדול כוֹח̇כ̇ה אש̇]ר נ[שׁאת]ה̇]	8
לאבותינו בהמרותם א̇ת פיכה ותתאנף בם להשמידם ותחס	9
עליהמה באהבתכה אותם ולמען בריתכה כיא כפר מ̇ושה	10
בעד חטאתם ולמען דעת את כוחכה הגדול ואת רוב חסדכ]ה]	11
לדורות עולם ישוב נא אפכה וחמתכה מעמכה ישראל ‏עלכול חט]אתם]‏ וזכרתה	12

---

36 Text and translation are from "4Q504 (4QDibHamᵃ)," ed. M. Baillet, DJD 7; and E.G. Chazon, in *The Dead Sea Scrolls Electronic Library* (ed. E. Tov; Leiden, 2006). The text is identical in *DSSEL* and *DSSR* 5 (see n. 16 above).

אֵת נפלאותיכה אשר עשיתה לעני גוים כיא נקר° שמכה עלינו 13

[   ] [ל]°בֿנו בכול לב ובכול נפש ולטעת תורתכה בלבנו 14

[לבלתי סור ממנה ללכת [מ]ימין ושמאול כיא תרפאנו משגעון יעורן ותמהון 15

[לבב] הן בע[ו]נותינו נמכרנו ובפשעינו קרתנו 16

[   ]°° והצלתנו מחטוא לכה 17

[   ]°ת ולהביננו לתעודות 18

8. Please, Lord, act as is Your character, by the measure of Your great power. Fo[r] You [for]gave

9. our fathers when they rebelled against Your command, though You were so angry at them that You might have destroyed them. Still, You had pity

10. on them because of Your love, and because of Your covenant (indeed, Moses had atoned

11. for their sin), and also so that Your great power and abundant compassion might be known

12. to generations to come, forever. May Your anger and fury turn back from Your people Israel [at all [their] sin[s]]. Remember

13. the wonders that You performed while the nations looked on–surely we have been called by Your name.

14. [These things were done] that we might [repe]nt with all our heart and all our soul, to (im)plant Your law in our hearts

15. [that we turn not from it, straying] either to the right or the left. Surely You will heal us from such madness, and [blindness] confusion.

16. [Behold,] we were sold [as the price] of our [in]iquity, yet despite our rebellion You have called us.

17. [   ]   Deliver us from sinning against You,

18. [   ]   make us understand the testimonies.

B. *Apostolic Constitutions 8.6.5–8*

5. Let us all earnestly entreat God on behalf of the catechumens: That the one who is good and loves mankind will kindly hear their prayers; and having received their supplication, may assist them and grant them for their good the requests of their hearts; that he may reveal to them the Gospel of his Christ, illumine them, and give them understanding, educate them in the knowledge of God, teach them his ordinances and judgments, implant in them his pure and saving fear, open the ears of their hearts to engage in his Law day and night;

6. and that he may establish them in piety, unify and number them among his holy flock, grant them the washing of regeneration, of the garment of incorruption, of real life; and that he may save them from all impiety, and give place to no adversary against them; and that he may cleanse them from all pollution of flesh and spirit, and dwell in them, and walk (among them) through his Christ; and bless their comings in and their goings out, and guide their affairs for their good.

7. Let us still earnestly supplicate for them, obtaining remission of their trespasses through initiation, that they may be deemed worthy of the holy mysteries and remaining constantly with the saints.

8. Arise, catechumens, request the peace of God through his Christ, that the day be peaceable and free from sin, even the entire time of your life, that your end be Christian, that God be gracious and kind, the forgiveness of trespasses. Dedicate yourselves to the only unbegotten God through his Christ. Bow down and receive a blessing.[37]

5. Ὑπὲρ τῶν κατηχουμένων πάντες ἐκτενῶς τὸν Θεὸν παρακαλέσωμεν, ἵνα ὁ ἀγαθὸς καὶ φιλάνθρωπος εὐμενῶς εἰσακούσῃ τῶν δεήσεων αὐτῶν καὶ τῶν παρακλήσεων, καὶ προσδεξάμενος αὐτῶν τὴν ἱκεσίαν ἀντιλάβηται αὐτῶν καὶ δῷ αὐτοῖς τὰ αἰτήματα τῶν καρδιῶν αὐτῶν πρὸς τὸ συμφέρον, ἀποκαλύψῃ αὐτοῖς τὸ εὐαγγέλιον τοῦ Χριστοῦ αὐτοῦ, φωτίσῃ αὐτοὺς καὶ συνετίσῃ, παιδεύσῃ αὐτοὺς τὴν θεογνωσίαν, διδάξῃ αὐτοὺς τὰ προστάγματα αὐτοῦ καὶ τὰ δικαιώματα, ἐγκαταφυτεύσῃ ἐν αὐτοῖς τὸν ἁγνὸν αὐτοῦ καὶ σωτήριον φόβον, διανοίξῃ τὰ ὦτα τῶν καρδιῶν αὐτῶν πρὸς τὸ ἐν τῷ νόμῳ αὐτοῦ καταγίνεσθαι ἡμέρας καὶ νυκτός,

6. βεβαιώσῃ δὲ αὐτοὺς ἐν τῇ εὐσεβείᾳ, ἑνώσῃ καὶ ἐγκαταριθμήσῃ αὐτοὺς τῷ ἁγίῳ αὐτοῦ ποιμνίῳ, καταξιώσας αὐτοὺς τοῦ λουτροῦ τῆς παλιγγενεσίας, τοῦ ἐνδύματος τῆς ἀφθαρσίας, τῆς ὄντως ζωῆς· ῥύσηται δὲ αὐτοὺς ἀπὸ πάσης ἀσεβείας καὶ μὴ δῷ τόπον τῷ ἀλλοτρίῳ κατ' αὐτῶν, καθαρίσῃ δὲ αὐτοὺς ἀπὸ παντὸς μολυσμοῦ σαρκὸς καὶ πνεύματος, ἐνοικήσῃ τε ἐν αὐτοῖς καὶ ἐμπεριπατήσῃ διὰ τοῦ Χριστοῦ αὐτοῦ, εὐλογήσῃ τὰς εἰσόδους αὐτῶν καὶ τὰς ἐξόδους καὶ κατευθύνῃ αὐτοῖς τὰ προκείμενα εἰς τὸ συμφέρον.

7. Ἔτι ἐκτενέστερον ὑπὲρ αὐτῶν ἱκετεύσωμεν, ἵνα ἀφέσεως τυχόντες τῶν πλημμελημάτων διὰ τῆς μυήσεως ἀξιωθῶσιν τῶν ἁγίων μυστηρίων καὶ τῆς μετὰ τῶν ἁγίων διαμονῆς.

8. Ἐγείρεσθε, οἱ κατηχούμενοι· τὴν εἰρήνην τοῦ Θεοῦ διὰ τοῦ Χριστοῦ αὐτοῦ αἰτήσασθε, εἰρηνικὴν τὴν ἡμέραν καὶ ἀναμάρτητον καὶ πάντα τὸν χρόνον τῆς ζωῆς ὑμῶν, χριστιανὰ τὰ τέλη ὑμῶν, ἵλεω καὶ εὐμενῆ τὸν Θεόν, ἄφεσιν πλημμελημάτων· ἑαυτοὺς τῷ μόνῳ ἀγεννήτῳ Θεῷ διὰ τοῦ Χριστοῦ αὐτοῦ παράθεσθε. Κλίνατε καὶ εὐλογεῖσθε.

C. Eighteen Benedictions, abbreviated version, b. Ber. 29a
(cf. y. Ber. 4:3, 8a)

הביננו ה' אלוהינו לדעת דרכיך ומול את לבבנו ליראתך ותסלח לנו...

Give us understanding to know your ways; circumcise our heart to fear you; Forgive us...

---

[37] Fiensy, *Prayers Alleged to be Jewish*, 92–95; cf. 7.26.3 (ibid., 46–47): "you implanted a law in our souls." The Greek text is quoted from M. Metzger, *Les Constitutions Apostoliques* (Paris, 1987), 3:152–54.

D. *Eighteen Benedictions, full version, Seder Rav Amram Gaon*[38]

4 אתה חונן לאדם דעת ומלמד לאנוש בינה וחננו מאתך דעה בינה והשכל.
ברוך אתה ה' חונן הדעת.

5 השיבנו אבינו לתורתך וקרבנו מלכנו לעבודתך והחזירנו בתשובה שלימה
לפניך. ברוך אתה ה' הרוצה בתשובה.

6 סלח לנו אבינו כי חטאנו מחול לנו מלכנו כי פשענו. ברוך אתה ה' חנון
המרבה לסלוח.

4. You favor man with perception and teach mortal man insight. O favor us
   with perception, insight and wisdom from You. Blessed be You *God*, gracious Giver of perception.

5. Lead us back, our Father, to Your Torah, and draw us near, our King, to
   Your service, and cause us to return in perfect repentance to Your presence. Blessed be You, *God*, Who takes pleasure in a repentant return.

6. Forgive us, our Father, for we have sinned; pardon us, our King, for we
   have transgressed, for You pardon and forgive. Blessed be You, *God*, Who
   is gracious and Who forgives abundantly.

---

[38] Edited by D. Goldschmidt (Tel-Aviv, 1971), 24. The English translation is from
S.R. Hirsch, *The Hirsch Siddur* (Jerusalem, 1978), 134–37.

LITURGY, POETRY, AND THE PERSISTENCE OF SACRIFICE*

Michael D. Swartz

I. From Prayer to Sacrifice

This volume is dedicated to reexamining the premise that underlies much historiography of the early rabbinic period—namely, that the destruction of the Temple in 70 CE brought about profound changes in the nature of the Jewish people and of Judaism as a religion. This essay addresses one aspect of this paradigm: the idea that Judaism was transformed in the first several centuries of the Common Era from a religion of sacrifice to a religion of prayer. This idea can be reexamined by interrogating the concept of sacrifice and its relationship to prayer in Judaism in late antiquity through one key source that acts both as a discourse on sacrifice and as a ritual on its own terms.

It is generally understood that Judaism as it ultimately emerged from the catastrophe centered on the individual's study and performance of the *mitzvot* and worship in synagogues. In descriptions of the history of Judaism in late antiquity, this transfer of ritual from Temple sacrifice to synagogue prayer is often portrayed as a swift and complete transformation, occasioned by the trauma of the destruction of the sanctuary and perhaps anticipated by the Second Temple synagogue. By these accounts, Judaism evolved from a religion of sacrifice to one of prayer: that is, from the physical, ritualistic, and institutional Temple cult, to the so-called "sacrifice of the heart"—spiritual, heartfelt, and personal.

Jonathan Klawans, in his *Purity, Sacrifice, and the Temple*, shows the degree to which this narrative was informed by a theologically conditioned ideology of antisacrificial triumphalism that can be traced to medieval philosophy but that emerged in its fullness in the nineteenth and twentieth centuries.[1] In fact late antiquity, far from being a time when sacrifice was obsolete, was a period when sacrifice was still

---

* All translations in this article are mine, unless otherwise noted.
[1] J. Klawans, *Purity, Sacrifice, and the Temple: Symbolism and Supersessionism in the Study of Ancient Judaism* (Oxford and New York, 2006).

pervasive in religions. We can sharpen this point by remembering that at the beginning of the fourth century there were only two communities of any consequence that were not performing sacrifices: Jews and Christians. Recently, in a ground-breaking theoretical study, Katherine McClymond has argued that in the nineteenth and twentieth centuries theorists of sacrifice became fixated on the concept of sacred violence as the defining characteristic of sacrifice.[2] She argues that if we look at the concept of sacrifice through the lens of ancient Jewish and Hindu sources we must expand that concept to other physical and verbal offerings. This conception is relevant to the question of whether sacrifice really ceased when the slaughter of animals on the altar in Jerusalem was no longer possible. We must therefore ask how early—and how complete—the transformation from sacrifice to prayer really was, and indeed, whether the idea of a dichotomy of sacrifice and prayer applies to late antiquity.

II. The Evidence

Several Jewish sources complicate the conventional picture of spirituality after the destruction of the Second Temple considerably.[3] The Mishnah itself, the first systematic statement of the rabbis' worldview, devotes two of its six major divisions, *Qodashim* and *Teharot*, to the sacrificial system and its implications—not to mention major portions of such tractates as *Pesaḥim*, *Yoma*, and *Ḥagigah*.[4] Likewise, the discovery of dozens of synagogues in the Galilee has revolutionized our understanding of Palestine in the Talmudic period. These synagogues abound in Temple imagery, from simple panels depicting *menorot* and incense shovels to the synagogue mosaic in Sepphoris, which depicts the Temple rituals almost in their entirety: sacrificial bulls and sheep, showbread and first fruits, and—as we can see from a fragment—Aaron

---

[2] K. McClymond, *Beyond Sacred Violence: A Comparative Study of Sacrifice* (Baltimore, 2008).

[3] A recent study that seeks to understand the larger forces in the Mediterranean world that contributed to this phenomenon in their complexity is G. Stroumsa, *The End of Sacrifice: Religious Transformations in Late Antiquity* (Chicago, 2009).

[4] For one theory of the place of sacrifice in the Mishnah see J. Neusner, "Map Without Territory: Mishnah's System of Sacrifice and Sanctuary," *HR* 19/2 (1979): 103–27. On conceptions of sacrifice in *Mishnah Yoma* see M.D. Swartz, "The Topography of Blood in Mishnah *Yoma*," in *Jewish Blood: Metaphor and Reality in Jewish History, Culture, and Religion* (ed. M. Hart; London, 2009), 70–82.

serving in his full regalia of vestments. This discovery has occasioned a debate about the place of Temple imagery in the ancient synagogue and whether it reflects a greater level of cultic and priestly concerns than previously thought.[5] This question can be illuminated by showing how deeply rooted the conception of sacrifice was for Jews in Palestine well into late antiquity. The evidence presented here is a major source for Jewish understandings of sacrifice in late antiquity: the *Avodah* piyyutim of the third to sixth centuries. It will be argued, based on both the themes of these compositions and their formal characteristics, that they constitute an example of the persistence of conceptions of sacrifice and evidence for the ongoing centrality of sacrifice to Jewish conceptions of ritual in late antiquity.[6]

III. The Avodah

The *Avodah* service grew out of a custom of reciting the mishnaic tractate *Yoma* on Yom Kippur.[7] The tractate's narrative style made it

---

[5] For the debate on the Sepphoris mosaic and its implications see Z. Weiss, *The Sepphoris Synagogue: Deciphering an Ancient Message through Its Archaeological and Socio-Historical Contexts* (Jerusalem, 2005). For a critique of this thesis see S. Fine, "Art and the Liturgical Context of the Sepphoris Synagogue Mosaic," in *Galilee through the Centuries* (ed. E.M. Meyers; Winona Lake, 1999), 227–37.

[6] This paper draws on some of my previous research on the *Avodah* and related genres; see especially M.D. Swartz, "Sage, Priest, and Poet: Typologies of Leadership in the Ancient Synagogue," in *Jews, Christians and Polytheists in the Ancient Synagogue: Cultural Interaction During the Greco–Roman Period* (ed. S. Fine; London, 1999), 101–17; idem, "The Power and Role of Hebrew Poetry in Antiquity," in *Continuity and Renewal: Jews and Judaism in Byzantine–Christian Palestine* (ed. L.I. Levine; Jerusalem, 2004), 542–62; and idem, "Judaism and the Idea of Ancient Ritual Theory," in *Jewish Studies at the Crossroads of Anthropology and History: Authority, Diaspora, Tradition* (ed. R. Boustan, O. Kosansky, and M. Rustow; Philadelphia, 2011), 294–317.

[7] For an introduction to the *Avodah*, as well as texts and translations of the major early *Avodah* compositions, see M.D. Swartz and J. Yahalom, *Avodah: Ancient Poems for Yom Kippur* (University Park, Pa., 2005); all translations of *Avodah* piyyutim cited here are from this volume. See also I. Elbogen, *Jewish Liturgy: A Comprehensive History* (trans. R.P. Scheindlin; Philadelphia and New York, 1993), 174, 217, 238–39, and 249–50; D. Goldschmidt, ed., *Maḥzor le-Yamim Nora'im [Ashkenaz]* (Jerusalem, 1970), 2:18–25; and E. Fleischer, *Hebrew Liturgical Poetry in the Middle Ages* (Jerusalem, 1975), 173–77 (in Hebrew). An important edition of a major *Avodah* piyyut, with an extensive introduction, is J. Yahalom, *'Az be-'En Kol: Seder ha-'Avodah ha-Ereṣ-Yisraeli ha-Qadum le-Yom ha-Kippurim* (Jerusalem, 1996). A comprehensive study of the *Avodah* service and piyyutim from the perspective of the history of Hebrew literature is Z. Malachi, "The *Avodah* for Yom Kippur: Its Characteristics, History, and Development in Hebrew Poetry" (Ph.D. diss., Hebrew University, 1974 [in Hebrew]). See also idem, *Be-No'am Siaḥ: Peraqim mi-Toledot Sifrutenu* (Lod, 1983), 46–113. An

conducive to liturgical recitation.[8] Apparently by early postmishnaic times, a liturgical version of the tractate had evolved, known as called *Shivʿat Yamim*.[9] This version follows the Mishnah closely with a few changes. By the fourth or fifth century the custom had grown into a full-fledged poetic genre with a distinct formal structure. This structure is best exemplified in two early masterpieces: *ʾAz be-ʾEn Kol*, a massive anonymous piyyut;[10] and Yose ben Yose's *ʾAzkir Gevurot ʾElohah*.[11]

The *Avodah* piyyut is an epic form. The poems customarily begin with an account of creation, and then describe each major generation, culminating in the selection of Aaron as priest. While the description of the sacrifice forms the culmination of the poem, the preamble reinforces the centrality of the Temple cult in its interpretation of history, for example, by describing how the Temple Mount was the original locus of creation; how plants and animals were created with indicators of purity and impurity; and how Israel's genealogy produced Aaron and his clan. After this mythic-historical preamble the service in the Temple is described, according to the order in the Mishnah. In these piyyutim, practically every major detail of the Mishnah is treated poetically, from the sequestering of the high priest in the Temple complex seven days before Yom Kippur;[12] to the story of how the priests used to rush up the ramp to deliver the daily sacrifice early on that morning, leading to violence among priests;[13] to the ten separate times the high priest washes his hands and feet.[14] The *Avodah* thus stands out

---

important early discussion is found in I. Elbogen, *Studien zur Geschichte des jüdischen Gottesdienstes* (Berlin, 1907); cf. also A. Zeidman, "Matbeaʿ Seder ha-ʿAvodah le-Yom ha-Kippurim," *Sinai* 13 (1944): 173–82, 255–62. For further elaboration of some of the arguments made here see M.D. Swartz, "Ritual about Myth about Ritual: Toward an Understanding of the *Avodah* in the Rabbinic Period," *Journal of Jewish Thought and Philosophy* 6 (1997): 135–55; and idem, "Sage, Priest, and Poet."

[8] See *b. Yoma* 36b and 56b, which describe a prayer leader who recites his version of the Mishnah before the Amora Rava on Yom Kippur. It is unclear whether *b. Yoma* 36b refers to full recitation of the Mishnah. See Z. Zohar, "U-Mi Metaher ʾEtkhem—ʾAvikhem ba-Shamayim: Tefilat Seder ha-ʿAvodah shel Yom ha-Kippurim: Tokhen, Tifqud u-Mashmaʿut," *AJS Review* 14 (1989): 4–5 (Hebrew Section).

[9] Published in Elbogen, *Studien*, 103–117; cf. the edition in Malachi, "Avodah," 2:127–31. For a translation see Swartz and Yahalom, *Avodah*, 53–67.

[10] Yahalom, *ʾAz be-ʾEn Kol*; Swartz and Yahalom, *Avodah*, 96–219.

[11] A. Mirsky, *Piyyute Yose ben Yose* (2d ed.; Jerusalem, 1991), 122–72; Swartz and Yahalom, *Avodah*, 221–89.

[12] Cf. *m. Yoma* 1:1.

[13] Cf. *m. Yoma* 2:2.

[14] Cf. *m. Yoma* 3:3.

for its emphasis on both the details and the cosmic centrality of the sacrificial system.

The *Avodah* is not unique in its use of the stylistic devices common to piyyut, but its explicit evocation of the sacrificial system reminds us of how this style serves the purpose of what the rabbis called the *miqdash me'at*, the "lesser sanctuary." It must also be remembered that the *Avodah* represents the greatest portion of the extant works of Yose ben Yose. Furthermore, other works dealing with the cult are attributed to him, such as *'Emet Mah Nehedar*, a rhapsody attached to the *Avodah* on the effulgence of the High Priest's face as he emerged from the Holy of Holies,[15] and *'En Lanu Kohen Gadol*, a confessional lament for the Temple.[16] In fact, recently Michael Rand has argued that the *Avodah* served as the inspiration for other genres of piyyut, including the *Seder Beriyot* and the Shavuot *Qedushta* of the classical era.[17] There is therefore evidence that the *Avodah* was not simply one liturgical genre among many. Rather, it constituted a dramatic high point of the High Holiday liturgy and may have been designed to be the showpiece of the early *payetan*.

A. *Themes*

The *Avodah* poems are based on the Mishnah's narrative, but differ dramatically in their methods and emphases. They precede the account of the sacrifice with an epic description of world history, in which God's creation of the universe leads dramatically to the foundation of Israel's Temple cult. The Temple Mount is described as one of the first things created in the world, the place "on which the entire world's beauty is founded."[18] God is described as having created animals expressly for ritual slaughter, and the great beasts, Leviathan and Behemoth, for enjoyment in the world to come.[19] In describing the

---

[15] Goldschmidt, *Maḥzor* 2:483–84; Swartz and Yahalom, *Avodah*, 343–47. The composition has its origins in Ben Sira 50; see M.Z. Segal, *Sefer Ben Sira ha-Shalem* (Jerusalem, 1976), 340–42; see also J. Yahalom, *Poetry and Society in Jewish Galilee of Late Antiquity* (Tel-Aviv, 1999), 15–16 (in Hebrew); and P.W. Skehan and A.A. Di Lella, *The Wisdom of Ben Sira: A New Translation with Notes* (New York, 1987), 546–55.

[16] Mirsky, *Piyyute Yose ben Yose*, 210–17; Swartz and Yahalom, *Avodah*, 351–65.

[17] M. Rand, "The *Seder Beriyot* in Byzantine-Era Piyyut," *JQR* 95 (2005): 667–83.

[18] *'Az be-'En Kol*, line 739, based on an interpretation of Ps 50:2 found in *t. Kippurim* 2:14.

[19] See for example Yose ben Yose's *'Atah Konanta 'Olam be-Rov Hesed* in Mirsky, *Piyyute Yose ben Yose*, 175, lines 18–20.

patriarchs and early Israelites, the poems often proceed directly from the patriarch Jacob directly to Levi, Amram, and Aaron, sometimes omitting Moses entirely and highlighting God's selection of the ancestors of the priesthood.[20]

More strikingly in contrast to the Mishnah, these compositions glorify the high priest and emphasize his heroic actions in purifying the sanctuary, and by extension, the nation. Whereas the Mishnah depicts the high priest as a passive agent of Pharisaic sages and sometimes ignorant of Torah,[21] the *Avodah* piyyutim portray him as a pious and conscientious man who, in the words of the anonymous early piyyut *'Atah Konanta 'Olam me-Rosh*, "perform[s] the commandment in awe and fear" and "rejoice[s] in the commandment to uphold the law."[22] More than this, the piyyutim portray the high priest as a physically splendid person, clad in glorious garments and heroic in his performance of the demanding sacrificial procedure. Thus, for example, *'Az be-'En Kol* marvels at how

> His stature
> rose to the height of a cedar
> when he was fit with embroidered garments
> to ornament his body.[23]

Yose ben Yose's *'Azkir Gevurot 'Elohah* describes him in heavenly terms, relating him not only to Israel, whom he represents before God, but perhaps, to the appearance of the divine habitation itself:

> Wrapped in a blue robe,
> as bright as the firmament,
> his rounded arms
> filled the sleeves.[24]

---

[20] See M.D. Swartz, "Chains of Tradition in the Avodah Piyyutim," in *Judaism, Christianity, and the Roman Empire* (ed. N. Dohrmann and A.Y. Reed; Philadelphia, in press). M.E. Stone, "The Axis of History at Qumran," in *Pseudepigraphic Perspectives: The Apocrypha and Pseudepigrapha in Light of the Dead Sea Scrolls* (ed. E.G. Chazon and M. Stone; Leiden, 1999), 133–49, has shown that in the apocryphal Levi literature and the *Book of Jubilees* the patriarchs are depicted as transmitting the explicit knowledge of sacrificial ritual to their students, who then constitute a priestly chain of tradition.

[21] See *m. Yoma* 1:1–5.

[22] Goldschmidt, *Maḥzor*, 2:20 (Hebrew numbering), lines 8–9.

[23] *'Az be-'En Kol*, lines 551–552.

[24] *'Azkir Gevurot*, lines 165–166.

Here the bright blue robe not only evokes heaven, but echoes the brilliance of the "pavement of sapphire" on which God appears enthroned in Exod 24:10. The vestments of the high priest become the subject of extensive excurses in the piyyutim, which describe each item of the high priest's garments and detail the significance of each as a signifier of Israel and as a token of the high priest's glorious role as an intermediary between God and the people.[25]

Another important element in the structure of the *Avodah* is the high priest's confession, said over the sacrificial animals. This occurs three times in the service. This recurring moment is an important one, for at some point it became customary for both prayer leader and congregation to prostrate at the report of the high priest's recitation of the divine name. At this point, the ritual becomes most mimetic, enabling as much as possible the reenactment of the people's experience in the Temple.

B. *Substance and Style*

Although for centuries it has been understood that the aesthetics of the Byzantine era constituted a distinctive style, the full implications of this aesthetic for the history of culture in late antiquity have not been recognized until recently. One of the pioneers in this recognition has been Michael Roberts. In his book *The Jeweled Style: Poetry and Poetics in Late Antiquity*, Roberts penetrates the sensibility behind the techniques used by late Latin poets such as Ausonius and Paulinus, and links this poetic sensibility to the art of the same period.[26] He describes an overall aesthetic of late antiquity—one that governs poetry, art, and literary criticism. Roberts argues that in that period, the goal of the arts was to dazzle the reader or viewer with the interplay of details rather than to express an elegant whole. As he puts it, "Late antique taste did not tolerate the plain and the unadorned; brilliance of effect, the play of contrasting colors, is all."[27] In his view, this aesthetic was not confined to poetry but can be found as well in the arts and literary

---

[25] See for example *'Azkir Gevurot*, lines 151–182; *'Az be-'En Kol*, lines 553–566. On depictions of the vestments see M.D. Swartz, "The Semiotics of the Priestly Vestments in Jewish Tradition," in *Sacrifice in Religious Experience* (ed. A.I. Baumgarten; Leiden, 2002), 57–80.

[26] M. Roberts, *The Jeweled Style: Poetry and Poetics in Late Antiquity* (Ithaca, 1989).

[27] Roberts, *Jeweled Style*, 118.

criticism. Thus late Latin poetry abounded in artfully composed lists of distinct parts and elaborations known as *leptologia*, the lavish description of details in the course of a poem or narrative.

Since the appearance of Roberts' study, this understanding of the late antique ethos has been extended into broader areas of cultural history. In her recent book *The Corporeal Imagination*,[28] Patricia Cox Miller relates Roberts' insights on late antique aesthetics to contemporary Christian art and literature. As she shows, Christian poetry, hagiography, and sarcophagi of the fourth century reflected an "aesthetics of discontinuity" in which narrative unity is secondary to the display of disparate elements. By extending Roberts' insights beyond the realm of late Latin Poetry and its proximate environment, Miller's study can be read as an argument for a deeper understanding of a Late Antique *mentalité* in which ornamentation is not simply an overlay to meaning but a form of meaning itself. This sensibility governed the composition of such diverse media as mosaics, monumental sculpture, and dress. The prevalence of mosaic art during this period is particularly instructive: just as the stones of the mosaic were set in such a way as to please the eye in their brilliance, so each detail in Late Antique poetry was meant to delight or enlighten the listener.

The relevance of this line of research should be apparent to students of piyyut in the Byzantine period. Each piyyut was designed to ornament a specific liturgical unit, such as the *Qedushah* or the *Amidah*, or a specific lectionary selection (*parashah*). Furthermore, such stylistic characteristics as metonymy (*kinnui*), intricate wordplay, and the practice of enumerating scriptural examples and other items can be cited as evidence that the aesthetic described by Roberts and Miller affected Hebrew poetry of the same era.

The tendency of poetry of late antiquity to linger on details for the sake of ornamentation finds expression in two techniques common to piyyut in general and to the *Avodah* in particular. One is the use of *kinnui*, in which no major detail, persona, or symbol is allowed to stand on its own but is represented by a substitute. By doing this, the poet emphasizes the special character of each word, calling attention to each object and person in the picture on its own. Another is the

---

[28] P. Cox Miller, *The Corporeal Imagination: Signifying the Holy in Late Ancient Christianity* (Philadelphia, 2009); see also her *The Poetry of Thought in Late Antiquity* (Aldershot, 2001).

payetanic method whereby discrete episodes in the narrative or stages in the sacrificial procedure are treated poetically.

Among the more striking examples of the *Avodah*'s use of ornamentation are the extensive excurses on the priestly vestments as described in Exodus 28 and 39. In the *Avodah*, the description of the vestments serves the theme of the glorious physical appearance of the high priest. In these passages, the poet treats every detail of each garment poetically, enlisting several criteria: material and color, for example; and by using a well-attested midrashic pattern that interprets each vestment according to a specific sin for which it atones. In one of these passages in *'Az be-'En Kol*, the author enumerates each stone according to the tribe it is supposed to represent. First the poet sets out the setting and theological reason for the stones:[29]

סִדֵּר >בְּ<תוֹכוֹ
שְׁתֵּים עֶשְׂרֵה אֶבֶן
לְהָסִיר לֵב אֶבֶן
מִשְׁאֵרִי(ס) [ת] (אבן)[תָּם]

סְכוּכוֹת יְרַקְרַק
בְּכַנְפֵי יוֹנָה
מְפוּתָּחוֹת שֵׁמוֹת
שְׁנֵים עָשָׂר שָׁבֶט

נְתוּנִים בְּטוּרִים
שְׁלֹשָׁה שְׁלֹשָׁה
לְהַזְכִּיר לְכוּלָּם
[צֶדֶק] שְׁלוֹשֶׁת הוֹרֵיהֶם

He arranged in it
twelve stones
to remove the heart of stone
from the remnant of the mild man.[30]

Sheathed in gold
like the wings of a dove[31]
engraved with the names
of the twelve tribes.

---

[29] Swartz and Yahalom, *Avodah*, 180–81.
[30] Israel, according to Gen 25:27.
[31] Lit., "in the wings of a dove"; cf. Ps 68:14.

They were arranged in rows
three by three
to remind the people
of the righteousness of their three ancestors.[32]

At that point the poet enumerates each stone and its corresponding tribe:[33]

נִיתָּן רִאשׁוֹן אוֹדֶם
>לְשֶׁ<ם (אל) [אוֹן]
לְהַלְבִּין א>וֹדֶם<
וְלֵ[י]שֵׁיב בְּרֹאשׁ מְתָיו

נִטְבַּע שֵׁינִי
בְּמַטְבֵּעַ פִּטְדָה
לִפְטוֹר שֵׁבֶט שִׁמְעוֹן
מֵעֲוֹן שִׁטִּים

מְאוֹר הִבְהִיק
שְׁלִישִׁי כְּבָרֶקֶת
כְּמַהֲרוֹ בַּמַּחֲנֶה
לִהְיוֹת צִיר כִּבָרָק

To the first[34] was given (the color) red
for the first fruit of his vigor[35]
to make scarlet white[36]
and so that he may sit at the head of his tribes.

The second[37] was stamped
with the impression of topaz
to absolve the tribe of Simon
from the sin of Shittim.

The third one[38] gave off
light like the morning star
as he hurried in his camp
to do his mission like lightning.

The poem continues through the twelve tribes. The passage relies on a pattern of wordplay between the name of each gem and the characteristics of the tribe it represents.

---

[32] The patriarchs.
[33] Swartz and Yahalom, *Avodah*, 182–83.
[34] Reuben.
[35] See Gen 49:3.
[36] See Isa 1:18.
[37] Simeon.
[38] Levi.

An interesting counterpart to these passages can be found in Roberts' *Jeweled Style* in the example that gives the book its title. In the *Heptateuchus*, an early fifth-century biblical poetic paraphrase attributed to Cyprianus Gallus, the author lingers on an enumeration of the precious stones on the high priest's breastplate according to Exod 28:17–20.[39] This attention to the jewels stands in contrast to the author's tendency to elide a great deal of legal material in Exodus. Here he lists the precious stones in succession:

> First in position is the carnelian, and emerald along with the topaz; then comes the sapphire, with which the carbuncle blazes, and the jasper is green and shines with tawny gold. Third place is taken by amber, and along with it the agate and amethyst, with its bright purple hue. Fourth the chrysolite, and onyx next to the beryl.[40]

As Roberts admits, this passage is not likely to appeal to the modern reader. But in its time, the subject of the jeweled breastplate served as an excellent opportunity to demonstrate the poet's literary skill, both because of its very difficulty as a subject for poetic treatment and because of the dazzling picture of splendor and ornamentation that it presents. In effect, each of these poets, the Jewish and the Christian, is polishing, as it were, each precious stone on his poetic garment.

But the poet's art can be detected in simpler lists as well. In the piyyut *'Atah Konanta 'Olam me-Rosh*, one of the earliest and simplest of the *Avodah* piyyutim, the anonymous composer details the steps in the Yom Kippur sacrifice in very direct language. This passage consists of a series of nouns that culminate in verbs only after five stanzas:[41]

צִיץ וּמְעִיל
כְּתֹנֶת וּמִכְנְסֵי בַד
חֹשֶׁן וְאֵפוֹד
מִצְנֶפֶת וְאַבְנֵט

קָרְבְּנוֹת פָּרִים
וְעוֹלוֹת כְּבָשִׂים
וּשְׁחִיטַת עַתּוּדִים
וְנִתּוּחַ אֵלִים

---

[39] Roberts, *Jeweled Style*, 10–13, discussing Cyprianus Gallus, *Heptateuchus E*, lines 1098–1103.

[40] Translation in Roberts, *Jeweled Style*, 11.

[41] Swartz and Yahalom, *Avodah*, 74–75.

רֵיחַ מְרְקַחַת
וּבְעוּר גֶּחָלִים
וּסְפִירַת יֹשֶׁר
וּזְרִיקַת דָם

שׁוְעַת קְטֹרֶת
וּתְפִלַּת אֱמֶת
וּקְדֻשָּׁתוֹ
מְכַפֶּרֶת עֲוֹנוֹתֵינוּ

תֹּכֶן בּוּץ
וַעֲרִיכַת אֶבֶן
מְחֻגַּר בְּכֻלָּם
כְּמַלְאָךְ מְשָׁרֵת

תִּכַּנְתָּ כָּל אֵלֶּה
לִכְבוֹד אַהֲרֹן
כְּלֵי כַפָּרָה
לְיִשְׂרָאֵל שַׂמְתּוֹ

Diadem, robe,
tunic and linen breeches,
breastpiece, ephod,
royal headdress and sash;

sacrifices of bulls
and burnt-offerings of sheep
and the slaughter of goats
and the cutting-up of rams.

the perfumed aroma
and the burning of coals
correct enumeration[42]
and the dashing of blood;

supplication at the incense
and true prayer;[43]
and his holiness,
which atones for our sins;

the measurement of fine linen
and arrangement of jewels—
he is girded in all of these
like a ministering angel.

You ordained all these
for the glory of Aaron

---

[42] Of the times the blood is sprinkled.
[43] See *m. Yoma* 5:1.

You made him for Israel
the instrument of atonement.[44]

On the face of it, this would seem to be a dry listing of objects and actions. However, there is significance in the list itself. For the audience, it serves as a reminder of the elements of the sacrifice, and gives as well a swift overview of the Yom Kippur ceremony. But the list also serves the prosody of the composition: the nouns are arranged by twos according to the four-foot rhythm of the stichs. The last six lines break this pattern. In the second half of the fifth stanza,

מְחֻגָּר בְּכֻלָּם כְּמַלְאַךְ מְשָׁרֵת

He is girded in all of these like a ministering angel

the poet loads both the holy vestments and ritual obligations onto the person of the high priest, who is likened to an angel. In the last stanza, in which the poet turns to the second person,

תִּכַּנְתָּ כָּל אֵלֶּה לִכְבוֹד אַהֲרֹן
כְּלִי כַּפָּרָה לְיִשְׂרָאֵל שַׂמְתּוֹ

You ordained all these for the glory of Aaron
You made him for Israel an instrument of atonement

the word "ordained" functions as a kind of *zeugma*, a verb used to tie together the objects that preceded it. This line reminds the listener of God, who is the source of the sacrificial law and the object of the worship service as well. Thus the poet accomplishes one of the central goals of the *Avodah* piyyutim: the praise of the high priest and his intimacy with God.

In these examples we have seen some of the salient characteristics of the style that Roberts maps out. In the Hebrew poet's description of the precious stones on the breastplate, each stone stands, poetically, as an object reflective of Israel as it stands before its God. At the same time, each is made to shine as a reminder of the physical splendor of the Temple service.

IV. FUNCTIONS OF THE AVODAH

These formal and thematic features of the *Avodah* piyyutim suggest some of the ways in which they functioned in the context of the

---

[44] MSS add: "and you placed the forgiveness of sins in his hand."

ancient synagogue. Documentary sources indicate that piyyut was quite a popular genre in antiquity and the early Middle Ages, despite the intricacy of the language it employed—or perhaps because of this very intricacy.[45] Thus, besides the more solemn religious functions this genre might have fulfilled, it might also have functioned as a form of entertainment, in an age when the synagogue had to compete with other forms of popular culture available to Jews and non-Jews alike in the Roman world.[46] In addition, the *Avodah* may have fulfilled yet other functions in the ancient synagogue:

A. *Ritual Discourse*

Most obviously, this genre functions as a discourse on the nature of sacrifice. The *Avodah* represents, among other things, a form of ritual theory. Ritual theory only evolves in certain times and places, particularly when a ritual system undergoes a crisis.[47] The *Avodah* reflects a conception of sacrifice as a world-sustaining activity, for which both the responsibility and glory devolve upon an extraordinary individual—the high priest. Such a discourse accomplishes a number of things. It helps the community find meaning in the opaque rituals laid out in Leviticus and the Talmud. It also shows that such questions were of interest to the community centuries after the cult's presumed obsolescence. At the same time, it could be said that such discourse helps keep the ritual, its institutions, and its personnel alive in the consciousness of the community.

---

[45] On the popularity of piyyut and the resistance of the authorities to it, see L.A. Hoffman, *The Canonization of the Synagogue Service* (Notre Dame and London, 1979), 66–71; and S.D. Goitein, *A Mediterranean Society: The Jewish Communities of the Arab World as Portrayed in the Documents of the Cairo Geniza* (Berkeley and Los Angeles, 1971), 2:159–62. S. Elitzur, "The Congregation in the Synagogue and the Ancient *Qedushta*," in *Knesset Ezra: Literature and Life in the Synagogue* (ed. S. Elitzur, M.D. Herr, A. Shinan, and G. Shaked; Jerusalem, 1994), 171–90 (in Hebrew), argues that Yannai and Haduta structured their poems so as to make the meaning clear for a less educated audience while leaving much to be interpreted for intellectuals, thus appealing to a variety of constituencies.

[46] See C. Hezser, "Towards the Study of Jewish Popular Culture in Roman Palestine," in *"The Words of a Wise Man's Mouth Are Gracious" (Qoh 10,12): Festschrift for Günter Stemberger on the Occasion of His 65th Birthday* (ed. M. Perani; Berlin and New York, 2005), 267–97; and G. Veltri, "Magic, Sex, and Politics: The Media Power of Theatre Amusements in the Mirror of Rabbinic Literature," in Perani, *"Words of a Wise Man's Mouth,"* 243–56.

[47] For this argument for the Avodah as a form of ritual theory see Swartz, "Judaism and the Idea of Ancient Ritual Theory."

B. *Participation*

The active ritual and liturgical function of the *Avodah* is exemplified by the confession of the high priest, which allows the congregation to interact and reenact a key moment in the Temple ritual. This confessional rite contains two key elements that link the Temple ritual with the synagogue: the confession itself, which stresses the postexilic elements of sin and atonement; and the recitation of the name of God, which is virtually performed through the word *"ba-Shem"* ("in the name [of God]") and accompanied by the descriptions of the people's prostration, and the congregation's recital of the doxology *"Barukh shem kevod malkhuto le-'olam va'ed"* ("Blessed is the glory of His Majesty forever and ever"). The most explicit expressions of the power of the name of God in Judaism are found primarily in the magical tradition; from that tradition we can find many instances where the presence of the name makes up for the lack of a Temple. In a curious text known as *'Inyan Soṭah*, magical names are used to recreate the biblical ritual of the accused wife (*Soṭah*) in the absence of the Temple.[48] In the *Avodah*, the drama of the recitation of the Name introduces a dimension of active participation into the synagogue ceremony.

C. *Dramatic Empathy*

Another important way the *Avodah* recreates the Temple ritual is through the creation of dramatic empathy, almost Aristotelian in its purpose, with the high priest in the person of the prayer leader.[49] The narrative of the composition lends itself to this identification, taking the listener along with the high priest as he performs every step of the ceremony. Indeed, in so doing the piyyut takes the synagogue congregation further than the real Temple ceremony did. In the *Avodah*, the congregation stands with the high priest as he slaughters the animals

---

[48] The text first appeared in A. Marmorstein, "Beiträge zur Religionsgeschichte und Volkskunde," *Jahrbuch für jüdische Volkskunde* 25 (1924–1925): 377–83; it was also published in P. Schäfer and S. Shaked, *Magische Texte aus der Kairoer Geniza* (Tübingen, 1994), 1:17–45. For analyses of the text see G. Veltri, "*Inyan Sota*: Halakhische Voraussetzungen für einen magischen Akt nach einer theoretischen Abhandlung aus der Kairoer Geniza," *FJB* 20 (1993): 23–48; M. Idel, *Golem: Jewish Magical and Mystical Traditions on the Artificial Anthropoid* (Albany, 1990), 61–63; and Swartz, "Sacrificial Themes in Jewish Magic."

[49] On the role of empathy and the emotions in Greek drama see E.S. Belfiore, *Tragic Pleasures: Aristotle on Plot and Emotion* (Princeton, 1992). On epic poetry see C.M. Bowra, *Heroic Poetry* (London and New York, 1966).

and collects the blood; peeks behind the linen sheet as he changes from his glorious golden garments into his humble white ones and prepares to enter the Holy of Holies; goes with him into the inner sanctuary; stands with him as he offers the incense and pleads on behalf of the community; prostrates themselves as he recites the divine name; and witnesses him as his face shines from the reflection of the divine presence.

D. *Verbal Sacrifice*

Finally, the prayer ritual can be seen as a form of sacrifice itself. The question of what actions can substitute for sacrifice is the subject of many statements in rabbinic literature.[50] Two stand out as particularly relevant to this study. The first is that the memorization, repetition, and study of sacrifice can substitute for the act of sacrifice itself.[51] The second statement, which deserves our attention not as a direct source for the piyyutim but as a touchstone by which we can think about their ritual function, declares: "What is the sacrifice of the heart? (*avodah she-ba-lev*)? It is prayer."[52] This statement is well known, but it is worth paying attention here to its implications. An old phenomenon, noted especially by biblical scholars, has to do with the close relationship between sacrifice and verbal acts, especially praise and thanksgiving, regardless of whether the sacrifices themselves were accompanied by psalms or liturgy.[53] This proximity takes two forms. One is exemplified by a familiar rhetorical figure in Hos 14:3, pledging to God *neshalle-mah parim sefatenu*, "we will pay the oxen of our lips." Another way in which this phenomenon can be observed is in the strong formal and verbal parallels, noticed already by Hermann Gunkel and documented by several scholars since, between the language of steles and votive

---

[50] On substitutes for sacrifice in rabbinic thought see M. Fishbane, *The Exegetical Imagination: On Jewish Thought and Theology* (Cambridge, 1998), 123–219; and N. Goldstein, "Sacrifice and Worship of God in Rabbinic Thought after the Destruction of the Temple," *Daat* 8 (Winter 1982): 29–51 (in Hebrew).

[51] See for example *'Avot de-Rabbi Natan* A ch. 4; *b. Megillah* 31b; *b. Menahot* 110a.

[52] See *Sifre Deut. 'Eqev* 41 (ed. Finkelstein, 87–88); *y. Yoma* 4:1 (7a).

[53] See J.L. Kugel, "Topics in the History of the Spirituality of the Psalms," in *Jewish Spirituality from the Bible to the Middle Ages* (ed. A.A. Green; New York, 1987), 113–44; G.A. Anderson, "The Praise of God as a Cultic Event," in *Priesthood and Cult in Ancient Israel* (ed. G.A. Anderson and S.M. Olyan; Sheffield, 1991), 15–33; H.L. Ginsberg, "Psalms and Inscriptions of Petition and Acknowledgment," in *Louis Ginzberg Jubilee Volume* (ed. American Academy for Jewish Research; New York: 1945), 159–71 (English Section).

inscriptions, and biblical expressions of praise and thanksgiving.[54] In predominantly oral cultures, where spoken vows and commitments in fact carry more weight than written texts, devotional poetry can be understood as a full equivalent of the presentation of an animal or erection of a monument to the god.

This dynamic is related to the elaborate literary form of piyyut. The ornamental and recondite aesthetic of the genre—in other words, the "jeweled style"—was not only a matter of literary or aesthetic fashion. Rather, it constituted a way of presenting a perfect verbal offering before the Lord. As the bull and sheep must be flawless and the choice of their flock, and as the priest himself must be a superb physical specimen, so must the verbal offering—the only one possible in this era—impress the audience as the finest available. To the late antique ear, this meant that it should be encrusted with linguistic gems, multifaceted in their implications, arrayed one after another.

But what exactly does one sacrifice when one gives verbal offerings? It must be remembered that liturgical poetry was composed, memorized, and sung by the composer in the framework of oral presentation. This activity is in fact parallel in many ways to that of the memorization, recitation, and analysis that constitute talmudic scholastic praxis.[55] As we know from several sources, such activity was physically and mentally demanding.[56] We may therefore ask whether the *avodah she-ba-lev* may not consist of such a "sacrifice" of one's time and effort. An analogous argument has been made by David Sansone, who argues that Greek athletics were a "sacrifice of the athlete's expenditure of energy before the gods."[57]

If this is a valid way of understanding discourse on sacrifice in the ancient Mediterranean world, we can also look at well-known rabbinic statements that specify effective substitutes for sacrifice in a new way. Michael Fishbane, in an essay on substitutes for sacrifice in rabbinic literature, draws our attention to a striking passage in *b. Berakhot* 17a.[58] There Rav Sheshet offers a prayer that equates his fast to sacrifice in the most physical way:

---

[54] See the previous note.

[55] On the role of orality and memory in rabbinic tradition see M. Jaffee, *Torah in the Mouth: Writing and Oral Tradition in Palestinian Judaism, 200 BCE–400 CE* (Oxford, 2001).

[56] See M.D. Swartz, *Scholastic Magic: Ritual and Revelation in Early Jewish Mysticism* (Princeton, 1996), 33–50.

[57] D. Sansone, *Greek Athletics and the Genesis of Sport* (Berkeley, 1988), 62.

[58] Michael Fishbane, *Exegetical Imagination*, 129–30.

> Master of the Universe, it is known before you that when the Temple
> was standing one who sinned could offer a sacrifice, and even if all that
> was offered of it was fat and blood, it could atone for him. Now I have
> sat fasting and my fat and blood have been diminished. May it be Your
> will that my fat and blood which have been diminished be as if they were
> offered on the altar, and favor me.

As Fishbane points out, this statement is remarkable because it reverses
the so-called substitution theory of sacrifice, whereby the animal and
its death is a stand-in for the death of the sacrificer. Instead, the human
worshipper sacrifices his own flesh and blood in hopes that it will be
accepted as a legitimate substitute for the animal.

V. Towards a Sacrificial Paradigm

The *Avodah* thus provides evidence that discourse on sacrifice and the
Temple should be understood in normative or foundational terms. That
is, the sacrificial system should be seen as a kind of "default mode" for
ritual, underpinning a broader range of actions in late antiquity than
we are accustomed to seeing. By this view, verbal ritual actions, especially liturgical prayers, are a *subclass* of sacrifice—not a metaphor or
even a substitute for sacrifice. That is, while to call something a metaphor is to say that the speaker acknowledges its difference in kind, to
call it a subclass is to say that it participates, even if to a diminished
degree, in the same reality as the larger category.[59]

Moreover, sacrifice itself did not disappear from the Mediterranean
in late antiquity. In the fourth century, the time when the *Avodah*
genre began to take definitive shape, sacrifice was a reality for several sectors of the Greco–Roman world, even after the establishment
of Christianity as the religion of the Roman Empire. The Samaritans
were still sacrificing at their sanctuary on Mt. Gerizim; Robin Lane
Fox has shown how vigorously polytheistic ritual institutions persisted
well after the supposed triumph of Christianity.[60] Indeed, Julian's
ritual program, directed toward covering the empire with sanctuaries
and aggressively promoting sacrifice, shows how easy it was to revive
or enliven the practice. It is certainly possible that hopes for restoration of the Temple were rendered less unrealistic because of Julian's

---

[59] I owe this point to Professor Steven Wasserstrom of Reed College.
[60] R.L. Fox, *Pagans and Christians* (New York, 1986).

attempt to rebuild the Temple.[61] Philosophers such as such as Iamblichus also sought to underpin sacrifice and the local cults with deeper spiritual significance.[62] Christianity too understood itself in sacrificial terms and considered sacrifice to take place in the Eucharist.[63]

Indeed, actual sacrifices did continue, especially in magical traditions.[64] An expiatory sacrifice of a fowl, onto which an individual's sins are transferred, survives to this day in the *Kapparot* ritual for Yom Kippur, which dates back at least to the Middle Ages.[65] Such a transfer of sacrificial ritual to magic, a process that Jonathan Z. Smith has called the "miniaturization" of sacrifice, has been documented for the religions of the ancient Mediterranean in general.[66] At the same time, the ancient synagogue itself preserved much of what was available of the cult after 70: the *menorah*, the *shofar*, the *lulav* and *etrog*, and, according to recent evidence, some form of incense.[67] These objects are common in the iconography of the ancient synagogue.[68] In addition, the Torah shrine in the synagogue focused the congregation on the Temple site because of its customary orientation towards the

---

[61] For a survey of sources, see D.B. Levenson, "The Ancient and Medieval Sources for the Emperor Julian's Attempt to Rebuild the Jerusalem Temple," *JSJ* 35 (2004): 409–60. On possible Jewish responses see J. Schwartz, "Gallus, Julian, and Anti-Christian Polemic in Pesikta Rabbati," *TZ* 46 (1990): 1–19; cf. W Bacher, "Statements of a Contemporary of the Emperor Julian on the Rebuilding of the Temple," *JQR* (o.s.) 10 (1897): 168–72; and J.H. Levy (Lewy), *Studies in Jewish Hellenism* (Jerusalem, 1960), 221–54 (in Hebrew).

[62] See especially Iamblichus, *On the Mysteries* (*Iamblichus: De Mysteriis* [ed. E.C. Clarke, J.M. Dillon, and J.P. Hershbell; Atlanta, 2003]), 5.227–279; and N. Beylache, "Sacrifice and the Theory of Sacrifice during the 'Pagan Reaction': Julian the Emperor," in Baumgarten, *Sacrifice in Religious Experience*, 101–26. On the philosophical challenges that occasioned these defenses, cf. Stroumsa, *The End of Sacrifice*, 57–63.

[63] See F.M. Young, *Sacrifice and the Death of Christ* (London, 1975). On the influence of Jewish ideas of sacrifice on early Christianity see D. Stökl ben Ezra, *The Impact of Yom Kippur on Early Christianity: The Day of Atonement from Second Temple Judaism to the Fifth Century* (Tübingen, 2003).

[64] See M.D. Swartz, "Sacrificial Themes in Jewish Magic," in *Magic and Ritual in the Ancient World* (ed. M. Meyer and P. Mirecki; Leiden, 2002), 303–15.

[65] See J.Z. Lauterbach, "The Ritual for the Kapparot Ceremony," in idem, *Studies in Jewish Law, Custom, and Folklore* (New York, 1970), 133–42.

[66] See J.Z. Smith, "Trading Places," in *Ancient Magic and Ritual Power* (ed. M. Meyer and P. Mirecki; Leiden, 1995), 13–27; S.I. Johnston, "Sacrifice in the Greek Magical Papyri," in Meyer and Mirecki, *Magic and Ritual*, 344–58.

[67] See L.V. Rutgers, "Incense Shovels at Sepphoris," in Meyers, *Galilee through the Centuries*, 177–98.

[68] On this point see especially Fine, "Liturgical Context." While Fine argues against the predominance of Temple concerns in the synagogue of late antiquity, this article does emphasize the correspondence of images and liturgical objects.

Temple as the proper direction of prayer; in addition, depictions of the shrine may have been meant to evoke the Ark of the Covenant or the Temple sanctuary.[69] Nor did the priests themselves disappear. There is mounting evidence of the presence and vitality of priestly families in the Galilee in the period covered by the *Avodah* piyyutim. Stuart Miller has shown how Sepphoris was both a center for the rabbinic class and for priestly families.[70] There is evidence that the priestly "watches," or *mishmarot*, that is, the families of priests who had served on a rotating basis in the Temple, preserved their identity and genealogy as they settled into villages in the Galilee after 70. Several of the poets of the ancient synagogue were priests; indeed, some wrote poems based on the family names of the priests of the *mishmarot*.[71]

For many Jews in late antiquity, sacrifice was not solely a utopian notion but rather a foundational concept that deeply informed the way they saw worship and the human connection with the divine. Prayer, the "sacrifice of the heart," should therefore be understood not as a substitute for sacrifice, but an act of sacrifice itself. In a world where sacrifice was a pervasive mode of ritual, scholars studied the laws of the lost cult because no system of ritual was complete without them. The synagogue, or "lesser sanctuary," was adorned with implements recalling the Temple and its symbols, although it could not replace that Temple as a sacred center. The very virtuosity of the poet of the synagogue, manifest in the recondite language and specific techniques of piyyut, served ritual function of adorning the sacred space with the choicest of offerings. The synagogue thus formed an appropriate setting where the messenger of the community, evoking the high priest, offered a perfect verbal sacrifice on Yom Kippur.

---

[69] On this structure as a Torah ark see Hachlili, *Jewish Art*, 272–85; and S. Fine, *This Holy Place: On the Sanctity of the Synagogue during the Greco-Roman Period* (Notre Dame, 1997), 112–21; cf. E.M. Meyers, J.F. Strange, and C.L. Meyers, "The Ark of Nabratein: A First Glance," *Biblical Archaeologist* 44 (1981): 241, who identify the Torah shrine as an "architectural structure devised as successor to the biblical Ark of the Covenant"; for an earlier interpretation of the Torah shrine as a "portal to heaven," see B. Goldman, *The Sacred Portal: A Primary Symbol in Ancient Judaic Art* (Detroit, 1966). One of the advantages of iconography is that a given object could represent more than one thing; thus the Torah ark could also be made to recall the Tabernacle and Temple.

[70] See S.S. Miller, *Studies in the History and Traditions of Sepphoris* (Leiden, 1984). Cf. Z. Weiss's evaluation of the archaeological record in this volume; and Miller's own assessment, "Priests, Purities, and the Jews of Galilee," in *Religion, Ethnicity, and Identity in Ancient Galilee: A Region in Transition* (ed. J. Zangenberg, H.W. Attridge, and D.B. Martin; Tübingen, 2007), 375–402.

[71] See Yahalom, *Poetry and Society*, 112–16.

PART V

COMMUNAL DEFINITION—POMPEY, JESUS, OR TITUS:
WHO MADE A DIFFERENCE?

SETTING THE STAGE: THE EFFECTS OF THE ROMAN CONQUEST AND THE LOSS OF SOVEREIGNTY[1]

Nadav Sharon

Our Scholion group's work has centered on the common scholarly convention that ancient Judaism revolved around the Temple in Jerusalem until it was destroyed in 70 CE, and thereafter became a religion with no geographical focus, or, perhaps, with several. One way or another, this thesis assumes that much of what we know about ancient Judaism can meaningfully be organized around the destruction of the Second Temple and understood as reflecting its existence or destruction.[2] A different scholarly view sees the evolution of rabbinic Judaism not so much, or not only, as a result of the Temple's destruction, but rather as a response to the rise of Christianity.

One might ask, however, how it was that this religion and its people, if in fact they were focused on the Temple to such an extent, were able to overcome the incredible catastrophe of its destruction so as to develop the concepts, attitudes, and institutions which enabled their survival in the new and completely changed reality. It is my aim in

---

[1] This paper is an early product of my doctoral studies under the guidance of Prof. Daniel R. Schwartz, conducted while I was a fellow of the research group, "On Religions of Place and Religions of Community" (2006–2009), at the Scholion Interdisciplinary Research Center in Jewish Studies at the Hebrew University, Jerusalem.

[2] For example, H. Graetz's dividing line between the third and fourth volumes of his *magnum opus (Geschichte der Juden)* is the "Untergang des jüdischen Staates," which, for him, happened with the destruction of the Temple. Note also his definition of the second period of Jewish history as the Second Temple period, ending with the Destruction in 70, and the third period—the period of exile—as beginning thereafter; see his, "Die Konstruktion der jüdischen Geschichte," *Zeitschrift für die religiösen Interessen des Judenthums* 3 (1846): 81–97, 121–32, 361–80 (repr. [as a book]: Berlin, 1936; citations refer to the reprint edition). For Graetz's problematic definition of the Second Temple period, see D.R. Schwartz, "Jews, Judaeans and the Epoch that Disappeared: On H. Graetz's Changing View of the Second Temple Period," *Zion* 70 (2005): 293–309 (in Hebrew), as well as his contribution to the present volume. For the view by which the state came to its end only with the destruction of the Temple, see below, at nn. 5–8. For more examples see G. Alon, "The Impact of the Great Defeat," in idem, *The Jews in Their Land in the Talmudic Age (70–640 CE)* (trans. and ed. G. Levi; Jerusalem, 1980), 1:41–55; A. Bertholet, *Das Ende des jüdischen Staatswesens* (Tübingen, 1910). For the rabbinic view of the destruction of the Second Temple as a watershed see the frequent idiom משחרב הבית (e.g., *t. Menaḥot* 10:26 and *t. Taʿanit* 2:3).

this paper not to argue with those views noted above, but rather to draw scholarly attention to a somewhat neglected series of events that I believe set the stage for that survival and for some of those post-70 developments. I am referring now to the events of 67–37 BCE and their aftermath.

A NEGLECTED ERA

Despite the enormous amount of scholarly work on the Second Temple Period it seems to me that the period of 67–37 BCE, and the dramatic change it brought upon Judea, have been somewhat neglected in modern historical study. The events of this period brought about the end of the eighty-year-old independent and sovereign Judean state, established by the Hasmoneans in the aftermath of Antiochus Epiphanes' religious decrees and the ensuing revolt. In fact, these events resulted in the almost complete annihilation of that prestigious priestly house. In 63 BCE the independent Hasmonean state, with its large territorial gains, found itself suddenly under the domination of the expanding world empire, Rome, and downgraded to a small semiautonomous vassal state.

Admittedly, at some points during its subsequent history, when it had its own kings, this state enjoyed independence to a greater degree—under Herod the Great and, after a few decades, Agrippa I. However, these kings were none the less vassals, appointees of the Romans, and however one looks at them their kingdoms were very far from independent. (This is, of course, excluding the short-lived kingship of Mattathias Antigonus [40–37 BCE], the last Hasmonean king, who was brought to power by the Parthians.) True, one might justifiably argue that objectively, in terms of independence, the situation after 63 BCE was probably not any worse than it had been prior to the Hasmonean revolt, and was perhaps even better when those Herodian kings were in power. However, when seen subjectively, through the eyes of Judeans who had just enjoyed eighty years of independence, the events of 63 BCE were probably perceived as not much less than a complete loss of independence.

This perception is exemplified in Josephus's speech to the besieged in Jerusalem during the Great Revolt: "Whence did we begin (our) servitude? (πόθεν δ' ἠρξάμεθα δουλείας;) Was it not from party strife among our forefathers, when the madness of Aristobulus and

Hyrcanus...brought Pompey against the city, and God subjected to the Romans those who were unworthy of liberty?" (*J.W.* 5.395–396).[3] This was also the Roman point of view, as is made clear by Cicero's statement regarding Jerusalem, just four years after Pompey's conquest: "...how dear it (i.e., Jerusalem) was to the immortal gods is shown by the fact that it has been conquered, let out for taxes, made a slave" (*Flacc.* 28:69).[4]

It seems to me safe to assume that a change such as the loss of sovereignty must have had a tremendous impact on Judean religion and society. However, as already observed, historical study has relatively neglected this period, and has focused on the destruction of the Temple, not on the loss of independence, when reflecting upon the evolution of ancient Judaism. Various studies have been written on Herod's rule and on the first century CE as background to the Great Revolt or to the rise of Christianity, but on the early Roman Period (63 BCE–70 CE) in general, as the background to understanding post-Destruction Judaism, very little has been done.

This neglect comes hand in hand, whether as cause or result, with a situation wherein numerous scholarly studies express themselves as if the end of the Jewish state came only with the Destruction in 70 CE, as exemplified in the following quotations (my emphasis added in each):

> It is remarkable that the *fall of the state*, the conflagration that destroyed the Temple, did not at all make the same terrible impression on those who lived through it as did the death of the first *state*. (Graetz, 1846)[5]

---

[3] Translation by Thackeray in LCL, substituting "we begin (our) servitude" for his "our servitude arise." (All translations of Josephus in this paper are, unless otherwise noted, from *Josephus* [trans H.St.J. Thackeray et al.; 10 vols. LCL; Cambridge, 1926–1965].) See also Josephus's lament in *Ant.* 14.77. The *Pesher Habakkuk* scroll from Qumran might also be implying this view: [והיתה הארץ] במנששלת הכתיאים ("[The land shall be] under the rule of the Kittim"; 1QpHab 2:13–14; trans. M. Wise, M. Abegg, and E. Cook, with N. Gordon, in *The Dead Sea Scrolls Reader, Part 2: Exegetical Texts* [ed. D.W. Parry and E. Tov; Leiden, 2004], 81). However, as is often the case, the words crucial for establishing this argument are missing from the scroll, and various other reconstructions have been suggested in place of the words והיתה הארץ, which is the reconstruction of M. Abegg (ibid., 80). Nevertheless, the equation of the Kittim (i.e., Romans) with the Chaldeans (i.e., Babylonians) in this text (2:11–12), and in others, might also hint at this view.

[4] *GLA* 1:198. Cf. Titus's speech to the besieged in Jerusalem: "Ever since Pompey conquered you by force (εἷλεν ὑμᾶς κατὰ κράτος) you never ceased from revolution" (*J.W.* 6.329; translation mine—N.S.).

[5] Graetz, *Konstruktion*, 48.

After the destruction of the Second Temple in the year 70 CE the Jews
were deprived of their *political independence*. (Zeitlin, 1945)[6]

The Destruction put a final end to Jewish *political independence*. (Alon,
1954)[7]

The failure of the [Great—N.S.] revolt led to the destruction of the last
independent Jewish state in Palestine until the establishment of Israel.
(Goodman, 1987)[8]

There is no doubt that these scholars knew very well that the Roman
occupation of Judea began in 63 BCE, and that that is when the independent and sovereign Judean state actually came to its end; but still,
this is the picture reflected in various scholarly works.[9] The reasons for
this phenomenon (and for the neglect of the period of 67–37 BCE in
general) are not my subject here. However, it seems that in addition
to the neglect of that period, this picture in turn has also made it seem
all the more natural for scholars to emphasize the Destruction as the
basis for understanding later Judaism and to overlooking the impact
of the loss of independence and the beginning of Roman dominion
of Judea.

It is, therefore, my contention here that some conceptual and institutional developments which were crucial for the development of
post-Destruction Judaism are to be understood more appropriately
against the background of the loss of independence and the beginning
of Roman rule in Judea.[10] These developments have usually either been

---

[6] S. Zeitlin, "The Political Synedrion and the Religious Sanhedrin," *JQR* 36 (1945):
126.

[7] G. Alon, "The Talmudic Age," in idem, *The Jews in Their Land in the Talmudic
Age*, 1:5. For a similar formulation see ibid., 1:206. Note, however, that the reference
at p. 5 to the "final end," which implies this is the conclusion of a process, softens the
formulation of the original Hebrew version, which speaks here of the loss of political independence upon the destruction of the Temple (G. Alon, *Toledot HaYehudim
be-Erets Yisra'el bi-tekufat ha-Mishnah veha-Talmud* [Tel-Aviv, 1953–55], 1:4).

[8] M. Goodman, *The Ruling Class of Judaea: The Origins of the Jewish Revolt Against
Rome A.D. 66–70* (Cambridge, 1987), 4. See also S. Talmon, "Textual Criticism: The
Ancient Versions," in *Text in Context: Essays by Members of the Society for Old Testament Study* (ed. A.D.H. Mayes; Oxford, 2000), 152. To these may be added numerous
references to the Destruction as the end of the independent state in popular literature
and media.

[9] D.M. Goodblatt ("The Jews of Eretz-Israel in the Years 70–132," in *Judea and
Rome: The Jewish Revolts* [ed. U. Rappaport; Jerusalem, 1983], 155–84 [in Hebrew])
notes this scholarly view (p. 155) and points out the fact that from 63 BCE Judea was
a mere vassal state, and that it was annexed to Rome in 6 CE (p. 161).

[10] Some scholarly studies do indeed see the early Roman period as a transitional
time, wherein Judaism was already on its way to its post-Destruction developments

attributed to the aftermath of the Destruction or been taken as long-standing Judean phenomena that existed throughout all or most of the Second Temple period. In contrast, I suggest that we consider the notion that the period of the loss of independence and the inception of Roman rule in Judea is when the seeds of these developments were sown, or was at least a major factor in shaping them.

This paper offers some preliminary steps in this direction. First, the case will be made that the early Roman period marked the first fundamental separation between the state and religious authority in Judea. Then I will discuss some institutional innovations in this period. Finally, the possible impact of the developments of this period on the centrality of the Jerusalem Temple will be discussed, along with the possible effects that impact may have had on the development of another institution, namely, the synagogue.

Religion and State

Judean Jews of the post-Destruction era had to get used to the idea that the religious aspect of their lives had turned into a communal issue, divorced from the authority of the state. Political power was now, for the most part, fully in the hands of the foreign empire and had nothing to do with the religious authority. This situation is similar to that already faced by Diaspora Jews during Second Temple times.

It has previously been recognized, however, that preliminary steps toward the separation of religion and state in Judea had already taken place while the Temple was still standing. Daniel Schwartz has shown that the Hasmonean conquest of Gentiles eventually led the Hasmoneans to add the royal title to their high-priestly title so as to enable them to "[call] upon the Gentile subjects to render obedience to them not as religious figures but rather only as temporal overlords."[11] However, this separation, which distinguished Hasmonean priestly and political authority, was still only nominal, since both spheres of power were still in the hands of the same person. It is true that during Alexandra's reign (76–67 BCE) the titles were split between

---

(see L.L. Grabbe, *Judaic Religion in the Second Temple Period: Belief and Practice from the Exile to Yavneh* [London, 2000], 333–34).

[11] D.R. Schwartz, *Studies in the Jewish Background of Christianity* (Tübingen, 1992), 12.

two individuals. However this separation was forced upon Alexandra because as a woman, she could not hold the high-priestly office; it was not really a full separation since the high priest whom she appointed was her son, Hyrcanus II. Indeed, as soon as she died the two titles were once again united, first in the person of Hyrcanus II (67/66 BCE), then in the person of his younger brother, Aristobulus II (67/66–63 BCE).

It is with the Roman occupation of Judea that the distinction turned into a true separation of powers, since throughout virtually the entire early period of Roman rule in Judea, from its inception until the Destruction, the Romans or their agents exercised political authority, leaving religious authority in the hands of the high priest.[12] The Romans tried various methods of governing Judea. At first they reinstated Hyrcanus to the high priesthood, but without kingship and with almost completely diminished political power (63 BCE; *J.W.* 1.153, 157). Later, Gabinius divided the country into five districts, each with its own council (57 BCE; *J.W.* 1.170: *synodoi; Ant.* 14.91: *synedria*), which exercised civic authority, leaving only the Temple to Hyrcanus's charge. After the Parthian invasion and Antigonus's assumption of the kingship (40 BCE), and probably in response to this development, the Romans appointed Herod as King of Judea, just as they later did with Agrippa I (41–44 CE)—but these vassal kings could not, by definition, be high priests. Finally, in the years 6–41 CE Judea came under direct Roman rule, and after Agrippa's short-lived kingship Judea became a Roman province.[13] A major common denominator in all these "experiments"[14] is the separation between political power and religious authority.

---

[12] Ibid., 13. Of course, this might be seen as not really new, since it is similar to the pre-Hasmonean state of affairs. However, even without noting the differences between these two eras, in the present context suffice it to say that since we are asking what set the stage for the post-70 era, conceptions held prior to the founding of the sovereign Hasmonean state are hardly relevant.

[13] For the difference between Judea's status in 6–41 CE, when it was under direct Roman rule, probably not a province but rather subordinate to the province of Syria, and its full provincial status in 44 CE or later, see the first part of H.M. Cotton, "Some Aspects of the Roman Administration of Judaea/Syria-Palaestina," in *Lokale Autonomie und römische Ordnungsmacht in den kaiserzeitlichen Provinzen vom 1.–3. Jahrhundert* (ed. W. Eck; Munich, 1999), 75–91.

[14] On the Romans as "experimenting" with different political arrangements for Judea see A.I. Baumgarten, "How Experiments End," in *Jewish Identities in Antiquity: Studies in Memory of Menahem Stern* (ed. L.I. Levine and D.R. Schwartz; Tübingen, 2009), 147–61.

Thus, notwithstanding the scholarly tendency mentioned above, the Judean state had in effect been lost, and only the religious sphere remained, embodied by the Temple.[15] So too, any significance that the Temple might have held as the seat of a sovereign was in reality lost.[16]

This new situation which the Judeans suddenly found themselves facing is illustrated in Jesus' saying: "Render to Caesar the things that are Caesar's, and to God the things that are God's" (Mark 12:17// Matt 22:21//Luke 20:25). This bespeaks a situation very similar to the reality of Jewish life in the Diaspora—on the one hand, subject to a foreign power that held all political authority; and on the other hand, needing to govern their own daily communal and religious life. In fact, the only real difference between the Judeans and their brethren of the Diaspora, in this respect, was their proximity to the Temple.

In my view, it is this "semi-Diaspora" situation in Judea, and the adoption or invention of concepts and institutions which fit this situation, that in some respects set the stage for the Temple-less life of post-Destruction Judea—i.e., a virtually complete Diaspora reality within Judea itself.

POLITICAL INSTITUTIONS

I. *The Ethnarch*

One interesting method of governing Judea with which the Romans experimented might seem to bespeak a continued linkage of state and religion. I refer to the appointment of Hyrcanus II as *ethnarch*, during some part of his tenure (see *Ant.* 14.190–195). He held this title, which literally means "head of the *ethnos*/nation," in addition to his title of high priest. Thus, the highest Jewish religious authority also had, under Roman auspices, some official measure of political

---

[15] As noted above, the kingships of Herod the Great and Agrippa I should not be counted against this, as they were only temporary. Moreover, the Herodians were perceived as usurpers and Roman vassals; Herod especially was seen, at least by some Judeans, as a foreigner or a "half-Jew" (*Ant.* 14.403). On Agrippa I, see *Ant.* 19.332; *m. Sotah* 7:8 with *t. Sotah* 7:16; and D.R. Schwartz, *Agrippa I: The Last King of Judaea* (Tübingen, 1990), 157–71. Furthermore, direct Roman rule was apparently preferred by some Judeans to being ruled by the Herodian house (*J.W.* 2.84–91; *Ant.* 17.304–314).

[16] Which explains why it would become a major springboard for later revolts. See Schwartz, *Jewish Background*, 9–10.

authority. However, this was not a return to the early Hasmonean unity of state and religion, in which the high priest ruled the state. Rather, it is more closely akin to the late Hasmonean situation, wherein the two titles, king and high priest—now *ethnarch* and high priest—show that the political and the religious powers are differentiated, despite the fact that they are held by the same person. This is demonstrated by the case of another Second Temple period persona known to have held the title of *ethnarch*—Archelaus, son of Herod (*J.W.* 2.93; *Ant.* 17.317), who was not high priest.

Nevertheless, the fact that Hyrcanus held both titles is, to some extent, a temporary step away from the separation of state and religion. However, another implication of the title of *ethnarch* should be noticed: Those rulers who are named *ethnarchs* are demonstratively denied the royal title.[17] This is most explicit in the case of Archelaus, who came to Rome in order to obtain Augustus's approval of his kingship; instead, the latter "appointed Archelaus not king indeed but ethnarch..." (*Ant.* 17.317).

What is the difference between kings and *ethnarchs*? Kings, by definition, rule territories.[18] This seems to have been obvious in antiquity. *Ethnarchs*, on the other hand, as is evident from the word itself, rule people.[19] The non-territorial aspect of the *ethnarch*'s rule is evident from the fact that we find an *ethnarch* over the Jewish community in Egypt (*Ant.* 14.117—Strabo, quoted by Josephus; 19.283—a Claudian edict;[20] see also Strabo, *Geogr.* 17.1.13).[21] Hence, although the innovation of the *ethnarch* is to some degree a step back in terms of the separation of

---

[17] Despite this, it seems that at least some Judeans still referred to the *ethnarchs* popularly as kings (Hyrcanus—*J.W.* 1:202–203, 209, 212; *Ant.* 14:157, 168; Archelaus—*Ant.* 18.93; *Life* 5; Matt 2:22).

[18] See, for example, the first definition of "king" in *Webster's Third New International Dictionary of the English Language, Unabridged* (Springfield, Mass., 1976), 1244.

[19] D.R. Schwartz, "Herodians and *Ioudaioi* in Flavian Rome," in *Flavius Josephus and Flavian Rome* (ed. J. Edmondson, S. Mason, and J. Rives; Oxford, 2005), 68; and see the literature mentioned there.

[20] This *ethnarch* seems to be identical with the *genarch* mentioned by Philo, *Flacc.* 74.

[21] Note that Hyrcanus "is recognized as 'ethnarch of the Jews' (e.g., *Ant.* 14.191— N.S.) and not of Judea, while Archelaus is later called by Augustus 'ethnarch of half the territory that had been subject to Herod...'" (M. Pucci Ben Zeev, *Jewish Rights in the Roman World: The Greek and Roman Documents Quoted by Josephus Flavius* [Tübingen, 1998], 49. See also ibid., 49–50, with further references.) However, while the evidence for Hyrcanus's ethnarchy is found in official documents quoted by Josephus, that for Archelaus is in the narrative only.

state and religion, reflecting "experimentation," it is an innovation that fits a Diaspora setting, or a state-less setting, and its implementation set the stage in Judea for post-Destruction existence.[22]

II. *Synedria*

I have already mentioned how Gabinius reformed Judea's administration by dividing the country into five districts, each governed by its own council (*J.W.* 1.170: *synodoi*; *Ant.* 14.91: *synedria*). Due to the enormous amount of research on this subject, and on the relation of the *synedria* to "the Sanhedrin," I will merely outline here the main views.

The majority of publications about the Sanhedrin, especially those of earlier eras, but also in more recent research, have seen this institution as existing throughout all or most of the Second Temple period.[23] Thus, Josephus's claim that Alexandra entrusted the administration of the kingdom to the Pharisees (*J.W.* 1.110–112; *Ant.* 13.405, 408–409) is understood, in some studies, as if she gave over to them the control of the Sanhedrin.[24] These scholars argue that the different terms we find in our sources (*gerousia, synedrion, boulē*) all refer to the same single institution, which may have had a different name at different times.[25] Some of them view the Sanhedrin as a leading national institution,[26] while others view it more as an advisory council to the ruler—the king

---

[22] For more on the title *ethnarch* see my, "The Title *Ethnarch* in Second Temple Period Judea," *JSJ* 41 (2010): 472–93.

[23] For example: E. Schürer, *The History of the Jewish People in the Age of Jesus Christ (175 BCE–135 CE)* (ed. G. Vermes et al.; 3 vols.; rev. English ed.; Edinburgh, 1973–1986), 2:200–206; V.A. Tcherikover, "Was Jerusalem a Polis?" *IEJ* 14 (1964): 67–78. S. Zeitlin ("The Political Synedrion," 120–26) sees the origin of the post-Destruction Sanhedrin in the coalescence of a Bet Din (supposedly established at the accession of Simon in 143 BCE), which dealt with religious issues, with the *synedrion*, which was supposedly an ad hoc gathering of Herod's friends convened to deal with issues of the state.

[24] So, for example, Schürer, *History*, 2:204; F.M. Abel, "Le siège de Jérusalem par Pompée," *RB* 54 (1947): 244. Cf. K. Atkinson, *I Cried to the Lord: A Study of the Psalms of Solomon's Historical Background and Social Setting* (Leiden, 2004), 93–94.

[25] G. Alon, "The Original Sanhedrin: Retrospect," in idem, *The Jews in Their Land in the Talmudic Age*, 1:189; Stern, *GLA* 2:376; Tcherikover, "Was Jerusalem a Polis?" 70–73. L.L. Grabbe ("Sanhedrin, Sanhedriyyot, or Mere Invention?" *JSJ* 39 [2008]: 1–19) also claims that all these terms refer to the same institution; he suggests that the variation is not a consequence of change over time, but rather of different sources using different terms. See also Grabbe, *Judaic Religion*, 145–46.

[26] So Schürer, *History*, 2:200–206; Atkinson, *I Cried to the Lord*, 93.

or high priest, as the case may be.[27] Other scholars, on the contrary, doubt the credibility of the evidence about the Sanhedrin and view this body as no more than an occasional gathering of advisors convened by rulers on an ad hoc basis.[28]

Scrutinizing in depth all of the relevant data is far beyond the scope of this paper, although I hope to do that in the future. I would like, however, to note here some important aspects of the evidence:

1. *Synedrion in the Pre-Roman Period*: The term *synedrion* appears several times in the Septuagint translation of the books of the Hebrew Bible. Often it seems to be a relatively close rendering of the Hebrew original, drawing on one or another of this Greek term's standard meanings (e.g., "court" in Prov 22:10, rendering דין; "council" or "place of meeting" in Jer 15:17, rendering סוד).[29] Apart from its occurrences in the Septuagint the term *synedrion* is scarcely found prior to the Roman era. In texts of the Second Temple period it is found in Ben Sira, which is likewise a translation from the Hebrew; there it either renders a verbal form of סוד (42:12) or takes the similar meaning of "to be/sit among/together" (11:9; 23:14) (as in LXX Ps 25:4, for example). In my view, the character of Ben Sira, the fact that it is a translation (probably made outside of Judea), and the contexts and rarity of the term's appearance speak against viewing it as evidence for an actual institution in Judea.[30] The term does not appear in a historical text such as 1 Maccabees, and it occurs only once in

---

[27] Grabbe, "Sanhedrin, Sanhedriyyot."

[28] D.M. Goodblatt, *The Monarchic Principle: Studies in Jewish Self-Government in Antiquity* (Tübingen, 1994), 108–13.

[29] See ibid., 108. For סוד as meaning "council" in the Bible see F. Brown, S.R. Driver, and C.A. Briggs, *A Hebrew and English Lexicon of the Old Testament* (Oxford, 1907), 691. For this usage in Qumran see, inter alia, 1QH^a 12:25; 4Q181 1 ii 1; and especially the idiom *sod hayaḥad*, which refers to the sect itself (e.g., 1QS 6:19; 4QS^e [4Q259] 3:17–18).

[30] The term also appears once in Susanna (28), whose date, place, and language of composition are disputed (see G.W.E. Nickelsburg, *Jewish Literature Between the Bible and the Mishnah: A Historical and Literary Introduction* [2d ed.; Minneapolis, 2005], 24 and 347–48 n. 28; idem, "Stories of Biblical and Early Post-Biblical Times," in *Jewish Writings of the Second Temple Period* [ed. M.E. Stone; Assen, 1984], 38). It likewise appears once in the *Psalms of Solomon* (4:1), which is also a translation from the Hebrew; and in any case, at least some of its psalms were composed after the Roman occupation (see below, n. 84). Moreover, this verse, "Why are you, profane man, sitting in the *synedrion* of the holy?" (trans. mine—N.S.), appears to be using biblical language, such as appears in Jer 15:17, for example (לא ישבתי בסוד משחקים); Ps 89:8 (בסוד קדשים); or Ps 111:1 (בסוד ישרים).

2 Maccabees (14:5)—referring not to a Judean institution, but to a *synedrion* of the Gentile king, Demetrius.[31]

In Josephus the term appears only twice, in contexts prior to the Roman occupation. One occurrence is in the rewrite of the *Letter of Aristeas*, in *Ant.* 12.103. This part of the sentence is a fairly close rendering of *Aristeas* 301, which also has the term *synedrion*. In this narrative, the term refers to a meeting of the elders who came to Alexandria to translate the Bible and has nothing to do with a Judean institution. The second time the term appears is in *Ant.* 13.364, where it refers to a meeting of the city council of Gaza.

2. *Synedrion in the Roman Period*: In Josephus's historical narrative a *synedrion* in Judea first appears in the narration concerning the above-mentioned reforms of Gabinius (*Ant.* 14.91).[32] However, in the parallel narrative in the *Jewish War*, the term *synodoi*, and not *synedria*, appears (*J.W.* 1.170). These terms are similar, and one can imagine that one or the other derives from scribal error or creativity. Nevertheless, I think we can discern that *synedria* is the correct term for the institutions Gabinius established.[33] Although both terms share the meaning, "a meeting," *synedrion* also has the meaning of "council,"[34] whereas definitions of the term *synodos* seem to imply one-time gatherings or meetings, usually not an institution that is both formal and permanent.[35] Indeed, this sense of one-time meetings or general gatherings fits the way Josephus himself regularly uses the term *synodos* (e.g., *J.W.* 1.585; *Ant.* 4.290; 8.133); this sense does not, however, seem to fit the intent of Gabinius's administrative reforms. The term *synedria*, meaning councils—a meaning that is also clear from the fact that

---

[31] See also J. Efron, "The Great Sanhedrin in Vision and Reality," in idem, *Studies on the Hasmonean Period* (Leiden, 1987), 310.

[32] Gabinius's reforms resemble the Roman partition of Macedonia into four regions, each governed by its own council, approximately a century earlier (Livy, *History*, 45.29.5–9). See A. Schalit, *Roman Administration in Palestine* (Jerusalem, 1937), 32–37 (in Hebrew); Goodblatt, *Monarchic Principle*, 110; Efron, "Great Sanhedrin," 310.

[33] As Reinach suggests in connection with the *War* passage. See note *a* on *J.W.* 1.170 in the LCL.

[34] LSJ, s.v. συνέδρα, 1704.

[35] LSJ, s.v. σύνοδος, 1720. It also takes the meaning of association, which often served religious purposes. See further A.D. Nock, "The Gild of Zeus Hypsistos," in idem, *Essays on Religion and the Ancient World* (ed. Z. Stewart; 2 vols.; Oxford, 1972), 1:430–32.

Polybius and others used this term to refer to the Roman Senate[36]—
on the other hand, fits the context of the reforms perfectly.[37]

3. *Gerousia*: The term *gerousia* appears a few times in the Septuagint (e.g., Exod 3:16; Num 22:4; Josh 23:2). However, as David Goodblatt has shown, this term does not have to be understood as referring
to a formal council, and might be no more than an equivalent of
gerontes, i.e., זקנים, elders.[38] Moreover, even if Goodblatt's suggestion
is not accepted, occurrences of this term in Greek translations of the
biblical books should not be taken as evidence for historical reality in
Second Temple Judea, for they may reflect the diasporan *Sitz im Leben*
of the translators.[39] The term also appears often in Josephus's rewriting
of the Bible, including contexts where the term does not appear in the
Septuagint.[40] However, after his treatment of the biblical period the
term appears only rarely; such occurrences as there are, in his writings
and elsewhere, are generally limited to a very short period of time,
200–143 BCE.[41] Even regarding that period, however, the term appears
in Josephus's writings only in two documents that he cites. Of these,
the first (*Ant.* 12.138–144) is a bill of rights given by Antiochus III
to the Jews, which, even if authentic,[42] might at most be a reflection

---

[36] H.J. Mason, *Greek Terms for Roman Institutions: A Lexicon and Analysis* (Toronto, 1974), 123–24.

[37] Livy (*History*, 45.32.2) uses *synedros* to refer to the members of the regional councils set up by the Romans in Macedonia (see n. 32 above).

[38] Goodblatt, *Monarchic Principle*, 92–99.

[39] For the existence of (non-Jewish) *gerousia* in Egypt from Ptolemaic times, at least in Alexandria, see M.A.H. El-Abbadi, "The Gerousia in Roman Egypt," *JEA* 50 (1964): 164.

[40] Goodblatt (*Monarchic Principle*, 94–97) sees in Josephus's usage of this term fur-ther support for his suggestion that *gerousia* is merely a translation of "elders," which need not entail a formalized council. On this point, however, I do not accept his view. The numerous occurrences of *gerousia* in Josephus's retelling of the Bible that are *not* paralleled in the Septuagint, and especially *Ant.* 5.135, where *gerousia* seems to be the manifestation of the type of government which Josephus terms "aristocracy"—that is, rule by a council—imply that Josephus saw the *gerousia* as a formal council. In my M.A. thesis ("Kingship, Aristocracy, and Domitian: The Evolution of Flavius Josephus's Thought on Kingship and Rule" [The Hebrew University of Jerusalem, 2006, in Hebrew]) I suggested that Josephus was promoting a specific pro-aristocracy (i.e., pro-*gerousia*) agenda in the *Antiquities*.

[41] Goodblatt, *Monarchic Principle*, 89–90, 98.

[42] On the question of the letter's authenticity, see Appendix D in the LCL *Josephus*, vol. 7. M. Stern ("The Documents in the Jewish Literature of the Second Temple," in idem, *Studies in Jewish History: The Second Temple Period* [ed. M. Amit, I.M. Gafni, and M.D. Herr; Jerusalem, 1991], 372–73 [in Hebrew]) accepted it as authentic.

of Greek perceptions and not of actual Judean institutions;[43] and the
second (*Ant.* 13.166–170) is merely Josephus's version of a letter of
Jonathan to the Spartans found in 1 Maccabees 12, which in turn has
its own problems. Namely, although the letter is said to have been sent
by Jonathan, the *gerousia*, the priests, and the rest of the Judeans to the
Spartans (1 Macc 12:6), since the reply of the Spartans (14:20) mentions only "elders" (*presbyteroi*) and no *gerousia*, it is very possible—as
Goodblatt noted—that at 12:6 *gerousia* is only a product of translation
and the Hebrew original really had no more than *zᵉqenim*, "elders."[44]
Apart from Josephus and 1 Maccabees the term also appears in three
passages in 2 Maccabees (1:10; 4:44; 11:27).[45] That is not much, and of
those three passages the first and the last are of limited value: for 1:10
comes in a letter added to the book and might, therefore, be based
on the other two;[46] and 11:27 is in a letter sent by Antiochus (IV or
V), which might, again, be no more than a reflection of Greek perceptions.[47] Hence, altogether there are good reasons for Goodblatt's
skepticism as to the existence of a formal council termed *gerousia*.[48]
However, even if we do not accept this skepticism, we are still left with
evidence for the existence of the *gerousia* only during a short period
of time; it disappears from our sources more than eighty years before
the *synedrion* first appears.[49]

4. *Boulē*: The term *boulē* is also sometimes viewed as another term
for the *synedrion*. Again, I do not take into account the few instances

---

[43] Goodblatt, *Monarchic Principle*, 85–86.

[44] Goodblatt, *Monarchic Principle*, 97–98. A similar phenomenon is found in 3
Maccabees, where the sole occurrence of *gerousia*, in 1:8, seems to be equivalent to
geraioi in 1:23 (see ibid., p. 94 n. 39). A good illustration of this occurs in another
work that mentions the *gerousia*—the book of Judith, which is also a translation from
the Hebrew. The term appears there in three verses (4:8; 11:14; 15:8) and is usually
taken to refer to a council. However, according to Y. Grintz (*Sefer Yehudit* [Jerusalem,
1986], 105 [in Hebrew]) the Syriac version reads סביא = elders. Accordingly he translates "זקנים" in all three places, but in his notes he writes that it refers to a national
council, the Sanhedrin. The problem is also illustrated in the King James Version,
which has "ancients" at 4:8 and 15:8, but "senate" at 11:14.

[45] On 11:27 see Goodblatt, *Monarchic Principle*, 17–18.

[46] Ibid., 89–90.

[47] Ibid., 98.

[48] Ibid., 83–99.

[49] See also Goodman, *The Ruling Class*, 113–14, who nevertheless speaks of the
variety of names this council had after the Roman occupation, including *gerousia*; for
which, however, he cites only Acts 5:21. On that text, which is the only occurrence
of this term in the New Testament, and on Philo's usage of *gerousia*, see Goodblatt,
Monarchic Principle, 90–91.

where *boulē* appears in the Septuagint, for in those cases too it seems to be a relatively close rendering of the Hebrew original (most often עצה; e.g., Judg 20:7) usually conveying the meaning of "counsel, plan." Among books of the Hellenistic period, the term appears only in 1 Maccabees. Even there it appears only once with reference to a council (14:22)—and that council is in Sparta; in a similar fashion, *bouleuterion* is used of the Roman Senate (8:15, 19; 12:3). In the New Testament the term *bouleutēs* appears in parallel accounts in reference to one Joseph of Arimathea (Mark 15:43//Luke 23:50), who is, accordingly, often viewed as a member of the Sanhedrin.[50] However, this seems to be rooted more in our common perceptions of the Sanhedrin, and the tendency to find it everywhere, than in the actual evidence.[51] The verse in Mark is ambiguous and could equally mean that Joseph was a member of the city council of Arimathea;[52] even if the reference is not specifically to the council of Arimathea it should probably be understood, as we shall soon see, to mean that he was a member of the Jerusalem *city* council and not of a national council/Sanhedrin.

In Josephus the term *boulē* (and its derivatives), with the meaning of council, appears in several places in reference to various foreign cities (e.g., *J.W.* 7.107; *Ant.* 14.190), always denoting city councils and not national councils, except for references to the Roman Senate (e.g., *J.W.* 1.284; *Ant.* 13.164). Thus, we also find a *boulē* at the time of the Great Revolt, as the city council of Tiberias (e.g., *J.W.* 2.639; *Life* 64). For this reason it seems that when *boulē* does refer to a Judean council (*J.W.* 2.331, 336, 405; 5.144, 532; 6.354), it is a city council of Jerusalem that is intended, not any national institution.[53]

---

[50] Schürer, *History*, 2:206; C.S. Mann, *Mark: A New Translation with Introduction and Commentary* (Garden City, N.Y., 1986), 657; J. Nolland, *Luke 18:35–24:53* (Dallas, 1993), 1163.

[51] Cf. Efron, "Great Sanhedrin," 325.

[52] A. Yarbro Collins, *Mark: A Commentary* (Minneapolis, 2007), 777; and see n. 55 where she proposes that Luke's understanding is an inference from Mark. Also note that in Matthew and John he is not said to be a *bouleutēs* or anything similar. The location of Arimathea is uncertain (Nolland, *Luke*, 1164).

[53] Contra Grabbe, "Sanhedrin, Sanhedriyyot," 17, and Tcherikover, "Was Jerusalem a Polis?" 67–70. Cf. Goodblatt, *Monarchic Principle*, 17–18. One further possible reference to a *boulē* is found in *Pss. Sol.* 8:20: ἀπώλεσεν ἄρχοντας αὐτῶν καὶ πάντα σοφὸν ἐν βουλῇ, which R.B. Wright (*The Psalms of Solomon: A Critical Edition of the Greek Text* [London, 2007], 119 and n. 148) translates: "He killed off their leaders and each wise man in the council." One should, however, note both that this text, too, is a

Two more factors about the appearance of *boulē* as council in Josephus should be noted. First, all references to a *boulē* in Jerusalem or Judea are found in the *War*. None is found in *Antiquities* or *Life*.[54] In fact, the first reference to the Jerusalem *boulē* in *War* is chronologically later than the end of the narrative of *Antiquities*. There is one exception to this rule—in *Ant.* 20.11. However, this sole reference appears in a formal letter sent to the Judeans by Claudius, and it seems to be a standard opening formula for such letters, as is clear by its similarity to the openings of letters to other cities (e.g., *Ant.* 14.190; 16.172);[55] therefore it should not be viewed as evidence for the institution's actual existence.[56] Second, all of these references to a Jerusalem or Judean *boulē* are from the time of the Great Revolt or immediately prior to it. They are later, both in the narrative and chronologically, than the latest references to a Judean *synedrion* (*J.W.* 1.620—Herod's days; *Ant.* 20.216–217—Agrippa II's days).[57]

Hence, I do not think *synedrion, boulē*, and *gerousia* should be associated with one another. The temporal gap between the evidence for *gerousia* and that for *synedrion*,[58] and the scanty and chronologically

---

translation from Hebrew, and that although the context makes it likely that the phrase indeed refers to a council, this is far from certain. In fact the phrase σοφὸν ἐν βουλῇ, which I have not found in any other text, occurs once more in these Psalms (17:37), and there it is impossible to understand it as referring to a council. Wright translates there: "wise in intelligent counsel" (p. 197), and indeed others have offered the same translation for 8:20 (Atkinson, *I Cried to the Lord*, 57; M. Stein, "Psalms of Solomon," in *Hasfarim Haḥizonim* [ed. A. Kahana; Tel-Aviv, 1956], 1:448 [in Hebrew]); and even Wright himself, for his translation in *OTP* 2:659. Moreover, even if this phrase is nevertheless taken to be a reference to a council, the context, which repeatedly mentions Jerusalem, makes it clear that it should not be seen as anything more than a city council.

[54] Not to mention *Against Apion*, which employs none of the various terms we are discussing.

[55] See also imperial letters to various cities in F.F. Abbott and A.C. Johnson, *Municipal Administration in the Roman Empire* (Princeton, 1926), nos. 30, 36, 54, 68, etc.

[56] Tcherikover ("Was Jerusalem a Polis?" 75) views this as merely a case of the usage of Greek terminology for traditional Jewish institutions, in accordance with his view that the various terms all refer to a single traditional Jewish institution in existence throughout the Second Temple period (see above at n. 25).

[57] There are two seeming exceptions: 1) *J.W.* 4.213, where, however, the verbal form need not imply any institution at all; and 2) *Life* 62—concerning which see the doubts expressed by D.R. Schwartz, *Flavius Josephus, Vita: Introduction, Hebrew Translation, and Commentary* (Jerusalem, 2007), 78 n. 103 (in Hebrew). Elsewhere in the *Life* Josephus refers to a body he terms "*to koinon*," but see Schwartz, ibid., 79 n. 107.

[58] Cf. S.B. Hoenig, *The Great Sanhedrin: A Study of the Origin, Development, Composition and Functions of the Bet Din Hagadol during the Second Jewish Commonwealth*

isolated evidence for a *boulē*, in addition to the fact that it seems to
denote a council that is municipal, not national,[59] speak against viewing these terms as synonymous. Moreover, if they are to be viewed as
synonyms, the abrupt changes in terminology need to be explained.
Therefore, whether the other two institutions existed or not does not
have a bearing on the issue of the *synedrion*.

According to the evidence just noted this institution existed during the early period of the Roman occupation of Judea (57 BCE–ca.
66 CE).[60] But did this institution actually exist? Despite numerous
ambiguities as to the history and nature of the *synedrion* in Judea, a
number of factors point to the existence of such a body:

1. There is no good reason to doubt that Gabinius established *synedria* in Judea, especially given the precedent set in Macedonia. These
must have been real and permanent institutions. And since this is the
first unambiguous mention of any *synedrion* in Judea, and from here
on it appears often, it seems that the body continued to exist throughout the period, despite various changes in its nature and authority.[61]

(Philadelphia, 1953), 11; who, however, claims that the Sanhedrin was established in
the interim (23), in the days of Simon (25–26). For the suggestion that the *hever* is
the link between the *gerousia* and the *synedrion* see Tcherikover, "Was Jerusalem a
Polis?" 72; but for the uncertainty of this term's meaning, see Goodblatt, *Monarchic
Principle*, 99–103.

[59] J. Efron ("Great Sanhedrin," 316) also notes that there is no connection between
the Talmud's Sanhedrin and its concept of *boulē*.

[60] E.J. Bickerman ("The Sanhedrin," *Zion* 3 [1938]: 356–59 [in Hebrew]) suggested
that since the early *gerousia* was not dependent on them, the Hasmoneans replaced it
by a *synedrion*, imitating the practice of Hellenistic kings. However, the only evidence
he adduces for a *synedrion* in the Hasmonean period, prior to the Roman conquest,
is a citation from *Megillat Ta'anit* for the 28th day of Tevet, which Bickerman takes
as a reference to the days of Alexander Jannaeus and his wife Alexandra. In fact, their
names and the reference to the Sanhedrin are found, not in the text itself, but rather in
a later *scholium*. The nature of the event mentioned in the scroll is not at all clear, nor
the time at which it occurred, nor what the scholiast really knew. See further V. Noam,
Megillat Ta'anit: Versions, Interpretation, History with a Critical Edition (Jerusalem,
2003), 107–109, 277–79 (in Hebrew).

[61] Contra Goodblatt (*Monarchic Principle*, 108–13), who, as already noted above,
denies the existence of such an institution and interprets most occurrences of this
term in Josephus as referring to "an ad hoc assembly of friends and advisers convened
by an official to assist in policy decisions or in trying a case" (p. 109); he downplays
the importance of the remaining occurrences that seem to refer to an actual permanent council. Goodblatt, however, does not deal with the fact that all occurrences
of the term *synedrion* concern a period subsequent to Gabinius's reforms, which
Goodblatt admits established permanent councils (p. 110). If this term refers to an
ad hoc assembly as Goodblatt claims, why is it applied only at this period? Had the

2. In his descriptions of Gabinius's reform Josephus (or his source) declares quite roundly that:

> The Jews welcomed their release from the rule of an individual and were from that time forward governed by an aristocracy. (*J.W.* 1.170)

> And so the people were removed from monarchic rule and lived under an aristocracy. (*Ant.* 14.91)

I find it hard to believe that Josephus (or his source) would make such pronouncements if these *synedria* had disappeared completely only two years later when Gabinius again reorganized the government in Judea (*J.W.* 1.178; *Ant.* 14.103), or even ten years later when Caesar settled the affairs in Judea (*J.W.* 1.199–200; *Ant.* 14.143).[62] It is rather more likely that the *synedrion* continued to exist,[63] although it need not be assumed that it remained static and unchanging. Among the often-changing government and power centers in early Roman Judea it is most natural to assume that the *synedrion* went through many changes as well. Thus, the regional councils were probably abolished during either of the above-mentioned reorganizations, that of Gabinius or that of Caesar, but one general council seems to have remained. Its powers must have been diminished when there was a powerful king such as Herod, and were probably strengthened when there was no king. Likewise, we can assume that at times it functioned on a more ad hoc basis and at others it was more permanent. In any case, it seems that at least through most of the period, the *synedrion* was neither independent nor fully authoritative and was rather subordinate to the king or high priest.[64]

Hasmoneans and other officials never previously convened "friends and advisers" for consultation?

[62] See E. Bammel, "The Organization of Palestine by Gabinius," *JJS* 12 (1961): 159–62, and E.M. Smallwood, *The Jews Under Roman Rule: From Pompey to Diocletian* (Leiden, 1981), 31–36.

[63] Contra Goodblatt, *Monarchic Principle*, 110–11. Note also that Josephus defines the constitution of Judea following Archelaus's rule (6 CE) as an aristocracy (*Ant.* 20.151); as noted above (n. 40) aristocracy in Josephus means rule by council/s. For this meaning see also D.R. Schwartz, "Josephus on the Jewish Constitutions and Community," *SCI* 7 (1983/84): 32–34.

[64] As L. Grabbe ("Sanhedrin, Sanhedriyyot," 3) correctly points out, even Goodblatt's view of monarchic rule would not deny the actual existence of a council, only that it was a leading, national institution. See also S.J.D. Cohen, *From the Maccabees to the Mishnah* (2d ed.; Louisville, Ky., 2006), 103; Goodman, *The Ruling Class*, 114–15.

3. In addition to the evidence from Josephus, the *synedrion* is often mentioned in the Gospels (e.g., Matt 5:22; Mark 13:9; Luke 22:66; John 11:47) and Acts (e.g., 4:15), and the Sanhedrin is frequently discussed in rabbinic literature. Doubtless we cannot fully rely on these sources (nor for that matter, on Josephus) to discern the exact nature, authority, and makeup of this institution. However it seems to be more than mere coincidence that both types of sources use the same term we find in Josephus. After all, the Gospels could have used a different Greek term (*boulē, gerousia*),[65] and it is hard to believe that the rabbis would have utilized such a Greek term if the institution had not previously existed.[66]

Thus, to summarize this section, just as we saw with the office of *ethnarch*, here, too, we see an innovation of the Roman era. And this innovation can similarly be understood as conforming to an essentially diasporan situation. Like the office of *ethnarch*, there is nothing essentially territorial about a council. Thus, there were councils among the Jewish Diaspora communities in Egypt (although, admittedly, they were not called *synedria*, but *gerousia*).[67] It seems natural that in the post-Destruction reality Judeans would have taken this subordinate, pre-Destruction institution as a model and tried to transform it into a leading institution, and this seems to be what the rabbis tried to do.[68]

---

[65] As mentioned already the term *gerousia* does appear once (Acts 5:21); but see above, n. 49. We do encounter the term *presbyterion* in the New Testament in two places (Luke 22:66; Acts 22:5), both from the same diasporan author. Furthermore, regarding Luke 22:66, note that the *presbyterion* seems to be only one component of the *synedrion*, and in fact the parallel narratives (Matt 27:1; Mark 15:1) speak of *presbyteroi*, i.e., elders, not a *presbyterion*. Cf. Goodblatt, *Monarchic Principle*, 121–22.

[66] Goodblatt (*Monarchic Principle*, 126–28) denies this explanation for this rabbinic borrowing of the Greek term, but does not decisively resolve the question.

[67] See *J.W.* 7.412; Philo, *Flacc.* 74. For the organization of the Jewish community in Alexandria as a *politeuma* see A. Kasher, "The Jewish *Politeuma* in Alexandria: A Model of Communal Organization in the Hellenistic-Roman Diaspora," in *Center and Diaspora: The Land of Israel and the Diaspora in the Second Temple, Mishna, and Talmud Periods* (ed. I.M. Gafni; Jerusalem, 2004), 57–91 (in Hebrew); for its *gerousia* see p. 75. For a suggestion that the Jewish community of Rome was similarly organized, and likewise had a governing council, see M. Williams, "The Structure of the Jewish Community in Rome," in *Jews in the Graeco-Roman World* (ed. M. Goodman; Oxford, 1998), 215–28, esp. 221–27.

[68] Cf. Schürer, *History*, 1:525–26; 2:209.

The Centrality of the Temple

A common perception of Second Temple Judaism is that the Temple in Jerusalem was central to almost the entire Jewish people, both Judeans and Diaspora Jews.[69] According to this view only the Dead Sea Sect and other marginal groups rejected the contemporary Temple on the grounds of theological and/or halakhic disputes; yet they still expected the future building of the "real" Temple (which would of course accord with their views), and in the interim formed some sort of substitute for the Temple. Some groups or individuals may have had disputes with the Temple authorities but did not completely reject the institution. Other views contend that Diaspora Jews, due to their distance from the Temple, had formed their own local substitutes for the Temple—synagogues and prayer. Accordingly, although they did not fully oppose or reject the Jerusalem Temple, nevertheless it was not immediately central in their lives.[70] Yet, it seems that both views agree that the Temple was central to all Judeans, and that only after the Destruction did they adjust their lives to the new Temple-less situation. However, I would like to suggest that already the earliest period of Roman rule in Judea had significantly qualified the centrality of and all-encompassing reverence for the Temple.

First, let us observe a number of phenomena:

1. With the *de facto* loss of the state in 63 BCE the Temple in effect lost any significance it may have had as the seat of a sovereign.[71]

2. Within a span of just thirty years the Temple came under serious threat numerous times. The Temple was placed under siege four or five times: according to *Ant.* 14.5, in the initial battle between Hyrcanus and Aristobulus in 67/66 BCE, Hyrcanus captured some of his enemies in the Temple, and the narrative seems to imply that subsequently Hyrcanus was besieged there by his brother;[72] in 65 BCE, Hyrcanus and Antipater together with Aretas besieged Aristobulus (*Ant.* 14.19–28);

---

[69] See, for example, the papers in this volume by J. Leonhardt-Balzer (on Philo) and by M. Goodman (on Judaism in general), along with Goodman's "The Temple in First Century CE Judaism," in *Temple and Worship in Biblical Israel* (ed. J. Day; London, 2005), 459–68.

[70] See, for example, M. Tuval's contribution to this volume.

[71] See Schwartz, *Jewish Background*, 9–10.

[72] *J.W.* 1.121, however, reports only that Hyrcanus took Aristobulus's wife and children as hostages in the Antonia citadel, and does not mention the Temple.

in 63 BCE Pompey besieged the supporters of Aristobulus who were
entrenched on the Temple mount (*J.W.* 1.143–153; *Ant.* 14.58–72);
a generation later, Herod's army besieged some of its enemies in
the Temple in 40 BCE (*J.W.* 1.251, 253; *Ant.* 14.335, 339) and Herod
and the Roman general Sossius did the same to Antigonus in 37 BCE
(*J.W.* 1.347–352, and cf. 354; *Ant.* 14.470–480, and cf. 482–483). Two of
these sieges ended with the Temple being taken violently (by Pompey,
and by Herod and Sossius). What is more, if Josephus's account is to
be believed, during Pompey's conquest the Temple was overrun and
the priests were massacred even as they were performing the Temple
rites (*J.W.* 1.148; *Ant.* 14.65–68). To these sieges we may add, moreover, the rebellion of Aristobulus's son Alexander in 57 BCE, who, it
seems, took Jerusalem and even tried to rebuild the wall destroyed by
Pompey (*J.W.* 1.160; *Ant.* 14.82–83). In the aftermath of this rebellion
Gabinius had to reinstate Hyrcanus in the Temple, which implies that
the Temple, too, had been taken (*J.W.* 1.169; *Ant.* 14.90). Furthermore, the Temple was robbed by Crassus in 54–53 BCE (*J.W.* 1.179;
Ant. 14.105–109). These events could well have undermined notions
about the special sanctity adhering to the Temple, a process further
intensified by the fact that Hasmonean high priests played unsavory
roles in some of them.[73]

3. Martin Goodman has already claimed that the prestige of the
high priests was greatly diminished after Herod came to power in 37
BCE, since from this point he nominated the high priests, and in effect,
they were his puppets.[74] Herod not only nominated the high priests
but also deposed them freely—and unlawfully, since the high priesthood had traditionally been a lifetime appointment (*Ant.* 15.39–41).[75]

---

[73] In this context the thrice-repeated narrative of the Babylonian Talmud (*Soṭah*
49b//*B. Qam.* 82b//*Menaḥ.* 64b) of Hyrcanus's siege of Aristobulus may be of significance. In that narrative Hyrcanus's party violated its oath and instead of the sacrificial
animals they had promised to send up to the besieged in the Temple, they sent a
swine. The swine, which is not mentioned in Josephus's narrative, apparently symbolizes the Roman Empire (e.g., *b. Pesaḥ.* 118b; *'Abot R. Nat.* version A, 34). As a result
of this evil deed the Land of Israel was afflicted by an earthquake. Compare the somewhat similar story (which is, however, seemingly related to Titus's siege in 70 CE) in
the Jerusalem Talmud (*Taʿanit* 68c//*Ber.* 7b), according to which the swine's touching
of the Temple Mount's wall is explicitly connected to the Temple's destruction.

[74] Goodman, *The Ruling Class*, 111–12. For the disapproval, by at least some of
the Judeans, of Herod's choice of a high-priest and the claim that the appointee was
unworthy see *J.W.* 2.7; *Ant.* 17.207. See also *Ant.* 20.247–250.

[75] See G. Alon, "Parʾirtin," in idem, *Jews, Judaism and the Classical World: Studies
in Jewish History in the Times of the Second Temple and Talmud* (trans. I. Abrahams;
Jerusalem, 1977), 48–88, esp. 59–61; Goodman, *The Ruling Class*, 112.

It seems, however, that the reduction in the prestige of the high priests was not only a result of Herod's practices, but had already begun from the onset of Roman intervention in Judea, long before Herod's reign. From the outset high priests depended on the recognition of the Romans.[76] Thus, at the height of the civil war between Hyrcanus and Aristobulus, in 65 BCE, the latter retained the position due to Scaurus's intervention in Judea (*J.W.* 1.128; *Ant.* 14.30); later, in 63 BCE, Hyrcanus was reinstated to the prestigious position thanks to the decision of Pompey (*J.W.* 1.153; *Ant.* 14.73). Later as well, it was by the decisions of Roman officials that Hyrcanus retained this office (*J.W.* 1.169//*Ant.* 14.90 [Gabinius]; *J.W.* 1.199//*Ant.* 14.143 [Caesar]). This practice of intervention in the appointment of the high priests continued throughout the days of Herod and Archelaus as well as under the Roman procurators.

There can be no doubt that these developments served as major incentives for subsequent revolts against the Romans. Indeed, the numerous revolts during the early years of the Roman occupation of Judea were not aimed exclusively against the Romans; they were also aimed, to no less an extent, against Hyrcanus the high priest. This is clear by the fact that the leaders of most of these revolts were Hasmoneans, Aristobulus and his sons, who obviously wanted to claim the high priesthood for themselves; and they were able to attract many Judean followers.[77]

However, in addition to these revolts, we may assume a priori that this state of affairs—especially the fact that the high priests governing the Temple did not receive that position due to their virtue or pedigree and were not elected to it by the nation or its institutions, but were appointed by the Romans and their agents—had another effect: Many Judeans who had formerly held the Temple in high esteem might now, at least until—as they hoped—some drastic change of this situation occurred sometime in the unknown future, become estranged from the Temple establishment. Such a tendency will have been further enhanced by the failure of the various revolts, as the Judeans came to

---

[76] Cf. Grabbe, *Judaic Religion*, 109.

[77] An indication of this might be the fact that, despite his status as king, Mattathias Antigonus used only the high-priestly title in the Hebrew legends on his coins. Cf. Y. Meshorer, *A Treasury of Jewish Coins: From the Persian Period to Bar Kokhba* (trans. R. Amoils; Jerusalem and Nyack, N.Y., 2001), 52–53; who is skeptical, however, on the question of whether the Greek legend, reading "king," was aimed toward foreigners whereas the Hebrew legend, reading "high-priest," was aimed towards his Jewish subjects.

realize the overwhelming power of the Romans and the impossibility of defeating them in the foreseeable future. Such a partial withdrawal from the contemporary Temple, without a complete rejection of it, would have been analogous to the situation of Diaspora Jews. Hence, to the extent that such a withdrawal indeed occurred, it would point again to the early Roman era as a period that set the stage for post-70 life—for a Temple-less reality.

Can we, however, discern some real evidence for such a withdrawal from the Temple? I believe there are some indications:

1. Daniel Schwartz discusses[78] the phenomenon of prophets and other leaders who, in the first century CE, led people into the desert and promised salvation from there. Schwartz asks why these leaders launched their rebellions in the desert and not in Jerusalem, and suggests that the withdrawal to the desert served, for these groups, the same function as the Qumran sect's withdrawal to the desert: they felt that holiness had left Jerusalem and relocated in the desert.[79] He further argues that, although these groups might be understood against the background of Qumran,[80] it rather seems that the perception that holiness had left Jerusalem was more general. Schwartz posits three factors, all dating from the Hasmonean era, for this perception: (a) The nominal separation of state and religion which was the consequence of the Hasmoneans' assumption of the kingship in addition to the priesthood, as discussed above. This was intensified by Roman rule. (b) Growing criticism as to the very legitimacy of the Hasmonean priesthood, and growing moral criticism of this priesthood. The moral criticism of the ruling priesthood was increasing in the Roman era,[81] and, as demonstrated above, it is most likely that there was also a deepening of the criticism of the high priests' legitimacy. (c) The growing influence of Hellenism.

While it seems to me likely that indeed these factors dating from the pre-Roman era laid the foundations for this withdrawal from the

---

[78] See Schwartz, *Jewish Background*, 38–43.

[79] Compare the request of rebels who survived the destruction of the Temple to be allowed to retire to the desert (*War* 6.351).

[80] For the desert as the place of divine revelation for the Qumranites, see most recently A. Schofield, "The Wilderness Motif in the Dead Sea Scrolls," in *Israel in the Wilderness: Interpretations of the Biblical Narratives in Jewish and Christian Traditions* (ed. K.E. Pomykala; Leiden, 2008), 37–53.

[81] See Schwartz, *Jewish Background*, 39 n. 30.

Temple, it must be remembered that these withdrawals to the desert are all from the first century CE, i.e., the early Roman period, and not earlier. As noted, Schwartz, too, sees an escalation of some of these factors in the Roman era. Thus it seems to me that this perception developed fully only in the early Roman period as a consequence of the stimuli noted above.

2. It seems that at least two texts that are commonly perceived as originating in Judea in the early years following the Roman occupation do not attribute importance to the Temple: The Parables of Enoch (*1 Enoch* 37–71), which includes what seems to be a reference to the Parthian invasion of 40 BCE (56:5–7) and is therefore usually dated not long after,[82] seems hardly to mention the Temple, altar, or sacrifices.[83] Similarly, the *Psalms of Solomon*—which clearly alludes to the initial Roman invasion of Judea led by Pompey (*Pss. Sol.* 2; 8; 17) and is dated not long thereafter[84]—includes only a few references to the Temple, altar and sacrifices (e.g., 2:2–3; 8:12, 22), and the author does not seem to be very interested in them. Indeed, where one would expect to find references to the Temple, the sacrifices, or the priesthood, such references are missing. Thus, at the end of Psalm 8 (vv. 27–30) the psalmist prays for future redemption, asking that God's mercy be upon Israel, and that he gather the Diaspora; but not a word is said of the Temple, which only a few verses earlier was said to have been profaned (v. 22). So, too, Psalm 17 criticizes the Hasmoneans for assuming the kingship, which rightly belongs to the House of David

---

[82] For the dating of the Parables see J.C. Greenfield and M.E. Stone, "The Enochic Pentateuch and the Date of the Similitudes," *HTR* 70 (1977): 51–65; and recently the essays by D.W. Suter, M.E. Stone, and J.H. Charlesworth in *Enoch and the Messiah Son of Man: Revisiting the Book of Parables* (ed. G. Boccaccini; Grand Rapids, 2007). It seems that there is almost a consensus that the text should be dated to around the turn of the era. For the view that 56:5–7 reflects the Parthian invasion see these papers and also the papers by A. Luca and H. Eshel in the same volume. The one dissenting view in this book is Suter's; he sees this reference as an apocalyptic myth more than history, but does not deny that it might be based on an old memory of the invasion (pp. 420–22).

[83] In fact the only possible reference to the Temple seems to denote the heavenly Temple and is found in chapter 71, which some scholars view as a late addition (see M.E. Stone, "Apocalyptic Literature," in *Jewish Writings of the Second Temple Period* [ed. M.E. Stone; Assen, 1984], 399, 401, and 403 n. 106).

[84] 2:26–27 alludes to Pompey's murder in Egypt on September 28, 48 BCE, and thus Psalm 2 should be dated to sometime after that. Some scholars view Psalm 17 as alluding to Herod's ascension to the kingship; according to them this psalm should be dated to after 37 BCE. See Schürer, *History*, 3:194; Atkinson, *I Cried to the Lord*, 2–6.

(vv. 4–6), but does not make a point of similarly criticizing them for unjustly assuming the high priesthood, which rightly belongs to the descendants of Zadok. The same psalm also has a somewhat detailed portrayal of messianic expectations (vv. 21–46), but again the Temple and sacrifices remain unmentioned.[85] Similarly, in passages where we might have expected to find allusions to sacrifices, we find, instead, references to prayer and fasting (e.g., 3:8; 9:6; 10:6; 15:2–4; 18:2). In general, in fact, prayer is a major issue for the psalmist,[86] just as, for that matter, it is important for the Parables of Enoch (see e.g., chapters 47; 61).[87]

THE SYNAGOGUE IN JUDEA

The issue of prayer leads us to another important institution: the synagogue. There is an abundance of studies on the synagogue in antiquity and its origins, including the origins of this institution in Judea, which is the subject at hand. The scope of the present paper does not permit dealing with all aspects of and views on this issue, and I will limit myself to a brief discussion. The first part of this discussion mainly

---

[85] See further A. Büchler, *Types of Jewish-Palestinian Piety from 70 B.C.E. to 70 C.E.: The Ancient Pious Men* (London, 1922), 140–42; 170–74.

[86] K. Atkinson (*I Cried to the Lord*) actually sees the context of the *Psalms of Solomon* as similar to that of the Qumran sect (but does not suggest that they were authored by this sect, and avoids identifying the collection with any particular sect or group [pp. 7–8]): the group polemicized against the halakhic positions of the Temple authorities, rejected the contemporary Temple cult, and replaced the sacrifices with prayer and fasting (p. 2). I do not see such outright polemic and rejection, but rather a diminished interest in the world of the Temple and sacrifices (cf. Büchler, *Types of Jewish-Palestinian Piety*, 170–74). In contrast to the Temple and that which concerns it specifically, *Jerusalem* appears to be particularly important for the psalmist (e.g., 2:19–22; 8:4, 15–22; 17:22, 30). Jerusalem also seems to be prominent in the recently published, so-called *Gabriel Revelation*, which is dated to the turn of the era as well; at least in its surviving portions, this text similarly does not allude to the Temple and its world. See the original publication by A. Yardeni and B. Elitzur, "A First-Century BCE Prophetic Text Written on a Stone: First Publication," *Cathedra* 123 (2007): 155–66 (in Hebrew); and also I. Knohl's reading in "Studies in the *Gabriel Revelation*," *Tarbiz* 76 (2007): 324–28 (in Hebrew).

[87] The question of Jesus' and his early followers' attitudes towards the Temple is beyond the scope of this paper, but see the beginning of the paper by Jörg Frey in this volume, where he argues that the message of Jesus (and John the Baptist), and the early Christians, was independent of the Temple, distanced from it, and included some criticism of it.

follows the lines of a 1988 study by Lester L. Grabbe;[88] later discoveries and scholarship will also be adduced, but in my view they have not altered Grabbe's fundamental conclusions.

Numerous theories have been proposed as to the time and place of the synagogue's origin: in the Land of Israel during the late First Temple period; in Babylon during the exile; in Jerusalem after the return from that exile; in third-century BCE Egypt; and in Hasmonean Judea.[89] If we follow the evidence closely and refrain from getting carried away by assumptions and theories, we find that the earliest evidence for synagogues is supplied by references to *proseuchai* (places of prayer) in inscriptions from third-century BCE Egypt.[90] In contrast, there is no evidence for the existence of synagogues in the Land of Israel until post-Hasmonean times. In earlier sources the terms *proseuchē* and *synagōgē* do not seem to refer to this institution (but rather to "prayer" and "gathering/assembly," respectively); Grabbe finds especially important, in this context, the fact that in our main narratives of Antiochus IV's persecutions and the subsequent Maccabean revolt (1 and 2 Maccabees, and Josephus) there is no mention of any synagogues. Had synagogues existed we would have expected to hear something about their desecration or at least about disruption of worship in them. The earliest literary evidence for synagogues in the Land of Israel comes from the Gospels (e.g., Mark 1:21–29; Luke 4:16–30), Acts (e.g., 6:9), and Josephus's narrative of the first century CE (*J.W.* 2.285–289; *Ant.* 19.300–305; *Life* 277–280).[91] The archaeological data accord with

---

[88] L.L. Grabbe, "Synagogues in Pre-70 Palestine: A Re-Assessment," *JTS* 39 (1988): 401–10.

[89] On the different theories see R. Hachlili, "The Origin of the Synagogue: A Re-Assessment," *JSJ* 28 (1997): 34–37; L.I. Levine, *The Ancient Synagogue: The First Thousand Years* (2d ed.; New Haven, 2005), 22–28. Levine proposes a different theory: the synagogue developed, through a more subtle and prolonged process, out of the city-gate of the biblical era and its functions (ibid., 28–44). For a suggestion that synagogues as buildings emerged only after the Destruction, see H.C. Kee, "The Transformation of the Synagogue after 70 CE: Its Import for Early Christianity," *NTS* 36 (1990): 1–24; but see also the decisive rejections of that argument by, among others, P.W. van der Horst, "Was the Synagogue a Place of Sabbath Worship Before 70 CE?" in idem, *Japheth in the Tents of Shem: Studies on Jewish Hellenism in Antiquity* (Leuven, 2002), 55–62; and J.S. Kloppenborg Verbin, "Dating Theodotos (CIJ II 1404)," *JJS* 51 (2000): 243–80.

[90] Grabbe, "Synagogues," 402–3.

[91] See also L.I. Levine, "The Pre-70 C.E. Judean Synagogue: Its Origins and Character Reexamined," in *Tehillah le-Moshe: Biblical and Judaic Studies in Honor of Moshe Greenberg* (ed. M. Cogan, B.L. Eichler, and J.H. Tigay; Winona Lake, 1997), 156*–57* (in Hebrew).

the literary evidence: the Theodotus inscription from Jerusalem, which mentions a synagogue, is usually dated to the first century CE, pre-70;[92] and the few pre-70 synagogues from the Land of Israel (of which the most famous are those of Masada, Herodium, Gamla) are all dated to the first century CE, or the end of the first century BCE at the earliest.[93] Therefore, it seems that in the Land of Israel the synagogue is a phenomenon of the early Roman period.[94]

Grabbe notes how the development of this institution set the stage for post-Destruction Judaism:

> The rise of the synagogue was a fortuitous but vital development which paved the way for a post-temple Judaism which became necessary

---

[92] In a recent and very thorough paper John S. Kloppenborg Verbin ("Dating Theodotos") firmly rejects views which date this inscription to well after the Destruction, and concludes that it should be dated to the Herodian or early Roman periods, prior to 70 CE.

[93] For a survey of the evidence for Judean synagogues of the pre-70 era, see Levine, *The Ancient Synagogue*, 45–74. Ehud Netzer has identified a building in Jericho from the beginning of the first century BCE as a synagogue (E. Netzer, Y. Kalman, and R. Loris [sic], "A Hasmonean Period Synagogue at Jericho," *Qadmoniot* 32 [1999]: 17–24 [in Hebrew]). In a later article he dates the building to 75–40 BCE (E. Netzer, "A Synagogue in Jericho from the Hasmonean Period," *Michmanim* 20 [2007]: 16 [in Hebrew]). Also see the excavation's final report: E. Netzer, R. Laureys-Chachy, and Y. Kalman, "The Synagogue Complex," in *Hasmonean and Herodian Palaces at Jericho, 2: Final Reports of the 1973–1987 Excavations* (ed. E. Netzer; Jerusalem, 2004), 159–92, where the excavators date the building's main phase to the days of Alexandra (p. 159) and offer a detailed discussion explaining its identification as a synagogue (pp. 184–88). I am persuaded, however, by Lee Levine's doubt as to the identification of this building as a synagogue; see L.I. Levine, "The First-Century Synagogue: New Theories and Their Assessment," in *Studies in the History of Eretz Israel Presented to Yehuda Ben Porat* (ed. Y. Ben-Arieh and E. Reiner; Jerusalem, 2003), 187–88 (in Hebrew); and idem, *The Ancient Synagogue*, 72–74. See also U.Z. Maoz's critique of this identification, "The Synagogue that Never Existed in the Hasmonean Palace at Jericho: Remarks Concerning an Article by E. Netzer, Y. Kalman, and R. Loris," *Qadmoniot* 32 (1999): 120–21 (in Hebrew); and E. Netzer's reply, "The Synagogue in Jericho—Did it Exist or Not? A Response to U.Z. Maoz's Remarks in *Qadmoniot* XXXII, no. 2 (118) 1999," *Qadmoniot* 33 (2000): 69–70 (in Hebrew). In general, it seems that when dealing with early buildings, dated to periods concerning which we do not have literary or epigraphic evidence supporting the institution's very existence, we should be wary of classifying them as synagogues rather than just as ordinary public buildings.

[94] Grabbe, "Synagogues," 404–8. Cf. Grabbe, *Judaic Religion*, 173–74; Cohen, *From the Maccabees*, 107. Levine (*The Ancient Synagogue*, 41–42) admits the lack of evidence for synagogues in Judea prior to the first century BCE, and therefore views that century as an advanced step in his proposed reconstruction of the development of the synagogue.

after 70.... Synagogues were not planned as a substitute for the temple but they were a useful vehicle to make the transition.[95]

We must ask, however, how it is that this institution, which had already existed in the Diaspora for a few centuries, arrived in Judea only now? In a different essay Grabbe remarks that "[i]t was mainly during the Roman period that developments within Diaspora Jewish communities started to have a significant influence on religion in the homeland."[96]

However, Grabbe does not seem to see this influence as an intrinsic effect of the Roman era. He mainly remarks on the growing population of the Diaspora, which by this time may have been larger than the Judean population, and the fact that many Diaspora Jews made pilgrimages to Jerusalem. While these factors for the growth of Diaspora influence on Judea seem likely, we should take notice of one direct outcome of the Roman conquest of Judea and the entire Middle East, which was probably a major factor in the growth of Diaspora influence on Judea: It brought into a single, Roman, framework Jews who previously had been divided among different states (Judea, Ptolemaic Egypt, Seleucid Syria, Greece, Italy, and more). Thus, for the first time in a long time the Judeans were in fact ruled by the same empire as a large portion of their Diaspora brethren (not including the Mesopotamian Jews under Parthian control).

Although the growing influence of the Diaspora communities on Judea might be reason enough for the appearance of this institution in Judea at this point in history, I think we should still look for an additional factor. For it seems that there were always connections between Judea and the Diaspora. It is interesting to note that most theories as to the origins of the synagogue view it as emerging because of the absence of the Temple (those who propose that it emerged in the Babylonian exile) or the distance of the community from the Temple (those who propose that it emerged in the Diaspora of the Second Temple period), and, obviously, post-Destruction synagogues are usually viewed as fulfilling the void made by the Temple's destruction. However, when dealing with the synagogue in late Second Temple period

---

[95] Grabbe, "Synagogues," 409–10. Cf. J.N. Lightstone, "Roman Diaspora Judaism," in *A Companion to Roman Religion* (ed. J. Rüpke; Oxford, 2007), 367–68.

[96] Grabbe, *Judaic Religion*, 113, and see pp. 113–14; 328–29. In this context it is noteworthy that Acts 6:9 explicitly associates a Jerusalem synagogue, or several synagogues, with Diaspora Jewry; see Levine, *The Ancient Synagogue*, 55–57.

Judea, scholars refrain from ascribing a similar role to the Temple. Thus, even Grabbe, who explains the emergence of the synagogue in the Diaspora as a result of distance from the Temple,[97] explicitly says that it was not planned as a substitute for the Temple.[98] I would like to suggest, nonetheless, that the appearance of an institution such as the synagogue might not have occurred had there only been the above-noted Diaspora influence. Rather, for that influence to have its effect in Judea it must have filled some vacuum there, and I propose that this vacuum is similar to that which was filled by synagogues in the Diaspora (or by similar substitutes in the Qumran community), i.e., the distance from the Temple.[99] Of course, this does not mean a geographical distance from the Temple (or: only a geographical distance), but rather a growing sense of moral, religious, spiritual, and/or political alienation from it, brought on by the factors discussed above.[100]

But whether or not the appearance of the synagogues in Judea derived from a growing sense of distance from the Temple, the opposite will have been the case; namely, to the extent that synagogues appeared in Judea they will have played a role in marginalizing or undermining the Temple and its cult. After all, as time went by, the

---

[97] Grabbe, "Synagogues," 403.

[98] See above, at n. 95. See also Hachlili, "Origin of the Synagogue," 46–47.

[99] P.V.M. Flesher ("Palestinian Synagogues before 70 C.E.: A Review of the Evidence," in *Approaches to Ancient Judaism, Vol. VI: Studies in the Ethnography and Literature of Judaism* [ed. J. Neusner and E.S. Frerichs; Atlanta, 1989], 67–81) likewise accepts the Egyptian origin of the synagogue and its post-Hasmonean appearance in Judea, and assumes an inherent difference between the Judaism of the Temple and that of the synagogue. He further surveys the evidence for pre-70 synagogues in Judea, and concludes that all such evidence pertains only to Galilee, not to Judea proper. The only exceptions are the synagogue(s) of foreigners mentioned in Acts 6:9, and possibly the synagogues at Herodium and Masada, which were established only during the Great Revolt, i.e., very close to the Destruction. The reason for this difference is, according to Flesher, that in Galilee, like in the Diaspora, people had no immediate access to the Temple, whereas in Judea proper the Temple was the main religious focus. Responding to Flesher's theory, however, we should note the following. First, for his case Flesher is obliged to accept scholarly opinions that reject the historicity of other passages in Acts that attest to the existence of synagogues in Jerusalem (22:19; 24:12; 26:11). Second, at least two buildings, which were excavated some years after Flesher wrote his paper and whose location is quite close to Jerusalem, have been identified by their excavators as synagogues—Qiryat Sefer and Modi'in (for which see the brief survey and bibliography in Levine, *The Ancient Synagogue*, 69–70). Further, it is telling that the literary sources, and especially the Jerusalem-born priest, Josephus, refer to the synagogues naturally without any hint that it was a phenomenon foreign to native Jerusalemites.

[100] This does not have any definite bearing on the question of whether regular gathering for prayer actually took place in the synagogues.

synagogue and the worship therein would probably have been viewed as worthy functional substitutes for the Temple and its cult, even if they were not meant as such when established. The more we are convinced that, as Esther Chazon argues elsewhere in this volume, fixed prayer was indeed developing during the Second Temple period, the more we will expect that to have been associated with the synagogues. But whatever we believe about communal *prayers* in the synagogues, it is well established that Scripture was regularly read and studied in the synagogues. As Martha Himmelfarb shows in her contribution to this volume, the more Scripture becomes accessible to the general public, the more the authority of the priests is undermined. One way or another, as result or cause or both, synagogues in pre-Destruction Judea indicate additional early Roman stage-setting for post-70 Temple-less existence.

Conclusion

The proposal made in this paper is that while we should not deny the extraordinary effect of the destruction of the Temple, at least some of the developments of post-70 Judaism are rooted in the period prior to the Destruction. This view was promoted earlier by Grabbe:

> Many of the particular features of Judaism which became characteristic after the fall of the Second Temple were those which we find already developing in the Diaspora religious practices.[101]

> With hindsight we can see how certain pre-70 trends were highly important in meeting the post-70 situation without temple or priestly leadership.... Other elements giving direction to the new situation were those aspects of Judaism that had evolved to meet the Diaspora situation: the synagogue, prayer, and the study of written Scriptures. These had already started to have an effect on Palestinian Judaism even before 70. The seeds were sown for a Judaism *sine templo*; even if the temple had not been destroyed, Judaism might well have developed in new directions anyway.... Even without the Roman Destruction, Judaism was likely to have developed a new shape which placed more emphasis on these "para-temple" practices.[102]

---

[101] Grabbe, *Judaic Religion*, 179.
[102] Ibid., 333–34.

Grabbe correctly emphasizes the similarity between the post-Destruction situation and that of the Diaspora of the Second Temple period. However, in addressing developments in Judea similar to those in the Diaspora he tends to view the former only as the result of Diaspora influence, rather than as reflections of and responses to conditions and developments in Judea itself prior to the Destruction.

In this paper, in contrast, I have suggested that in fact these developments were intrinsic to Judea itself and to the situation following the Roman occupation and the end of the independent Hasmonean state. The Roman conquest brought about the unification of Judeans with their Diaspora brethren, which enhanced the ability of the Diaspora to influence Judea. More significantly, however, it placed the Judeans in a situation very similar to that of their brethren abroad. The state of affairs in Judea itself, following the Roman occupation, was to some extent an exile-like,[103] or semi-Diasporan, situation.[104] Therefore, concepts and institutions which developed in Judea in this period were inherent to the situation in Judea, even if they were sometimes influenced by the Diaspora.

For this reason, while Grabbe views the appearance of the synagogue as a result of a growth in the influence of the Diaspora, in this paper I focus upon the Roman conquest of Judea as a condition and catalyst for that influence. Judean Jews were receptive to the synagogue because of a Temple-related vacuum created by the Roman conquest and its aftermath. I have similarly tried to show that in addition to the synagogue, this period instilled in the Judeans some of the basic

---

[103] For an understanding of the term "exile" in rabbinic literature as meaning, not physical deportation, but rather subjugation and a state of mind, see C. Milikowsky, "Notions of Exile, Subjugation, and Return in Rabbinic Literature," in *Exile: Old Testament, Jewish, and Christian Conceptions* (ed. J.M. Scott; Leiden, 1997), 266–78. For the Diaspora-like identity of the Qumran sect see N. Hacham, "Exile and Self-Identity in the Qumran Sect and in Hellenistic Judaism," in *New Perspectives on Old Texts: Proceedings of the Tenth International Symposium of the Orion Center for the Study of the Dead Sea Scrolls and Associated Literature, 9–11 January, 2005* (ed. E.G. Chazon, B. Halpern-Amaru, and R.A. Clements; Leiden, 2010), 3–21.

[104] That some Judeans of the period regarded their situation as "exilic" may be implied by the above-mentioned phenomenon of men who led Jews into the desert promising salvation (see above, at nn. 78–80). This is clear at least in the case of Theudas (*Ant.* 20.97–98), who promised his followers that the Jordan River would part at his command, following the biblical precedent of Joshua; his actions implied an understanding of their current situation as exilic. See further C.A. Evans, "Aspects of Exile and Restoration in the Proclamation of Jesus and the Gospels," in Scott, *Exile*, 300–305.

concepts of the post-70 (and Diaspora) reality: the absorption of the fact that they were living under foreign subjugation; the separation of religion and state; and the decline in the centrality of the Temple. I have also tried to show that at least two political institutions, the *ethnarch* and the *synedrion*, which probably developed only in this period, are also appropriate to a Diaspora, or post-70, situation. For the present purpose it is not important to what extent these institutions were actually adopted in post-70 Judea; what is important are the perceptions that they instilled in the people.

Finally, I hope that this paper has shown the great effect of the end of independence and the importance of the early Roman era in Judea, not only for the background of Christianity and the Great Revolt, but also for a better understanding of post-Destruction Judaism and how it was able to adapt and survive. Further study may uncover additional ways in which this period set the stage for developments that came to fruition after the Destruction.

TEMPLE AND IDENTITY IN EARLY CHRISTIANITY AND IN THE JOHANNINE COMMUNITY: REFLECTIONS ON THE "PARTING OF THE WAYS"[1]

Jörg Frey

Was the year 70 CE really a watershed for emerging Christianity?[2] How did early Christian communities, both Jewish and Gentile, react to the destruction of the Jerusalem Temple; and how did that event affect the formation of their identities[3] as communities, or the identity formation of their individual members? These questions are embedded in the general debate on the relevance of the year 70 CE, the end of the Jewish War, and particularly the destruction of the Herodian Temple, for the history of Judaism. Within this context, the development of

---

[1] I am grateful to my friend Prof. Daniel R. Schwartz for the invitation to the Scholion conference. Thanks are also due to numerous other colleagues and friends in Jerusalem for the fruitful discussion of my paper. The article was written during my fellowship at the Alfried-Krupp-Wissenschaftskolleg in Greifswald during the academic year 2008/09, and I owe thanks to the Krupp Foundation for honoring me by granting me this prestigious and valuable scholarship. I am especially indebted to Ruth Clements for numerous suggestions regarding content and language and for her meticulous editorial work.

[2] Since the term "Christianity" can be used only *cum grano salis* for the early Jesus movement, I use the term (as well as the term "Judaism") without presupposing any fixed dogmatic "system" or presuming a mutual exclusiveness of both terms. In any case, the note in Acts 11:26 that the members of the Jesus group in Antioch were called Χριστιανοί suggests that already at an early stage this community was visible to outsiders as a group that could in some way be distinguished from the local synagogue, with some Χριστός making the difference. Similar processes might have happened elsewhere.

[3] "Identity" is one of the most debated terms in current cultural studies. Of course I cannot enter into the theoretical discussion here, but I refer the reader to the most relevant literature. See for general discussions, P. du Gay, J. Evans, and P. Redman, eds., *Identity: A Reader* (London, 2000); and S. Hall, ed., *Questions of Cultural Identity* (London, 2007). On early Judaism see M. Konradt and U. Steinert, eds., *Ethos und Identität in hellenistisch-römischer Zeit* (Paderborn, 2002); and J. Frey, S. Gripentrog, and D.R. Schwartz, eds., *Jewish Identity in the Greco-Roman World* (Leiden, 2007). On early Christianity, see J.M. Lieu, *Christian Identity in the Jewish and Graeco-Roman World* (Oxford, 2004); B. Holmberg, ed., *Identity Formation in the New Testament* (Tübingen, 2008); and idem, ed., *Exploring Early Christian Identity* (Tübingen, 2008).

emerging Christianity, which started as a Jewish Messianic movement,[4] deserves special consideration. Did the destruction of the Jerusalem Temple affect Christians as well as Jews, and potentially not only in Palestine but all over the Mediterranean Diaspora?[5] And how is the so-called "parting of the ways,"[6] the process of separation between the emerging church and the synagogue, related to the events of the year 70 CE and the loss of the cultic center of early Judaism?

These issues call for consideration of a wide range of texts and problems, which cannot be dealt with in detail in a single contribution. In the present article, I will first give a brief and general sketch of the relationship between the Temple (and eventually its destruction) and early Christian identity formation. For that purpose, I will mainly draw on the distinction between pre-70 and post-70 writings. In the second part, I will focus on the Johannine corpus, i.e., the Gospel of John and the three Epistles, as a test case for identity formation in Asia Minor in the post-70 period. Here we will ask what factors contributed to the split between the local synagogues and the Johannine communities and what was decisive for the particular community identity developed within the Johannine tradition.

We will see that the impact of the destruction of the Jerusalem Temple on early Christian identity was rather limited.[7] Other factors

---

[4] See M. Hengel, "Early Christianity as a Jewish-Messianic, Universalistic Movement," in M. Hengel and C.K. Barrett, *Conflicts and Challenges in Early Christianity* (ed. D.A. Hagner; Harrisburg, Pa., 1999), 1–41.

[5] See M. Goodman, "Diaspora Reactions to the Destruction of the Temple," in *Jews and Christians: The Parting of the Ways AD 70 to 135* (ed. J.D.G. Dunn; Tübingen, 1992), 27–38.

[6] On the paradigm of the "parting of the ways," see J.D.G. Dunn, *The Partings of the Ways Between Christianity and Judaism and Their Significance for the Character of Christianity* (London, 1991); and J.M. Lieu, "'The Parting of the Ways': Theological Construct or Historical Reality?" *JSNT* 56 (1994): 106–9. On the recent interrogation of this paradigm, see A.Y. Reed and A.H. Becker, "Introduction: Traditional Models and New Directions," in *The Ways that Never Parted* (ed. A.H. Becker and A.Y. Reed; Tübingen, 2003), 1–33; and see further D. Boyarin, "Semantic Differences; or, 'Judaism'/'Christianity,'" ibid., 65–85; and M. Goodman, "Modeling the 'Parting of the Ways,'" ibid., 119–30.

[7] The views developed here differ widely from those of S.G.F. Brandon, *The Fall of Jerusalem and the Christian Church* (London, 1951), who tended to place the decisive turning point within early Christianity in the events of the year 70 CE, when Jewish Christianity lost its center. But his dichotomy between Palestinian Jewish Christianity and Pauline Gentile Christianity was already outdated when the book appeared and cannot be maintained in the light of more recent research. A very different approach was taken by L. Gaston, *No Stone on Another: Studies in the Significance of the Fall of Jerusalem in the Synoptic Gospels* (Leiden, 1970), who presupposes that the first

seem to have been more influential—not only the development of Christology, but also the structural development of the emerging communities and the wider political contexts in which they lived. Even in John, where the temple motif is used quite frequently, the direct impact of the destruction of the Temple seems to have been rather weak, whereas other aspects of the Jewish War might have influenced Johannine theology at least indirectly. This paper is an attempt to trace the interplay between Temple, temple imagery, and cultural context in early Christian writings, particularly the Gospel of John.

I. The Jerusalem Temple, Its Destruction, and Early Christian Identity

Let me start with some brief and necessarily superficial glimpses of the relevance of the Jerusalem Temple for the emerging Jesus movement. These might set the stage for investigation of the Temple theme within the later writings.

1. *The Constitution of an Identity Unrelated to the Temple*

1.1. Disregard of the Temple in Jesus' Message, and Temple Criticism in the Early Jesus Tradition

The Jesus movement[8] originated in Galilee as a religious and social group phenomenon, initiated by a charismatic personality who exorcised, healed, and proclaimed the imminent and already-beginning Kingdom of God.[9] Jesus was not of priestly descent, nor did he act

---

Christians had participated in the Temple cult, and that the criticism of the Temple, e.g., in Mark 14:58, is already a consequence of the Destruction and reflects a Markan interpretation of the event as a divine punishment. But in the light of a more thorough source-critical analysis of Mark, such a simple division between a pre-Markan positive view of the Temple and a Markan negative view is unconvincing. For criticism, cf. S. Lücking, "Die Zerstörung des Tempels 70 n. Chr. als Krisenerfahrung der frühen Christen," in *Zerstörungen des Jerusalemer Tempels* (ed. J. Hahn; Tübingen, 2002), 140–66 (esp. 141–44).

[8] This term is used here because it unites the pre-Easter and parts of the early post-Easter period in a sociological perspective. Cf. the title of G. Theissen, *Die Jesusbewegung: Sozialgeschichte einer Revolution der Werte* (Gütersloh, 2004); on the term, see ibid., 11–12.

[9] For the categorization of Jesus as a charismatic healer, see especially G. Vermes, *Jesus the Jew* (London, 1973). A thorough and up-to-date treatment of the issue of the "historical Jesus" can be found in J.P. Meier, *A Marginal Jew* (4 vols.; New York,

in a priestly or even ritual manner. His message, as far as we can reconstruct it from the earliest sources,[10] was relatively unrelated to the Jerusalem Temple and its cult. This is not due merely to the Galilean context, because the Galileans, too, were strongly connected with that religious center of the Jewish world. Rather, the heart of Jesus' preaching, the kingdom of God, is not explicitly related to the earthly sanctuary,[11] nor are any of the exorcisms and healings narrated in the gospels linked with the Temple.[12] In disregard of purity and other religious and ethical issues, Jesus accepted invitations to eat in the houses of tax-gatherers and sinners (Mark 2:15–16), and offered fellowship to outcasts such as the crippled or the leprous (cf. Luke 14:13; Luke 7:22 par. Matt 11:5, etc.). Moreover, it is said that he assured people of divine forgiveness of their sins without any reference to the sacrificial cult (Mark 2:1–12).[13]

1991–2009); and M. Hengel and A.M. Schwemer, *Jesus und das Judentum* (Tübingen, 2007).

[10] According to a broad consensus in Jesus research, the passages from John have to be left aside, at least to begin with, when we are seeking the "historical Jesus." Although some Johannine elements may represent a historical tradition, as a whole the Johannine story and language are secondary developments. The Johannine Temple scenes (which are much more numerous than the Temple scenes in the Synoptics) must be explained, therefore, on the basis of the Johannine agenda and theology, not as part of the "real" history of Jesus. On the establishment of this "classical" consensus, see J. Frey, *Die johanneische Eschatologie* (3 vols.; Tübingen, 1997), 1:38–39. That consensus has been called into question in recent years, but only at the expense of floating a much more hypothetical and uncertain construction; see, for example, P.N. Anderson, *The Fourth Gospel and the Quest for Jesus* (New York, 2006).

[11] Whether apocalyptic imagination thought of a heavenly temple in God's coming kingdom or of a renewed and eschatological Temple on the renewed earth is not relevant for the present argument. Both options are possible for the proclamation of Jesus, and a decision cannot be made.

[12] In Luke 17:14, the healed lepers are to present themselves to the priests, but this cultic act is unrelated to the Temple itself. Even in John 5:14, where Jesus "finds" in the Temple the person he had healed, and one might suppose that he was there to bring a thank-offering, the healing itself had happened elsewhere, at the pool of "Bethesda," without connection to the Temple. In John 9, Jesus meets the man born blind outside the Temple (cf. 8:59); and the healing, using the "medium" of clay from spittle, is performed without any reference to the Temple and its cult. Moreover, the man is commissioned to wash himself in the Pool of Siloam (Shiloach)—a noncultic washing that must be symbolically interpreted as "the one who is sent."

[13] The authenticity of this passage is disputed, but the designation of vv. 5–10 as a secondary addition to a more original healing story (so, for example: Bultmann, *Die Geschichte der synoptischen Tradition* [9th ed.; Göttingen, 1979], 13) is largely due to a dogmatic view that Jesus as a mere human being could not have acted in such a fashion. In my view, this argument is not compelling.

Correspondingly, there is, remarkably, no tradition about Jesus observing particular purification rites in the week before Passover.[14] Whatever we might speculate about Jesus' and his followers' religious lives, knowledge of the Scriptures, participation in local synagogues, or additional festival journeys to Jerusalem,[15] the basic elements of his message and of discipleship seem remarkably unrelated to, and therefore independent of and distant from, the Temple.[16]

In his distance from the Jerusalem Temple and its cult, Jesus appears in a striking parallel with his "teacher" John the Baptist, whose message and eschatological purification rite were also unrelated to the Temple and its "official" cult. Of course, there is no explicit criticism of the Temple ascribed to the Baptist, and to interpret his immersion rite as such might be an overstatement. But he was not simply indifferent towards the Temple cult.[17] Rather, by actively offering a rite of atonement and purification without any sacrifice he actually established a "rival enterprise" which inevitably questioned the Temple as institution—not only because of the apocalyptic expectation of imminent judgment upon all those who would not repent, but also because of the means via which purity and atonement could be achieved.[18]

---

[14] On the contrary, the apocryphal gospel fragment, *P.Oxy.* 840, reports the charge that he entered the Temple area without the required immersion. Cf. also John 13:10, etc.

[15] According to the Synoptic account (i.e., Mark), Jesus went to Jerusalem only once, at the Passover of his death. This may be a simplifying construction. John relates several journeys to Jerusalem for different festivals. Furthermore, Luke tells the legendary episode of the young Jesus in the Temple disputing with the learned authorities; and more generally, his narration of Jesus' and John the Baptist's births is full of references to the Temple. Whatever the historical value of those episodes may be, it is quite probable that Jesus was in the area of the Temple not merely once but more frequently, both before the beginning of his public ministry and possibly also during that period—which was probably not as short as Mark's one-year chronology suggests.

[16] Cf., among others, G. Theissen and A. Merz, *Der historische Jesus* (Göttingen, 1996), 380–81. Cf. also F. Siegert, "'Zerstört diesen Tempel...!' Jesus als 'Tempel' in den Passionsüberlieferungen," in Hahn, *Zerstörungen des Jerusalemer Tempels*, 108–39 (127), who describes Jesus' relation to the Temple using the term "Unabhängigkeit."

[17] Thus F. Avemarie, "Ist die Johannestaufe ein Ausdruck von Tempelkritik? Skizze eines methodischen Problems," in *Gemeinde ohne Tempel: Zur Substituierung und Transformation des Jerusalemer Tempels und seines Kults im Alten Testament, antiken Judentum und frühen Christentum* (ed. B. Ego, A. Lange, and P. Pilhofer; Tübingen, 1999), 395–410 (esp. 407).

[18] Cf. M. Ebner, *Jesus von Nazareth in seiner Zeit: Sozialgeschichtliche Zugänge* (Stuttgart, 2003); and Hengel and Schwemer, *Jesus und das Judentum*, 316: "Das Wirken des Täufers setzt einen Konflikt mit dem Tempelkult und der diesen beherrschenden Priesteraristokratie voraus.... Für den Priestersohn aus der Ordnung Abia spielte der Kult offenbar keine wesentliche Rolle mehr."

This link with the eschatological message and viewpoint of the Baptist could at least partly explain the disregard of the Temple in Jesus' Galilean activity. Here are the roots of the later establishment of a religious identity at a distance from the Jerusalem Temple among Jesus' followers.

In Mark's gospel, the Temple is not mentioned before Jesus' entry in Jerusalem. Mark 11:11 simply states that "Jesus entered Jerusalem and the Temple and looked around at all things." Then, Mark tells of the cursing of the fig tree[19] and the so-called "cleansing" of the Temple. The last days of Jesus are then filled with debates in the Temple and with religious authorities, until Jesus' final arrest.

But when looking at the historical Jesus, we cannot draw only on Mark's composition; we must rather consider the complex picture presented by the Synoptic tradition as a whole. According to a broad scholarly consensus, at least two elements related to the Temple may be considered to belong to the pre-Markan stratum of the Jesus tradition:[20] first, a prophecy of the destruction of the Temple (Mark 13:1–2 and parallels), which is referred to in a different form in the Markan Passion narrative (Mark 14:58);[21] and second, the episode of the so-called "cleansing" of the Temple (Mark 11:15–17 and parallels), which provides the reason for Jesus' later arrest and death. Regardless of the precise interpretation of this episode,[22] the most original form of the

---

[19] Mark 11:12–14, 20–25. The episode forms a frame for the "cleansing" of the Temple. In Mark, the fig tree episode "is probably a comment on the bankruptcy of the institution"; thus C. Rowland, "The Temple in the New Testament," in *Temple and Worship in Biblical Israel* (ed. J. Day; New York, 2006), 469–83 (470).

[20] This is cautiously phrased by E.P. Sanders, "Jesus and the Temple," in *The Historical Jesus in Recent Research* (ed. J.D.G. Dunn and S. McKnight; Winona Lake, 2005), 361–81 (362): "It is overwhelmingly probable that Jesus did something in the Temple and said something about its destruction."

[21] Some form of this logion is probably authentic, since it occurs in all strata of the Synoptic and non-Synoptic Jesus traditions (cf. Mark 13:1–2; 14:58; Matt 26:61; Luke 13:34–35; John 2:19; Acts 6:14; *Gos. Thom.* 71). There is debate as to whether Mark 13:2 is based on an authentic prophecy of the destruction of the Temple or whether this saying is just a weakening of the "more original" version of Mark 14:58. Cf. K. Paesler, *Das Tempelwort Jesu: Die Traditionen von Tempelzerstörung und Tempelerneuerung im Neuen Testament* (Göttingen, 1999); and more recently, A. Yarbro Collins, *Mark: A Commentary* (Minneapolis, 2007), 600–601.

[22] E.P. Sanders, *Jesus and Judaism* (Philadelphia, 1985), 61–76, interprets the episode as a prophetic sign of the impending destruction of the Temple. Other interpreters, e.g., B.F. Meyer, *The Aims of Jesus* (London, 1979), 198–200, view it as a messianic revelation implying the aspect of eschatological restoration. An even stronger theological interpretation is provided by J. Ådna, *Jesus und der Tempel: Die Tempelaktion und das Tempelwort als Ausdruck seiner messianischen Sendung* (Tübingen, 2000),

Temple logion, and the relationship between the two, these elements of the earliest Jesus tradition demonstrate that there was a potential for criticism of the Temple in Jesus' ministry that goes beyond a mere disregard of or independence from the institution.[23]

The development of the Temple logion in the pre-Markan tradition[24] is further evidence for a continued or even increasingly critical stance towards the Temple within the early Jesus movement. The distribution of the logion shows that the criticism expressed here was considered important already before 70 CE. When the Temple was actually destroyed in 70 CE, Jesus' prophecy could appear to have been confirmed. Thus, the logion became even more important and was subject to further interpretation in the later gospels and in Acts.[25]

1.2. *The Cultic Interpretation of Jesus' Death and Temple Criticism in the Early Communities*

It is furthermore important to note that Jesus' death did not happen in a cultic context. Although the Temple authorities probably played an active role in his arrest, denunciation and conviction, his crucifixion was far from being a sacrifice. There is hardly any greater contrast than that between a sacrificial act in a sanctuary and the most shameful form of execution in the Roman world—that of crucifixion by Roman soldiers.

The mode of Jesus' death presented a problem for its later interpretation in sacrificial terms. The Epistle to the Hebrews, in particular, takes numerous and complicated exegetical steps to interpret Jesus as

---

who views the episode as an intervention against the sacrificial cult that is prophetically linked to Jesus' own atoning death.

[23] On the other hand, there is no explicit questioning of the legitimacy of the Temple, if one does not interpret Mark 14:58 to mean that the coming of the Kingdom of God is to bring the Temple cult to an end. From a sociological perspective, it has been suggested that the Galilean outlook, and a tension between rural and urban populations, might have contributed to the genesis of such Temple criticism; see G. Theissen, "Die Tempelweissagung Jesu: Prophetie im Spannungsfeld von Stadt und Land," in idem, *Studien zur Soziologie des Urchristentums* (Tübingen, 1979), 142–59.

[24] On this, see Paesler, *Tempelwort, passim.*

[25] After 70 CE, the notion that Jesus himself would destroy the Temple (Mark 14:58: "I will destroy…") was either omitted (in Luke 21:6; but Luke uses the saying in Acts 6:14 as a charge against Stephen, though reported by false witnesses); corrected (in Matthew 26:61: "I am able"); or metaphorically transferred to Jesus' body (John 2:19, 21).

himself both high priest and, at the same time, atoning sacrifice.[26] Such an interpretation presupposes an extensive process of reinterpretation in which cultic terms were increasingly adopted, primarily for expressing the salvific effects of Jesus' death. The process was probably inaugurated by Jesus' own comments on his imminent death (according to the traditions on the Last Supper),[27] and it later intensified when his death had to be understood and explained in the light of the Easter events and the Scriptures.

One of the earliest post-Easter traditions in which the cultic category of atonement is used to interpret Jesus' death is adopted by Paul in Rom 3:25–26. But notably, this earliest explicit utilization of atonement terminology does not compare Jesus with the sacrificed animal, nor is his death compared with the sacrificial act as such. Instead, he is paralleled with the ἱλαστήριον, the *kapporeth*, as the place of God's gracious presence.[28] Although it is debated whether this imagery already implies a notion of the "replacement" of the atoning cult, it inaugurates a line of interpretation in which the Temple is viewed as being "replaced" at least in some respect by the (body of the) crucified and resurrected Jesus.[29]

This line was continued and developed in various ways in the early Judean community of Jesus followers, at first in Jerusalem. From the

---

[26] The nonpriestly origin of Jesus (Heb 7:14) is a reason for the author to look (in the Scriptures) for another priesthood, not from Levi, but from Melchizedek (Heb 7:1–18); and, in a strange combination of images, Jesus is described as having entered the heavenly sanctuary as high priest to sacrifice his own blood (Heb 9:24–26).

[27] Although there is an extensive debate on the origin and precise phrasing of the words of Jesus in the account of the Last Supper (Mark 14:22–25; Matt 26:26–29; Luke 22:15–20; 1 Cor 11:23–25), it is plausible that Jesus himself offered some kind of verbal reinterpretation of his action, in anticipation of his imminent death (cf. Mark 14:25). On the reconstruction of these words in the context of the Passover see the classical contribution by J. Jeremias, *Die Abendmahlsworte Jesu* (4th ed.; Göttingen, 1967). The literature on these issues is vast and cannot be cited here.

[28] Cf. W. Kraus, *Der Tod Jesu als Heiligtumsweihe* (Neukirchen-Vluyn, 1991), 21–32; D.P. Bailey, "Jesus as the Mercy Seat: The Semantics and Theology of Paul's Use of *Hilasterion* in Romans 3:25" (Ph.D. diss., Cambridge, 1999); P. Stuhlmacher, *Biblische Theologie des Neuen Testaments* (2 vols.; 3d ed.; Göttingen, 2005), 1:192–94.

[29] See, e.g. Kraus, *Tod Jesu*, 233: "wird die jetzt erfolgte 'Aufhebung' des irdischen Heiligtums angesagt." The point is put differently by D. Stökl ben Ezra, *The Impact of Yom Kippur on Early Christianity* (Tübingen, 2003), 202–4. It is true that the aspect of abolition is not expressed openly in the formula; but the idea that God had merely "instituted an *additional* eschatological Yom Kippur" (Stökl ben Ezra, *Impact*, 204, italics mine), is in my view too weak. Later, especially in the Gospel of John, the analogy between the Temple and the body of the Crucified One is made explicit (cf. John 2:19; 7:37–38; 19:34–35), together with the motif of substitution.

scanty evidence, as preserved primarily in the first chapters of Acts, we can see that the early Jewish followers of Jesus in Jerusalem still visited the Temple at least for prayer (Luke 24:53; Acts 3:1–26; 5:19–21, 42),[30] although the form and extent of their participation in the sacrificial cult is unclear. But there are good reasons to assume a further participation even in the sacrifices themselves, at least by parts of the community.[31]

On the other hand, we can see that the line of Temple criticism was also continued, or even intensified. It is probably not a mere coincidence that the critical distance seems to be rooted in the circle of the so-called "Hellenists" (cf. Acts 6:1), i.e., the Greek-speaking followers, who were at least loosely linked with the Jewish Diaspora—which was a greater distance from the Temple, practically speaking. Thus, the stance vis à vis the Temple is already divided among the earliest communities in Jerusalem and Judea.

Elements of Temple criticism which are also thoroughly rooted in Jewish tradition can be studied in Stephen's speech in Acts 6–7, given—so we read—after members of the Diaspora synagogues of Jerusalem charge Stephen with speaking "blasphemous words" against Moses and God (Acts 6:11), and also against the Holy Place and the Law (Acts 6:13). According to Luke, there are even "false witnesses" who quote a saying ascribed to Stephen (Acts 6:14), which is actually a version of Jesus' Temple logion from Mark 14:58.[32] In his speech, Stephen retells the history of Israel down to Solomon and then adopts the universalistic view "that the Most High does not dwell in houses made by human hands" (Acts 7:48–49). Although this simply recalls what is known from the Bible (1 Kgs 8:27), the use of χειροποίητος in connection with the Temple "must have been highly offensive in Jewish ears."[33] The passage, therefore, shows the greater distance from

---

[30] According to Acts 22:17, Paul had a vision while praying in the Temple. According to Luke, Paul visits the Temple to pray as a matter of course.

[31] One piece of evidence for this is the later polemics against sacrifice found in Jewish-Christian traditions, cf. the *Gospel of the Ebionites* frg. 6 (= Epiphanius, *Panarion* 30.16.4–5): "I came to do away with sacrifices, and if you cease not sacrificing, the wrath of God will not cease from you." Cf. also Epiphanius, *Panarion* 28.1.4 and 29.1.6; and *Ps.-Clem. Homilies* 3.56.4 and *Recognitions* 1.39.

[32] The parallel might be due to Luke's desire to connect the martyrdoms of Jesus and Stephen. Mark 14:58 is interestingly omitted in Luke's version of the Passion account, although Luke certainly knows the saying.

[33] Thus C.K. Barrett, *A Critical and Exegetical Commentary on the Acts of the Apostles* (2 vols.; Edinburgh, 1994–1998), 1:373; see also Rowland, "The Temple in the New Testament," 473–75. An analysis of the concept of Temple criticism and

the Jerusalem Temple and its cult, probably connected with a more "universalist" viewpoint, among the "Hellenists" in Jerusalem.

It thus seems that already in the early preaching of this group, as also in their further mission after being scattered from Jerusalem (Acts 8:1; 11:19), an early form of Hellenistic Jewish "Christian" identity took shape which was even more independent from Jerusalem and the Temple. In the tradition of the Hellenists we can also locate the interpretation that Jesus metaphorically represents or even "replaces" the place of God's gracious presence in the Temple (cf. Rom 3:25). And it was within a community established by their mission (see Acts 11:19–21), in Antioch, that Gentiles were admitted without being circumcised. Moreover, such an admission of Gentiles was practiced programmatically, with the consequence that ritual purity could only be observed in a reduced degree when Jews and Gentiles joined for the communal meals. The community members from Jewish descent were obviously expected to accept such a "liberal" position. Most probably, all the leading figures in the community at Antioch were Jews, and they certainly found scriptural reasons for their policy. But the common meals necessarily engendered difficulties, and the conflict became obvious when other Jewish followers of Jesus, used to a more rigid praxis of purity, visited the community.

What Paul describes in Gal 2:11–14 is, therefore, a conflict of emerging identities which led to the separation between Paul and his older "colleague" Barnabas, and also between himself and the whole community of Antioch that had engaged him for the mission among Gentiles. The incompatibility of these identities ultimately led to a further "parting of the ways."[34]

The emergence of the term Χριστιανοί as a designation of the members of the community in Antioch (Acts 11:26) may already point to a form of identity that could be recognized as separate by others.[35] Although the community in Antioch was still Jewish, a new and distinctive form of identity is emerging which is no longer (or only just) defined by the identity markers Temple, Torah, and purity. Rather, as

---

its background in Jewish tradition is given in G. Fassbeck, *Der Tempel der Christen* (Tübingen and Basel, 2000), 90–110. The attempt of E. Larsson, "Temple-Criticism and the Jewish Heritage," *NTS* 39 (1993): 379–95 (esp. 393–95) to explain away all offenses against the Temple is far from plausible.

[34] On the problems see J. Frey, "Paulus und die Apostel," in *Biographie und Persönlichkeit des Paulus* (ed. E.-M. Becker and P. Pilhofer; Tübingen, 2005), 192–227.

[35] See Barrett, *Acts* 1:556–57; J. Jervell, *Die Apostelgeschichte* (Göttingen, 1998), 326.

the term Χριστιανοί indicates, that identity is primarily based on the belief in Jesus as Χριστός.

2. *Paul's Jewish Identity and Identity Formation Independent of the Temple in the Pauline Communities*

The only corpus of early Christian writings which can be dated with certainty to before 70 CE are the authentic Pauline letters, written largely in the 50s and addressed to communities in the Jewish Diaspora: in Macedonia (Philippians, Thessalonians), Achaia (Corinthians), Asia Minor (Galatians, possibly Philemon), and Rome (Romans). All other New Testament writings were written either around 70 (Mark, possibly Colossians) or later.[36] These writings might point to the situation influenced by the events of 70 CE. But the formation of a "Christian"[37] identity largely independent of the cultic center of Judaism started long before 70 CE, as we can see from the writings of Paul.

2.1. *Paul's Jewish Identity*
There is no need to discuss Paul's own religious identity here. His background of education and thought was unquestionably Jewish,[38] as is obvious not only from some autobiographical passages (2 Cor 11:22; Rom 9:1–5; 11:1)[39] but also from the patterns of thought used in his letters. Notably, Paul never ceased considering himself a Jew, strongly linked with his "brethren," and his "kinsmen in terms of the flesh" (Rom 9:3–5). As a consequence, he maintained his commitment to preserve unity with the community in Jerusalem, despite all the tensions. He was even eager to himself deliver the money collected for the "poor" in Jerusalem, despite the dangers he was aware of before that journey (Rom 15:31). It is plausible that he visited the Temple,[40] as

---

[36] This is the majority view maintained in the critical introductions. There is still some debate on the authenticity and possible early dating of James, Colossians and 2 Thessalonians, but this cannot be discussed here.

[37] I am well aware of the danger of anachronism in the use of this term for the Pauline period. See above, n. 2.

[38] On this, see J. Frey, "Paul's Jewish Identity," in Frey, Gripentrog, and Schwartz, *Jewish Identity*, 285–321. See also K.-W. Niebuhr, *Heidenapostel aus Israel* (Tübingen, 1992); and A.L. Hogeterp, "Paul's Judaism Reconsidered: The Issue of Cultic Imagery in the Corinthian Correspondence," *ETL* 81 (2005): 87–108.

[39] Even the passages where Paul states a contrast between then and now (Gal 1:13–15; Phil 3:3–6) demonstrate his thoroughly Jewish roots—which he never abandoned.

[40] It is debated whether and in which context Paul himself undertook the vows of a Nazirite. See J. Koet, "Why did Paul Shave his Hair (Acts 18,18)? Nazirite and

reported by Luke. However, the accusation (Acts 21:29) that he brought a Gentile into the Temple may mirror suspicion against him, at least among some circles in Jerusalem that viewed his mission among the Gentiles as a fundamental dissolution of essential boundary markers of their tradition.

In Paul's mission and theology, there is a remarkable double tendency. On the one hand, he was able to abandon the restrictions of purity and other laws in order to be to those outside the law as if he were outside the law in order to win them (1 Cor 9:21).[41] Against the "Judaizers," he vigorously defends the unrestricted membership of the believers from the Gentiles without circumcision (e.g., in Galatians). On the other hand, he also defends the lifestyle of the Jewish community members in Rome who keep dietary restrictions and special "days" (Rom 14:1–15:13).[42] Thus, Paul cannot be accused of simply neglecting Jewish identity markers. His view is based rather on a redefinition of the requirements for the Gentiles to participate in the promise, and a "reconfiguration" of basically Jewish convictions[43] which he could argue for from Scripture, interpreted in the light of the Christ event. Although his mission and thought contributed much to the (lengthy and complicated) process of the so-called "parting of the ways," and some fellow Jews might even have considered him an apostate, he would have never thought that he had ceased being a Jew; and until his death, he hoped for the unity of Jewish and Gentile believers in the communities.

There are some hints, especially in Romans, that Jerusalem still remained at the center of Paul's imaginative and spiritual world (Rom 15:19, 25). The message of salvation had its origins in Jerusalem, and it was from Zion that the savior was expected (Rom 11:26; cf. Isa 59:20–21). According to Rom 15:16, the believers from the Gentiles

---

Temple in the Book of Acts," in *The Centrality of Jerusalem: Historical Perspectives* (ed. M. Poorthuis and C. Safrai; Kampen, 1996), 128–42; and F.W. Horn, "Paulus und der Herodianische Tempel," *NTS* 53 (2007): 184–203 (esp. 197–98).

[41] It is important to note, however, that he adds in a parenthesis that he is actually not "outside the law" but *under* Christ's law (1 Cor 9:21)—which supports the view that the law is eschatologically reinterpreted or even renewed by the Christ event.

[42] On these conflicts and Paul's interventions see V. Gäckle, *Die Starken und die Schwachen in Korinth und Rom* (Tübingen, 1995), 292–436.

[43] Cf. T.L. Donaldson, *Paul and the Gentiles: Remapping the Apostle's Convictional World* (Minneapolis, 1997), 215–48.

are even a kind of "offering" to the God of Israel,[44] although the Temple to which such sacrifices are normally brought is not mentioned in this context. According to Paul's thought pattern, "Jews…and Jerusalem…are always at the center"; the consequence of this, however, is not that non-Jews had to become Jews, but rather that non-Jews have to join *as* non-Jews when they are adopted as members of the people of God.[45]

2.2. *Identity Formation in the Pauline Communities*

For the members of the communities founded or influenced by Paul, first in Syria and Cilicia (including Antioch), and then in the different areas of his mission in Asia Minor and Greece, the connection to Jerusalem might, however, have been very different. Of course, the numerical proportions of Jewish and non-Jewish members in these communities cannot be ascertained, and in some of the communities there were probably a considerable number of Jewish believers with a certain degree of influence. But in time the number of Gentile believers grew, and according to some passages in the Pauline Epistles, they were soon the majority at least in some of the communities (Thessaloniki, Philippi, Corinth: see 1 Thess 1:9–10; 1 Cor 12:2; Acts 16:33). Although at least partly influenced and impressed by Paul, these Gentile believers did not share Paul's own education and Jewish worldview; and some problems discussed in Paul's letters are obviously due to the different thought patterns, e.g., regarding resurrection, ethics, or other aspects of communal life.

Even for former "God-fearers" who were probably well acquainted with the Scriptures and other aspects of Diaspora Judaism, the Temple in Jerusalem could never become an element of central or even practical relevance. Although these fellow travelers could participate in the Temple cult in various ways,[46] by sending gifts, by pilgrimage, and by prayer, they were barred from unlimited participation, and access to the sanctuary was ultimately restricted to Jews. Although Jerusalem

---

[44] Cf. Horn, "Paulus und der Herodianische Tempel," 200–202; see also M. Vahrenhorst, *Kultische Sprache in den Paulusbriefen* (Tübingen, 2008), 314–20.

[45] Cf. the terminologically cautious distinctions by A. Runesson, "Inventing Christian Identity: Paul, Ignatius, and Theodosius I," in Holmberg, *Exploring Early Christian Identity*, 59–92 (esp. 82).

[46] See S. Krauter, "Die Beteiligung von Nichtjuden am Jerusalemer Tempelkult," in Frey, Gripentrog, and Schwartz, *Jewish Identity*, 55–74.

with its Temple was an impressive religious center and one of the most important places of pilgrimage in the Mediterranean East, it could never practically affect the religious identity of Gentile sympathizers with Judaism (or of Gentile Christians) in their everyday lives.

For former God-fearers or other Gentiles who had been addressed by the Pauline mission and baptized, the situation had changed. Now, by faith in Jesus, they were accepted without being circumcised and without any further obligations. Most notably, their new identity as members of the eschatological people of God was established without any particular reference to the Temple or its cult. There is no evidence that Gentile believers ever tried to pay the Jewish Temple tax. Thus, for the growing group of Gentile Christians the Jerusalem Temple never became a decisive part of their religious identity.

Paul may have viewed support for the poor brethren in Jerusalem as a kind of "equivalent" to the Temple tax or as a similar sign of relatedness.[47] But the passages in his letters in which he discusses the collection show how difficult it was for him to convince his addressees to give the support for which he had asked. They did not feel so strongly linked with Jerusalem—even with the fellow believers in the Jewish-Christian community there—let alone with the Temple.

Thus, it is most probable that the Temple played no major role in the constitution of their new identity, which was decisively defined by the relationship with Christ. Being "in Christ" (2 Cor 5:17) or living through Christ (cf. Gal 2:20) was the most distinctive expression of this identity.[48] The addressees of the Epistles are called "beloved of God" (Rom 1:7), "saints" (1 Cor 1:2; 2 Cor 1:1; Phil 1:1), "sanctified in Christ Jesus" (1 Cor 1:2), or "community" (ἐκκλησία: 1 Thess 1:1; Gal 1:1). Their status is characterized by mention of the gospel (εὐαγγέλιον) (1 Cor 15:1–2; cf. Rom 1:16–17; Gal 1:6–9), which is then explained in confessional formulae as the message of the saving death and resurrection of Christ (1 Cor 15:3–5). Their conversion is described in 1 Thess 1:9 in terms that originate in the language of the Jewish Diaspora: "…how you turned to God from the idols, to serve

---

[47] The organization of Paul's collection "bears remarkable similarities to the gathering of the Temple tax" (thus M. Tellbe, "The Temple Tax as Identity Marker," in *The Formation of the Early Church* [ed. J. Ådna; Tübingen, 2005], 19–44 [34]). See 34–35 for further details.

[48] See also V.H.T. Nguyen, *Christian Identity in Corinth* (Tübingen, 2008) who stresses the element of "Christ-like identity."

the living and true God…"; and the initiating act is baptism, which inaugurates being "in Christ" as a "new creation" (2 Cor 5:17). Remarkably, there is no mention of the Temple in any of these phrases.

Of course, the Pauline letters show extensive use of cultic terms, but the notion of purity or holiness is always used metaphorically, without any concrete reference to the Jerusalem Temple. Cultic language qualifies the status of the community and its members as "holy," as "belonging to God," or even as a "temple" (cf. 1 Thess 3:13; 1 Cor 3:16–17; 2 Cor 6:16), in which God or his Spirit dwells, and such a qualification has consequences for an ethical lifestyle (Rom 12:1).[49] But such a metaphorical use of temple language is not primarily applied to Jewish-Christian readers, nor is it linked with any aspect of ritual purity.[50] Since the notion of the sanctity of a temple was quite common in the ancient world, Paul's metaphors could be understood even by readers without any Jewish background.[51] Although it is true that the temple metaphors in the New Testament Epistles are evidence of the remaining relevance of Temple theology,[52] there is no direct or even practical link to the Jerusalem Temple in the authentic Pauline Epistles.

3. Temple Imagery and the Issue of Identity in the Deuteropauline and Catholic Epistles

The first explicit reference to the Jerusalem Temple in the Pauline corpus occurs, interestingly, in a deuteropauline letter—in the apocalyptic passage 2 Thess 2:3–4, where it is said that the "man of lawlessness" will "take his seat in the Temple of God, proclaiming himself to be God." This does not sound like a reflection of the destruction of the Temple, but is rather a general apocalyptic idea in the tradition of the end-times tyrant, and there is no clear indication as to whether this passage presupposes the presence or the destruction of the Temple in Jerusalem.

---

[49] See Vahrenhorst, *Kultische Sprache*, 346–47; as well as Horn, "Paulus und der Herodianische Tempel," 186.

[50] See Horn, ibid., 191.

[51] See J.R. Lanci, *A New Temple for Corinth: Rhetorical and Archaeological Approaches to Pauline Imagery* (New York, 1992). See also Vahrenhorst, *Kultische Sprache*, 339.

[52] This is emphasized by W. Horbury, "Der Tempel bei Vergil und im hellenistischen Judentum," in *Gemeinde ohne Tempel*, 149–68 (esp. 166). Cf. Horn, "Paulus und der Herodianische Tempel," 192.

In the other deuteropauline and Catholic Epistles we can observe a similar situation. Although probably all of them were written after 70 CE, none of them has an explicit reference to the destruction of the Jerusalem Temple.

In conservative scholarship this factor was often used as an argument for an earlier dating of these writings,[53] but there are numerous other arguments for the critical consensus that Ephesians, the Pastoral Epistles, Jude and Second Peter are actually pseudonymous writings from the end of the first century or beginning of the second.[54] Although there is still some debate concerning Colossians, Second Thessalonians, First Peter and James,[55] a post-70 date is probable for those writings as well. The same is true for Hebrews, where the cult is described as if it were present (see Heb 8:3–4; 9:8; 13:11); but what the author has in view here is the cult of the Tabernacle as described in the Septuagint, not the contemporary cult practiced in the Herodian Temple.[56]

For the pseudo-Apostolic writings from the time after 70 CE, the silence about the destruction of the Temple may be explained by the authorial fiction, according to which an open reference to the events of the year 70 CE would be inappropriate. But the fact that these writings are silent not only about the destruction of the Temple but also more generally about the city of Jerusalem and its cult[57] may point to the limited role the Jerusalem Temple played for the communities addressed.

Like the Pauline Epistles, these later writings, too, were written for communities in the Diaspora somewhere outside of Palestine, and there is no evidence for any significant difference from the authentic

---

[53] Thus, programmatically, J.A.T. Robinson, *Redating the New Testament* (London, 1976). See similarly, for the Synoptics, B. Reicke, "Synoptic Prophecies on the Destruction of Jerusalem," in *Studies in New Testament and Early Christian Literature: Essays in Honor of Allen P. Wikgren* (ed. D.E. Aune; Leiden, 1972), 121–34, who attempts to demonstrate that none of the Synoptic Gospels knows of the Jewish War, which would suggest a date before 70 CE for all of them. In my view this is unconvincing for Luke and Matthew, where references to the Destruction are very clear.

[54] On Jude and Second Peter see my commentary: J. Frey, *Der Judasbrief und der zweite Petrusbrief* (Leipzig, 2012, forthcoming).

[55] Cf., e.g., M. Hengel, "Der Jakobusbrief als antipaulinische Polemik," in idem, *Paulus und Jakobus: Kleine Schriften 3* (Tübingen, 2002), 511–43.

[56] Cf. the cautious argument by M. Karrer, "Der Hebräerbrief," in *Einleitung in das Neue Testament* (ed. M. Ebner and S. Schreiber; Stuttgart, 2008), 474–95 (esp. 485).

[57] With the sole exception of Hebrews (cf. the reference in the previous footnote).

Pauline writings in terms of their attitudes towards the Temple. Obviously the Temple did not play a major role for the identity of the Christian communities in those regions, nor is its destruction mentioned in these writings.

A remarkable but late exception is a writing which is roughly contemporary with the latest writings of the New Testament canon: the *Epistle of Barnabas*. There, the Destruction is mentioned and "historically" explained as having been caused by the fact that the Jews themselves instigated war (with the Romans) (*Barn.* 16:4).[58] The Destruction is put in the context of accusations (cf. *Barn.* 16:1–10) of idolatrous trust in the Temple (*Barn.* 16:1), and of the view that God had handed the earthly Temple over to destruction (*Barn.* 16:5) so that people should seek a spiritual temple. But this writing, featuring an abundant use of Scripture and broad debate about its true interpretation, differs significantly from most of the canonical Epistles[59] and points much more to the later *adversus Iudaeos* literature. Here, the challenge of Judaism is countered by an interpretation of the destruction of the Temple as caused by God's initiative and a hint that the Romans now "rebuild" it (*Barn.* 16:4b), which probably points to the erection of the temple of Jupiter in Hadrian's time.[60]

In the canonical Epistles, in contrast, the destruction of the Temple is not yet discussed. There is only a continued and intensified use of temple metaphors: In Ephesians, First Peter and also in the Pastoral Epistles, temple metaphors are related to the community or more generally the church, which is now described as a temple or dwelling place of God (Eph 2:20; 1 Tim 3:15), a spiritual house and—at the same time—a holy priesthood (1 Pet 2:5). In 1 Tim 3:15 the church is even metaphorically compared with architectural elements of the Temple: it is the "pillar and foundation of the truth."

In a similar manner, sacrificial metaphors are used to describe ethical living, which is described as "spiritual sacrifice" (1 Pet 2:5; cf. Eph 5:2; Heb 13:16). This is largely a continuation of the earlier metaphorical use of the temple motif in the authentic letters of Paul (1 Cor 3:10–17;

---

[58] "For through their going to war, it was destroyed by their enemies." Cf. H.-M. Döpp, *Die Deutung der Zerstörung Jerusalems und des zweiten Tempels im Jahre 70 in den ersten drei Jahrhunderten* (Tübingen and Basel, 1998), 236.

[59] Cf. R. Hvalvik, *The Struggle for Scripture and Covenant* (Tübingen, 1996), 330: "The theological profile of the work is...without clear parallels."

[60] Thus Hvalvik, *Struggle*, 20–21. For another interepretation of this passage, see R. Clements, "70 CE after 135 CE—The Making of a Watershed?," 522–24 in this volume.

6:19). The metaphors are used to point out the holiness of the community and its ethical consequences, with only some minor changes in intention from earlier usage: Whereas Paul had used the motif for marking the boundaries of the holy community and emphasizing the danger of transgression (1 Cor 3:16–17; 6:19), Ephesians uses the same imagery to express the notion that the borders have been removed and the dividing wall is now broken down (Eph 2:14);[61] thus, this usage emphasizes the unity of Jewish and Gentile Christians[62] and the open access to God that is now granted to those who were formerly excluded. But not even the mention of the removal of the dividing wall causes the author to hint at the destruction of the Temple.

We can conclude that (with the exception of *Barnabas*) none of the post-Apostolic letters gives any hint of the destruction of the Temple, and that there is also no evidence that this event affected the identity of the addressees in a thoroughgoing manner.

Remarkably, this is also true for Hebrews, where we find the most extensive use of temple imagery and cultic language in the New Testament. But—without going into detail—the author draws completely here on the scriptural passages that allude to the sanctuary in the wilderness; he does not refer to the Temple of Solomon, let alone the Herodian Temple. He introduces the scriptural construction of a priesthood according to Melchizedek (cf. Ps 110:4), superior to the priesthood of Levi, in order to cope with the problem that Jesus, who is "high priest" according to the traditional confession (Heb 2:17), was not of priestly descent (Heb 7:14). In the comparison with the higher, heavenly and true eschatological temple, priest, sacrifices, and covenant, the earthly counterparts are seen to be a mere shadow of their eschatological counterparts and are even said to be ineffective and unable to sanctify completely (Heb 10:1–4). In adopting the biblical tradition of criticism of the sacrifices (Ps 40:7–9), the author provides a complete transformation of the sacrificial tradition, according

---

[61] Cf. Fassbeck, *Der Tempel der Christen*, 193–214. See also p. 233: "Es geht Eph…nicht darum, Grenzen (von Heiligkeit) zu etablieren, sondern darum, eben diese aufzusprengen."

[62] Cf. also John 17:21. The unity motif, applied to the unity of Jewish and Gentile followers of Jesus, is also used in John 10:16 and 11:52; on this, see J. Frey, "Heiden—Griechen—Gotteskinder," in *Die Heiden* (ed. R. Feldmeier and U. Heckel; Tübingen, 1994), 228–68; and especially U. Heckel, "Die Einheit der Kirche im Johannesevangelium und im Epheserbrief," in *Kontexte des Johannesevangeliums* (ed. J. Frey and U. Schnelle; Tübingen, 2004), 613–60.

to which the sacrifices of "every priest" (Heb 10:11) are irrelevant for the addressees' status, which is only determined by the sacrifice that was brought once and forever by the true high priest in the heavenly sanctuary (Heb 10:14).

Thus, through the most condensed use of temple theology and cultic thought structures in the New Testament, Hebrews provides the strongest form of Temple criticism.[63] After the sacrifice of Christ, which saves once and forever, no other sacrifices are necessary or even possible (Heb 10:18). But this fundamental principle is unrelated to the actual cessation of worship in the Jerusalem Temple (of which the author probably knows), nor is there any hint that the addressees had formerly participated (or were inclined to participate) in its cult. The cultic thought structure seems to be developed at a distance from, and probably in disregard of, the institution of the Temple in Jerusalem. In the scriptural world of Hebrews there is no consideration of the earthly Temple. From this point of view, Hebrews fits quite well with what we saw in the Pauline and post-Pauline Epistles.

4. *The Synoptic Gospels and the Reaction to the Destruction of the Temple*

Whereas the New Testament Epistles are directed to communities in the Diaspora and address their situation with only a very limited reference to the story of Jesus and the community beginnings in Jerusalem, the Gospels tell a story situated in Jewish Palestine, in which Jerusalem and the Temple play an important role at least in the context of Jesus' passion and death. But due to the indirect mode of communication in the Gospels, interpretation has more difficulties to face and uncertainties remain with regard to both the addressees and also the date of the four works.

4.1. *Mark, the Temple and the Crisis of the Jewish War*
While most interpreters suggest a date around 70 CE for the Gospel of Mark, the precise dating is a matter of debate and depends on the interpretation of Mark 13,[64] especially the prophecy of destruction in

---

[63] Cf. Fassbeck, *Der Tempel der Christen*, 44.

[64] Of course, the problems of Mark 13 and its possible sources or literary development cannot be discussed here. For Mark's authorial intention, the redactional text is most important.

Mark 13:2 and the "desolating sacrilege" (βδέλυγμα τῆς ἐρημώσεως) in Mark 13:14. In my view, a date slightly before 70 CE is preferable.[65]

Scholars favoring a date after 70 CE argue that the logion in Mark 13:2, compared to its parallel in Mark 14:58, matches the events of the War, insofar it mentions the destruction of the larger buildings of the Temple district (as reported by Josephus) and is silent concerning any hope for the building of a "new" Temple.[66] These scholars also read the mention of the "desolating sacrilege" as a reference to the destruction of the Temple. But this reading seems to underestimate the strong links with Daniel (Dan 9:27; 11:31; 12:11) and the apocalyptic tradition here, and also to ignore the wording in Mark 13:14. The phrase "but when you see the desolating sacrilege *set up where it ought not to be…*" does not really fit the Destruction; it points to a different situation. And when the text, explicitly addressing its readers,[67] suggests fleeing to the mountains, this is hardly conceivable after the destruction of the Temple, but rather points to an earlier, precarious situation.[68] The reference to the "desolating sacrilege," who (!) is "set up" (or "stands") could either derive from the apocalyptic tradition;[69] or be influenced by Gaius Caligula's attempt to place his statue in the Temple in 40 CE;[70] or point to some other event in the Jewish War, before the Destruction;[71] or forecast an ultimate

---

[65] Cf. M. Hengel, *Studies in the Gospel of Mark* (London, 1985).

[66] Thus, M. Ebner, "Das Markusevangelium," in Ebner and Schreiber, *Einleitung*, 154–83 (170–71); cf. also G. Theissen, *Lokalkolorit und Zeitgeschichte in den Evangelien* (Göttingen, 1989), 271. For more recent suggestions of a post-70 date of Mark see E.-M. Becker, "Der jüdisch-römische Krieg (66–70 n. Chr.) und das Markus-Evangelium: Zu den 'Anfängen' frühchristlicher Historiographie," in *Die antike Historiographie und die Anfänge der christlichen Geschichtsschreibung* (ed. E.-M. Becker; Berlin, 2005), 213–36; T. Gray, *The Temple in the Gospel of Mark* (Tübingen, 2008). See also Lücking, "Zerstörung," 157–62.

[67] See the parenthetical imperative ὁ ἀναγινώσκων νοείτω.

[68] See also the argument in J. Marcus, *Mark 8–16* (New Haven and London 2009), 890–91.

[69] See the argument in B. Pitre, *Jesus, the Tribulation, and the End of the Exile* (Tübingen, 2005), 302–7.

[70] Cf. the argument by H.-M. Döpp, *Die Deutung der Zerstörung*, 249–51. The wording of Mark 13:14, and especially the personalization of the "abomination of desolation" by the masculine participle ἑστηκότα (which goes beyond the tradition from Daniel), suggest a link to Caligula's attempt to erect his statue in the Temple, and the author seems to expect a similar profanation in the near future.

[71] Possibly the cessation of the sacrifices or the occupation of the Temple by the Zealots. Thus, e.g., J. Marcus, "The Jewish War and the *Sitz im Leben* of Mark," *JBL* 111 (1992): 441–62 (esp. 454), who suggests that the reference to the "abomination of desolation standing where he should not" "in its Marcan context…reflects…

desecration of the Temple[72] that was expected on the basis of earlier experiences. However, "none of the…events often cited as an explanation actually offers a parallel to v. 14."[73] But neither is Mark 13:2 actually so close to the events that it may *only* be read as a detailed reference to the events of 70 CE. There is good reason to view Mark 13:2 as a pre-Markan tradition that is not an abbreviation of Mark 14:58 but rather the earliest form of the Temple logion, which might go back to Jesus himself.[74] The wording "no stone on another" is not really a description of the Destruction but a general statement that could well be phrased in anticipation of events. It is, therefore, far from plausible to interpret Mark 13:14 as a reflection of the actual destruction of the Temple.

Uncertainties remain,[75] but a date of Mark before 70 CE (probably after the start of the war) seems to be most plausible. The perspective of the evangelist does not yet presuppose the destruction of the Temple but rather reflects an earlier situation: The turmoil in Galilee and Judea had activated apocalyptic tensions and fears (Mark 13:7–8); and regardless of its earlier ingredients, Mark 13 is evidence for such a situation, including the expectation of a final tribulation.[76] Mark aims at reducing the eschatological tension by the affirmation that the wars are "not yet the end" (Mark 13:7); that the birth pangs are only beginning (Mark 13:8); that the good news must first be proclaimed to all nations (Mark 13:10); that there is yet time to "endure until the end" (Mark 13:13)—and by the separation of *all* these events from the coming of the Son of Man (Mark 13:24–27).

---

specifically the occupation of the Temple by Eleazar son of Simon in the winter of 67–68." See ibid., n. 59: "In the putative pre-Markan apocalyptic discourse, however, the reference may very well have been to Caligula's plan to erect an image of himself in the Temple in AD 40."

[72] See Pitre, *Jesus*, 300: "As in Daniel, the desecration of the Temple is part of the end and precedes the final period of unparalleled tribulation (cf. Dan 9:25–27; 11:35–12:1)."

[73] C.A. Evans, *Mark 8:27–16:20* (Nashville, 2001), 319.

[74] See the reconstruction by Paesler, *Tempelwort*, 81–92.

[75] It is even uncertain as to where to locate the readers of Mark. There is much to commend the traditional view that Mark was written in Rome, but one may well ask whether especially ch. 13 does not presuppose a greater proximity to the events of the Jewish War. Cf. Marcus, "The Jewish War and the *Sitz im Leben* of Mark," 460–62.

[76] The prayer that the events should not happen during the winter (Mark 13:18) is hardly conceivable after the Destruction.

This view is confirmed by the observation that Luke and Matthew change Mark's text in light of the events now past.[77] In contrast to those later gospels, Mark does not yet reflect or even comment on the destruction of the Temple. Nor is the Temple in its cultic function really important in this situation: The flight to the mountains (Mark 13:14, 18) was to happen, not because of the end of the Temple cult, but because of the tribulation and persecution that was expected, together with the final desecration of the Temple.

But is there any positive role and function of the Temple for Mark? We should not ignore the important narrative role the sanctuary plays in the closing chapters of this gospel (chs. 11–15), where, once Jesus had arrived in Jerusalem and at the Temple and "looked around at everything" (Mark 11:11), he then "cleansed" the sanctuary.[78]

According to Mark 14:58a, the Jerusalem Temple is made by hands (χειροποίητος, cf. Acts 7:48), and its destruction as foretold by Jesus (Mark 13:2; 14:58a) is to be followed by the erection of another Temple, "*not* made with hands" (ἀχειροποίητος, Mark 14:58b). Although the saying is introduced as a "false" accusation, it is probable that "Mark believed that it contained a vital truth."[79] Thus, Mark not only shares the criticism of the "Hellenists" against the "handmade" Temple but also envisages a metaphorical transfer of the idea of a new temple, originating in God, most probably with the resurrection of Jesus.[80]

Accordingly, the theme of the "cleansing" story in Mark is not simply the destruction of the Temple but its "restoration" according to its original design as a place of prayer for all nations (Mark 11:17).[81] But when we ask where in the narrative such an inclusion of the Gentiles is rooted, we are pointed to the Passion, when at the time of Jesus' death the veil in the Temple is torn in two (Mark 15:38), thus opening the

---

[77] Cf. Luke 21:20–24 against Mark 13:14–20 and Matt 22:7 against Mark 12:1–12. Significantly, Luke omits Mark 13:18 (the prayer that the flight should not be in the winter). Luke also omits the charge against Jesus (from Mark 14:58a) that he predicted that the Temple would be destroyed.

[78] Cf. P.W.L. Walker, *Jesus and the Holy City* (Grand Rapids, 1996), 4: "Jesus' coming to the Temple must be seen as a 'divine inspection'—the Lord coming to that which was his own to see what was being done in his name."

[79] Walker, ibid., 9–10.

[80] The phrase διὰ τριῶν ἡμερῶν in Mark 14:58b should probably be understood as pointing to the resurrection (thus Walker, ibid., 10).

[81] Cf. C. Wahlen, "The Temple in Mark and Contested Authority," *BibInt* 15 (2007): 248–67 (esp. 254): "The temple is cleared not from sacrifice but from commercialism."

access to God—an event which is immediately followed by the confession of the Gentile centurion (Mark 15:39).

Thus, the perspective adopted in Mark 11:17 is not simply the anticipation of a restoration of the "handmade" Temple and its cult in a less commercialized manner.[82] Rather, the author envisages a redefinition of the House of Israel itself which is to open its doors to "*all* the nations."[83] But if this is true, the temple motif is also used metaphorically.

As far as we can see, the readers of Mark's gospel are no longer linked with the Jerusalem Temple, but share the distance we have already observed for the audience and addressees of Paul. The episodes of Jesus and the Temple are related to the vision of salvation for all nations, opened up through Jesus himself; the tribulations in Judea and the impending destruction are understood to be simply a step towards eschatological salvation and the erection of another temple not made with hands.

4.2. Reactions to the Destruction of the Temple in Luke and Matthew
The later Synoptic Gospels, Luke and Matthew, presuppose and use Mark, including the report of the Temple cleansing and the apocalyptic discourse. Both evangelists change the references to the destruction of the Temple and "correct" sayings from Mark in the light of later events: A comparison of the reference to the Destruction in Matt 22:6–7 with those in Luke 21:20–24 and 19:41–44 shows that Luke still writes from proximity to the catastrophe and "still seems to be deeply moved by it,"[84] while Matthew views the events already from a greater distance. But in reverse of this chronological sequence, I will start here with Matthew who, "with two exceptions…, alludes to the Jewish War and its consequences only where the motif is provided for him by Mark."[85]

---

[82] But where Wahlen (ibid., 266) conjectures that the author of Mark simply thought here of the community of his readers and its assemblies, this is also daring and implausible.

[83] Ibid., 267.

[84] Thus M. Hengel, *The Four Gospels and the One Gospel of Jesus Christ* (London, 2000), 189. For his whole discussion of the chronological priority of Luke over Matthew, see ibid., 186–205.

[85] Hengel, ibid., 194.

In Matt 24:1–2, the evangelist abbreviates Mark 13:2, and in Matt 24:15 (= Mark 13:14) he changes the masculine ἑστηκότα into the grammatically correct neuter and the enigmatic ὅπου οὐ δεῖ ("where it should not [stand]") into ἐν ἁγίῳ τόπῳ, which points more clearly to the Temple square or the holy city.[86] But in the parable of the great supper (Matt 22:1–14), Matthew inserts a passage (vv. 6–7, also dependent on Mark 12:6) that focuses on the destruction and burning of Jerusalem without mentioning the Temple (Matt 22:7). The Destruction is explained by the anger of the king about "those murderers" who killed his servants and ignored his invitation to the meal: "and he sent his armies, destroyed those murderers and burned their city." Thus, for the first evangelist, the destruction of Jerusalem is a divine punishment, not only for the rejection of Jesus but more generally for the shedding of innocent blood—the killing of the prophets (Matt 23:30–31, 34, 37) and other righteous men down to the present time, from Abel to Zechariah the son of Barachiah (Matt 23:35),[87] also including Jesus (cf. Matt 27:4, 19, 23–25). In his lament over Jerusalem Jesus expresses the verdict, mentioning the Temple: "your house (οἶκος) is left to you, desolate" (Matt 23:38).

The Temple logion in Matt 26:61 is also altered in order to avoid the idea of Jesus predicting that he will rebuild the Temple. Here, he simply has the power to do so (δύναμαι). There is no further expectation of a renewed or "spiritual" temple. Instead, the gospel adopts the prophetic criticism that God calls for mercy, not for sacrifice (Matt 9:13; 12:7; cf. Hos 6:6). The idea of God's presence is transferred to Jesus himself. He is the "Immanuel" (Matt 1:23; cf. 28:20), the presence of God dwelling among his people and wherever the disciples gather in his name (Matt 18:20). Thus, he is even "greater than the Temple" (Matt 12:6).

In his situation, already presupposing the prominence of Pharisaic Judaism,[88] Matthew reflects on the Jewish War from a considerable historical distance. Without looking backwards, he merely mentions

---

[86] Cf. Hengel, ibid., 316 n. 753.

[87] According to Josephus, *War* 4:333–334, a Zechariah ben Bareis was killed by the Zealots in 68/9 CE. It is probably that this incident is alluded to in Matt 23:35. Cf. Döpp, *Die Deutung der Zerstörung*, 22–23.

[88] Cf. Matt 23:1–12 and, especially, the stereotyped address in Matthew 23: "woe to you, scribes and Pharisees…." Cf. H.-J. Becker, *Auf der Kathedra des Mose: Rabbinisch-theologisches Denken und antirabbinische Polemik in Matt. 23,1–12* (Berlin, 1990).

the destruction of the city and the Temple as a divine act of judgment, while focusing much more on controversies with his Jewish
contemporaries. But whereas the issue of the law is heavily debated,
the destruction of the Temple and its cult seem to be no reason for
lamentation for Matthew's (still Jewish) "Christian" community.

Concerning the reasons for this stance, we can only speculate. There
was some geographical distance from Jerusalem, but even in Antioch the Jews were probably not unaffected by the destruction of the
Temple. Thus it seems that the Temple had ceased to be a significant factor for the religious identity of the Jewish-Christian groups
Matthew addressed. Did they have a closer connection with the
Temple as long as it existed? Or had they too dissociated themselves
from the Temple cult much earlier? There is no real basis for an answer
to these questions.

Things are different in Luke(-Acts), where the Temple is much more
prominent than in Mark and Matthew.[89] It is particularly important in
the Lukan birth stories, which reflect a piety linked with the Temple
and the expectation of Israel's salvation:[90] Simeon and Anna are linked
with the Temple (Luke 2:27, 36–7), and the young Jesus debates with
the teachers in the Temple (Luke 2:46). In Luke's version of the trial,
correspondingly, Jesus answers the high priests that he was with them
daily in the Temple (Luke 22:53). The earliest community in Jerusalem
gathers in the Temple (Acts 2:46; 5:42), Peter and John go there for
prayer and proclamation (Acts 3), and Paul reports having received a
vision there (Acts 22:17). Finally, Paul is arrested there during his last
visit in Jerusalem (Acts 21:27–30). Thus, the Temple is closely linked
in Acts with the piety of the earliest community, although it is unclear
what this might mean for Luke's own addressees.

In Acts, the first Christian historian describes an idealized formative
period, but he is well aware that his addressees lived somewhere in the
Diaspora and that the sanctuary in Jerusalem no longer existed. Thus
the relevance of the Temple for Luke's readers should not be overesti-
mated. In Luke-Acts, the Jerusalem Temple is, rather, a narrative element that marks the continuity between the salvation history of Israel
and the new eschatological work of salvation. It helps to describe the

---

[89] On the Temple in Luke, see further H. Ganser-Kerperin, *Das Zeugnis des Tempels: Studien zur Bedeutung des Tempelmotivs im lukanischen Doppelwerk* (Münster,
2000).

[90] Cf. Luke 1:9.

Jewish roots of Christian identity and to explain the dissociation of the Christian and the Jewish communities that the author observed in his time.[91] Luke's story of Jesus and his account of the earliest community are firmly linked with the history and the expectations of Israel (cf. Luke 2:29–32), and even the new community of Jesus-followers starts from the Temple; but the Temple is also the place of the conflict where Paul has to face open aggression (Acts 21:27–30). The closing of the doors of the Temple (Acts 21:30) signifies the Jews' definitive refusal to accept the new message.[92]

The destruction of the Temple is referred to more precisely than in Matthew. In the context of the "cleansing" of the Temple, Luke inserts a passage that describes the events of the Jewish War more extensively and more accurately than any other passage in the New Testament: "For the days shall come upon you, when your enemies will cast up a bank about you and surround you, and hem you in on every side, and dash you to the ground, you and your children within you, and they will not leave one stone upon another in you; because you did not know the time of your visitation" (Luke 19:43–44). In this passage, the author "clearly alludes to the Roman *circumvallatio* in the siege of the city and depicts its complete destruction and the sorry fate of its population."[93]

In the eschatological discourse, Luke avoids the Danielic term "desolating sacrilege" but mentions again the encirclement of Jerusalem by the Roman army as the sign of imminent devastation (Luke 21:20–21). Whereas Mark (followed by Matthew) had phrased the expectation of the appearance of the eschatological enemy of God, Luke "depicts in a very concrete way the real situation in the Jewish mother country immediately before the siege and capture of Jerusalem."[94] A few verses later, there is again a very clear picture of what had happened in 70 CE (Luke 21:24): "And they will fall by the edge of the sword, and be led captive among all nations; and Jerusalem will be trodden down by the Gentiles, until the times of the Gentiles are fulfilled." The Son of Man is expected only after the fulfillment of the καιροὶ ἐθνῶν,

---

[91] Cf. Ganser-Kerperin, *Zeugnis*, 375.

[92] Cf. also Acts 22:22–23; 28:24–25.

[93] Hengel, *Four Gospels*, 313 n. 728. The logion of the stones crying in the preceding passage (Luke 19:40) might also refer to the ruins of the city (ibid., 190), but it could already be derived from prophecy after 586 BCE (e.g., Jeremiah).

[94] Ibid., 190.

the times[95] of the Gentiles, thus the eschatological expectation is rather open-ended.

In contrast to the heated tone of expectation in Mark, Luke's attempt to calm down any kind of time calculation might be viewed as a reaction to the apocalyptic movements active during and stimulated by the Jewish War. And, also in contrast to Mark, the announcement of destruction is not only part of an esoteric teaching for the disciples but is embedded into Jesus' public teaching in the Temple;[96] the awareness of the Destruction is not an eschatological mystery but openly pronounced and also linked with the event of Jesus' death.

But in this regard, Luke's explanation also differs widely from Matthew's. Although Luke blames the Jerusalemites for not knowing the time of their visitation (Luke 19:43), and thus interprets the Destruction as God's punishment (cf. Luke 13:35), he does so from a perspective of compassion and with the expression of mourning and grief (cf. Luke 23:28) for the fact that Israel did not recognize its salvation.[97]

Of all New Testament authors, Luke is the most concerned with the capture of Jerusalem, and he gives the most accurate and even compassionate account of the events. This suggests not only that he is still relatively close to these events, but also that he still felt affected. But the observation that in the report of the Destruction in Luke 19:43–44, the focus is more on the city of Jerusalem than on the Temple, suggests that the Temple and its cult should not be considered too central for the identity of his own readers. Wherever Luke's addressees can be located, they are somewhere in the Diaspora, and their situation, including the factors determining their identity, might have been quite similar to those of the addressees of the deuteropauline Epistles.

---

[95] Cf. ibid., 315 n. 739 on the Danielic background of the phrase, which could be also translated by "years of the Gentiles."

[96] The narrative setting for Luke 21 is provided in Luke 20:1.

[97] Cf. P. Dschulnigg, "Die Zerstörung des Tempels in den synoptischen Evangelien," in *Tempelkult und Tempelzerstörung (70 n. Chr.): Festschrift für Clemens Thoma* (ed. S. Lauer and H. Ernst; Vienna, 1994), 167–87 (esp. 176). Whether the Temple is also a symbol of hope for an eschatological restoration (thus, with reference to Acts 26 and 28:23–27, Ganser-Kerperin, *Zeugnis*, 375) may be left open here.

II. TEMPLE, CHRISTOLOGY, AND THE PARTING OF THE WAYS:
THE JOHANNINE COMMUNITY AS A TEST CASE

From here, we can now move on to the "Fourth Gospel" or, more broadly, to the Johannine corpus and the community or school which can be assumed to have produced the Gospel of John and the three Johannine Epistles.

In John, the Temple is mentioned almost as frequently as in Luke's gospel,[98] and temple imagery seems to be even more frequent. And like the readers of Luke, the Johannine school is located in the Diaspora in the period after the destruction of the Temple—which is also referred to in John (11:48). From the perspective of the foregoing sketch of the development of an early Christian identity in disregard of and at increasing distance from the Jerusalem Temple, we can now explore how the temple motif is used in John, how the identity of this particular community has been shaped and what factors have contributed to such an identity as separate from the local synagogue. This will help us assess whether and in what way the events of 70 CE had an impact on the identity and life of the Johannine community members.

1. A Few Introductory Issues

A few very brief remarks must suffice here to sketch the overall view of the Johannine literature presupposed in the following argument.[99]

a) Numerous elements of language and theology suggest that the gospel "according to John" and the three Epistles "of John" are closely connected; whereas the fifth "Johannine" writing, the Apocalypse or Revelation "of John," must be treated separately, because it was certainly not written by the same author and probably points to a different circle.[100]

b) In contrast to earlier research, scholars have become more cautious and reluctant regarding far-reaching theories on the composition and redaction of the gospel. Due to the remarkable uniformity

---

[98] In comparing these two gospels we may leave aside the Book of Acts.

[99] Cf. generally M. Hengel, *The Johannine Question* (London, 1989). Expanded German edition: M. Hengel, *Die johanneische Frage: Ein Lösungsversuch, mit einem Anhang zur Apokalypse von Jörg Frey* (Tübingen, 1993).

[100] On the complicated relationship see my essay, ibid., 326–429.

of the Johannine language,[101] none of the classical theories of sources and redactional additions is supported by clear philological observations. Instead, most of the hypotheses appear to be based largely on ideological criteria (*Tendenzkritik*) or dominated by the interpreter's view of the subject matter. According to a growing number of scholars, no earlier stratum or source apart from the Synoptic tradition can be firmly established; neither for the miracle stories, nor for the speeches of Jesus, nor for an independent account of the Passion.[102] The last chapter, John 21, is probably an addition of the editors (cf. John 21:24–25), but there are no compelling reasons to consider major portions of John 1:1–20:31 to be later redactional additions.[103] Thus, the work must primarily be interpreted as a compositional unity under cautious consideration of its historical and rhetorical context.

c) In view of the common language and style, the three Epistles and the gospel can be ascribed either to one single author or to different authors within a common milieu, group of communities, or "school."[104] Drawing on traditional material, including a particular school tradition (cf. 1 John 2:18, etc.) and apparently also including further discussions from within the "school," these writings reflect particular problems of an early Christian circle of communities. This is evident in the Epistles,

---

[101] Cf. Frey, *Eschatologie* 1:429–45; cf. also E. Ruckstuhl and P. Dschulnigg, *Stilkritik und Verfasserfrage im Johannesevangelium: Die johanneischen Sprachmerkmale auf dem Hintergrund des Neuen Testaments und des zeitgenössischen hellenistischen Schrifttums* (Freiburg [Switzerland] and Göttingen, 1991).

[102] Cf., e.g., U. Schnelle, *Einleitung in das Neue Testament* (6th ed.; Göttingen, 2007); and M. Lang, *Johannes und die Synoptiker* (Göttingen, 1999), who demonstrates that the Johannine account of the Passion can be totally explained on the basis of Mark and Luke.

[103] See for criticism of current redaction theories Frey, *Eschatologie* 1:266–97 and 365–87; and more recently J. Frey, "Grundfragen der Johannesinterpretation im Spektrum neuerer Gesamtdarstellungen," *TLZ* 133 (2008) 743–60.

[104] Thus U. Schnelle, *Einleitung*, 471–76; and, most influentially, R.E. Brown, *The Epistles of John* (New York, 1982), and idem, *The Community of the Beloved Disciple* (New York, 1979). On the Johannine school see R.A. Culpepper, *The Johannine School* (Missoula, Mont., 1975). The analogy of other ancient philosophical schools may be inappropriate at some points, cf. the criticism by C. Cebulj, "Johannesevangelium und Johannesbriefe," in *Schulen im Neuen Testament* (ed. T. Schmeller; Freiburg, 2001), 254–342. As a useful way of distinguishing between the different terms, it has been suggested that we view the "school" as the group of "theologizing" persons, preachers, and teachers dependent on the Johannine tradition or influenced by its formative tradition-bearers or witnesses, whereas "community" should include all circles or local communities under this influence (cf. U. Schnelle, *Das Evangelium nach Johannes* [Leipzig, 1998], 3: "Zur Gemeinde zählen alle joh. Christen, zur Schule hingegen nur die, die aktiv an der joh. Theologiebildung beteiligt waren").

where a particular crisis in the school, caused by the secession of some former members, is directly addressed, but it can also be assumed for the narrative communication of the Gospel.[105]

d) According to the traditional view, all four writings were composed and edited in Asia Minor, in or around Ephesus, and there is no compelling reason to distrust the tradition here.[106] This means that the Johannine writings were composed in an area of the Jewish Diaspora, and, most notably, also in a region where the mission of Paul had been effective. We can assume that the communities shaped by the Johannine school lived in the vicinity of the addressees of Revelation, and possibly also of other communities shaped by the Pauline or post-Pauline tradition, although there is no clear evidence in the New Testament writings of any interaction between these different groups.[107]

e) On the other hand, the Johannine school was not a closed "sectarian" circle unaware of other early Christian traditions. There is evidence that the author of the gospel knew and (critically) drew upon Mark and probably even Luke. The author or his circle are aware of Peter's martyrdom (John 21:18) and of the destruction of the Temple (John 11:48).

f) These observations, along with the fact that the theological language of the gospel and especially its developed Christology also point to the end of the first century, support the view that John was the last of the four canonical gospels to be written, around the end of the

---

[105] This does not preclude the notion, however, that the gospel was edited with a wider circle of readers in view, as especially Richard Bauckham has argued; see R. Bauckham, "For Whom were Gospels Written?" in *The Gospels for All Christians: Rethinking the Gospel Audiences* (ed. R. Bauckham; Edinburgh, 1998), 9–48.

[106] Although the earliest New Testament manuscript, a small papyrus fragment with parts from John 18 (John Rylands Library P52), was found in Egypt, there is no compelling reason to locate the gospel there. Scholars who thought of a Gnostic origin or influence favored Syria, where Gnosticism is said to have developed, but a Gnostic influence is in my view unlikely. The entire ancient tradition points to Asia Minor, where John (the apostle) was later highly esteemed as a hero of the local church. Although the author is most certainly not the apostle, the son of Zebedee, but rather another teacher, possibly with the same name, the testimony of Irenaeus and, already earlier, of Polycarp and Papias, confirms the view that the gospel was composed in Ephesus or nearby. Some of its traditions may point back to Palestine and to the time before 70 CE, but it is not possible to reconstruct a written source that could come from that region.

[107] Cf. P. Trebilco, *The Early Christians in Ephesus from Paul to Ignatius* (Tübingen, 2004).

first century CE.[108] At the least, we can say that all the writings from the Johannine School were composed after 70 CE, and that in spite of the traces of Palestinian Jewish tradition and a closer knowledge of Jerusalem evidenced by the gospel (which may point either to a particular tradition or to the background of the author himself), we have hardly any chance of getting back behind the post-70 period and the Diaspora context to an earlier period or situation of the Johannine communities.

g) Regardless of the details of their composition history, the writings of the Johannine corpus give evidence of a particular group identity. Elements of this identity include: the self-designation as "children of God" (John 1:12 etc.); belief in Jesus as the Messiah and Son of God or, quite remarkably, "the Son," but also an indebtedness to an authoritative leader figure; a particular "school" or community tradition (cf. 1 John 2:18) and a developed theological language; and an ethos of love and communal solidarity. Communal solidarity and a critical distance from the "world" of pagan cults[109] are elements in common with, and that might be adopted from, the Diaspora synagogue.

On the basis of such a brief characterization of this community, the issue now before us is whether, and to what degree, its identity and that of its members was still linked, not only with the Scriptures and the Jewish tradition, but also more directly with the Temple in Jerusalem, and what can be said about the foundation and development of this identity. For this purpose we must also take into account the mention of the Ἰουδαῖοι in the gospel; the textual hints pointing to conflict with the synagogue and the alleged expulsion of the Johannine community members; and the conflicts on developing Christology.

2. Explicit References to the Jerusalem Temple and Its Destruction[110]

In John, there are more references to the Jerusalem Temple than in the other gospels (with the exception of Luke), and the "narrative space" devoted to the Temple and Temple scenes is much more extensive. This may be explained by the number of festival journeys narrated

---

[108] This is in accordance with Irenaeus' view that John (in his view, the apostle, the son of Zebedee) lived in Ephesus until the time of the Emperor Trajan (98–117 CE).

[109] Cf. 1 John 5:21; 3 John 7.

[110] On the issue see generally A.J. Koestenberger, "The Destruction of the Second Temple and the Composition of the Fourth Gospel," in *Challenging Perspectives on the Gospel of John* (ed. J. Lierman; Tübingen, 2006), 69–108.

in this gospel. In Mark, the Temple is not mentioned before Jesus'
entry in Jerusalem, and the works of Luke and Matthew also follow
this pattern (with the notable exception of the scenes in Luke 2 and in
the temptation episode of Luke 4:9). John, however, follows a different temporal and spatial pattern. Here, the episode of the "cleansing"
of the Temple is programmatically placed at the beginning of Jesus'
ministry (John 2:14–22), and from that point, the narrative unfolds
with continuous reference to the Temple and the opponents of Jesus
in Jerusalem.

2.1. Jesus' Festival Journeys and the Narrative Relevance of the Temple

As a consequence of the "transfer" of the cleansing episode to the
beginning of the narrative, Jesus travels to Jerusalem for Passover twice
within three years (John 2:13; 12:1).[111] He goes there once for Sukkot
(John 7–8), and from that point he seems to stay in Jerusalem until
Hanukkah (John 10:22). There is mention of another unnamed feast
(5:1), possibly Shavuot,[112] and of two Sabbaths (5:10; 9:14, 16)—on
which Jesus engages in healing and thus arouses opposition to himself
due to his allegedly unlawful acts.

During Sukkot, Jesus extensively teaches in the Temple (John 7:14,
28; 8:20, 59; cf. 8:2), and on Hanukkah he is walking in Solomon's
porch (10:22). In Jerusalem, people can find him in the Temple
area, where he preaches and teaches (John 7:14), and he also "finds"
others there (John 5:14). In the trial he points to his public teaching "in
the synagogue and in the Temple where all the Jews come together"
(John 18:20). The Temple is the public space of the "Judeans" or—
since the term includes also the crowd in Galilee—the "Jews";[113] it is

---

[111] Between those two years, around the time of Passover, Jesus is said to be in
Galilee (John 6:4). However, the episode of John 6 is not precisely dated.

[112] Cf. R.E. Brown, *The Gospel according to John* (2 vols.; New York, 1966), 1:225,
who reasons that in John 5 the Torah is discussed. But a firm decision cannot be made,
and the vagueness might be deliberate.

[113] I am not convinced of the attempt to translate οἱ Ἰουδαῖοι by the simple geographic term "Judeans." For some interpreters this seems to be politically correct,
marking a difference from present time Jews, but philologically the translation is
very questionable. Cf. D.R. Schwartz, "'Judaean' or 'Jew'? How Should We Translate
Ioudaios in Josephus?" in Frey, Gripentrog, and Schwartz, *Jewish Identity*, 3–27. The
Galileans in John 6:41 and 6:52 cannot be called "Judeans" without difficulties, and
Jesus is, according to John 4:9, not a "Judean," but a Jew from Galilee.

the place which is quite normally used for teaching when Jesus is in Jerusalem.[114]

Thus, the Fourth Gospel conveys a relatively detailed image of the Jerusalem Temple and its celebrations. In a remark of "the Jews" there is even mention of the time taken to complete the "building" or renovation of the Herodian Temple (John 2:20). Such details suggest that the author drew on a larger tradition of reliable information, especially concerning Jerusalem and the situation there.[115]

In the Johannine narrative, the Temple becomes the starting point for the opposition against Jesus. Here, Jesus "provokes" the authorities by his rather violent "cleansing" act, and it is in the Temple district that the most polemical accusations are pronounced (John 8:44, 48). In addition to this, there is an extensive use of temple imagery which is metaphorically related to Christ or "his body" as temple (John 2:21), or, more broadly, with a new form of veneration of God "in Spirit and Truth" (John 4:23) that is to replace the older forms of veneration on Mt. Gerizim and also in Jerusalem. But apart from the metaphorical usage, the narrative relevance of the temple motif is obvious. The links with the Jewish festival calendar and the numerous encounters within the Temple precincts are remarkable in view of the limited space devoted to the Temple and the limited mention of the different Jewish festivals in the other gospels.

2.2. The Reference to the Destruction of the Temple and the Advice of Caiaphas

The author also indicates clearly that he is well aware the events of the year 70 CE. The destruction of the Temple is presupposed in the advice of Caiaphas in the passage on the assembly of the *synhedrion* (designated as "the high priests and Pharisees") in which the decision is made to put Jesus to death (John 11:47–53).[116]

---

[114] The synagogue meant in John 18:20 is probably that of Capernaum (cf. John 6:59).

[115] Cf. also the mention of Bethesda in John 5:2, and the more precise distinction between the parties in John's narrative about the trial of Jesus. See also M. Hengel, "Das Johannesevangelium als Quelle für die Geschichte des antiken Judentums," in idem, *Judaica, Hellenistica et Christiana: Kleine Schriften 2* (Tübingen, 1999), 293–334.

[116] According to John, it is not the cleansing of the Temple but the ultimate demonstration of Jesus' divine power, the resurrection of Lazarus, which provides the real reason that Jesus is finally put to death.

The episode is shaped in a deeply ironic literary design which calls for different levels of understanding:[117] The Jewish leaders gather after the resurrection of Lazarus, Jesus' greatest miracle or "sign." In face of the growing number of Jesus' followers, the leaders discuss the political consequences: "If we let him continue like this, all men will believe in him, *and the Romans will come and take away both our place and our nation*" (John 11:48: ἐλεύσονται οἱ Ῥωμαῖοι καὶ ἀροῦσιν ἡμῶν καὶ τὸν τόπον καὶ τὸ ἔθνος).The wording clearly suggests not only that the author knew what had happened in 70 CE, but that he presupposes that his readers in Asia Minor did also.[118] True, in the present narrative setting, this could only be phrased as a "prophecy." But the phrase precisely points to what had actually happened: The Jewish leaders lost control over the "place" (מקום) and their influence on the Jewish nation (here: ἔθνος) due to the "coming" of the Romans, but nevertheless they did not let Jesus continue.

A second statement from the leaders' discussion is quoted: the advice of Caiaphas, who is said to be the high priest "of that year" (John 11:51). The advice is repeated later (John 18:14) and thus emphasized, so that the readers are strongly called to look for a deeper meaning: Caiaphas asks the assembly to consider "that it is expedient for you that one man should die for the people, and that the whole nation should not perish" (John 11:50). On the surface level, this sounds as a cynical political calculation: Better one to die than the whole nation. However, the Johannine author stimulates his readers to consider a second level of meaning when he explains that Caiaphas "did not say this of himself; rather, he prophesied, for he was high priest in that year." Thus the readers are led to the christological and soteriological dimension of the saying. The high priest as the authority for validating sacrifices declares Jesus' death to be a vicarious self-sacrifice by which the nation should be saved and the scattered children of God should be brought together as one (11:52).[119]

---

[117] See my interpretation in Frey, "Heiden—Griechen—Gotteskinder."

[118] Cf. Walker, *Jesus and the Holy City*, 195. The indirect mode of reference is not an argument for a pre-70 dating of John, for it is the only possibility within the given narrative setting.

[119] This is the same literary device used when Pontius Pilate, as the Roman authority for legal judgment, declares three times that he cannot find any blame in Jesus. Jesus is not guilty, even though he is crucified, and this is confirmed by the supreme judge, just as the efficacy of Jesus' self-sacrifice is confirmed by the high priest.

Leaving aside for this moment the soteriological dimensions, we can see the deep and calculated irony of the saying: The leaders think that an extension of Jesus' ministry could lead to the intervention of the Romans and the destruction of the Temple. They consider Jesus politically dangerous—an idea which is strictly rejected later in the dialogue with Pilate (John 18:36). On the basis of their understanding of the situation and their fear for their own privileges, they see the need to arrest and hand over Jesus, even though—as Pilate later confirms—no political case can be made against him (John 18:38).

But in contrast to the view reported as that of the Jewish leaders, the author and his readers know that Jesus' earthly ministry was actually brought to an end, and that the destruction of the Temple had happened in spite of this. Caiaphas' reasoning is obviously wrong; the leaders are discredited as a cynical group of politicians who sacrifice an innocent life for no benefit. On the other hand, the Johannine readers are urged to see that there is another benefit to Jesus' death "for" the nation and the scattered children of God. But of course, Caiaphas and his colleagues remain unaware of this dimension.

In a remarkable difference from Matthew and also from Luke, the destruction of the Temple is not explained by the hostility of the Jewish leaders against Jesus, nor by the refusal of "the Jews" to accept Jesus' message and authority. Although John blames "the Jews" for their rejection of Jesus and for their hatred of the disciples, the destruction of the Temple is simply alluded to, not interpreted as a divine punishment. It is just an historical fact; but since John is less concerned with historical events than is Luke, for example, and rather focuses on the deeper soteriological meaning of the story, the hint at the destruction of the Temple is simply used in order to express the idea of Jesus' vicarious death "for" others and to illustrate the ignorance and cynicism of the leaders of the Jewish nation.

2.3. A New Temple Built by Jesus and Jesus as the New Temple: The Christological Application of the Temple Motif

From the passage discussed, it is quite clear that the author and his audience are well aware of the destruction of the Temple. Thus, the sanctuary as mentioned in the Johannine text represents a past and remote situation. It is part of the narrative world of Jesus and his followers in Jewish Palestine, which is, of course, distant from the world of the Johannine readers. What, then, is the relevance of the Temple or the temple motif for the readers of John?

Although the Johannine Jesus is seen remarkably often in Jerusalem and in the Temple district, there is no indication in the Johannine text that the same holds true for his post-Easter followers (as is reported of the early Jerusalem community in Acts), nor that the Johannine community or any members of it had visited the Temple or even participated in its cult in earlier times. This may be due to the particular perspective in John, where there is no effort to draw a "historical" picture of community beginnings, as especially Luke does, in Acts. But this factor is also significant for the meaning the Jerusalem Temple had for the gospel's addressees in the contemporary Johannine community. The sanctuary in Jerusalem is a past phenomenon; the Johannine Jesus already envisages the "hour" when worship in Jerusalem will cease (John 4:21)—yet that "hour" to come "is" already now. This may point to the situation of the community, in which the veneration of God in the Jerusalem Temple has already been replaced by universal veneration "in Spirit and truth" (John 4:23).

The Jerusalem Temple is an element of the narrative world in which Jesus lived and acted. As such, it is transported into the world of the readers, and within the Johannine narrative, the temple motif is used in various metaphorical dimensions:

a) The first and foremost of these dimensions is a christological one: Jesus is linked with the Temple as the place of God's presence on earth. This is already prepared in the prologue when it is said that the "Logos" "tabernacled among us" (John 1:14),[120] and also by the use of the Bethel imagery when it is said that the disciples shall see "the heaven open and angels of God ascending and descending upon the Son of Man" (John 1:51)—which hints at equating Jesus with the "house of God" (Gen 28:12, 17). The link between Jesus and the Temple is then explicitly established in the passage on the "cleansing" (John 2:14–16), which is programmatically placed at the beginning of Jesus' ministry. This passage is not only a sign that the conflict between Jesus and the authorities in Jerusalem overshadows his whole path; it is also a strong statement about Jesus *as* (the new) temple.

There are remarkable differences between the Johannine Temple "cleansing" episode and the Synoptic accounts.[121] In the Fourth Gospel,

---

[120] Thus the translation in C.S. Keener, *The Gospel of John: A Commentary* (2 vols.; Peabody, 2003), 1:408.

[121] John 2:13–17; cf. Mark11:15–17, par Matt 21:12–13 and Luke 19:45–46.

Jesus' action is described in a more violent manner. Only here is a whip mentioned, and Jesus not only overturns the moneychangers' tables (as in Mark and Matthew), but also pours out the vessels with the coins (John 2:15). More importantly, the "cleansing" scene is connected with the Temple logion known from Mark 14:58, which is adopted here in a modified form as Jesus' own interpretation of his action (John 2:19).[122] Thus, in contrast with the Synoptic tradition, the Temple action and the Temple logion are now unified in one composition.

The connection is subtle: The action is followed by a challenge from the Ἰουδαῖοι, who ask for a sign of authority (John 2:18).[123] Jesus replies with the Temple logion, which is presented here as an imperative: "Destroy this Temple, and in three days I will raise it up" (John 2:19); this pronouncement is then crudely misunderstood by the contemporaries, but remains enigmatic for the disciples as well (cf. John 2:22). Only the readers are told: "He was speaking of the temple of his body" (John 2:21).

The form of Jesus' saying with the remarkable imperative has caused some speculation about who was to destroy the Temple, and how actively this was to be done.[124] But the phrase should not be over-interpreted. The stress is clearly on the second part of the statement: "in three days I will raise it up."

Jesus' saying implies the idea of a "new" temple, different from the Herodian Temple, which is to be built by Jesus himself. But the precise reference is left open for the moment, and only explained for the readers in a narrative aside. However, such asides comprise one of the

---

[122] On the Temple action and the Temple logion in John see recently K.S. Fuglseth, *Johannine Sectarianism in Perspective: A Sociological, Historical, and Comparative Analysis of Temple and Social Relationships in the Gospel of John, Philo and Qumran* (Leiden, 2005), 117–76.

[123] Cf. Mark 11:27–28; Matt 21:23; Luke 20:2. There the groups are mentioned more precisely: The high priests, the scribes, and the elders ask Jesus by what authority he acts. But in contrast with the Synoptics (cf. Matt 16:4; Luke 11:29), the demand for a sign of authority is not plainly rejected in John (cf., however, John 4:48), probably due to the different connotations of the term "sign" (σημεῖον) in this text. From the context, it is suggested that Jesus' "building" of the "new" temple in three days, i.e., his resurrection, is the true sign of his power, which gives him also the right to "cleanse" the Temple.

[124] Is the form an imperative (cf. R. Bultmann, *Das Evangelium des Johannes* [Göttingen, 1941], 88 n. 4; with reference to Amos 4:4 and Isa 8:9–10) or an indicative, as a kind of prophecy ("you will destroy this Temple"; cf. W. Bauer, *Das Johannesevangelium* [3d ed.; Tübingen, 1933], 48, with reference to Isa. 37:30)? Cf. H. Thyen, *Das Johannesevangelium* (Tübingen, 2005), 177–78.

most significant literary features in John. They convey the clues for understanding the Johannine story in its intended meaning—that is, in the light of Jesus' death and resurrection. In listening to the explanations of the narrator, readers follow the insights of the "beloved disciple," who claims to be the most genuine interpreter of Jesus and who provides the true meaning of what he did and said: "He was speaking of the temple of his body."

With these explanatory asides, the author notes that the insight into the "real" meaning of Jesus' words, works, and fate was not given during the life of the earthly Jesus but only received through the disciples' post-Easter remembrance. The whole "Johannine view" of Jesus, Christology, and other concepts is linked with the "remembrance" of the disciples after Easter, or, in other words, with the explanatory and "remembering" work of the Spirit in the post-Easter community (John 14:26). Thus, the author shows an awareness that he is not simply narrating "events" from the time of the "historical" Jesus, but that he is deliberately adopting an interpretive viewpoint that stems from post-Easter times. Deviation from the older tradition and, of course, from historical "facts," is thus defended as legitimate, because these alternative interpretations developed under the guidance of the Spirit (cf. John 14:26; 16:13).[125]

Thus, in post-Easter times, the Johannine community seems to have considered Jesus' body as a "new temple" which in a certain manner replaced the Jerusalem Temple. However, the precise way in which Jesus was to function as a temple remains unclear,[126] nor can the imperative λύσατε be interpreted as a real call to actively destroy the physical Temple. Nonetheless, the reader gets the idea that the "first" Temple is to be replaced by a "new" one and that Jesus himself—already in his earthly appearance—is the "place" where God dwells and may be encountered. The body of Jesus is itself called a temple, and later it is said that "from his body rivers of living water shall flow" (John 7:38)—obviously an allusion to the Temple river of Ezekiel 47. The body of Jesus, or even more strongly, the body of the crucified and

---

[125] In my view, by these deliberate remarks on the "remembering" activity of the Spirit (cf. John 14:26) and the fundamental relevance of the disciples' remembering for their understanding, the author indicates an actual awareness of the fact that this logion was not spoken by the earthly Jesus but rather developed in the growing insights of the post-Easter community.

[126] Cf. also C.R. Koester, *Symbolism in the Fourth Gospel: Meaning, Mystery, Community* (Philadelphia, 1995), 82–85.

risen one, is the place where humans can find grace and communion with God.

Due to the Johannine emphasis on the physical, bodily reality of the incarnate one (cf. John 1:14), the function of the Temple as place of divine presence is particularly focused on Jesus' body (John 2:21; 7:38). In the Johannine perspective, this implies the body of the crucified and resurrected Jesus, as is demonstrated by the Thomas episode (John 20:24–29) where the resurrected one shows the wounds of his crucifixion, leading Thomas to the climactic confession "My Lord and my God!" (John 20:28). The one who sees him, sees the Father (John 14:7, 9), and the invisible God is made accessible through him (John 1:18). In the Johannine view, Jesus is the unique place of the divine revelation.[127] Contemplation of the image of the crucified one (which is compared to the image of the serpent in the wilderness)[128] is necessary to attain salvation (cf. John 19:36–37). In this respect, Jesus' body replaces the Temple as a place of God's presence and as a source of salvation.

2.4. *Further Metaphorical Applications of the Temple Motif in John*

Yet another christological use of the temple metaphor occurs in the "cleansing" pericope. More than in the Synoptics, the Temple appears to be one of the major concerns of Jesus in John's account of the episode. Whereas in Mark, Jesus comes to Jerusalem and looks around as if he had to get acquainted with everything, the Johannine Jesus is zealously engaged in favor of "the house of his father." The scriptural quotation in John 2:16, "do not make my Father's house a house of merchandise," claims not only close affinity with the Temple but also an intimate connection with God, including a unique power to define the Temple's function. This is further intensified by the quotation from Ps 69:10 in John 2:17: "Zeal for your house will consume me."[129] Jesus

---

[127] Cf. especially J. Rahner, *Er sprach aber vom Tempel seines Leibes: Jesus von Nazaret als Ort der Offenbarung Gottes im vierten Evangelium* (Bodenheim, 1998).

[128] Cf. John 3:14–15. On this episode, see J. Frey, "'Wie Mose die Schlange in der Wüste erhöht hat…': Zur frühjüdischen Deutung der 'ehernen Schlange' und ihrer christologischen Rezeption in Johannes 3,14f," in *Schriftauslegung im antiken Judentum und im Urchristentum* (ed. M. Hengel and H. Löhr; Tübingen, 1994), 153–205.

[129] In a characteristic modification of the LXX text, the quotation is transferred to the future tense. Thus, the psalm is not only referring prophetically to Jesus' time; in the view of the author it also refers to the later event of Jesus' death in which he will actually be consumed due to the "zeal" for God's house. This is the only reason

is depicted as "zealous" "for" (not against) God's house, which is, at least on the surface level, the Temple of Jerusalem, and in his Temple action he enacts his authority as the Son of the Father.

In the Johannine perspective, however, such "zeal" is not simply oriented towards the earthly Temple, let alone its purification or restoration; rather, it is oriented toward the "house of God" in a wider sense. And the idea that such "zeal" should "consume" Jesus (which is a hint at his death, as caused by the conflict with the authorities) points again to the soteriological dimension that through his death, the "zeal" will come to its completion. This, in turn, points to further ecclesiological and eschatological dimensions of the usage of the temple motif in John.

In the farewell discourses there is a remarkable saying about the many mansions in "my Father's house" (John 14:2–3). This saying probably adopts a tradition from the Johannine community in which the heavenly realm of God was viewed in terms of a heavenly temple or palace with many rooms or mansions.[130] The idea is linked with a parousia tradition comparable to 1 Thess 4:16–17, although the idea is much more focused in John. Rather than the apocalyptic imagery of the heavenly temple, the new communion of the disciples with Jesus is in view. They shall dwell where Jesus is (John 14:3); i.e., in the "house of the Father." Apocalyptic temple imagery, personalized eschatological expectation, and the idea of the post-Easter community are intensely connected here in order to provide comfort for the disciples in their distress about the farewell of Jesus, or later, his absence.

In the discourse of John 14, this apocalyptic tradition is further interpreted: The disciples shall not only be where Jesus is, they are already now "in Jesus" (John 14:20), yet Jesus and the Father will dwell "in" those who love him (John 14:23). This mutual interiority shows a widening of the temple motif. Now, the Temple is not only related to Jesus' body (i.e., to Christology) and to the expectation of a heavenly abode (i.e., to eschatology), but also to the community of believers who are "in" Jesus and who also experience the "indwelling" of God and Jesus. The *Shekhinah* motif from John 1:14 is intensified here, and

---

why the tense is changed from the aorist to the future tense. Cf. Frey, *Eschatologie* 2:71–73.

[130] On this saying and its background in the apocalyptic tradition see Frey, *Eschatologie* 3:134–48. Cf. also G. McCaffrey, *The House with Many Rooms: The Temple Theme of Jn 14:2–3* (Rome, 1988).

the disciples who love Jesus and listen to his words are themselves made a place of God's dwelling.

Thus, the reference of the temple motif shifts from Jesus to the community:[131] The disciples shall dwell in the house of the Father, i.e., belong to the new temple or even form a new temple where God dwells. As already in Paul, the community and its individual members are metaphorically addressed as a kind of "temple."

Such a complex imaginative world is typical for John's gospel, where metaphorical networks are created and developed in which the readers can dwell and move.[132] The extensive use of temple imagery in John is not only superficially generated by the number of Jewish feasts narrated in John but strongly motivated by the theological interest in depicting Jesus as the fulfillment of a large number of Jewish eschatological expectations. Temple imagery is used to express the christological idea of God's revelatory presence in Jesus (cf. John 14:7, 9), but it is also used to designate the community of disciples. In all these references, the application of the temple motif is far removed from the concrete Temple in Jerusalem and from any idea of participation in its cult.

Although John mentions numerous "historical" features of the Jerusalem Temple (cf. John 2:20), the link between the author or his addressees and the past phenomenon of the Temple in Jerusalem is rather loose and is getting even looser. This is most clearly visible in John 4, when Jesus tells the Samaritan woman, in an explicit distancing from the sanctuaries on Mt. Gerizim and in Jerusalem: "But the hour is coming, and now is, when the true worshipers will worship the Father in spirit and truth, for such the Father seeks to worship him" (John 4:23). Although Jesus clearly takes the Jewish perspective over

---

[131] This is the main thesis of the work of M.L. Coloe, *God Dwells in Us: Temple Symbolism in the Fourth Gospel* (Collegeville, Minn., 2001). Cf. p. 3: "The Temple functions in the narrative as the major christological symbol that gradually shifts its symbolic meaning from the person of Jesus to the Johannine community in the post-resurrection era. In the time of Jesus' ministry, he is the focus of the cultic imagery of Temple and Tabernacle.... Within the narrative there are indications that what is said of Jesus, will, in a future time, apply to the community of believers."

[132] On the metaphorical networks cf. esp. J.G. van der Watt, *Family of the King: Dynamics of Metaphor in the Gospel according to John* (Leiden, 2000); on imaginative language in John see comprehensively R. Zimmermann, *Christologie der Bilder im Johannesevangelium: Die Christopoetik des vierten Evangeliums unter besonderer Berücksichtigung von Joh 10* (Tübingen, 2004); idem, "Imagery in John: Opening up Paths into the Tangled Thicket of John's Figurative World," in *Imagery in the Gospel of John: Terms, Forms, Themes, and Theology of Johannine Figurative Language* (ed. J. Frey, J.G. van der Watt, and R. Zimmermann; Tübingen, 2006), 1–43.

against the Samaritans (John 4:22: "we worship what we know"), even the Jewish place of worship is eschatologically devaluated by reference to the adoration "in spirit and truth." Yet the time of that adoration is said to be coming, and in fact, already to be here, i.e., because of the presence of Jesus. It follows that for those who adore the Father in spirit and truth by believing in Jesus (cf. John 14:1), the Temple has no real function any more.

This is confirmed by the observation that, within the Gospel narrative, Jesus' glory "is never experienced in the Temple,"[133] and on the other hand "those who respond to Jesus in faith do so outside of the Temple."[134] This is true for the post-Easter community—regardless of the existence or nonexistence of the Temple cult. In this respect, the events of the year 70 CE are not a watershed for Johannine theology.

However, this does not preclude the possibility that the destruction of the Temple as a historical event might have influenced the historical development of Johannine theology and thus—at least indirectly—the identity of the community members. Therefore, we have to look at the process of the "Parting of the Ways" as visible behind the Johannine texts.

3. Anti-Jewish Polemic: The Word ἀποσυναγωγός and Its Explanations

The clue to this process is the development hidden behind the remarkable word ἀποσυναγωγός in John 9:22, 12:42, and 16:2: the separation between the Johannine group of (Jewish) Christians and the local synagogue. To investigate this development, we have also to look at the image of "the Jews" in John and to consider the "dark" side of the gospel: the rather stereotyped polemics against "the Jews."

3.1. The Image of the Ἰουδαῖοι in John

It is a striking feature of the Gospel of John that it contains some of the most hostile anti-Jewish polemics in the New Testament.[135] The

---

[133] Cf. A.R. Kerr, *The Temple of Jesus' Body: The Temple Theme in the Gospel of John* (Sheffield, 2002), 5; with reference to J. Lieu, "Temple and Synagogue in John," *NTS* 45 (1999): 51–69.

[134] Kerr, *Temple*, 6.

[135] On this, cf. the volume *Anti-Judaism and the Fourth Gospel* (ed. R. Bieringer, D. Pollefeyt and F. Vandecasteele-Vanneuville; Louisville, 2001); also T. Nicklas, *Ablösung und Verstrickung: "Juden" und Jüngergestalten als Charaktere der erzählten*

polemical force is particularly strengthened by the fact that John mentions the Ἰουδαῖοι in a more uniform and stereotyped manner than Mark and Luke. Comparable with Matthew and his polemics against the Pharisees and Scribes, John seems to presuppose a process of stereotyping and a greater distance from the time of the events narrated. Only in the Passion narrative do we find a more variegated picture of the crowd, the "high priests" and their servants, and here we may assume that John draws on more accurate knowledge of the historical situation in Jesus' time.[136] But in most of the other parts of John, especially in the account of the public ministry of Jesus, the stereotyped use of οἱ Ἰουδαῖοι evokes the impression of a uniform and monolithically hostile group.[137]

Of course, there are also positive mentions of Ἰουδαῖοι.[138] Jesus himself is explicitly called a Ἰουδαῖος (John 4:9), and salvation, therefore, comes "from the Ἰουδαῖοι" (John 4:22).There are also sympathizers of Jesus among the Ἰουδαῖοι,[139] so that they cannot be viewed as a uniform group.

A number of passages use the term Ἰουδαῖοι in a more neutral manner.[140] But in the perspective taken by the evangelist, these Jews seem to be viewed at least from some distance. Their customs are explained as if they are unfamiliar (John 2:6, 13; 4:9 etc.), and their

---

Welt des Johannesevangeliums und ihre Wirkung auf den impliziten Leser (Frankfurt, 2001); R. Hakola, *Identity Matters: John, the Jews and Jewishness* (Leiden, 2005); L. Kierspel, *The Jews and the World in the Fourth Gospel* (Tübingen, 2006). Cf. also J. Frey, "Das Bild 'der Juden' im Johannesevangelium und die Geschichte der johanneischen Gemeinde," in *Israel und seine Heilstraditionen im Johannesevangelium: Festgabe für Johannes Beutler zum 70. Geburtstag* (ed. M. Labahn, K. Scholtissek, and A. Strotmann; Paderborn, 2004), 33–53. An expanded version of the latter is about to appear in idem, *Die Herrlichkeit des Gekreuzigten: Studien zum Johannesevangelium* (ed. J. Schlegel; Tübingen, 2011).

[136] See M. Hengel, "Das Johannesevangelium als Quelle für die Geschichte des antiken Judentums."

[137] On the translation of the term, see above, n. 113. Although the term sometimes refers also (geographically) to "Judeans," it is not possible to translate it consistently by that term. Especially with its symbolic overtones, the referent of the polemics is "the Jews" as a religious group that is not defined simply by a geographical location.

[138] Cf. John 4:9a, 22; 10:19; 11:19, 31, 33, 36, 45; 12:9, 11; 18:33, 39; 19:3, 19, 21 (2x).

[139] Cf. John 3:1; 8:31; 11:45; 12:11; 19:38; cf. 7:31; 10:19–21.

[140] Cf. John 2:6, 13; 3:1, 22; 4:9b; 5:1; 6:4; 7:2, 15, 22, 35; 8:22, 31;10:19; 11:55; 13:33; 18:12, 14, 20; 19:20, 21, 40, 42, although in some of these passages the context endows the reference with a negative connotation (cf. John 8:31 with 8:48–59; 10:19 with 10:24, 31).

feasts are mentioned as "feasts of the Jews" (John 5:1; 6:4 etc.). Even Jesus, when disputing with his contemporaries, speaks of "your law" (John 8:17; 10:34; cf. 15:25), as if he were himself excluded from the people addressed by the Jewish law.

In many passages, however, the term is used in the sense of a hostile group and burdened with strong polemical connotations. The opposition is already indicated in the first passage of the narrative when the Jews from Jerusalem send priests and Levites to ask the Baptist about his identity (John 1:19). With the cleansing of the Temple (John 2:13–22), the conflict is inaugurated, and Jerusalem is marked as the place where Jesus meets rejection. After the conversation with Nicodemus, who fails to understand Jesus (John 3:10), and the Samaritan episode (John 4:1–42), the narrative dynamic unfolds from chapters 5 to 12: Because of his unlawful action on the Sabbath, the Ἰουδαῖοι persecute Jesus (5:16) and seek to kill him (John 5:18).[141] The debates about his authority and his Messianic identity become increasingly polemical: the Ἰουδαῖοι call Jesus a demonized Samaritan (John 8:48), and he, for his part, questions their true descent from Abraham and calls them "children of the devil," who do the deeds of their father, the devil (John 8:44). This is the peak of the anti-Jewish polemic in John. The conflict comes to a final stage when the leaders decide to put Jesus to death (John 11:53). Accordingly, there are no real legal proceedings in the Passion story; after a single, final inquiry (John 18:19–28), without any new results or decisions,[142] Jesus is handed over to Pilate, accused of being a politically dangerous messianic pretender.

As the differences from the Synoptic accounts and the uniform use of the terms suggest, the Johannine image of "the Jews" and their narrative role is mostly the work of the evangelist and not a representation of historical realities in the time of Jesus. There is, however, lively debate concerning the extent to which the conflict narrated represents the situation at the time of the composition of the gospel, or whether it rather mirrors earlier stages of the community's history.[143]

---

[141] Cf. also John 7:1, 19; 8:22–24, 59; 10: 31, 33; 11:8.

[142] This is a conspicuous difference from Mark, where the decision is made in the final session of the *synhedrion*, and Jesus is sentenced to death because of blasphemy (John 14:62).

[143] On this, see more extensively my article "Das Bild 'der Juden.'"

The question can only be answered in view of the inner dramatics of the text, in which context the use of this term must be understood as a narrative device. Notably, the term "the Jews" does not occur in the prologue, nor (except marginally)[144] in the farewell discourses, nor in the Johannine Epistles. In all these passages another term takes the place of the opposing faction: "the world" (ὁ κόσμος), which is deployed with a very similar distribution of some uses that are positive,[145] some that are neutral, and a majority that are negative. This raises the question of how "the Jews" and "the world" are related to each other. Do "the Ἰουδαῖοι" just represent the unbelieving world, as some interpreters have suggested?[146] Such an interpretation treats "the Jews" merely as symbolic figures and seems to neglect the historical circumstances behind the Johannine text.

3.2. *The Word ἀποσυνάγωγος and Its Interpretation*
A usual point of departure for this inquiry is the Greek word ἀποσυνάγωγος ("excluded from the synagogue"). The three occurrences of the word in John mark its first documented appearance in Greek, a fact which may point to the significance of the events to which it points in the life of the Johannine community. In John 9:22 it is said that, "the Jews had agreed that anyone who confessed Jesus to be the Messiah would be put out of the synagogue"; in 12:42 there is mention of some Jews,[147] "even of the authorities," who "believed in him, but because of the Pharisees they did not confess it, for fear that they would be put out of the synagogue"; and finally in 16:2, in the farewell discourses, the disciples are told: "They will put you out of the synagogues. Indeed, an hour is coming when those who kill you will think that by doing so they are offering worship to God."

All three passages seem to point to a deliberate expulsion from some Jewish community. According to John, this situation is foretold by Jesus (John 16:2–3), but in the world of the narrative it is the

---

[144] John 13:33 is simply a link back to earlier passages. John 16:2–3 obviously refers to Jewish (synagogal) opponents, but interestingly the term Ἰουδαῖοι is not used.

[145] John 3:16; 4:42: the Savior of the world. On the analogy between οἱ Ἰουδαῖοι and ὁ κόσμος see Kierspel, *Jews, passim*.

[146] Cf. the classical statement in R. Bultmann, *Evangelium*, 59; E. Grässer, "Die Juden als Teufelssöhne in Joh 8,37–47," in *Antijudaismus im Neuen Testament*? (ed. W. Eckert, N. Levinson, and M. Stöhr; München, 1967), 157–70 (esp. 170).

[147] Notably, the word Ἰουδαῖοι is not mentioned here.

reason why some fellow Jews do not openly confess their faith in Jesus (John 12:42). John 16:2 even mentions further violence against the disciples, and it is suggested in this passage that such violence originates from synagogue groups or authorities. But the precise background of and reasons for that "expulsion," which might in some way provide an explanation for the Johannine polemics against the "Jews," are a matter of ongoing dispute.

Obviously these passages address, not the time or situation of Jesus, but rather the circumstances and experiences of the later community. It is, however, difficult to get back from the text and its narrative world to a particular historical situation. Such an inquiry poses numerous methodological problems due to the literary design of the Johannine text, which, as I have noted, is a deliberate retelling of the story of Jesus from the retrospective viewpoint of the later community.[148] Thus, the "horizon" of the time of the story told and the "horizon" of the reading community are deliberately blended so that the readers will find themselves in the image of the disciples, and the insights of Johannine theology are already uttered by the Johannine Jesus. The narrative and discourses in John, therefore, provide a "sandwich" of different levels: the level of the story of Jesus acting in Galilee and Judea and disputing with Jewish contemporaries (especially in John 5–12), and the level of the Johannine community at a later time, which is in conflict with contemporary Jews, and perhaps also with other, non-Jewish groups. It is almost impossible to separate these levels and to decide which elements of the text refer to the level of the community of addressees and which elements refer instead to another level of the tradition or even to the history of Jesus.

Different scholarly suggestions have been made regarding the historical setting of the text in order to explain the text in its present form—and especially its anti-Jewish polemics—on the basis of a tragic divide wherein the Johannine community was expelled or separated itself from the local synagogue.

---

[148] On the Johannine retrospective and the concept of the "blending of horizons," cf. Frey, *Eschatologie*, 2:247–61.

3.3. *Scholarly Theories of the History of the Johannine Community*

a) Most influential has been the reading presented by J. Louis Martyn.[149] According to him, John is "two-level drama,"[150] a simultaneous play on two stages.[151] Taking the story of the healing of the man born blind in John 9 as paradigmatic, Martyn suggests that this story tells not only how Jesus healed a blind man, but at the same time, how in the later community a blind man is healed by a Christian charismatic, confesses belief in Jesus, and is then expelled from the synagogue by "the Jews" because of this confession. Martyn suggests that in this chapter, "the Jews" or the "the Pharisees," investigating charges against Jesus and the blind man, represent synagogue authorities, as is only conceivable in the time after the destruction of the Temple and the Pharisaic restitution of the Jewish community. Thus he concludes that the term ἀποσυνάγωγος points to the situation of the expulsion of "heretics" from the Syngogue after 70, especially following the formulation of the *Birkat ha-Minim*, which (in theory) made it impossible for such groups to continue to participate in synagogue prayers.[152] On the basis of such a historical situation, Martyn explains the development of the anti-Jewish polemics in John. According to him, members of the community who had recently been expelled from the synagogue reacted with fierce accusations against "the Jews." But in the writing of the gospel, these anti-Jewish polemics, originally rooted in a particular post-70 CE conflict, were transferred into the narrative of Jesus' time and even put on Jesus' lips.

Martyn's reading provides a conceivable explanation of the polemical tone and also some kind of excuse for it, insofar as it thus originates in a situation of rejection or even traumatization of former Jewish Jesus-followers who were expelled from the synagogue because of their belief in Jesus.

---

[149] J.L. Martyn, *History and Theology in the Fourth Gospel* (2d ed.; Nashville, 1979; 1st ed. 1968); cf. D.M. Smith, "The Contribution of J. Louis Martyn to the Understanding of the Gospel of John," in *The Conversation Continues: Studies in Paul and John in Honor of J. Louis Martyn* (ed. R.T. Fortna and B.R. Gaventa; Nashville, 1990), 275–94.

[150] Martyn, *History and Theology*, 62, 129.

[151] Martyn, ibid., 37.

[152] Martyn also considers earlier conflicts between the synagogue and the early Christian community (e.g., Acts 18–19), but assumes that the formal separation only could happen as a consequence of the curse on the heretics (*History and Theology*, 48–66).

Building upon this reading, Martyn developed a view of the history of the Johannine community.[153] Founded by Jewish-Christian missionaries, it was at first part of a synagogue community (first stage). But when messengers from Palestine brought the wording of the *Birkat ha-Minim*,[154] the followers of Jesus were marked off and formed a separate Jewish-Christian group (second stage). The number of people being converted declined but did not stop, but followers of Jesus were not able to confess openly because of the threat of being excluded (third stage). From John 16:2–3, Martyn further concludes that the leaders of the synagogue finally threatened converts with death (fourth stage).

In this reading, the Johannine text is read as a true image of later contemporary situations and processes. Not only synagogue institutions and Christian theological convictions, but even the healing of the blind man, are read as part of the world of the Johannine community. In a second step, the data are then combined into a history of the "parting of the ways" between the synagogue and the developing Johannine community. From a methodological point of view, however, there are numerous questions against such a "mirror reading" of the text, one which takes into consideration neither the semantic autonomy of the narrative nor its inner dramatic movement.[155]

b) Adopting the *Birkat ha-Minim* hypothesis, Klaus Wengst[156] tried to locate the Johannine community in an area where he thought that synagogal authorities might have had the right to impose death penalties on community members.[157] Thus he suggested that the Fourth Gospel was composed in the realm of Agrippa II, in the regions of

---

[153] J.L. Martyn, "Glimpses into the History of the Johannine Community," in *L'Évangile de Jean* (ed. M. de Jonge; Leuven, 1977), 149–75.

[154] Martyn even speculates that reports from the local authorities of the synagogue might have influenced the decisions of Rabban Gamliel II at Yavneh to phrase or expand the *Birkat ha-Minim* and to use it as an instrument to identify Christians and other heretics (*History and Theology*, 65–66).

[155] Cf. the criticism by R. Kysar, "The Expulsion from the Synagogue: The Tale of a Theory," in idem, *Voyages with John* (Waco, Tex., 2005), 237–45.

[156] K. Wengst, *Bedrängte Gemeinde und verherrlichter Christus: Der historische Ort des Johannesevangeliums als Schlüssel zu seiner Interpretation* (Neukirchen-Vluyn, 1981). Cf. the third edition with a new subtitle: *Bedrängte Gemeinde und verherrlichter Christus: Ein Versuch über das Johannesevangelium* (München, 1990).

[157] Based on John 12:42, etc., Wengst even assumes a composition of the gospel (without John 21) before the reformulation of the *Birkat ha-Minim*, because he thinks that sympathizers, as mentioned here, cannot be imagined at a later juncture.

Batanaea and Trachonitis. One side effect of Wengst's theory was that he could now read the gospel totally within a Jewish context.[158]

The suggestion, however, is not very plausible. Even in the reign of Agrippa II, it is very improbable that synagogue authorities had the right to impose and carry out death penalties.[159] But there are two more general problems with the explanations mentioned.

The first problem is that the link between the expulsion from the synagogue as mirrored in the use of ἀποσυνάγωγος, on the one hand, and the decisions of the rabbis of Yavneh, on the other, has been strongly questioned in subsequent scholarship.[160] First, the construction of the so-called "synod of Yavneh"[161] coalesces various decisions made between the first and the second Jewish War into a single event, inspired by an anachronistic pattern ("synod") from church history. Second, the expansion of the curse on the heretics in the Eighteen Benedictions[162] was certainly not intended as an instrument to keep Jewish Christians away from the synagogue, but simply as a prayer for liberation from the oppressors and for the destruction of the heretics.[163] Furthermore, the expansion of the "curse" on the *minim* was hardly aimed at Jewish Christians, at least not in its earliest form. Rather, it was aimed against apocalyptic groups and all those who were perceived as having caused the catastrophe of the Jewish War. It is probably only in later text forms that the *noṣerim*, the Jewish Christians,

---

[158] This hermeneutical interest is also retained in his later commentary on John, where, however, the historical thesis concerning the place of composition is practically abandoned. See K. Wengst, *Das Johannesevangelium* (2 vols.; Stuttgart, 2000–2001); cf. my critical review in *BZ* 43 (2002): 137–40.

[159] Cf. Hengel, *Die johanneische Frage*, 288–306, also Frey, "Heiden—Griechen—Gotteskinder," 213–37; idem, *Eschatologie* 2:295.

[160] Cf. G. Stemberger, "Die sogenannte 'Synode von Jabne' und das frühe Christentum," *Kairos* 19 (1977): 14–21; P. Schäfer, "Die sogenannte Synode von Jabne," in idem, *Studien zur Geschichte und Theologie des rabbinischen Judentums* (Leiden, 1978), 45–64; R. Kimelman, "Birkat Ha-Minim and the Lack of Evidence for an Anti-Christian Jewish Prayer in Late Antiquity," in *Jewish and Christian Self-Definition* (ed. E.P. Sanders, A.I. Baumgarten, and A. Mendelson; London, 1981), 2:226–44; S.T. Katz, "Issues in the Separation of Judaism and Christianity after 70 C.E.: A Reconsideration," *JBL* 103 (1984): 43–76; W. Horbury, "The Benediction of the Minim and Early Jewish-Christian Controversy," in idem, *Jews and Christians in Contact and Controversy* (Edinburgh, 1998), 67–110.

[161] Cf. the works by Stemberger and Schäfer (previous footnote).

[162] Cf. Schäfer, "Synode," 48–52. Cf. the account in *b. Ber.* 28b.

[163] Thus Schäfer, "Synode," 52, against the influential view of I. Elbogen, *Der jüdische Gottesdienst in seiner geschichtlichen Entwicklung* (3d ed.; Frankfurt, 1931), 37–38.

came to be mentioned explicitly.[164] Finally, it is totally unclear how quickly and how far the decisions of the rabbis in Yavneh became normative.[165] For the Diaspora, especially in Asia Minor, this is very improbable in the early period.[166]

The second problem is that the environment of the Johannine community was not so completely Jewish as Martyn and Wengst assume from the ἀποσυνάγωγος passages. The explanations of the Jewish customs (John 2:6; 4:9–10, etc.), and the distanced mention of Jewish feasts (John 2:13; 5:1; 6:4; 7:2; 11:55) and Jewish law (John 7:51; 8:17; 10:34; 12:34; 15:25; 18:31; 19:7), point in a different direction. If we further consider the "Greeks" who want to see Jesus (John 12:20–22; cf. 7:35) and who point towards the Gentile world that is to be drawn to belief in Jesus in the post-Easter era,[167] we get the impression that the addressees or the community are at the very least mixed, including both Jewish and Gentile Christians.

This is also confirmed by the mention of "scattered children of God" (John 11:51–52) who are to be brought together into a unity by the death of Jesus and of the "other sheep, not from this fold" (John 10:16), who are to become members of the one flock of the Good Shepherd. Thus, at least a part of the community of the writer seems to come from Gentile origins. They were not so well acquainted with Judaism, nor had they lived at any time according to Jewish law. Nor, accordingly, were they really affected by the separation of the Jewish Christians from the synagogue.

---

[164] Cf. Schäfer, "Synode," 51. It is, therefore, unclear on which texts or practices Justin bases his discussions of the "curse" (Justin, *Dial.* 16:93, 95, 108, 123, 133; cf. Horbury, "Benediction," 67).

[165] As G. Stemberger, "Jabne und der Kanon," in idem, *Studien zum rabbinischen Judentum* (Stuttgart, 1990), 375–89, states (388), the influence of the rabbis on the general Jewish population was rather limited during this period. This is, of course, a topic addressed by several of the studies in the present volume.

[166] *T. Meg.* 2:5 (ed. Lieberman, 349) mentions that R. Meir, when visiting Asia Minor, did not find a scroll of Esther. This indicates that practices standard among the rabbis may not have been recognized as normative there—all the more so in the late first century when John was composed, probably decades before R. Meir's trip. There has been some debate as to whether "Asia" in this text refers to Asia Minor, but that seems to remain the most probably identification; for a detailed defense of it, see B. Bar-Kochva, "Purim in the Second Temple Period and the Scroll of Esther in 'Asia': 'Historical Approach' and 'Orthodox History,'" *Sinai* 121 (1997/98) 55–70 (in Hebrew). I am grateful to Daniel R. Schwartz for this information.

[167] Cf. Frey, "Heiden—Griechen—Gotteskinder," *passim*.

c) This is taken into consideration in another influential reconstruction of the history of the Johannine community, by Raymond E. Brown.[168] With an awareness that the gospel shows traces of one conflict with "the Jews" and of another one with "the world," Brown took the narrative sequence in the gospel as the basis of his reconstruction. He assumed that after the dispute with the synagogue (as reflected in John 5–12) the community was in dispute with Gentile unbelief, as represented in the term "the world" (reflected in John 13–17).[169]

For Brown, this reconstruction is confirmed by the testimony of the Johannine Epistles, which he views as part of the later history of the Johannine community. As in the farewell discourses of the gospel, the Epistles, too, mention "the world" as the opposing faction, whereas "the Jews" are not mentioned at all. The conflict of which the Epistles give evidence seems to be not with "external" opponents, but rather with opponents from within the community itself. According to the most probable interpretation,[170] some former members broke off from the others, probably due to differences in their view of Christ (1 John 2:18–22; 4:2; 2 John 7).[171]

Regardless of how the compositional sequence between the gospel and the Epistles is viewed, however, there is evidence that the conflict with the synagogue resulting in the "expulsion" of the Jewish Christian members was followed by another conflict within the Johannine community. That second conflict seems to be closer to the time of composition of the Epistles and the edition of the gospel. At this time, the community was threatened by the separation of some possibly important members and, more generally, by the unbelief and the hatred of "the world" (as it is phrased in the Epistles and in the farewell discourse of the gospel). If this is true, the conflict with the synagogue, and the expulsion of Jewish-Christian members of the Johannine circle from

---

[168] Cf. his massive commentaries: Brown, *The Gospel according to John*; idem, *The Epistles of John*; idem, *The Community of the Beloved Disciple*.

[169] Thus Brown, *Community*, 63.

[170] There is a minority of scholars who interpret the formulae in 1 John differently and think that the secessionists were Jewish Christians who went back to the synagogue. Thus, e.g., H. Thyen, "Johannesbriefe," in *TRE* 17:186–200; idem, "Johannesevangelium," ibid., 200–225 (and again in his *Das Johannesevangelium*). If that reconstruction were accurate, we would expect some polemics against the synagogue or the Jews in 1 John—but, in fact, the Jews as opponents are totally absent.

[171] Cf. Hengel, *Die johanneische Frage*, 161–200.

the synagogue community, might have happened some years or even one or two decades earlier.

3.4. *Overlapping Conflicts in the Johannine Text*

In my view, not only the Epistles but also the gospel give evidence that this second conflict, the split in the Johannine community, had already happened. But whereas in the Epistles only the inner-Christian conflict is addressed, the gospel mentions the opposition of "the Jews" and of "the world." Thus different conflicts from the history of the community are fused in narrating the story of Jesus, and the literary design, with its blending of temporal horizons (see above n. 148), leads to some generalization of the dynamics of each.

Thus the basic narration of Jesus' encounter with his Jewish contemporaries is enriched by elements of later periods, including debates on the question of the Messiah which sound still rather inner-Jewish, and later debates on Christology. In the later situation of the community, the conflict between Jesus and his Jewish contemporaries is used as a paradigm for the conflict the word of God has to face when entering the world, a paradigm for the struggle between belief and unbelief. It is thus generalized, and so are "the Jews" as the opponents of Jesus. The opposition is further intensified by dualistic linguistic elements, such as the oppositions between light and darkness, truth and falsehood, life and death. Now the opponents ("the Jews" or "the World") are from below, whereas Jesus is from above. They represent darkness whereas he is the light of the world. This is the language which makes the Johannine text so dangerous and open for later use in anti-Jewish polemics.[172]

4. *The "Parting of the Ways" According to John and the Development of Identity in the Johannine Community*

How could the conflict with the synagogue have developed, and what were the factors that would have led to the expulsion or separation of the Jewish Christians from the synagogue? Without assuming an all-

---

[172] It should be noted, however, that the technique of generalization and the use of dualistic language affects not only the image of the Jews in John 5–12 but also the image of "the world" in the farewell discourses and that of the opponents in the Johannine Epistles.

too-closed community (and thus escaping the pitfalls of the so-called "community hypothesis"[173] as suggested by Martyn, Brown and others) we can at least identify some developments and factors.[174]

4.1. *The Debate on Christology*

In the christological debates of the Fourth Gospel, especially in John 7–8 and 10, there are traces of an inner-Jewish discussion on the identity and authority of Jesus. In this discussion, both sides draw on the Scriptures and on traditional views of the Messiah: Where is he to come from? What signs is he to do? And what do the Scriptures really say? There were Jews who believed in Jesus and others who were at least sympathizers. Those Jewish "Christians"—who should not yet be called "Johannine" Christians—shared the post-Easter belief in Jesus' resurrection or exaltation and viewed him as the true "king of Israel" (John 1:49), whereas the majority of their fellow Jews rejected the claim of his messianic authority. Both sides cited "Moses" or "the Scriptures" as their authority.[175] And even at a later stage of development, the Johannine argument is still strongly focused on the proof of Jesus' messianic identity from the Scriptures. These textual elements point back to an earlier inner-Jewish debate about Jesus and about the true way of Israel.

There is a discussion in scholarship as to whether the high Christology of the Johannine community, the view of Jesus as a divine being, developed only after the expulsion from the synagogue, as a kind of reaction to that expulsion,[176] or instead developed earlier, and thus contributed to the sharpening of the conflict.[177] Or in other words: Is the high Christology a non-Jewish, Gentile element which only developed in opposition to "the Jews," or could it have developed while the community was still within a Jewish context? In my view, the latter

---

[173] Cf. Kysar, "The Expulsion from the Synagogue"; also Koestenberger, "Destruction," in Lierman, *Challenging Perspectives*, 69–91 (esp. 72–78).

[174] See the more thorough discussion in my "Das Bild 'der Juden.'"

[175] For the Johannine view, cf. John 5:39, 44, and 10:34–36, where Moses and the Scriptures are invoked as the basis for the true understanding of Jesus' divine authority.

[176] Thus the suggestion by J.L. Martyn, *History and Theology*.

[177] Thus Brown, *Community*, 173 (against Martyn's proposal). However, Brown thinks that a second group of Jews and Samaritans, with a critical attitude towards the Temple, will have enhanced the christological development (ibid., 36–37).

is much more plausible, since most elements of Johannine Christology, including the titles (Messiah, Son of God, Son of Man, Logos), phrases ("I am"), and images (vine, shepherd, temple, etc.) used for Jesus, draw on the Scriptures and other Jewish tradition.

But the gospel also gives evidence for the problems caused by such a christological view. The adoration of Jesus could be considered a blasphemy at least by some fellow Jews, and this is confirmed by elements of the Johannine text: In John 5:18 "the Jews" infer that Jesus makes himself equal to God, and in John 10:33 they even *say* that he makes himself God; this is repeated in John 19:7 and linked with the sentence that Jesus has to die.

From these passages it can be concluded that at least some elements of the so-called "High Christology" in John should be assumed to account for the ultimate split between the synagogue and the Johannine Jewish Christians. Thus, this developing Christology might be one of the most important reasons for the expulsion of the Johannine Jewish Christians from the synagogue, as reflected in the unique use of the term ἀποσυνάγωγος in the Gospel of John.

For Jewish Christians, this would have meant a very stark change in their whole social life. Not only had they lost their social network, supply of food and all the other things of everyday life, but also the relative security and privileges granted to the Jews by the Roman emperors. When separated from the local synagogue they entered into a legal condition that was much less secure. Moreover, they had to redefine their identity, and probably the retelling of the story of Jesus and his disputes with his fellow Jews could help them define such an identity as one linked with the fate of Jesus.

At a distance from the synagogue, the Gentile Christian influence could further intensify. An increasing number of community members might now be unaware of Jewish customs and might never have observed the Jewish law. Such a mixed community is presupposed in the Johannine texts.

4.2. *Additional Factors: The Influence of the* Fiscus Iudaicus

But it would be too one-sided if we only considered the theological or christological motivations for the split. Most probably there were other factors from the social and political context that supported such a development.

With regard to Asia Minor one factor is often neglected:[178] the imposition of the *fiscus iudaicus* on all Jews in the Roman Empire. This was probably the most important effect of the Jewish War and the destruction of the Temple upon the well-established Jewish communities in Asia Minor.[179] Instead of the former tax of a *didrachmon* that had to be paid by men between 20 and 50 years old for the upkeep of the Temple of Jerusalem, now all Jews—men, women, and children, from age 3 to age 62—were required to pay the same amount for the temple of Jupiter Capitolinus in Rome. A special authority was established for collecting the tax and deciding on related matters. This meant that now, for the first time, Jews had to be registered as such, their names appearing in the appropriate tax lists.

It is quite conceivable that some Jews might have tried to go without paying the humiliating tax to the pagan deity. On the other hand, Suetonius reports that under Domitian the tax was collected with all rigor (*acerbissime*), both from those who had adopted a Jewish lifestyle (perhaps proselytes or also God-fearers) and from those who had denied their Jewish origin[180] (thus apostates, but perhaps also Jewish Christians).[181] In any case, there was a great uncertainty about who was liable to pay the tax and who was not, especially under Domitian, and the end of the situation was celebrated when Nerva became emperor.[182]

The new tax and the praxis of its collection had an important effect on the issue of who was considered a Jew.[183] Before that period,

---

[178] On the following see now the comprehensive work by M. Heemstra, *The Fiscus Judaicus and the Parting of the Ways* (Tübingen, 2010), see earlier P. Hirschberg, *Das eschatologische Israel: Untersuchungen zum Gottesvolkverständnis der Johannesoffenbarung* (Neukirchen-Vluyn, 1999).

[179] Cf. Hirschberg, *Israel*, 55–58. On the regulations see E.M. Smallwood, *The Jews Under Roman Rule* (Leiden 1981), 373.

[180] Suetonius, *Dom.* 12:2: *praeter ceteros Iudaicus fiscus acerbissime actus est; ad quem deferebantur, qui velut improfessi Iudaicam viverent vitam vel dissimulata origine imposita genti tributa non pependissent.*

[181] Koestenberger, "Destruction," 82.

[182] See Cassius Dio, *Roman History*, 68.1.2; also note the coins from the reign of Nerva with the text, *FISCI IUDAICI CALUMNIA SUBLATA*, H. Mattingly, *Coins of the Roman Empire in the British Museum* (London, 1963), 3:15 (No. 88) and 17 (No. 98).

[183] Cf. also M. Goodman, "Nerva, the Fiscus Judaicus and Jewish Identity," *JRS* 79 (1989): 40–44.

membership in a synagogue community was simply an issue of mutual agreement or of acceptance by the community. Now it became a matter of concern to the Roman administration as well. This could lead to a growing awareness of the special position of the Jews within the Roman Empire. But it could also affect and enhance the ongoing separation between the old and self-confident synagogues in Asia Minor and the originally Jewish but more and more Gentile Christian communities. Gentile Christians could point to the fact that they had never been Jewish, but Jewish Christians could also try to avoid paying the tax by distancing themselves from the local synagogue. The public suspicion against the Christians as a "new" religious group could also encourage the synagogue authorities to keep their distance from members who were inclined to follow such a suspicious teaching. Especially in the case of denunciations,[184] Christians, Jewish or Gentile, could come under increased pressure either to sacrifice to the Roman gods and the emperor, or to suffer persecution—as the letters of Pliny demonstrate for Bithynia in the beginning of the second century. Possibly they could even blame the synagogue for causing persecution or "offering worship to God" by doing so (John 16:2).

Of course, such a scenario cannot totally explain the split between the synagogue and the developing Christian communities, nor can it provide an excuse for the anti-Jewish polemics in John, or quite similarly, in Revelation (cf. Rev 2:9; 3:9). But in addition to the ideological reasons, especially the view of Christ and the issues of Jewish law, of circumcision and of purity, the social and political context could affect and stimulate the process of separation and thus produce a situation in which Jewish Christians might see themselves as expelled from the synagogue.

5. What, Then, was Decisive for the Identity of the Johannine Community?

It is obvious that these processes all contribute to the collective identity of the Johannine community. There is a collective memory of the dispute with the synagogue and of the so-called "expulsion," even though the precise history of that process of separation cannot be reconstructed in detail anymore. The process of separation as such

---

[184] Cf. Hirschberg, *Israel*, 99.

was probably enhanced by the destruction of the Temple in 70 CE. However, contrary to influential patterns in scholarship, an immediate influence of the so-called *Birkat ha-Minim* cannot be assumed. Rather, a political consequence, the imposition of the *fiscus iudaicus*, might have promoted a process of identity definition within or apart from local Jewish groups.

5.1. *The View of Christ and the Identity and Ethos of the Community*
The identity of the Johannine community and its members is primarily characterized by its faith in Christ, or—more precisely—by its distinctive view of Christ: a high Christology according to which Jesus is the eternal Word, God's unique Son and—even more—God (θεός: John 1:1, 18; 20:28). In a remarkable dialectic, the high Christology is linked with the idea that Jesus was sent from the Father; "came in the flesh" (1 John 4:3; cf. 2 John 7), i.e., assumed true humanity (cf. John 1:14); and was crucified, but "glorified" and "exalted" by the Father. In the Johannine Epistles, this Christology is used as a criterion for the true faith (which was not kept by the people who left the community according to 1 John 2:18–22 or 4:2–3).

In the gospel, the christological views and also the particular interpretation of Scripture are closely connected with a distinctive awareness of the Spirit or "Paraclete"[185] who is given to the community, actively supporting its testimony (John 15:26), strengthening its faith (John 16:7–11) and authorizing its testimony (John 20:23). The reference to the Spirit as source of "remembrance" (John 14:26) and of the disciples' post-Easter understanding (John 2:22; 12:16) points to the self-consciousness of the Johannine community as a community taught by God Himself (John 6:45).

The most important self-designation of the community members is "God's children" (John 1:12; cf. 3:3, 5 etc.; frequently in 1 John). Those who believe in Jesus are "born from above" (John 3:3). Their status as members of the "family of the king"[186] is rooted in the work of Jesus, or—more precisely—in his death and resurrection (cf. John 20:17). God is their father (John 20:23), they belong to the "household" of God

---

[185] Cf. the Paraclete sayings in John 14:16–7, 26; 15:26; 16:7–11, 13–15; see also John 20:22–23.

[186] Thus the title of van der Watt's study, *The Family of the King* (above n. 132).

(John 14:2), and community members can be called simply "brothers" (John 21:23). The "family of God" is viewed in opposition to any other family or affiliation.

Family metaphors also point to an important aspect of the ethos of the gospel.[187] Children do as their fathers do (cf. John 8:44), and actual behavior points to the identity or to the true origin of a person. Love is a sign of discipleship and points to affiliation with God, whereas hatred proves that someone actually belongs to darkness or to the devil (cf. 1 John 1:9; 3:7–12, 15). The Epistles show that such love has a practical dimension. Being brothers and sisters implies and demands mutual help and support, and the refusal of such support (cf. 1 John 3:17: "closing one's heart") is a violation of the love commandment, indeed—proof of "hatred" and of nonaffiliation.

These elements of the particular group ethos are also paralleled in Diaspora synagogues (and other ethnic and religious associations); together with the distance from pagan cults (cf. 1 John 5:21), such a group ethos of mutual solidarity and support may well be adopted from synagogal structures.[188]

But it is most remarkable that all the elements that make up the identity of Johannine community members as expressed in the Epistles are developed without reference to the Temple and also without explicit reference to "the Jews." Therefore one cannot say that their identity was primarily gained by separating themselves from a counterpart, although the memory of conflicts and disputes is alive in the Johannine narrative. It is rather positively constituted by a particular view of Jesus and faith in him, and the temple motif is mostly used to express the status of Jesus as the unique "place" of God's revelation and salvific presence and—dependent upon that—of the community as the "place" of God's indwelling in the world.

---

[187] On "ethos" cf. J.G. van der Watt, "Preface," in *Identity, Ethics and Ethos in the New Testament* (ed. J.G. van der Watt; Berlin and New York, 2006), vii; see also J. Frey, "'Ethical' Traditions, Family Ethos, and Love in Johannine Literature," in *Early Christian Ethics: Jewish and Hellenistic Contexts* (ed. J.W. van Henten and J. Verheyden; Leiden, 2011, *in press*).

[188] Cf. Frey, "'Ethical' Traditions."

5.2. Johannine Theology in Reaction to the Events of the Jewish War
Some elements of Johannine theology might be interpreted as a reaction not just to the destruction of the Temple but in some way to the Jewish War or the developments caused by the war:[189]

a) First, mention should be made of the obvious transformation of apocalyptic traditions in the Fourth Gospel. Although apocalyptic elements are not totally absent from the Fourth Gospel (and are even more visible in the Johannine Epistles),[190] those elements are strongly reinterpreted. There is no more any immediate interest in apocalyptic imagery or in the apocalyptic expectation as such, but all those traditional elements are now brought into a close relation with the view of Jesus or with the present of the community. As such they serve as a confirmation of Jesus' salvific authority and of the status of the community, and thus as an element of comfort for the readers in their situation of distress. As already in Luke, the apocalyptic tension is reduced, which may be an effect not only of the delay of the parousia (cf. John 16:16–19) but also of the turmoil in Palestine in the late sixties of the first century CE.

b) The reinterpretation of apocalyptic elements is closely linked with the distancing of Jesus "from a political construal of his messianic claims."[191] Of course, in the evangelist's view Jesus is not a messianic pretender, as "the Jews" think, but the true Messiah, the Son of God (John 20:30–31). But the concept of the Messiah is distanced from other current concepts of messianism in Second Temple times: It is decidedly nonpolitical and nonviolent. Jesus enters Jerusalem on a donkey (John 12:15) and rejects any kind of activism in defense

---

[189] Cf. Koestenberger, "Destruction," 85–92; but his heading, "John's Gospel as a Jewish Response to the Destruction of the Temple" is, in my view, overstated.

[190] Cf. Frey, *Eschatologie* 3:23–30, 68–70. In the Johannine writings, there are numerous elements from early Christian apocalyptic tradition, such as the expectation of the Parousia (cf. John 14:2–3; 16:16–19; see also John 21:22–23; 1 John 2:28); of eschatological judgment (1 John 4:17; cf. 2 John 8) and the resurrection of the dead (John 5:28–29; 6:39, 40, 44, 54); and of a transforming vision of God or Christ (1 John 3:1–2). In addition, elements of specifically Johannine Christology are plainly apocalyptic, such as the notion of the Son of Man as a heavenly being. See now B.E. Reynolds, *The Apocalyptic Son of Man in the Gospel of John* (Tübingen, 2008).

[191] Cf. Koestenberger, "Destruction," 86, with reference to E.W. Stegemann, "Zur Tempelreinigung im Johannesevangelium," in *Die Hebräische Bibel und ihre zweifache Nachgeschichte: Festschrift für Rolf Rendtorff zum 65. Geburtstag* (ed. E. Blum, C. Macholz, and E.W. Stegemann; Neukirchen-Vluyn, 1990), 503–16.

of himself (John 18:10–11). Although he is truly a king, and in his kingdom the kingdom of God is realized,[192] his kingdom is conceived of as a "spiritual" one which does not compete with the "kingdom" of the Roman emperor as represented by Pontius Pilate. Jesus' kingdom is "not of this world" (John 18:36); and the denunciation of "the Jews" against him, the idea that his royal claims could endanger Roman rule, is demonstrated to be false when Pilate himself attests to his innocence in political terms: "I find no guilt in him" (John 18:38; cf. 19:4).

J.A. Draper interprets John as an "introversionist response" to the failed millenarian hopes of the Jewish War.[193] This may be an over-statement, but it does point the correct direction. In a daring anal-ogy from church history, A.R. Kerr speaks of a "quietist eschatology,"[194] as opposed to any kind of "activist" eschatology. Although there may be a subtle antithesis between Jesus as king and the claims of the Roman emperor, which is expressed in the use of titles such as σωτήρ τοῦ κόσμου (John 4:42) or κύριος and θεός (John 20:28), the Gospel of John avoids any plain political antithesis. In this, John is in marked contrast to the Johannine Apocalypse (cf. Revelation 13 or Revelation 17).

c) Other aspects sometimes mentioned in this context are more questionable. And if Andreas Koestenberger[195] wants to read the gos-pel primarily against the background of the destruction of the Temple, he overstates the case. There is no clear evidence that the Johannine community mainly tried to answer "the agonizing problem of the post-70 period: how can we re-shape our lives without the Temple?"[196] As demonstrated above, this was not the main problem of early Chris-tian communities in the post-70 period. They lived in the Diaspora far from Jerusalem, had a considerable number of Gentile Christian mem-bers, and could draw on an earlier tradition in which the temple motif was already used metaphorically, e.g., to designate the community of

---

[192] Cf. Frey, *Eschatologie* 3:271–75; also M. Hengel, "The Kingdom of Christ in John," in idem, *Studies in Early Christology* (Edinburgh, 1995), 333–57.

[193] Quoted by Koestenberger, "Destruction," 86.

[194] Kerr, *Temple*, 65–66, speaking by analogy to some early Jewish responses to the destruction of the Temple (cf. *2 Bar.* 6:3–7:1).

[195] Koestenberger, "Destruction," 94–95.

[196] Thus S. Motyer, *Your Father the Devil? A New Approach to John and 'the Jews'* (Carlisle, 1997), 41 (quoted by Koestenberger, "Destruction," 90), who reads the gospel (based on John 20:30–31) as a work with a missionary purpose.

believers. And strategies of coping with the distance from the Temple or doing without the Temple had already a number of forerunners and parallels in Second Temple Judaism.

In John, the christological use of the temple motif is most remarkable and most significant. This is due to the author's interest in displaying the authority of Christ using elements of biblical and Jewish tradition and presenting Jesus as the fulfillment of a variety of biblical messianic and eschatological expectations. But such use is quite independent of the actual existence or nonexistence of the sanctuary.

III. Conclusion: Who Made the Difference: Jesus or Titus?

The conclusion is unavoidable: The direct impact of the destruction of the Temple of Jerusalem on the Fourth Gospel and on the development of the identity of the community members as "children of God" is remarkably small.[197] The question put by the organizers of this conference, as to whether Jesus or Titus made the difference, must be answered clearly in the sense that the difference was primarily made internally, by the developing Jesus tradition (and Christology). The consequences of the year 70 CE further stimulated the already ongoing separation between the local synagogue and the emerging Christian communities in the Mediterranean Diaspora.

---

[197] Cf. the general statement by K. Berger, *Die Urchristen* (München, 2008), 13: "Doch ist es nicht erkennbar, dass dieses Jahr eine entsprechende [scil. epochemachende] Bedeutung für die frühen Christen hatte."

RELIGIOUS REACTIONS TO 70:
THE LIMITATIONS OF THE EVIDENCE

Martin Goodman

That the year 70 marked a turning point in the history of Roman attitudes to Jews,[1] in the Jewish leadership of Judea,[2] and in the economy of Jerusalem and its environs,[3] is not in doubt. Harder to pin down is (perhaps surprisingly) the most obvious change to be expected as a result of the destruction of the Temple—that is, a change within Judaism.

It is of course clear that at some time in late antiquity, some rabbis began to assert that, despite the clear injunctions in the text of the Torah for Jews to worship through sacrifices, incense, and other offerings in the place specified by divine command (which rabbis, like other Jews, took to be the site where the Temple had stood in Jerusalem),[4] there were other ways to worship which were just as effective. Later tradition ascribed to Yohanan b. Zakkai, in the aftermath of 70, the claim that deeds of loving-kindness are just as effective as sacrifices as a way of atonement.[5] By the time of Maimonides, it was possible to view the sacrificial rituals of the Temple as a necessary but now otiose stage in the religious development of Israel.[6] But the question is when such ideas, which ran directly counter to the centrality of sacrificial ritual in most cultic practice in the ancient world, were first adopted by Jews—and, in particular, whether such ideas did in fact occur to Yohanan, or indeed to anyone in the traumatic sixty years

---

[1] M. Goodman, *Rome and Jerusalem: The Clash of Ancient Civilisations* (London, 2007), chapter 12.

[2] See J. Choi, *Jewish Leadership in Judaea after 70 CE* (Leiden, 2012).

[3] On the pilgrimage economy, which came to an end in 70 CE, see M. Goodman, *Judaism in the Roman World: Collected Essays* (Leiden, 2007), chapter 5. But note that the establishment in Jerusalem of a legionary garrison, which Josephus gave as a reason for his lands there becoming unprofitable (*Vita* 422), should in fact have provided a ready market for those Judean farmers who survived the war.

[4] On the sacrificial cult in Jerusalem in general, see E.P. Sanders, *Judaism: Practice and Belief, 63 BCE–66 CE* (London, 1992), chapters 5–8.

[5] *'Abot R. Nat.* 4.21.

[6] For Maimonides on sacrifices, see *Guide of the Perplexed*, 3.32, 46.

which followed the Destruction. Is it, perhaps, rather the case that they were historically retrojected onto the post-Destruction generation by religious thinkers of much later centuries—who had had time to come to terms with the need to survive without the Temple?[7]

For any Jews to think they could live and worship satisfactorily without a Temple is in many ways surprising. In the years before 70 CE, while the Temple still stood, it would have been hard to overestimate the significance for all Jews of the public cult, carried out on behalf of all Israel by the priests, in daily, festival, and Sabbath offerings, and the solemn ritual of the Day of Atonement. So long as such offerings were made, it was possible to remain secure in the hope that Israel remained under divine protection. When the cult came under attack, as in the horrendous plan of Gaius Caligula to intrude his statue into the Temple, Jews across the world—including Philo and Agrippa in Rome—dedicated themselves to saving the sanctuary from sacrilege,[8] and the Jews of Judea presented themselves in open opposition to the might of the emperor, suicidal though such opposition might be expected to be.[9]

And once the Temple was destroyed, its memory loomed large in the religious mentality of all Jews. A large proportion of the Mishnah discusses the service in the Temple in purely practical terms. In the year 358/9 CE the grieving relatives of a Jew who was buried in Zoʻar, on the southern edge of the Dead Sea in the province of Arabia, dated his death to "year 290 after the ḥurban."[10] And in the centuries after this tombstone was erected, synagogue mosaics in different parts of Palestine recalled the Temple service in their imagery of the Temple utensils, such as incense shovels, and via the depiction of the Temple itself, albeit in the service of a new liturgy.[11] In the light of such evidence, can one really imagine that Jews already in the time of Yohanan ben Zakkai were seeking new forms of Judaism to substitute for the sacrificial cult enjoined by the Torah?

---

[7] For the creation of later legends about Yohanan, see J. Neusner, *The Development of a Legend: Studies on the Traditions Concerning Yohanan ben Zakkai* (Leiden, 1970).

[8] Philo, *Legat.* 203–333; Josephus, *A.J.* 18.289–301.

[9] Ibid., 18.279–288.

[10] H.M. Cotton and J.J. Price, "A Bilingual Tombstone from Zoʻar (Arabia)," *ZPE* 134 (2001): 277–83.

[11] S. Fine, *Art and Judaism in the Greco-Roman World: Toward a New Jewish Archaeology* (Cambridge, 2005), 189–205.

The first method to be tried by historians who wish to investigate such issues must of course be to examine the evidence from the period immediately after 70 to see whether sources untainted by later redaction contain the same ideas as those ascribed to Yohanan ben Zakkai in later rabbinic texts. There is indeed nothing wrong with such an approach, but, as will emerge, the simple collection and analysis of such evidence can be of only limited value in ascertaining the religious reactions of Jews between 70 and 135. It is not that evidence is lacking—on the contrary, we can find out a good deal about Jewish history in this period from the earliest stratum of the rabbinic tradition, from Christian sources, from pseudepigrapha, documents, inscriptions, archaeology, and Josephus—but that none of these sources tells us quite what we are looking for in a form from which we can extrapolate with confidence to the attitudes of other Jews.

Not least disappointing in this regard are the documents from the Judean Desert.[12] Those which can be firmly dated to this period ought, in principle, to provide the basis of historical reconstruction of Jewish life in this period, and writing such a history of the social, economic and cultural life of the (or a) Jewish community between the wars may well indeed be possible on the basis of such texts; but the documents reveal oddly little about the *religious* lives of these Jews beyond the (negative) fact that the marriage and other private legal systems under which they operated strongly suggest that they lived in a world not dominated by rabbinic authorities like Yohanan ben Zakkai and his successors.[13] It is legitimate to infer from this evidence that rabbinic authority did not hold sway among wealthy Jews who lived by the Dead Sea, but not necessarily that rabbis equally lacked religious authority elsewhere. The value of these documents is greatly enhanced by the fact that, in many cases, they can be precisely dated by their contents. It is worth noting that the convention by which the undated religious texts found in the caves near Qumran are all assumed to have been composed before 70 CE is indeed, essentially, only a convention, based on assumptions about the relationship of the scrolls

---

[12] See in particular the texts edited in: P. Benoit, J.T. Milik and R. de Vaux, eds., *Les grottes de Murabbaʿat* (Oxford, 1961); and H.M. Cotton and A. Yardeni, eds., *Aramaic, Hebrew and Greek Documentary Texts from Naḥal Ḥever and Other Sites* (Oxford, 1997).

[13] See H.M. Cotton, "The Rabbis and the Documents," in *Jews in a Graeco-Roman World* (ed. M. Goodman; Oxford, 1998), 167–79.

in the caves to the other artefacts in the caves, including the pottery,[14] and to the Qumran site, which was destroyed in 68 CE (although it may well have been resettled by other Jews after 70).[15] If some of the scrolls which belong in the later bands of carbon-14 dates were in fact copied after 70 (as is quite possible, given the imprecise nature of dating by this method),[16] and if they were abandoned in the caves not in the aftermath of 70 but some years later, then the corpus of religious documents produced by Jews after 70 will be rather larger than it is commonly assumed to be—although the representativeness of these Jews also will remain in question.

Dated to the decades after 70 with more probability is the pseudepigraphic apocalypse *4 Ezra*, in which the vision of the eagle (11:1–12:51) makes best sense as an allusion to Roman rulers from Julius Caesar to the end of Domitian's reign. But even that dating, which is now fairly universally accepted,[17] leaves some very puzzling issues unresolved—not least the identity of the eight kings represented by the eight secondary wings which became small and feeble, indicating that their times will be brief. The *dramatic* date of the apocalypse is of course the thirteenth year after the *first* destruction of Jerusalem, as a result of which Ezra is in Babylon, and earlier scholarly theories that the text was composed in the first century BCE are not wholly unfounded, even if they lack supporters nowadays.[18]

The only other extant Jewish apocalyptic work generally ascribed to this period is *2 Baruch*, which again presents itself as a reaction to the destruction of the first Temple rather than the second. A literary relationship with *4 Ezra* is plausible, but it is impossible to tell which borrowed from which, or whether they relied on a common source,[19]

---

[14] J. Magness, *The Archaeology of Qumran and the Dead Sea Scrolls* (Grand Rapids and Cambridge, 2002), 43–44.

[15] J.E. Taylor, "Kh. Qumran in Period III," in *Qumran: The Site of the Dead Sea Scrolls: Archaeological Interpretations and Debates* (ed. K. Galor, J.-B. Humbert, and J. Zangenberg; Leiden, 2002), 133–46.

[16] On carbon-14 dating see G. Doudna, "Dating the Scrolls on the Basis of Radiocarbon Analysis," in *The Dead Sea Scrolls after Fifty Years: A Comprehensive Assessment* (ed. P.W. Flint and J.C. VanderKam; Leiden, 1998-1999), 1:430–71; J. Atwill, S. Braunheim and R. Eisenman, "Redating the Radiocarbon Dating of the Dead Sea Scrolls," *DSD* 11 (2004): 143–57.

[17] On the dating of *4 Ezra*, see M.E. Stone, *Fourth Ezra: A Commentary on the Book of Fourth Ezra* (Minneapolis, 1990), 9–10.

[18] On these earlier theories, see E. Schürer, *The History of the Jewish People in the Age of Jesus Christ (175 BCE–135 CE)* (ed. G. Vermes et al.; 3 vols.; rev. English ed.; Edinburgh, 1973–1986), 3:299.

[19] See Schürer, *History*, 3:752–53.

and the only strong internal reason for placing the composition of *2 Baruch* after 70 is the apparent hint at 32:2–4 that there had been two destructions—but that passage was considered by R.H. Charles to be an interpolation by a later Christian copyist.[20] It is of course in any case impossible to tell how many other Jews shared the musings of these two authors, whose works (especially *4 Ezra*) were to prove very popular among Christians, who had their own theological reasons for being interested in the destruction of the Temple.[21] These writings may never (for all we know) have had any *Jewish* readers at all.

It is worth noting that the *Liber Antiquitatum Biblicarum*, sometimes dated to the years after 70 CE on the (not very strong) basis that it places the destruction of the First Temple by Nebuchadnezzar on 17 Tammuz,[22] a date which might (but need not necessarily) reflect the Destruction in 70,[23] does not in fact make any direct allusion at all to the more recent catastrophe.[24] The dating of this text is too uncertain for anyone to attempt the argument from silence that its failure to mention the catastrophe suggests that this was seen as unimportant, but there have been claims that another text, the *Fourth Sibylline Oracle*, which was certainly redacted after 79 CE (because the author refers to the eruption of Vesuvius in that year),[25] shows an attitude toward the Jerusalem Temple that is radically different from that found in other *Sibyllines*. The author of this text launched a general polemic against animal sacrifice,[26] and although the argument is doubtless directed essentially against pagan cults it is nonetheless striking that it does not specifically exempt from the polemic the worship in Jerusalem which had so recently come to an end. If silence in this case is significant, it will have distinguished the author of the *Fourth Sibylline* from that of the *Fifth*, who may have written a good deal later, perhaps in the early

---

[20] R.H. Charles, *The Apocrypha and Pseudepigrapha of the Old Testament in English* (Oxford, 1913), 2:499.

[21] On the general problem of distinguishing Jewish from Christian material in the pseudepigrapha, see J.R. Davila, *The Provenance of the Pseudepigrapha: Jewish, Christian, or Other?* (Leiden, 2005).

[22] Ps.-Philo, *L.A.B.* 19.7.

[23] See Schürer, *History*, 3:328–29.

[24] H. Jacobson, *A Commentary on Pseudo-Philo's Liber Antiquitatum Biblicarum* (Leiden, 1996), 1:199–210, denies any significance to this silence and argues strongly for composition between 70 CE and the end of the second century.

[25] *Sib. Or.* 4.130–36.

[26] *Sib. Or.* 4.29.

years of Hadrian,[27] since the *Fifth Sibylline* quite explicitly laments the Temple's destruction.[28]

The Christian texts from the decades after 70, which include of course much of the New Testament as well as such treatises as the *Epistle of Barnabas* and the *Didache*, have in many cases much to say about Jews and about the destruction of the Temple, but the value of their testimony is inevitably compromised by the stances they took towards Judaism, as they, or at least some of them, began to define themselves in opposition to Jews. Indeed, the parting of the ways between Judaism and Christianity is better understood as part of the process of self-affirmation by nascent Christian communities than as a development within Judaism,[29] and it is unlikely that Christian writers felt any great need to describe accurately the religious attitudes of non-Christian Jews.

As for the rabbinic evidence for Judaism between 70 and 135—there is no reason to doubt the general accuracy of those attributions of sayings to named rabbis in the tannaitic sources when the arguments ascribed to one generation follow on logically from those ascribed to their teachers in a fashion which would have been hard to achieve through pseudepigraphy.[30] But these early texts are strikingly uninformative, revealing little more than that Yohanan ben Zakkai permitted the sounding of the *shofar* and the waving of *lulavim* in places outside Jerusalem now that the Temple was no longer standing.[31]

Only one major source of evidence for Jewish reactions to 70 remains for discussion, but it should be emphasized how remarkable it is that the writings of Josephus can be placed and dated with a degree of precision during the years 70 to 100,[32] and that the author so often turns to precisely the question at issue: how Jews should react to the disaster which had taken place in 70. Here is a real, identifiable Jew, known from contemporary non-Jewish sources,[33] who set himself to describe

---

[27] For dating of *Sib. Or.* 5, see J.J. Collins, *The Sibylline Oracles of Egyptian Judaism* (Missoula, Mont., 1974), 73–95.

[28] *Sib. Or.* 5.150, 397–413.

[29] J.M. Lieu, *Christian Identity in the Jewish and Graeco-Roman World* (Oxford, 2004).

[30] So J. Neusner, *Judaism: The Evidence of the Mishnah* (Chicago and London, 1981), 14–22.

[31] *M. Rosh HaShanah* 4:1, 3.

[32] P. Bilde, *Flavius Josephus between Jerusalem and Rome: His Life, his Works and their Importance* (Sheffield, 1988).

[33] Suetonius, *Vesp.* 5.6.

Jewish society and customs to outsiders precisely because of the disaster in 70. It is true that in his earlier works the focus of his attention was on the history of Jews before 70, but he made frequent reference in passing to his own day and his own views,[34] and his last great work, *Contra Apionem*, portrayed itself as composed quite specifically to counter contemporary slurs against Jews and Judaism.[35] Josephus' evidence may not be without its own problems of interpretation— to what extent, as an apologist, did he idealise Judaism? did he magnify the role of priests because he was a priest himself? how much did he change material that he found in his own sources, or did he take over from such sources descriptions of Judaism (such as the centrality of the Temple cult) which he knew to be irrelevant in his own day? did any of his fellow Jews share any of his views, or were his writings only ever of interest to the Christians who preserved them?—but it is odd how often a straightforward statement by Josephus, such as his oft-repeated assertion that there are (in his day, so *after* 70) three philosophies in Judaism,[36] is ignored by historians, who assume that he really meant to refer to the period *before* 70.

Much more could of course be said about each of these sources of evidence for religious reactions to 70 (not least about what reactions these sources themselves display), but enough may have been said to suggest that a simple collation of the evidence is not going to provide a very satisfactory understanding of the issue. Each of these literary sources reveals (if its composition is indeed securely dated to the correct period) that the religious reaction attested in the text was possible for at least one Jew. How widely this reaction was shared is unknowable. The archaeological and epigraphic evidence, which in some respects enables wider generalisations to be made about Jewish *society*, is not very helpful when it comes to analysis of religious ideas. Historians may feel at the mercy of the later Christian and rabbinic traditions, which placed great (if different) emphases on the significance of 70, and which preserved precisely the texts on which their own analyses relied.

---

[34] This was precisely the thesis underlying the study by S. Schwartz, *Josephus and Judaean Politics* (Leiden, 1990).

[35] See now the fine commentary by J.M.G. Barclay, *Flavius Josephus: Translation and Commentary, 10: Against Apion* (ed. S. Mason; Leiden, 2007).

[36] E.g. Josephus, *Vita* 10.

One response to these limitations would be (as that of students of the historical Jesus a few generations ago) to abandon the search for the real religious responses to 70 and to look instead at the presentation of those responses in the later rabbinic and Christian traditions. Such an approach would have the benefit of certainty and clarity, but for ancient historians, accustomed to the need to try to understand ancient societies with the benefit of only limited evidence, it may seem rather feeble. It ought to be possible to build a model of the expected religious responses to 70 based on the plentiful evidence from before 70 which suggests the reaction which might have been anticipated—from despair, to guilt, to a determination to keep the Torah better than in the past, to eschatological expectation, to a mundane hope for an early rebuilding of the Temple such as had been achieved after the destruction by the Babylonians. Such models, based also on knowledge of how other societies react to disaster, may or may not be dignified by theoretical abstraction or sociological theory, but they are entirely valid tools to help understand the inevitably partial evidence at our disposal. So long as such evidence as does survive can be explained within this model, it has a claim to being taken seriously.

Not that this is the end of the matter, for there will inevitably be debate as to how much of our evidence is directly relevant and ought to be incorporated into the model. Thus not all will agree with my proposal that the Diaspora uprising of 115–117 and the Judean revolt of 132–135 should both be understood within this context, in both cases directly relating to the frustrated desire of Jews to see their Temple rebuilt so that they could resume the worship that had been so precipitously brought to an end.[37] But these are at least real events which need explanation, and they involved many hundreds of thousands of Jews. Therefore I suggest that inclusion of such public events within a model that attempts to explain reactions to 70 may seem at least as reasonable as inclusion of the utterances of the individual authors whose writings have been preserved from this period by happenstance or due to the agenda of later Jews or Christians; let alone the much later traditions which tried to make sense of what was, by their day, an event that was not only of immense consequence, but which appeared to be unalterable—until, in the eyes of some rabbinic Jews at least, the coming of the Messiah.

---

[37] Goodman, *Rome and Jerusalem*, 476–91.

EPILOGUE:
70 CE AFTER 135 CE—THE MAKING OF A WATERSHED?*

Ruth A. Clements

There can be no doubt that, in terms of "facts on the ground," the destruction of the Jerusalem Temple was attended by a great deal more continuity than traditionally conceived of, in terms of religious life and institutions. Nonetheless, the fact remains that the rhetorical construction of 70 CE as a unique watershed event, in Jewish history or otherwise, has influenced everyone from church fathers and early rabbis to modern secular historians. This paper takes recent historical reconsiderations of 70 CE as a significant but not ultimately or universally disruptive event as a basis from which to reconsider the rhetorical crafting of the destruction of the Temple/Jerusalem as the event that "made all the difference." I argue in this paper that such a recrafting began among early Christians primarily in the wake of the (failed) Bar Kochba revolt. Justin, in particular, seems to have taken the lead in using a range of biblical texts to cast the events of 70, in conjunction with the aftermath of the Bar Kochba revolt, as a direct consequence of Jesus' crucifixion. The fall of the Temple, as punishment for the crucifixion, becomes the seal upon the fate of the Jews and the platform for the emergence of the Christians as the true people of God. Conversely, I suggest that this Christian construction of 70 becomes a shadow partner of the producers of the Mishnah and later rabbinic literature in conceptualizing what it means for *Jews* to be God's people.

Daniel Schwartz, in his paper in this volume, notes the difficulty that modern Jewish scholars (that is, beginning with Graetz) have had in

* This paper was presented at the 2009 Annual Meeting of the Society of Biblical Literature, held November 21–24 in New Orleans, Louisiana. It took shape in conversation with a number of papers presented at the Scholion conference, which had been held earlier that same year. I want to thank Jörg Frey, Martin Goodman, Martha Himmelfarb, Daniel Schwartz, and Nadav Sharon, who allowed me to read earlier versions of their papers.

pinning down the significance of 70 and the years surrounding it.[1] On the Christian side, the import of 70 has been just as elusive, though perhaps for different reasons. On the one hand, from the nineteenth century forward, constructions of the New Testament milieu and early Christian history generally tended to downplay the centrality of the Temple cult for most pre-70 Jews, on the grounds that by 70 the Temple had already been displaced by a religion of (Pharisaic) legalism (not a complimentary term)—the precursor to rabbinic Judaism.[2] On the other hand, as early as Luke-Acts, Christian historiography tended to equate the eclipse of Jerusalem, and the proliferation of the Jesus movement to other geographical centers, with the spread of the faith to the Gentiles and away from the Jews.[3] By the fourth century, the events of 70 CE had become both the definitive punishment of the Jews for their recent "crime against the Christ of God" and the beginning point proper for the story of how the apostles and disciples "were scattered over the whole world."[4]

---

[1] See Schwartz, "Was 70 CE a Watershed in Jewish History? Three Stages of Modern Scholarship and a Renewed Effort," especially 1–5.

[2] See, for example, A. von Harnack, *The Expansion of Christianity in the First Three Centuries* (2 vols.; New York, 1904–1905), who states that "for generations there had been a gradual neutralising of the sacrificial system proceeding apace within the inner life of Judaism" (1:10)—a process that von Harnack relates to the extraordinary success, as he holds, of Judaism's transformation into a proselytizing religion. He asserts that "the destruction of the Temple by the Romans really destroyed nothing; it may be viewed as an incident organic to the history of Jewish religion. When pious people held [that] God's ways at that crisis were incomprehensible, they were but deluding themselves" (1:13). R. Bultmann, *Theology of the New Testament* (2 vols.; New York, 1951–1955; 1 vol. repr.: Waco, Tex., 2007), can assert that the Temple and its cult "had essentially lost its original meeting in [Jesus's] time," with the emphasis switching to "observance" and focused in the synagogue, so that "Judaism, borne up by the synagogue and the scribes, survived the fall of the Temple without disaster" (17). I point out that this aspect of the Christian historical construction is nearly identical to that of Jewish historians of the same period, from Graetz onward; see Nadav Sharon's sampling and discussion in this volume, "Setting the Stage: The Effects of the Roman Conquest and the Loss of Sovereignty," 417–418. The difference between the two lay in the interpretation of this construction as positive or negative.

[3] See Hans Conzelmann, *Die Mitte der Zeit: Studien zur Theologie des Lukas* (Tübingen, 1954; English: *The Theology of St. Luke* [trans. G. Buswell; London, 1960]), for the "classic" modern delineation of the historical movement of Luke-Acts in to and then out from Jerusalem; that center is the setting for the rejection and death of Jesus (then later Stephen, and finally, Paul; see also n. 11 below), as well as for the movement of the community of believers away from the Jewish framework and to the Gentile world.

[4] Eusebius, *Hist. eccl.* 3.1–8; quotes from 3.5 and the lead-in to 3.1, respectively. The translation used in this paper is that of G.A. Williamson, *Eusebius: The History of the Early Church* (rev. and ed. Andrew Louth; London, 1989 [1st ed. 1965]).

The discovery of the Qumran documents, among other things, has irrevocably changed the first part of this construction.[5] The fundamentally priestly (even if separatist) nature of the sectarian scrolls has brought back into focus questions about both the vitality of the Jerusalem cult in its own right and the religious vitality of the priests in relation to their supposed Pharisaic rivals. Furthermore, the rich library of nonsectarian texts found at Qumran testifies in turn to the vigor of the life of the spirit as more broadly configured in Second Temple Palestine. Thus, the Judean Desert texts require that we reformulate the question of the significance of 70 in terms of its impact on a diversity of strong and active players.

One more element to be added to the mix, in my view, is the recent scholarship of historians of early Christianity and Christian-Jewish relations, which has reread the patristic sources in particular through the lens of a "hermeneutics of suspicion,"[6] and so paid closer attention to the rhetoric of theological historiography in patristic writing.[7] This methodological approach has in turn problematized the notion of a one-time, cataclysmic, social/religious "parting" between Christians and Jews in the early centuries of the Common Era, and opened Christian historiography to less cataclysmic readings of both 70 and 135—a point of view in which this paper participates.

So, the watershed question is best seen, then, not as a matter of "yes" or "no," but rather as a question of within which framework(s) the significance of 70 is assessed. The current paper is an attempt to tease out the Christian theological substratum underlying many of the modern frameworks through which this question is addressed.

---

[5] See the discussions of Goodman, Himmelfarb, Schwartz, and Sharon in this volume.

[6] I use the phrase here in a way similar to its use in feminist biblical scholarship (see classically, for example, E. Schüssler Fiorenza, *In Memory of Her: A Feminist Theological Reconstruction of Christian Origins* [New York, 1983]), to denote a mode of reading texts *against* the rhetorical agenda of the "historical winners" who produced the texts. In the case of early church history, this hermeneutic reads to recover the history of (or perhaps better said, the history of conflict with) Jews, Jewish Christians, Gnostics, and other "Others" whose history is presumed to have been suppressed or marginalized in the recounting of Christian origins and Christian truth as set forth in the writings and historical documents of the "fathers of the church." See now as well the methodological discussion of S. Matthews, *Perfect Martyr: The Stoning of Stephen and the Construction of Christian Identity* (New York, 2010), 27–30.

[7] See, for example, from different angles, Judith Lieu, *Image and Reality: The Jews in the World of the Christians in the Second Century* (Edinburgh, 1996); and Daniel Boyarin, *Border Lines: The Partition of Judaeo-Christianity* (Philadelphia, 2004).

Jörg Frey suggests that, as a Galilee-centered movement based on a nonpriestly, charismatic figure, the earliest Jesus community developed its identity apart from a close relationship to Temple and cult.[8] Aside from a few specific New Testament literary contexts that can otherwise be closely related to Jewish circles,[9] the Temple and the status of Jerusalem (threatened, destroyed, restored, or otherwise) play a minimal role in New Testament writings. True, the earliest stratum of the gospel tradition contains a strand of Temple criticism;[10] the prophecy of the Temple's destruction, however, is associated in Mark with more general apocalyptic upheaval and the beginning of the end-times. In Luke, the most "Temple/Jerusalem-centered" of all the gospels, we find the only hint of punitiveness related specifically to Jesus; that is, the Romans descend upon the city "because you did not know the time of your visitation" (Luke 19:41–44).[11] However, even here, it is important to note, what is at issue is the Jerusalemites' failure to recognize Jesus as the Messiah. Neither here nor in the other gospel contexts is an explicit link made between the crucifixion and the Destruction, or between the Destruction and the constitution of Jesus' followers as a "new people."

Similarly, the Jerusalem Temple plays no significant role in either Paul's (pre-70) letters or in the epistolary literature following him,

---

[8] For this point and much of the discussion that follows, see also Frey's paper in this volume, "Temple and Identity in Early Christianity and in the Johanninine Community: Reflections on the 'Parting of the Ways,'" 447–507. Note that Frey frames the significance of the destruction of the Temple in relation to the dynamic of separation between early Christian and Jewish communities.

[9] E.g., the apocalypses (Mark 13, Revelation) and the Letter to the Hebrews; although, as Frey observes, the references to the high-priestly service in Hebrews are entirely drawn from the biblical description of the wilderness Tabernacle and its cult ("Temple and Identity," 464–65).

[10] I.e., the Temple-cleansing narrative (Mark 11:15–17 par); the prophecy of the Temple's destruction (Mark 13:1–2 par). See Frey's discussion, "Temple and Identity," 452–57.

[11] Note on the one hand the Temple focus of Jesus' early life in Luke 1–2, which is paralleled by the beginnings of the mission of the apostles, centered on Jerusalem and in the Temple (especially Acts 1–5); and on the other, the characterization of Jerusalem as the place that kills the prophets (Luke 13:34–35; par Matt 23:37–39), embodied by the parallel narratives of the crucifixion of Jesus (Luke 22–23) and the stoning of Stephen (Acts 6–7): see Frey, 455 and n. 32. For a detailed discussion of the function of these parallels, especially in relation to the deaths of Jesus and Stephen, see D.P. Moessner, "'The Christ Must Suffer': New Light on the Jesus-Peter, -Stephen, -Paul Parallels in Luke-Acts," *NovT* 28 (1986): 220–56; and more recently, Matthews, *Perfect Martyr*.

which may be presumed to postdate 70.[12] Slightly later, neither the letters of Ignatius nor the *Didache* concern themselves for or against the restoration of the Jerusalem Temple.[13]

There are two general ways one might construe such a lack of emphasis: 1) the plain fact that the Temple already had, at best, minimal spiritual significance for most Jews by the late Second Temple period, and that its destruction merely left the way clear for a fuller expression of law-based observance (which had already captured the central position in Jewish religiosity);[14] or 2) an underlying, taken-for-granted assumption of the continued centrality of Jerusalem and its Temple, within which the fact of the Roman destruction has yet to attain anything other than a temporal and temporary significance.[15]

I suspect the second construction is the less anachronistic, and I want to explore my suspicion through an investigation and comparison of, 1) the only early postcanonical work that concerns itself explicitly with interpreting the destruction of the Jerusalem Temple, i.e., the (pre-135) *Letter of Barnabas*; and 2) the post-Bar Kochba formulations of Justin Martyr. Both authors read the Destruction through an exegetical lens, and both construe the event as formative for Christian identity, but in very different ways. I want to suggest, in fact, that it

---

[12] On temple imagery in the letters of Paul, see for example J.R. Lanci, *A New Temple for Corinth: Rhetorical and Archaeological Approaches to Pauline Imagery* (New York, 1997). Lanci argues persuasively that Paul's use of such imagery draws on the presence and function of temples in the cultural environment of his Corinthian audience, and is not meant to convey the idea of a replacement for the Temple in Jerusalem. On the later Epistles, see Frey, "Temple and Identity," 461-63, who notes that, although this lack of mention may be part of the authorial fiction of apostolic authorship, it also may well be due to the minimal role that the Jerusalem Temple played in the diasporan, largely Gentile/God-fearer social milieux of the audiences of these letters.

[13] Although "temple" language appears in the letters of Ignatius, it is used in a metaphorical sense (like that of the temple imagery in the letters of Paul) to refer to the believers—in the case of Ignatius, to the holy individual "temple-bearer." The use of such imagery is not predicated on the "replacement" of the Temple in Jerusalem (or any other temple) with the believer-temple (cf., e.g., *Eph*. 9, *Magn*. 7).

[14] This seems to be an assumption at the root of various nineteenth- and twentieth-century Christian constructions of the pre- and post-70 period. See, for example, the citations from Harnack and Bultmann, given in n. 2 above.

[15] A number of the papers in this volume explore the ways in which the "absent presence" of the Temple before 70 was felt (or compensated for) by diasporan communities. Many of the earliest Christian communities took shape in social contexts that relied on such strategies, which were buoyed up by the certainty of the physical Temple's presence, albeit at a distance. See Frey, "Temple and Identity"; and Goodman, "Religious Reactions to 70."

is the defeat of Bar Kochba that proves the real "watershed" here, and
that the exegetical links made by Justin, particularly, between 70, 135,
and the crucifixion, became historiography for later writers.

THE LETTER OF BARNABAS: THE TRUE TEMPLE

The discussion of the destruction of the Temple in *Barnabas* 16 is such
an anomaly among its predecessors and contemporaries that it has
become a crux for such questions as the dating and social location of
the letter.[16] At the beginning of the chapter, the author states:

> 1. And finally, concerning the Temple. I will show you how those
> wretched men, when they went astray, placed their hope on the building
> and not on their God who created them—as though God has a house!
> 2. For, roughly speaking, they consecrated him by means of the Temple,
> as the pagans do! 2b. But how does the Lord speak when he sets it aside?
> Learn! "Who measured the heaven with a span, or the earth with a hand?
> Was it not I, says the Lord? [Isa 40:12] The heaven is my throne, and the
> earth is the stool for my feet. What sort of house will you erect for me,
> or what place for me to rest? [Isa 66:1][17] 2c. You knew that their hope
> was vain! 3. Furthermore, he says again: "Behold, those who tore down
> this Temple will themselves build it" [οἱ καθελόντες τὸν ναὸν τοῦτον
> αὐτοὶ αὐτὸν οἰκοδομήσουσιν].[18] 4. It is happening. For because of their

---

[16] Both dating and provenance continue to be subject to scholarly disagreement;
see discussion below.

[17] This is part of the arsenal of texts already marshaled by the author of Acts in
Stephen's speech, at Acts 7:49; in other words, part of an already traditional *topos*
of Temple criticism. See the discussion in J. Carleton Paget, *The Epistle of Barnabas:
Outlook and Background* (Tübingen, 1994), 172 and n. 334.

[18] As is the case with a number of authoritative quotations in *Barnabas*, this precise
quote is not found in scripture. P. Prigent and R.A. Kraft (*Épître de Barnabé* [Paris,
1971], 190) suggest two possibilities as the source of the citation: 1) a paraphrase of
Isa 49:17: καὶ ταχὺ οἰκοδομηθήσῃ ὑφ' ὧν καθῃρέθης καὶ οἱ ἐρημώσαντές σε ἐκ σοῦ
ἐξελεύσονται; "And soon you will be built by those by whom you were destroyed,
and those who made you desolate will go forth from you" (Greek text: *Septuaginta*
[ed. A. Rahlfs; Stuttgart, 1979]; *NETS* translation); and 2) Esdras 6:15–19, which notes
that while Nebuchadnezzar destroyed the House (τόν τε οἶκον καθελόντες), Cyrus
commanded the rebuilding (οἰκοδομῆσαι). In both contexts, the point is the same.
Notwithstanding the two correspondences to Esdras, the Isaian possibility seems to
me more likely, both because of the brevity and form of the *Barnabas* passage, and
because of the concatenation of Isaianic citations just prior to this. Carleton Paget
accepts the Isaianic identification but notes that this is an uncharacteristically loose
use of Isaiah on the part of our author; he suggests that it represents the author's
manipulation of the biblical verse to suit his own agenda, rather than use of previously
crafted traditional material (*Barnabas*, 20 and notes). It seems certain in any case, that
the verse was not part of the "Temple criticism" unit just cited. It may be significant

fighting it was torn down by the enemies. And now the very servants of the enemies will themselves rebuild it [νῦν καὶ αὐτοὶ οἱ τῶν ἐχθρῶν ὑπηρέται ἀνοικοδομήσουσιν].[19]

5. Again, it was made clear that the city and the Temple and the people of Israel were destined to be abandoned. 5b. For the scripture [ἡ γραφή] says: "And it shall be at the end of days that the Lord will abandon the sheep of the pasture, and the sheepfold, and their watchtower to destruction!"[20] 5c. And it happened just as the Lord announced![21]

The allusion to rebuilding the Temple has given rise to several conjectures concerning the dating of the letter. One plausible conjecture is that the passage refers to the (proposed) building of a temple of Jupiter along with the reestablishment of Jerusalem as Aelia Capitolina.[22] A second is that it refers to a hope of rebuilding the Temple associated with the rebellion under Trajan. The problem with both of these possibilities is, on the one hand, the lack of any allusion to contemporary political turmoil or Roman punitiveness against the Jews (as might be expected in the aftermath of 117 CE or the Bar Kochba revolt); and

---

in terms of later developments, though, that in its prophetic context Isa 49:17 refers to the desolation and rebuilding of "Sion" more generally, not to the Temple per se; see the discussion below of Justin's reapplication of similar postexilic oracles.

[19] Prigent and Kraft, *Épître*, 190, note that this reading is shared by mss. HGL; but S has "they and the servants." This seems to be the reading followed by the *ANF*, which, however, translates, "They, *as* the servants of their enemies, shall rebuild it" (*ANF* 1:199; page numbers cited according to the online edition of the Eerdmans reprint: http://www.ccel.org/ccel/schaff/anf01.html). Note that "they *and* the servants" can indicate a partnership in the positive sense; it is taken in this sense by Carleton Paget (*Barnabas*, 18–19), and connected with the possibility of the dating in the time of Nerva. "They *as* the servants" conveys an adversarial relationship, and so the *ANF* seems to understand the passage, relating it to Hadrian's founding of Aelia Capitolina (*ANF* 1:180 n. 1442).

[20] The prooftext brought here "[does] not occur in Scripture," as the *ANF* note says, 1:199 n. 1677. However, the prooftext fits very well the context and tone of *1 Enoch* 89–90, and likely came to our author from a version of that work or an underlying document; several other quotations in the letter appear to have come from the Enochic tradition or similar sources. Cf. Prigent and Kraft, *Épître*, 192; and Carleton Paget, *Barnabas*, 9–10 and n. 38.

[21] This translation is based on that of R.A. Kraft, *Barnabas and the Didache* (*The Apostolic Fathers: A New Translation and Commentary* [ed. R. Grant; New York: Nelson and Sons, 1965], c. R.A. Kraft, 1991; subsequently updated online edition: http:// www.sas.upenn.edu/religious_studies/rak/publics/barn/barndidintro.htm#barntrans. For the critical edition of the Greek text see Prigent and Kraft, *Épître*.

[22] This view has a long scholarly pedigree. See, e.g., Frey, "Temple and Identity," citing the argument of R. Hvalvik, *The Struggle for Scripture and Covenant* (Tübingen, 1996), 463. Carleton Paget, *Barnabas*, 22–27, discusses both the grounds for maintaining such a date and the difficulties with the arguments advanced in its favor.

on the other hand, the seeming tone of cooperation between Romans ("their enemies") and Jews. The only clear datum of political conflict is the destruction of the Temple in 70 CE itself. M. Shukster and P. Richardson argue that the historical circumstances that best account for this picture of seeming political accommodation are those of the time of Nerva (96–98 CE). They contend that Nerva's determination to correct the abuses of his predecessor—particularly, in relation to his Jewish subjects, the abuses that had come to be associated with the "Jewish tax"—might naturally give rise to hopes (or expectations) that the Jerusalem Temple would also soon be rebuilt.[23] I am inclined to accept their argument, particularly in view of the fact that the notion of "rebuilding" expressed in the text does not easily seem to fit the circumstances of the *replacement* of the Jewish Temple with a pagan one.[24]

The discussion of the Temple provides a climax and conclusion to the exegetical expositions of the preceding chapters. In the prior chapters, the author has set forth: 1) the errors of Jewish scriptural interpretation; 2) the true (spiritual) meaning of fundamental Jewish observances, such as circumcision and dietary laws; and 3) the ways in which Christ was prefigured in the Scriptures. The centerpiece of the exegetical argument comes in chapter 12, where the author offers several prophetic prooftexts for the crucifixion itself, based not on verbal prediction but on a pictorial typology.[25] In chapters 13 to 15, the author then goes on to show (again, based on scriptural prooftexts)

---

[23] M.B. Shukster and P.R. Richardson, "Barnabas, Nerva, and the Yavnean Rabbis," *JTS* (1983) 34/1: 31–55. The authors take Chapter 16 as a key to the book and argue on its basis for a dating to the reign of Nerva. In a second article, "Temple and *Bet Ha-midrash* in the Epistle of Barnabas," in *Anti-Judaism in Early Christianity, Vol. 2: Separation and Polemic* (ed. S.G. Wilson; Waterloo, Ont., 1986), 17–31, they develop a case for Syro-Palestinian provenance.

[24] See also the extensive discussion in Carleton Paget, *Barnabas*, 9–28. Similar conclusions are accepted by S.G. Wilson, *Related Strangers: Jews and Christians, 70–170 C.E.* (Minneapolis: Fortress, 1995), 133–35; and E.B. Aitken, "The *Basileia* of Jesus is on the Wood: The *Epistle of Barnabas* and the Ideology of Rule," in *Conflicted Boundaries in Wisdom and Apocalypticism* (ed. B.G. Wright III and L.M. Wills (Atlanta, 2005), 197–213.

[25] That is, he finds pictorial representations (and thus predictions) of the cross in two biblical narratives: that of Moses lifting his arms in the battle with Amalek (Exodus 17) and that of Moses lifting up the serpent in the wilderness (Numbers 19). See my discussion of the significance of this essentially new hermeneutical strategy in, "Lifting Moses' Elbows: Or, How Do You Know a Polemic When You See One?" in *Proceedings of a Conference at Beit Morashah* (ed. A. Goshen-Gottstein; forthcoming).

that it is the Christians, not the Jews, who are the true heirs of the covenant. Finally, in ch. 16, Barnabas portrays the destruction of the Temple as a result of the Jews' mistaken trust in the physical presence of the Temple itself, rather than in God. Carleton Paget notes that this chapter forms an *inclusio* with Chapter 2, where the author stresses that God does not need physical, "man-made" sacrifices, but rather spiritual ones.[26] Here, similarly, the author argues that the true Temple of God is not physical, not "made with hands," but spiritual.[27]

Because the Jews "placed their hope" in the physical building (presumably to keep them safe), and went to war, argues the author, that building was destroyed. Note that both the war and the Destruction are here portrayed as purely political events. The author nowhere connects the Destruction with either the crucifixion itself or the replacement of the Jews by the Christians as the new people of God. Each of the steps in the argument is established independently via scriptural proof; the entire thrust of the argument in chapter 16 is that the destruction of the physical Temple had been previously predicted by Scripture, which in this way laid the biblical foundation for the construction of the true spiritual Temple in the hearts of believers.[28] As in the previous chapters, the polemic is directed against the obtuseness of the Jews, in their failure to understand the true Temple. The possibility of the rebuilding of the Temple seems to have been seen by the writer as a real, contemporary threat; chapter 16 along with the rest of the letter is an assertion that, such a threat notwithstanding, it is not Jewish but Christian observance that constitutes true and proper worship of God.

JUSTIN MARTYR: THE TEMPORARY TEMPLE

The writings of Justin, composed after 135 CE, present a very different story. Within the framework of Justin's extant writings, he first makes his case concerning the destruction of the Temple as part of the argument of his first *Apology*, not in the context of the *Dialogue with*

---

[26] Carleton Paget, *Barnabas*, 172.
[27] At ibid., 107, Carleton Paget notes that ἀνθρωποποίητον at *Barnabas* 2:6 is a *hapax*. He likens the term to χειροποίητος in, e.g., Mk 14:58; Acts 7:48. The phrasing in chapter 16 is different, the image used metaphorically (φθαρτὸν καὶ ἀσθενές, ὡς ἀληθῶς οἰκοδομητὸς ναὸς διὰ χειρός), but equally negative (the temple made with hands is weak, full of idolatry and demons).
[28] Note the occurrence of the same imagery in chapter 6.

Trypho—that is, the Temple discussion is fundamentally shaped by Justin's attempts to establish the legitimacy of Christian claims in the eyes of the Roman authorities. The heart of the *Apology* is a scriptural exposition that runs from chapter 31 to chapter 53. O. Skarsaune has demonstrated that the exposition itself is crafted from two blocks of traditional material, one of which is set within the other.[29] Chapter 31 introduces the exposition by establishing the authority of the Hebrew prophets (in their Greek translation) for predicting the general contours of Jesus' life (and death) history. Significantly, the chapter also makes a programmatic statement about the persistence of the Jews' refusal to understand the prophecies and consequent hatred of the Christians, which Justin illustrates by reference to Bar Kochba's punishments of Christians in "the Jewish war which lately raged."[30] Thus, the Bar Kochba revolt is an explicit historical datum in Justin's framing of the Jesus testimonia.

Justin first makes the connection between the crucifixion and the Destruction in chapter 32, through an interpretation of Gen 49:10–11, which he cites as follows:

> A ruler shall not be wanting from Judah, nor a leader from his thighs, until He comes for whom it is laid up (ἕως ἂν ἔλθη ᾧ ἀπόκειται); and He shall be the desire of the nations, binding His foal to the vine, washing His robe in the blood of the grape.[31]

---

[29] O. Skarsaune, *The Proof from Prophecy: A Study in Justin Martyr's Proof-Text Tradition: Text-Type, Provenance, Theological Profile* (Leiden, 1987); see especially Part Two: "Testimony Clusters and the Disposition of *1 Apol.* 31ff. and *Dial.* 11–141." Skarsaune is by no means the first to have recognized the different strands being brought into play, but his analysis most clearly articulates both the coherence and the different tendencies of the two set of testimonia.

[30] Translations of Justin are taken or adapted from *ANF* vol. 1. I refer to the edition of the Greek text of the *Apology* by C. Munier, *Justin: Apologie pour les Chrétiens* (Paris, 2006).

[31] *ANF* 1:230 (altered); Justin's citation here, as also at *1 Apol.* 54.5, differs from the LXX. The enigmatic Hebrew עַד כִּי־יָבֹא שִׁילֹה of Gen 49:10 is translated by the LXX as ἕως ἂν ἔλθη τὰ ἀποκείμενα αὐτῷ, "until the things stored up for him come" (*NETS*); in this formulation, αὐτῷ most easily goes back to Judah, whereas in Justin's phrasing, the prophecy may look forward to a different (messianic) figure. In the first citation of the verse in the *Dialogue* (52.2), the LXX reading appears; but in *Dial.* 1.120.3, Justin discusses the two readings, and asserts that "the Seventy" follow his "messianic" version, which points to the Christ. See the discussion of Justin's uses of this passage in Skarsaune, *Proof from Prophecy*, 25–29 and n. 34. The Hebrew is also interpreted messianically in rabbinic tradition; see, e.g., *Targum Onkelos* and Rashi, *ad loc.*, and *Gen. Rab.* 99:8. On the history of the interpretation of this verse, see A. Posnanski, *Schiloh: Ein Beitrag zur Geschichte der Messiaslehre* (Leipzig, 1904). More recently, on postbiblical exegesis of the verse, see J.L. Kugel, *Traditions of the Bible* (Cambridge,

Justin continues by asking "up to whose time" the Jews had a king of their own. He answers that it was with the *appearance* of Jesus that the Romans "began to rule the Jews," and that with the *crucifixion* their conquest was complete: "For of all races of men there are some who look for Him who was crucified in Judea, and after whose crucifixion the land was *straightway* (εὐθύς) surrendered to you as spoil of war."[32] In terms of strict historical accuracy, this is a bit problematic: apart from the telescoping of time between the crucifixion and the events of 70, Judea had conclusively lost its independence to the Romans by 63 BCE, some ninety years before the crucifixion.[33] Exegetically, though, the proof might sound very elegant a century plus after the crucifixion and nearly seventy years after the Roman victory; and this is a verse and a point to which Justin will have recourse in several other contexts.[34]

Justin's discussion of the Destruction proper comes in chapters 47–49 of the *Apology*. These chapters form the conclusion of the "great insertion"; that is, the second unit of traditional material identified by Skarsaune, which runs from chapter 36 through chapter 49.[35] At the close of chapter 46, Justin states that he is now going to move on

Mass., 1998), 469–74; and see also the discussion of later rabbinic interpretation of this passage by S.J.D. Cohen, "Does Rashi's Torah Commentary Respond to Christianity? A Comparison of Rashi with Rashbam and Bekhor Shor," in *The Idea of Biblical Interpretation: Essays in Honor of James L. Kugel* (Leiden, 2004), 449–472, 452–55.

[32] *1 Apol.* 32; emphasis mine.

[33] Cf. Sharon, "Setting the Stage," 416–18.

[34] Cf. *1 Apol.* 53; *Dial.* 52. In *1 Apol.* 32 and *Dial.* 52, in particular, it functions as a programmatic introduction to an exposition of the scriptural predictions of the coming, life, death, and resurrection of Jesus, and the belief of the Gentiles in him. The Genesis text provides the basis for the historical circumstances of Jesus' advent. Skarsaune argues that this programmatic usage of the text comes to Justin from a previously existing testimonia collection, and he contrasts Justin's use of the text in the *Apology* with his use in the *Dialogue*, where the quoted version of the text matches the LXX more closely than does his citation in this passage (*Proof from Prophecy*, 27–29). With that in mind, it is important to note that the framing of Jesus' life events in relation to the Roman conquest of Judea seems *not* to have been part of Justin's source. Rather, it seems to have been crafted by him for the apologetic context. In *Dial.* 52, it is the breaking off of the kingly and prophetic successions, rather than the coming of the Romans, that confirms the fulfillment of the prophecy. Interestingly, in this second exposition, Herod's pedigree as an "Ashkelonite" is mentioned to confirm that rulers "have ceased from Judah"; and Justin mentions the dismantling of the First Temple(!) and the Babylonian exile to drive home the point that not even at that time did prophecy cease as it now has (with the advent of John, the last prophet). See further on this passage, n. 41 below.

[35] See Skarsaune, *Proof from Prophecy*, 160–62.

to "urgent" matters. He uses two prophetic prooftexts to establish that the destruction of Jerusalem had been foretold:[36]

> That the land of the Jews, then, was to be laid waste, hear what was said by the Spirit of prophecy: "Zion is a wilderness, Jerusalem a desolation. The house of our sanctuary has become a curse (Ἐγενήθη ἔρημος Σιων, ὡς ἔρημος ἐγενήθη Ιερουσαλημ, εἰς κατάραν ὁ οἶκος, τὸ ἅγιον ἡμῶν);[37] and the glory which our fathers blessed is burned up with fire, and all its glorious things are laid waste: and You restrain Yourself at these things, and have held Your peace, and have humbled us very sore" (Isa 64:9–11). And you are convinced that Jerusalem has been laid waste, as was predicted. And concerning its desolation (ἐρημώσεως), and that no one should be permitted to inhabit it, there was the following prophecy by Isaiah: "Their land is desolate (ἔρημος), their enemies consume it before them, and none of them shall dwell therein."[38] And that it is guarded by you lest any one dwell in it, and that death is decreed against a Jew apprehended entering it, you know very well.[39]

There are several important things to note about the argument here:

1) Isaiah 64:9–11 LXX, the leading prooftext, focuses on Jerusalem (referring in context, of course, to the earlier destruction of city and Temple by the Babylonians). The LXX text is parsed as follows:

> 64:9 πόλις τοῦ ἁγίου σου ἐγενήθη ἔρημος Σιων ὡς ἔρημος ἐγενήθη Ιερου-σαλημ εἰς κατάραν; 10 ὁ οἶκος τὸ ἅγιον ἡμῶν καὶ ἡ δόξα ἣν ηὐλόγησαν οἱ πατέρες ἡμῶν ἐγενήθη πυρίκαυστος καὶ πάντα τὰ ἔνδοξα συνέπεσεν; 11 καὶ ἐπὶ πᾶσι τούτοις ἀνέσχου κύριε καὶ ἐσιώπησας καὶ ἐταπείνωσας ἡμᾶς σφόδρα.

> Your holy city has become a wilderness; Zion has become like a wilderness, Jerusalem a curse. The house, our holy place, even the glory that out fathers blessed, has been burned by fire, and all our glorious places have fallen in ruins. And for all this you have restrained yourself, O Lord, and have kept silent and have humbled us severely. (*NETS*)

Justin's citation (whether at his own initiative or that of his source)[40] omits the initial subject of the biblical citation ("your holy city") and

---

[36] Cf. also the use of Isaiah 63–64 in *Dialogue* 25.

[37] See Munier, *Apologie*, 252, for the Greek text. He translates: "Sion est devenue un désert, Jérusalem comme un désert; la demeure qui était notre sanctuaire est vouée à la malédiction."

[38] This is actually a composite quotation drawn from Isaiah and Jeremiah; see following discussion.

[39] Translation as in *ANF* 1:239, slightly modified.

[40] At *Dial.* 25 he cites the verses correctly, within the context of a longer citation of Isaiah.

thus shifts each succeeding verb onto a different subject, so that it is the "house of our sanctuary" that has become "a curse" (rather than Jerusalem, as in the LXX); this then sharpens the contrast with "the glory that our fathers blessed," which has been destroyed by fire.

2) Justin then fills out the meaning of "desolation" by way of another quotation, attributed to Isaiah but actually combining Isa 1:7 and Jer 50:3. This pronouncement speaks only of "the land," not city or Temple. The first part of the quotation, from Isa 1:7, is in the second person plural in its biblical context, addressed by the prophet to the people of Judah and Jerusalem ("your land," "your enemies"); the Jeremian part, "and none of them shall dwell therein," actually comes from an exilic oracle against *Babylon*, which predicts measure-for-measure punishment against that empire for what it has done to Judea.[41]

3) The "misapplied" passage from Jeremiah—"none of them shall dwell therein"—then becomes the pivot of Justin's entire argument. Justin applies this imagery of exile *from the land* to the Hadrianic ban against Jews entering *Jerusalem*,[42] "slipping" between 70 (destruction of the Temple) and 135 (banishment from Jerusalem), and linking the latter to the former as a kind of completion of the prophecy.

---

[41] Skarsaune notes that Justin's uncritical use of this quote suggests that he got it from a testimony source (*Proof from Prophecy*, 160–62). When Justin reuses this sequence of arguments in the *Dialogue with Trypho*, the Jeremian phrase is missing; *Dial.* 52 alludes very briefly to Isa 1:7–8 to describe the situation "after the manifestation and death of our Jesus Christ in your nation" (*ANF* 1:369), but without making an explicit cause-and-effect connection between these events and the desolation, or mentioning the Romans as its agents. See also the discussion below on *Dial.* 16.

[42] The historicity of, and the relationships between, various pieces of Hadrianic legislation related to the Jews and Judea, and to the Bar Kochba war is a matter of continuing debate. On the expulsion of Jews from Jerusalem and its surroundings as a punitive measure, see classically R. Harris, "Hadrian's Decree of Expulsion of the Jews from Jerusalem," *HTR* 19/2 (1926): 199–206. Harris does not question the historicity of some form of expulsion, but he does call attention to the fact the language in which it is reported in the Christian sources is exegetically and theologically driven. D. Rokéah, building on Harris's work, argued in 1966 that the entire account of the expulsion should be held suspect: "Comments on the Revolt of Bar Kochva," *Zion* 35 (1966): 122–125 (in Hebrew). In general, the current view seems to be that some sort of ban was in effect, although its contours, enforcement, and duration are debatable. See, e.g., O. Irshai, "Constantine and the Jews: The Prohibition against Entering Jerusalem—History and Hagiography," *Zion* 60 (1995): 129–35 (in Hebrew); Y. Tsafrir, "Numismatics and the Foundation of Aelia Capitolina—A Critical Review," in *The Bar Kochba War Reconsidered: New Perspectives on the Second Jewish Revolt* (ed. P. Schäfer; Tübingen, 2004), 31–36, who takes the expulsion as historical fact; and also, again, Rokéah, *Justin Martyr and the Jews* (Leiden, 2002), 56–57 and n. 53, who alludes to his earlier article but seems to concede that such a ban "was promulgated" (57).

The following passage, chapter 48, consists mainly of citations of
Isa 35:6 and 57:1, which form an "outline" of prooftexts for the life
work of Jesus and his death as the persecuted "Just One," with the Jews
as the implied perpetrators of his death.[43] This discussion is followed
closely (in chapter 49) by Justin's argument that the same prophet
(Isaiah) who foretold the Destruction had also foretold Jesus' rejection by the Jews and acceptance by the Gentiles (Isa 65:1–3); thus,
persecution/rejection, Destruction, and substitution (of a new people),
while not joined here in an explicit cause and effect relationship, are
nevertheless closely linked. Skarsaune argues, looking at parallel configurations in *Dial.* 16–17, 24–25, and 119, that a single testimonia
collection, shaped in a Gentile context, is behind all these passages.[44]
It seems to have been Justin's contribution to have tied that configuration to the aftermath of the Bar Kochba revolt.[45]

In ch. 53, Justin again invokes the "desolation" imagery, this time
to straighten out the matter of inheritance. Referring to Isa 54:1 ("For
the children of the desolate one [τὰ τέκνα τῆς ἐρήμου] will be more
than the children of her that has a husband"), Justin casts the Gentiles as formerly "desolate" (ἔρημα) of God; most Jews and Samaritans
(who had previously possessed the inheritance) are now themselves
like Sodom and Gomorrah (invoking Isa 1:9)—cities of the ungodly,
overthrown with fire, their entire country remaining desolate, burned
and barren (τὴν πᾶσαν αὐτῶν χώραν ἔρημον καὶ κεκαυμένην οὖσαν
καὶ ἄγονον μένουσαν). Although the connection with Jerusalem is not
made explicit, the implication is clear: the destruction of "ungodly"
Jerusalem is tied to a change of heirs.

---

[43] Skarsaune argues that Isa 57:1 (and perhaps the following verses) are again part
of a testimonia collection, accusing the Jews of killing the "Just One" and proclaiming
(or forecasting) their punishment. See *Proof from Prophecy*, 30–31, 160–61.

[44] *Proof from Prophecy*, 161.

[45] Skarsaune himself is somewhat ambivalent concerning the extent of Justin's editorial initiative in working with his received materials. He seems eventually to concede
that the post-Bar Kochba twist might in fact be a product of Justin's own rhetorical-
theological agenda. See *Proof from Prophecy*, 429. It is perfectly plausible that such a
prophetic unit, synthesizing texts on the persecution of the "Just One," retribution,
and the rise of a new (Gentile) people, might have developed in the wake of 70 among
the fledgling Gentile Christian communities. Rokéah attributes the circumcision-
expulsion connection to Justin, but frames it in a larger context of the defense of
the Torah's integrity against heretics: Torah is both curative and punitive, and this
punishment was laid up for the Jews *from the beginning* (in other words, he sees the
theological as antiheretical, rather than anti-Jewish; see *Justin Martyr and the Jews*,
58–60.

In the *Dialogue with Trypho*, written some time after the *Apology*, although Justin again has recourse to the proofs from Isaiah, he also introduces a new line of Deuteronomistic thinking. In chapter 16, Justin develops the notion that circumcision "according to the flesh" is a *negative* sign: it was instituted in Moses' legislation solely

> so that you alone may suffer that which you now justly suffer; and that your land may be desolate, and your cities burned with fire; and that strangers may eat your fruit in your presence, and [referring to the Hadrianic decree] not one of you may go up to Jerusalem.[46]

This passage combines the Isaianic imagery of desolation with related imagery from Leviticus 26 and Deuteronomy 28 to interpret the aftermath of the Bar Kochba war. Although the exegetical "hook" of Jer 50:3 is missing from the context, Justin again invokes the Hadrianic decree as the mechanism for exile from/desolation of the city, and once again, this expulsion is portrayed as a just punishment for having slain the "Just One." Significantly, Justin then goes on to sharpen the argument in two ways. First, he configures circumcision, the distinctive marker of belonging for the Jewish people, as a sign that sets the Jews both apart "from us" and apart for punishment. Second, Justin ties the accusations of persecution of the Just One in the past to the persecution of "us" in the more recent past and the present; in particular, he makes here for the first time the accusation that the Jews "curs[e] in your synagogues, those who believe in Christ."[47]

---

[46] *ANF* 1:319; Justin will come back to this argument in ch. 92.

[47] The accusation of cursing Christ or cursing Christians is raised again in chapters 93, 95–96, 108, 123, and 133. Traditionally, it has been presumed that Justin is here referring to the institution of the *Birkat ha-Minim*. The debate on this point, spurred by and revolving around the article of R. Kimelman, "Birkat Ha-Minim and the Lack of Evidence for an Anti-Christian Jewish Prayer in Late Antiquity" (in *Jewish and Christian Self-Definition* [ed. E.P. Sanders, A.I. Baumgarten, and A. Mendelson; London, 1981], 2:226–44), is in my opinion, not conclusive. See on the issue in general Frey, "Temple and Identity," 495–96, esp. n. 164. It should be pointed out that the theme of cursing is complex in the *Dialogue*; the topos of cursing Christ/Christians is peripheral to the larger problem; namely, that Jesus died by a means that, according to the Torah, renders the corpse accursed (Deut 21:22–23; see *Dial.* 32 [the problem as first raised by Trypho]; 89–96 [Justin's main exposition]; 111 [recapitulation of the longer argument]). A part of Justin's exposition is that the "curse" of Deuteronomy prefigures the "curse" with which the Jews would persecute the Christians in Justin's own present (*Dial.* 96); and the practice of cursing Christians becomes an example of how the Jews persist in their folly: "even when your city is captured, and your land ravaged, you do not repent, but dare to utter imprecations on Him and all who believe in Him" 108).

In Ch. 40, as he begins to answer Trypho's request for proof that the crucified man, Jesus, should be thought of as the messiah, Justin takes a different Deuteronomistic tack, advancing the Passover as the first in a series of types of the Passion.[48] In what is for him an unusual move, he associates the validity of the type with the temporary nature of the biblical injunction. First he notes that God permits the Passover lamb to be sacrificed only in "the place (ὁ τόπος) which the LORD will choose, to make his name dwell there" (Deut 16:2).

> knowing that the days will come, after the suffering of Christ, when even the place (ὁ τόπος) in Jerusalem shall be given over to your enemies, and all the offerings, in short, shall cease; and that lamb which was commanded to be wholly roasted was a symbol of the suffering of the cross which Christ would undergo.[49]

That is, 1) The Passover may only be sacrificed at the Temple in Jerusalem; 2) The Temple has now been destroyed; 3) Since the biblical injunction restricts the sacrifice to the Temple, the destruction of the Temple thus proves that the physical Passover sacrifice was always meant to be temporary; 4) Thus, the *real* purpose of the command to sacrifice the Passover was to provide a typological prediction of the future sacrifice of Jesus. Justin then goes on to discuss the Yom Kippur sacrifice, which, he argues, is equally Temple-bound and therefore equally temporary and equally symbolic.

There are several striking things about this argument: 1) Justin makes clear that the destruction of 135 and the cessation of sacrifice is a permanent, not a temporary, phenomenon, an assumption which is missing in Barnabas and irrelevant to other earlier sources. 2) God had planned it this way all along, by setting up the sacrifice in a place he foreknew would be destroyed. 3) Trypho is portrayed as "buying" the main point of the argument.[50]

---

[48] This is the earliest explicit use of the image in this way.

[49] The innovative explanation that follows alludes to the form of a lamb as it is fixed on a spit, with limbs splayed, i.e., a "pictorial" type like those marshalled by Barnabas; later in ch. 111, Justin will derive a more exegetically-based paschal type, by interpreting the blood placed on the doorposts.

[50] Several chapters and proofs later, at ch. 46, Trypho concedes that in fact, it *is* impossible now to keep the whole law, given ("as you said") that the offerings are impossible to perform. He then gives a "short list" of what it *is* possible/essential to perform: "To keep the Sabbath, to be circumcised, to observe months, and to be washed if you touch anything prohibited by Moses, or after sexual intercourse" [it is interesting that *kashrut* is not on Justin's list here]—transferable command-

Thus, Justin's argument brings the prophetically-driven complex of the slaying of the "Just One" and the punishment for this, together with the "recent history" of 70 and 135 CE and Justin's own theological-political agenda of legitimizing the historical roots of the Christians. His historical argument has three pillars: first, that the Roman conquest of the city and destruction of the Temple follows directly from the crucifixion of Jesus, on the Jews' responsibility; second, that the historical events of the Bar Kochba war have put the seal on, validated, and made permanent the state of desolation; third, that these events prove that the central (Temple) observances which constitute or validate the covenant between God and the Jews were *always* meant to be temporary, as thus the covenant was also. The merging of the two disasters makes possible a historical-theological continuum of crucifixion, punishment (by way of destruction of the Temple and banishment from Jerusalem), and confirmation—of the end of the covenant with the Jews and the institution of the Christians as God's people.[51]

---

ments, all of which are recognized in other literature of the Second Temple period as marking the distinctiveness of Diaspora Jews. See further the discussion below on Marc Hirshman's account of the concept of "portable" commandments as deployed in Justin and the *Mekhilta of Rabbi Ishmael*, in idem, *A Rivalry of Genius: Jewish and Christian Biblical Interpretation in Late Antiquity* (trans. Batya Stein; Albany, 1996).

[51] In later second-century authors, the implied or stated focus is more on 70, but the crucifixion-Destruction axis remains constant. The slightly later *Peri Pascha* of Melito of Sardis connects the current "bitter" situation of the Jews ("once precious, now made void") with the accusation that "You killed your Lord in the midst of Jerusalem" (93; cf. 72 and 94, where "all the families of the nations" are called upon to take note). The puzzling "in the midst of Jerusalem," however, is likely crafted with an eye towards Lamentations' reflection on the destruction of the First Temple (4:12–13): "The kings of the earth, and *all the inhabitants of the world*, would not have believed that the adversary and the enemy should have entered into the gates of Jerusalem. This was *for the sins of her prophets, [and] the iniquities of her priests, that have shed the blood of the Just in the midst of her*" (translations from the edition of S.G. Hall, *Melito of Sardis: On Pascha and Fragments* [Oxford, 1979]).

Tertullian, taking a different exegetical tack, reads the book of Daniel (mainly 9:24–27) as predicting the conjunction of the "extermination" of Christ and the "extermination" of Jerusalem under Vespasian, along with the end of "vision and prophecy" for the Jews, who "all" killed Jesus. Notably, Tertullian calculates (using Daniel's times) the date of the storming of Jerusalem to correlate with the exact date of the crucifixion (*On the Jews*, ch. 8).

FROM THE RABBINIC SIDE: COVENANT AFTER THE TEMPLE

Finally, a brief suggestion concerning rabbinic responses to the events of 70. The Mishnah, our oldest potential witness, contains, on the one hand, fairly straightforward reporting of Temple ritual, whether this is for the purpose of the historical record or for the purpose of easy reference in the event of a still-expected restoration.[52] On the other hand, in some significant tractates (*Pesaḥim*, for example, as Baruch Bokser pointed out), the Mishnah rhetorically creates a deceptively seamless join between its historical record of Temple practice and observance for the post-Temple era.[53] A more self-conscious response can be seen in the Mishnaic tractate *Abot*, which describes the handing down of the Torah through the generations without even a mention of the Temple. As Daniel Schwartz notes, the structure of the first chapter most explicitly illustrates the movement from a conception of the world with the Temple at the center to a conception of the world without the Temple at all.[54]

Schwartz suggests that the Temple-less dynamic of *m. Abot* derives from the Pharisaic response to the Jewish loss of sovereignty already articulated much before 70; namely, the willingness of the Pharisees to "prescind from territory as that which grants identity."[55] It is also possible, however, to read the Mishnah's account on a broader scale (as Bokser did *m. Pesaḥim*) as responding, at least in part, to precisely the kind of argument raised by Justin—that is, the idea that Jewish rituals were meant from the outset to come to an end, since they were mandated to be carried out in the "place" that God knew would one day be destroyed. Similarly, just a short time later than the Mishnah, the compilers of the *Mekhilta*, in Marc Hirshman's compelling formulation, can be seen responding indirectly to arguments such as those raised by Justin, by placing, in their turn, "portable" commandments

---

[52] See S. Safrai, "Jerusalem and the Temple in the Tannaitic Literature of the First Generation after the Destruction," in *Sanctity of Time and Space in Tradition and Modernity* (ed. A. Houtman, M.J.H.M. Poorthuis, and J. Schwartz; Leiden, 1998), 135–52, p. 151.

[53] See B. Bokser, *The Origins of the Seder: The Passover Rite and Early Rabbinic Judaism* (Berkeley, 1984).

[54] See D.R. Schwartz, "Josephus on the Pharisees as Diaspora Jews," in *Josephus und das Neue Testament* (ed. C. Bottrich and J. Herzer; Tübingen, 2007), 137–46, pp. 143–44; see also more briefly, his introduction to this volume.

[55] Schwartz, "Josephus on the Pharisees," 143.

such as Sabbath, circumcision, Torah study, and ritual immersion on
a list of commandments to die for, while relegating the Temple itself
to an aspect of Jewish observance that Jews were *not* willing to die for,
and which was therefore, not preserved (and thus, by implication, *not*
essential to the continuation of the people's relationship with God).[56]

CONCLUSIONS

So, where does that leave us? I have suggested that up through the
composition of the Mishnah, Jewish sources, including the apocalypses
and Josephus, operate on the assumption that "normative" Judaism
has the Temple at its center, whether this entails the consciousness of
a functioning cult or the expectation of its imminent or eventual reestablishment. Both Josephus and the Mishnah, in their different ways,
craft their arguments with an eye towards the potential conceptions of
outsiders (for Josephus, Roman pagans; for the Mishnah, perhaps both
pagans and Christians) concerning what that event might mean for the
continuity of "the Jews."

The earliest Christian writings, I argue, start off with the same
assumption. For Mark 13 and parallels, and for Revelation, the destruction or reestablishment of the Temple/Jerusalem, respectively, serves
as a marker for the end-times. The element of punishment for the
death of Jesus is missing from these writings. Similarly, *Barnabas* characterizes the Temple's destruction (which the author hopes is permanent and perhaps fears is not) as the kind of cap on the series of proofs
that the true meaning of Jewish observances and texts is their spiritual
or prophetic interpretation by Christians. Although the spiritual blind-
ness of the Jews, and their consequent disinheritance, is a constant in
Barnabas's account, any specific element of the Destruction as punishment for the crucifixion is missing. It is Justin, in particular, who,
in the wake of Hadrian's war, begins to work a sea change, joining
together an edifice of prophetic exegesis built especially on Gen 49:10,
Deuteronomy 16 and 28, Isa 1:7 and ch. 64, with the events of 70 and
135, to create a seamless historiography of loss of Jewish sovereignty,

---

[56] *Shabbata* ch. 1; see Hirshman, *Rivalry of Genius*, 55–58 and n. 50 above; note also
Mekhilta of R. Ishmael Baḥodesh 6 on (portable) commandments to die for. For the
text of the *Mekhilta*, see *Mechilta d'Rabbi Ismael* (ed. H.S. Horovitz and I.A. Rabin;
2d ed.; Jerusalem, 1970), 343 and 227 respectively.

desolation in and expulsion from land and city, and dissolution of the covenant, in immediate retribution for Jesus' death. By the time of Eusebius' *Ecclesiastical History*, the story of the war itself can be told via excerpts from Josephus, corroborated by Jesus' "predictions" as recorded by Luke; the "total destruction" of the city (both in 70 and again somehow in 135), as punishment for the crucifixion, has become a historical (and historiographic) datum.[57]

Early rabbinic strategies of de-emphasis, as in the passage from the *Mekhilta* mentioned above, may be read at least in part as efforts to counter what may have seemed, to some, the historical compellingness of the arguments of Justin and his successors. Counters the *Mekhilta*: if the Temple is *not* "to die for," and, instead, Torah observance (to which Temple is irrelevant in this conception) is at the center of covenant and connection to God, then the destruction of the Temple, while a tragedy to be mourned, is at best a minor blip on the radar screen of the ongoing relationship between God and his people.

For later Christian writers, though, who found in Justin's historiography an irrefutable justification for Christian self-identification as the *true* People of God, the continuity of Jewish life in the face of this "history" persisted as a disturbing theological conundrum, which needed to be addressed ongoingly. This paper implies that the modern historical construction of 70 CE as a "watershed" participates, to an extent, in the same theological problem-solving process.

---

[57] Quotations from Josephus form a large part of Eusebius's account of the end of the Second Temple period and the fall of Jerusalem in *Ecclesiastical History*, Books 2 and 3, interspersed with theological commentary on the events as punishment for the crimes of the Jews against Jesus, James, and/or the Christians; see, e.g., *Eccl. Hist.* 3.7.1. Also note that in Eusebius's historical sweep, 135 (with Hadrian's ban) marks the end of the bishops and church of the circumcision (4.5–6), as well as the establishment of the church triumphant, "all over the world and to the limits of the human race" (*Eccl. Hist.* 4.7.1).

INDEX OF ANCIENT NAMES AND TOPONYMS*

---

* Index prepared by Mordechai Schwartz.

INDEX OF MODERN AUTHORS*
